John Durand

Sporting magazine

or, monthly calendar of the transactions of the turf, the chase and every other diversion interesting to the man of pleasure

John Durand

Sporting magazine

or, monthly calendar of the transactions of the turf, the chase and every other diversion interesting to the man of pleasure

ISBN/EAN: 9783741112898

Manufactured in Europe, USA, Canada, Australia, Japa

Cover: Foto ©Stingray / pixelio.de

Manufactured and distributed by brebook publishing software (www.brebook.com)

John Durand

Sporting magazine

THE Sporting Magazine,
OR
MONTHLY CALENDAR
of the
TRANSACTIONS OF
THE TURF THE CHACE
And every other Diversion
Interesting to the
Man of Pleasure, Enterprize & Spirit.
VOL. 17.

LONDON.
Printed for the PROPRIETOR and Sold by J. WHEBLE,
N°. 18, Warwick Square, Warwick Lane, near S!. Pauls.

THE SPORTING MAGAZINE;

OR,

MONTHLY CALENDAR

OF THE

TRANSACTIONS OF THE TURF, THE CHASE,

And every other Diversion interesting to the

MAN OF PLEASURE, ENTERPRIZE, AND SPIRIT.

For OCTOBER, 1800.

CONTAINING,

	Page		Page
Extra Sporting Intelligence	3	Cruelty and Avarice Outwitted	24
A Bidding to a Wedding	4	Sportive Moralities	25
Diamond and Warrer	ibid	Cricket Matches	26
A Case of Poaching	5	Trial for Sedition	31
Account of a new Entertainment, called Wilmore Castle	6	Sporting Intelligence	31
Journal of a Gamester	7	Feasts of Wit	38
Death of Mr. Weltjie	8		
Thoughts on the Means of acquiring the Vete in my Science	9	**POETRY.**	
Pedigree and Performances of Alfred	11	The Watering Place	41
Treatise on Horses	12	The Dippers	ibid
Humourous Account of the late Sweating Sickness	14	Ups and Downs	42
Curious Regulation for Household Servants	15	Ode on the Death of Mrs Montague	43
Ferocious Wolves in France	16	London's Summer Morning	ibid
Chronicle of Eccentricities	17	Epigram on reading the Execution of a Malefactor	44
Instructions in the Manner of Dean Swift	22	Lines on a Poor Author	ibid
		Invitation to Joy	ibid
		Epitaph by W. H. Reld	ibid
		Racing Calendar	1—12

[Embellished with a beautiful Engraving, by Scott, of Mr. Durand's JOHNNY, by King Fergus, and an Etching of the FOX and his PREY, by Howit.]

London:

PRINTED FOR THE PROPRIETORS;

And Sold by J. WHEBLE, Warwick Square, Warwick Lane, near St. Paul's; C. CHAPPLE, 66, Pall-mall, opposite St. James's Place; J. BOOTH, Duke Street, Portland Place; JOHN HILTON, at Newmarket; and by every Bookseller and Stationer in Great Britain and Ireland.

W. JUSTINS, PRINTER, PEMBERTON ROW, GOUGH SQUARE.

TO CORRESPONDENTS.

OUR Oxford Correspondent is informed, with regret, that the sealing of his Letter having injured a considerable part of the sentence, included in a parenthesis, we are under the absolute necessity of leaving out the whole, and to pass on to the next period. Besides, a *personal censure* is implied; of the propriety of which, we are not competent judges.

THE very humourous Devonshire Epistle, from our old Correspondent, J. J. B. shall appear in our next.

WE are apprehensive that the Epitaph upon Munday Hodges, transmitted from Newmarket, has appeared in print before.

THE SPORTING MAGAZINE,

For OCTOBER 1800.

MR. DURAND'S JOHNNY, BY KING FERGUS.

THE Exploits of Johnny will most likely appear in a future Number of our Magazine; at present we shall only offer his Portrait, from a Painting by Sartorious, engraved by Scott.

EXTRA SPORTING INTELLIGENCE.

To the EDITORS of the SPORTING MAGAZINE.

Oxford, Oct. 14.

GENTLEMEN,

FOR the better information of our Sporting Bucks, who are already arrived, and those who are on the point of entering at our celebrated University, (for no one can presume to enter the lists at Bibury, or Newmarket; or make a distinguished figure in the field, without first undergoing the corrections, revisings, and additions, necessary for a complete Buck at this famed Seminary), I beg leave, as a Subscriber, and a Lover of Field Sports, to acquaint them, and the rest of the Sporting World, with the alterations, &c. &c. in the different hunts in this neighbourhood. The long-established and famous Pack of the Rev. Mr. Loder, (a worthy old divine) hunt as usual the Bagley Woods, Wytham Woods, &c. the Stow Wood, Shotover Hill, Rycote, and Nuneham Parks. Sir Thomas Mostyn has taken the hunt of Lord Sefton, who took to the celebrated Pack of Messrs. Wards, at Bicester. The Duke of Beaufort hunts as usual the Wichwood, Ditchley, Norton, and Begbrook, with Blenheim Covers. A Pack, late Sir William Rowley's, hunt for the first season, the Faringdon, Pusyfurze, Coxwell's Woods, and Tubney Warrens, which, with two Packs of Harriers within seven miles, will afford ample satisfaction to all Lovers of the Horse and Hound, and who follow the adage of "Go along, and never stop, till death crowns with victory."—F. H. S.

A CHANCE SHOT.

A SERVANT of Lord Inverury, being out snipe-shooting, on the 1st of October, marked a snipe down, at which he fired upon the ground, and killed it. When he went to pick it up, he was surprized to find a brace more than he expected, killed by the same shot. *Chifoith House, Aberdeenshire, October 2, 1800.*

ON Thursday, the 25th ult. as John Kinglin, of Modbury, Devonshire, was fastening a screw of his gun-lock, it unfortunately went off, and lodged the contents (nail-shot) in the body of his mother, who languished about twelve hours in great agony, and then expired.

A melancholy accident lately happened near Plymouth.—A man being employed to clean a fowling-piece,

piece after washing it, put in a large nail, red hot, to dry it, which set fire to some powder left in the barrel, and the nail being consequently forced out, entered the side of his head. He languished two days and expired.

Barnstaple, Oct. 11.—On Thursday last one of the Fremington Volunteers having taken his firelock to be repaired, borrowed one for the day from the Quarter-master; on inspection, the piece was found to be extremely dirty, and the officer ordered him not to fire it. He neglected to obey, and on firing the fifth round, it burst, and a splinter flying off, penetrated the man's chest who stood in front of him, pierced his heart, and killed him in a few minutes.

An ostler, lately watering some horses in the river Taw, at Barnstaple, and falling from his seat, was in danger of being drowned; when a large Newfoundland dog, belonging to the Golden Lion Inn, caught him by the shoulder, brought him to the bank, and remained by him, till his barking attracted assistance, by which the man was restored to life. The poor man has had a silver collar (engraved with the account of this event) put on the neck of his preserver.

A BIDDING TO A WEDDING.

To the EDITORS *of the* SPORTING MAGAZINE.

GENTLEMEN,

THE following is a genuine invitation to what is called in this as well as some other of the western counties, and in Wales, a *Bidding*. It exhibits a custom, which, though extremely common throughout these parts, will, I presume, be entertaining to many of the numerous readers of your justly admired Magazine

Yours, &c. J. J. B.

" As we intend entering the nuptial state, we propose having a *Bidding* on the occasion, on Thursday, the 23d of October instant, at our own house on the Quay, where the favour of your good company will be highly esteemed; and whatever benevolence you please to confer on us, shall be gratefully acknowledged, and returned on a similar occasion, by your most obedient humble servants,

" THO. BILLINGER, and
" ELIZABETH KAYTON.
Barnstaple, Oct. 9, 1800.

" N. B. The young man's uncle, (Thomas Peak), and the young woman's mother, (E. Kayton), will be thankful for all favours conferred on them that day.

" Them that are pleased to favour Thomas Peak with their company, and to attend the bride and bridegroom in procession to church that morning, are desired to meet at Mr. Langdon's, the Greyhound, the corner of Back-lane, in Boulport-street.

NEWMARKET FIRST OCTOBER MEETING.

DIAMOND AND WARTER.

IT is the general opinion that the attention of the Sporting World was never more strongly excited, than by the race between Mr. Cookson's Diamond, and Mr. R. Heathcote's Warter, which was to have been run at Newmarket.

Diamond was got by Tattersall's Highflyer, whose blood is in general requisition; and he is supposed to have won Mr. Cookson a clear 60,000l.—Warter was got by King Fergus, the Sire of Hambletonian, and was bred by the Rev. Mr. Withers, of Doncaster, in Yorkshire, of whom he was purchased by Mr. R. Heathcote, his present owner. The exploits of these those excellent horses are too well known to require any comment.

The severe contest between Diamond and Hambletonian must be in general recollection, as well as Warter's race with that uncommon horse, called Timothy. Betting was never more equal, nor were the Sporting Men ever more at a loss how to dispose of their money to the best advantage.—Warter having beat Diamond the Oatland stakes last year, the latter received 7lb. weight in the present race. This, as the Knowing Ones conceive the lead of the utmost importance, rendered Diamond the favourite, particularly as his *backers* flattered themselves with the opinion, that one of Warter's legs would fail him in running, and that consequently they were *on the right side*. Till about a fortnight before the Meeting, betting was equal; three to two was then betted in favour of Diamond, which was at first very cautiously accepted.

So highly was the *Gambling Mania* roused, that, till a late hour on Saturday night, previous to the Meeting, all the Sporting Houses near St. James's, and even more to the eastward, were crowded with betters of every description. The bolder sort dashed at the odds, whilst others more cautiously hedged, and all awaited the event with the most anxious expectation.

The whole of Sunday the Newmarket road was crowded with carriages and cattle of every description, from the dashing curricle to the humble buggy, and from the pampered hunter to the spavined hack.

At length arrived—

" The great and important hour."

When lo! when every mouth was opening to bet, and expectation was on tiptoe, it was declared in the Coffee-room, that Warter, by reason of a kick, had *declared forfeit*, and Mr. Heathcote, in consequence deposited 250 guineas.

At two o'clock a race was run between Lord Grosvenor's colt, by John Bull, and Sir Frank Standish's Spread Eagle. A very bad race, for the latter being beat before she had run 300 yards, gave up the contest.

The next race between Mr. R. Georgiana and Mr. Panton's Grey Falcon, afforded all the satisfaction the Gentlemen of the Turf could expect. They ran the Abinger Mile, and though the mare was the youngest by a year, and gave 7lb. yet the horse was the favourite. They started in high style, and running up the hill, the mare appeared beaten, when five to four was betted on the horse; but recovering herself, she headed him in about 100 yards, and keeping her position, she won by half a neck—an exceeding good race.

Owing to Warter having paid forfeit, many bets, which were made, play or pay, were in consequence lost; and Mr. Heathcote is reported to be engaged for 1400l.

POACHING.

THE following case was, on Monday, October 6, investigated by Mr. Henderson, a respectable Magistrate at Bedfont, Middlesex.—A few days since, Mr. Carter, an attorney, of Kingston, and a Mr. Cotterell, of the same place, dined at Hampton Wick, with Mr. William Hill, one of the keepers of Hampton Court Park. They drank rather freely after dinner, and about eight o'clock in the evening, Hill, the keeper, having reason to expect poachers in the park, borrowed a stick, and went out, saying to Mr. Bishop, the master of the house, that if Mr. Carter enquired for him, he would be be back in less than hour, and in his hurry he left a very famous terrier, which always accompanied him, sleeping by the fire in the room where they had dined.—About ten o'clock, Carter and Cotterell having enquired for Hill, said they would go and assist him; and having left the house, were called back by Bishop, the landlord, and desired them to take Hill's terrier and leave it at his house, as they must pass it on their way home.— This they assented to, and passing through a paddock belonging to Bushy Park, they heard the report of a gun, and conceiving it to be Hill, immediately made to the place. —On their way, Hill's terrier leaped upon a hare on her form, and having killed it, Carter imprudently took it up, and proceeded along with it, hanging over his shoulder. They had not proceeded above a hundred yards, before they met 2 of the keepers of Bushy Park, named Elphing, who having taken their address, laid an information before Mr. Henderson, by whom the affair was impartially investigated on the day above-mentioned, at his house in Bedfont.— Two questions appeared to rise from the facts stated by the keeper: —First, Whether the hare was found in the possession of Carter, aided by Cotterell?—Secondly, Whether the hare was killed in such a manner, as to render Carter and Cotterell liable to be punished as poachers?—The hare was granted to be in their possession, which warranted Mr. Henderson in fining Carter 20l. and Cotterell 10l. but the poaching could not be proved, as Hill, the keeper, swore he left his dog by accident; and Bishop, the landlord, said, that after they had left the house, he called them back to take the terrier with them, which they had no previous intention of doing. Mr. Henderson conducted himself with propriety, temper, and impartiality, during the examination; and after he had paid the informer 15l. being a moiety of the conviction money, he rode over to Hampton-Wick, for the purpose of requesting the overseers to expend the remaining 15l. in purchasing a stock of coals, for the relief of the poor in the approaching winter.

THEATRE-ROYAL,
DRURY-LANE.

ON Tuesday, October 21, a new entertainment called *Wilmore Castle*, was performed for the first time.

The business of the piece is engrafted upon the following story:

Mr. Wilmore, a respectable London merchant, determines from an object of parliamentary interest, to wed his son and daughter with *Alderman Marrowfat* and sister. This he appears resolved to accomplish, however militating with his children's inclinations. Discovering that the latter were on the point of marrying a *Mr. Harley* and sister, *Wilmore* dispatches his son and daughter to *Wilmore Castle*, the country residence of his brother *General Wilmore*—with an injunction to him to confine them till his arrival in the country with the *Marrowfats*.—The *Harley's* pursue their lovers, and get by stratagem into the Castle, under a fictitious name. Interviews between the young people take place—and who ultimately effect, by a special licence they had previously obtained in town, their marriage in the Castle Chapel, just at the moment almost that *Wilmore* arrived with the Alderman, &c. This denouement was actually accomplished from the Alderman's staying to dine in the vicinity of *Wilmore Castle*.

There certainly is not much novelty of character, or force of humour

mour in this entertainment. It is rather of a negative kind; there is nothing to displease, but, on the other hand, there is nothing to strike. An *Old Maid*, the sister of the *Wilmore's*, is a character too trite in the design, and too feeble in the representation, to lend any great weight to the production. Bannister played the part of a postillion, after having been a man-milliner, and a good deal of satire is thrown out with some effect against this class of people. This character is intended as the principal support of the humour of the entertainment: he is a coxcomb, however, of but slender parts, with little capacity for the intrigue which he asserts, and scarce wit enough to raise a laugh at the expence of those he is formed to ridicule. A City Alderman, whose delight is in a good dinner, introduces some jests at the expence of the *good livers*, which are neither very new nor very pointed; upon the whole, indeed, there is a languor in the piece; there is no whim or incident in it; of smart dialogue, there is but a scanty portion, and the plot is neither conceived with ingenuity, nor conducted with skill. The audience is neither interested by the story, nor amused by the dialogue; there is not enough of spirit and strength, to engage the favour of an English audience.

The music of some of the songs is pleasing; the first song by Miss Stephens particularly, which was encored—she sung it very well. A song by Bannister, describing the character of a cockney, had some humour, and was likewise encored. —All the performers did what their parts permitted

The piece was received throughout in several places with applause, and without any disapprobation. At the end, however, a considerable opposition appeared, and it was some time before Bannister could be heard, in giving it out for a second representation.

JOURNAL OF A GAMESTER.

ROSE at four—Dreamt had thrown crabs all night, and could not nick seven for the life of me—had some strong green tea, and threw a tea cup at my wife, because she asked for money to buy the children's shoes.—My stomach being queer, and my hand unsteady, toss'd off a half pint bumper of brandy, and sauntered down to the billiard-table—Saw two ill-looking fellows at the corner of the Haymarket—Was afraid they were bailiffs, so shirked 'em, by dodging 'em behind a coach—*Memorandum* —The first lucky run to change my lodgings—Lost fifteen guineas at billiards, and borrowed one of a friend to pay my dinner—Won a hit or two at backgammon, but lost again at piquet—Ordered some turtle and claret for ten, at a guinea a head, and sent my wife two shillings and sixpence to buy some victuals for herself, five children, and the maid — Housekeeping damn'd expensive, and no end to woman's extravagance — Heard good news—A famous Pigeon expected to dinner—A young *West-Indian*, and rich as Cræsus—Was resolved to be prepared, and leave nothing to luck; so loaded a couple of the Doctors for throwing a seven and nine.

After dinner, plied the young *Creole* with wine, and shammed Abraham to avoid the glass; but nevertheless pretended to be drunk —About eleven o'clock, the tables were set, cash deposited, and the sport began—By three o'clock, had won 5,000l.—Was high in spirits —thought myself a made man, when the Devil deserted me, and put it into the head of my opponent

nent to examine the dice!—To make short of my story, I was detected, compelled to refund, and, finally, kicked out of the room, with my ears slit, and my hair docked.

In my way home, these cogitations offered themselves—What can I do? I am expelled society—I cannot game—I cannot apply to habits of industry—What is to become of me?—I have it—A thought strikes me—The *New Philosophy* says death is an eternal sleep—There's horror in the thought! but ....

By five o'clock arrived at home, and found my wife in tears, and my children crying for bread! Gave 'em a hearty curse—Drank a pint bumper of spirits, and went to bed!!!

Death of Mr. Weltjie.

SUDDENLY, on Thursday evening, Oct. 24, died, at Chiswick, while drinking tea with Mrs Mayersbach, widow of the celebrated Water-Doctor of that name, Mr. Louis Weltjie, late clerk, cook, and purveyor to the Prince of Wales. Weltjie appeared to be in good health during the course of the day and the evening; but just as he began to drink the second cup, he suddenly fell back and expired. Being a very gross and corpulent man, it is supposed his death was occasioned by a stroke of the apoplexy.

The history and fortune of this man are somewhat singular: he was by birth a German, and formerly sold cakes and gingerbread about the streets. By what means he got recommended to the notice or favour of his Royal Highness the Prince of Wales, we know not; but, after he received the appointment of Chief Cook and Clerk of the Kitchen, he soon became Purveyor to Carlton-House, and the Pavilion at Brighton, in which situation he acquired a considerable fortune.—Some years since, his daughter having taken a liking to a young cook, the subordinate of Weltjie, she married him, which greatly excited the indignation of her father, who preferred his complaints to his Royal Patron. He represented with great indignation, the *disgrace* and *degradation* of *his* family, by so humble an alliance, and warmly solicited the dismissal of the offender. The good sense of his patron saw the matter in a very different light, which induced him to observe, that the *inequality* was not so great as to outrage the *feelings*, or wound the *pride* of a man, who could not entirely forget his own former situation. He was, therefore, advised to make the best of the affair, and reconcile himself cordially with his son-in-law and daughter. Instead of prudently adopting this counsel, the enraged father persisted in urging the discharge of the offender, against the *dignity of his family*, threatening to consign both husband and wife to indigence; to prevent which, the illustrious person alluded to, discharged Weltjie himself, and put the son-in-law into his lucrative situation.

THE FOX AND HIS PREY.

IN this Etching, by Mr. Howit, we have Reynard descending from a Hen and Duck-house—having made free with a Drake, the wary plunderer is marching off with his prey, fast holding, and with cautious steps, until he has fairly quitted the premises—then to his repast, voraciously devouring his feathered prize, while the farmer's wife, on *finding* her *loss*, exclaims with bitter curses against the general enemy of her poultry and herself.

THOUGHTS

THOUGHTS ON THE MEANS OF ACQUIRING THE VETERINARY SCIENCE.

To the EDITORS *of the* SPORTING MAGAZINE.

GENTLEMEN,

IN consequence of the awakened attention of the public mind, the Veterinary Science is now become a matter of universal enquiry; and its importance and utility so evident, that the species of contempt that was annexed to the idea of a farrier, is now giving way to the credit and respect due to the able veterinary practitioners. It is not a little surprising, that in a country where the breed, and other circumstances attending the improvement of this valuable animal, has been a subject of investigation to the most eminent men, and attended to by those of the highest rank with an ardour few other subjects have commanded; that the prevention and cure of his diseases has been suffered to remain in the same hands that forge his shoes, or, at least, in those of equal ignorance. The attempts of a few enlightened individuals, as Bracken, Osmer, Gibson, &c. have done little more towards improving this branch of knowledge, than that of meliorating his treatment in the stables of ingenious men, who choose to undertake the management of their own sick.

Ignorance and presumption ever accompany each other, and always bear a relative proportion; hence the farrier, who can hardly read or write, despises that knowledge he does not understand; his stock of learning consisting, generally of an old manuscript, with the names of a few diseases, and as many remedies, has been received from his father, who had it carefully delivered to him by his grand-father, with strict injunctions never to show it, as it contained many rare secrets. Upon these grounds, and with these authorities, are the various diseases of the animal in question attempted to be removed; nor can it be wondered at, that want of success invariably marks their practise, or that sending for a farrier is analagous to sending for death, with additional consolation of paying dearly for the mischief he brings.

Few sciences immediately practical, (if I may so express myself) ever arrive at any great perfection, until they become objects of general enquiry. In the aggregate of mankind, the stimulus of interest must be applied to assist scientific research; therefore the Veterinary Science has remained in obscurity, notwithstanding the efforts of some ingenious writers and practitioners, till a public seminary has been established, the mode of acquiring the necessary knowledge reduced to a system, and held out to those who are able or willing to avail themselves of it. It is now, therefore, when every eye is opened upon their errors, and that thereby they lose their best practice, that farriers are compelled to alter their plan, and to wish to obtain some other information than is contained in their receipt book. But even yet the operation of the College in disseminating knowledge must be slow; for it will be long before every county, or great town, is supplied with an eleve from that school properly qualified; and the mode of obtaining a competent knowledge without a residence there, is difficult: for the groundwork is not laid, there is no helping hand to the first step; every thing, therefore, is confused and unintelligible, and the inquisitive, but ignorant mind, turns with disgust from the rugged path: and yet the acquiring

acquiring of sufficient knowledge to form not only a tolerable, but able veterinary surgeon, is by no means difficult, when the first steps are pointed and made clear, and the future gradations marked out. But information conveyed in this manner must be multifarious; it must comprize a vast variety of subjects, and must be fitted to very different capacities. It is necessary it should be at once scientific, yet plain and intelligible.

From the relative connection between animal and human medicine, regular-bred surgeons have hitherto been the only persons who have distinguished themselves in this art; and indeed so connected are they, that a good surgeon has gone three-fourths of the way towards making a good veterinarian; yet without a general knowledge of horses, of the modes in use with regard to them, of the peculiar nomenclature attending the description of their diseases, such a one would be very much at a loss; and he who at the road side might appear a paraulsus, in the stable would personate a blockhead.

It is not difficult to mark the hindrances to our improvement in veterinary medicine, but it is more so to remove them: the establishment of a public school is the first great step, yet, as I have before observed, it will be long before its influence can become very extensive; and far the greater number of those who do at present, or intend to practice as farriers, cannot avail themselves of this advantage.

There appears to me three classes of persons to whom the Veterinary Science would be acceptable, but who from various circumstances, cannot embrace the opportunity offered them: these are surgeons who are already settled, and wish to combine the two practices of human and animal medicine together; but for want of a general knowledge of horses, of the few differences that exist between the horse and the man, with their relations to their several diseases, and a total ignorance of what some veterinarians would term stabularian usage, are afraid to attempt such a junction.

The next kind of persons are those who are at present in the practice of farriery, but who are totally ignorant of the internal formation of the animal they profess to cure, who have no knowledge of medicine, and by attending to symptoms only, confound one disease with another, and who, as soon as it receives its name, apply invariably the same remedy through every stage of it.

The third kind are young men, who either wish to qualify themselves, or whose relations resolve on this profession for their children, but whose means are not equal to the placing them at the college. These latter would find it useful to attach themselves to some enquiring and intelligent farrier, or to a surgeon who was engaged in these pursuits.

I have before mentioned, and am fully convinced, that each of these three classes of persons may fit themselves to act as able veterinarians, without any residence at the college; but it must be by a well laid down system communicated in the clearest and ablest manner.

When an already qualified surgeon turns his attention to this branch of science, he finds he has to acquire a thorough knowledge of comparative anatomy, and the principal differences that exist between the formation of the animal and human frame, especially such as lead to the greatest varieties in the diseases, and their consequent treatment; such as the horizontal situation

ation of the one, so unlike the perpendicular position of the other, and affecting materially all medicines intending to operate on the alimentary canal.

He will acquaint himself by these means, that in his treatment of diseases in the horse, he cannot avail himself of a very powerful medium of assistance in various affections of the human, namely, that of the sympathetic effect of a nauseating stomach on remote organs, as no such effect can be produced in the animal. Purgatives he has to learn are likewise of less use in acute diseases, or those whose termination is rapid, as they are so long in producing their effect: he must therefore more usually employ clysters. The great strength of the arterial system must ever be present to his imagination; by this he will learn how much more prone to inflammatory diseases is the horse, and how much sooner such diseases is seen through their stages from this cause, and consequently how much more active and decided must be the treatment; if he waits for directing symptoms, gangrene stares him in the face, and ends the unhappy animal. But one of the grand anatomical differences he has to enquire into, is the formation of the feet: from this arises a long train of diseases that have but little analogy to any thing met with in the human. He must consider the great vascularity of these parts, their aptitude to inflame, and under inflammation, to take on a diseased formation; whereby incurable lameny is produced. This class of diseases our enquirer will find most difficult, as no analogy helps him; the names are arbitrary and various, nor seldom can any certain prognostic be formed: an intimate knowledge of the formation, and a careful observance of symptoms, will prove his best guides.

But what more particularly embarrasses a surgeon when he first sets out in his pursuits of this nature, is his ignorance of the nomenclature and idiom, if I may so call it, used among grooms and farriers, and of the general knowledge of the stable, with the observance of certain forms, by which these kind of people can at once tell whether you are habituated to horses; which can only be acquired by constant attention to them in general. By this conversance, an experienced groom, from the manner only, can tell the seat of complaint with greater certainty, than the ablest physician, or most scientific surgeon, unaccustomed to sick horses. There are circumstances still more trifling, but which must be nevertheless overcome: the proper mode of examining a horse must be attended to—when the action, the arteries is most conveniently detected as under his jaw; how to judge of the coldness of his extremities, by his legs, feet, ears, and muzzle; and how to distinguish impeded or accelerated respiration by his flanks; and when respiration is only quickened from a general affection, or when the abdominal muscles only act with force to relieve local affections, as in diseases of the chest, broken wind, &c.

(*To be continued.*)

PEDIGREES and PERFORMANCES OF ALFRED.

HE was bred by John Wastell, Esq. of Arnderly Steeple, near Northallerton, Yorkshire, and foaled in 1770. Got by Matchem: dam by Snap, Cullen Arabian, Greenwood's Lady Thigh, by Partner, Greyhound, Sophonista's dam, by the Curwen Bay Barb, Lord d'Arcy's Chesnut Arabian, White-
shirt,

shirt, Old Montague Mare. Alfred was own brother to Conductor, Ainderly, Georgina, Dictator, Receiver, Scorpion, and Laurustinus: his dam also bred Coaxer, &c. &c.

Alfred, when first in training, was the property of Lord Bolingbroke; and at Newmarket First Spring Meeting, 1774 he received 200gs from Lord Farnham's Flirt, and Mr. Vernon's Sophy.

In Second Spring Meeting, Alfred walked over the B. C. for the Clermont Cup, value 120gs, and 400gs in specie: he also walked over B. C. for a subscription of 175gs.

Alfred then became the property of Mr. Vernon; and at Newmarket July Meeting, he won the Grosvenor Stakes of 700gs, beating Sir C. Bunbury's Alexis, Lord Grosvenor's Gillkicker, Duke of Grafton's Magnet, and two others.

At Newmarket Second October Meeting, Alfred walked over D. C. for a Sweepstakes of 200gs, and won a Sweepstakes of 105gs, weight or age, B C. beating Duke of Ancaster's Transit, Mr. Strode's Rebus, &c. He also received 100gs compromise from Lord Abingdon's Tuzzimuzzy, to whom he was to have allowed 9lb.

He was afterwards a stallion at Ainderly Steeple, at 5gs each mare; and was sire of Columbus, Elfledo, Snowdrop, Gayler, Robin-Hood, Steeple, Ransom, Imperatrix, Balloon, Cheshire Round, Nancy, Black-Eyed Susan, Columba, Doctor, Shipton, Blemish, Miss Judy, Tickle Toby, and several other good racers, and hunter's plate horses: his stock were likewise celebrated for being capital hunters.

Of JUPITER.

HE was bred by the late Colonel O'Kelly, and foaled in 1774. Got by Eclipse, out of Col. O'Kelly's well-known mare by Tartar; her dam by Mogul, Sweepstakes, Bay Bolton, Curwen Bay Barb, Old Spot, Vintner Mare. Jupiter is own brother to Antiochus, Venus, Adonis, Lilly of the Valley, Mercury, Volunteer, Commyface, and Queen Mab, &c.

In 1777, Jupiter won the three yrs old stakes at Lewes, of 800gs; received a forfeit of 200gs in September, at Abingdon: at Newmarket October Meeting, he won a Sweepstakes of 1000gs, H. M. beating Lord Bolingbroke's Comet, and six others.

In 1778, at Newmarket, Jupiter won the Fortescue Stakes of 300gs, D. I. beating Dilettante, Athenais, Tuscan, Magna Charta, and three others.

He was afterwards a stallion at Thornville Royal, Weatherby, Yorkshire, at 10gs each mare; and a sire of Halkin, Curdock, by Jupiter, Mr. Parkhurst's Welter, who won the Welter Stakes this year at Bibury, of 20gs each p. p. (44 Subscribers) 13st. each, 3 mile heats, and many other very capital hunters, some of which have been sold for amazing high prices.

A PHILOSOPHICAL *and* PRACTICAL TREATISE *on* HORSES, *and on the* MORAL DUTIES *of* MAN *towards the* BRUTE CREATION.

BY JOHN LAWRENCE.

UPON IMPROVEMENTS IN THE ART OF SHOEING CART-HORSES.

BY a strange absurdity, as cart-horses are shod in a more unnatural and preposterous method than any other description, so there is infinitely less occasion, and less excuse for it. Although the pure, dry,

dry, and elastic air of some parts of Asia, so hardens the hoofs of horses, that they are tough enough to endure the ground with very slight, perhaps sometimes without any shoes, yet the nature of the hoof in that race is essentially changed by the heavy and moist air of our northern climate, and we find the feet of our horses, generally tender in proportion to their blood, and tougher as they approach the cart-breed. Most cart-horses are provided in an ample measure, with quarters and frogs sufficiently capacious to support their weight, and which would for ever do that office in the fullest manner, were they not constantly pared down, to make way for an artificial and delusive support of iron. This pretended iron support is much more destructive to their feet, than either their own weight, or the hard ground; for instead of encouraging the natural growth of horn upon the foot, destined to sustain the shoe, it is daily abrading and wearing that necessary substance away. The plea, that heavy horses require such ponderous shoes to support their weight, is totally unfounded and absurd; since those horses, as well as all others, are never so firmly supported, or their feet so strong and sound, as when running abroad without shoes; and if it be urged, that in such case they do not labour, the answer is as just as it is ready; that during the season of labour and carrying weight, a heavy covering, which weakens and destroys the feet, can never be a proper support for the body. What would a porter say to the artist, who should propose to him to pare away the hard skin of his heels, and to make amends for the loss of natural substance, by an additional thickness of shoe?

I will however grant, because I know it from long experience, that almost all horses require a certain substance of shoe, sufficient to preserve their feet from the concussion of the ground in exercise; and for this any person may find an analogy in his own feelings, when running over hard ground with thin-soled shoes; but this consideration by no means affects draft-horses, in the degree it does those which are obliged to move quick; and the circumstance of the former being confined to a walk, is extremely favourable to any necessary amendment in their shoeing, even when their feet may have been crippled, and worn tender by weight of iron.

If there be really no necessity for these heavy oval shoes, beyond a paltry saving in the price of iron, and a gratification of the ridiculous prejudices of ignorant smiths, surely the concerned will no longer suffer their own interests, and the feelings of their cattle, to be so idly sacrificed. Excluding all ideas of risk and damage, let it be simply considered with what ease a couple of horses, properly shod with flat narrow-webbed shoes, and having their soles entire, and their frogs in their natural state to cling to a slippery surface, would take a load up-hill over the pavement, to what they would be able to do with the common large and oval shoes. It must at least make a horse difference in four; but in the view of humanity, the difference is immense. Taking it as a mere point of interest, and supposing that the amendment cannot be compassed without an additional allowance to the farrier, there is nothing more obvious, than that it would be infinitely to the advantage of the keepers of cart-horses to comply; of the truth of which, they may be very cheaply and easily convinced.

The reader, desirous of information, will have made his own inferences from the principles I have
laid

laid down; without being any great connoisseur in horse-shoeing, he has, I dare say, found them accordant with common sense, which has much more to do in the right management of all things, than professional mystics willingly allow. As has been said, the reformation must come from the personal exertions of people of property. In such consists the lawful and meritorious influence of wealth. Little is to be effected, as ages have shewn in this particular case, from the feeble efforts of authors, who, to use a phrase of the schools, are poor by custom, and therefore little attended to. But whoever shall set about this necessary reform, will have an immense load of prejudice to counteract in grooms and farriers in general, by no means undeserving the character bestowed on them, by the discerning Earl of Pembroke. A bold zeal for antiquated forms, and an invincible attachment to precedent, right or wrong, are not confined to the superior professions.— The late professor, St. Bel, assured me, that one of his workmen left the service of the College, although his wages were higher, and his labour less, than elsewhere, rather than submit to be taught any other method of shoeing than that which he had learned in his youth, and which, for that good reason, he was sure must be the best: and I was within these few days informed, by a friend, of a dairy-man in Buckinghamshire, well known to the said informant, who always weighs his butter for market with a family stone, although the said stone weighs several ounces above a pound; giving the following sage reason for the practice—"that as " his father before him, weighed " with the stone, and did well, be- " sure it did not become him, to " be wiser than his father!"

HUMOUROUS ACCOUNT OF THE LATE SWEATING SICKNESS.

AMONGST the annals of our public calamities, there is none more distinguished than the ravages which were caused a few centuries ago in the population of the country, by a dreadful and peculiar distemper, which, from its fatal symptoms, was called the *Sweating Sickness*.

This horrible epidemy has never visited any other parts of Europe, notwithstanding their nearer proximity to the sun, so that its causes have justly been considered as local and peculiar; and its return cannot be watched or prevented with too much vigilance and anxiety.

It is with infinite concern that we feel it our duty to announce some very suspicious and formidable symptoms of this malady, which have lately made their appearance in various quarters of the town, and amongst the most opposite classes of society.

The first signs which we have been enabled to trace, broke out on the 9th ult. in several great houses at the West end of the town. *Lady Galina* ——, who had worn her characteristic undress during all the severity of the winter, was amongst the first who were attacked. Her disorder broke out in a violent elastic black velvet, with an incrustation of gold net, from head to foot; and the *Hon. Mrs. Figleaf* herself was not to be known by her nearest friends, being covered all over with a terrible eruption of pink sarsnet and black satin. Many sweet dancers were discovered to be privately afflicted with flannel and callico, and to have assumed articles of male attire; while others were ascertained to have taken the infection at the bosom, by the quantity of infected cotton, which made the

the sufferers look like so many wet-nurses.

In the progress of the sickness the patient has been known to take her cat or lap-dog into bed with her; and some have asked their friends to provide them with good bed-fellows for life.

The present calamity, however, is not confined to the fair sex. It is in every sense epidemical, and affects not only natural but political bodies. A hundred red-hot Deputies from another country have been invited to sit in a room, in which for a century there has never been space enough for two-thirds of its own Members. They are designed to contribute to the heat of the Assembly, as many of them are known to take fire upon the slightest occasions, and others are now baking in a certain oven, after which they intend to wrap themselves in ermine for the rest of their lives.

The worst symptoms, however, have appeared in the market places, where a class of persons called *middle men*, composed of the *warmest* Citizens, have encreased the sweating sickness to such a dreadful paroxysm, as to threaten the whole kingdom, with consumption. It is certain, that thousands of families have already been sweated down to skeletons. The same is the case with any thing they touch, whether it be meat, bread, or corn. If they lay their hand upon a bushel, it instantly sweats itself down to a peck; and a quartern loaf has been known to waste by their deleterious heat, down to the size of a two-penny-roll.

Their art of *sweating the people* is so complete, that some persons have thought they actually *ground the faces* of their patients. But we shall have to speak more of this symptom of the sickness at another opportunity. At present, it is our duty to caution the public particularly against taverns and post-chaises, in which the infection is violently taken, and the perspiration sudden and profuse. The very bottles in some inns have sweated themselves down to pints—but the most dangerous circumstance one has yet heard of, is a combination in one of the branches of a most respectable profession, to sweat the gross. They have been known to order seven sweats at a time, and encrease the effects of their prescription by a new and violent species of action.

CURIOUS REGULATION FOR THE HOUSEHOLD SERVANTS OF AN ENGLISH BARONET, ABOUT THE YEAR 1568.

I. THAT no seruant bee absent from praier, at morning or euening, without a lawfull excuse, to be alledged within one day after, vpon paine to forfeit for euery time 2d.

II. That none swear anie othe vppon paine for euery one 1d.

III. That no man leaue any doore open that he findeth shut, without theare bee cause, vppon paine for euery tyme 1d.

IV. That none of the men be in bed, from Our Lady-day to Michaelmas, after 6 of the clock in the morning; nor out of his bed after 10 of the clock at night; nor from Michaelmas till Our Lady-day, in bed after 7 in the morning, nor out after 9 at night, without reasonable cause, on paine of 2d.

V. That no man's bed be vnmade, nor fire or candle-box vncleane, after 8 of the clock in the morning, on paine of 1d.

VI. That no man make water within either of the courts, vppon paine of euery tyme it shall be proued 1d.

VII. That no man teach any of the

the children any unhoneſt ſpeeche, or baudie word, or othe, on paine of 4d.

VIII. That no man waite at the table without a trencher in his hand, except it be vpon ſome good cauſe, on paine of 1d.

IX. That no man appointed to waite at my table be abſent that meale without reaſonable cauſe, on paine of 1d.

X. If anie man break a glaſſe hee ſhall aunſwer the price thereof out of his wages; and if it bee not known who breake it, the butler ſhall pay for it, on paine of 12d.

XI. The table muſt be couered halfe an houer before 11 at dinner, and 6 at ſupper, or before, on paine of 2d.

XII. That meate be readie at 11 or before, at dinner, and 6, or before, at ſupper, on paine of 6d.

XIII. That none be abſent, without leave or good cauſe, the whole day, or anie part of it, on paine of 4d.

XIV. That no man ſtrike his fellow, on paine of loſſe of ſeruice: nor reuile or threaten, or provoke one another to ſtrike, on paine of 12d.

XV. That no man come to the kitchen without reaſonable cauſe on paine of 1d. and the cook likewiſe to forfeit 1d.

XVI. That none toy with the maids, on paine of 4d.

XVII. That no man weare foule ſhirt on Sunday, nor broken hoſe, or ſhooes, or doublett without buttons, on paine of 1d.

XVIII. That when any ſtrainger goeth hence, the chamber be druſt vp againe within 4 hours after, on paine of 1d.

XIX. That the hall bee made cleane euery day, by eight in the Winter and leauen in the Summer, on paine of him that ſhould doe it 1d.

XX. That the court-gate bee ſhut each meale, and not opened during dinner and ſupper, without juſt cauſe, on paine the porter to forfeit for every time, 1d.

XXI. That all ſtayrs in the houſe, and other rooms that need ſhall require, bee made cleane on Fryday after dinner on paine of forfeyture of euery one whom it ſhall belong vnto 3d.

All which ſommes ſhall be duly paide each quarter day out of their wages, and beſtowed on the poore, or other godly uſe.

Ferocious Wolves in France.

FRANCE is at preſent very much infeſted with wolves, which the late roaring of artillery has driven from the foreſts of Germany. On the 29th of Auguſt one of theſe furious animal iſſued about eight in the evening out of the foreſt of Claimount, and met with two children coming from gleaning: the firſt of whom it let paſs, and tore the other. It next fell upon a woman, and tore her in the body and the hand, Purſuing its courſe, it caught a little girl keeping cows, and tore her in the head, biting alſo her brother, who ran to her aſſiſtance. It then attacked a horſe, and ſnapped a piece of its neck off, and afterwards proceeded towards a neighbouring farm. The night, which began to grow dark, prevented two domeſtics, who came forth at the cries of *help! help!* from ſeeing the beaſt till it was upon them, and lacerated one in a moſt cruel manner; the other brought it to the ground with a muſket ſhot, but did not kill it, for it roſe again to renew its ravages until a ſecond ſhot effected the buſineſs. All this paſſed in the ſpace of a quarter of an hour. Three of the wounded are in the moſt deplorable condition. The Prefect has ſent them medical aſſiſtance, but it is feared that it will be to little purpoſe.

CHRONICLE

CHRONICLE OF ECCENTRICITIES.

A BEGGAR, whose appearance bespoke the extreme of poverty and wretchedness, was lately apprehended in Bond-street, by the parish officers, and conveyed to the Police Office, Marlborough-street. Upon searching him, there were found upon his person Stock receipts to the amount of 630l. in the 3 per cents. 52l. in cash, besides a quantity of half-pence. For a considerable time past, it appeared, he had slept under a bulk in Davies-street, Grosvenor-square. No wretch could look more miserable than he did: his short, ragged coat, was tied round his body with a string, and he was partly covered with part of an old carpet; in his pocket was a piece of beef-steak. He was committed as a vagrant to Tothilfields Bridewell; and the Stock receipts and money were ordered to be delivered to the custody of the overseers of the parish of St. George, Hanover-square.

A wit observes upon this occasion, that the enemy must ever despair of ruining the finances of this country, when they hear that even our *beggars* in the streets are *stockholders*, and that *Scrip receipts* are found in the wallets that formerly contained mouldy bread and cheese.

Another writer observes, that in several cases where persons have been struck with lightning, it has been attracted by the *money in their pockets*. The Schedule of the Income Tax, he however supposes, would act as a very good *conductor* on such an occasion.

The following curious Address to the King of Candia is a genuine article of the Eastern hyperbole—

To the fortunate person endowed with all good qualities; possessed of firmness, like the Golden Mountain; adored by Mandalay swami (i. e. Rulers of Countries); taker of Tributes from the Foreign Powers; the most learned of the Magicians; Enjoyer of Pleasures like the Guardian Deities; studious of Mouna Montra (i. e. mental Contemplation of the Supreme Being); a Warrior surrounded with an Army of intoxicated Elephants; the most eminent of the Ruling Princes; a Deity crowned with a Royal Diadem, shadowed by an Umbrella resembling the full Moon; the lucky Prince of Lanka, sitting on a gemmed Throne, and wearing a shining Crown; a Descendant of the Solar Race, entitled Vootuma Paria Teroovausal.

Fatal Fondling with a Bull.—An Inquest was lately held at Mumble, on the body of Mr. John Hailes, farmer, who was killed by his bull. It appeared that the deceased was very fond of the bull, and highly valued him, had been feeding him in the fold-yard with some oats in the straw, out of his hand, and afterwards was scratching his head and talking to him, when the bull, who had before shewn symptoms of wildness, ran at him suddenly. He for some time sheltered himself behind a brick pillar; but being closely pursued, he endeavoured to get under a cart-dray, in doing which, the bull struck him so violently against the dray; as to occasioned his death. The bull was immediately driven to some distance, while the body was removed, but soon returned to the spot in pursuit of the unfortunate object. He was afterwards shot.

Surprising Adventure!—A few days ago, a very large Herring-Hog being

ing observed in Comber river, by James M'Dowall, of Castle-espie, blacksmith, he undressed, armed himself with a pitchfork, and went into the water to meet the fish returning down Channel, and closely pursuing a shoal of herrings, he, in the midst of them, drove the fork into its head. Not being able to bring it on shore, the force of the animal, and the swell of the water, having lifted him from the bottom, he was obliged to swim along side to the opposite shore, still, however, holding by the fork. Nearly worn out with fatigue, he resolved on leaving it; but drawing the fork out of the wound, it instantly turned round, open mouthed, when, in his own defence, he dashed the fork into it. The animal gave a tremendous roar, threw up the water, and tumbled over on its back: M'Dowall still holding by the fork, was tossed over also, and fell several yards distance. The fork broke in this attack; however, on examining, he found it was dying, and by means of the broken fork, he was enabled to force his hard-earned prize farther in shore, where the tide in a short time left it quite dry. It is in length thirteen feet and a half, in circumference nine, tail three feet broad, fin on the back twenty inches high, had five rows of large teeth; weighed nine cwt. and three quarters, and has produced twenty-nine gallons of pure oil.—*Belfast News Letter.*

The Biters Bit.—Some French papers say, that a farmer, near Lyons, proposing to attend a fair the next day, had selected thirty sheep for sale, which he put into a stable. — Towards the evening, which proved a very stormy one, a fellow knocked at the door, and entreated lodgings for himself and his humble companion, a *bear*, with which he was also going to the fair. The farmer had compassion on him. But as there was no place in which *Bruin* could be well secured, he turned the sheep out, placed the shaggy gentleman in their stead, and took the *bear-leader* into his house. During the night, the family was alarmed by most horrid groans. Two of the *neighbours* had broken into the stable, with intent to steal the sheep!— *Bruin* had dispatched one of them. His master arrived in time to save the life of the other thief,—and the honest farmer, by this exercise of hospitality—*saved his sheep.*

A London paper, jesting, describes a new Fashionable Club at the West end of the town, to be composed of Irish Noblemen and Gentlemen, members of the Legislature. After observing, that it is a measure taken in consequence of the *Union*, the writer says,— " Two *surgeons* in ordinary, a *gunmaker*, and a *sword-cutler*, are to be placed on the establishment; *pistols*, *powder*, and *ball*, will be kept in the house, ready at all times; and a part of Hurlington Gardens is to be inclosed, as a *field of honour*; where disputes may be quickly settled, that no malice may exist for a minute in the club."— Some years ago a burlesque advertisement appeared in a Dublin paper, describing a club in that city, (celebrated for the *duels* it occasioned) of which the accommodations seemed to be still more *complete*;— for the gentlemen were informed that an assortment of *coffins* and *shrouds* were constantly on hand, and there was an *undertaker* at the next door.

Another account says, since a Club of these Gentlemen has been formed in London, the first thing called for by the Chairman, is for the waiter to bring in a plate of powder and ball, to lie upon the table in readiness to accommodate disputes.

A curious and splendid Toy has been presented by the Grand Choulaa

Choules to the Portuguese Governor at Macao, as a token of friendship on his preferment to the high station of Prime Minister of China. It consists of a snuff-box of gold, set with pearls and diamonds, worth 1000l. It has the most curious mechanism concealed within, by means of which, on touching a little spring, a lid, or little trap-door opens, a bird jumps up, moves his bill, and flutters his wings, and after having sung his little song, returns himself to his hole, and draws the trap down after him.

The *Property Man* belonging to one of the *Winter Theatres*, has lately dispatched to a Provincial Manager the following *Cargo of Stage Effect*—

"6 Bottles and a half of Lightning—14 Black Wigs, 7 pair of Whiskers, and a quantity of Cork to burn—A large quantity of Quills and Peas for Showers of Rain.—A barrel of the very best Thunder—47 Tooth-Brushes for the Ladies, very little used—The Dress of a *Spectre*, consisting of a White Dress, discoloured with Blood, and a quantity of Chalk.—N. B. The Dress wants Washing.—36 Daggers, that only want sharpening."

A quantity of *Brimstone* was likewise sent, but returned by the Manager, there being a sufficiency of that commodity in the country.

A noble Lord is said to have appeared at Blandford Races with no less than nine different equipages upon the course. What a pity he could not ride in them all! The hospitable nobility of earlier reigns displayed their magnificence in the number of their tenants and retainers. In earlier times, when a Lord was *at home*, the country round him perceived his presence. His neighbours, his tenants, were welcome and entertained, and the poor were fed from his table. In this *enlightened age*, when *a Lady is at home*, a couple of hundred flirts of fashion, whose faces are scarce known to her, are crammed with all the luxuries of the season. The expence, the distinction is the same. Both have displayed their wealth and magnificence.—The difference is, that formerly they did good with it;—one fed a province for a month; the other spends in a night what would feed it. This keeps nine carriages, that keep as many parishes.—The first contributes by his vices to the revenue; the other upheld the manners and the political system of the country by his virtues.

There is, in the Burgh of Kirkby-Kendal, a ludi magister, or pedagogue, *familiarly* called a bum-brusher, doup skelper, or schoolmaster—

Who, in his noisy Mansion skill'd to rule,
oft boasts of his never changing his *taylor*, his *barber*, nor his *shoemaker*.

—For five-and-twenty years, his galligaskins have been made by the same needle-jerker, his chin scraped by the same beard-cutter, and his brogues fashioned by the same leather-slasher! A *cobler*, who had just begun business, offered to do his work at half-price—but *Holofernes* is a man of his *word*, and of course refused him.

The following is a correct copy of a curious sign-board, which was placed over a door in a certain street in the city. We give it to our readers as a specimen of *eccentricity*—

"Maugling done here every day in the week, except Sundays, Mondays, Wednesdays, and Fridays."

A country Magistrate, who had a culprit brought before him for robbing an orchard, was at a loss what punishment to inflict upon him, and said to his servant, (whose name was John) "Take down *Burn*."—"Yes, Sir," replied John, when his Master desired him to look for *Orchard*.

The following curious circumstance may be relied on as a fact:—A short time since several gentlemen being on a visit to a friend in Essex, one of them wishing to take a little diversion in fly-fishing, procured a guide to point out a part of the river, where he might expect to find some sport. The man conducted the gentleman to a spot where there were good fish: the rod and line of course were prepared; but when about to cast the fly, the gentleman found the hook (as he thought) had caught the bushes, and was giving the second pull to extricate it, when the man, who stood behind, bawled aloud—"the hook has caught my nose!" The gentleman perceiving this, endeavoured all in his power to relieve him, but without effect, and the poor fellow was under the necessity of walking five miles with the hook in his nose to a surgeon, where the hook and his nose were separated, to the great joy of the much-alarmed sufferer!

A man named George Simmons, a shoemaker in the neighbourhood of East-Smithfield, for the trifling wager of two quarts of beer, undertook to cleanse a grocer's shop of the flies. He was accordingly attended by a numerous train of taylors, hackney-coachmen, &c. from the public-house, to a grocer's on Tower-hill, and making the shopman acquainted with the bet, he obtained three pieces of paper, spread with treacle: one he placed on his head, and one on each hand; then walking to and through the shop, he contrived a humming sound like that of a large fly, and in the space of three minutes, the man's head was entirely enveloped in a cloud of flies. In this manner he walked as far as the Tower stairs, where he lodged his airy companions in the bar of a small gin-shop, to the no little astonishment of a great concourse of people.

A flight of strange Storks of enormous size lately made its appearance near Cardillac, in France, one of which was taken in the following manner:—The stork alighted near a village by the side of a boy, where it seemed to be watching for some prey. A young peasant beheld it with astonishment, drew near, examined, drew back, advanced a little closer, and then hesitated again. The bird, oppressed no doubt with heat and fatigue, stretched itself, and spread its wings, when this young observer at once lost all temper: he takes to his heels, makes the sign of the cross, starts at every noise, and looks about at every step to see if he is about to be devoured. His comrades meet him, ridicule his fears, and with much entreaty prevail on him to go back: they fire at the bird, wound it slightly, seize on him with caution and trembling, and soon obtained the victory. The conquerors then bore off their prisoner in triumph, fed it, healed its wound, and since feast most luxuriously on the numerous eggs it lays.

Thick Skulls and thin Skulls.—Dr. Crichton, in his enquiry into the cause of Mental Derangement, has the following striking passage:—" It is very remarkable," says the Doctor, " that a great majority of the skulls of such patients are very *thick*, or very *thin*. Among 216, whose heads were opened, 167 were thick, and 36 only thin, one of which was thick on the right side, and thin on the left. Among 100 raving mad, 78 were thick, and 20 quite thin, *one* of which was quite *soft*. Among 26 epileptic persons, who were raving, there were 19 thick, and four thin. Among 46 idiots, and 20 epileptics, there were 38 thick, six thin; and

and one *thick*, *thin*, and a part *soft*. Among 24 melancholy patients, 18 had very thin skulls."—It may therefore be fairly inferred, that all wars, bloodshed, and devastation, derive their origin from thick, thin, and soft skulls.

In the Masquerade at Margate, on the 21st of August, the first characters that entered the lists, were a *Cobler* and a *Ballad-singer*, a happy pair, of considerable professional talents: the former, however, waxed warm in the work, and his *home-spun* wit being soon brought to an *end*, took to his *pumps*, and ran away. The *Ballad-singer* proved more constant; and though not possessed of all the melody of the nightingale, shewed more versatility by giving a Cranburn-alley duet, in the best style of the best originals. Two clowns had been for some time annoying the company by their bluntness and vulgarity. Even *Bears* from the Alley, of whom there were several present, denied their kindred and acquaintance, and a *Pantaloon* at length turned them out, to the great joy of the whole society. At this moment, a shriek was heard from a remote part of the scene: on enquiry, it was found to issue from an *East-India Nabob*, terrified out of his senses at the appearance of *Tippoo Sultaun*. An *Old Tar*, alarmed for the *Nabob's* safety, undertook to undeceive him, and immediately put a variety of interrogatories to the Prince of Mysore. From this it appeared, that the Black Hero knew no more of Seringapatam, than Sir Richard Glynn's lamplighter, who represented that city, on the front of the Mansion-house, as taken by the English navy. From the acuteness of the examination, some supposed that Mr. Garrow had come down from the Cliff to personate the old tar, but on enquiry, we found there was no ground for that opinion. The Hon Mr. W. at first occasioned some confusion, being supposed from his dress to be a *Sans-Culotte* just arrived from France. The *Bulls* and *Bears* pressed round, to know whether the signing of the preliminaries was yet officially announced in *The Moniteur*. The Ladies wished to be informed, what were the *vast designs* which Bonaparte had just conceived; and *Justice Midas* went to a corner to make out his *mittimus*, when it was at last discovered, that the stranger was only a poor *Highlander*.—Among the other characters most deserving of notice, from the spirit with which they were supported, were an old *Admiral*, a *Poet*, a *Country Bumpkin*, *Dicky Gossip*, a *Match Girl*, &c.

At another Masquerade on the night of the 27th, the most prominent, and by far the best supported character, was that of an *Irishman* by Mr. L——d: although he swore he had just come over the *Herring Pond*, to look what sort of a *Husband* they had got for his own dear *Mother (Ireland)* in the green gown, and whether he had ever seen such a fruit as a *potatoe*, yet he seemed to know every body, and have something appropriate to say to each person in the room.

Next in point of excellence, was a *Jerry Sneak*. A Pill and Potion Monger, not far from Middlesex hospital: thinking himself completely concealed by an old coat, and an ugly mask, attempted to be witty, but his jokes smelt so strong of *his shop*, that he soon exposed himself.

The *female characters* were few in number: two tolerable *Gypsies* attracted some attention.

INSTRUCTIONS

INSTRUCTIONS IN THE MANNER OF DEAN SWIFT,

For Gentlemen of moderate Fortune, Half-Fashion Gentlemen, &c.

AS the Winter is now approaching, and the Court and people of the *Haut Ton* are about to return to town, it becomes necessary for you also to think of a removal from your *Summer Campaigns, Watering Excursions,* and *Shooting Parties;* and, indeed, like the tail of a Comet, you ought ever to be found in the train of your superiors. Let not the *lowring prospects* and *melancholy situation* of your affairs, discourage your revisiting the *gallant, gay* Metropolis of our *renowned Isle;* the place is large and wide, and affords many a hiding-place to the *moneyless wight.* It is infinitely better adapted for persons of your description, than your small towns and villages, where the prying eye of vulgar curiosity spies out the least circumstance that concerns you: you may dine in one Eating-house to-day, and another to-morrow, and so on, for a mere trifle, the whole Winter round; but be sure never to go twice to the same place, *as you might be known, or your taylor or boot-maker might dog you*—which your own prudence will point out to you, might be attended with *inconvenience.*

When you meet with any of your more wealthy acquaintance, you may pretend you have an engagement to dine out with Lord B——, Colonel C——, Captain G——, &c. and who on no account would admit of an apology for your absence: Thus he will look on you as a great man, having a large circle of acquaintance, and by this means you will get rid of his solicitation to dine with him at *Ibbotson's, Stevens's, British, George's,* Richardson's, Maurice's, Spring-Gardens, &c. where, you know, every one (according to the custom of this country) pays for himself.

Should you go to the play *on an order* from any of the performers, be sure to *look sharp* out for a box where *some Dowager* is alone, or at least where there are no *blands of fashion;* you may introduce yourself to the Lady in the usual manner, *by treading on her train* when she attempts to stand up. This will make an opening for you to beg *at least ten thousand* pardons. You may then proceed to make observations on the performance and performers:—" How you saw that piece much better acted at Bath, &c." You may also observe to the Lady, that if you are not much mistaken, you met with her a few nights since at the Opera, or that you met with her at *Cheltenham, Weymouth, Brighton,* or any other fashionable Summer retreat; but do not attempt to mention *Margate,* as that place is quite vulgar, and only frequented by *Cits, Jews,* and *the natives* East of Temple-Bar.

You may affect to be half-seas over also; but you may soften it down by one of your *neat, studied apologies,* that you dined with a party of intimate friends, who never stop short of *three bottles;* and, provided you do not *carry the joke ion far,* the Ladies are not displeased at seeing the Gentlemen *hearty,* well knowing that if they sacrifice copiously to *Bacchus* in full libations, they will not forget their *humble devotions at the shrine* of Venus.

Between the acts, and between the play and the farce, you may entertain the Lady or Ladies with the relation of your Military Adventures. How you were at the taking of the *Helder* with His Royal Highness; that you were one

one of the advanced Guard that entered *Alkmaer*; and, as there will be little danger of your being found out, you may say that Captain D—— was shot dead at your side; that the colours were shot away, and dashed in your face; and that *the blaze* from the mouth of one of the enemy's cannon, at the storming of one of their batteries, burnt off *both your whiskers!* This will give the Ladies a high idea of your courage, and, like a *second Othello*, you may win her heart with *a relation of your adventures.*

Should one, or any of these females be a *kept mistress*, a connection with her may not be amiss, as her keeper being *past active service*, you may have a chance of becoming *the favourite*, and entering into *present pay, and free quarters*, which, lo! one is *your situation*, would be no bad speculation.

You may now and again—*if you can raise the wind*—sport a *hired curricle* and pair. This will raise you very high in the opinion of the Fair Sex; and many an adventurer *has succeeded* in this way.

Whenever you hire horses, let them be the best hacks you can find; it will be only a few shillings more; and you may take *the worth of your money* out of them, by riding all day *slap dash* through the most public streets. This day's ride will serve you for a month; and as spurs cost nothing for keep, you may appear every day in *a formidable pair of Smorrow's*; and should your boots not keep the appearance of riding a great deal, you may *scratch* them with a two-penny file kept *on purpose.* One thing be very particular in, never to give your address where you lodge, as your *private situation* might not correspond with your *public pretensions.*

You may fix on some fashionable coffee-house, and give the waiter half-a-crown now and again to take your letters, and to say (should any enquiry be made) that you are one of the most *dashing fellows* in town; by this means you will also avoid being found out by your cards, as in such case your tradesmen might be inclined to pay you some *unpleasant* morning visits — Notwithstanding all this precaution, you may be *touched* on the shoulder, and be presented with a *scrap of dirty paper*, but you must run all chances, and you know he is a good General who is *never defeated*; so never be discouraged for what may follow; a man may as well die in prison as in his bed; it will be just the same in 100 years: besides, by shewing *a little spirit*, you may make your fortune for life.

If at any time you should dine at a Coffee-house, be sure you take on you all the airs of a man of fashion; but above all, *find fault* with every thing that is brought before you; down the waiter in *a military style*, find fault with every thing, and swear in a commanding military *demi-use*, that were it not out of respect to the company, you would fling every thing on the table at his head. Though you can scarcely judge between good wine and *syllabub*, assert in the most *knowing manner*, that you never tasted worse in your life, and jocosely observe to the waiter, that you think his master has his wine from the house of *Alder, Sler, and Co.* you will thus raise a laugh at the expence of the waiter and his master, and come off as a man of wit and humour.

After spending the evening until late with your friends, if any of them should request to see you home, assure them that you have an engagement with a Married Lady *of great consequence*, whose character you could not think *of exposing*, or that you mean to take part of a bed with the *cara sposa* of some Noble Duke, whose *variety of amours* calls him *on duty* in another quarter; thus you will get rid of your troublesome companions, and pass for a man of great gallantry.--Should the town at last become *too hot* for you, and you should be obliged to quit it at a *short notice*, you may *take French leave*—be off like a shot—get into some of the large country towns—advertise for board and lodging in some genteel family *where no other lodgers* are admitted; the chance in this case is in your favour, as you may either *gull* your landlord, or some of his richer neighbours, and obtain in the country what all your address could not procure for you in town.

CRUELTY AND AVARICE OUTWITTED.

THE following extraordinary fact has been communicated to us from undoubted authority:— A poor labourer, with a large family, who worked for a farmer not 100 miles from Bridgnorth, during the present extravagant price of all the necessaries of life, applied to his master, entreating him to let him have the amount of his week's wages in corn or flour. Having been employed by this man between 20 and 30 years, he hoped he would give it him under the market price. The farmer, ashamed to demand that price from the labourer, and yet not inclined to let him have it for less, refused the request. Upon the poor man's complaining of the distress of his family, who were starving, the master wantonly told him that if he could not *buy*, there was nothing left for him but to *steal*. The poor fellow, irritated by the inhumanity of his employer, and driven to despair by the miserable situation of his wife and children, literally followed the advice given him, and at different times purloined to the amount of two bushels of corn from his master's barn. The thief was advertised, with a reward of five guineas for the discovery. Alarmed at this step, the man went voluntarily to a neighbouring Magistrate, and confessed the fact, relating all the circumstances attending it. The farmer was sent for, and informed that the Magistrate had received certain information of the offender; but that he must deposit the five guineas reward, which he had offered, before he should be put in possession of the particulars. This condition being complied with, the Magistrate acquainted him with the name of the party, who, he told him, had only followed the advice given by his hard-hearted employer, and that if he chose to prosecute him, the whole of the case must of course be laid before a Court of Justice.—The farmer not chusing this public exposure, declined a prosecution, and the worthy Magistrate, after seriously admonishing the labourer, who had always borne an irreproachable character, and who had been driven by cruel distress, and the inhumanity of his master, to commit this unjustifiable depredation, ordered the amount of the reward to be laid out in food and clothing for his half naked and half-starved children.—*(Salopian Journal)*.

Note by the Editor.—This story might be deemed incredible, if it was not corroborated by other melancholy instances of excess to which great numbers of the poor have been driven by the wanton and infamous rise of every necessary of life.—One poor woman, as a kind of public testimony, rushes out

out of her lodgings in Holborn, and cuts her throat, declaring she had three children, whom, not being able to maintain, she could not bear to see starve.

Another wretched female, near Cambridge, (and we know it to be true) within a very few days past, first hung her two infants, and then herself, being put off in her application to an overseer of the parish for relief.—These, it may be objected, by some cold-blooded calculators, are only *individual instances*; but as Mr. Durant expressed it in the Common Hall on Friday, the 3d instant—" Hundreds and thousands of people may now be seen starving in Spitalfields." Let then, all the opulent dealers in provision, who are the causes of this crying calamity, especially those whose pretended religion makes it an enormous sin to *pay tithes to the establishment*. Let them, we repeat it, read these relations and tremble. Equally the enemies of God and man.—Such, though their external conversation may be *yea, yea, and nay, nay, are only whitened Sepulchres full of dead mens bones and rottenness; ravening wolves in sheep's cloathing, who devour widows houses.*

SPORTIVE MORALITIES.

THE following history of Thomas Palmer, who lately died in America, and who was an active naval officer during the late war, is extracted from his log-book—

" First part of the voyage * pleasant, with fine breezes and fair winds—all sail set. Spoke many vessels in want of provisions—supplied them freely.

" Middle passage.—Weather variable — short of provisions—spoke several of the above vessels our supplies had enabled to refit—made signals of distress—they up helm, and bore away. †

" Latter part.—Boisterous, with contrary winds—current of adversity setting hard to leeward—towards the end of the passage it cleared up—with the quadrant of honesty had an observation; corrected and made up my reckoning; and, after a passage of 50 years, came to in Mortality Road, with the calm, unruffled surface of the Ocean of Eternity in view."

German Epitaph on a Postmaster.—Traveller! hurry not as if you were going post-haste;—in the most rapid journey you must stop at the Post house. ¶ Here repose the bones of M. Mathias Schulzen, the most humble and most faithful Postmaster of his Majesty the King of Prussia, at Salzwedal, during the space of twenty-five years. He arrived 1655; by holy baptism, he was marked on the post-map for the celestial land of Canaan.—He afterwards travelled with distinction in life's pilgrimage, by making courses in the schools and universities. He carefully performed his duties as a Christian, in his employment, and the purposes annexed to it. When the post of misfortune was come, he behaved according to the letter of divine consolation. In the end, his body being enfeebled, he kept himself ready to attend the signal given by the arrival of the post of death.—His soul set off on her journey the 2d of June, 1711, for Paradise; and his body was afterwards committed to this tomb. . . . Reader! in thy pilgrimage, always be mindful of Death.

* Alluding to the early part of his life.

† Those whom he had formerly befriended, now, in his distress, refuse him assistance.

CRICKET MATCHES.

On Monday, August 11, and following day, a Grand Match of Cricket was played, in Lord's Ground, at Mary-le-bone, between Twelve Gentlemen of England, against Nineteen Gentlemen of Kent, for One Thousand Guineas.

KENT.

FIRST INNINGS.		SECOND INNINGS.	
Hooker b. Lord Fred. B.	3	c. Hammond	2
Goddard c. Robertson	1	c. Ray	7
Crawte b. T. Walker	7	c. Fenex	3
Horne c. Ray	10	b. Wells	6
Smith c. Hammond	9	stumpt Hammond	4
Read c. J. Wells	6	c. Lord Fred. B.	0
Bennet c. Small	1	c. T. Walker	0
Goodhew c. Ditto	0	c. Ray	10
Crowhurst c. Lord Fred. B.	0	b. Wells	12
Ward b. Wells	0	c. Beldam	2
Dorrington c. T. Walker	0	b. T. Walker	1
Larken c. Beldam	10	run out	5
Hulks c. Ditto	0	run out	0
Best c. Fennex	0	b. Wells	3
Bassett c. Ray	17	b. Lord Fred. B.	12
Boxall b. Wells	4	c. Fennex	2
Longhurst b. T. Walker	4	run out	1
Coulter c. Robertson	4	stumpt Hammond	0
Taylor not out	4	not out	3
Byes	0	Byes	0
	82		75

ENGLAND.

FIRST INNINGS.		SECOND INNINGS.	
T. Walker c. Goodhew	12		
Freemantle leg before wicket	35		
Beldam b. Ward	17		
Lord Fred. B. b. Read	20	c. Coulter	2
R. Whitehead, Esq. b. Boxall	9	b. Boxall	10
Hammond b. Ditto	2		
T. Walker c. Ditto	5		
Robertson b. Ditto	9	not out	17
Wells b. Ward	0		
Small c. R	6		
Ray not out	0	not out	7
Fennex c. Bennet	1		
Byes	6	Byes	0
	122		36
			On

Cricket Match—in Marshe's New Ground, Rochester.

On Monday, August 18, and three following days, a Grand Match was played, on Marshe's New Ground, Rochester, between Twelve Gentlemen of England, against Nineteen Gentlemen of Kent, for One Thousand Guineas.

ENGLAND.

FIRST INNINGS.		SECOND INNINGS.	
T. Walker b. Read	0	c. Pryer	19
H. Walker stumpt Ward	4	b. Read	3
Beldam c. Bennet	6	b. Taylor	8
Hammond c. Larken	8	c. Read	21
Lord Fred. B. b. Boxall	0	b. Taylor	14
Robinson b Ditto	2	c. Ditto	29
Wells c. Read	17	c. Hoxall	5
Small c. Ward	1	b. Read	1
Freemantle b. Read	3	b. Taylor	0
Whitehead, Esq. b Ditto	9	not out	6
Fennex b. Boxall	9	c. Basset	14
Ray not out	0	b. Ward	12
Byes	5	Byes	
	58		130

KENT.

FIRST INNINGS.		SECOND INNINGS.	
Read b. Wells	9	c. Lord Fred. B.	0
Smith c. H Walker	0	b Fennex	15
Horne run out	2	c. Ray	0
Bennet c. Lord Fred. B.	7	c. Beldam	11
Larken hit wicket	0	not out	0
Hooker stumpt Hammond	0	b. Wells	8
Crawte c. Wells	12	stumpt Hammond	1
Hulks c. Lord Fred. B.	21	b. Wells	0
Coulter c. H. Walker	2	run out	7
Goddard c. Wells	18	c. H. Walker	2
Taylor leg before wicket	4	b. Fennex	0
Basset b. Fennex	16	not out	8
Ward run out	2	b. Lord Fred. B.	2
Goodhew b. Beldam	17	b. Wells	0
Crowhurst c. H. Walker	6	b. Fennex	5
Selby b. T. Walker	6	c. Robinson	0
Pryer b. Hammond	1	run out	1
Dorrington not out	9	b. Fennex	3
Boxall b. Hammond	0	c. Hammond	0
Byes	0	Byes	14
	132		77

Cricket Match—in Lord's Ground, Mary-le-Bone.

On Thursday, August 28, and the two following days, was played a Grand Match of Cricket, in Lord's Ground, Mary-le-bone, between Twelve Gentlemen of Surrey, against Fourteen Gentlemen of England, for One Thousand Guineas.

ENGLAND.

	FIRST INNINGS.		SECOND INNINGS.
Crawte	3 run out		
Small	5 c. Waller		
Freemantle	28 c. H. Walker	0	b. Wells.
Ld. F. B.	10 c ditto	20	c. Wells.
Ward	9 b. Wells		
Fennex	1 b. ditto		
Hammond	52 c. Robinson		
Barton	22 b. Wells	18	b. Wells.
Ray	12 b T. Walker		
J. Weller, Esq.	0 c. Waller		
Bennet	1 c. Wells		
Ayling	7 run out	0	not out.
Reade	6 c. Chetty	3	run out.
Boxall	0 not out		
Byes	1	Byes	1
Total	157	Total	42

SURREY.

	FIRST INNINGS.		SECOND INNINGS.
J. Walker	0 b. Ward	8	c. Reade.
G. Beldam	7 c. Small	0	c. Ld F. B.
T. Walker	2 b. Boxall	26	b. Reade.
Robinson	22 c. Hammond	28	run out.
W. Beldam	1 b. Boxhall	5	b. Ward.
Wells	0 b. Ward	4	b. Boxall.
H. Walker	4 run out	13	b. Ld F. B.
Hampton	5 stumpt Hammond	0	run out.
Lord	7 c. Ayling	0	stumpt Hammond.
Hon. H. Tufton	0 b. Ld. F. B.	0	b. Fennex.
Waller	6 not out	5	c. J. Weller, Esq.
Chetty	0 b. Ld. F. B.	0	not out.
Byes	1	Byes	2
Total	55	Total	93

England won by 9 wickets, and 51 runs.—5 to 4 on Surrey at starting.

Cricket Match—on Lexon Heath.

On Saturday, August 30, was played a grand match of Cricket, on Lexon Heath, between nine of the Herts Militia, with the Hon. General Lenox, and Lieutenant Mathews, of the Royal Artillery, against eleven of the town of Colchester, for 1000 guineas.

COLCHESTER.

FIRST INNINGS.			SECOND INNINGS.	
Kempster	-	9 b. Porter	6 c. Hoggins.
Burres	-	4 c. Hoggins	0 b. ditto.
Bloomfield	-	2 c. ditto	12 c. Dowrer
T. Pasford	-	2 run out	1 run out.
J. Pasford	-	5 Leg bef. wick.	7 c. Hoggins.
Hewett	-	1 b. Sibley	7 not out
King	-	2 c. Porter	0 c. Rist.
Cooper	-	1 b. ditto	2 c. Sibley.
Simmons	-	1 c. Hoggins	4 c. Lawrance.
Myrks	-	0 b. Porter	0 b. Hoggins.
Rogers	-	0 Not out	1 b. Sibley.
	Byes	2	Byes	6
	Total	29	Total	46

HERTS.

FIRST INNINGS.		
Lieut. Osman		6 b. J. Pasford
Porter	-	17 b. ditto
G. Sibley	-	34 c. Hewett
H. Gen. Lenox		45 not out
Hoggins	-	0 b. Pasford
Lieut. Mathews		1 c. Bloomfield
Lawrance	,	7 c. Myrks
Law	-	1 c. Bloomfield
Hibbett	-	6 b. J. Pasford
Nichols	,	0 b. ditto
Rist	-	0 b. ditto
	Byes	10
	Total	127

Hon. General Lenox won by 1 inns and 51 runs.—Five to 4 on Colchester at starting.

MASONIC

MASONIC MUMMERY.

Without meaning any offence to any good Mason, and under the idea of exhibiting an account of all fashionable diversions, we give the following, partly for a warning, and partly for the amusement of our readers. It is rather unfortunate for those who ridicule Professor Robinson, and others, for what has been said of the Infidel Societies, that here is a new case in point, either contemptibly weak, or desperately wicked; because, to prepare or harden the minds of the Members for some purposes not in the common course of life, religious objects have been burlesqued, and sacred authorities degraded, either for mere amusement, or worse purposes.

TRIAL FOR SEDITION AT AYR CIRCUIT COURT.

Wednesday, September 17.

THIS day came on the trial of John Andrew, shoemaker, in Maybole, some time teacher of a private school there; and Robert Ramsay, cartwright there.

The libel charges them as being guilty of the crime of sedition, and administering unlawful oaths, importing an obligation not to discover crimes, which it is the duty of every good citizen and loyal subject to divulge and bring to light, in so far as they did, under the shew and pretence of a meeting for masonry, some time in the year 1796, at Maybole, along with others, their associates, most of them from Ireland, form themselves into an illegal club or association, stiling itself, "*The Grand Assembly of Knights' Templars;*" which club, under the pretence of initiating into the ceremonies of masonry, did admit various persons as members; and did at said admission perform various ceremonies, partly with a view to vilify and undermine the established religion, and partly to represent the Government of the country as oppressive and tyrannical; and did, with this view, oblige those who were admitted, to take, and did administer to them, an oath, binding them, among other things, "*to conceal the secrets of the Order of Knights Templars, murder and treason not excepted,*" or an oath of such import and tendency; and, more particularly, charges them with administering, or causing to be administered, such oath on certain occasions libelled in the year 1796.

Mr. Clerk, Counsel for the pannels, made no objection to the relevancy of the indictment; upon which the Court pronounced the usual interlocutor, and the Jury were named and sworn in.

Evidence for the Prosecution.

Quintin M'Adam, Esq. of Waterside, said, he was Master of a Lodge of Free Masons, at Maybole, of which the pannels were members, but separated themselves from it.

He was shewn the following papers; one entitled—*Regulations of the Grand Assembly of Knights Templars, held at Maybole,* and a printed copy of *Paine's Age of Reason,* having the name of John Andrew printed on it. The above papers being libelled on, were identified by this witness.

Wm. Hamilton, Mason in Maybole, said, he was a member of a lodge at Maybole, Royal Arch, No 264. When he was admitted a member, a pistol was fired, and some person called out, *put him to death.* He was blindfolded at first when brought into the room, and the covering being afterwards taken from his eyes, he was shewn a stone jug in the corner of the room, and a bush in the jug, and a candle burning in it. He was told by the

the pannel Andrew, that it was the representation of God Almighty in the midst of the burning bush.—Andrew was master of the lodge, and was reading the 3d chapter of Exodus. The witness was desired to *put off his shoes, as it was holy ground he stood on*; the covering was put down again on the witness's face, and he was led under an arch, and, after passing under the arch, he was desired to find the book of the law; it was taken up by some other person in the lodge, who was called *High Priest*, and who said, he would explain it. The witness was desired to put money on the book to pay for explaining it to him; the book, he was told, was the Bible. The witness put money on the book as desired, and John Andrew made observations on the chapter as he read it, but the witness does not positively remember any of them. Recollects that part of the chapter where the children of Israel are said to be in bondage.

The passport for a Royal Arch Mason was, *I am that I am*.

After the above ceremonies, the witness being taken out of the room, had his coat taken off, and tied on his shoulders in a bundle, and was then brought in; a carpet with a rent in it was called the *veil of the Temple*. He was led through it, and round the room. A sword was put into his hand, and he was ordered to use it against all who opposed him as a Knight Templar. John Andrew read the 4th chapter of Exodus; the witness was desired to throw down the sword, and was told it was become a *serpent*; after which he was desired to take it up again, and told it was again a *rod*. Andrew poured ale and porter on the floor, and called it *blood*. He was shewn *thirteen burning candles*, one in the middle he was told represented *Jesus Christ*, the other the *Twelve Apostles*. Andrew blew out one of the candles, which he called *Judas, who betrayed his Master*; one of them was dim, and was called *Peter, who denied his Master*. Something on a table, under a white cloth, being uncovered, was perceived to be a *human skull*, which the witness was desired to take up, and view it, and was told, it was a real skull of a brother, called Simon Magus. Porter was poured into the skull, which the witness was desired to drink; he did so, and it was handed round to the whole Knights. Andrew put the point of the sword into it, and then touched the witness's head with it, saying—*I dub thee in the name of the Father, Son, and Holy Ghost.*

He took an oath to "*keep the secrets of the Knights Templars, murder and treason not excepted;*" the penalty for revealing was, that *his body would be rented up like a fir deal*.

John Andrew was master at this admission, and at two others where the witness was present.

The witness's impression was, that the ceremonies used were a scoffing at religion; and, though he cannot say positively, he thought they had a tendency to overturn the Government.

Quintin Stewart, tailor in Maybole, said, he went through some parts of masonry with John Andrew, when he had no charter. He was prepared to be a Royal Arch Mason, and taken to the door, where a man in the inside called out, *Put him to death*, and a pistol was fired; he was blindfolded and brought into the room, and the covering removed, that he might *see the great sight, the Lord in a flame of fire in the bush, and it not consumed*; this was read by Andrew. He was commanded to *put off his shoes, as the place was holy ground*. He saw a thorn bush in a corner a corner of the room, and a candle in the heart of it burning. Andrew said, *Go and deliver the children of Israel from their bondage and the burthen of their task-masters.* He was taken round their royal encampment in the middle of the room, and was then put into what they called a *dark vault*, in search of the book of the law, and a book was thrown down on the floor, and afterwards put into his hand; he was asked to explain it. The High Priest came and said he could do it, upon being paid for it. The High Priest had a carpet round him; his name was William Moor, an Irishman; witness gave money, and the High Priest explained the law. Thirteen candles were burning on a table; they were called *our Saviour and his twelve Apostles.*

Witness was taken out of the room to be prepared to be a *Knight Templar.* His coat was tied in a bundle on his back, and a staff put in his hand, to travel through the *sandy deserts.* He passed through the *first and second veils of the Temple.* He was ordered to cast his staff on the ground, so as it might become a *serpent, &c.* He was taken round their royal assembly two or three times; then to a table where something was lying covered; he was ordered to uncover it, and he found it to be a human skull, which he was told was the head of a brother, who once tasted, heard, and smelled, as we do now. Andrew poured porter into it, and gave it to the witness to drink; he drank a little of it, as did the rest. Andrew took a sword, and put the point of it into the porter, and touched the witness's head with it, and said, *I dub you, I dub you, I dub you.*

The witness was shewn thirteen small wands, or rods, in a jug, which they called again *our Saviour and his Twelve Apostles.* Andrew, the master of the lodge, commented a little on

them, and then took the witness's obligation to keep his secrecy. The words of the oath were *to keep the secrets of a Knight Templar, murder and high treason not excepted.* To the best of the witness's knowledge, these were the words.

Evidence in Exculpation.

John M'Clure, jun. in Kirklandhill, denied most of the circumstances urged by these witnesses.

John M'Clure, schoolmaster at Craigencroy said, murder and treason were excepted in his oath.

Several persons gave Andrew and Ramsay good characters.

Mr. Clerk, Counsel for the pannels, replied, and said, the facts charged are not in the nature of *malum in re.*

Lord Justice Clerk summed up the whole evidence with great perspicuity and candour. His Lordship observed, that he could have wished that this prosecution had been brought sooner; but this could not be imputed to the prosecutor, for it did not appear that he had delayed bringing his action after he got the information. Though this species of crime may not have occurred in our law before, still the law may be applied to remedy it when it does occur. The special law enacted in regard to it does not infringe on the law as it stood before. The oath is not innocent, even as limited by the witnesses for the pannels; and though there is no proof that the pannels had entered into a design of leading the persons they admitted into their society to seditious practices, yet the oath may be employed for that purpose. His Lordship said, he could not believe that any such ceremonies were employed in other Mason Lodges, because they are so abominable and impious; it rather appeared that this was a new oath introduced by the pannels, and not in use before in admitting Masons.—Verdict, *Not Guilty.*

SPORTING

SPORTING INTELLIGENCE.

THE bet of one hundred guineas, which was to have been decided on the 10th inst. upon the Bath road, has terminated without a trial. A Gentleman of fortune betted a post-master the above sum, that he rode his blood horse fifty miles (twenty-five out, and twenty-five in) in less time than his opponent should go the same ground with a post-chaise and four, changing horses and chaise as often as he pleased, both in *going* and *coming*. At the first blush of the business, the horse became the favourite; but when it was found the post-masters on the road individually partook of the bet, and entered more spiritedly into the *professional execution*, reducing it to *certainty* in three hours and twenty minutes, the owner of the horse paid forfeit.

A match between Sir H T. Vane's Cockfighter, and Mr. Wilson's Champion, has been settled to be run at Newmarket the next Spring Meeting for 2000 guineas. Cockfighter is the favourite, though, from the uncommon speed and bottom which Champion shewed at Epsom, when he won the Derby stakes, a very severe and well-contested race is expected.

Eight thousand guineas were lost at one match of Billiards this summer at Margate. The money has been paid, and the loser did not drown himself.

Fashionable *gambling* has also been very prevalent at *Brighton*! A young heir to a large north country property, being received into what is called *good company* only for one evening, found the demand upon him the next morning, for his supper and *desert* 2500 guineas!

Sir Wheeler Cuffe, after the Newmarket Meeting, rides his bay horse Old England, by Sir Peter, against Mr. Parkhurst, who also rides his Welter, by Jupiter, thirteen stone each.

The Batavian *Budget of taxes* announces a tax on pleasure-horses —*pleasure-horses* in Holland! and *Dutch jockies!* what an age of Revolutions!

Colonel Hanger's *retreat* from the *Racoon Porta*, (mentioned in our last Number, p. 259) is now spoken of by military men, as one of the best conducted manœuvres of the present day. We shall hear less of Moreau's skill in *retreats* after this!

It appears by some old charters, that the Citizens of London have a *right* to *hunt* or *shoot* within ten miles of the metropolis, without any licence.—No mention is made of their being *qualified!*

Mr. Heathcote's Warter, who is matched at Newmarket against Mr. Cookson's Diamond, in October, is to run the first Spring Meeting against Sir Harry Vane Tempest's Cockfighter. Warter is rather the favourite against Diamond; but the odds are against him with Cockfighter, who has beat at York several horses of acknowledged excellence.

In the successive variance of feminine amusements, *foot-ball* is fast going out, and *leap-frog* is now the full sport of the day: a famous match was played a short time since in Greenwich-park, by an *athletic* Duke, and three *elastic* women of fashion, to the astonishment of the veteran corps of *Pensioners*, who agree that a Whitsun roll down the hill, in point of *exhibition*, is nothing to be compared with it!

A more

Sporting Intelligence.

A mare belonging to Mr. Robson, of Little Britain, was matched last month to trot seventeen miles in fifty-six minutes, with Mr. Marsden, who betted Mr. Robson four hundred to one she did not do it, Mr. Marsden thinking it impossible any horse, mare, or gelding, could do it. She performed the match with great ease in three minutes and ten seconds within the time given. She also had an engagement with Mr. Dyson, of Park-lane, who betted Mr. Robson 2000 guineas to 100, she did not trot nineteen miles in one hour; but on her last performance, Mr. Dyson being called on to cover, chose to forfeit the money down, rather than make the stakes good. This mare is blind of one eye, 17 years of age, and was lately purchased for 10 guineas. She is again matched to trot 19 miles within the hour.

Archery.—The Quiver given by Lady Horton to the three Lancashire Societies, viz. the Lancashire Bowmen, Broughton Archers, and Middleton Archers, to be shot for six years, and on the seventh to be shot for by those gentlemen who had won it once, was finally contested on the 10th inst. in Sir Watts Horton's park, at Chaderton, by Thos. Palmer, Esq. Joseph Thackeray, Esq. and Samuel Hobson, Esq. the only archers entitled by the regulations to shoot for it (Mr. Thomas Marriot being out of England.) The prize was won by Mr. Thackeray, who had 267 cast—Mr Hobson, 268—and Mr. Palmer, 212.

A *Frenchman* gained his bet of fifty guineas, by eating last month 22 dozen, or 243 of the *largest oysters*—raw from the shell—which he swallowed *will in an hour*, together with two bottles of sherry, and 2lo. of white bread!!! This wonderful Frenchman may be seen at a certain great house in Piccadilly, and is since known by the name of the *Oyster Monster!!!*

A man, named John Taylor, a few mornings since, ran for the wager of a guinea, at Ewell, in Surrey, a mile in five minutes, which he easily performed: many bets were pending, though a Mr. Fitz and Lieut. Plum were the principal winners.

An odd coincidence occurs in a late Transfer of Property. A Mr. *Spererib* has sold his estate at *Ham*, to a Gentleman of the name of *Porker*, a relation of Mr. *Gammon*.

The French Papers state that the Prince of Bourbon Conti, sent out of France, lives happily near Barcelona. His pension is paid regularly, and he consoles himself for the loss of his dignities with a good table, a few capital horses, and the pleasures of the chase.

A very severe and scientific *set to* lately took place in the Broadway, near St. Clement's Church, between two of the *Fair Inhabitants* of the softer sex, who reside in the delightful retreats of *Lewkner's-lane.* After a contest of ten minutes, one of the amazons thought proper to give in, and the *conqueress* behaved so generously on the occasion, that she not only exchanged *fists* in token of amity, but treated in a very handsome libation of that *fashionable* liquor, called *flashes of lightning!*

Fatal Duel.—Abuse of the Point of Honour!—(from a Dublin paper of the 10th inst.) " Yesterday morning two of the *fair sex* in the occupation of carrying baskets, had a misunderstanding in Pill-lane, opposite the fish-market. Much time was not devoted to investigation or disquisition—they engaged in a twinkling, *beak* and *claws.* One of them bit a piece completely out of the cheek of her antagonist—while the other returned the compliment

pliment by tearing out an eye of her dressers.

Mr. Ward, Miller, of Uppingham, in Rutland, lately lost his life by fighting with a brother miller, servant to Mr. Sewell, of that place, whose mill is situate about an hundred yards from the deceased's.—We understand the combatants agreed to meet half way between the two mills to decide the quarrel; that they fought for above an hour, during which time they stopped several times to drink each other's health—set to again, till at length Ward was obliged to give it in, and died from the bruises he had received in the battle. His opponent lies dangerously ill.

Lately as the coach from London to Chester was leaving Littleworth, the driver was alarmed with the cry of fire from the inside, when he found that a loaded pistol, deposited in the pocket of the coach-door, had gone off, as is supposed, by the shutting of the door, shot a gentleman, who was a passenger, in the leg, with a brace of bullets, and set the garments of a lady on fire.

On Wednesday, September 24, the Kentish-town Association, commanded by the Honourable Captain Fitzsimon Frazer, had their last Field-day for this season; when they fired at a target for a subscription silver cup. The firing of the corps, in general, was remarked for extraordinary precision, and did credit to their discipline. The prize was adjudged to Mr. Cantel, jun. who put in two excellent shots out of three; one of which was in the centre of the bull's eye.

Edward Oates, under-gardener to the Archbishop of York, lately attempting to disturb and take a nest of young hawks, was so violently attacked by the dam and her mate, that he fell from the tree, and was killed upon the spot.

Eccles Wake.—This motley assemblage of noise and barbarism commenced on Monday Sept. 1: bull-baiting in all its purity—racing by quadrupeds and bipeds—four and two-legged brutes—asses in various shapes. A hand-bill, giving a list of these rational amusements, has been weekly circulated in Manchester: the bill closes with "God save the King, and long life to the Honourable Secretary at War!"

Lady Dinsdale has had a *Route*, which ended in the company receiving three black eyes, four cracked craniums, and two bloody noses!

A trotting-match by two ponies, for 100 guineas, was lately performed on the race course on Barham Downs, the property of Mr. Lee, of Temple-bar, London, and Mr. Quihampton, of Ashford. The match was made to trot six times round the course, which is twelve miles, and was performed in rather more than 49 minutes. At starting the odds were in favour of Mr. Lee's poney, who kept the lead till the third time of coming round, when getting into a gallop, he was obliged to return to the former ground where he first changed his pace, and after that period could not regain upon his adversary; the match was in consequence won by Mr. Quihampton, and the *knowing Gentlemen* greatly taken in.

Chatham, Oct. 6.—A few days past, some carpenters employed on board the Lazaretto, in Sandgate creek, went ashore to amuse themselves in shooting birds; not having any shot, they loaded their guns with pieces of old lead; in returning on board, the last man who had a piece in his hand not discharged, in getting into the bow of the boat, his foot slipt, he fell down, and with the fall, the gun went off, shot one man that was in the boat who died soon after, and wounded another

Sporting Intelligence.

in his thigh, that an amputation was obliged to take place.

A curious circumstance happened on a market-day, at Croydon:—A great number of people assembled to dispose of their commodities; geese were offered for sale at nine shillings, butter at fourteen-pence, and every other article dear in proportion. Just as the market had opened, the Brighton mail coachman drove into town, and told the market people that an amazing mob was within half a mile of them, whose intention it was to oblige them to sell geese at four shillings, fresh butter at twelve-pence, and every article cheap in proportion.— The market-folks held a consultation, and imagining that the mob would arrive before they could pack up, agreed to sell for the low prices. There was no mob, and the coachman drove off, happy at being the cause of the "knowing ones being taken in.

Puppyism. — A young, dashing blade, the other day, in London, stept into a haberdasher's to buy a watch-ribbon, which came to fourpence; he laid a shilling on the counter, the man immediately gave him 6d. only, without recollecting that 2d. more was due to him: so, after some time, when this Bondstreet Lounger had looked at the man, and the man at him, " Fellow," says he, " FATIGUE me with my TWOPENCE!!"

" *O tempora! O mores!*"

Some gentlemen who were at Canterbury Races, have been visiting the principal towns in that neighbourhood, and being tolerably expert at *card-playing*, have carried off a large sum of money. At Sandwich, on the Wednesday evening, they collected upwards of 200l.; an old man in the wool trade, with a farmer from the country, soon had their pockets emptied by playing at cribbage with them; one of the gentlemen betted the *man of wool* two guineas that he did not produce 100l. in half an hour; the stapler, about 75 years old, hobbled out, and came back with bank notes to the amount within the limited time, but alas! he had better left them at home, for he not knowing the game, his notes were easily obtained by the gentlemen, who said they did not make a practice of sitting up late, very politely wished them a good night, and took their departure.

A great number of salmons have come up the river Ouse, several miles above Lewes, in Sussex, for the last two or three years; but the variety of nets that are daily used in this river, some of them with meshes small enough to catch a sprat, is enough to destroy the fishery of the finest river in the kingdom. The water-bailiff, or other officer whose province it may be, should prevent the use of those destructive engines.

A certain *dashing Sprig of Fashion,* who resides not far from *St. James's Square,* is stated some time since to have returned from a watering-place, for the purpose of eloping with the daughter of a tradesman in B—nd-street. The youthful couple had reached, in all the joys of expectation, the distance of 35 miles westward of London, when they were overtaken by the enraged brother of the fair fugitive, who, regardless of the breach of privilege, bestowed a very handsome remembrance on the shoulders of Nobility, and returned to town in triumph with his disappointed sister.

Another maiden Lady in St. Clement's, has had a favourite *Cat* interred in a *patent* coffin.

On Monday, Oct. 6, a match was run from Dewsbury to Markham-Moor, near Tuxford, and back, distance 100 miles, by Mr. Thomas

Thomas Whitaker's grey horse, Shillito, carrying 11st. against Mr. W. Spedding's grey horse, Jack-a-Rattle, weight 7st. which was won by Jack-a-Rattle, performing it in 13 hours, and Mr Whitaker's in 14 hours.—Jack-a-Rattle only had about three pints of ale during the journey.

A race-horse belonging to an officer in Norwich barracks, some days since, run away with a boy who rode him, and on reaching Tombland, near the passage into the church-yard, precipitated himself into the cellar of a basket-maker. The boy, in the act of falling, caught the floor above: there were three men and a boy at work in the cellar; and although the aperture by which the horse entered was so small, that it was with great difficulty he could be got out by it, neither he, nor any of the people were in the least hurt.

An American recruiting Serjeant, in his advertisement, calls upon the following description of persons to join him--and, indeed, it appears very probable, that they may afford the United States a considerable body of troops:—" Those persons whose wives are not blessed with a lamb-like disposition; whose fathers have not a *quantum sufficit* of parental affection; whose creditors are rapacious; or whose sweethearts have proved too frail, will do well to embrace this opportunity of joining the army, where they will be treated with kindness, and have every attention paid to them as men and soldiers."

The following anecdote shews that there are *sharps* and *flats* in Paris, as well as in London:—" A person applied to a man very rich, and credulous, with a proposal of selling him a secret, by which he would win considerable sums at play. The bargain was struck for the secret, at a consideration of 24,000 francs paid down in cash, a bill for 80,000 francs, and the cession of a property valued at about 50,000 more. The agreement was made, and the instruments, both of obligation and sale, were regularly drawn up, and signed in the presence of a public man. The new possessor of the pretended secret was soon after introduced by his instructor to a gaming-house, where they suffered him to win some thousand francs: but his good fortune did not last long; the fourth and fifth sittings were fatal to the player, who then began to suspect an imposition. Ashamed of being made the dupe of a man without the necessaries of life, he proposed to the seller, that he should retain the 24,000 francs, together with the property, valued at 50,000, he had received; but that he should give up the bill for the 80,000. This the sharper refused to do; and the matter has been brought into a court of justice."

Some time since, a well-dressed sharper observing a gentleman arrive on horseback at Mr. Cockburn's stables, in King-street, Glasgow, and hearing him ask the ostler where another person lived, he, in the ostler's hearing, said to the gentleman, as if acquainted with him, " We'll go and have a dram," and seemingly went along with him to Mr. Cockburn's house. Shortly after, the sharper came to the stable, and ordered the ostler to give the horse sixpenny-worth of oats. He then went away, but returned fully equipped, mounted, and rode off with the horse.

A Mr. C. Crunch, a young farmer, of Barford, lately shot a fine hen bustard on Salisbury-plain, which measured from tip to tip of the wings six feet, and above three feet from the beak to the tail.

FEAST

FEAST OF WIT; OR, SPORTSMAN's HALL.

A BLACK man, in Jamaica, some time ago was taken up by his Master for buying goods, knowing them to have been stolen. He was tried, found guilty, and sentence passed upon him. The Judge pronounced—"Take and flog that black rascal." The prisoner begged to be heard, which was granted. Says he, "If white man buy tolen goods, will you order white rascal a flog? (Yes, to be sure, said the Judge). Dere is my Massa, he buy tolen goods, he know I was tolen when he bought me; hold um fast."

The Ladies, says a Punnical Correspondent, have all been lately in a *flutter* about a *Secret Expedition* to *Breast Harbour*.

Nervous susceptibility is not wholly confined to the fashionable and titled Dames, as we are credibly informed, that the *melting' rib* of a *buckish butcher*, not far from Knightsbridge-Green, has such a dread of being insulted by naughty men, that after sunset she never ventures beyond the shop-door, without the *feminine* accompaniment of a *brace of bull-dogs*

The rumoured determination of sending all Aliens out of the country who shall be found *gambling* in our *funds* can be considered as no great hardship. Few men, we believe, ever complain of those who relieve them from the *stocks*.

The enemy's ships must keep a sharp look out now that the Botany Bay navy is on the watch. The colonists will *steal* upon them before they are aware.

No man ever succeeded so suddenly in making proselytes, as Mr. Howard, of Old-street, during the late riots. No sooner were his men turned loose, than the whole were converted into *Quakers*.

It now appears that Mr. Howard, of Old-street, was a forestaller of *legs*. This accounts for his being attacked by so many *cripples*. Every man, who assembled in the mob, before his house, might plead a *lame* excuse.

The common cry of *scarcity* extends even to the *game*. We are confidently assured, that not a *partridge* has been seen in any of the *brick-fields* near London.

The dispositions of the Courts of Sweden and Denmark were sufficiently shewn in the names of the Officers whom they selected for opposing our right of visiting neutral ships, in conformity to the Right of Nations. The name of the one is *Wrangle*, and of the other *Krabbe*.

A ministerial paper represents the French Officers as so many *ci-devant* valets-de-chambre — This accounts for their *dressing* the Austrian Generals so well.

The *accoucheurs* will be happy to hear from the Agricultural Reports, that several distinguished Gentlemen are *breeding*.

The Ladies, who complain so loudly against the near approach of the *naked Gentlemen* at Ramsgate, seem to think the fashion of nudity the *exclusive privilege* of the fair sex.

The French Philosopher, who pretends to have discovered that a part of the human body possesses the quality of *wood*, has in fact proved nothing that is new. We have long known that British sailors are *hearts of oak*, and *wooden heads* are surely no novelty in any country!

The

The belief in *ghosts* is fast decaying in this country. When the Magistrates of Bath were told the other day, that a ghost haunted the purlieus of one of the churches of that city, instead of sending for a *clergyman*, they commissioned a *constable* to *lay* it, which he did—in the *watch-house!*

An officer, in the Expedition to Holland, obliged to surrender to a superior party of the enemy, called out, *Je me rends*, i. e. I surrender. From that time the soldiers ludicrously called him *Jemmy Round*.—We are far from throwing the least blame on an officer, who behaved in the most gallant and honourable manner; we only mean to point out the humour of our men.

An Irishman was met lately in the Borough by a Gentleman who recollected him in the Rebellion, and who asked him what brought him here?—the fellow replied—" Please your Honour, you know I was hanged."—" Hanged," said the Gentleman, with some surprise, " Yes, Sir, hanged, that is, I was cast for death, and made my escape, which is the same thing, as you know I am a *dead man* by the *law*, though now I earn a very honest *livelihood*."

A poor fellow who was sentenced to be hanged a few weeks ago in Ireland, when he came to the gallows, observed, that the Judge did not say he should be hanged by the *neck*, and therefore demanded to be suspended by the *heels*. The Sheriff observed, that at all events he must be hanged until he was dead. " Och then," says Pat, " if that's the case, neck against heels for ever—hang away, Mr. O'Mullihane!"

A woman in the neighbourhood of Ormskirk, in Lancashire, went a few weeks ago to the shop of a tallow chandler, to purchase a pound of candles, for which she tendered the sum she had sometimes before paid for the same quantity—" This is not enough," said the shopkeeper, " candles are advanced in price, and you must pay me another halfpenny!"——" And pray, Sir, what is the reason of this advance in the price of candles?"—" Oh!" replied the chandler, " this war, this war,"—" What!" said the woman, " are they then gotten to feight on by candle leet?"

A few weeks ago, at a town in Warwickshire, one of the members of a distressed company of comedians prevailed upon a *blacksmith*, with a stentorian voice, to undertake the song of *The Early Horn*, by way of making a little *variety*, and " raising the wind" at his *benefit*. The blacksmith came upon the stage, and began to clear his pipes, with a *tye—tum—tarra*.—" D—n your *tye—tum—tarx*," cried a fellow from the gallery.—" Why, d—n *you* then," returned the blacksmith, " and d—n *me* if I sing *any more*."—Thus ended the blacksmith's song before it was *begun*. The audience grumbled much at their disappointment; and the *actor*, rather than meet their reproaches, marched off with the *cash* received at the door, and left the *expences* of the house to be *shared* by the company.

The paucity of lamps in Chester has been so great, that a Gentleman, who lodged at an inn in Northgate-street, not being able to procure a lanthorn, was obliged one night to give the waiter half a crown to walk before him, with his shirt skirt hanging out of his breeches, as a *mark* for him to follow to his hotel.

It has been thought extremely hard that Mr. Kemble was ill-treated by the Livery, merely on account of his *size*, as if a man could not *talk* of scarcity without producing

producing a *sample*. This *truly great* man is indignant at such treatment, and declares it will be some time before he *pitches his load* again in Common Hall.

The proverb of, "There is truth in wine," was lately verified in a novel manner: Dr. Wade, of Dublin, having frequently lost money from a sort of press in which he deposited it, placed a bottle of port uncorked against the door, so that it must fall out when the press should be opened. In a few minutes after he had set this trap, he found his maid servant all covered with the contents of the bottle, which was unfortunately decanted in her bosom.

The French Commandant of Malta might have conveyed his whole garrison to France as part of Dolomieu's Cabinet of Natural History. They had suffered so much from famine, that they might have passed for *mummies!*

A Correspondent at Margate relates the following curious circumstance:— A Gentleman and servant lately staid at one of the boarding-houses here until his bill amounted to 25 guineas, besides considerable debts which he contracted at other places. He then went off, and left his servant behind, who joined in the general execrations uttered against his master. The Gentleman, however, returned in about a week, when all parties agreed in praising him as an honourable man. But now mark the change! he staid another month, and then taking his servant with him, went off without paying a shilling of his increased debts!

FASHIONS.—*Dialogue between a Lady and Man Milliner at Paris.*— "Citizen, I am just come to town; pray have the goodness to inform me how I must appear, to be in the fashion!"—" Madame 'tis done in a moment; in two minutes I shall equip you in the first style.—Be pleased to take off that bonnet." " Well."—" Off with that petticoat."—" There it is."—" Away with these pockets."—" There they go."—" Throw off that handkerchief."—" 'Tis done."—" Away with that corset and sleeves." —" Will that do?"—" Yes, Madame, you are now in the fashion. —'Tis an easy matter you see.— To be *dressed* in the fashion, you have only to *undress!*"

Hadfield, on his removal from Newgate, expressed much reluctance to change his situation; dismal as was that of Newgate, he did not wish to exchange it for scenes of untried being; and to Mr Kirby's reasonings on the matter he coolly replied, "You talk very finely, Master Kirby—but mad as you think me to be, do not imagine that I am to be convinced by such *Newgatory* arguments."

" Several works of the *immortal* Shakespeare," says an Irish correspondent, " are to be *revived* at Drury Lane this season."

The Emperor Paul wishes to take one of his daughters *from her husband*. How many men of fashion in England would wish to have such a father-in law.

Some time since, as an Irish Gentleman met with an acquaintance in town, he informed him, he was at a loss how to spend his evenings, and enquired what was the Play at Drury-lane Theatre?— " There is an excellent performance there this evening." said the other, " I assure you, for I have seen the Play-bill; and that is—*The Birth-Day*, and *Lodoiska.*"—" *Load of Whiskey!*" replied the Irish Gentleman, very hastily, " then, by J—s, I'll be there, for I have not tasted a drop of *whiskey* since I came from Dublin."—The other jocosely wished him a good day, and hoped he would *relish* it.

POETRY.

POETRY.

THE HIGH COURT OF DIANA.

THE WATERING PLACE.

FROM London driv'n by Phœbus'
  scorching ray,
The sick and healthy, wing their eager
  way.
The Youths of Fashion urge with sound-
  ing thong
Their well-bred steeds, who dash like
  wind along.
The *Margate Hoy* each day is fully stow'd,
And *Boulton's Coaches* fill the *Brighton Road*.
Mister and Mistress Tape, a loving pair,
Now leave *Cheapside*, all in their own *ow-bus
  chair*,
Forgetting not their vehicle to cram
With bottl'd porter, chickens, cake, and
  ham.
In bran-new boots, and mounted on a hack,
On Ludgate-hill th' Apprentice turns his
  back;
Smacks his smart "*Whip*," and curls his
  long spurr'd boot,
And damns the "*Vaiters*"—cause—'tis
  to *pieced*.
The artful Gamester, as he onward plods,
Lays the deep plot, and calculates the odds.
The *Lady Abbess* shews her well-drawn
  plan,
And tells each *pupil* how to know her man.
At length appears the wish'd-for spot in
  view,
And all arrived, their different schemes
  pursue.
When Sol's bright beams first dance upon
  the wave,
Both high and low their limbs promiscuous
  lave.
Then at the libraries, the rattling dice
The old, the young, the rich, the poor, en-
  tice;
Gentle and simple own their itch for play,
And *routing* proves the Order of the Day.
But Blades of Spirit scorn such narrow
  bounds,
And set the *Caster*—for a thousand pounds.

Cry, "Seven's the Main! What odds that
  I don't nick!"
And her cool hundreds on a card or trick;
Some pay devotion to the generous wine,
And others bow at love's seducing shrine.
Th' *unthanks* CIT, sent out for *change of
  air*,
Finds in a coffee-room some easy chair,
Where, 'midst the joys of porter, punch,
  and smoke,
He tells, with shaking sides, the worn-out
  joke,
Whilst his *plump dame* displays her brawny
  fist,
In playing "*Commerce*," or a game at
  "*Vist*;"
And *Miss* and *Master* join their *dear Mama*,
In spending guineas—earn'd by *poor Papa*.

Such is the scene, till Winter's chilly
  looks
Drive away *Ladies, Nobles, Pigeons, Rooks*;
And empty pockets force the *trading fop*
To quit *gaming*, and mind his *shop!*
                                     SMOKER.

THE DIPPERS.

SINCE dipping's the fashion with old
  and with young,
Since all must dip Ocean's green billows
  among,
Attend, ye *fair dippers*, attend to my lay,
Nor by dipping too often drive prudence
  away.

Ye young wealthy *Nellys*, of dipping beware,
Nor dip into scenes where the wily can
  snare;
Yet dip in the streams which all fountains
  surpass,
For the soul must expand when dipp'd
  deep in the glass!

Ye *Misers*, forbear, when you dip the
　　pure ore,
And remember time passes—but turns
　　back no more!
And, while dipping amid the rich stream-
　　lets of gold,
Beware, lest your follies, in youth, should
　　be old!

Ye *Topers*, who dip in the nectar divine,
Of dipping be careful—for truth is in
　　wine;
And, 'tis said, that the brain of the wise
　　or the fool
Will always be shallow, when noddles are
　　full.

Ye *Poets*, ye *Satirists*, pause, while ye
　　think,
Nor dip your pens rashly in Ridicule's ink,
Lest your names down the river of Lethe
　　should glide,
And the dipper be sham'd, when by dip-
　　ping he died.

Ye *Gamesters*, who dip in the vortex so
　　strong,
And dip, without conscience, the gudgeons
　　among;
Beware, lest a *shark* in the current you
　　find,
Who will *dip you*, in turn, and avenge all
　　mankind.

UPS AND DOWNS!

SEE *Kate* the bewitching, in splendid
　　array,
The pride of the simple, the toast of the
　　gay;
She is haughty and fierce as the greatest
　　Bashaw,
Her smile is enchanting, her pleasure is
　　law,
She mocks humble merit, to genius un-
　　known,
While the praise of the servile and base is
　　her own;
But when fickle Fortune has ventur'd to
　　frown,
She is humble and gentle—for then she is
　　DOWN.

See bold *Mistress Staring*, with jewels
　　and lace,
Looks Virtue and Modesty full in the
　　face!
She talks of her pedigree, boasts of her
　　pelf—
And remembers all things, but her vain-
　　boasting self.

With a thousand strange fancies she scat-
　　ters her gold,
And at last she discovers that Fame is not
　　sold;
Since, by Fortune set up, she amuses the
　　town,
And the gazer remembers, how low she
　　was DOWN.

The Gamester, who rattles the dice-box
　　all night,
Who makes Hazard his trade, and Picquet
　　his delight;
With his curricle, dashing to Brighton re-
　　pairs,
And, while feasting; for others nor cares
　　nor cares;
Now he's up, he is fit for the highest a
　　guest,
And his cook and his valet ne'er peacefully
　　rest;
Tho' should Chance in a whimsical mo-
　　ment e'er frown,
He'll be kick'd out of doors, and hence-
　　forward—is DOWN!

The *Dowager Dimple*, who once was
　　the Queen
Of the Balls, and the Baths, and the
　　Course, and the Stein;
Who adorn'd her fair form in the habit of
　　taste;
Who was toasted as Venus, and little more
　　chaste;
Now she strolls all the morning, neglect-
　　ed, forlorn,
Of Puppies the sport, and of Matrons the
　　scorn;
And her conduct is censur'd by Nymphs
　　of renown,
Who with smiles and grimaces—are run-
　　ning her DOWN!

There is fair *Lady Lovely*, with graces
　　and charms
Enough to set kingdoms and Kings up in
　　arms;
She is scouted and scorn'd, tho' not many
　　months since
She was thought a fit Tut'ress for States-
　　man or Prince—
She was *up*, as 'tis said, and so high she
　　was thrown,
That the sun-shine of fashion and taste
　　were her own;
But now the horizon is mark'd with a
　　frown,
And the cold glance of Courtiers pro-
　　claims—she is DOWN.

Then since 'tis the *ups* and the *downs*
　　that can give
The zest to all pleasures, which teach us
　　to live—

Let

Let those who are *up* be with modesty
　blest,
And let those who are *down* learn in quiet
　to rest;
Let the *fav'rites of Fortune* remember the
　day
When they scarce had a dinner—or money
　to pay—
And should Fate on the splendour of life
　again frown,
They will laugh at the *highest*, tho' THEY
　may *be* DOWN!
　　　　DERRY DOWN, DOWN.
Brighton.

AN EXTEMPORE IRREGULAR
ODE
On the DEATH of Mrs. MONTAGUE.

" —— Cui pudor, et justitiæ soror
" Incorrupta fides, nudaq; veritas
" Quando ullum invenient parem?
" Multis illa flebilis * flebilis occidit,
" Nulli flebilior quam—*to ye, Little
　Sweeps!*†"　　　　　　　　Hor.

MOURN, hapless, sooty, little
　　Sweepers! mourn
Your banish'd feast and tinsell'd laurels
　torn!
The swinging knell proclaims your hostess
　down
To those blest realms to wicked wights
　unknown:
No more your teeth, so purest ivory white,
Shall her old English beef and pudding
　bite.

　No more shall ye, with joy elate,
　　From yonder chimnies scream;
　Ah me! what sad reverse of fate!
　　MAY now no MAY will seem.

No more the brush and shovel's sound
Shall urge your feet to beat the ground,
　In measures light and airy;
While some solicit those that pass
The tribute small of humble brass,
　Of greater presents wary.

In the lov'd Square no festive boards are
　spread,
Previously garnish'd with huge loaves of
　bread,
To meet old England's boasted pride,
With smoaking puddings by its side,
(That erst the board of ancient monarchs
　grac'd,
But since, alas! for meagre cates dis-
　plac'd;)

* The metropolitan corps of Chimney-
Sweepers, annually treated by Mrs. Montague in Portman-square.
† For "*tibi Virgili?*" making similar
metre.

With flaggons of porter and sorry-brew'd
　ale,
Fit for those of the dray, and that work
　with the flail
Permit us, heav'nly Cherubim! to moors
In solemn step around thy sculptur'd urn;
And deck its polish'd sides with many a
　wreath,
Wont their sweet scents from votive plate
　to breathe.
Though black our hands, our hearts are
　pure as snow,
From which unceasing gratitude shall flow,
For you *first* taught us, whilst you gave
　us bread—
" Not to yourself, but God to give the
　praise;
" For He alone the drooping soul can raise,
" If we his holy paths with steadfast virtue
　tread."
Sept. 5, 1800.　　　　　　WOWSKI.

LONDON's SUMMER MORNING.

WHO has not wak'd to list the busy
　　sounds
Of SUMMER's MORNING, in the sultry
　smoke
Of noisy London? On the pavement hot
The sooty chimney-boy, with dingy face
And tatter'd cov'ring, shrilly bawls his
　trade,
Rousing the sleepy housemaid. At the
　door
The milk-pail rattles, and the tinkling
　bell
Proclaims the dustman's office, while the
　street
Is lost in clouds impervious. Now begins
The din of hackney-coaches, waggons,
　carts;
While tinmans' shops, and noisy trunk-
　makers,
Knife-grinders, coopers, squeaking cork-
　cutters,
Fruit-barrows, and the hunger-giving cries
Of vegetable venders, fill the air.
Now ev'ry shop displays its varied trade,
And the fresh sprinkled pavement cools
　the feet
Of early walkers. At the private door
The ruddy housemaid twirls the busy mop,
Annoying the smart 'prentice, or neat girl
Tripping with band-box, lightly. Now
　the sun
Darts burning splendour on the glitt'ring
　pane,
Save where the canvas awning throws a
　shade
On the gay merchandise. Now, spruce
　and trim,

In shops (where beauty smiles with in-
  dustry).
Sits the smart damsel, while the passenger
Peeps through the window, watching ev'ry
  charm.
Now pastry dainties catch the eyes minute
Of humming insects, while the limy snare
Waits to enthral them. Now the Lamp-
  lighter
Mounts the tall ladder, nimbly vent'rous,
To trim the half-fill'd lamp; while at
  his feet
The pot-boy yells discordant 'all along
The sultry pavement, the old-clouthsman
  cries
In tone monotonous, and side-long views
The area, for his traffic. Now the bag
Is slily open'd, and the half-worn suit
(Sometimes the pilfer'd treasure of the base
Domestic spoiler), for one half its worth,
Sinks in the green abyss. The porter now
Bears his huge load along the burning way,
And the POOR POET wakes from busy
  dreams
    To paint the Summer Morning.

EPIGRAM.

ON READING OF THE EXECUTION OF
A MALEFACTOR WHOSE NAME WAS
VOWEL.

VOWEL! quoth NED, with sigh pro-
  found,
  The forfeit now is paid;
Thy num'rous crimes have justice found,
  Tho' justice was delay'd.
"True" (says his friend) "but cease,
  I pray—
Suppress at once your sigh,
Since, thank our stars, no one can say
  'Tis either U or I."
Near the 'Change.   W. BIRCH.

LINES ON A POOR AUTHOR.

IN IMITATION OF MR. POPE'S ODE
ON SOLITUDE.

HUNGRY the wretch, and torn with
  care,
  With scatter'd papers strew'd around,
Who groaning breathes the garret air,
    That whistles round.

Who lacks of gold, who wants e'en bread,
  Whose bureau yields him no attire,
Whose roof 'gainst heat affords no shade,
    Nor hath a fire.

Curs'd he whose wretchedness doth find
  Hours, days, and years thus drawl
    away;
Whose starving body, worn-out mind,
    Doth curse the day.

No sleep by night, by day no ease,
  Each pass'd alike in expectation,
Least growling duns should come to tease
    His meditation.

Thus starves the man by fame unknown,
  Unpitied thus the author sighs;
Driv'n from the world, no friendly stone
    Tells where he lies.
          SOUBLERICUS.

INVITATION TO JOY.
(FROM THE GERMAN.)

SAY, who would mope in joyless plight,
    While youth and spring bedeck the
      scene,
And scorn the proffer'd gay delight,
    With thankless heart and frowning
      mien?
See Joy with becks and smiles appear,
    While roses strew the devious way;
The feast of life she bids us share,
    Where'er our pilgrim footsteps stray.

And still the grove is cool and green,
    And clear the bubbling fountain flows,
Still shines the night's resplendent queen,
    As erst in Paradise she rose;
The grapes their purple nectar pour,
    To 'suage the heart that griefs oppress;
And still the lonely ev'ning bow'r
    Invites and screens the stolen kiss.

Still PHILOMELA's melting strain,
    Responsive to the dying gale,
Beguiles the bosom's throbbing pain,
    And sweetly charms the list'ning vale;
Creation's scene expanded lies:—
    Blest scene! how wond'rous bright and
      fair!
Till Death's cold hand shall close my eyes,
    Let me the lavish'd bounties share!

EPITAPH.

CY git Broc, qui tout sa vie
  Eut tant d'aversion pour l'eau
Que a du sein des morts il vous crie,
  Ne pleurez pas sur mon tombeau.

Here lies a Sot, who while upon the ground
Detested water, lest he should be drown'd;
Nor would he think he'd yet escap'd his
  doom,
Should you let fall one tear upon his tomb.
          W. H. REID.

THE SPORTING MAGAZINE;

OR,

MONTHLY CALENDAR

OF THE

TRANSACTIONS OF THE TURF, THE CHASE,

And every other Diversion interesting to the

MAN OF PLEASURE, ENTERPRIZE, AND SPIRIT.

For NOVEMBER, 1800.

CONTAINING,

	Page		Page
King's Stag Hounds	47	Curious History of the Dogs at the University of Gottingen	70
Sporting Articles	ibid	A curious Devonshire Epistle	72
Nimrod on various Pedigrees	48	Thoughts on the Means of acquiring the Veterinary Science	73
Deaths of Racers, &c.	49	Late Tippo Sultaun's Wardrobe	76
Observations on a strange Quere	50	Treatise on Horses	77
Law Case—Bunbury v. Southcote	ibid	Origin of Cropped Hair in England	80
Trait Hits upon Agricultural Societies	53	American Longevity	81
An Extraordinary Character	54	Heraldic Custom	ibid
Horse-stealing	ibid	Feast of Wit	82
Curious Advertisement	55	Sporting Intelligence	85
Aquatic Excursion to Margate	56	POETRY.	
Instructions for Shopkeepers, &c.	57	Song and Recipe for killing a Wife	89
Pertinent Pleasantries on the Price of Corn	58	Piccadilly's Complaint	ibid
Submersion of Swallows	61	Stanzas on Poaching	90
Theatricals	63	Olla Podrida, an Œnigmatical Epitaph	ibid
Guy Faux	67	A Cambridge Song	91
Journal of Modern Characters	ibid	Bless my Heart! How hot it is	ibid
Cash Account of a pretty French Woman	68	Epitaph on the late Hodges	92
On Trotting Horses	ibid	On the Death of a Flying Barber	ibid
A dangerous Woman	69	Racing Calendar	13—20

[Embellished with a beautiful Engraving, by SCOTT, of Col. Kelly's DUNGANNON, beating the Prince of Wales's ROCKINGHAM; and an Etching of HERONS and ROOKS, by HOWIT.]

London:

PRINTED FOR THE PROPRIETORS;

And Sold by J. WHEBLE, Warwick Square, Warwick Lane, near St. Paul's; C. CHAPPLE, 66, Pall-mall, opposite St. James's Place; J. BOOTH, Duke Street, Portland Place; JOHN HILTON, at Newmarket; and by every Bookseller and Stationer in Great Britain and Ireland.

W. JUSTINS, PRINTER, PEMBERTON ROW, GOUGH SQUARE.

Dungannon beating Buckingham at Newmarket.

THE SPORTING MAGAZINE,

For NOVEMBER 1800.

EXPLANATION OF THE PLATE.

COL. O'KELLY'S DUNGANNON, beating His Royal Highness the PRINCE OF WALES'S ROCK-INGHAM, over the B. C. Newmarket.

[An ENGRAVING by SCOTT, from a Painting by Sartorius.]

THIS famous race was between the two first horses of the day, about twenty years since. It was won by Dungannon, swerving against Rockingham; however, it was fair. Mr. Wilson has the original picture. The Prince lost a great deal of money.

ROYAL CHASE, &c.

THE stag hounds afforded on Saturday, Nov. 22, the best run this season; the deer was turned out at Maidenhead Thicket before a very numerous field; making the circle of which, he pointed for Hare Hatch, through the woods to the right, passed Marlow, and over a good racing country, to the Thames; the hounds having laid well at him, and running breast high *without a check*, obliged him to the only alternative of crossing, which he did above Crookham, where the *Charon* of that ferry had for an hour incessant employ; places were never more anxiously solicited from the hand of a minister, than those in the different boats; during which, the hounds, and those who were first over, ascended the towering hills of Bucks, through Wickham Woods, where full forty horsemen were thrown out, and back to Hall Barns, through Mr. Burk's Park, and he was run into, and unintentionally, but unavoidably killed, in a wood near Pen-House, after a terrible run of three hours; Sir Henry Gott, the father of the field, Lord Sandwich, Johnson the huntsman, and four others, being the only ones *completely in at the death*, though full fourscore were present, when the hounds were first drawn up to the scent.

SPORTING.

AT the Malton Meeting on the 19th inst. the long-expected match, which at Flexton had been undecided, between Mr. Plumer's white dog, Speed, and Major Topham's black dog, Snowball, was run over Whartam. Never had any match of greyhounds excited equal expectations; as it was supposed, that Speed was the fleetest dog in England; and the bets at starting were in his favour. After a severe course, in which Snowball from the first starting, shewed a decided superiority through the whole running, the match was declared in his favour. Snowball killed the hare. As soon as the course was over, the owner declared that Snowball should never again run in public, but be kept only for his breed.

The hounds lately disposed of by Sir G. Heathcote (when he purchased Sir W. Lowther's), are now in the possession of his Highness of York, affording excellent sport in the neighbourhood of Oatlands; so severe was the chase one day last week, that the horse of the whipper-in died in consequence.

Exclusive of the necessary court attendants upon his Majesty, the stag-hounds have very few *sporting* followers. Turning out the deer so constantly at the same place not only removes the pleasing idea of variety, but, it being a country entirely open, and *without leaps*, it affords very little chance of *breaking a neck*; without which (to a juvenile and emulative mind) there can be no *sublime* enjoyment of the chase.

On the 14th inst. a hare being found near to the Round Course at Newmarket Heath, a match for twenty guineas was run for between Mr. Clough's black dog, Snap, and Mr. Mitchell's dun bitch Mouse, which, after a well contested course of two miles, terminated in favour of the former.

The Duke of Hamilton has been particularly fortunate at Dumfries races; his Grace's bay colt won all in four heats.

Wednesday the 20th, the *Chess Club* had its first meeting this winter, at Parsloe's, St. James's-street.

A grand shooting party is now at Earl Cholmondley's, in Norfolk.

Three farmers some evenings since returning home from Ipswich market, two of them previously agreed to frighten the other by attempting to rob him on the road. On pretence of being in a great hurry, one of them set off full speed, while the other kept behind. The one who was to act the robber, having given his horse in charge to a man, disguised himself in a great coat, and in a resolute tone stopped his companion, and demanded his money. The farmer taking him for the character he assumed, knocked him down, and rode over him. He was shortly after taken up, but the man to whom he entrusted his horse, had rode off with it, and the adventurous wit was, with aching bones, obliged to be conveyed home in a post-chaise.

NIMROD ON VARIOUS PEDIGREES, &c.

To the EDITOR of the SPORTING MAGAZINE.

SIR,

YOU must pay 8d. for neglecting to inform yourself of the true breeder of Warter, the celebrated racer. He was bred by Mrs. Pennington, of Warter-Hall, near Pocklington, in Yorkshire, got by King Fergus, dam by Snap, &c. &c.—And no one ever heard of a Mr. Withers as a breeder or a sportsman.

It is hoped you will gratify us with other engravings and performances, than those of Play or Pay, Johnny, &c. &c. and endeavour to procure those of Cockfighter, Champion, Aniseed, and Sophia, who deserve a place in your excellent publication.

Your readers wish to find from you next month, a full and accurate detail of the affair at Brighton, between Sir G. Southcoat and others.

Your's, &c; NIMROD.

[We are regardless of postage in cases where valuable communications are sent us—Shall be glad of this Correspondent's favours at all times—and if he will tell *how* and *where* to procure the portraits of the horses he names, we will endeavour to obtain them.

DEATHS

DEATHS OF RACERS, &c.

EARLY in this month, died, in the 31st year of his age, at Aldburgh, near Masham, Yorkshire, the celebrated stallion, Young Marsk, the property of Mrs. Hutton, widow of the late James Hutton, Esq. Marsk was a good runner, and sire of many capital racers, brood mares, and hunters.—*For his pedigree, &c. vide one of the late Sporting Magazines.*

Lately, died, at the Upper Hare Park, Newmarket, aged 27, the famous stallion Potso's, the property of Mr. Golding, who purchased him at one of Lord Grosvenor's sales a few years since, at Newmarket, for fifty guineas. He was sire of Capsicum, Cayenne, Druid, Canterbury, Champion, Sebedoni, Waxy, Mealy, Worthy, Duchess of Limbs, Coriander, Coheiress, &c. &c.

Last week died, at Lowther-Hall, in Westmoreland, aged 29 years, that well known racer, Ajax. He was sire of many capital hunters in the north of England. We are informed, that Pleader, aged 30, is still alive.—In one stable at Lowther-Hall, it is said, a few years ago, there were six stallions, whose ages amounted to 144 years.

On Thursday, Nov. 19th.—A match against time was decided on the road between Newcastle-upon-Tyne, and Morpeth, for a bet of 100gs; a brown gelding by Dunce, the property of Lieut. Col. Orde, of Holywell, near Durham, went the distance of 70 miles in six hours and ten minutes. He was allowed seven hours to perform the distance in. He carried seven stone, and was rode by three boys alternately. Foreriders cleared the way, to prevent any accident happening.

YORK AUGUST MEETING, 1801.

Saturday before the Meeting—Mr. Wentworth's chesnut horse, Barnaby, by Stride, dam by Eclipse, 8st. against Mr. Baker's bay horse, Jonah, by Escape, out of Lavender, 8st. 5lb. both then six years old—4 miles. 200gs h. ft.

Sir T. Gascoigne's bay colt, Doodle, by Restless, out of Tippet, 8st. against Lord Darlington's chesnut colt, Muley Moloch, by John Bull, out of Missehoe, 8st. 5lb. both then three years old—2 miles for 200gs h. ft.

SATURDAY IN THE AUGUST MEETING.

A Sweepstakes of 50gs each—colts 8st. fillies 7st. 12lb.—2 miles.

Lord Darlington's chesnut colt, Muley Moloch
Sir T. Gascoigne's chesnut colt, Lenox, by Delpini, out of Violet.
Sir H. T. Vane's brown colt by Traveller, out of Shuttle's dam.
Mr. Wilson's bay filly, Sephia, by Buzzard, out of Huncamunca.
Mr. G. Crompton's chesnut roan colt, Quiz, by Buzzard, out of Huby's dam.

NEWCASTLE-UPON-TYNE RACES, 1801.

First Day.—Sir H. Williamson's bay colt, Ruby, by Walnut, out of Lavinia, 8st. against Mr. Riddell's chesnut colt by Walnut, dam by Young Marsk, 8st. 5lb.—4 miles. 100gs h. ft.

Mr. Baker's bay colt, Jack's Alive, by Walnut, dam by Eclipse, against Mr. Storey's brown colt by his Arabian dam, by Fortitude, 8st. each.—2 miles. 100gs h. ft.

Mr. C. Graham's bay horse, Duncan, by Stride, dam by Young Marsk, then 6 yrs old, 9st. against Mr. Fletcher's chesnut horse, Master Robert, by Star, dam by Young Marsk, aged 9st. 8lb.—4 miles. 200gs p. p.

Mr. Fletcher's brown colt, Lethe, by Sir Peter, out of Queen Mab, then 4 yrs old, 7st. 7lb. against Mr. C. Graham's brown horse, Bryan — by Aston, dam by Le Sang, 5 yrs old, 8st. 3lb.—2 miles.

To the EDITORS of the SPORTING MAGAZINE.

GENTLEMEN,

IN perusing the back pages of your amusing Chronicle, a favourite diversion with me, I was struck with the following strange query—strange, on account of the sort of *professional* character of the signature, Tally-ho! which surely ought to belong to a Sportsman: it was (No. 96, Sept. p. 273) whether a horse had ever been known to walk one mile in five minutes? Certainly never, the thing being impossible, since such speed is at the rate of twelve miles per hour, and it is well known, that six miles in one hour, is the utmost, in the walking pace, ever performed by a horse; and walking being the slowest pace, in course, speed and continuance must be in the nearest possible approximation, and the horse will walk the whole hour through, at nearly the top of his speed. You had, however, amply provided, Sir, for a solution of all questions of this nature, by a frequent quotation of the *Philosophical and Sporting* Treatise on Horses, where every querist may be satisfied, as to their actual and probable capabilities of exertion in every pace. I have the honour to be, Sir, your obedient servant,

ANOTHER SUBSCRIBER.
Newmarket, Nov. 20th.

BILLIARD PLAYING.
BUNBURY, v. SIR THOMAS SOUTHCOTE.
Court of King's Bench, Nov. 7.

MR. Garrow moved for a Rule to shew cause why a warrant of attorney given by the defendant should not be set aside, and the Marshal of the King's Bench ordered to discharge the defendant out of custody as to this suit. Mr. Garrow said, that he moved the Court upon the matters of an affidavit made by Sir Thomas Southcote, Baronet, the particulars of which were as follows:—

Sir Thomas being some time since at Brighton, a Mr. Whaley; whom he then considered to be his friend, came to him, and informed him that he had engaged to play a match at billiards with Mr. Bunbury, that he, Sir Thomas, must play for him, and that he would back him. Sir Thomas consented to play for his friend, and accordingly met Mr. Bunbury, in company with Mr. Hill Darley. Mr. Whaley proposed, as the Rooms at Brighton might be exceedingly full, that they should play at a table at Lewes. They accordingly repaired to this table, where the marker was told they had come to play for a guinea a game, when in fact they were to play for several hundreds. After playing some time, Mr. Whaley contrived to get the marker out of the room, and kept the mark himself, pretending to be Sir Thomas's friend. The luck and skill run considerably against Sir Thomas, and Mr Whaley lost about two thousand guineas, which he paid at the table. Sir Thomas having lost so much for his friend, now played for himself, and in the end lost to Mr. Bunbury six thousand guineas. Sir Thomas returned to Brighton, and set out for London, but had proceeded

Billiard-Playing.

proceeded not more than ten miles when he was arrested at the suit of Mr. Bunbury, and made to sign a warrant of attorney for the payment of the money, on which warrant he had since been confined in the King's Bench. The affidavit of Sir Thomas further stated, that he believed the whole transaction to have been a concerted plan between Whaley, Darley, and Bunbury, to take him in, and that the money which Whaley appeared to lose was afterwards returned to him. They applied to him to accommodate matters, but Sir Thomas had rejected their offers.

Lord Kenyon said it was highly proper to reject all overtures of accommodation, and cheerfully granted a rule to shew cause.

In a paragraph sent a few days after the trial to most of the newspapers, we observe, that Colonel Whaley has in a great measure disowned any knowledge of the parties, and farther, asserted his ignorance of this gambling transaction.

And, on Monday Nov. 24, Mr. Law shewed cause against a rule obtained by Mr. Garrow, to shew cause why a warrant of attorney, given by Sir Thomas Southcott, for 1,788l. 19s. should not be set aside; and why Sir Thomas, who had been taken in execution under the said warrant, should not be discharged out of the custody of the Marshal of the King's Bench prison. The affidavits of Col. Whaley and some others were read, stating, that their meeting with Sir Thomas was not through design, but merely accidental; that the whole consideration of the warrant of attorney was for money borrowed by Sir Thomas of Mr Whaley, and no part of it was for money won at play. There was also 215l. for two horses which Sir Thomas had purchased of Mr. Whaley.

Mess. Erskine, Law, and Raine, hewed cause against the rule, and Mr. Garrow supported it.

Lord Kenyon said, there was a statute which imposed severe penalties on persons sending challenges, in consequence of quarrels at play, it may not be improper that the law respecting an offence which seems to be advancing with gigantic strides should be promulgated. The statute 9th Anne, c. 14, and sect. 8, enacts, ' that for preventing such quarrels as shall and may happen on account of gaming, any person or persons whatsoever, who shall assault and beat, or shall challenge or provoke to fight, any other person or persons whatever, upon account of any money won by gaming, playing, or betting, such person or persons assaulting, beating, challenging, or provoking to fight, on the account aforesaid, who shall be thereof convicted upon an indictment or information, to be exhibited against him or them, for the purpose aforesaid, shall forfeit to her Majesty, her heirs and successors, all his goods, chattels, and personal estate whatsoever: and shall also suffer imprisonment, without bail or mainprize, in the common gaol, or county, where such conviction shall be had, during the term of two years. We sit here for very little purpose indeed, if we are to adopt as true, every thing witnesses, think proper to put on paper. If difficulties occur in wresting the truth from the contrary affidavits of witnesses, it is no new thing to send the matter to that tribunal by which those difficulties may be best disentangled, and the rights of the parties discussed. The case made out by the defendant is this—he is a gentleman who appears to be entitled, some time or other, to come into possession of his mother's jointure: the plaintiff, it also appears, knew of this circumstance—he meets him, as he says, by accident, and, being very benevolent and dealing out his

his

his good offices to every body in want of them, thinks proper to lend him. From time to time, various sums of money, amounting together, as I have taken them, to 1761l. Upon looking into the security taken from him, it is most apparent that it was prepared with a blank for the sum to be inserted; to that security there appears the name of a gentleman as the subscribing witness—it is singular that there is no account from him of this transaction, the charge of which imputes to the parties concerned in it, a conspiracy to plunder.

Those who were actuated by a wish to present themselves in Court with a favourable aspect, one would have thought, would naturally have endeavoured to have got the testimony of a person who came from an unsuspected quarter. These persons, the defendants, on the contrary, introduce themselves to our acquaintance, by admitting they are gamesters. One of them swears he is not a *notorious* gamester: he says he is acquainted with men of great fortune, and keeps the company of persons of the first rank. I know, when I meddle with this subject, I go on tender ground; I know by long experience, that gamesters are *genus irritabile*; I know that they are not only very sore themselves when they are attacked, but that great names, men of rank and title, are ready to step forward and place a shield before them; they are sorry for their honourable friends, and cannot bear they should be exposed. All this makes me sensible I am treading upon tender ground; but I hope my own conscience, and the rectitude of my intentions, will bear me out. What is it that is asked? Not that the Court shall decide, but that the Jury shall tell me, what I confess appears suspicious, how it was this person, who is represented as a beggar, should be able upon his *no* credit, to borrow within two or three days 500l. from a man who only knew him by accident, and who is so disinterested, that he requires no security from him at the time. I wish a Jury to ascertain the truth of the facts which have been sworn to so categorical a manner. I think we should forget the duty we owe the public, if we did not send this to the consideration of a Jury. I desire the parties to appear before the Jury in *puris naturalibus*. Let the plaintiff bring forward the checks upon his banker, which he says he advanced to the defendant. God forbid I should impute to him that he cannot bring them forward, or that from any thing I have said, his character should not stand fair with the public. My opinion is, that the warrant of Attorney should remain, and that the plaintiff should bring an action up to the extent of his judgment."

Mr. Justice Grose thought the circumstance of the case too suspicious not to require the intervention of a Jury.

Mr. Justice Le Blanc said, it was impossible the Court could refuse to open a door to the investigation of this business; if the war of attorney was permitted to stand, the defendant would be excluded the means of obtaining redress. The Court would not do its duty to the public, if it did not direct an inquiry.

Mr. Garrow moved, that Sir Thomas should be discharged out of custody, but this the Court refused.

HERONS AND ROOKS.
An Etching by Mr Hewit.

FOR an elucidation of the causes and consequences of the conflict, represented in this plate, we must refer our readers to page 67 of our Magazine for November 1799.

TRAIT

TRAIT HITS UPON THE AGRICULTURAL SOCIETIES.

MR. EDITOR,

IT is needless to tell you, how much we have been lately obliged to *talk* about scarcity, and how often, and how uselessly, we have discussed the important question, as to the *real* or *artificial* nature of this scarcity. Every ten or fifteen years, these topics are renewed, debated with ardour, and sent into oblivion. Real improvement in the mean time stands still. Experience shews, that we are not better than our ancestors, nor, I am afraid, much wiser.

But, Sir, in this war of words, I have been led to consider the many Agricultural Societies established among us, (not to speak of the Agricultural Board) and I have enquired how it comes about, that the combined wisdom of all the *clever* men in the kingdom, hath produced so little change for the better? This seems a kind of paradox, but if we look into the transactions of those societies, as regularly given in the newspapers, &c. our surprise is considerably lessened. They seem to be *agricultural* only in name, but should rather be called Societies for experiments in *Natural History*, for making sheep as big as oxen, and oxen as big as elephants. Lord Bacon says, that he deserves to be called a philosopher, who makes a blade of grass grow where grass never grew before; and our ambition is to make three inches of fat grow, where half an inch would be quite sufficient. It is not to produce *two* sheep, where there was but *one* before, but to produce one sheep as big as *two*, and with no more meat that is eatable than *one* would produce.

Such are the *pursuits of agriculture*: but surely one may ask, and not ask impertinently, *cui bono?* Is the perfection of cattle their containing a quantity of *fat* that is useless? Are these animals bred for the tallow chandlers, rather than the butchers? And are we to see their produce in our candlesticks, rather than in our plates? I will ask, what do the public reap from the ingenuity of a gentleman, who produces the largest ox that ever was seen, whose flesh (that is, the eatable part) is sold at two shillings, or half-a-crown per pound, to gratify the curiosity, or connoisseurship of those, who may think it an honour to be able to tell their children, and their childrens' children, that they eat a beef-stake from the rump of an ox, that was shewn at a shilling a-piece! Really, Sir, this may do very well for Smithfield, during *Bartholomew Fair:* but how does this help the market at any other period of the year. We expect substantial benefits from breeders of cattle, and they give us only something to look at. Is all this as it should be? It is, I grant, a very curious thing, that a man can breed cattle, not only to any size, but almost to any shape that he pleases, that he can place the fat on the rump, or on the back, or about the loins, wherever he thinks fit it should grow. This is all mighty curious, and he receives great applause, perhaps a reward of a medal, or some such great testimony of the Society's approbation; and this manufactory of animals, out of nature's plan, goes on from meeting to meeting; but, again I ask, how are the public benefited? If the term Agricultural Society, means any thing, is it not fair to suppose, that it means a Society of men, who unite their wisdom and experience to produce plenty and *moderate prices*, to improve our land, and our beef, but not to improve the latter to a degree of uselessness? Such,

I should humbly presume, must have been the original aim of such Societies. How far it is now pursued, let their annals tell. It would be something to improve the breed of cattle, so as to bring more to market, and effect a reduction of price, but to bring, now and then, an ox that shall cost as much as three or four, the meat of which must be sold at three or four times the market-price, seems to me as egregious trifling, as it Mr. Astley should boast of the perfection to which he had brought English horsemanship, because he can ride upon his head, or make a horse pick up a handkerchief. It is very curious to see a man ride full gallop on his head, while his horse picks up a handkerchief, but *cui bono?* Who wishes to ride upon his head?

I am, Sir,
Your humble servant,
A FRIEND TO REAL
IMPROVEMENT.

P.S. I have now before me an article in a newspaper, stating, that at an Agricultural Meeting held in Yorkshire, a man received the reward of *two guineas*, for bringing up twelve children without Parish assistance! There is *liberality!* Two guineas for *twelve children!* What would he have had for *twelve sheep* so *fat*, that nobody could eat them?

EXTRAORDINARY CHARACTER.

THERE is an officer now in town, who declares himself to be a *Free-Man*; (whether of the *City of London, Town Corporate*, or *Borough* of any other part of this kingdom, is not yet known,) but who is better recognized by the title of *General Fly-Flapper*. He, no doubt, has at least heard, or read much of real service, and has seen *some* blood spilled in his life-time; that he has been accustomed to *see blood flow*, there can be but little doubt, as the wainscots of several coffee-houses, west of Temple Bar, bear ample testimony. This son of Mars's propensity to the destruction of the poor flies, is unparalleled, to the very great annoyance of several visitors of those useful houses. Millions have perished by his merciless hands, and each blow with his flapper, is accompanied with "d—n ye, I wish you were all Frenchmen." This is the hero's amusement till the clock strikes four, on which he rises, marches, wheels, and marches again, till he disappears, but only to renew the bloody combat on the succeeding day. Some description of this *Great General* may not be unacceptable: he measures eight feet! not in height —five from his foot to the crown of his head; and three from hip to hip. His complexion sallow; a tolerably good eye, but a brow that terrifies when in action; wears a cocked hat; that in the front is of an extremely sharp acute angle, sufficiently pointed to convey a draught of water to the mouth of the most diminutive eel, or to take a pearl from the eye of a Scotch piper. Having given some description of his stature, I wish I could conclude with that of the dimensions of his coffin. Your's, &c.

AID DE CAMP.

HORSE-STEALING.

JAMES Thwaites was indicted for stealing a horse, the property of Edward Burgess.

William Barrow, a horse-slaughterer in Tothil-fields, Westminster, swore, that about the middle of September last, the prisoner came to him with a horse into the yard, and said, he brought it from a person of the name of Bowman, at Kensington Gravel Pits; that he was to have it killed, and that he was to take back the ears to the owner, to prove to him that the horse was killed. The witness told the

the prisoner, "that he should not kill the horse, neither should the horse be delivered back to the prisoner, until it should be ascertained to whom the horse belonged," for the witness suspected the prisoner had stolen the horse: he therefore determined to make inquiry, whether there was such a person as Mr. Bowman at Kensington. Accordingly, he sent his boy some time afterwards to make this inquiry, the result of which was, that no such person was met with. In the mean time, the prisoner went away, saying, "he would come again for the horse, or the value of him." The witness having looked at the horse a good deal, found on it the Hackney-Marsh mark. On the Friday week following, the prisoner came to the house of the witness, as he said he would; in the mean time, the witness had caused the horse to be advertised, but nobody came under that advertisement to claim it. The prisoner said, he wanted the money for the horse, for he said he thought the horse was dead; but the witness told him, the horse was not dead, but that he had advertised it; and that he had sent his boy to fetch a constable, upon which the prisoner ran away directly; the witness pursued, took, and with some difficulty, secured him, and gave him into the charge of a constable; he was taken to the Public Office at Bow-street, and committed. In consequence of some advice, the witness took the horse to the neighbourhood of Hackney, supposing that he might belong to somebody thereabouts, as he had the Hackney-Marsh mark, and that he might possibly find his way home and be owned; accordingly, being let loose, the horse walked for about three miles, and the witness followed him until he came to the house of Mr. Burgess, to whom he belonged, and who had had him for about four years; the horse walked into the yard, and his master knew him immediately.

The prisoner said, he bought the horse of Mr. Bowman, of Kensington, but he called no witness.— *Guilty, Death.*

Curious Advertisement.

THE following curious advertisement is actually to be found in a Hamburgh Paper:—The lady, who is the advertiser, is Wilhelmina Henrietta Antonia, of Altona. It has been so often repeated since that period, that there can be little doubt of the sincerity of her wishes to find a proper companion.

"As I have not yet found a man," says Miss Antonia, "whom I can love, I have contracted a general desire to please, either by politeness, by following the fashions, or by a spirit of malice, which, however, never degenerates into genuine coquetishness. An invincible love for liberty, and a certain taste for idleness and ease, which renders every kind of authority insupportable to me, have prevented me hitherto from marrying. I have not yet found any man so superior as to command me, so suitable as to enslave me, so void of character as to be my slave, so discreet and so faithful as to be my friend. I have a mind too elevated, a heart too timid, and an imagination too ardent for me to be the subject of a long continued delusion. I neither wish to command, or to obey any man. I wish for a friend with whom I may pass my life, and divide my fortune, united by the purest, the truest, and the most virtuous sentiments, without constraint, and without reserve, without false delicacy, and without vanity; music, interesting reading, the society of some well-informed and high-educated man would fill up our lives.

"If, therefore, there is to be found a woman between the age of 20 and 30, of a good constitution and moral character, well brought up, who, together with a pure and sensible heart, a reasonable and unaffected mind, and a correct taste, possesses politeness, feminine qualities, prudence, and that sincerity which the common intercourse of society requires, I should be happy to offer her my friendship and my house. I should wish that she should neither be ugly, nor absolutely poor. If the particulars which I have enumerated are found to answer, I hope she will, with a noble frankness, acquaint me through the medium of the *Affiches des Empire*, with her good qualities, and even with her failings, and that she will consent to partake with me the pleasures and the pains of life; she will find in my house an income of 4000 marks annually, a commodious and extensive apartment, with a fine view over a large garden towards the Elbe, entirely at her own disposal. My carriage and my servants shall be entirely at her command. She shall eat by herself when she pleases. We shall make trial of each other's dispositions for three years. All I stipulate is, that she shall be neither a French woman, a Jewess, nor a Lady of Quality."

AN AQUATIC EXCURSION TO MARGATE.

WE left Billingsgate on board the British Queen, wind N.E by E. about half after one o'clock on Monday last. Our party amounted to one hundred and sixty, the principal of whom were Ladies. — Expectations of much pleasure during their excursion, and other causes, produced the most perfect harmony for several hours; and many excellent songs were sung with much spirit. We had not been on board above an hour, before dinner commenced in the cabin, when all the female part of the company appeared to enjoy their provisions with a good appetite. They next expatiated on the inconveniences attendant on the voyage, as if they were only ideal. The seamen on board encouraged their hopes. "We shall be down in seven hours and a half; perhaps it may be nine—at any rate in twelve," was the general opinion. This, however, was not the opinion of the Captain, and the result was as he expected. The wind at five o'clock was due East, and we were then only at Northfleet; at seven, we got off Gravesend, having made tacks for above an hour, and lost ground every tack. We then cast anchor until the next tide, having the mortification of remaining five hours on that station, till high-water commenced at twelve o'clock. The steward providing the ladies with hot water, and the gentlemen being very attentive in waiting, tea was drank on deck by every judicious person on board; for those who preferred the cabin, soon experienced the ill effects of it; and then "the joys of a sailor's life" appeared no more. We soon understood the situation of those below, by the effect on the deck. After we weighed anchor, a strong gale sprung up: it was then that sickness was the order of the day. The births in the cabin were full in a moment, and every place occupied under hatch. From their being crowded, convulsions succeeded sickness, and the scene of horror was heightened by the whistling of the wind, and the washing of the decks; all above board

board were inundated, and all below lying over each other, huddled together by the rolling of the ship. Every passenger on board was sick, even the ship's steward.—The morning appeared with a watry sun; a sure indication of wet weather. At six o'clock, we were off Yantlet, at the Nore—the atmosphere pouring down a torrent of rain.

A council was held among the ladies (the gale continuing), when it was resolved to petition the captain to put back to Gravesend; and on their knees they requested the gentlemen to back their intreaties. A scene of more general misery never appeared on a pleasureable excursion. A twenty-pound note was tendered by one lady to the captain, who, being a good-natured fellow, said, if the majority of the company wished to return, he would comply. This being the case, we tacked about, at seven o'clock, the wind being still N.N.E.; at eleven, we got back to Gravesend, where thirty-five ladies went ashore, and several gentlemen. Here we left them, to procure post-coaches to Rochester, from whence they proposed taking any casual conveyance to Margate. At one o'clock we set sail, to traverse the same course we had left; the wind having veered round to the west, we scudded along rapidly, and in half an hour Gravesend was out of sight. The favourable gale continuing, we continued on one tack till ten o'clock at night, when a dead calm succeeded, being then off the Sisters, about nine miles from Margate. The lights on the Piers, and at the Duke's Head Inn, were clearly perceptible. A light shower, attended by lightning, which was extremely vivid, was succeeded by a gale of wind, and at a quarter after twelve, we reached Margate Pier, and then every one endeavoured to secure a bed, after being thirty-six hours on our passage. The town, however, being full, no beds at that hour could be procured; we were, therefore, necessitated to remain on board for another night. We passed it in the manner of the preceding one, lying on the deck as close to each other, for the sake of warmth, as possible: however great our inclination might be for sleep, the cold prevented its taking place. When day-light appeared, we walked round the Cliffs, and on the Pier, until the innkeepers arose at six o'clock, when we breakfasted, and concurred in one general opinion on the *pleasures* of a Margate hoy.

The parties who left us at Gravesend, got into Margate at twelve o'clock, fatigued almost to death with the journey, and put to the expence of five guineas for a chaise, the distance from Gravesend to Margate being fifty miles.

Margate was never known to be so full; beds are three shillings a night, garrets are cheap at half-a-guinea per week. The ordinary is two shillings and sixpence a-head; last year it was two shillings, and beds one and sixpence. The extravagant charges will do no good to the place.

This morning left us the New Rose in June (the old one has been broken up). The passengers amounted to 120, returning to London.——*Aug.* 22, 1800.

INSTRUCTIONS FOR SHOPKEEPERS, APPRENTICES, &c. IN THE MANNER OF SWIFT.

WHEN a Shopkeeper first enters on business, he ought to advertise for a partner in trade, with at least 1000*l.* and in so doing, set forth that the profits will clear 40 or 50 *per cent*, and that the advertiser will take on himself the *active* part of the business; by this is understood, every thing relating thereto, more especially *money matters*. When he gets up in the morning, let him dress off in the *sprucest style*—nankeen trowsers very wide, made *a-la-Turque*, as the size of a Turk's *inexpressibles* are very convenient, and much admired by the *fair sex*; have your hair cropt in the neatest manner, the hair rather close, which will give the head the elegant small appearance of the *Apollo of Belvidere*. The little hair that is left, should be distracted in a variety of directions, so as to affect the natural carelessness of an *Orlando Furioso*; but by no means wear any powder, as it will dirty your clothes, and give you the appearance of a *barber* or a *miller*. Your cravat should come up to your ears, and be filled out with a stiffner *large* and *strong*, which will give you the appearance of great strength, a natural qualification, and *useful* to the ladies in *a variety of ways*. You must always imitate your superiors as nearly as possible; and, as it is the humour among our *capricious islanders*, for the peasant to *tread on the kibes of the Peer*, you are by no means to forget the privilege. Let your waistcoat be *very short*, which will answer one elegant purpose, and two very laudable ones; the first is, it will shew the fascinating *contour* of your hip; the second, save cloth, and consequently expence; and, lastly, you will mortify *Snip*, by injuring the luxuriance of his *cabbage*. Be sure you follow the same plan in your coat; have the buttons on the hip set very close, which will help to give you the appearance of a manly breadth in the shoulders; and let the tail be cut as sharp away, as a *jack-daw's*, or *a fighting cock's*, when he is spurred and chipt out for battle. The Shopmen and grown-up Apprentices may observe the same rules as their young *airy* masters, but with the additional caution, never to be seen, like *Warty Cockney*, sweeping the shop in a white apron; this part of your business will be readily taken off your hands for a few coppers. Thus equipped, get behind your counter about twelve o'clock, and take care that you *handle your yard* in a genteel stile, as nothing so much pleases the ladies, as to observe your address *in this way*. Keep the lady in close conversation; catch the *amorous glances* of her eye with a most *significant look*; and you must know a look speaks *silent and most expressive language*; and be sure to *touch* her fair hand, which conveys a wonderful sympathy; and to know the effect of such, you need only read the amours of *Uncle Toby* and *Widow Wadman*, who carried on their courtship by similar touches, in tracing out the parallels in his plan of the *siege of Dunquerque*; by *touches* he gained the widow's heart, and a *Shopkeeper* may come off as well in *the field of Venus*, as a *Soldier*. As the *lone fish* are now coming *up the rivers*, to take shelter about the *luxuriant shores* of the venerable Thames for the winter, your shops to a certainty will be, no doubt, much frequented by them, which will give you the finest opportunity of selecting a most agreeable acquaintance among them: they will be easily distinguished by the *keenness* of their *salamander looks*; and one great thing in your favour is, that ladies of the above description always shew a marked partiality for those, who can furnish them with articles at an *easy rate*. From the great variety that frequents your shops, your amours may be regulated in the most agreeable manner —a few yards of muslins, &c. and *a gig of a Sunday*, will *frank you* for the

the whole week; and you will obtain for those trifles what the *hoary Peer, the man of large fortune,* and the *fat* and *greasy Citizen,* retired from business, must pay hundreds for. Should the sums attending your *gallantry,* the chances of the *hazard-table,* and a variety of concurring expences, render a *bankruptcy* inevitable, do it in as masterly a stile as possible; the more you take in, the less loss will it be to each, and you will be called a d——d *clever fellow,* instead of the miserable appellation of a *paltry rogue;* and you need not blush at paying them with *a shilling in the pound,* as you have numerous examples to follow in this respect. One thing I would particularly recommend, let your shop be very large; buy a cart-load of straw, and plenty of brown paper; make up neat parcels, with a small diamond cut in front of each, to which may be pasted a scrap of different cloths: thus your shop will make a most respectable appearance; and as grocers set off their shops with *empty canisters,* apothecaries with *bladders and empty bottles to make up a show,* you have a right to do the same; but above all, a few days before you break, have your house *fresh painted.*   G.

PERTINENT PLEASANTRIES *upon the* PRICE *of* CORN.

To the EDITORS *of the* SPORTING MAGAZINE.

GENTLEMEN,

HAVING occasion to visit a friend a few miles out of town, I stept into one of those inviting vehicles, called *Short stages,* and soon found myself one of six " agreeable companions," who resolved to shorten and sweeten their journey by a familiar exchange of sentiments. The *scarcity* occurred to us before we were off the stones. " It is all owing," said a grave looking gentleman, " it is all owing to the *war* in which we are engaged." " Nay," interrupted a young gentleman in a smart uniform, " it can't be owing to the war; you have had wars before, and no scarcity; and besides, *what should we have done without the war.* In my opinion, the *monopolizers* are at the bottom of the whole business." " *Monopolizers!*" quoth a third person, in a drab coat, " that is easier said than proved? where are these monopolizers to be found? No, no; it is owing to the *millers.*" — " The *millers,* indeed!" exclaimed a very pretty country-looking woman, who seemed to be possessed of the *clack;* " the millers, indeed! I wonder people will allow their tongues such freedoms with large bodies of men; there have always been millers, and I should be glad to know besides, *what you would do without millers?* It is very clear it is all owing to the *great farmers.*" " I don't know, Ma'am," said the fifth person in our collection, " why the great farmers are to be blamed; a man may surely be a great farmer, without being a great rogue: people are not to bring their corn in handfuls to market: there have always been great farmers; besides, *what would you do without great farmers?* For my part, I have no doubt the root of the evil lies in Mark-lane; look at your *corn-factors,*" added he, with an air of triumph, and looking at me, as if he expected my opinion. I said it might be so, I was unacquainted with the subject; where all parties are blamed, it is probable some deserved it. The military spark, recollecting himself, declared he would be d——d if the *bakers* had not a share in this business; but the bakers won

even found an advocate in the pretty female, who pleaded the cause of the millers; and who exclaimed, "The *bakers!* Lord help them! the worst-used people on the face of the earth: when did you hear of a baker that was rich? Besides, *what would you do without bakers?*"

This gave me an opportunity to sum up the evidence, by observing, that as *we could not do* without *corn*, nor without *millers*, nor without *great farmers*, nor without *cornfactors*, nor without *bakers*, we had nothing left but to sit down quietly, and submit to our grievances; as, notwithstanding so many persons are desirous of throwing the blame, it is impossible to make it stick anywhere. This seemed tolerably agreeable to all parties (each reserving his own opinion to himself), and peace was restored upon a tolerable footing, when an unlucky question, started by one of my companions, again split the coach into parties. This was no other than " Was the scarcity *real* or *artificial?*" The officer, and the enemy to *cornfactors*, maintained with great powers of vociferation, that the scarcity was *artificial*. They had travelled; they had beheld the harvest; they had seen things with their own eyes; they were convinced, that all the world should not make them think otherwise.

On the other hand, the advocates for the *millers,* the *great farmers*, and the *bakers,* maintained, with equal strength of lungs, that the scarcity was *real*. They too had travelled; they had beheld the harvest; they had seen things with their own eyes; they were convinced, and all the world should not make them think otherwise. The latter party, however, trusted that I would not be silent on this question; for as there had been riots in London, undoubtedly I must know something of the matter;" and, I perceive, Sir," said the pretty lady, " I perceive, Sir, by the buttons on your coat, that you belong to one of the *corps*; so you must know something!"

I assured my hearers, that neither my situation in the *corps*, nor my residence in London, had qualified me to talk upon this subject; on the contrary, I was afraid that these circumstances were against me; for I had not, like them, " travelled, beheld the harvest, nor seen things with my own eyes;" that I had often heard the subject canvassed as it had been to-day, in which assertion was placed against assertion, hearsay against hearsay, and eye-sight against eye-sight; but that I remained as ignorant as before of the question in dispute, and feared I should ever remain so.

It appears to me, Gentlemen, rather a hard case, that we cannot go into company without being obliged to listen to discussions, which arrive at no conclusion; where opinions are given in lieu of arguments, and mere assertions substituted for proofs; and of which discussions, the only object seems to be, to prove how much a man can talk on a subject which he does not understand. Prejudice, too, is a gainer on such occasions; and I am afraid much, of what we call a social interchange of sentiments, tends only to the confirmation of certain pre conceived opinions.

But to return to the causes of scarcity. Is not this way of tracing effects to causes rather common in other cases? Ask what is the cause of the scarcity of morals, and you will be referred to the remissness of the *magistrate*.—No, says the magistrate, I am not remiss, but the *laws* are deficient: the *legislature* never knows how to strike at the root of an evil.—The *legislature?*

tore! exclaims a member of Parliament, what cant is all this? What can the legislature do? Is not our statute-book already crouded with penalties? Is there a crime untouched? We may punish the guilty, but can we prevent their *crape?* Can we make men honest?

To descend from great things to small, what is the cause of the scarcity of good plays? Ask the *manager*, and he will tell you, that no good plays are offered to him, and appeals, as he justly may, for proof of this assertion, to such as do appear.—But ask our *dramatic writers*, and they will tell you, the managers afford no encouragement to good writing, and prefer pantomimical namby-pamby, or translations, which can be *got up* cheap, to the *genuine English drama*. But ask the managers and writers when they happen to be together, and cannot abuse one another, and they will jointly assure you, that the *town* is in fault, that the public taste is vitiated, and that good plays will not go *down*; besides, they add, *in confidence*, that there is a most piercing scarcity of *good actors*. And the actors, when consulted apart from either managers or writers, will assure you there is no encouragement to good acting; such trash given them to perform as does not require, and cannot therefore be supposed to draw forth, a display of genius!

Thus, Gentlemen, I presume, the scarcity of bread will not be a matter of greater difficulty to understand, than the causes why *wars* are begun, and why not sooner-ended. But, on this subject, I am afraid to trust myself, lest I not only trespass on your time, but add one to that happy number, who mistake fancies for facts, and are inclined to triumph as much when they make a bold assertion, as when they advance a striking proof. And so I remain in my usual state of ignorance and uncertainty, as to all the topics alluded to in this letter, and know only for certain that

I am, Sir, your's, &c.
SCEPTICUS.

The SUBMERSION *of* SWALLOWS.

Decided from the Testimony of Mr. POLLOCK, *a respectable character, and an inhabitant of New-York, as follows:*—

"ON the afternoon of the 24th of August, 1798, I was sitting in my parlour, which looks towards the North river, about fifty feet from the bank, in company with our mutual friend, Mr Jacob Sebor. Our attention was attracted by numerous flights of birds, which appeared to come across the town from the eastward, and descend immediately into the river. So singular an appearance excited our particular observation. We went out and stood close to the bank, and then perceived, that what we at first imagined to be blackbirds, were actually swallows; and that as soon as the various flocks had cleared the houses, and got directly over the river, they plunged into the water, and disappeared. This was not confined to the vicinity of the place where we stood, but was the case as far as the eye could reach, up and down the river, and continued without cessation for nearly two hours, when the closing of the evening prevented our farther observation.

"Aware of the importance of affording any additional information on this long-disputed question in the natural history of the swallow, I procured a telescope, and watched attentively many of the flocks from their first appearance, until their immersion, continuing my eye fixed upon the spot long enough to be fully

fully convinced, that not one of the birds returned to the surface again. Indeed, one flock of about two hundred birds plunged into the water within thirty yards of us, and instantly disappeared, without the least appearance of opposition that might be expected to arise from their natural buoyancy; and, at the same time, the evening was so serene, and the river so unruffled, that no deception of our sight could possibly have occurred.

"When the birds first came in view, after crossing the town, their flight was easy and natural; but when they descended near to the water, they appeared much agitated and distressed, flying in a confused manner against each other, as if the love of life, common to all animals, impelled them to revolt against this law of nature imposed upon their species. "As some time has elapsed since the above-mentioned facts occurred, I thought it proper, before I gave you Mr. Sebor's name, as having been a witness to them, to consult his recollection on the subject, and I have pleasure in assuring you, he distinctly remembers every circumstance I have recited, and of which I made a memorandum at the time."

"It may be worthy of remark, that as far as my observation went, the swallows totally disappeared on the 24th of August, 1798; for, during the remainder of that year, I did not see one.

"H. POLLOCK."

New-York, 18th July, 1800.

THEATRICALS.

COVENT-GARDEN THEATRE.

ON Saturday, Nov. 1, was introduced to the stage, Mr. Reynolds's new comedy, called *Life*, and which experienced, from a brilliant audience, a no less favourable reception than the best of his former productions. The principal *dramatis personæ*, and fable of this piece, are as follow:

Sir Harry Torpid	Mr. Lewis,
Clifford	Mr. Farley,
Primitive	Mr. Munden,
Marchmont	Mr. Murray,
Lackbrain	Mr. Fawcett,
Crafty	Mr. Emery,
Mrs. Belmont	Miss Chapman,
Mrs. Decoy	Mrs. St. Ledger,
Rosa Marchmont	Miss Murray.

The scene is laid at a fashionable watering-place, and the most prominent characters consist of the description of people in the habit of frequenting such a resort. Among these, *Sir Harry* is one of those loungers, so much the subject of ridicule of the present day, who, over-run with *ennui*, fly from one scene of dissipation to another, in vain, for amusement. At last, he meets with *Rosa*, the beauteous and amiable daughter of *Marchmont*, a gentleman in pecuniary distress, and falls in love with her. This proves a stimulus to his mind, and a sovereign cure for his *ennui*. He becomes at once a man of activity; seeking his own happiness in the attainment of his mistress, and also endeavouring to promote the felicity of others. In the number of these, is *Mrs. Decoy,* a fortune-hunting impostor, who contrives to draw *Lackbrain,* an unpolished country Squire, into a marriage.

Just at this period, *Primitive,* the uncle of *Lackbrain,* returns from the West-Indies with a large fortune. He is delighted to hear of his nephew's marriage, and of the taste of the young couple for simple rustic life. On examination, however, he finds it a scene of intrigue, dissipation, and debauchery; and takes under his care and protection, *Mrs. Belmont,* an amiable and distressed woman, on whose person, *Clifford,* a young Templar, entertains a dishonourable design.

The

The *denouement* consists in the discovery, that *Mrs. Belmont* is the wife of *Marchmont*, and mother of *Rosa*, and his own daughter, whom he had disowned on her marriage against his approbation, and whom *Marchmont*, her husband, had also afterwards abandoned to the world, giving himself up to dissipation. A reconciliation takes place between the husband and wife, and *Rosa* is united to *Sir Harry*.

The *comic* object of Mr. Reynolds, in this play, seems more that of satyrizing the existing follies of the day, as they attach to individuals, than in delineating a *general picture of life*—The *extortion* and dissipation of the lower order of watering-places, receive from his hand most liberal and well-deserved castigation.

The story of this play, so far as it is made the vehicle of sentiment, is drawn up altogether after the German model, and therefore, perhaps, it savours more of romance than real life; but, as the morality it conveys, is altogether sterling English, we consider ourselves obliged to the author for divesting, what is at present a popular kind of writing, of some of its most offensive peculiarities.

The character given to Lewis, is not so rich in humour as some from the same pencil; but it has touches of nature, which makes it more welcome to the heart. Of the actor's success in sustaining it, it is unnecessary to speak. Miss Murray was extremely interesting in the amiable daughter of *Marchmont*; as was Miss Chapman, in the persecuted wife. Munden's benevolent old man was very forcibly drawn; and Fawcett, in *Lackbrain*, was highly entertaining. Mrs. St. Ledger was buxom and gay in the intriguing fortune-hunter, but somewhat coarse. We thought Murray rather laboured; and Emery was much too starched in the *Librarian*. The second and last acts of this play are the best; a strong interest is, however, kept up throughout; and it was altogether loudly applauded.

Several new scenes have been painted for it, some of which are local portraits. The prologue and epilogue, spoken by Whitfield and Munden, have little to recommend them. The latter ridicules crops of every description; the best point of which, is the mistake of a traveller, who, in the bustle of changing horses at an inn, gives the half-crown he had intended for the post-chaise-boy, to a natty Peer!

COVENT-GARDEN THEATRE.

A NEW musical entertainment, in three acts, intituled *Il Bondocani*, was performed here on Saturday, November 15. The characters were—

Haroun Alraschid —	Mr. Townsend,
Chebib —	Mr. Emery,
Abdalla —	Mr. Hill,
Hassan —	Mr. Farley,
Haseb —	Mr. Whitfield,
Mesrour —	Mr. Blanchard,
The Cadi of Bagdad —	Mr. Fawcett,
Mabsud —	Mr. Beverly,
Corrib —	Mr. Claremont,
Officer —	Mr. Atkins,
Captain of the Guard —	Mr. King.
Viziers, Emirs, Agas, Soldiers, &c.	
Camira —	Miss Dixon,
Darina —	Mrs. Mills.

The advertisement candidly admits, that the story is taken from the *New Arabian Tales*; but even the *New Arabian Tales* cannot pretend to originality, for the two principal characters, the *Caliph* and the *Cadi*, are borrowed from *Measure for Measure*.—The scene is laid at Bagdad; the Caliph of which place, concealed under the assumed name of *Il Bondocani*, and, in the disguise of an Arabian dress, mixes with his subjects in search of a lady worthy to share his throne. In the course of his adventures, he discovers that his *Cadi* is a corrupt judge; *Hassan*, a principal lord of his court, a contemptible coxcomb; and *Dorina*, the daughter of *Gebib*, a poor, but honourable man, the very woman he sought for. The fable is very complete, as it consists of the commencement, the progress, and the completion of the *Caliph's* plan, developed in scenes and incidents of the sprightly, or the ludicrous cast, and judiciously blended with an under-plot of the serious, sentimental kind; the interest of which is produced by the filial piety of *Abdallah*, the son of *Gebib*, who, for the purpose of relieving his father's wants, falsely charges himself with the crime of having carried off a lady from the haram, and thereby obtains the reward offered for the discovery of the offender. In the investigation of this charge before the *Caliph*, who has by this time resumed his proper character, the lady who was carried away, proves to be *Selima*, the mistress of *Abdallah*, of whom he had been in pursuit. Her father now appears, and insists he is the real offender; but the *Caliph*, happy himself, resolved that the joy should be universal, forgives all the parties, and thus concludes his adventure.

The texture of this plot is far superior to the generality of flimsy productions of the same class, which have been recently produced. The author (Mr. T. Dibdin) does not seek to avail himself of the pitiful apology so often made for deficiency in this particular, and therefore looks to something more than the praise of having contrived " a sufficient vehicle for the music." All the scenes form a well-connected whole, and all the characters a well-connected company, embellished with much chaste sentiment, sprightly humour, and several situations of highly comic effect. Of these latter, the last act, for which the author seems to have reserved his strength, possesses by much the greatest portion. The prison-scene, particularly, where the *Cadi* attempts to exercise upon others the art of corruption, which had been so often practised upon himself with success, produces a very good effect, and is managed with great address. But while we allow this just praise to the life, the spirit, the interest, and construction of the piece, it is impossible not to notice the gross absurdity, however common, of exhibiting the citizens of Bagdad in English customs, manners, and modes of thinking. The scene, no doubt, is laid at Bagdad, very properly, for the introduction of the great variety of magnificent dresses, in which the manager has been liberal in the extreme; but, surely, for the sake of consistency, of the delusion, if such were intended, the author should have drawn his characters with some regard to the manners of their country, and not like so many English at a masquerade. The defect is principally observable in the character of the *Cadi*, the great support of the piece. This Chief Justice of Bagdad is made to speak and act precisely as an English attorney, who had stood in the pillory for mal-practice. To produce strong ludicrous effect, characters must, we admit, be forced from their natural situations, and exhibited in improbable points of view; but, if an author would transport the imagination of his audience to Bagdad, he must not insist upon setting it down at the Old Bailey. In point of spectacle, the piece is very rich, and the music, in quantity, just sufficient for embellishment, without retarding the progress of the plot, or disjointing the scenes, and thus frittering away all the interest. It is, we understand,

understand, the joint composition of Messrs. Moorhead and Attwood. The overture abounds in variety of movements. Mrs. Mills has two pleasing airs, the first of them a very delicate one, which she executed with taste. Mr. Fawcett, in the *Cadi*, has also two of a humourous, lively stile, well written for the character, in which he was encored. The audience was the most brilliant and numerous of the season; and the piece, which did not experience the slightest disapprobation during the performance, was announced for a second representation with loud applauses.

Of the poetry, the following was among the best, executed very happily by Mr. Townsend:

Thus when the mariner, inclin'd to sleep,
On a deceitful calm relies,
Sudden the awful thunder roars,
Sudden the forked lightning flies,
And the loud storm appals the distant shores,
    Whirlwinds and cataracts unite,
    To fill the wretch with dire affright,
And wanton o'er the bosom of the deep.

Or when the Indian, careless of his foes,
    Marches secure beneath the forest's shade,
Too soon the adverse shout he knows;
    In vain he mixes in the strife,
    Tho' dear, the warrior sells his life,
He falls, and eyes with gore the hostile blade.

FRENCH THEATRE.

A NEW Piece, called the *Prisoner for Debt*, has lately been produced, of which the following is the plot:—*Amelia* is beloved by M. *Sainville*, her uncle, but she prefers *Edward* to him, who is a young painter, very much captivated with her, and who comes to paint M. *Sainville*. While drawing the picture of the uncle, he drew, by stealth, the features of the niece, and in place of one portrait he made two. They are almost finished, and *Edward* prevails on *Amelia* to place herself behind her uncle, who was to sit to him for the last time. M. *Sainville* over-hearing this conversation, is confirmed in the opinion of the love of *Edward* and *Amelia*, which he had hitherto only suspected. He does not derange their plan, but seats himself, suffers his niece to take her station, and it is not till the middle of the sitting, that, seizing the hand of the latter, he informs the two lovers that he is not their dupe. After having possessed himself of the portrait of *Amelia*, he dismisses *Edward*, whom he refuses to pay, under the pretence that his portrait is not like. The latter keeps it, and retires, projecting some means of vengeance. Soon after, *Germain*, valet to M. *de Sainville*, comes to inform his master, that the painter, in order to avenge himself, has drawn over his portrait, the grated bars of a prison, and has put at the bottom this inscription—*The Prisoner for Debt*—and has exposed it in this state in the hall of the Museum; that every person has recognized him, and that he is become the laughing-stock of the public. M. *Sainville*, quite furious, determines to go to the Museum to destroy the picture.—His niece prevents him, and advises him rather to send to *Edward*, and treat amicably with. The uncle follows this advice, but the young painter raises difficulties, and rejects the money offered him to suppress the picture. M. *Sainville* asks *Edward* what he wants, and even goes so far as to propose restoring to him the portrait of his niece. The painter declares, that he will not withdraw the picture, except on condition of the hand of her whom he loves, being promised to him. The uncle hesitates, and at last consents. Immediately, *Edward* causes the portrait to be brought, upon which there

there is in reality painted the grate of a prison, but which had not been exposed in the Museum. *M. Sainville* sees with great pleasure, that *Edward* only wished to frighten him, and he unites the two lovers.

When we read of forty-five new plays being produced on the theatres of Paris, in the course of a single month, we *must* suppose many of them are like that which was a *great* favourite of the *great* Cardinal *Richelieu*. The *dramatis personæ* were only *three*;—and Mr. Dibdin, in his History of the Stage, describes the *plot* of it as follows:—

Turlupin grows jealous of his friend *Guguille*, and is determined to cut off his wife's head!. He seizes her by the hair, with a drawn sabre in his hand, whilst she, upon her knees, conjures him, *by every thing dear to him*, to abate his anger. She reminds him of their *past loves:* how she *rubbed his back*, when he had the *rheumatism;* and how charmed she was, when he wore his *flannel night-cap*. But all in vain. "Will nothing move thee?" cries this *amiable* female, (a character personated by a man of the name of *Gros Guillaume*, who was almost as broad as long) in the last accents of despair. "Oh, cruel!—Think, "think on the bacon and cabbage "I fried for you yesterday."— "Oh, the sorceress!" cries *Turlupin*, "I cannot resist her. She "knows how to take me by my "foible. The bacon!—the fat is "now rising in my stomach.— "Live,—my cabbage,—and be du- "tiful."

Among the multitude of new pieces which the French Theatre now almost daily produces, it would be strange if nothing of merit were to appear. Now and then, however, something like good Comedy is to be found.

An author lately produced a piece, which had considerable success, which is admired as a specimen of genuine Comedy. The object of the writer is to prove, that the misconduct of wives is generally the fault of the husband. This truth he has chosen to illustrate by wit and ridicule, rather than by grave morality, and by scenes of distress.

The piece is called *The Three Husbands*. One is jealous to excess, alarmed at every step of his wife, even the most indifferent, every moment dreading a stain upon his honour: the other is equally in the other extreme, careless of his wife's behaviour from vanity, judging it impossible that he should be injured, and thus from security and presumption, he neglects the attention and kindness which his spouse expects: the third husband having lost two wives, had married a third, who is lost, but not feeling his enjoyments impaired, he is at no pains to recover her; this character is a sort of go-between to the other two; he is their professed friend and comforter, while in reality his interference contributes chiefly to augment their chagrins, and to add to their perplexities.

Two Wives are represented as plain, honest City Dames, displeased with their husbands, and choosing a whimsical course to obtain redress of grievances. They consult in their difficulties a Female Conjurer of great address, who, instead of calling in the aid of the Black Art, employs her talent for intrigue, and her knowledge of life to correct the errors of the Husbands, and to give them the lesson they require.

A foolish Pretender to gallantry is introduced, paying his addresses to both the Wives at once; and the Sybil plays him off, to produce the effect she wishes upon the Husbands. She instructs the Wives how they ought to act.—The one endeavours to rouse the jealousy of
the

the confident and secure Husband, the other to quiet the alarm of the jealous. For this purpose, the pretender is encouraged; assignations are made and discovered; perplexed and comic situations succeed, till at last both Husbands are corrected, and all parties rendered happy in the married state. The third Husband in the Sybil, recovers his lost Wife, and, after having been employed to produce the general contentment, the foolish gallant is dismissed to contempt and ridicule.

It is evident, we think, that the author, M. Picard, has had *The Merry Wives of Windsor* in his eye:—the jealousy of *Ford*, and the security of *Page*, are imitated in the two first Husbands, and the foolish gallant is a parody upon Sir *John Falstaff*. M. Picard has, however, introduced much novelty and variety in the plot of his Drama, and the Dialogue is said to be replete with wit and humour. The Piece ranks among the pleasantest which the French stage has for some time produced.—The French, indeed, have not had much to boast of lately: they have been forced, like ourselves, to subsist often upon their own eminent writers, first tortured and disfigured by German manufacturers, and then produced still more meagre in a translation.

GUY FAUX.

ON the 5th instant, Guy Faux was led in procession, according to ancient custom, by the boys of the metropolis, and the contributions were levied as usual to defray the expence of a *decent execution*. In the west end of the town, the culprit was carried round in a cart, to the solemn sound of a band of marrow-bones and cleavers. He was attended by a clergyman, who read prayers to him, earnestly exhorting him to think seriously of his awful situation. The wretch, however, appeared very *hardened*, and was perfectly *deaf* to the advices of his ghostly attendant. Being desired to confess his crimes, he refused to answer. During all the ceremony, he observed a most impenetrable silence. It must be admitted, indeed, that he did not follow the example of many incorrigible criminals, in scoffing at religion, damning the parson, or kicking Jack Ketch. He was quite resigned and composed. The shouts of the populace never deranged his equanimity, though the joltings of the cart seemed to render his posture somewhat uneasy. Considering the badness of the times, he was decently attired, and the reversion of his gala suit may be a perquisite worth half-a-crown, to be equally divided between the ordinary and the hangman.

The clergyman, indeed, was scarcely canonical in his appearance. He was dressed in a very becoming wig, well powdered. In contempt of the malefactor, however, he had, instead of his surplice, a drayman's frock, which, it ought in justice to be stated, had been scowered on purpose for the occasion. Though Guy could not have been insensible to this insult, he discovered no symptoms of resentment; and it is universally allowed, that he finished his career in perfect charity with all mankind

JOURNAL OF MODERN CHARACTERS.

A BON VIVANT.

ROSE at twelve with a most confounded head ache—Eyes sunk in my head—My mouth dreadfully parched—My pulse feverish—Could'nt eat any breakfast, so drank a bumper of brandy to *set me to rights*—About two o'clock, sauntered down to the Coffee-house, and had a bason of vermicelli, with
three

three glasses of noyau—At half past two, eat a devil'd kidney, and drank two glasses of Madeira—Half an hour afterwards, took a glass of nervous restorative cordial, and washed it down with a dram.

About five, finding my appetite very lax! la! took two glasses of bitters, and, at half past six, sat down to dinner—Couldn't eat a morsel—What the devil ails me?—A gentleman said, I must go to bed sooner; take more exercise, and never touch any thing between meals—Hate these prating fellows—How the devil can I lead a more regular life?—Don't I live every day the same?—However, though I couldn't eat a dinner, I made amends by drinking; for, before the cloth was taken away, I had dispatched a bottle of Madeira, and three bumpers of brandy, by way of *settling my stomach!*

At eight o'clock, sat in to drinking, and by two in the morning, had taken to my own share three bottles of Port, and five devil'd biscuits.

At three o'clock, got home, and, finding myself rather queer, took two glasses of hot brandy and water, half and half, and, having nothing else to do, undress'd myself as well as I could, and went to bed?

Of how many in the metropolis is this Journal the epitome? Oh that men, possessing the attributes of reason and intellect, should clothe themselves in the sensual habits of brutes!

CASH ACCOUNT OF A PRETTY FRENCH WOMAN.
(From a French Journal.)

DEBTS AND EXPENCES.—To the baker I owe 60 francs; for a box at the Italian Theatre, paid 30 louis; to the butcher, for six months meat, owe 224 francs; given on account 12 francs; for a hen turkey, with truffles, paid two louis; to the grocer, for sugar, coffee, wax, &c. owe 129 francs; to *Berthelemet*, for comfits, pastilles, &c. paid seven louis; for water, I owe 36 francs; for *liqueurs* paid 100 crowns; to the apothecary, for remedies in my last cold, I owe 107 francs. To the perfumer for scents, rouge, and virgin milk, paid 10½ louis; to my cook owe two years wages; to my dancing-master, for three months lessons, paid nine louis; to my milliner, for gloves, laces, &c. I owe four hundred francs; for three hats bought of *Lervi*, paid 12 louis; to my mantua-maker, I owe for five robes, 126 francs; to the jeweller for my solitaire, paid 46 louis; to my upholsterer, for beds and other furniture, I owe 25 louis; to the music seller, for a harp paid, 700 francs; to the painter, for my portrait, paid six louis; to my shoe-maker, I owe 200 francs; for refreshments and decorations at my last ball, paid 500 francs.

There are other articles in this account, nearly similar to the foregoing; but this is sufficient to show, what a pretty woman at Paris pays for, and what she does not. I have passed over several articles written in abbreviations, which I cannot decypher. They are, without doubt, what may be called secret expences. Several were indicated only by the initials; but all were paid for ready money.

ON TROTTING HORSES.

To the EDITORS *of the* SPORTING MAGAZINE.

GENTLEMEN,

YOU lately stated (correctly enough) that an old one-eyed mare trotted over the Huntingdon road seventeen miles, in about

about fifty-seven minutes; also, that the same mare trotted afterwards the like distance in less than fifty-three minutes. The truth of the matter is, the losers, supposing the first performance so surprising, and suspecting (no unfair supposition in these cases) that *the bull had been thrown over the bridge*, paid their money with much reluctance, and immediately betted four hundred pounds to one, that the mare did not trot seventeen miles in fifty-six minutes.

Now, to look into this matter with sporting eyes, there is really nothing very extraordinary in it, only something new. It sounds high to trot seventeen miles in one hour; but it may really be a performance of much greater ease to a horse, than to trot fifteen in the same time, according to the old rules. The mare in question carried a jockey-boy, weighing only five stone, or 90l.; whereas, of late, it was uncommon for a racing trotter to carry so little as ten stone, or double the weight, besides seldom having the advantage of a good rider.

This change in the trotting system has been effected, in consequence of the advice given by Mr. Lawrence, in his Treatise on Horses, although it was an end, which, with his utmost efforts, he could never previously compass. Many years ago, a dealer, with whom I had some connections, was a party concerned in a trotting match, no weight specified, according to immemorial custom, it was to perform sixteen miles in one hour; but, although I took great pains to represent to this person Mr. Lawrence's opinion of the horse, which was, that he could, with six stone, trot eighteen miles in one hour unhurt—I could not prevail, nor even make the man comprehend, that weight made any difference in trotting, notwithstanding his great repute as a knowing one. With the choice in his own hands, he actually set on horseback eleven stone twelve pounds, exclusive of saddle and bridle, in preference to six stone!

These remarks are made to put the unwary on their guard, and if we must have trotting matches, it is surely infinitely less injurious to the poor animals going over the hard road at such an amazing rate, to carry a light than a heavy weight. On this, and numberless other useful particulars, the keepers of horses of all sorts, would act much for their own interest, by taking the advice of the very humane writer abovementioned. I have the honour to be, with much respect,

Sir, your's, &c.
EQUESTRIUS.

Brentford, Nov. 1.

A DANGEROUS WOMAN.

THAT a word may be a two-edged sword, the following circumstance will illustrate:

The daughter of a barrister, at the death of her father, found herself in possession of a small competence. She was tenderly attached to a feeble mother, who lived a retired life; yet her own excellencies gave her an enlarged circle of acquaintance; but when she appeared in family or private parties, unhappily, she was too much distinguished. The other females were neglected, and, in proportion as the men admired, the ladies, of course, *hated*.

They sifted her conduct for a pretext to have her abandoned, but in vain. A maiden of fortune, who, from her riches, was allowed to give the tone to the opinions of her acquaintance, declared that Miss * * * was a *very dangerous woman*.

The word hit: they severally pronounced with a shake of the head in all their parties, that *such a one*, although very elegant, and very engaging, was a dangerous woman. The girls said this to their brothers, and the wives to their husbands; and they only spoke truth, for when she was present, they were all in danger of being overlooked. Coolness soon turned to estrangement, and this superior creature found, at three and twenty, every door shut to her. A female *friend*, to sooth her uneasiness, told her the cause—" You are believed to be a dangerous woman."

The word was a death stroke to her heart. What could parry it? It implied every thing, without specifying any thing. Had they imputed any vice to her, the whole tenor of her life would have been its refutation. Sinking under the blow, she pined in secret, and her constitution was undermined. Had she made the just translation of this invidious word, she would have been less bitterly affected; for, when they called her dangerous, they only meant that she was *attractive*.

Her wretched mother, by advice of the physician, carried her to Bath. Change of objects and amusement, restored her spirits, her health, and her charms: but, that she might not lose her reputation of being dangerous, a man of affluent fortune declared himself in danger of losing his peace on her account. She withdrew the reserve which had chilled him; marriage followed, and this DANGEROUS WOMAN now moves in a circle far above that from which she was chased; and when the women pursue her with their envy, she takes refuge in the arms of a doating husband.

VERAX.

CURIOUS HISTORY OF DOGS AT THE UNIVERSITY OF GÖTTINGEN.

AT many of the German universities, it has long been a fashion among the students, to be continually surrounded with an unsuitable number of dogs. Even in the lecture-room appears many a beardless Telemachus.

At Göttingen, especially, had this indecorous practice become prevalent: to bring at least one dog into the lecture-room, was considered an indispensable mark of distinction for a young student of rank and fortune. The professors had expressed their displeasure at it, specially *Pütter* and *Michaelis*: the former was particularly expert in hurling down by a well-aimed kick of his foot, such of the canine intruders as chanced to ascend his professional pulpit, so that they flew howling far beyond the seats of the auditors: the latter could not do this, as he delivered his lectures sitting only behind a table. He, however, frequently expressed his indignation, and said, " Can you be answerable to me and the other auditors, if any of those dogs should be going mad, and the madness break out just in this place, that he shall not bite one of us, and thus cause our death, or at least the loss of our reason? It would be better, if at home you repeated and prepared yourself for the lecture, instead of losing your time, by amusing yourself with your dogs. And if you have much bread left, are there not many poor people to whom you may give your superfluity, and who will be thankful for it? but the dog is merely your parasite. The first dog that causes here any disagreeable disturbance, I shall kill with my own hand." And an opportunity soon after occurred

curred to put his threat in execution.

Whether it happened in the winter of 1778, or 1779, I cannot now with certainty recollect. During a very severe frost at that time, a Livonian Baron had brought a greyhound with him into the lecture-room. The professor, as usual, ordered a good fire to be kept up: the warmth was very agreeable to the dog, who lay stretched out under the almost red-hot stove: but soon the animal was convulsed, and began to howl, to pant, and to foam at the mouth. One of the auditors exclaimed, "The dog is mad." At once a dreadful death-silence reigned throughout the lecture room, and dismay sat on every countenance. Suddenly, one half of the auditors thronged towards the door; some flew up the stairs to the loft; others hurried precipitately into the street, and lost their inkstands, hats, and cloaks. The greater part jumped upon the tables, and prepared, as well as they could, for defence; and there I, too, took refuge. Michaelis alone stood before his table, undaunted, like a man; held with uplifted arms in both hands, a huge folio (I believe it was Norden's Travels through Egypt) ready to be hurled at the foe, and smiled at our timidity. With unaverted eye, he observed the motions of the animal, and, having watched an opportunity, marched, as usual, with a firm step, out at the door: but, immediately returned with a servant holding a drawn sword in his hand; and ordered him to kill the furious animal.—Immediately, one of the students exclaimed, Hold! it's a pity to kill the dog.—To whom does it belong? asked Michaelis.—To me!—Well then, take your favourite in your arms, carry him out, and give him some medicine.—Excuses and repugnance were here of no avail: the Baron was obliged to retire with his patient. When he was gone, Michaelis said with a smile, "That gentleman is a great genius, indeed! he should be employed in secret expeditions, for he has his heart upon his tongue." He then made useful reflections and applications, shewed us how with only his folio, he would have been able to defend himself, and related to us the following incident:—
"During my travels, when I was one day walking by the side of the Thames, near London, a mad dog, whom they were pursuing, jumped towards me. On this side of me was the Thames, on that another water; it was impossible to escape from the animal, except by jumping into the water, which I accordingly did without much hesitation."

Some of the students had one night broken his windows with stones, for the purpose of having some *fun*, at the expence of the professor in the morning: but Michaelis did not wait till morning, but had the windows mended in the night. What he had expected, happened. The perpetrators of the blackguard deed, who came early in the morning to divert themselves, passed by disappointed, chagrined, and ashamed: but Michaelis opened his window, and in a friendly manner saluted them. From that time, no one ever threw stones at his windows. In the winter of 1781, there was so little snow, that the students could not enjoy the usual diversion of making excursions on sledges. Some Englishmen, however, would not leave unemployed the bells and decorations, which they had purchased at a great expence: they accordingly hired two wheeled cabriolets, and had the tinkling apparatus put on the horses. Thus they drove through the town in the midst of the rain. Michaelis was just reading

ing his lectures, and he, as well as his auditors, was astonished at hearing the unexpected winter-music, as they drove past his house. He rose very calmly from his seat, looked out at the window, and said with a smile, "'Tis the foreign birds of passage. The storks are travelling after the dog-days!"

A DEVONSHIRE EPISTLE.

Vor Maaster zecretary VEEBLE, *in Warickt Square, Lunnun.*

Barnstable, Devonshere, the zeventh day of October, one thousand eight hundred.

If you pleazeth,

CHE wou'd beg yaur divershon vor zayiug, whot 'cham going to convorme your worship conzarning. But, virst ant voremost, che must zay one thing (and that's not two) and that iz, az touching yaur Magazine, that cums here onze a munth: it iz zo witty, and zo huge clever, that aul the tawne liketh it, and zay, that zartainly you must be vazily lorned, and aul that; and when Ize redeeth it to my wife Joane, we both laff tell we are both reddy to bepiz ourselves vor joy. But that iz not what Ize writith about to yau, only that by the by; ant to make zhort o' my ztory, Ize must convorme yau, that my spouze and me have gotten betwixt uz one only sun, who iz kalled Nathan, and who commeth twenty-three next grass. Ant thoft we zayeth it, he iz az sprunny a buoy az iz in the tawne of Barnstable, or vive miles raund it.

Now, az he iz my only cheeld, Ize have brost'n up a schollard, ant Ize thort vor to zend to the versity a Knnibridge, ant make a doctor of visick on', but only Ize thoft he had too much larning vor that; vor he haz gone through, in speech, *qui, qux, qued, di, do, dum,* ant all those kind of things; ant haz lately laarn'd, *ais in per centum,* ant properly, *que marybus,* ant *Quem Janzzs* ant hiz measter zayeth, he can larn'un no varder. Bezidez all this, he can rite zo az vor many people to read it; ant can vigger, ant cast countz main well: he understands distraction, and part ov the multiplication tabel, zo var az vour times vour, ant zeven times two, which you'll zay iz a vilthy deal to larn in zix weeks time. The buoy haz partz ant a woundy memory; vor lazt zabbath-day, when parsun Law's preach'd to aur church, ant took hiz text out of the gozpell of *Bell* ant the Dragon, he zaide a deal about Genesiz ant the Revalationz, ant about *Belzhazzar, King of Babalon;* ant *Zimm Magzi,* ant Lot's wife; ant circumcizion; ant Jerico ant Jeruzalem. Ant che heard measter Metherall, ant Asq. Shepperd, our Mare, zay, that they never herde zuch a braave zarmond in all their borne dayez. Vor my own part, Ize dan't much understond zarmondz, but Ize beleeveth, twaz a speciall good one, vor it made the old women cry: but what elce bringeth this story vor, iz, that Nathan took the hodz ant tailez ov it in his memory, ant repeated a good deal of it *extumpere* that evening, at the Valiant Soger, in Bedport, to above ten volk that were smoking and drinking there.

Now may hap, Zir, what does aul this mugnify? Why, if you'll have patience, Ize will tell ye; Nathan knoweth hiz own accomplishmentz, that he haz larning ant aul that; ant haz had hiz nativity cazt in coffee-groundz by Dame Drake, the cunnin woman that telleth vorturez, ant she zayeth, Nathan is boarn to great varment, if he goeth to Lunnun. Zo now, nathing runneth in hiz head but Lunnun, Lunnun; ant ov all things he hankereth avter being a hortbur, the cheeld hath a proud stomach (he taketh avter his mother vor that) and aymeth at grate thingz.

He hath now an offer to zecretary to a brick-kilner, (vor az he iz known to have wit at will, and to be a schollard, every body iz vor katching at'n) but nothing will zurve hiz turn, but to Lunnun he will go, and be an horthur; or, if we won't let'n do that, he woweth most bitterly that he will go to zea. Now, you muzt know, that him iz my wivez doting piece, and she feareth, if he should go to zea, that him wou'd be a kaptain, ant zo he kill'd as dead az a doore naile. And whereaz, whervore, ant therevore, my Woife deszireth, in ordur to make Nathan an horthur, your worship to tak'n prentice; ant now the zecret iz out, ant e'en let it goo.

If you'll tak'n, no money shall peart uz, ant my loan will zend you a couple of rabbitz, ant a new milk cheeze. She doth knaw, that with a little matter ov showing, in a little time the buoy wou'd ov his own zelfe, be able to rite Magarzines ant Newspapers uz fazt az hops: therevore, if you'll tak'n, zay zo by the next poast. Ize be a mon of zome zubstance, ant keepeth nine kowez, ant a boare; ant our Ioane maketh butter ant cheeze, ant eggs, and thicky kind of thingz; ant, moreover, ant likewise, Ize liveth in mine own houze, and payeth scott ant lott, hath been twize constable, ant am now churchwarden over the highwai. Che huv likewize two hundred good shillingz in a bag in my hutch, ant do owe no mon a vour-penny piece, nor do care one zingle zixpence vor measter Shepperd, our Mare, to be my unkle; but that be huge glad, if you'd make my zon Nathan, an horthur. The buoy's fingerz itch to be with you; but uz shall expect you'll bind'n an horthur at zum hall, that he mey vreeman to Lunnun. Zo no more at prezant, but cham vary wondervully, yaur zarvant, ant zo vorth,

ROGER WIMPLE.

P.S. Che vargott to tell ye, (ant che was to blame vor it) that besidez the buoy's latine, him understands something of strology, and can tell (within an haure or two) what tiz a clock by the almanack; ant zayeth, that if him had but Iohnson's Dicktionary, ant Esop's Fables with cutts, him believeth, that him cauld vind out the longitude; vor him iz az sharp onmoost az a new-ground hatchet, and zo vitty, that uz feareth him will not live. W. R.

THOUGHTS ON THE MEANS OF ACQUIRING THE VETERINARY SCIENCE.

(Concluded from p. 11.)

OUR practitioner must ever keep in mind, that as in diseases of children, so an accurate attention to symptoms is his only guide, as neither the one or the other are enabled to tell their complaints. The regulation of the materia medica, with the proper doses of medicines for the animal, must be well understood; this bears no proportion to the relative sizes of the two subjects, for he will find that six or eight times, and often more, of the quantity of many medicines may be given to the one, than to the other, and perhaps with little effect: nor does the analogy of the materia medica hold good in other respects, besides quantity; opium, a most powerful remedy in the human, has not so salutary an effect on the horse, yet it is not to be neglected.

As it is probable it would be difficult to learn the more trivial forms, and the lesser operations from a common farrier, for they are
not

not in general very communicative, a surgeon will find himself much puzzled in these particulars: as unless they are conducted according to the true stable usage, the groom, and very likely his master, will have but a very indifferent opinion of his abilities; such as bleeding, rowelling, purging, firing, raking, castrating; with nicking, docking, giving a ball or drench. All this a veterinary practitioner, however great his note, must be able readily to do; for though in gentlemens' stables, the grooms are in general expert at the lesser matters, yet it will be necessary sometimes to show he can do them himself, and often he will find that there is not any other person who can. It appears a trifling circumstance, but it is more than probable, that a veterinarian attempting the examination of a horse on the off side first, would for ever damn his reputation, and convey a very indifferent opinion of his abilities to the bye-standers; and yet an ingenious operator, unacquainted with the customary forms of a stable, might readily do this. Many circumstances equally inconsiderable in themselves, yet convey very strong impressions to those around, and are therefore carefully to be avoided. A practitioner in human medicine, from his more extended education, will probably have it in his power to read the French authors on this science, which country has undoubtedly been a parent to it. The most celebrated of these are, Lourgelat, Vitet, the elder and younger La Fosse. The first of these was eminent in his time, but has introduced some errors; the second seems to have patronized all the mistakes of the former, with the addition of many of his own, which Monsieur La Fosse the younger, in his most excellent dictionary d'Hyppiatrique, has been at the pains of correcting. This last-mentioned work contains almost all that is known in the science, and is alone capable of forming a good practitioner, out of an already able surgeon. Our best English authors are Bracken, Gibson, and Osmer. Of later date, we have some excellent lights thrown on the subject which he should carefully study. Stubbs gives an accurate knowledge of the muscles, and some blood vessels and nerves. The elegant plates of Blaine's work, will be found highly useful in conveying a true picture of the viscera, and will prove an excellent *vade mecum* in anatomical research. On the formation and diseases of the feet, St. Bel, Freeman, and Coleman, may be satisfactorily read: the former of these is nearly a literal translation of the younger La Fosse. With these helps, a surgeon may safely combine the practice of veterinary with human medicine, and I will venture to predict, that not long hence it will be very generally done, to the great benefit of not only the animal, but to our own diseases, the knowledge and cure of which are greatly accelerated by analogy and comparative anatomy.

With the farrier, whose present stock of knowledge is very confined, it is hard to lay down instructions, which he will follow; for it requires a considerable stock of strength of mind, to determine to throw aside old prejudices and old habits, and above all, to be forced to acknowledge we know nothing. The commencement must be by possessing himself of all the modern anatomical works on horses: by these he must learn to know and distinguish parts by their true anatomical names, forgetting the old obsolete terms of former farriers, as the rim of the belly for *peritonium*;

nium; cawl for omentum; gullet for œcophagus, &c. &c. With these descriptions, he must compare the parts of such dead bodies as fall under his notice, in which he will be fortunate, if he can obtain the assistance of some ingenious surgeon: he should dissect with the description before him, tracing parts from their source or origin, by which means he will not mistake them. These anatomical enquiries should be conducted from the lesser to the greater parts, from those more easily learned, to those more difficultly acquired; beginning with the muscles, he may proceed to the principal component parts of the feet, at which time he should endeavour to articulate a skeleton, which he may easily do by means of Poole's Anatomical Instructor: he will then be gaining a knowledge of the bones, and furnishing himself with a useful reference. From the viscera of the chest and belly, he may trace the origin and termination of blood vessels and nerves, which knowledge he must apply to the parts he has already but impartially gone over. Lastly, the brain, lymphatics, &c. &c. should occupy his attention. Above all, he should banish his receipt-book, and learn, in all instances, to act from reason and science. Obsolete and old works, as Markham's Master-Piece, the Farrier's Dictionary, &c. &c. should be equally avoided, and Gibson, Bracken, and other good authors, carefully studied. When he has gained these first outlines, he must peruse the best treatises on physiology, with human medicine, which will habituate him to reduce his thoughts to system; and, lastly, all the modern works on farriery, comparing them with his late authors, by which he will perceive the improvements made in the science since their time. It must be strongly impressed on his mind, that he never attempts to act in any case without having first established a firm principle for his action. After a careful investigation of the symptoms of a complaint, he must conclude on its nature, and if possible, what it arises from, and how accounted for, and whether the indisposing causes still exist, or whether the disposition to the diseased action only remains; from these datas he will be enabled to act from a scientific ground, and to produce a proper reason to himself and others for his conduct. A new world will now open to him, and he will look back with astonishment on his former ignorance: from the obstinate, ignorant, and hurtful farrier, he will be metamorphosed to the ingenious, scientific, and useful veterinarian. This is no ideal character, nor is this a fancied scheme: I have myself seen all these effects produced, and as great change by the meritorious and indefatigable attention of now a most enlightened man residing in Sussex; and I am convinced, that with the same attention, others might become as eminent.

Nearly the same mode must be pursed by the third class of persons; only it is absolutely necessary, that in this case it should be under the guidance of some ingenious farrier, or more properly a surgeon.

Thus, Mr. Editor, I have thrown together a few hasty thoughts on this subject; they may, perhaps, give some hints to those who are disposed to possess themselves of information, or stimulate some more ingenious persons to lay down those gradatory steps at length, to the improvement of the science, and advantage of the public at large.

EQUINUS.

TIPPOO'S WARDROBE.

GREEN WAR DRESS.

THIS dress (which belonged to Tippoo Sultaun) is called a cheita, a Persian word, implying forty folds. The inscription in the inside, however, states, that there are forty folds in the body of the dress. The turban has been dipped in the waters of the fountain of Zum Zum, at Mecca, and is hence supposed to be invulnerable. It is a tubernock, or holy gift.

The nose-piece of the turban has several Arabic inscriptions in letters of gold, and taken chiefly from the Koran; they are all invocations to the prophet Mahomed, to protect the wearer. This dress was taken from the Tippoo's own wardrobe, which contained no other but the clothes or armour in constant use.—The above are intended for his Royal Highness the Duke of York.

MUSICAL TIGER.

This piece of mechanism represents a Tiger in the act of devouring a prostrate European. There are some barrels in imitation of an organ within the body of the tiger; the sounds produced by the organ are intended to resemble the cries of a person in distress, intermixed with the roar of a tiger. The machinery is so contrived, that while the organ is playing, the hand of the European is often lifted up, to express his helpless and deplorable condition.

This piece of mechanism was found in a room of the Palace at Seringapatam, appropriated for the reception of musical instruments.

TIGER'S HEAD.

This head formed part of the throne of Tippoo Sultaun. It is made of wood, and is covered with plates of the purest gold about one-tenth of an inch in thickness. The teeth are of rock crystal, and the eyes of the same material. The throne was of an octagonal form, and entirely covered with similar plates of gold, marked with the tiger stripes (which was the distinguishing mark of Tippoo and his family.) Over the throne was raised a canopy of gold, supported by eight light but strong pillars; there was a friuge of pearls round the top of the canopy, of about four inches in depth, and the whole was crowned by a *herma* made entirely of precious stones, and sent to England in August, 1799.

This head with four legs, representing the legs of a tiger, was placed under the throne. The seat of the throne was about four or five feet from the ground, and the height of the canopy eight or nine feet. The head is accompanied by a small, but rich and beautiful carpet, used by Tippoo upon his Musnud, on days of state.

THE BEDDING OF THE SULTAUN

Is adorned with two green war helmets, dipped in the waters of Zum Zum, at Mecca, and thence supposed to be invulnerable. One peitre or cuirass, to cover the body —are likewise presents to the King.

THE RED WAR DRESS

Falls to the share of the Prince of Wales.

This war-dress was worn by Tippoo, in his campaign in Adoni, in 1786, against the Nizam and Mahrattahs. He was then in the plenitude of his power. Rajah Cawn, the Sultaun's favourite slave, knew the dress immediately on its being shewn to him, after the reduction of Seringapatam, and confirmed the fact above stated.

A PHILO-

A PHILOSOPHICAL and PRACTICAL TREATISE on HORSES, and on the MORAL DUTIES of MAN towards the BRUTE CREATION.

BY JOHN LAWRENCE.

UPON IMPROVEMENTS IN THE ART OF SHOEING CART-HORSES.

(Continued from page 14.)

WITH respect to those farriers who are intelligent, and desirous of improvement, the best method an employer can take with them is to put Osmer's book into their hands. No man of tolerable understanding can read that treatise without learning something of horse-shoeing; and I have recommended it to several young farriers of merit, both of town and country, who have acknowledged their obligations to it. Farther every one who wishes to have justice done to his horses, must insist upon the following preliminaries with his smith, which are entirely within the cognizance of common sense—namely,

That he never weaken the foot of the horse, by paring away the sole and frog, nor destroy the bars, under pretence of opening the heels.

That he make use of none but the best, hard and well-wrought iron; that he set the horse upon a flat and even surface, and never make the shoe project beyond the heel.

That he never suffer a burning hot shoe to be fitted to the horse's foot.

The above directions may be made general, almost without exception.

I am sorry to say that the villainous custom of fitting the shoes red-hot, and of burning the crust of the foot to a level with the shoe, instead of hammering the iron to the shape of the foot, subsist in full force at this instant. The mischief done by this lazy custom, to the feet of horses, is incalculable; a pregnant example of which, is the case of Hue-and-Cry, the trotting stallion; which horse lost both his fore-hoofs by it; and, as I have been informed by the owner, the late Mr. Bevan, the farrier sat up three nights with the horse, using his utmost endeavours to prevent a mortification from seizing his feet.

The hammers of the smiths are, in general, too large and heavy, that they cannot drive a nail with that truth and accuracy which the case requires, and where the smallest deviation may occasion disagreeable consequences. The brutal treatment also, which horses experience from too many of the men of this description, ought here to be pressed upon the remembrance of proprietors. It is well known, and indeed every day seen, that the miserable animals, flinching under the torture inflicted by these Vulcans, are cruelly beat about the head and body with their massy hammers. There is also a gross abuse in the affair of twitching; when a horse is twitched to excess, the mark is over shot, and the intention of thereby holding a horse in a quiet state is destroyed. I once saw a mare in foal twitched to such excess, by a stupid, heavy-handed fellow, that her lip burst asunder, and the mare threw herself on the ground in a state of desperation, and would not rise until the cord was loosened.

It is here necessary to give the reader a caution against the too usual error of precipitate measures of improvement. A gentleman finds his horse constantly tender-footed, flinching and stumbling. The farrier is applied to, he makes great promises, and every shoeing the horse goes worse. The owner now, with his favourite author in his hand, takes up the foot of his horse, and perceives with indignation that he is shod right wrong, in the very teeth of orthodoxy. The farrier is again sent for, and damn'd for a thick-headed son of a bitch, not worthy to shoe Balaam's ass; and in fine, ordered, at his peril, to shoe immediately and strictly according to the given pattern. The fellow shakes his wise noddle, grins, and makes his bow. The nag being shod, according to order, is mounted by his sanguine and delighted master, who now supposes all his troubles at an end; but, alas! he has only made an exchange of errors, his horse goes like a cat in pattens, he can't trot a yard. The poor animal, as if he were in fault, is now checked with the curb, spurred, cursed, abused, and rode home again. Another meeting takes place with the farrier, who now assumes airs of consequence, on account of his superior skill and lore-knowledge of what had happened. They both join in ridiculing book-knowledge in the art of shoeing, and the folly of authors who pretend to shoe all horses by one common standard. The nag is shod again in the old way, goes better immediately in consequence of the change; but in a very short time, having no feet to go upon, is sold for a few pounds to the mail coaches, where they are made to go, whether they can or not.

The error lies in supposing a horse able to go well in proper shoes, or indeed any shoes at all, whose soles, frogs, and heels are so reduced, as to be scarce able to bear his own weight. In such case, the only remedy is to turn him instantly to grass, with narrow plates upon the walls of his hoofs, to prevent their being broken, until his hoofs and frogs shall have grown to their natural state, and then to put him into the hands of a skilful farrier, who may always preserve them in that state, by strictly following the rules of Osmer and Clarke, supposing the hoofs to be naturally sound; if otherwise, I have nothing better to propose, than to repeat my own favourite method of the bar-shoe. But of all things in the world, let no man put faith in farriers, or their pretended cures by shoeing, in cases like these. There is only one farrier equal to the task, which is Nature; and she always performs her operations *sub jove*, abroad.

I think I cannot too much recommend the practice, hinted at in the beginning of this chapter, of hammering the external surface of the shoe somewhat concave; its great use in securing a horse's footing over convex stones, must strike every one, and it is unattended by any countervailing disadvantage. On a reference, I find it mentioned by Sollysel, as well as that ancient author whom I quoted. It must be of infinite use to town cart-horses more particularly, but I think it a practice which merits universal adoption.

Respecting the single calkin, or usual turning up of the hinder shoe of the saddle horse, I must acknowledge I see nothing in it either of prejudice or utility. If the horse have the use of his frogs upon the ground, he will want nothing else to preserve him from slipping; and if otherwise, he slips with his toe not his heel. As to calkins upon the fore heels, I am convinced nothing results from them but mischief and danger in any case. In frosty weather, or upon a chalky or slippery country, sharp-headed, sharp-edged ice nails, made of the hardest stuff, are the only security; unless, as an additional one, it be thought proper to indent the welts and

and toes of the shoes, which may have considerable effect. In this affair, there is certainly an exception to be made with regard to cart-horses, which are obliged to back with heavy loads, an exertion in which the stress materially lies upon the heels, and most of all the hinder ones. The case is the same with the shaft-horse, in going down hill. It is a question, whether their frogs would, in those respects, be sufficient; if not, calkins behind might, as usual be adopted, but not at any rate before.

To recapitulate, all horses with good feet should, and well and safely may, be shod with flat, light, narrow-webbed shoes, made of the hardest iron; these shoes should be formed thickest at the toe, and thinnest and narrowest at the heel, that the animal may have that equal and steady base, which nature intended him.

I shall conclude this chapter, with the best professional advice I have been able to procure upon certain practical and operative parts of the subject.

St. Bel proposes the following weights, each shoe, for the respective descriptions of horses, which, at any rate, form a good general outline, to be varied according to circumstances, at the discretion of the operator.

For the heaviest cart-horses 2 lb. 12 oz.

For the lighter ditto, 1 lb. 12 oz.

For the heaviest coach-horses 1 lb. 12 oz.

For the lighter ditto, 1 lb. 4 oz.

For the saddle-horses in general, from 1 lb. 2 oz. to 10 oz.

For racers 3 oz. to 4 oz.

The fairest opportunity of making trial of the true principles of the art, is that presented by the colt at his first shoeing, when his hoofs are in a state of natural perfection, and previous to his being habituated to any particular custom. This occasion ought to be zealously embraced, in particular if the present owner means to keep the horse for his own use; and, indeed, if it were possible to diffuse such ideas among our breeders, that circumstance alone would have a most powerful tendency towards the necessary reformation. As the matter stands, the feet even of our four and five year olds, are too generally put out of a state of speedy amendment.

I have given my opinion as to the dependance which ought to be placed on the operations of farriery, for the recovery of thin, weak, and damaged feet: I have not a whit more respect for the various manœuvres practised with the intent of curing convex or pomiced feet—of the different modes of shoeing in use to prevent interfering—or of the operation of unsoling, and of various others which might be named. As to any tampering with pomiced feet, or those where the soles belly out, and the horse is obliged to walk upon them, it is attended with constant pain, without hope of amendment, to the animal: the shortest and cheapest way is to knock him on the head, or suffer him to take his chance abroad. I have no reverence at all for the memory of the inventors of the different kinds of shoes, the use of which, in different cases, has been so ostentatiously set forth by writers; they appear to me ingenious contrivances, without use, and I generally full of cruelty. The usual methods of shoeing, taken to prevent a horse from cutting, generally give him an uneven, and consequently unsafe position upon the ground; and after all, he continues to interfere. Drawing the sole, I look upon to be an abominable,

abominable, and to the best of my knowledge, ever an useless operation I speak not on my own experience, for although farriers have more than once proposed it to me, I never would permit it; but I have made it my business to enquire for many years past, and I have never yet heard of a horse which was worth nine pence after it.

The general directions are, never to pare the sole, frog, or binders, any more than to cut them level, and strip them of rotten and scaly parts; but I must confess I have seen feet so exceedingly luxuriant in growth, and so tough, that they would bear, nay perhaps require some little paring; but the danger to be apprehended from the want of paring, was ever a feather when weighed against that of trusting a smith to perform it at discretion, butress in hand.—In this case, I have generally stood over the operator myself, ready to cry out—No more doctor. The directions, however, do not extend to the crust or wall, which in deep, concave, hard feet, must be at any rate taken down because its growth continually binds and contracts the quarters, dries up the frogs, and prevents their necessary contact with the ground. The size and strength of the feet, and the situation of the frogs, are the best measure for the due performance of this.

Whenever it becomes absolutely necessary to cut the bars or frogs, never suffer it to be presumed in the usual way of blacksmiths, that is to say, inwards or downwards, one of the most destructive of all their manœuvres, but always let them be shaved horizontally, or flat; and it is so dangerous to cut too near in the frog, that in case of a considerable bulk in that part, it is even better to thicken the shoe-heels a trifle, and so to bring them and the frog upon a level and even bearing. For a foot in a sound and natural state, the breadth of the shoe at the heels, should be one-half of its breadth at the toe, and its substance decrease by degrees from the toe, so as to be one-half thinner or weaker at the extremity of the heels; notwithstanding this decrease of width at the heel of the shoe, it will be still wide enough to stand out somewhat beyond the crust, and thereby be prevented from getting within the heel as it grows.

(To be continued.)

REAL ORIGIN OF CROPPING HAIR IN ENGLAND.

A Very ancient writer has asserted, that when Henry the Eighth took it into his head to crop his hair short at the solicitation of Anna Bullen, the nobility and yeomanry of England instantly followed his example, and continued it for some months, till the Barbers Company, being sorely aggrieved at the measure, went in a body to that inflexible monarch, and petitioned him, in terms of the utmost humiliation, to desist from the adoption of a custom that was fraught with the entire ruin of so respectable a company. The King was melted by their prayer, took their unfortunate case into his princely consideration, ordered a new flaxen wig from one of the wardens of the company, and issued his royal mandate, that no man should be entitled to the benefit of the clergy that did not make his prostration at the altar in a wig of British manufacture.

During the Civil wars between Charles I. and his Parliament, it is well known, that cropped heads were introduced to distinguish the Republican from the Court party;

nor is it less remarkable, that the same destinction has subsisted between the Royal and the Republican parties since the French Revolution, both in France and Ireland.

AMERICAN LONGEVITY.

THERE is now living at Knoydart, in Ulst, Long Island, a poor man of the name of Macdonald, who has attained the great age of 111 years.

He served in all the wars of the House of Hanover—was in Flanders under the great Marlborough—fought two weeks in the present war on the Continent—has had five wives, of whom the last is a young woman of singular beauty, and affectionately devoted to her hoary husband.

The children of the first marriage consisted in all of 13, six were sons. By his three succeeding wives he had eleven children; one of the sons by the last of these is an admirable player on the bagpipe, and was some years ago among the successful candidates for the annual prizes of the society at Edinburgh, for encouraging that ancient Highland music. His present wife (Mary) is the mother of two fine boys and a girl; the youngest of the lads is in his sixth year, and the old man assures his neighbours, that "neither is the soil fallow, nor the seed unfit to sow."

Hufeland, a German writer has published a work, entitled *The Art of Prolonging Life*, in which he gives the following description of a man, who, from physical and moral causes, is most likely to live to a great age:—"He should be of the middle size, well proportioned, hair chesnut-colour, head rather large than small, veins strong, shoulders round, breast large, voice manly, sense exquisite, pulse slow and uniform, stomach excellent, appetite keen, fond of the table, without giving himself up too much to its pleasures, eating sparingly, rarely thirsty; an ardent thirst being a sign of a rapid consumption; countenance serene, eye quick; heart accessible to love, to hope, and to joy, but inaccessible to hate, to choler, and to envy; very fond of business, meditation, and agreeable reveries: an optimist, in the full force of the term; friend of nature, and of domestic happiness, without ambition, without avarice, without inquietude: a man thus formed, will live from 110 to 140 years."

HERALDIC CUSTOM.

HOWELL ap Einion ap Griffith, commonly called Sir Howell y fwyall (*i. e.* Sir Howell, with the battle axe) dismounted the French King at the battle of Poictiers, cutting off his horse's head with his battle axe, and after that he took him prisoner. In commemoration of this exploit, it is said that he bore the arms of France, with a battle axe in bend sinister, argent. Moreover he received of the black Prince, by gift, the Constableship of Chester and Crickett Castles, and also the rent of the Dee Mills and a mess of meat to be served before his battle axe for ever, in memory of his good services. This mess of meat was afterwards given to the poor, and had eight yeomen attendants found at the King's charge, which were called Yeomen of the Crown, and they had eighteenpence a day. This establishment was continued to the beginning of Queen Elizabeth's reign.

FEAST

FEAST OF WIT; OR, SPORTSMAN's HALL.

A PUN.—Some persons broke into the stables of a troop of light horse, and cut off their tails. A brother officer advised the troop to sell them by *wholesale*, for, says he, you can never *re-tail* them.

It was said of a poor fellow who hanged himself lately, from *disappointment in love*, that he was very appropriately buried in *cross* roads!

Mr. Sturt's singing "*Cease rude Boreas,*" at the moment he expected to be swallowed up by the billows, was a very pretty *swan-like* idea, and it seems was not without its effect upon that "blustering sailor," who, in the end was so complaisant, as not to put the singer quite *out of tune.*

A theatrical correspondent at Dublin, says, we are surprised to hear of a scarcity of *Actors* in this city; but to this we reply, where are the *Gentlemen* who acted the *Heroes,* the *Patriots,* &c. on those nights when the *Union* drew such crowded houses in that city?

The art of transmutation, says a wit, is likely to be revived in the new invention of manufacturing paper from *grass*. In time, therefore, we shall not be surprised to find a lady's bonnet very consistently converted into *fools-cap*.

The following curious description of an heroine, occurs in one of the sentimental productions of the day: "Vivacity in her manners; a *voluptuous* grace; fulness in her figure; a soul-darting expression in her eye; a *wild luxuriance* in her hair; an *impassioned* sensibility in her smile; and an exquisite *fervor* in her more meditative expression of countenance."

Of all the *stars in the firmament,* the most *northern* is the only one that never changes its place; but, respecting the Russian sovereign, the most *northern Monarch—under the firmament—* he is observed to be the most changeable of all.

Repartee.—M. de la Farre had been long an admirer of Madame de la Sabliere. Upon a visit one morning, as he approached her, he exclaimed:—"My G—d! Madame, what ails your eye?"—"Ah! La Farre," answered the lady, "you no longer love me—I have had this defect my whole life, and you never perceived it until this day."

The following curious bill was lately delivered to the representatives of the Radnor family, for repairs performed by a tradesman (a statuary we suppose) of Truro, in Cornwall, on a monument of that family, in Truro church. The public may depend on the authenticity of it:—

Miss B——, Dr. to W—— L——.

	£ s. d.
To putting one new foot to Mr. John Roberts	0 2 6
Mending his other	0 0 6
Putting seven new buttons to his coat	0 0 8¼
A new string to his breeches knee	0 0 3
Two new feet to Philippa, his wife	0 6 6
Mending her eyes, and putting a nosegay in her hand	0 2 6
Two new hands and a nose to the Captain	0 5 2
To two new hands, and mending the nose of his wife	0 4 10
Repairing her eyes, and putting a new cuff to her gown	0 1 8
To making and fixing two new wings on Time's shoulders	0 5 9
Making a new great toe	0 1 0
Mending the handle of his scythe, and putting a new blade to it	0 1 6¼
	1 15 6

Feast of Wit; or, Sportsman's Hall.

The numerous company necessary to form a fashionable rout, renders it also necessary to make some alteration in the house of the receiver. One nobleman, we find, has built *three* street-doors to his mansion, to correspond, we presume, with *pit, box,* and *gallery!*

The fat bishop of Evereux travelling from Falaise to Caen, in Normandy, was benighted, and calling to a peasant who was yet at plough, asking him if he could get *into* the town that night. Why, it may be so, says the peasant, unless they have narrowed the gates, for I came through with a load of hay this morning, and I think you may *get through* without one!

The letters from the army in the Mediterranean, mention the troops to be in excellent *health*. This, says a wit, surely is not to be ascribed to the loss of all the *medicines*, which fell into the hands of the Spaniards!

During the civil war between the Catholics and the French Protestants, a Huguenot Chief took a castle belonging to the Catholics, and condemned the soldiers that had defended it, to jump from the top of one of the towers to the ground. One of the soldiers advanced to the edge of the precipice twice, and retired, which the Chief observing, said, if you do not do it this time without hesitation, I shall give you a much harder task. Sir, replied the soldier, if you will undertake the jump, I will give you four times to do it in. This repartee pleased him so well, that he immediately desisted from his resolution.

A few years ago, a mountebank happening to be at a village in the west, a farmer's servant maid in a neighbouring village, hearing much talk of the merry pranks of Mr. Andrew, had a vast desire to see him, but never could obtain an opportunity. Happening, however to be at church on Sunday, she heard the minister utter the following words:—" *Thursday next being the feast of Saint Andrew, is appointed to be kept holy.*"—Home goes the girl, with a heart full of joy, and sure, at length, of having the pleasure of seeing Mr. Andrew—" Nancy," says she, to her young mistress, " what do you think? the *Andrew* is a coming here next Thursday."— " No, that he is not,' says Nancy, " for he goes to S—— every Thursday."—" Well, but I am sure he is a coming here next Thursday," replies the girl, " *sir* the parson *said so* at church; and as how he has appointed to keep a *said to.*"

A Florentine having caught a prodigious large pike, was resolved to present it to the Grand Duke of Tuscany, who had a great taste for extraordinary curiosities: he went to the gates of the palace with his pike, and demanded admittance to speak to the Duke, which he could not gain, unless he promised one of the guards the half of what the Duke should make him a present of. To this he consented, and was accordingly admitted. The Prince and the whole Court admired the pike, and ordered the man that brought it one hundred ducats. The man overhearing the order, said, no, my lord, one hundred stripes of the stick, and not one hundred ducats!—The Duke, astonished at such an extraordinary answer, demanded for what reason? —It is, my Lord, replied the man, that I have not been able to gain admittance, without promising one of your highness's guards, the half of what you should give me. So, I pray you give me fifty, and him the remainder:—No, replied the Duke, it shall not be so; you shall have the hundred ducats, and he the bastinado.

A French

A French preacher preaching on the Feast of Mary Magdalen, enlarged so much upon the bad life of that woman, and threw out some fine things upon her conversion—Then directing his discourse to the ladies, there are many, said he, among you, that come here more for diversion, than devotion; and of all the women that are here present, I do not know whether there could be found one only, who would repent like the Magdalen. What do I say? Who would repent like her? No! but who may have the least remorse for their sins. I do not speak of all the ladies present, but of one in particular, who is unworthy to be found along with virtuous women—she is the most wicked and most impudent woman in the world. It is not a great while ago, since she renewed her every year's promise to her confessor, to live like an honest woman; however, she still goes on in the same way, always the same!—Since, then, her sin does not tend to make her ashamed, it is right that we should: it is said in the scripture, if thy brother commit a fault, reprove him once, or twice; but if he does not amend the third time, tell it to the church. Since, therefore, exhortations are not capable of bringing back this female sinner, it is not right to cover her shame, but publicly expose her infamy, and even name her before this assembly. Yes, Sirs, I am going;—I am going to name her—It is—(here he stopped) and then began again. I shall name her, I ought to do it; but, however, —No, I ought not—But why not? This salutary exposure may reclaim her from her wickedness—I shall name her—It is——However, I shall not name her—her name is so infamous, that it is a shame even to pronounce it.—Still it is necessary to make her known: there she is, right opposite to me, making up a sanctified face! I am going to throw my prayer-book at her— Take good care—it will fall upon her.—Then raising his arm, and making believe to throw it, all the women popped down their heads— O times, O manners! said the preacher; I thought among you there was only one of that sort, but now I find the number to be great indeed!

ECCENTRICITIES.

A Sailor's demand upon a Slop-seller—

A Shappo	—	Hat
A Mappo	—	Wig
A Flying Gib	—	Handkerchief
An In-defender	—	Shirt
An Out-defender	—	Small Jacket
A Cold defender	—	Flushing Coat
Up-haulers	—	Trowsers
Down trampers	—	Shoes
Trappings & Gaskets for the same	}	Shoestrings and Garters

An Irish mate of a West-Indiaman now lying in the river, having been many years at sea, had his Captain's leave for a few days cruize upon the town. On his return on board, being questioned by the Captain what he had seen, he mentioned the Play-houses, amongst certain *other houses*, as the scene of his amusements. He said he had made two *successful voyages* to the Play-house, and at first saw *Bob Scratchem* and *Solomon's Razor*; and the next night, *Gimlet Prince of Dunkirk*, and *Duffy's Elixir!* The reader scarcely need be informed, that honest Patrick meant no other than the Beaux Stratagem, with Selima and Azor; and, Hamlet, Prince of Denmark, with Daphne and Amyntor. *Related by Capt. B.*

SPORTING

SPORTING INTELLIGENCE.

DIARY OF A BRIGHTON BLOOD.

ROSE at nine—Rumpled my wig, and stood before the glass an hour endeavouring to give myself a sloven-like appearance—Having at length succeeded in making myself a complete blackguard, walked to the Bathing Place—Lady *Dashaway* told me I had been up all night—Smiled assent—Memorandum, always affect the Rake; its stylish, and the women like it—Took my position on the cliffs so as to prevent the Ladies bathing—Damned good fun! though the other morning got my nose pulled by a crusty old Gentleman, *merely* for asking to bathe in the machine with his daughter—Dull Dog—Not one of us could take such a joke, so passed it over, though a shameful report was circulated at the Libraries that I declined, because the old man was a notorious *fighting* character—All a hum! can hit a card at ten paces when my nerves are steady, and an't frightened.

At twelve o'clock, knowing the Libraries and the Steine crowded, went with a party of *spirited witty* Dogs and bathed in view of the Ladies! though a damned unluckly accident happened, for a party of Wags having seized on our cloaths bribed the old Bathing Woman to follow us into the water—We made for shore, could not find our cloaths—What the devil was to be done?—Boys pelted us—Women hissed us—Dogs barked, children shouted, men swore—At last hearing a sour fellow talk of the pillory, made a precipitate retreat, and, covered with mud, rotten eggs, and other sweet scented accompaniments, arrived at home, departed quick for London, and left my *bills unpaid*, and my character behind me!

Sir William Lowther's hunters have been sold at Tattersall's for two thousand three hundred guineas.

In the mortuary of a provincial paper we read the following death:—" At the great age of 31, *Young* Marske, the sire of so many capital horses."

The Surrey fox-hounds have had some sharp runs, and repeatedly *blooded* the pack in good stile.—These frequently boast a large field, to which the *Cross*, the *Lane*, and the *Acre*, contribute a snug and friendly little party. *Lotions*, *Potions*, and *Patent Coffins* may not unfrequently be seen at *a Death*.

A wager for five hundred guineas was decided a few days since at Northleach, in Gloucestershire, as follows:—A Mr. John Spencer of that place, betted a Mr. Richard Botting, from London, that he (Spencer) would walk blindfolded from the middle of a certain field, across some inclosures, to a barn about half a mile distance, in twelve hours, which he performed with ease in three, to the great discomfiture of the Londoner and his friends, who were completely taken in; very considerable sums over and above the original wager having been laid.

On the morning of the 10th, a heavy road mare started from the Town-hall, at Lewes, in a gig, carrying two persons, to go to the Golden

Golden Cross, Charing Cross, in ten hours, for a bet of twenty guineas, on her performance of which many other bets were depending. Bets of five guineas to two were also repeatedly taken: she performed the journey in nine hours.

Another race occurred in the same place in the course of the month; viz. the *Duchess of Limbs*, and *Miscreant*, two valuable racing fillies, in foal, by capital horses, the property of Sir F. Poole, were mounted and rode from their pasturage near Lewes, by jockeys who, though at present unknown to the Baronet, may hereafter receive from him, the reward of their voluntary services, at the goal of Horsham, if not at the goal at Newmarket.

The Duchess of Limbs and Miscreant, in their last race from Lewes, owing to the skilful management of their riders, proved much too fleet for their pursuers, who are all returned, of course, much mortified, at being *double distanced*.

An account from Lewes, of the 8th, says, the business of horse-stealing was never more brisk in this neighbourhood at the height of the career of the notorious Jigg than it is at present. It therefore behoves persons who have valuable horses, and who wish to keep them, to shut them up at night.

A singular charge of swindling was exhibited within these last few days, before the sitting Alderman, at Guildhall, by a gentleman, against a woman of the name of Leicester, whom he charged with defrauding him of 10l. The account given by the gentleman was to the following effect:—That about ten or twelve years ago, he had a son, whose conduct was of so irregular a nature, as rendered it necessary that he should be sent out of the kingdom, to avoid worse consequences. Of the fate of this son, he had since heard nothing; but some time since received a letter, purporting to be from the long-lost prodigal. The letter stated, that he had been many years a slave amongst the Algerines, where he underwent all the hardships attendant on that vile and degraded condition; that he afterwards escaped to Malta, and after that island had surrendered to the English, he was permitted to take his passage home, and was just landed at Portsmouth. He expressed his contrition for those former irregularities, which he hoped he had expiated by long scenes of misery and begged his father to remit him 10l. that he may be enabled to equip himself in a suitable manner, 'to appear amongst his friends. The father very joyfully complied with the request, remitting the 10l. in the manner directed; but after some time, the prodigal not making his appearance, the disappointed father proceeded to make further enquiry. The result was, that the letter was discovered to have been forged on board one of the convict ships at Portsmouth, on board of which was the husband of Mrs Leicester, into whose possession it was traced.

Mrs. Leicester said, she received the letter from the convict, her husband, and was committed for further examination.

One morning lately, about seven o'clock, a young man entered a gentleman's house through the area, in Chatham place, Blackfriars, went to the pantry, fed himself, and filled his pockets, when he was observed by a servant just risen out of bed, who questioning him about so early and unexpected a visit, he replied, that extreme want impelled him to come over the iron rails to get a good meal; the servant forgave this species of theft, but on searching him, found he had stolen a silver

Sporting Intelligence.

a silver spoon. He was secured, and conveyed to the Compter to be examined.

On the 6.st dull day we have had this month, five *Bond street Beaux*, who dined together, cast *dice* which of them should *shoot Limself*, each binding himself on his *honour* to abide by the cast. The lot happening to fall on a well-known *swaggering Lobby-Lounger*, he blubbered and wept, and actually promised a rump and dozen to be let off!

On Saturday, November 8, died, at the Upper Hare Park, near Newmarket, aged 27 years, the celebrated stallion Potso's, the property of Mr. Wm. Gulding. He was got by Eclipse, out of Sportsmistress, and was unquestionably one of the best-bred sons of that *memorable horse*. His performances on the turf are too well known to amateurs, to need a repetition here.

It is with much concern, we announce the death of Mr. Thomas Carter, on Saturday, November 8, at his house in Thornhaugh street—a victim in early life to the fatal ravages of the liver complaint. This gentleman, in whom the *harmonists*, and various musical societies, have lost the "choicest feather of their wing," was, perhaps, better known as the inseparable companion of Sam Maynard, of Doctor's Commons. Those who have had the good fortune to hear their duets, may well boast of having been regaled not only with the *flow of soul*, but the *perfection of harmony*. Mr. Carter, who had only attained his 52d year, has left an amiable widow to lament his loss.

A letter lately received from a gentleman in the East-India Company's Civil service at Bencoolen, contains a remarkable account of a Malay fisherman having brought in his prow, from Buffaloe Point, one of the largest sharks ever seen in that part of the world, which attacked the Malay as he was swimming round the head of his prow to clear his tackle, and was killed by the man's dexterity. It measured near nine feet in length, and was an old shark, which had been remarked by the fishermen. The Malays, when provided with their weapons, are so fearless, from being inured to the water in their infancy, that some of them will voluntarily attack this formidable creature, and seldom fail to subdue him in his own element.

A Yorkshireman, a noted poacher, was carried before a meeting of Justices in that county, on a charge of seditious words, in saying, that he wished the French would land in Filey Bay. The chairman asked the fellow in an angry tone, how he could be so wicked as to wish for the landing of the enemy, and particularly in a place where he had himself a family and relations, to be sacrificed to their fury— " No," said the culprit, scratching his head, " I did not mean that, your worship; all the reason I had for wishing the French to land was, *that your worship might take their guns from them, as your worship knows you have done to me more than once.*"

The poet Kotzebue, though now flattered by the Emperor of Russia, seems not inclined to trust himself in his dominions.—This reminds one of the *monkey* belonging to a King of Spain, and a great *favourite*, that had his head broke for beating his master at a game of chess—The wise beast would never after venture to beat his master, who felt himself much mortified at not being able to obtain a confidence which he had deservedly forfeited.

Cloak-dropping at the theatres is become the fashionable *divertisement* between the acts, in the upper boxes

boxes. It is an admirable device for drawing the attention of the house, and displaying the female form in a new *attitude*. A *loose fish* at Drury-lane, lately observing a lady *angling* in this new style, with a *rod* composed of a long arm, and a *line* of handkerchiefs, exclaimed, "I wish I could catch my cloak so easily, which I dropped last night at the *Three Blue Balls*.

A young man going into a place of public entertainment, was told that his dog could not be permitted to enter, and the latter was accordingly left with the guard at the door. The young man had scarcely entered the lobby, when his watch was stolen. He returned to the guard, and prayed that his dog might be admitted, as through his means he might discover the thief. The dog was suffered to accompany his master, who intimated to the faithful animal that he had lost something: the dog set out immediately in quest of the strayed article, and fastened on the thief, whose guilt on searching him was made apparent. The fellow had no less than six watches in his pocket, which being laid before the dog, he distinguished his master's, took it up by the string, and bore it to him in safety.

They were audacious rogues who robbed the *batteries* of a college at Oxford, and it is wonderful how they found their opportunity—Had they broke into the library, or the chapel, one would not have wondered!

The King has declared his determination not to hunt the *tigers* sent by the Marquis of Wellesly, for fear of their attacking his subjects;

A Cork Paper informs us, that *horse-stealing* in the neighbourhood of that city, is become a common practice among the *light-fingered* gentry.

The *soi-disant Captain*, the terror of the *Nursery Maids* and young *Misses* of Brighton, has taken the hint given him by *Mrs. Smoaker* and Co. the bathing nymphs, at his last public exhibition, and has fallen in *love* with retirement; *alias*, does not shew his face.

On the night of November 1, as three of the King's keepers were traversing the New Forest, in the neighbourhood of Lyndhurst, as is customary, they discovered two dogs pursuing a deer, both of which they shot, when immediately five men, armed with fire-arms, came up within a short distance, and, after discharging their pieces, ran away. They were pursued, and one of the miscreants was taken. Mr. Allen, one of the keepers, received two slugs in the middle part of his thigh.

A ludicrous incident is related in the last Paris Papers, of a citizen of some respectability being taken up by the patrole, rather intoxicated, and conveyed to the guard-house, having been found *whistling* at the corner of a street, at two o'clock in the morning, and calling violently, *Bacchanal! Bacchanal!* These were deemed sufficient proofs that he was a house-breaker, found in the act of inviting his accomplices. The citizen was held in close custody, and even treated with contumely, until his dog *Bacchanal*, who was rather more *sober* than his master, found his way into the *corps de garde* covered with mud, and, by explaining the circumstances, effected the release of his master.

At a village near the metropolis, on Sunday, the banns of marriage were published; but as soon as prayers were over, the couple, who were in church, marched up to the altar, and desired to be married. The clergyman assented, and the infant was just born in *wedlock*.

POETRY.

POETRY.

THE HIGH COURT OF DIANA.

A SONG AND RECIPE, FOR KILLING A WIFE.

By J. Bisset, *Museum, Birmingham.*

OH! now botheration to all your fine singing,
Your Fortes, Pianos, your quick time and slow,
Attend to my Song, and I'll after be bringing
A grand *secret* out—for the *Bon Publico*.
'Tis a secret so great, that *a parent* should follow,
That after you're dead, will make blessed your life:
For I swear by the beard—of the beardless Apollo,
I've found out the secret—of killing a wife.

Of Rumford's fam'd stoves, with his *patent* prevention,
For curing of chimnies that us'd for to smoke,
It cannot come up to my famous invention—
Oh, no, botheration—'tis all a mere joke.
Smoky houses, they say, is a cursed vexation;
But that's a mere flea-bite to conjugal strife,
And can't be compar'd to what cursed taxation,
A man surely finds with a shrew of a wife.

"A house that is smoky, with ease you may cure it;
As easy as twisting a bit of thin wire;
Because do ye see—if you cannot endure it,
You've nout lag to do, but to set it on fire!
But wives that love scolding—oh bless the dear creatures—
They make you unhappy the whole of your lives.

But I've found out a secret—will alter their natures,
A Grand Panacea—for killing of wives.

Thro' all parts of Europe, I'll send my prescription;
East, West, North, and South—round the world shall it sail;
All mortals shall know it—I'll have no restriction—
I'm sure 'tis an antidote—never can fail.
My name, soon will top all the famous empyrics,
Your Solomons, Brodums, Chings, Leakes, Hills, and Clives;
Their Lotions and Potions, may cure them hysterics,
But a dose of my secret, will kill all your wives.

My secret is this then, not founded on fiction;
For deep penetration, of this makes me sure,
That women can't live long, without contradiction.
Give your wives then their way, for their life there's no cure.
If you think they have faults, sure it must be your blindness;
The sweet lovely creatures know better than you,
If you wish to kill wives, let it be by your kindness;
This is the grand secret you all should pursue.

PICCADILLY's COMPLAINT.

NO more the wheels quick rattle thro' my street,
No more pedestrian's blazing flambeau meet;
Fled is all fashion, spirit, life, and ton,
Since their great leader, lovely Gordon's gone.

Oh! then, ye World of Fashion mourn,
And pray for Gordon's quick return.

No more smart John's smack the sound-
ing thong,
And now the back moves undisturb'd
along;
No more do powder'd footmen crowd the
stairs,
No more's the street blockaded up with
chairs.
  Oh! then, ye World of Fashion, mourn,
  And pray for Gordon's quick return.

No more the drawing-room's strew'd o'er
with flow'rs,
No more the vase it's od'rous incense
show'rs;
No more the patent lamp sheds dazzling
light,
And Piccadilly's wrapt in sombrous night.
  Oh! then, ye World of Fashion, mourn,
  And pray for Gordon's quick return.

The hall which echo'd with the footman's
knock,
Witnesses now the ticking of the clock;
The mourning cricket chirps the night
away,
And rats, and mice, have now free room
to play.
  Oh! then, ye World of Fashion, mourn,
  And pray for Gordon's quick return.

Clos'd is each window; in sepulchral
gloom
Are wrapt the splendours of each gorgeous
room;
And to keep out th' effects of sun and air,
Each chair and sofa's cover'd o'er with
care.
  Oh! then, ye World of Fashion, mourn,
  And pray for Gordon's quick return.

When shall I hear the rattling sounding
noise,
The harbinger of wit and sportive joys?
When will the steeds with dirt all cover'd
o'er,
Dash thro' Hyde Park, and stop at Gor-
don's door?
  Oh! then, ye World of Fashion, mourn,
  And pray for Gordon's quick return.
                    PICCADILLY.

STANZAS ON POACHING.

I.
O Ye Poachers beware,
  How in catching an hare,
Ye offend the irascible Squire;
  For if you are caught,
  O then you'll be taught,
That it is no lay snares made of wire.

II.
For the forests afford,
  Both to Peasant and Lord,
All food of most exquisite flavour;
  And 'twill plainly appear,
  That woodcocks and deer,
Sent best with sauce of rich savour.

III.
But Poacher shew thy sense;
  And take out a licence,
And let honour reign in thy mind;
  For the Law has much force,
  Man's schemes to divorce,
And with fetters all villains to bind.

OLLA PODRIDA.

AN ENIGMATICAL EPITAPH.

HERE lie entomb'd
the ashes, earthly parts, and remains
of a bright and aspiring genius;
who,
in his youth, it must be confessed,
discovered some *sparks*
of a light and volatile nature;
but was, in maturity,
of a steady, grateful disposition,
and diffusive benevolence.
Though naturally
of a *warm temper,*
and easily *stirred up,*
yet was he a most shining example
of a fervent and unreserved benignity.
For though he might have been
the most dangerous and dreadful
of enemies;
yet was he the best and kindest
of friends.

Nor did he ever look *cool,*
even upon his enemies;
Though his friends too often,
(And shamefully indeed!)
Turned their backs upon him.
Oh! undiscerning and incendious times,
when such illustrious examples,
such resplendent virtues,
are thus wantonly made *light of,*
thus basely *blown upon!*

Though rather the promoter
of a cheerful glass in others,
and somewhat given to *smoaking,*
yet was he himself never seen
in liquor,
which was his utter abhorrence.
Raking, which ruins most constitutions,
was far from spoiling his;
Though it often threw him into
inflammatory disorders.

His

His days, which were short,
were ended by a gentle gradual decay.
His strength wasted, & his substance spent,
a temporal period was put
to his future existence;
which was some immediately effected
by his being seized with a severe cold,
and no help administered,
in some of the warm days
in the fatal month of May.

His loss and cheering influence
is often feelingly regretted,
by his sincere admirers,
who
in grateful remembrance
of the benefits received
from his endearing virtues,
have erected this monument
to his memory.

A CAMBRIDGE SONG.

COME ye good college lads, and attend
 to my lays,
I'll shew you the folly of poring o'er
 books;
For all ye get by it is mere empty praise,
Or a poor meagre fellowship and sallow
 looks!

CHORUS.

Then lay by your books, lads, and never
 repine;
 And cram not your attics
 With dry Mathematics—
But moisten your clay with a bumper of
 wine!

The first of mechanics was old Archi-
 medes,
 Who play'd with Rome's ships as he'd
 play cup and ball;
To play the same game I can't see where
 the need is—
Or why we should fag Mathematics at
 all.
 Chorus—Then lay by your books, &c.

Great Newton found out the Binomial
 Law,
 To raise $x-y$ to the power of b;
Found the distance of Planets that he ne-
 ver saw,
And which we most probably never
 shall see.
 Chorus—Then lay by your books, &c.

Let Whiston and Ditton star-gazing en-
 joy,
 And taste all the sweets Mathematics
 can give;
Let us for our time find a better employ;
And, knowing Life's sweets, let us learn
 how to live!
 Chorus—Then lay by your books, &c.

These men no absurd conclusions may
 draw;
Perpetual Motion they never could
 find:
Not one of the set, lads, could balance a
 straw—
And Longitude seeking is hunting the
 wind!
 Chorus—Then lay by your books, &c.

If we study at all, let us study the means
To make ourselves friends, and to keep
 them when made;
Learn to value the blessings kind Heaven
 ordains—
To make other men happy, let that be
 our trade.

CHORUS.

Let each day be better than each day
 before;
 Without pain or sorrow
 To-day or to-morrow,
May we live, my good lads, to see many
 days more!

BLESS MY HEART! HOW HOT IT IS!

LET the Sage look around him, he'll
 speedily trace,
With the folks of our isle, a rude mur-
 muring race,
Discontented and peevish, and always
 ine in'd,
Whatever falls out, to receive it unkind;
They pine at our Winters, too cold and
 too long,
And when Summer revives us (attend to
 the song,)
 Then in courts and cottages,
  With low and high,
  This is the cry,
 Bless my heart! How hot it is!

When Sirius attends on the Chariot of
 Day,
And the earth yields its tribute to make
 the heart gay;
When beneath the deep shade, by the
 spring in the grove,
Young Damon leaves Phillis the lessons of
 Love;
When the Wren o'er the stream sings her
 lay on the reed,
And the rest of Creation is charming
 indeed,
 Then in courts and cottages,
  With low and high,
  This is the cry,
 Bless my heart! How hot it is!

When

When balloon-belly'd Cits about noon get
    astride,
And the fam'd Cuckold's-round *, for
    fresh appetites ride,
While the page and the poultry fly out of
    their way,
Like fear, apprehensive of falling a prey;
At this brow-tanning time, while a las-
    situde reigns,
Over cities, farms, hamlets, vales, moun-
    tains, and plains,
  Then in courts and cottages,
    With low and high,
    This is the cry,
  Bless my heart! How hot it is!

When the lady in lawn, that out-silvers
    the swan,
Sits incessantly courting the zephyrs to
    fan;
When windows are open, and fires are put
    out,
And green rushes thick scatter'd the
    chimnies about;
When the wasp hunts for sweets, and in
    every room
The bow-pot refreshes with matchless
    perfume,
  Then in courts and cottages,
    This is the cry,
    With low and high,
  Bless my heart! How hot it is!

When the Kine stand breast high in the
    slow gliding brook,
Where the Angler all indolent hangs o'er
    his hook;
When the stream tempts the Schoolboy all
    hazards to run,
And Ephemeron rises and dies with the
    Sun;
When the ripe clust'ring vine tempts each
    lip that it meets,
And the lap of Pomona runs over with
    sweets,
  Then in courts and cottages,
    This is the cry,
    With low and high,
  Bless my heart! How hot it is!

In this sultry season, Fate, be it my lot,
While the woodbine and jessamine shelter
    my cot,
No comfort to lack, and be lib'ral to yield
To the wants of the rustic that toils in
    the field;
May the bounty of Heaven still add to
    my store,
To cherish the stranger that faints at my
    door,

* From London to Highgate through
Hampstead to London again, so called
time immemorial.

All in courts and cottages,
    Should cool the lip,
    Of such a trip,
  When e'er they cry, How hot it is!

May my mind be resign'd to the fortune
    that's sent,
Be it good let me smile, be it evil content;
Tho' Summer assails with the heat of the
    line,
Or the Winters be long, let me never re-
    pine,
But rail at impatience, and teach it in song,
That gratitude ever should govern the
    throng—
  Hence in courts and cottages,
    Go take what's sent,
    And live content,
  Nor murmur once,—How hot it is!

EPITAPH ON THE LATE HODGES,
A well known Sportsman.

ON Virtue, Birth, and Fame, this
    marble's dumb;
Of Wealth, he'd more than you by half
    a plumb.
All days, e'en Sabbath he profan'd, save
    one day,
This selfish care was to provide for Mon-
    day †;
In riches great, ungrateful to mankind,
One mark of gratitude in grav'd, we find,
By *Turf maintain'd*, he courteously ret. ed;
And Atlas like, he now the *Turf* sup-
    ports.
On friends he call'd, to ward Death's fa-
    tal blow,
Crying, *Bar Eb;* then sinking, cry'd,
    Bar Obt.

* His name was, Munday Hodges.
† He was a well-known E O Table-
keeper, and spoken of as a man that is
called (in the flash way) a *knowing sinker.*

On the Death of the FLYING BARBER.

WEEP, Barbers, weep, your mutual
    loss deplore,
The good, the skilful Easter shaves no
    more;
Neglected now the silver bason lies,
To worth like his, a just, a well-earn'd
    prize.
Men of Clare-hall, your chins with sor-
    row tell
That Peers and Briggs will ne'er shave
    half so well,
Though they the Razors use, so often tried
By Barbar-Surgeon Foster, e'er he died,

THE SPORTING MAGAZINE;

OR,

MONTHLY CALENDAR

OF THE

TRANSACTIONS OF THE TURF, THE CHASE,

And every other Diversion interesting to the

MAN OF PLEASURE, ENTERPRIZE, AND SPIRIT.

For DECEMBER, 1800.

CONTAINING,

Page		Page
Journal of the Royal Chase — — 95		Crim. Con. Duckworth v. Butt — 130
Anecdote of one Faulkener — — 97		Anecdotes of the Emperor Paul — 135
Specimen of Yankee Wit — — ibid		Account of the new Tragedy of Antonio; or, The Soldier's Return 137
Boxing Match — — — — ibid		A Proper Blow-up — — — 139
Account of Harlequin Amulet — 98		A Legal Duel — — — — ibid
——— Harlequin's Tour; or the Dominion of Fancy — — 100		Fox Hunting — — — — ibid
Humourous Suggestions of Medical and Surgical Punishments — 102		Feast of Wit — — — — 140
		Sporting Intelligence — — — 142
Norwegian Corps of Skaiters — 104		POETRY.
Upon the Abuse of Gaming — 106		Lines over the Door of a Penny Barber — — — — — 145
Some Account of Jerusalem Whalley 108		The Muck-Bird and Red Bird — ibid
Theatricals in Edinburgh — — 109		Epitaph — — — — — 146
New Pantomime — — — 111		The Way of the World — — ibid
Curious Abstracts from original Wills 114		Epigram — — — — — ibid
Magnificent Ruins in Egypt — 115		The Poet's Garret — — — 147
Treatise on Horses — — — 116		On the Marriage of Mr. J. Bacchus, aged 97, to Miss Watson, aged 27 ibid
Pedigree and Performances of Walter 120		
Swiftean Advice to the Collegians of Dublin — — — — — 121		The Greyhound, a Fable — — 148
		The Sportsman's Morning — — ibid
Crim. Con. Hoare, Esq. v. Allen, Esq. — — — — — 122		The Sportsman's Eve — — — ibid

[Embellished with a beautiful Engraving of a FARRIER's SHOP, by SCOTT, and an Etching of a WILD CAT and SPANIELS, by HOWITT.]

London:

PRINTED FOR THE PROPRIETORS;

And Sold by J. WHEBLE, Warwick Square, Warwick Lane, near St. Paul's; C. CHAPPLE, 66, Pall-mall, opposite St. James's Place; J. BOOTH, Duke Street, Portland Place; JOHN HILTON, at Newmarket; and by every Bookseller and Stationer in Great Britain and Ireland.

W. JUSTINS, PRINTER, PEMBERTON ROW, GOUGH SQUARE.

THE SPORTING MAGAZINE,

For DECEMBER 1800.

THE FARRIER'S SHOP.
[An Engraving by Scott, from a Drawing of Sartorious.]

THIS Plate requires not a word of explanation; it is a subject of fancy, and speaks for itself. As, however, it is customary to announce the plates of the month in some part of the Magazine, we here do it in respect to the FARRIER'S SHOP, and which, when our volume is bound, is to be placed opposite this page.

SPORTING INTELLIGENCE.

JOURNAL of the ROYAL CHASE.

ON Monday the 8th, the Berkeley hounds threw off at Bear Grove; after drawing which, and a considerable scope of country without success, they at length unkennelled within half an hour of sun-set, at Shottesbrook Great Wood, and went off in high stile to Billingbear, Binfield, the Hazes, Brick-bridge, White and Lawrence Waltham, to Kiln Green, where they killed, though so dark, that no one man in the field could see to ride up to the hounds.

On Tuesday the 9th, a deer was turned out at Maidenhead Thicket, before his Majesty, and upwards of one hundred horsemen: looking with the utmost contemptuous indifference upon so formidable an aggregate, he for a long time seemed to refuse the least compliance with the eager expectation and anxious wishes of the multitude; when having at length irritated the patience of some, and excited the curses of others, by taking to a pond in Birches Green, he bid them adieu; and, with the pack *close at him*, led them through the beechen woods of Assey-Hill, Hurley Park, on to Bear Grove; to the right over the open country to Lord Malmsbury's; leaving this to the left, he afforded some excellent racing to the seasoned horses, and more seasoned sportsmen, till reaching the Thames, he crossed it at Medenham, to the great regret and disappointment of numbers, for, as the ferry-boat could contain but eight, with safety, it was in vain for more than two freights to pursue; when the hounds were rising the hills of Oxfordshire, more than a mile on the other side. In this dilemma, the scene may be better conceived than described; numbers of the unfortunate were obliged to return in *dudgeon* to different parts of the country, while the more happy *few* continued the chase, till the deer was taken at Henley, after a most capital run of two hours and a half.

On Saturday, the stag-hounds hunted at Ascot Race-ground; and on the same day, the Berkeley hounds, during a *five hours incessant rain*, drew Bear Grove. Scarlet's Copse, Lord Braybrooke's, and Colonel

Colonel Vansittart's coverts, without a single note of preparation; but, throwing into Bisham Park on their way home, the *challenge*, the grand *crash*, and *a view*, instantly succeeded each other: disdaining an early shelter from his "native lodging place," he boldly crossed the open common to Cookham Deane, and Aldridge's woods, till nearly reaching the Thames at Stonehouse, where, finding the hounds gain fast upon him, he headed, re-crossed Cookham Deane, and reached Bisham great woods, where, affording a circle of breast-high running, he availed himself of the *stoppers* nocturnal negligence, and reached his *earth*, after a brisk and uninterrupted gallop of three-quarters of an hour.

The Duke of Cumberland hunted with the Berkeley hounds at East Burnham beeches, on Monday, Dec. 15, where the first fox was lost in a very little time after being unkenneled; this disappointment was however soon obliterated by a fresh fox, who, when found, had the pack so close upon him, that he had no alternative but to break covert with the whole body of hounds at his *brush*, which proved his almost immediate destruction, being run into and *killed*, after about a ten minutes racing burst, the most of it *in view*.

On Friday the 12th inst. Mr. Hanbury's hounds, attended by a great number of respectable sportsmen, turned out a fox, had an excellent day's running, and killed at Lady Wood, in great stile.—Monday following, met at Castle Hedingham, when, if possible, their sport exceeded that of the preceding meeting: after an hour, ran one fox to ground; found again, and run very hard for two hours, killing one horse in the pursuit; found a third fox, which ran them very hard till dark.—Capt. Towers, of the Guards, narrowly escaped the loss of a valuable hunter, which was near being drowned in crossing the river Colne.

The Duke of York's hounds, kept at Oatlands, were lately drafted from the Earl of Egremont's, and at first amused the neighbourhood with hunting hare: but plenty of foxes being found in the environs they constantly hunt fox, and are improving rapidly; they have had at Walton, Ockham, and Ripley, some good runs, and frequently kill. His Highness hunts as often as the extent of his official engagements will permit: this sporting department is under the superintending management of G. Lake, Esq.

We hear from Kinross, that the late coursing meeting there, was well attended, and that there was much good sport. The two silver cups and the purse were won by a dog called Spring, the property of Robert Wellword, Esq.

On Tuesday the 23d, Mr. Hounsom's bay mare Carnation, by Revenge, out of Superior's dam, by Highflyer, beat easy Mr. Sawyer's brown mare, two miles over Epsom, for 100 guineas, play or pay. The odds at starting were in favour of Mr. Sawyer, who had retained, and brought from Newmarket the celebrated Westlake, to insure a superiority of *jockeyship*; notwithstanding which step of sporting prudence, Carnation (in the language of the Duke of Queensberry) "took the lead and kept it," to the great credit of Fenwick's subordinate, who officiated as jockey in a most masterly manner upon the occasion.

The match of Tunbridge against time (from Westminster-bridge to Rochester, in two hours) ran on the 1st of October, is not yet settled, but will go to the Jockey Club for decision, upon a nice point

point of punctilio, respecting some informality in the precise time, or hour, of starting only, as the owner of the horse brings ample proof of his having performed the engagement.

A match was lately to have been run over Doncaster Course for 100 guineas, but one of the horses having been drawn, the other started alone to make good the bet, and after having gone about a mile, a greyhound bitch ran with her the other three miles, keeping nearly head to head, which produced a singular race; and when they arrived at the distance-post, 5 to 4 was betted on the greyhound, and even betting at the stand. The mare won by about a head.

ANECDOTE.

THERE was a man, named Faulkener, who went out about five years ago to Philadelphia, having purchased ten thousand acres of land in the western territory. He was boasting a great deal of his purchase, and happened to ask an old Quaker which was the way to his estates?—" Right through that gate, Friend," said the Quaker, " that's the way to thy settlement." " Why," replied the other, " that's the workhouse." —" Thou art right, Friend," replied the Quaker; and sure enough, the poor fellow found a home in that very house in less than twelve months after!

AMERICA.

THE following is a very droll specimen of Yankee wit:

TO BE SOLD BY
NICHOLAS BRANCH,

At his *Refectory*, west-end of the bridge, Providence,
SOLID ARGUMENTS,
CONSISTING OF
Bread, Butter, Cheese, Hams, Eggs, Salmon, Neats Tongues, Oysters, &c. ready cooked.

AGITATIONS.
Cyder, Vinegar, Salt, Pickles, Sweet Oil, &c.

GRIEVANCES.
Pepper, Sauce, Mustard, Black Pepper, Cayenne, &c.

PUNISHMENTS.
Wine, Brandy, Gin, Spirits, Bitters, Porter, &c.

SUPERFLUITIES.
Snuff, Tobacco, and Sugar.

N. B. Any of the above articles to be exchanged for

NECESSARIES, viz.
French Crowns, Spanish Dollars, Pistareens, Cents, Mills, or Bank Bills

CREDIT GIVEN FOR PAYMENTS,
30, 60, and 90 Seconds, or as long as a man can hold his breath.

RUDIMENTS, Gratis, viz.

Those indebted for	*Arguments*
Must not be	*Agitated*,
Nor think it a	*Grievance*,
If they should meet	*Punishment*
For calling for such	*Superfluities*,
And supposing it not	*Necessary*
To make immediate	*Payment*.

BOXING MATCH.

IN addition to the statement in page 142, we have to mention that Mr. Cullington, of Tottenham-court, was stake-holder to Gamble and Belcher, and also stake-holder for the majority of the adventurers in the ring, paying to several claimants in the field of battle on December 22, sums to the amount of 700l. He paid also in the evening to Dr. Moore, who
advanced

advanced the fighting-money for Belcher, the victor, his demands, extending to nearly 1200l.

Among those in the ring were, Lord Say and Sele, Colonel Ogle, Colonel Montgomery, F. Reed, Esq. Captain B. Captain Desmond, Squire Mountain, Cullington and Lee (Umpires), Kelly of Lisle-street, and also stake-holder in the ring, Mr. Aldridge, jun.; also the following professors of the pugilistic art— Jackson, Bark, Paddington Jones (who lately fought Belcher), Brown, Bell, Whitecombe, Gibbon, &c. &c.

The following statement of the winnings is circulated among the knowing few.

Two Great Personages	£.3000
Lord Say and Sele	100
Lord F.	500
Dr. Moore	600
Captain Desmond	500
Lord Y.	200
Mr. Mountain	350
Mr. Brown	500
Mr. Aldridge	200
Mr. H.	300
The Pub. in St. Martin-street	200
Jackson	100
Paddington Jones	20
Small betts paid on the spot	800

Among the losers were, Mr. Kelly, of Lisle-street; a green-grocer of Covent-garden, to the amount of 70 guineas; a *rabbit-merchant* to the tune of 200, and most of the *rabbit-merchants* in London, who on that day ceased crying "Rabbits," but cried loudly for their *loss*, as they were *all broke!*

On Sunday morning a desperate battle was fought in the fields near Hoxton, between two *ass-keepers*; who, if they did not display much skill, shewed an equal degree of obstinacy, and amused a very respectable assembly for upwards of an hour, when victory declared itself in favour of the *least* of them, and he was conducted from the field on his own ass, with every mark of honour; while his unfortunate competitor, like blind Belisarius of old, was left, almost alone, to grope his way to the first public-house he could find.

To the EDITORS *of the* SPORTING MAGAZINE.

GENTLEMEN,

BEING a subscriber to your Magazine, and knowing that all sports (the turf and chase in particular) are enlarged upon in your publication, I shall take it as a particular favour if you will, in the next Number, insert "The Laws relative to Coursing." My reason for writing to you is to oblige a friend of mine, who has made several matches with a favourite young greyhound, which are to be run in January. If you should not be able to gratify me by acceding to my request, I shall take it as a favour if you will publish this letter in the next Number, (making any alterations or additions which you may deem necessary) and perhaps some person will be so kind to answer it in a future Number.

I am, Gentlemen,
Your's, very truly,
ACTÆON.

*THEATRES.

DRURY-LANE.

THE Christmas holidays were preceded here, as usual, by a new pantomime, intitled *Harlequin Amulet*, of which we understand Mr. Johnson is the inventor.

It opens with a well-executed view of a subterraneous temple, where several Welch Bards had taken refuge from their persecutors, having

having been informed that *Mocar*, the evil genius of their race, had medidated their destruction. *Mocar* is seen through an aperture in the rock; the affrighted bards disperse, except the Chief, who, prostrating himself, invokes the aid of his patron. The storm that raged abates, a beautiful rainbow appears, and *Iris*, descending on the arch alights on the stage, and promises aid to him who shall venture to pursue her enemies. *Iris* then waves her scarf, a bright cloud appears, and *Harlequin* descends to the earth, accompanied by his attendant *Punch*. *Iris* gives a talisman to *Harlequin*, and informs him that *Columbine*, on beholding him, will quit her father's mansion, and follow his fortunes.

Mocar is apprised of the approach of *Harlequin*. He lights his wand with magic fire, which *Harlequin* soon extinguishes. *Punch* now discovers armour for his master—a fantastical figure drops from its sleeve, illuminated with rays of blue flame, while snakes twine around *Punch*, which are soon subdued by the talisman of *Harlequin*. *Pantaloon* next introduces *Punch* to *Columbine*, who becomes enamoured of his master's mistress—the perseverance of *Punch*, and the consequent defeats he endures from *Harlequin*, gives rise to much pantomimic merriment, which ends in the penitence of *Punch* and his master's forgiveness. *Columbine* being again at large, flies with *Harlequin* to a fisherman's cottage, and reward their hosts who, in return, provides them with a vessel to make their escape. The departure of the lovers furnishes an opportunity for a most beautiful view of the sea.— *Pantaloon* and his associates pursue the lovers, but fail in navigating their vessel, in consequence of the magic power of *Harlequin*. He next strikes a rock, a light-house springs out at the top, and they gain the shore.

Harlequin and *Columbine* are still closely pursued. He waves his wand, two beautiful figures rise out of another rock, which as soon as *Pantaloon* and his party approach, the latter become petrified. They are, however, released by *Mocar*. The piece then proceeds with the usual gambols of *Harlequin*, and the waggeries of *Punch*, with which are blended many striking and picturesque views of Wales, Castles, Sea Prospects, &c. *Harlequin* is again in jeopardy, but is released by the genius of the *Talisman*, who is discovered seated on a cloud, with a rainbow at a distance, and the enemies of the lovers are finally subdued.

The last scene represents a Gothic Hall, admirably well designed, and correctly executed. It is enriched with wreaths of laurels, banners, trophies, statues; the latter, by the magic of the *Talisman*, descend from their pedestal, and perform a warlike dance. The distance then opens, and discovers a correct and interesting view of London, St. Paul's, Carleton-House, &c. A brilliant rainbow appears. A grand procession enters in celebration of St. David's Day. *Harlequin* and *Columbine* are united, and the piece concludes.

The construction of this piece differs in some respects from the usual stile. There are very few metamorphoses, the variety and ingenuity of which generally constitute the leading feature. The artist has substituted in their room an immensity of scenes richly and beautifully coloured. The rapidity with which they succeed each other, some in motion scarcely affording time for the eye to rest upon them, assist very much the bustle and activity of the piece; but, owing to the great complexity of the mechanism,

mechanism, there were a few interruptions in the performance — This seemed to be the principal cause of a slight degree of disapprobation which marked the conclusion. There were also some parts, particularly the two Colossal figures, which produced a very indifferent effect. There was also a further variety in the introduction of several songs, among which Mrs. Mountain was best intitled to praise. The music, though not new, was very lively and pleasing.

COVENT GARDEN.

After the play of *Jane Shore*, a new pantomime was brought forward, entitled *Harlequin's Tour*, or the *Dominion of Fancy*. The scenery presented a great variety of picturesque views, faithfully and beautifully delineated. Among the principal are Margate, Dandelion, Charing Cross, Scarborough, Ulswater Lake, Bath, Tunbridge Wells, Weymouth, and many others of fashionable resort.

The air-built palace of Fancy in the first scene, and the pavilion of the same Goddess at the conclusion, are not surpassed by any specimens of scenic magnificence which we have ever witnessed — The most prominent of the mechanical metamorphoses are, a Doctor's Shop Window into his Chariot; a pair of Lamps into two Chinese Giants; a Milliner's House into a Caravan of Wild Beasts; a Military Target into an emblem of the Union; two Spruce Beer Bottles into a Mop and a Pistol; a Sign-post into a House; a Washing-tub into an old Woman; a Chest of Tea into a Pump.

The overture and most of the music are Moorhead's, the remainder Atwood's.

The Pantomime is the production of T. Dibdin, and got up with great effect by Bologna, jun. The managers have been most profusely liberal in every instance of expensive dress, mechanism, scenery, and elegant decorations.

Although not one of the most lively pieces of this class, it went off with much applause, except in one or two passages; the omission of which, with a few other slight alterations, will render it perfectly unexceptionable.

A compliment was paid to the Union by the introduction of various emblems appropriate to that approaching event; and Mr. Denman came forward to give a song suited, we believe, to the occasion; but the audience passed a premature sentence upon it, and demanded a substitute.

Mrs. Mills was the *Columbine* of the night, and gave a new and successful proof of the versatility of her powers.

The following Inscription is literally taken from a Shew-Board in a Country Village in Yorkshire.

WRIGHTEN, and Readden and *Tirw Spillen* and Alko Marchants Ackounts with dubble Entery

Post-skript Girlls and Buoys Boarded and good Youzitch for Chilldren.

WILD CAT AND SPANIELS.
[*An Etching by Mr. Howitt.*]

WE have not been furnished with any particulars of this subject of *The Wild Cat and Spaniels*, but presume the artist means no other sort of *Wild Cat*, than those that occasionally breed in woods, and are of the same species as the *House Cat*. Of this, however, we request information, that a more satisfactory account may be laid before our readers in some future Number.

HUMOUROUS

HUMOROUS SUGGESTIONS OF MEDICAL AND SURGICAL PUNISHMENTS.

To the EDITORS *of the* SPORTING MAGAZINE.

GENTLEMEN,

THE multiplication of penal statutes has given rise to many serious disquisitions on the wisdom of laws, their failure, and the difficulty of carrying them into execution; and some gentlemen of profound habits of thinking, have sunk so deep in this subject, as to assert, almost in plain terms, that penal laws are good for nothing; because crimes are as frequent after they have been enacted, as before. Others have inquired, and I confess with some propriety, into the right of any community to inflict the punishment of *death* upon its member; and, if I am not mistaken, this punishment is in America restricted to murderers of the worst class only.

Meditating upon these subjects a few nights ago, it occurred to me that the fault of our laws might perhaps consist in the punishments we inflict, not being properly proportioned to the crimes; or, in other words, that rogues have been far more fertile in devising new crimes, than honest men, or legislators (who, *ipso facto*, are honest men), have been ingenious in varying their means of punishment. To enumerate all the crimes for which the law ordains punishment, would require a much larger proportion of your Magazine, than you might be disposed to allow to such a purpose; but all the punishments in use may, I believe, be expressed in these few words, *death, banishment, imprisonment, whipping, pillory,* and *fines*. There are six punishments to at least six hundred species of crimes; and, by the bye, to save myself the trouble, I beg leave to refer the curious reader to Mr. Colquhoun's two volume on the London and Marine Police, where he will find the *genera* and *species* of rogues classified in a truly Linnæan system, and often with Linnæan names.

Perhaps, therefore, I say, the failure of our penal laws may proceed from the want of connection between the crime and the punishment. But it is not my intention at present to attempt to establish this connection: I leave that to wiser heads, and proceed to inform you, that, in the course of my meditations aforesaid, I recollected a plan put into my hands some years ago, for " commuting all punishments for *operations* of *pharmacy* and *surgery*." The worthy gentleman who proposed this scheme had principally in his eye the frequency of executions, which he thought disgraceful to a country boasting its humanity; and his idea was, instead of hanging so many felons, to make them submit to certain experiments and operations in physic and surgery. Hereby, said he to me, with all the enthusiasm of a schemer, science will be promoted, as well as crimes punished, by rogues being obliged to submit to operations, which, I am sorry to say, we can scarcely persuade honest men to undergo, although their lives are in danger; and I know so much of these operations, that I will venture to say, that, if my scheme be adopted, felons will understand what it is to suffer the *pains* of law better than ever they did.

This plan of my learned friend, however, did not succeed at the time it was proposed, and I know not why; I am, however, hopeful that it may meet with a more gracious reception from the public at present, when the invention of *sub-*

stitutes is greatly the fashion, and when we have ingenious men who undertake to find *substitutes* for almost every necessary of life, from a *militia man* to a *joint of meat*. Now, as it is notorious, that the punishment of felons is very expensive to government, and as government, like all other well-regulated families, must be sensible of the hardness of the times, I flatter myself I am performing an acceptable service, by proposing a cheap substitute for punishments.

It is almost needless to say, that the science of surgery is very much obstructed by the want of opportunities for operations and experiments, before the student arrives at actual practice upon his patients. It is a very awkward thing, and would be very shocking if it were known, that a surgeon should be able to say to a patient, "Sir, I am come to cut off your leg; but as this is the first time I ever performed the operation, you must excuse me, if I don't go through it as I could wish." This, Gentlemen, would surely be very shocking and very unsafe; whereas, it is obvious, that by the scheme I propose, at least twenty students may go through the whole series of operations in the course of one Old Bailey Sessions, greatly to their improvement, and to the furtherance of the law.

Another advantage would be, that, as the operations of surgery are very numerous, they might afford that variety of punishment, which seems very much wanted, in order to proportion punishments to crimes; and the antipathy of the lower classes to surgical operations is so strong, that I trust I need not expatiate on this as a powerful argument in favour of the scheme. The sight of a case of instruments would create more terror, than the sight of a cat-o'-nine-tails, which I am told there are various ways to evade. For slight offences, or first offences, it may perhaps be necessary to order the felon to be put under the hands of an apothecary's boy for a week or fortnight. Crimes of the next degree of atrocity, might be punished by a gentle dislocation; as we rise higher in offence, we ascend through the various degrees of fractures, simple and compound, up to the trepan, or lithotomy.

Methinks I hear the Recorder passing sentence at the conclusion of an Old Bailey Sessions, in this manner:

"You, John Glim, have been found guilty of house-breaking: it only remains for me, that I pronounce the sentence of the law; which is, that you be taken from thence to Surgeon's-Hall, in Lincoln's-Inn-Fields, in the city of Westminster, and county of Middlesex, and there be cut for a *fistula*."

"You, Thomas Vagrant, have been found guilty of stealing privately. The sentence of the law is, that your right hand should be cut off; but the court, in consideration of your having a numerous family, whom you maintain by your profession as a ballad-singer, hath been pleased to remit that part of your sentence, and orders that you be *qualified for the Opera House*."

This, Sir, would alter the face of things in Newgate; instead of rioting, drinking, and swearing, which are too much to be heard in all our jails, we should hear nothing but groans and screams, and the direful operation of boluses and juleps. The Newgate Calendar then would be a list of cases in surgery; and the keeper, if he found a prisoner refractory, might easily procure such advice from the first surgeon in the neighbourhood, as would effectually prevent his running away.

Upon highwaymen, footpads, and all such blood-thirsty fellows, I would have the various kinds of *styptics* tried; experiments might also be made with *gun-shot* wounds, a species of retaliation, which would admirably serve the purposes of science and justice. As to crimes committed in a state of intoxication; for the lesser species, a course of quack medicines might probably be severe enough; but for the more atrocious, it would be absolutely necessary to punish by tapping. Not that I mean that the sentence of the judge should be definitive. Alleviating circumstances ought still to appeal to the fountain of mercy, and in cases where the jury strongly recommended to mercy, his Majesty would no doubt remit the *trocar*, or the *bistoury*, as might seem fit. Very heinous offences committed by females, might be punished by operations incident to the sex, such as experiments on the nervous system, on the tongue, &c. or perhaps the *Cæsarian operation* might be ordered in lieu of *hanging*; and, if we may believe some learned professional men, who have lately tried that operation, it would not amount to much more than a respite for a week!

As to petty offences, bleeding and tooth-drawing would in general be sufficient, and perhaps as good for the morals, as beating hemp and blaspheming; or the apothecaries might be permitted to try the effect of some new-invented medicine. I fancy I shall some day or other, read in the newspapers a paragraph like the following:

" Yesterday three men and a woman were brought before the Lord Mayor, for getting drunk, and making a riot in a public-house at unseasonable hours; but, on their making a handsome apology for their conduct, and promising to behave better in future, his Lordship was pleased to order, that each should take a box of Dr. Humbug's Cathartic pills, and be discharged."

In this plan, I humbly presume, it is very obvious that various persons would be gratified. Men of science would be undoubtedly pleased with so extensive a range of experimental practice; and I trust there is enough in the scheme to satisfy those, who think that our punishments are in general too lenient. Executioners and jailors may be bribed, and there are various ways of softening punishments ordered by the law; but the gentlemen to be employed upon my plan, would have too much interest in its success to be swayed by any considerations of another kind, or to be prevailed upon to lay down the knife or the lancet, before law and justice had been fully satisfied. Besides, should a greater degree of severity be contended for in the case of certain crimes, than an expert operator might inflict, we have bungling surgeons and blundering apothecaries enough, whose handy work and prescriptions would amount to the full rigour of the law; or the numerous tribe of advertising doctors might be employed, and I hope none will say, that the punishment in that case would not be perfectly adequate to the crime.

Having suggested these hints, Gentlemen, I leave the consideration of the whole scheme to the examination of your readers; trust they will weigh it with impartiality and determine whether it is or is not entitled to a preference over the present system. I am, Gentlemen, your most obedient,

A FRIEND TO JUSTICE
AND SURGERY.

P.S. I have this moment read, that the Divorce Bill has been thrown

thrown out of the House of Commons. I am sorry for it. I think I could have recommended, in my plan, a trifling operation or two, which would have effectually prevented the increase of Divorces. *Sublata causa, tollitur effectus.*

June 13, 1800.

NORWEGIAN CORPS OF SKAITERS.

IT is well known, that Norway is, during four or five months, covered with snow, which, at some distance from the sea-coast, is so deep, that it becomes impossible for the traveler to quit the beaten road either on horseback or on foot. Even the road itself must be new beaten after each new fall of snow; and that operation is performed by means of a machine somewhat resembling a plough, pointed before, and gradually widening behind, which, being drawn by horses, cuts its way through, and levels at the same time.

Notwithstanding the difficulties which the Norwegian winters thus naturally present, the chase has ever been a favourite exercise with the inhabitants of the country, which formerly abounded with fierce animals, besides deer and smaller game.

To make the most of the short days in that climate, by traversing the forests with increased celerity, the Norwegians devised the use of skais, very different, however, from those which we use in our southern lands for the purposes of amusement.

The Norwegian skaits are a pair of boards, about four or five inches broad, from half an inch to an inch thick, slightly hollowed in the middle underneath, to prevent unsteadiness, and to advance in a straight line. The board for the left foot is ten feet long, the other only about six. They are both bent a little upward at the extremities, but higher before than behind.—They are tied to the feet with thongs fastened in the middle, where they are left higher and thicker than in the other parts. The skait for the right foot is often underlaid with rein deer skin or seal skin, which glides very smoothly along when the skaiter moves forward in the direction agreeing with the grain of the hair, but which presents a resistance when he presses his foot in a backward direction, causing the hair to bristle.

It is an ascertained fact, that a good skaiter, when the snow is tolerably firm, can travel more rapidly over a level country, and continue his rapid march for a longer time, than the best horse trotting on the finest road.

If he has to descend a mountain, he moves with such impetuosity, that he is obliged to moderate his first effort in springing forward, lest he should lose his breath in the descent. He ascends more slowly, and not without some difficulty, because he is obliged to mount in a zig-zag direction. Nevertheless, he reaches the summit in as short a time as would suffice for the best foot-man. And if the snow has acquired any small degree of consistency, he never sinks into it.

Experience having proved, that in spite of the multiplied obstacles arising from the severity of the winter, Norway had been repeatedly attacked by the enemy, during that season—and this mode of performing long excursions being in general use among the inhabitants—it was natural that the idea should occur, of forming a military corps of skaiters.

Accordingly, such a plan has been adopted; and the corps, consisting of 960 men, is divided into two battalions, one for the northern part

part of the country, the other for the southern.

Their present uniform consists of a short green jacket, a grey surtout with a yellow cape, pantaloons, and a black leathern cap.

Their arms are a carbine hung with a sling, which passes over the shoulder, a broad cutlass, and a staff three yards and a half long, an inch and quarter thick, having at the end an iron point, and at some distance from the extremity, a circular piece of iron. The principal use is to check the excessive rapidity of the skaiter's motion in descending heights. On these occasions, he places it between his legs, drags it after him, or he drags it by his side. On other occasions, he makes use of it to push himself forward in ascending: in short, he variously employs it according to circumstances. This staff serves him also as a support for his carbine, when he wishes to fire a shot; though, indeed, the Norwegian peasants in general shoot very well without any such aid, and seldom miss their aim.

To the exercise of skaiting, this corps unites also that of the ordinary chasseurs, or light troops, of which it is to be considered as constituting a part: it performs all the same functions as they, nor differs from them except in the circumstance of marching on skaits, which gives it a great advantage over the others. The skaiters, moving with great agility, and being secured by depth of the snow from all pursuit, either by infantry or cavalry, may safely hover round a hostile army on its march, may watch all its motions, harrass and gall it on each side of the road, without incurring any danger. Even discharges of cannon would produce little effect on a number of skaiters scattered at two or three hundred yards distance from each other, and whose movements besides are so rapid, that at the moment while the cannoneers fancy they still have them in sight, they have already vanished, to make their appearance anew when least expected.

If the enemy halt, that is the time when the skaiters enjoy their full superiority over them. Whatever precautions the hostile army may have adopted, they are momentarily exposed to the attacks of men, who do not stand in need of roads or paths, but indiscriminately traverse morasses, lakes, and rivers, provided that they only be covered with snow: even though the ice beneath should be too weak to bear either man or horse, the skaiter is safely wafted over it by the rapidity of his motion. Indeed, there is not any corps better calculated in the winter seasons for the service of reconnoitring, carrying intelligence respecting the enemy, or performing the office of couriers.

It may, however, be supposed, that they find a difficulty in turning round, on account of the great length of their skaits: but that is not the case. The skaiter draws back his right foot, to which is fastened the shorter skait, places it vertically to the left, then raises the left, and, placing it parallel to the right, he is turned. If he wishes to turn completely back, he has only to repeat the manœuvres.

In their ordinary winter exercises, the skaiters form themselves in three ranks, and three between the files; and, unless when they designedly scatter themselves, they exactly observe those distances, that they may not impede each other in the use of their skaits.—When they have occasion to fire, the middle and rear ranks advance close to the front; each file thus forming a little body apart.

The baggage and camp-equipage

page of this corps, is conveyed in sledges placed on the skaits. A single man easily draws one of these sledges by means of a leathern thong, which passes over his right shoulder, and crosses to his left side, like the sling for the carbine.

An improvement on this plan has been suggested—that of attaching to the corps a few pieces of light artillery, to be drawn upon skaits in the same manner as the baggage.

UPON THE ABUSE OF GAMING.

To the EDITORS *of the* SPORTING MAGAZINE.

GENTLEMEN,

SOME recent instances in the fashionable world, of *Gaming*, having ended in distress and self-murder, and the too general prevalence of that abominable vice among the higher orders, induce me to request you to republish the following Extract from Sir William Blackstone's *Commentaries on the Laws of England*. The information it contains may deter some, and the justice of the learned author's reflections may reclaim others, from a pursuit which is equally inconsistent with their interest and their duty. A. B.

" Next to that of luxury, naturally follows the offence of *Gaming*, which is generally introduced to supply or retrieve the expences occasioned by the former: it being a kind of tacit confession, that the company engaged therein do, in general, exceed the bounds of their respective fortunes; and therefore they cast lots to determine upon whom the ruin shall at present fall, that the rest may be saved a little longer. But, taken in any light, it is an offence of the most alarming nature; tending, by necessary consequence, to promote public idleness, theft and debauchery, among those of a lower class; and, among persons of a superior rank, it hath frequently been attended with the sudden ruin and desolation of ancient and opulent families, an abandoned prostitution of every principle of honour and virtue, and too often hath ended in self-murder. To restrain this pernicious vice among the inferior sort of people, the statute 33 Hen. VIII. cap. 9. was made; which prohibits to all, but gentlemen, the games of tennis, tables, cards, dice, bowls, and other unlawful diversions there specified, unless in the time of Christmas, under pecuniary pains, and imprisonment. And the same law, and also the statute 30 Geo. II. cap. 24, inflict pecuniary penalties, as well upon the master of any public-house wherein servants are permitted to game, as upon the servants themselves who are found gaming there. But this is not the principal ground of modern complaints; it is the gaming in high-life that demands the attention of the Magistrate;—a passion to which every valuable consideration is made a sacrifice; and which we seem to have inherited from our ancestors, the ancient Germans, whom Tacitus describes to have been bewitched with a spirit of play to a most exorbitant degree. " They addict themselves," says he, " to dice (which is wonderful) when sober, and as a serious employment; with such a mad desire of winning or losing, that, when stript of every thing else, they will stake at last their liberty and their very selves. The loser goes into a voluntary slavery; and, though younger and stronger than his antagonist, suffers himself to be bound and sold. And this perseverance, in so bad a cause, they call

call the point of honour: *ea est in re prava pervicaria, ipsi fidem vocant.*"—One would almost be tempted to think Tacitus was describing a modern Englishman. When men are thus intoxicated with so frantic a spirit, laws will be of little avail; because the same false sense of honour, that prompts a man to sacrifice himself, will deter him from appealing to the Magistrate. Yet it is proper that laws should be, and be known publicly, that gentlemen may consider what penalties they wilfully incur, and what a confidence they repose in sharpers; who, if successful in play, are certain to be paid with honour; or, if unsuccessful, have it in their power to be still greater gainers by informing: for, by the statute 16 Car. II. cap. 7. if any person, by playing or betting, shall lose more than 100l. at one time, he shall not be compellable to pay the same; and the winner shall forfeit treble the value, one moiety to the King, the other to the informer.—The statute 9 Anne, c. 14, enacts, that all bonds and other securities, given for money won at play, or money lent at the time to play withal, shall be utterly void; that all mortgages and incumbrances of lands, made upon the same consideration, shall be, and ensure to the use of the heir to the mortgager: that if any person at one time loses 10l. at play, he may sue the winner, and recover it back by action of debt at law; and in case the loser does not, any other person may sue the winner for treble the sum so lost; and the plaintiff, in either case, may examine the defendant himself, upon oath: and that, in any of these suits, no privilege of Parliament shall be allowed. The statute farther enacts, that if any person cheats at play, and at one time wins more than 10l.

or any valuable thing, he may be indicted thereupon, and shall forfeit five times the value, shall be deemed infamous, and suffer such corporal punishment as in case of wilful perjury. By several statutes of the reign of King George II. all private lotteries by tickets, cards, or dice, (*and particularly the games of faro, basset, ace of hearts, hazard, passage, rolly-polly, and all other games with dice, except backgammon*) are prohibited, under a penalty of 200l. for him that shall erect such lotteries, and 50l. a time for the players.—Public lotteries, unless by authority of Parliament, and all manner of ingenious devices under the denomination of sales or otherwise, which in the end are equivalent to lotteries; were before prohibited by a great variety of statutes, under heavy pecuniary penalties. But particular descriptions will ever be lame and deficient, unless all games of mere chance are at once prohibited; the inventions of sharpers being swifter than the punishment of the law, which only hunts them from one device to another. The statute 19 Geo. II. cap. 19. to prevent the multiplicity of horse-races, another kind of gaming, directs that no plates or matches, under 50l. value, shall be run, upon penalty of 200l. to be paid by the owner of each horse running, and 100l. by such as advertise the plate. —By statute 18 Geo. II. cap. 34. the statute 9 Anne, is farther enforced, and some deficiencies supplied: the forfeitures of that Act may now be recovered in a Court of Equity; and, moreover, if any man be convicted, upon information or indictment, of winning or losing at any sitting 10l. or 20l. within twenty-four hours, he shall forfeit five times the sum.—Thus careful has the legislature been to prevent this destructive vice; which may

drew

shew that our laws against Gaming are not so deficient, as ourselves and our Magistrates in putting those laws in execution."

Some Account of Jerusalem Whalley.

THOMAS WHALLEY, Esq. well known by the journey which he, eight or ten years ago, for a considerable wager, undertook to Jerusalem, and which has since obtained to him this appellation, was the son of a gentleman of very considerable property in the north of Ireland. His father, when advanced in years, married a lady much younger than himself, and left her a widow with seven children. Three years after the death of her husband, Mrs. Whalley married Mr. Richardson, a gentleman of respectable character in Gloucestershire, who is still living.

Thomas was the eldest son of Mr. Whalley, and had a property of 10,000l. per ann. left him by his father. At the age of sixteen he was sent to Paris, to learn the French language, and to accomplish himself in the arts of dancing, fencing, &c. He was placed under the care of a gentleman who had formerly been in the army; and who, having spent a good part of his life on the continent, was supposed to be a fit person to undertake the direction of young Whalley's studies. It soon, however, appeared that the tutor had not the ability to check the volatile disposition of his pupil: Mr. Whalley purchased horses and hounds, took a house in Paris, and another in the country, each of which was open for the reception of his friends. His finances, ample as they were, were found inadequate to the support of his extraordinary expences; and, with the hope of supplying his deficiencies, he had recourse to the gaming-table, which only encreased his embarassments. In one night he lost upwards of 14,000l. The bill which he drew upon his banker, La Touche in Dublin, for this sum, was sent back protested, and it became necessary for him to quit Paris. He returned to England, and his creditors (or rather the people who had swindled him out of this money) were glad to compound for half the sum.

After staying some time in London, he went back to Ireland, and took a house in Dublin, where he lived in the most expensive manner. Soon getting tired of the insipid sameness of the mode of life he was engaged in, he determined again to visit the continent. While he was still hesitating as to the exact place of destination, some friends, with whom he was dining, and who had heard that he was intending to go abroad, made inquiry of him whither he was going. He hastily answered, "To Jerusalem." Being convinced that he had no such intention, they offered to wager him any sum he did not go thither. Though, when he gave the answer to their enquiry, he had not the most distant idea of such an expedition, yet, stimulated by the offers made him, he accepted them to the amount of 15,000l. and on the following day he made preparations for his journey. He set out in a few days after he had made his engagements, accomplished the journey, and returned to Dublin within the time to which he was limited, claiming and receiving from his antagonists the reward of his unexpected exploits.

After staying some time in Dublin, he again went to Paris, and was witness to those very interesting scenes which occurred in the early part of the revolution in France. He staid in Paris till after the return of the King from Varennes;

rennes; and, when it became no longer safe for a subject of the King of Great Britain to remain in France, he returned to Ireland — Soon afterwards he became connected with a young woman of amiable disposition, who lived with him till the time of her death; and by whom he had four children, three of whom have survived him.

Not having employment sufficient for his active mind, he came to England, and frequenting the fashionable gaming-houses in London, at Newmarket, Brighton, &c. he soon dissipated a large part of his remaining fortune. He then retired to the Isle of Man, where he employed himself in cultivating and improving an estate he possessed there, and in educating his children. He at the same time drew up Memoirs of his own Life, with a view to their publication, written for the express purpose of preventing other young men from being led into similar errors with himself; and containing some excellent reflections on the folly of the life he had led, and on the small share of happiness he had, with the ample means he possessed, produced to himself or to others. —On the death of the lady above-mentioned, he married the Hon. Miss Lawless, sister to the present Lord Cloncurry. He died lately at Knutsford, while upon a journey, in the 33d year of his age.

THEATRICALS IN EDINBURGH.

To the EDITORS *of the* SPORTING MAGAZINE.

GENTLEMEN,

GOOD news from a far country, they say, is always welcome; you will therefore accept the following account of the present improved state of our Theatre.

You must know, then, that on Saturday the 22d ult. I was present at the opening of our Theatre. —The company now introduced to us by the veteran manager, Mr. Jackson, in conjunction with Mr. Aicken, is very strong and respectable. The Theatre has been improved and embellished, in a style equally creditable to the taste and liberality of the Manager. The side-doors are removed from the Stage, and the space thrown into elegant boxes: the pit is enlarged, and the whole house beautified with considerable effect. The orchestra, under the management of Bird, is creditable to the Theatre. "*Speed the Plough,*" and "*The Citizen,*" were got up on the first night of representation. The merits of the Comedy it is not my intention to discuss: neither it, nor most of the other productions of our modern Dramatists, can be analysed by the established rules of the Drama. It is sufficient to the Manager that this piece is (as it will be during the continuance of the present taste) a favourite with the public; and, as such, he judged rightly in bringing it forward. My object, at present, is to give a few observations on the merits of the principal performers.

Grant is considerably improved since his last appearance on this Stage. He is accused of a servile imitation of a respectable actor. For this opinion I see no grounds, and may with more justice give this gentleman credit for close and successful application to improvement in his profession. His figure is rather diminutive, and his voice limited; his action is, however, chaste and correct, and his articulation distinct. Low comedy I conceive to be the line best adapted to Mr. Grant's talents: in the higher walks, however, he is by no means contemptible. Little energy can be shown by the actor in the part of *Sir Philip Blandford*, except in the last scene, where the emotions of horror and remorse were depicted with considerable feeling. Mr. Grant supported the part of *Young Philpot* with great spirit; and displayed, in *Lessardo*, last night, in "*The Wonder*," a talent for broad humour that justifies the opinion I have expressed.

Mr. Toms performed *Henry*.—This character is, like the former, excessively insipid, the last scene excepted, in which Mr. Toms's powers were disclosed. He displayed great spirit and feeling in his expressions of indignation at the supposed crime of *Sir Philip*, and of love towards his beauteous daughter.

Mr. Young was deservedly applauded in *Young Handy*. He looks this character better than Macready, and does not suffer by a comparison with that favourite actor in other respects. He might make more of the unfortunate Ploughing-match, but spoke the soliloquy in the fifth act with feeling and judgment. Mr Young was also very successful in *Don Felix* last night, and promises to be an acquisition.

Mr. Rock's acting is "above all praise." I make no hesitation in pronouncing this deservedly popular performer one of the best Comedians on the British Stage. He was loudly welcomed by the audience, and played the parts of *Sir Abel Handy* and *Old Philpot* with inimitable humour. During his extravagant joy at parting with *Lady Handy*, the House was convulsed with laughter and applause.

I had not the pleasure of seeing Miss Walstein in *The Fair Penitent*, and consequently lost the only opportunity that has yet occurred of appreciating this lady's abilities. The part of *Miss Blandford* excites no interest, and affords no scope for the powers of a first-rate actress, which Miss Walstein is, and I doubt not justly, reported to be. She is one of the finest Stage figures I have seen, and is generally considered to bear a strong resemblance to Mrs. Siddons.—But, of this lady, who occupies a prominent situation in our company, I shall embrace the first opportunity to form such a judgment as I may venture to communicate.

Miss Duncan, from the York Theatre, has experienced a very flattering reception in the several parts attempted by her. She possesses an elegant person, a beautiful and expressive countenance, and a melodious rather than powerful voice. Her *Maria* was sprightly and interesting, and bears a strong resemblance to the acting of Mrs. Jordan. This lady exerts too much vivacity, even in those parts where most of it is required; and the *pruriency* of her acting is its only fault. The truth of this observation was strongly exemplified in her performance of *Nell*, in *The Devil to Pay*. Neither the *romp* nor the *ideot* are the features of this character, but a rustic simplicity, arising not from stupidity but from ignorance.—I have a high opinion of Miss Duncan's powers, and am prompted, by a wish to see them always exercised with judgment, to make this observation.

The inferior parts were performed, without any remarkable faults, by Mr. and Mrs. Turpin, Mrs. Ward, Mrs. Kennedy, Mrs. Egan, Mr. and Mrs. Duncan, Mr. Halliou, &c. of each of whom I shall speak on a future occasion.

On the whole, the company is excellent, and more numerous than any we have had for several years past. The Managers deserve more than "empty praise" for their arrangements, and I have no doubt will be amply rewarded. Several additions and alterations are wanting in the scenery.

I cannot close without reprobating, in the strongest terms, those critics, as they are called, on the performers and performances at the Theatre, which have been of late with great industry obtruded on the public. It is absurd to expect that any company whatever should be composed entirely of first-rate Players; and it is not to negligence or inaccuracy that these authors confine their invectives, but every Player is damned that is not absolutely perfect in every thing. A real lover of the Drama, desirous to see the Edinburgh Theatre on a respectable footing, would not, by these assassinations of character, attempt to deprive the industrious Actor of that encouragement and applause by which he is stimulated to fresh exertion, and modest merit is seen and rewarded—by which his abilities are gradually expanded, till, nursed by public favour and support, he becomes an ornament to his profession.

"These critics of the stage,
Who, like barbarians, spare nor sex nor age,"

would do much injury to our dramatic amusement, were not their writings so glaringly malicious as entirely to defeat their purpose, and so deficient in justice and true criticism as to have no weight with any discerning person.

"These censors in the pit,
Who think good-nature shews a want of wit.
Such malice! O, what must can undergo it!
To save themselves, they always damn the poet."

TERRACE, Nov. 28. VERUS.

NEW PANTOMIME!

THIS bastard species of theatrical amusement has been criticised by our Dramatic Censors perhaps too severely, as being incapable of gratifying tastes superior to those of Tradesfolks, Aldermen, Common-Councilmen, or children in the holidays. Exhibitions of this nature ought not, however, to be condemned *in toto*. There are a few that merit exemption from so general a censure; such, for instance, are those in which an interesting story may be expressed and understood by action only; and among this kind may be reckoned the Pantomime of "Robinson Crusoe." But that sort deserves the highest praise, which, to a story deeply interesting, adds the most wonderful feats of action, the most ingenious machinery, and the sublimest scenery. Of this last and most perfect species of Pantomime we never had it in our power to notice an example, before the present famous piece, intituled

HARLEQUIN IN ITALY;
OR,
A FLIGHT O'ER THE ALPS.

We proceed to give our readers a brief sketch of the plot, characters, and scenery, of this extraordinary representation. To impress a just idea of the merits and celebrity of the respective performers, collected as they have been from every nation in Europe, it is only necessary to present the following role of the *Dramatis Personæ*:

Harlequin, by	Prestissimo Bonaparte.
The Magician, by	Le Pere See-Eyes.
Sempervivus, Harlequin's Friend	Signor Mewloo.
Columbine's Father,	M. La Revolutionnim.
Columbine's Suitor,	The Baron Franciscus.
Pantaloon,	Count Paulo Pagivitz.
Scaramouch,	The Chev. Syallawath.

The Clown, by the same	Sieur Pitts.
Punchinello (Clown's Man)	Mister M'Dunderas.
Columbine, by the celebrated	Donna Victoria.

This Pantomime, at the opening, does not very materially differ from others. *Columbine*, wearied with the importunities of suitors, of whose addresses, notwithstanding the imperious commands of her father, she cannot approve, chooses for herself, in the excursions of fancy, an imaginary lover, with whom she becomes enamoured, even before he has existence. The *Magician*, knowing the state of her mind by his art magic, waves his wand, calls up his Familiars, and gives birth to a *Harlequin* exactly suited to her inclinations.— Here a variety of scenes are exhibited, *en Ombres Chinoises*, before the actual developement of the Drama. By these *Harlequin* is understood to have obtained a temporary possession of *Columbine*. The fair fugitive becomes wanton and capricious, and longs for a *Mamlouck*; upon which *Harlequin* begins his feats and adventures.— *Harlequin* performs his first spring from the feet of the Alps to the island of Malta, and from the island of Malta to the land of Egypt. This amazing jump reminds the classical reader of the hop, step, and leap, that *Neptune* makes, in the *Iliad*, from *Samothracia* to *Troy*.

" From realm to realm, three ample strides he took."

Harlequin's adventures in Egypt form a brilliant display of scenery and machinery. There, like his predecessor, *St. George*, he encounters several terrible Saracens, and sundry fiery Dragons. The *Clown*, however, (who, as in other Pantomimes, is the head and soul of *Harlequin's* enemies and pursuers) finds a way, some how or other, *haud passibus equis*, to come up with him; upon which the *Clown*, who is himself a Conjurer, and very clever withal, brings forward a trained Crocodile, which he sets at *Harlequin*, exactly as a Butcher sets his dog at a bull. The monster is then seen to open his enormous jaws, to make a snap at *Harlequin*, and, in fine, to swallow him up at a mouthful. The *Clown* then turns about to the audience and laughs, and all the audience laugh with him.—Poor *Harlequin* being thus disposed of, to all appearance for ever, the scene changes to the Alps, and exhibits *Columbine's* adventures in the absence of *Harlequin*. There she is several times entrapped by the *Lover* she detests; but, by the assistance of *Harlequin's* sprightly friend, *Sempervivo*, she contrives to escape. The *Lover*, finding himself likely to be foiled, calls in *Pantaloon*, and his man, *Scaramouch*, to his assistance. *Pantaloon* makes his *debut*, mounted on a pair of stilts (concealed by his long pantaloons) in order to appear grand. *Scaramouch*, however, is a much more formidable personage: he is furnished with an immensely fierce pair of mustachoes, and flourishes in either hand a huge carving knife and fork, with which he threatens to cut up, and eat, all the little children he can meet with. *Sempervivo*, no ways intimidated, performs a thousand astonishing capers: he skips about from Alp to Alp, like a Shamoy goat, and exceeds *Harlequin* himself in some of his vaulting: in fine, he rescues *Columbine* from *Pantaloon*, sends him off with a flea in his ear, shaves the whiskers of *Scaramouch*, and drives him blubbering after his master. At last, the *Clown* and the *Lover* lay their heads together: by the assistance of a black Knight, they once more recover

recover *Columbine*, and shut up *Sempervivo* in an enchanted castle.—Here, then, the audience are led to suppose that the piece must conclude, and that *Columbine* will be compelled to marry the lover of her father's choice. But now comes the *denouement* of the plot, which strikingly evinces the superior excellence of this Pantomime above every other; inasmuch as supernatural or miraculous methods are never employed, until nothing can be effected by ordinary means: the contriver thereby strictly adhering to the precept of Horace,

 "Nec Deus intersit nisi dignus vindice nodus."

The stage represents a scene at once beautiful and sublime—of the Alpine Coast of the Mediterranean. Enter the *Magician* from between two rocks, *solus*, and in all his awful parapharnalia; his *San-Bonito* cap on his head; his white wand in his hand; his sable robes, and his venerable beard "streaming like a meteor in the troubled air." He waves his wand over the sea, and begins his magical incantations; when, behold! an immense and terrific sea-monster is seen swimming towards him. In short, this monster proves to be the identical crocodile that had swallowed up *Harlequin* in Egypt; and he now vomits him up, safe and sound, on the shore.—After all, this surprizing incident does not shock probability very much. We have the best precedent for it in *Jonah* and the *Whale*. By the bye, it might have been a crocodile, and not a whale, that was concerned in the affair of *Jonah*. The text simply mentions "a great fish;" but of what *genus*, commentators have not yet been able to agree. *Harlequin* (like a fly escaped from a cobweb) having cleared himself from the gastric juice of the crocodile, prepares to take "flight o'er the Alp," to recover *Columbine*, and to release his friend *Sempervivo* from the enchanted castle.—Here the scenery of the piece produces the most awful and interesting effect. *Harlequin* is seen, sometimes gliding like a meteor among the glaciers, sometimes ascending the snowy pinnacles of the mountains, and sometimes opening for himself a passage through the perpendicular rocks of granite by a stroke of his sword. In fine, he arrives at the scene of action in less time than would be required circumstantially to describe the journey. He now becomes invincible. He completely baffles the black Knight, the Lover, the Clown, and the Clown's Man, releases his friend *Sempervivo* from the enchanted Castle, and carries off *Columbine* in triumph.

Such is the general outline of this celebrated Pantomime, in which, however, many subordinate characters and interesting episodes are introduced; but these could not be conveniently noticed without breaking the thread of the narrative.

In this piece, the contrast of characters, and the whimsicality of situations, are very remarkable.—In other Pantomimes, the Actor who plays the part of the *Clown* is generally equal, if not superior, in agility to the *Harlequin*; because, to perform these practical blunders, it requires more real address than the feats of mere activity. But the source of amusement, in this piece, arises from the downright and sincere attempts of the *Clown* to rival the gambols of *Harlequin*, the said *Clown* being crippled with the gout. For instance, when *Harlequin* takes his surprizing leap across the Mediterranean, the *Clown*, in imitation, attempts a running leap over a ditch, but not knowing his ground he he sinks up to his neck in a bog-hole, in which he would have been infallibly smothered, if *Harlequin* had not run to his assistance, and dragged him out in a curious pickle. At another time, when *Harlequin* jumps on the top of the Alps, the *Clown* essays to leap out of a ferry-boat on a rock; he jumps short, however, and breaks his nose and shins. But if the *Clown* be awkward on land, he is wonderfully active on water: put him in a wherry, with a sculler in each hand, and he'll shoot the falls of Niagara.

There is one remarkable droll incident in this Entertainment:— *Harlequin*, at one time, wishing to accommodate differences, sends his proposals to the *Clown* on two scrolls of *papyrus*, by way of compliment. The *Clown*, however, to shew his contempt, converts them to a very *curious* kind of use. Afterwards, *Harlequin* gets possession of the two scrolls, plentifully bedaubed, and makes the *Clown* eat them.— This laughable circumstance, notwithstanding, appears to have been borrowed either from the choleric *Flewellin* making ancient *Pistol* eat up the leek, in *Henry the Fifth*, or from the Sieur *Folliot's* swallowing the enormous carrots, which so much delighted the galleries, in *Harlequin and Oberon*.

Punchinello is a very amusing personage. There is a strain of shrewdness in all his blunders; and, as your dramatic *Drawcansirs* "Out-Herod Herod," so *Punchinello* out-clowns the *Clown*.

We regret to notice, that this Pantomime is likely to have but a short run. The principal Performer has so well succeeded, that, like his predecessor, Rich, he is about to turn Manager: and the other Performers, though excellent in their way, are all in embarrassed circumstances; so much so, that some of them must be contented to take refuge in the *Fleet*.

CURIOUS ABSTRACTS,
From Original Wills, proved in the Prerogative Court of Canterbury.

WILLIAM Williams, late of the island of Jamaica, Esq. deceased, proved Oct. 21, 1768. " I give and bequeath to that most abandoned, wicked, vile detestable rogue and impostor, who has assumed, and now does, or lately did go, by the name of ———— ————, pretending to be a son of mine, one shilling only, to buy him a halter wherewith to hang himself, being what he hath for a long, a very long while past, deserved from the law and hands of the hangman, for his great and manifold villanies."

John Goss, late of the city of Bristol, mariner, deceased, proved, May 19, 1796; " My executrix to pay out of the first monies collected unto my beloved wife, Hester Goss (if living) the sum of one shilling, which I give her as a token of my love, that she may buy hazel-nuts, as I know she is better pleased with cracking them, than she is with mending the holes in her stockings."

Stephen Church, late of the parish of St. Mary-at-Hill, London, lighterman, deceased, proved, Nov. 5, 1793: " I give and devise to my son ————, only one shilling, and that is for him to hire a porter to carry away the next badge and frame he steals."

John Davis, late of Clapham, Surrey, woollen-manufacturer, deceased, proved, Jan. 24, 1788. " I give and bequeath to Mary ———— (daughter of Peter Delaporte,) the sum of five shillings, which is sufficient to enable her to get drunk with, for the last time at my expence; and I give the like sum of five shillings to Charles Peter (the son of the said Mary,) who I am reputed to be the father of, but never had, nor never shall have any reason so to believe."

William Woddeson, late of Harlington, Middlesex, deceased, proved. Oct. 27, 1786. "*Item.* I commit my body to the earth, to be buried in a plain coffin, to be drawn, if not inconvenient, on my own one-horse chaise to the church, and then to be carried on the shoulders of six poor men, without any pall, or any funeral pomp whatsoever; and I order, that the said poor men be paid two shillings and sixpence each for their trouble. *Item.* I desire my corpse to be dressed in my last new shirt, and muslin neckcloth and nightcap, and my plaid night-gown, and my old rusty sword, which always lay by my bedside, in my right hand, and my Latin Testament in my left hand, and my little pillow in the pillow-case under my head."

MAGNIFICENT RUINS *in* EGYPT.

Extract of a Letter from Citizen Descotils.

CITIZEN Denon shewed us the numerous collections of drawings which he had made in his excursion. Those of Denderah strongly increased the desire, which we previously entertained of seeing these superb remains of the Egyptian arts. To gratify our curiosity, we had only to go about three-quarters of a league on the other side of the river. We repaired thither as soon as we procured an escort. We had formed a grand idea of those ruins; but their magnificence infinitely exceeded our expectations. The ruins of Denderah consist of three temples, and three detached gates; the grand temples, which is the most engaging, and in the best state of preservation, is 81 metres long, and very nearly 36 broad. It consists of two parts; the outer is a portico supported by 24 columns, which are ranged six in front and four in depth: the columns are nearly seventeen metres in height, and two in diameter above the capitals; they are conical; the pedestal is a cylinder of a larger diameter than the base of a column. Above are two thin pediments, the lower of which projects a few centimetres beyond, the upper, which is of a cubical form, and having its four vertical faces covered with basso' relievos. The second part of the temple, which is inferior in height and extent to the portico, contains several apartments communicating with each other, and lighted only by very narrow loopholes. Above these are several closets, which, with the complete building of the two other temples, and the three gates, are covered with hieroglyphics and figures. The most remarkable parts of the hieroglyphics, almost all of which project from their ground, are two zodiacs, one of which is sculptured on one of the upper closets, and the other on the cieling of the portico. The first is a circular belt, filled with figures of men, the inferior animals, &c. among which may be successively distinguished, a ram, a bull, two men close to each other, a crab-fish, a lion, a husbandman holding an ear of corn, a balance, a scorpion; a two-winged centaur with a sort of mitre on his head, and in the act of shooting an arrow from a bow of the same form, as those still sold in Cairo; an animal with the head of a he-goat and the body of a fish, a man having a vase in each hand, from which he pours out water, which is represented by zig-zag lines; this figure resembles that under which the sign Aquarius is still exhibited—and two fishes joined by the tails with a piece of ribbon: the other figures in the belt are, for the most part, studded round with stars, disposed in various orders. Around the circle are twelve figures, which seem to support this sort of celestial Atlas. The grand zodiac is disposed in perpendicular bands, and in the same order as the former: the lion holds the first place on the right, and is followed by five of the signs. The six others are on the left, and exhibit nothing striking, except with respect to the position of Cancer, which is placed a little above the feet of a singular figure, the body of which embraces the six signs on the right: the feet, the head, and hands of this figure, are wanting, but the rest of the body is seen, and it presents the same zig-zag which indicates water: the sun is placed close by the side of Cancer. This hieroglyphic seems to have some reference to the inundation of the Nile. These signs do not stand alone in the zone which surrounds them; there are many of the figures surrounded with stars, which are doubtless constellations. These objects give us a high opinion of the astronomical science of the Egyptians, and augment our regret for the loss of the hieroglyphic language. I do not think that a more extensive repertory can be any where found of it than at Denderah. All the walls, the cielings, the columns of the three temples, and the three gates, are covered with figures and hieroglyphics, frequently two or three centimetres only in height. The surface occupied with sculpture may, without exaggeration, be estimated at twelve thousand square metres: many of the figures have been destroyed with the chizzel. There is not a single figure on the capitals in an entire state; those on the walls have been to a great height destroyed with the same industry. Designs on the walls, similar to those which we sometimes meet with in France, representing men with crosses in their hands, induce the supposition that it is to Christian fanaticism, we have to ascribe the mutilation of one of the finest monuments in the world. The figures which have escaped destruction give us very high proofs of the talents of the artists. They contain many architectural ornaments, which were copied by the Greeks, such as the mascaron, palm-leaf, and that which has since been denominated the Grecian volute.

A PHILOSOPHICAL *and* PRACTICAL TREATISE on HORSES, *and on the* MORAL DUTIES *of* MAN *towards the* BRUTE CREATION.

BY JOHN LAWRENCE.

UPON IMPROVEMENTS IN THE ART OF SHOEING CART-HORSES.

(Concluded from page 80.)

THE form of the shoe must exactly correspond with the outline of the foot, and ever be made thickest externally at the rim, and gradually thinner internally next the horse's sole, a form directly opposite to the common concave shoe; this will leave just room enough (and there ought to be no more) between the edge of the shoe and the sole, for the introduction of the pecker, which is used to remove small stones and gravel accidentally lodged. Mr. Clarke says, he has frequently observed a swelling of the legs immediately above the hoofs, attended with

with great pain and inflammation, and a discharge of thin ichorous and fœtid matter, which he attributed to the compression made upon the internal parts of the feet, by the common concave, long, and heavy shoes; and that from the same cause chiefly proceed most of the diseases of the feet, founder, hoof-binding, narrow heels, foul thrushes, bleime, high soles, and the like. I have been long convinced of the truth of this observation.

As to the disposition of the nail-holes, every farrier knows that in the fore-feet, the toe is thickest and strongest; in the hinder feet, the heels; according to the French proverb, quoted by Blundeville, *devant derrier, derrier devant*—before behind, behind before.

There is a complaint of very ancient standing, against smiths, for needlessly multiplying nail-holes, and making their nails too large; by which the crust is so torn, as scarce to leave sound space to drive a nail. It is the case, even now, with many of our country shoers, who are not satisfied unless they *skewr* on the shoes.— Old Blundeville's directions herein are not amiss, who says, The nail-heads should be square, and not so broad beneath as above, but answerable to the pierced holes, which they should fill; and above which they should not appear more than the thickness of the back of a knife.—The shanks of the nails to be somewhat flat, stiffer towards the head than below, and the points sharp, without hollowness or flaw. —As to the number of nails in a shoe, the following table is according to the direction of Professor Saint Bel:

For Race-horses, six—three on each side.
— Hacks, Hunters, &c. seven; four on the outside, and three within; the inside quarter being weakest.

For Mail-coachers, Post-horses, &c. same number.
— large Horses, four on each side.
— heavy Cart-horses, five on each side.

Solleysel says, that common smiths, in order to prevent pricking the horse with their large nails, pierce the shoe too near the edge, which practice, in time, ruins the foot.

The shoe being fast nailed, the less there remains to be rasped the better; and that instrument should only be used as high as the rivets, but never above them, because, in the first place, it is unnecessary, and because the surface of the hoof is much injured, and disposed to dry, by being rasped. Furthermore, a heavy and careless hand is extremely apt to touch with the tool the origin of the nail, just beneath the coronet, where it is extremely sensible; the consequence of which is a small wound or bruise, ending frequently in a sand-crack.

Every foot should be kept as short at the toe as is consistent with the safety of the crust, and the proper shape of the foot. My Lord Pembroke's rule is, to cut the toe square, and afterwards round off the angles; and Laurentius Russius, who wrote some centuries before the noble Earl, says, that a short toe, and a narrow, light and straight shoe, make a large and strong hoof, and a firm leg. In taking down the toe, Solleysel forbids the use of the buttress, directing it to be done with a paring-knife after the shoe is fixed, which is to be purposely set back as far as necessary. This, he says, will occasion a derivation of nourishment backward towards the heels, and in time greatly strengthen and enlarge them; which salutary consequence is, indeed, well known to us. If the rasp is at all used in this

this business, it ought to be confined to the toe, and laid on in such wise as to render it as thick as possible, in tender-footed horses.

The only advantageous method that I could ever discover, of shoeing deep strong feet with *contracted narrow heels*, is that of La Fosse, with the half-moon shoes; the crust being previously taken down, as before directed. The horse being presumed already lame, will travel very little more so from his quarters being exposed; and, as being totally unfit, at any rate, for expeditious riding, a little tenderness and flinching may well be borne in a slow pace, since the short shoes will be daily contributing towards his cure, whilst large, hollow, and long ones, would only be aggravating the disease. The smiths render these feet finally useless, by rasping them and paring the soles, under pretence of giving them ease, which, in fact, causes them to dry and contract still more: the only means whence they can possibly get ease is, by the expansion of the quarters, to be attained from the animal's weight borne upon them; the frog also, which appears dried and shrunk up, will expand and increase in bulk from the same cause. Some feet of this description will be thus rendered good, and the remedy is pleasant, from being void of trouble or expence; but if the horn be of a certain peculiar hard and faulty contexture, or the bones and internal processes of the feet materially damaged, which will be discovered after a few times shoeing with the short shoes, all remedies hitherto proposed, from the days of Solleysel (the grand empiric for feet) to the present, are worse than the disease.

For the FLAT FOOT, the author just mentioned advises the following treatment:—Forge a shoe as straight as possible from the toe to the spunges, that is to say, not so circular as usual, with holes pierced very near the edge: after this shoe is nailed fast, there should be about half an inch of horn left to be cut with the knife from the toe, and in proportion round the sides. The shoe is, on no account, to be made concave next the foot, although it may rather touch the sole, but to be hammered hollow externally. The horse may be expected to flinch a little, from the shoe setting somewhat upon the sole; but beware he be not pricked. Every time of change, the shoes are to be made still straighter at the toe, which is to be kept short, but not at the quarters; and in three or four times changing, the author promises an amendment in the shape of the feet. I have never experienced this, nor have I much opinion of its utility, or of any measures tending to throw nature out of her destined course by violence. A foot naturally flat and thin, will be so still, or rendered worse by forcible attempts at amendment.—The only practice to be depended upon, I believe, in this case, is to keep the toe as short as possible, never to diminish the substance of the crust, sole, or binders, and to shoe always in bars, making use of the smallest nails. Our modern English bar-shoe is a judicious improvement of the ancient *planche*, or paneelet, of which Blundeville and others had so high an opinion, for strengthening and giving substance to weak feet. The late Doctor Snape, farrier to his Majesty, had a very ingenious hand at forging this kind of shoe, as I have often experienced.

Joint-shoes for all feet, vaulted shoes for pumiced or convex soles, patten-shoes, lunettes, or half-moons, thick at heel, those with a button or shouldering

shouldering on the inside, to stand clear of a false quarter, and those formed thickest on the inside, to prevent interfering, are very ancient inventions, and sufficiently known to farriers.

I have said, that interfering is usually occasioned by a preternatural turn or twist of the pastern joint, which gives the toe an oblique direction, either inward or outward; or, perhaps, the defect may not lie in the lower, but in the upper extremity of the leg: in this case, it ought to be considered, that those measures of shoeing, the aim of which is to give the foot a straight position upon the ground, must at the same time inevitably expose the ligaments to unusual straining; the consequences of which may be much worse than those of cutting or knocking.—Here follow, however, the best direction for shoeing a horse which interferes.

A careful farrier always examines and notes which branch of the old shoe is most worn, and acts accordingly. When the toe is turned outward, the stress lies chiefly upon the inward quarter; of course, the inward quarter must be left untouched, and the thickness of the shoe on that side increased, the external branch of the shoe being made thin, and that quarter of the hoof also reduced in proportion. The whole operation ought to be performed to such a nicety, that the foot may bear equally upon all parts of its circumference. To amend this position, farriers have formerly made the inner branch of the shoe excessively thick, and even raised it upon cramps; which must always have very ill consequences, particularly as the horse interferes with the heel, and the mischief is done with the foot lifted up; whence it follows, that the forced straight position on the ground is at last of no consequence to the main end.

When the horse is pigeon-toed, that is, turns his toes inwards, the mode of shoeing usually adopted is just the reverse of the above. After all, if any good can possibly be done in these cases, it must be from leaving nothing on the inner side, with which a horse can strike himself; but, with this view, an injudicious operator frequently reduces the hoof till it is irrecoverably weakened, the horse has an uneven position upon the ground, and still interferes.

For HAMMER AND PINCHERS, or over-reaching, short fore-shoes, and a reduction of the toes of the hinder-feet, is the method directed; after which, and supposing the horse can go with his quarters exposed, he will most probably still strike his fore-heels with what you have left of his hinder toes.

I have never seen, nor indeed at all considered, the form of the ox's shoe, so am unable to judge of the propriety of the following methods given by Saint Bel:—The ox is either shod with a flat plate of iron, having six or seven nail-holes on the outer edge, accompanied with a projection of four or five inches of iron at the toe, which, passing the cleft of the foot, is bent over the hoof; or with eight shoes, one under each nail; otherwise with four, one under each external nail; or only two, one under the external nail of each fore-foot.

To the EDITORS of the SPORTING MAGAZINE.

GENTLEMEN,

YOUR correspondent NIMROD is mistaken about the pedigree of Warter. I have copied it from Mr. Wetherby's Stud-Book, and sent it you. If you think it with his performances, worth inserting, you will oblige,

R. B.

Grantham, Dec. 5, 1800.

PEDIGREE OF WARTER.

WARTER was bred by the late Sir Joseph Pennington, Bart. of Warter-Hall, Pocklington, Yorkshire, and foaled in 1794. He was got by King Fergus: his dam (the dam of Sir H. T. Vane's Rolla, &c.) by 'Highflyer; his grand-dam, Platina, (the dam of Pavia, Magdalena, Recruit, Cavendish, Tom Tring, Hautboy, &c. and sister to Gnaw-post) by Snap; her dam (Miss Cranbourne) by the Godolphin Arabian, out of Miss Western by Sedbury; her dam, Mother Western, (the grand-dam of Eclipse) by Smith's Son of Snake, Montagu, Hautboy, and Brimmer.

HIS PERFORMANCES.

WARTER, when two years old, was sold by Mrs. Pennington to Gilbert Crompton, Esq. of Nunmonkton, near Boroughbrior, Yorkshire; and at three years old (1797) at York Spring Meeting, he won a sweepstakes of 20 guineas each, for three-year olds, colts 8st. fillies 7st. 12lb. last Mile-and-Half, (6 subscribers) beating Mr. G. Compton's Telegraph (afterwards Mr. Wentworth's Tartar) and Mr. Fenton's Dapple.—7 to 4 on Telegraph; 2 to 1 against Dapple; and 3 to 1 against Warter.

At Doncaster, Warter won 100l. in specie: for three-year olds, 7st. 5lb. and four-year olds, 8st. 7lb.; maiden colts allowed 2lb. and maiden fillies 3lb.; a winner of any subscription or sweepstakes carrying 4lb. extra; two-mile heats; beating, at six heats, the following horses:

Mr. G. Crompton's bay c. Warter, by K. Fergus, 3 yrs old - - - 3 0 3 1 0 1
Sir C. Turner's ch. c. Pepperpot, 4 yrs old - - 3 0 1 3 0 2
Sir F. Standish's br. c. Stamford, 3 yrs old - - 1 3 6 2 dr.
Mr. Wentworth's b. c. Cardinal, 4 yrs old - - 2 5 2 3 dr.
Lord A. Hamilton's b. c. by Trumpator, 4 yrs old - 7 4 4 4 dr.
Mr. T. Hutchinson's br. c. Hipswell, 3 yrs old - 6 6 5 dr.
Mr. Sitwell's ch. c. Commodore, 3 yrs old - 4 dr

5 to 2 agt Stamford, 3 to 1 agt Cardinal, and 5 to 1 agt Warter. After the different heats, the bets varied very much.

In 1798, at Preston, Mr. G. Crompton's Warter, 4 yrs old, won 50l. for 3 yrs old 7st. 2lb. and 4 yrs old 8st. 4lb. (a winner that year carrying 3lb extra, and for winning two, or more, 5lb. extra) beating, at two heats, Sir R. Winn's bay filly by Phenomenon, out of Ann of the Forest, 3 yrs old: Lord Derby's ch. colt by Diomed, and Lord Darlington's Ratz, 4 yrs old. —The same meeting he won 50l. for all ages, at four heats, each heat four miles, carrying 7st. 3lb. beating Sir H. T. Vane's Patriot, aged, 8st. 10lb. and Mr. Harrison's Trumpator, 5 yrs old, 8st. 3lb.

At Doncaster, Warter won 50l. carrying 8st. 5lb. beating extremely easy, at two heats, three miles each, Sir R. Winn's bay filly by Phenomenon, 3 yrs old, 5st. and Mr. Artley's Duchess, 3 yrs old, 5st. 4lb.—10 to 1, and after the

Swiftean Advice to the Collegians of Dublin.

the first heat 20 to 1, on Warter. He was then sold to J. Heathcote, Esq.

In 1799, at Newmarket First Spring Meeting, he won the Main of the Oatlands Stakes, of 100 gs each, D. I. (four subscribers) carrying 8st. beating

Mr. Turner's Oscar, 3 yrs old, 6st. 9lb. - - - 2
Mr. Cookson's Diamond, 6 yrs old, 9st. 7lb. - - 3
4 to 1 agt Warter.

At Stamford, carrying 8st. 7lb. he won the Gold Cup, value 100 guineas, and 80 guineas in specie, beating Crusade, Telegraph, and L'Abbe, all 4 yrs old, 7st. 7lb. each, four miles.—Even betting on Warter.

At Oxford, he won 50l. carrying 8st. 7lb. beating, at two 3-mile heats, Mr. Lade's grey horse Will, 6 yrs old, 9st.

At Burford, he walked over for the King's Plate of 100 gs, for 5 yr olds, 9st. each, 3-mile heats.

At Litchfield, he won the King's 100 gs, for 5 yr olds, 8st. 7lb. each, 3-mile heats, beating, at two heats, Mr. Bailey's Conon, Lord Sackville's Magic, and Lord Donegal's bay colt by Potsos, out of Trifle, 4 yrs old.—7 to 4; after the heat, 4 to 1 on Warter.

At Newmarket First October Meeting, Mr. Heathcote's Warter, carrying 8st. 5lb. won 50 gs, B.C. beating Mr. Durand's Johnny, 5 yrs old, 8st. 5lb. and Mr. Hallett's Stickler, 6 yrs old, 8st. 11lb.— 6 to 4 on Warter.

In 1800.—On Monday, in the First Spring Meeting, Mr. Heathcote's Warter, 6 yrs old, received forfeit from Mr. Cookson's Ambrosio, aged, 8st. 7lb. each, B.C. 500 gs each, h. ft.

On Monday in the Second Spring Meeting, Warter, 6 yrs old, 8st. 5lb. received forfeit from Mr. Cassans's

ch. horse Spoliator, aged, 8st. two middle miles of B.C. 200 gs each, h. ft.

In 1800.—At Newmarket Craven Meeting, on Monday, Mr. Heathcote's Warter, 6 yrs old, 8st. 7lb. agt Sir H. T. Vane's Cockfighter, 4 yrs old, 8st. two middle miles of B.C. for 1000 gs each, h. ft.

In July Meeting, on Monday, Mr Heathcote's Warter, 8st. agt Major Rooke's Jock Andrews, 6st. 13lb. both aged, first three miles of B.C. for 200 gs each, h. ft.

Swiftean Advice to the Collegians of Dublin.

HAVING been educated in this University, and having been a scholar of that house, are the reasons why I address myself to you, Gentlemen, as you are best known to me; but what I have to say to you will equally apply to the *sages* of Oxford and Cambridge, with this difference that after you have obtained your situations by long reading and a hard examination, you think yourselves intitled to great indulgence, consequently you sit down, " like the fat weed that roots itself in ease on Lethe's wharf," thinking, in your own opinion, that you have acquired the *ne plus ultra* of learning, the very *acme* of perfection; your learned brethren in England, obtaining their fellowships much easier, and not having received that *crop-full* surfeit that you have, and not being so much of that *jovial, warm, amorous, toping* disposition as you, they generally creep on, like Shakspeare's school-boy, " like a snail, unwillingly to school," and publish something to benefit society. But when you obtain your
Junior

Junior Fellowship, for all other academic honours follow of course, as "day the night," you become new men, you have your heads sufficiently crammed with Greek, Latin, and Logic; and, as this is the only learning requisite, together with a smattering of that *elegant, polite,* and *accomplished* language which is spoken by the *Old Clothes Men in Rag Fair,* you have nothing more to do but retail it out at your quarterly examinations, to the great astonishment of the *Gibs* and *Freshmen,* who look upon every thing you utter as delivered by the *Oracle of Apollo.* Be sure you teach your pupils enough of Greek and Latin; nay, more than enough; the living languages are nothing to the dead, and, as you have learned nothing else yourself, it could not be expected you would teach them any other. Logic you must not forget; you know how necessary it is to prove that *two contradictories cannot be true; that a man is not an ass; that the inferences of one is the negation of the other; that a man can laugh and an ass cannot*; and such other *learned* and *necessary* questions, which have occupied *philosophers* ever since the time of Socrates and Aristotle to the present day. As for *German, French, Italian,* &c. you have *nominal* professors of them; and that is enough; and though one might as well send a *goose* from *Dover* to *Calais* as you, still you may keep at home and live well, for which purpose you are learned enough; and notwithstanding your ignorance of the French, you can tell *good claret from bad,* as well as if you spoke the language equal to Voltaire, Montesquieu, or Rousseau. At the quarterly examinations, if you have any spite to any of the Students for *not taking off his cap to you,* or for *throwing any thing at you at dinner,* or such like offence, you have a fine opportunity to be revenged: put some of your *jaw-breaking questions* to him, which you are sure he cannot answer; you will thus pass him off as a great blockhead, write to his father, and should he be one of your public pupils, you may get him as a private one, with something snug for imparting to him some of your *great learning.* Be sure in all your studies, not to forget your devotions to the bottle: you know Horace was a great poet and a great drinker, so was Aristotle, who drank till he fell down dead, because he could not find out the cause of the ebbing and flowing of the sea; and should the like befall you, it will be attributed to abstruse study. Having no more time at present you will excuse me until some future occasion, when you, perhaps, may hear farther from me. I am, learned Gentleman, truly yours,

ACADEMICUS.

LAW INTELLIGENCE.

Court of King's Bench, December 4.

CRIM. CON.

HOARE, ESQ. *v.* ALLEN, ESQ.

THIS was an action for criminal conversation with the plaintiff's wife; and the damages were laid at Twenty Thousand Pounds.

Mr. Erskine, as Counsel for the plaintiff, commenced by soliciting that attention from the jury which their sense of justice, and the melancholy history he had to unfold, demanded. Before he proceeded to observe either generally, or with reference to this cause, he would adopt that course which had characterised his professional life. He was of opinion, and ever should be, there was something which peculiarly distinguished these causes, and

and that the damages a jury ought to give the injured party, depended on his sense of the injury; it was therefore the duty of a husband, when he presented himself before a Court, to have nothing to conceal, but to come forth in the face of God and his country; and if there were any circumstances from which his adversary might hope for a mitigation of damages, not to impose the proof of them upon that adversary, but to give them at once to the Court. Having premised thus much, he stated that the plaintiff, Mr. Hoare, a gentleman of fortune, character, and respectability, in the year 1787 married Miss Elizabeth Cook, a niece of Major Cook's. She was a lady, who, at her marriage, was without fortune, but possessed of unspotted morals; her mind was pure, her manners amiable, and her person beautiful; the disparity of their ages was inconsiderable — she was twenty-three, and the plaintiff a few years older. In April 1790, he was appointed Paymaster-General of the British forces in India, and went over to that country, taking his lady with him. There he became acquainted with the defendant, who was then a Captain, but had since been advanced, by his merits, to the rank of Major. He should not prove to the jury the obligations the defendant owed to the plaintiff, nor how he had conducted himself towards him and his family; the defendant should speak for himself, and in the terms in which he had pleaded his own cause before the injured husband. In 1793, Mr. and Mrs. Hoare returned to England, and that the jury might form an idea of the intimacy and strict friendship between them, he should shew them the letters transmitted by the defendant to the plaintiff in England. In the year 1800 Major Allen returned to this country, the whole period between that time and the plaintiff's previous departure from India having been filled up with a correspondence, in which the friendship of the defendant appeared to have been identified with the mutual affection of the plaintiff and his lady. He apprehended that honourable and moral men could entertain no suspicion of the intention of the defendant, during that period, to dishonour his friend. It was not his purpose to say when the unhappy connection took place — but he was to maintain this, that if any case deserved more the consideration of a jury in point of damages, it was one in which the injury a husband received in the dishonour of his wife was aggravated by its having been committed under the mask of friendship. No man could deny the power of beauty; but Heaven had wisely placed guards in the breast of man to operate against the effects of his passions, and prevent their destroying the peace and becoming the source of misery to others. Next to the prohibition of incestuous intercourse, stood the obligations of friendship, which dictated to a man to suppress and nip his rising passions in the bud, when the object of them was the wife of his friend. Were it otherwise, what misery would pervade social life? A man who was married could not contemplate his friend, seated at his hospitable board, without suspecting he was carrying on a secret correspondence to seduce his wife. It was a duty imposed by the laws of religion and morality, for a man to resist temptation, and it was not to be endured that any one should say he had been drawn in by the confidence of friendship to gratify his passions, at the expence of his friend's peace. When the defendant returned to England, the plaintiff invited him to visit him at his house

house at Twyford Lodge, in Hants; but his visits had not long continued, ere he observed a coolness in the behaviour of his wife towards him; he was conscious he had not deserved the change. What then must have been his feelings, when this beautiful woman, in whose society he had traversed the globe, and explored the remote corners of the earth, no longer return his affection? What must have been the torture that rent his soul, when addressing her in the language of the most tender love, and asking her whether her behaviour was ever to be thus? she replied—" Yes! I can no longer attempt to conceal from you that I have fixed my affections on Major Allen." He recoiled, and was at a loss to know in what manner to act with a woman who was capable of making such a declaration. Upon expressing that concern and resentment he must naturally be supposed to have felt upon such an occasion, she took out a bottle of laudanum, which she held towards him, threatening to destroy her life; she declared her resolution not to live, at the same time appealing to Heaven that she never had dishonoured his bed; that her affection was an affection of the mind; and that she had resolved, if God would give her strength, to tear it from her breast, and atone by her future conduct. This communication Mrs. Hoare, no doubt, told afterwards to the defendant, who had written a letter, which the plaintiff had received notice to produce. He was not bound to do so, but, as he wished to keep nothing back, he would produce it. At this time the defendant was on a visit at the plaintiff's at Twyford Lodge; he left the letter the morning of his departure; it was dated midnight, and was partly to this effect:—" that it was the first time he had ever sat down to write to the plaintiff except with pleasure, and God knew how much pain he felt at that moment; that the plaintiff could not be ignorant Mrs. Hoare had acquainted him with what she had communicated to the plaintiff; that he would not be so ungenerous as to add to his feelings if he could avoid it; that it would have been happy if they had never known each other, for that soon after Mrs. Hoare saw him, she conceived an attachment, which, pleased with her preference, he did not discourage; that unfortunately they were thrown too much in each other's way in India, but that he had never harboured a thought towards her he need to have been ashamed of communicating to her husband; that, after their departure, he had retained his friendship and affection for both of them, that, after his arrival in England, many weeks had elapsed before he came to the Plaintiff's house, notwithstanding the most pressing invitations; that judging from Mrs Hoare's letters she was unhappy, he had thereupon visited her; that he was concerned to find she still preserved her affection, and equally so to perceive her declining health, while he was conscious he was the innocent cause; that it was to be lamented she had ever come to his mother's, where they had but too many opportunities of being with each other. The letter added, that although he would not use any means to persuade her to leave her husband's house, yet, if she should take that step, he should think himself bound, by every principle of love and honour, to make her happy."—Still, observed Mr. Erskine, the Defendant had an opportunity of redeeming himself; he had never touched the person of the lady—he might have endeavoured to have rooted out her passion, and to have persuaded

persuaded her to return with chearfulness to the society of her husband, who would have forgotten and forgiven her unhappy lapse. She soon after did leave her husband's house, and threw herself into the arms of the defendant, and their platonic passion was converted into enjoyment. Mr. Erskine having pronounced a beautiful eulogium on the institute of marriage, and addressed the jury upon the subject of damages, which, he conceived, whatever might be their amount, would inadequately compensate for the injury, proceeded to call evidence.

The marriage was proved to have taken place at the parish church of St. Andrew, Holborn, in the year 1787.

William Cook, Esq. Sir Henry Mildmay, Sir Thomas Musgrave, and the Rev. Mr. Newbold, bore testimony of the harmony and affection that ever appeared to have subsisted between Mr. and Mrs. Hoare; they stated, Mr. Allen frequently had visited at Twyford Lodge, but that there was nothing in his conduct calculated to excite alarm: he frequently drove Mrs. Hoare out in his curricle.

The letters referred to by Mr. Erskine were proved, and read in evidence.

Miles Wallace, waiter at the Ship inn, Dover, said, that on Saturday the 15th of October last, two Ladies and a Gentleman came to his master's in the evening, and continued there the whole night, and for several nights afterwards; the Gentleman passed for Major Allen, and the Lady with whom he slept for his wife; they went away on the 23d, and returned again on the 27th.

Sophia Golding, the maid at the Ship, remembered the Gentleman and two Ladies coming to the inn. She took tea up to the Lady and Gentleman next morning; they were in bed.

George Graham, butler to Mr. Hoare, said, he was sent to Dover to identify Major Allen and Mrs. Hoare; they were the persons mentioned by the last witnesses.

Cross-examined by Mr. Garrow.

Had lived two years with Mr. Hoare, at Twyford Lodge; was there on the 10th of October last, when Mrs. Hoare went away; Major Allen had been some time at the Lodge; he had left it four days on the Sunday. On the Tuesday after his departure, Mr. Charles Hoare, the plaintiff's brother arrived, and dined with Mr. and Mrs. Hoare; the witness waited at table, but did not recollect Mr. Charles Hoare presenting the Lady with a glass of wine, and using this remarkable expression, "When shall we three meet again?" He remembered a Mr. John Clarke calling the day before Mrs. Hoare left the house, and believed he went away on horseback. Mrs. Hoare quitted the Lodge before six in the morning in a post-chaise; he did not know whether the chaise had been brought from Winchester by Mr. Clarke's servant. Mr. Hoare and his brother were up; they breakfasted together, and accompanied her to the chaise. Mr. Hoare himself handed her in, and took an affectionate leave of her; she was attended by her maid; he did not know where the chaise was ordered to drive, but had had no reason to expect she was not to return; she had a trunk with her; her maid had been busy the day before getting her things ready. Mr. and Mrs. Hoare had passed the preceding day amicably, and had slept together. He did not observe any thing remarkable on the Sunday when Major Allen went away; the evening before his

his mistress and the Major had retired from the tea-table to the drawing-room, and passed a considerable time in conversation.

Re-examined by Mr. Erskine.

He never saw any thing that generated the least suspicion of the catastrophe; he supposed, when his mistress went away, she was going to her uncle's, Major Cook's; the whole family thought the same.

—— Hall, Mrs. Hoare's waiting-maid, said, she had lived seven years in the family. On the 10th of October last, at five in the morning, they left Twyford Lodge in a chaise; she thought they were going to Enfield, to Major Cook's; when they came to London, they proceeded to a hotel in the west end of the town, and arrived there about three in the afternoon. Major Allen came in about half an hour, dined, and staid till ten o'clock. The witness asked her mistress's leave to go and see her friends, and during her absence she left the hotel. Major Allen came in a post-chaise, and took the witness to Acton, telling her on the way, that Mrs. Hoare was at his mother's house; she asked him for an explanation, for things had a very odd appearance; he said her mistress would give her an explanation. When they reached his mother's at Acton, he told the witness, as she supposed, by Mrs. Hoare's desire, that an attachment had for some time subsisted between them, and that she had left her husband's house, never to return. The witness expressed her regret, and declined remaining any longer with her mistress. She returned to Twyford Lodge. On her cross-examination she said, Major Cook had a house in Ormond-street. It appeared the Major was at that time confined by the gout, and had received no information of a visit from his niece.

Mr. Clarke, brother in-law to Sir Henry Mildmay, was acquainted with Mr. and Mrs. Hoare in India; he never knew man and wife live on better terms; it was on the 8th October last he first knew of her attachment to Major Allen; he was sent for by Mr. Hoare, and found him in the deepest distress; he went by his desire to Mrs. Hoare; she was walking about the room, apparently in the greatest agitation; he remained about two hours at the house; a servant and horse were sent for him, and he understood the same servant was to order a post-chaise.

It was admitted that the defendant was a man of fortune.

Mr. Law commenced by saying, that his learned friend had most honourably and ably conducted the present cause—no observation had escaped him, yet he had not exaggerated in one iota, the affliction of the respectable person for whom he stood forward the advocate; indeed his affliction, he had no doubt, was incapable of exaggeration. The law was watchful to protect the rights of husbands, but it was not watchful to protect those who owed their misfortune to their own negligence, or inattention. If the jury would carry back their minds to that period when the seeds of this calamity were ready to burst forth, they would perceive how easy they might have been destroyed, had the plaintiff displayed that manly firmness which it was incumbent on him to have shewn; he was himself answerable for the consequences of his infatuated wife's conduct; had he done that which, as an affectionate husband, jealous of his honour, he was called upon to do, this day would not have been

been occupied in unfolding the miseries of his unfortunate house. He had received from the defendant, Major Allen, a correct and candid representation of the antecedent conduct of his wife; had he, upon receiving that intimation, consulted the dictates of prudence—had he interfered, not with rigour or by harsh coercion, but had he used only common prudence, means might have been used by the friends of the lady, she might have had time to have recovered from that delirium of passion by which she was hurried away, and then what ruin and misery to all parties might have been prevented! The defendant was a gentleman, who had the advantage of one of the most prepossessing figures nature ever bestowed; his character the breath of calumny had never dared to sully, and his manners were characterised by extreme delicacy. Upon his arrival in England he was concerned to find that, after a separation of seven years, the same passion was lurking in the breast of Mrs. Hoare; he abstained from visiting her; it would have been betraying the cause of his absence had he resisted the pressing invitations he received. He visited the lady, found her health declining, and knew himself to be the cause. After such a scene as that in which Mrs. Hoare presented the laudanum, had taken place, what should Mr. Hoare have done? and what did Major Allen do? The latter had not departed by secret night—he had not left the house of his friend till he had apprised him of his danger, and called upon him to avert it. Had the husband acted as a wise and firm man ought to have done? Was a curricle a place in which he ought to have allowed his wife to sit in close and dangerous contact with her lover? Knowing that a man was within his walls who was the object of his wife's infuriated passion, he should have followed the communication of that passion by an immediate admonition to the defendant to depart; after his departure, and when he had collected his friends about him, should be not have checked her in quitting his house? By not doing so he had acceded to the act of separation, and it was an admitted proposition of law, that where an husband voluntarily parted with his wife for any adultery, afterwards he had no right to damages. Could there be any doubt of what was in agitation after that melancholy and ill-omened toast drank by Mr. Charles Hoare? Why did he suffer her to leave his house in a hired post-chaise at five o'clock in the morning in the month of October? Had she really been going to her uncle's, would he not have sent her in his own carriage? would he not have dispatched his brother with her, and under his protection have delivered her safe and immaculate into her uncle's hand? Besides, would he not have written to Major Conk to insure her reception? Under such circumstances, no husband had ever presented himself in a Court of Justice and obtained damages. If the plaintiff had not thought proper to have confined his wife to her house, at least he need not have found wings for her flight; he could not but know, after what had passed, she would hasten to the arms of the defendant. He had abandoned his rights, thrown her on the world at large, and for what had happened in consequence of his own ill-advised conduct, the defendant stood before the jury more an object of pity than of censure.

Lord Kenyon spoke to the following effect:—"Gentlemen of the Jury, I cannot say that I am prepared to follow the learned

Gentleman who has addressed you, on behalf of the defendant, in the observations with which he closed his otherwise very proper, and certainly, most able address to you. I am not prepared to be the panegyrist of Major Allen; but we are here enquiring into the right which the plaintiff, in this cause, has to ask for damages at your hands. I am afraid we are in a condition, state, and temper of society, which in many respects forbodes ill; whether any clouds are hanging over this kingdom, I will not presume to say, but if our moral and religious duties are neglected, punishment must fall, and fall heavily some day on us; and certain it is, that great is our neglect of many of our moral and religious duties, and perhaps the most melancholy part will be, that we shall find men, within and without doors, of certain well-known character and condition, vibrating between two extremes of opinion, of what our moral and religious duties are. I think it is happy for those, whose minds have taken up early habits which prepare them for their journey through life, to pursue a conduct founded on our moral and religious duties, such as by the laws of God and man, we are commanded to observe. If other doctrines meet with advocates any where, such advocates, whoever they may be, appear to be the worst enemies of mankind, pests of society, and a disgrace to human nature. But every person who comes here before us, has a right to have his cause fully discussed, to have every thing urged, *pro* and *con*, and to have the case completely sifted. An opinion which took possession of my mind some time ago, in the progress of this cause, I took care not to utter, and one good has resulted, to myself at least, by my observing silence, since it has enabled me to employ those faculties of mind, which God has been pleased to bestow upon me, in reviewing that opinion as the case proceeded. I have done so; I have looked at it, and examined that opinion, over and over again; and, by the best use I have been able to make of my understanding, I have not found it possible to change that opinion. When the learned counsel for the plaintiff opened the case, it came before us with great strength, feeling, and effect; such, indeed, as must be the effect of so much eloquence; it laid strong hold of my mind, and up to a certain stage, the evidence tended to confirm that effect, and my opinion then was, that the damages could not be too large; but we should examine the case to the end of it; and the material questions for you to ask yourselves are, Who the person who complains is? What his conduct has been? What are the circumstances of his case who calls for damages at your hands? I wish to speak tenderly of Mr. Hoare; I feel for him in his unhappy situation. I believe him to be a virtuous and an honourable, but mistaken man. The cases which have been alluded to by the learned Counsel for the defendant, were all decided upon the broad principles of common sense and plain justice. The first of them, however, had a different determination from the rest; it was the case of Theophilus Cibber, against, I think, Colonel Sloper, for criminal conversation with his wife, and upon that action, it appeared that the plaintiff had procured two pillows, and laid them on the bed where he knew the parties were going.—It was tried, I believe, before Lord Mansfield, and he, we all know, was a great ornament of our profession, he thought that a case for the smallest damages;

damages; he did not think the evidence took from under the plaintiff his very ground of action. He was taken by surprise; it was indeed extraordinary that a mind so illuminated as his should be taken by surprise at any thing, but so it was; but from that time the point has been uniformly settled, that the party himself, complaining, may either, by misguided judgment, or other means and conduct towards his wife, take away his own right of action. I have certainly so held, but my opinion I should not think worth quoting, if other Judges had not confirmed it, and therefore I may quote that opinion. I held that opinion in the case of the Duke of Hamilton at the suit of a Mr. Esten, and I do not find that any body has reprobated that opinion, which was, when the parties had separated by mutual consent, the action for subsequent adultery would not lie. How stands this case? We see that down to the month of October last, however, this unfortunate lady may have been fascinated by the sight of the defendant, it stands confessed by both parties there was no ground for the present action. But at that time we find the lady determined to leave her husband, communicates this to her husband; communicates it also to Major Allen, the defendant; he again communicates the same thing to the plaintiff, and upon that occasion he writes a letter to the plaintiff, which has been read to you, and which I will not read over again, the substance of it I take to amount to this: "I have not dishonoured you, I have an affection for you, I am sorry to find your wife's affection alienated from you, but by no fault of mine, for I give you my honour I have not disgraced you to this moment; but if she should separate from you, and be cast upon the world, and deserted, I feel myself bound in honour to receive her." I will not stop here to discuss the principles of honour here laid down; I hope my principles of religion, the sense I have of what I owe to Society, and my neighbour; but above all, of my duty to my God, would have taught me, I could learn no useful lesson in this School of modern Honour. But to return to the facts here: the Lady lives with her husband after these communications were made to him, both by her and by the defendant; she sits at the head of the table doing the honour of it in the usual way; she partakes of the same bed with him, and the domestics observe no alteration in either of them, every thing seems to go on in the usual train the day before she departs; it is true, Mr. Clark, the plaintiff's friend, finds both of them in great agitation, but that is a species of evidence which could not be allowed to be pursued. What then ought to have been the conduct of Mr. Hoare in this case?—Not to have allowed his wife to go out of his house, when he could not but know that the place of her destination was the house of the defendant, and could be no other, for the defendant told him she would lose the countenance of the world; and if she came away from the plaintiff, the defendant must receive and protect her. Thus the plaintiff had notice of four days before his wife's departure. The morning comes, a chaise is ordered, the plaintiff gets up at five in the morning of the 6th of October before day light; he and his brother, Mr. Charles Hoare, breakfast with this lady, and when she is about to depart, the plaintiff himself hands her into the chaise!——O! but she was then thought to be going to her uncle, Major Cook! Was the uncle prepared to receive her?

her? Nothing like it; for the uncle had heard nothing of the business. To whom then was this lady to go? No man upon earth could form any other conclusion, than that she must be going to the defendant. I will not add affliction to affliction. I will not bruise the broken reed. In a word, it is my opinion, that Mr. Hoare does not come here in the situation of a person, who has a right to a verdict, because she was not seduced from him, but he has suffered her to quit him, he knowing whither she was going; he has acted under some misguided judgment, by some means or other; he has contributed, I will not say to his disgrace, but his own misfortune. I cannot, however, do otherwise than reprobate the conduct of Mr. Allen. I should desert a main part of my duty, as a Judge, if I were to assent to any panegyric on him, I think his conduct unjustifiable. I know reports are going forth among some persons in this country, of my sentiments being too rigid on these subjects. I do my duty, God knows, without great abilities, but as well as I can, and I must not be deterred from doing so by any consideration on earth. I think that on this case, thus disclosed, the plaintiff is not entitled to a verdict."—Verdict for the Defendant.

CRIM. CON.

GUILDHALL, DEC. 18.

Sittings before Mr. Justice Le Blanc, and a Special Jury of Merchants.

DUCKWORTH v. BOTT.

MR. Wood opened the pleadings, from which it appeared, that this was an action for criminal conversation with the Plaintiff's wife.

Mr. Erskine, in the course of an eloquent speech, stated to the Jury, that his client, Mr. Duckworth, was an eminent attorney in the northern parts of this island, residing at Manchester; a man, he understood, of irreproachable character, greatly esteemed, not only in his profession, but in his neighbourhood, and a man of considerable property. He had been married to this wife many years, and had by her, living, three daughters and two sons, and no man living could have conducted himself more honourably in every thing that was connected with his domestic character and life.—He had been a most indulgent husband, and an honourable parent, attending assiduously to the education of his offspring; the defendant was a dentist, resident at Nottingham, but occasionally going to remoter parts of the country, in the exercise of his profession. He paid a visit to Manchester, where he was introduced to the Plaintiff, and employed in the way of his profession by him, and who also recommended him to his acquaintance. The recommendation of Mr. Duckworth, was most undoubtedly valuable to a person of that description, from the character he had long sustained in the neighbourhood, and from his acquaintance being almost universal. The Plaintiff, in order to shew his indulgence to his wife, and also to the Defendant, who was then in the exercise of his profession, had disbursed 150l. so that it was not at all wonderful that Mr. Bott had frequently described the Plaintiff, Mr. Duckworth, as his best friend. Mr. Bott was only introduced into the Plaintiff's family, in consequence of Mrs. Duckworth having bad teeth, which had been neglected in her youth, and required a great deal of care and attention; it was necessary also to have a number of artificial teeth made

made for her. He not only attended the Plaintiff's lady in the character of his profession, but as his appearance was that of a plain, fair, and candid man, and perhaps his religious persuasions which contributed to give him the air and character of simplicity, (he being a Quaker), tended to impose on Mr. Duckworth. He was therefore received in the double character of a person exercising his profession, and also in the character of a friend. This lady had been married ten years, and had five children as before stated, now living, and four that had been still-born. This Defendant also was a married man, and had a family of children. The Counsel adverted next to the principle on which actions of this sort ought to be tried, and to the nature of the evidence which he should be able to produce in this case. It was only circumstantial evidence, but not the less convincing on that account. Where a great variety of circumstances went all to prove the same point, it infallibly produced conviction on the mind. The Defendant had conducted his criminal intercourse with the Plaintiff's wife with so much address, that he never suspected her, till the lady herself, in a fit of despondency, revealed it to him: and from that time he no longer cohabited with her. The Gentlemen of the Jury after hearing all the evidence, would give to the Plaintiff such damages as they thought the justice of the case required.

Mr. Robinson was the first witness called on the part of the Plaintiff. He said, he was present at Mr. and Mrs. Duckworth's marriage, which was on the 25th of July, 1784. He knew Mr. Duckworth intimately, and had seen the manner in which he had conducted himself towards his lady; he had uniformly behaved to her as a kind, generous husband. On cross-examination, he thought Mrs. Duckworth might be about 44 or 45, and Mr. Duckworth about 40.

The next witness was John Wade, who said, he was at present in the Plaintiff's service, in the character of a groom: he had lived with him near six years. He recollected having seen Mr. Bott, the defendant, at his master's country-house, at Broomhill, about three miles and a half from Manchester: his master was then from home. He recollected a towel being put up across a parlour-window, to prevent any body who was walking on foot from observing any thing that passed in the parlour. He once passed that window on horseback, and could see over the towel: he observed Mr Bott and Mrs. Duckworth sitting together; he had his right hand round her neck, and was giving her a kiss. The witness looked at her, and she at him; her face was red, and she seemed to be very much *flurried*. This was in September or October, 1799; he was performing no operation on her teeth at that time; he had no instrument with him.

Mary Elliott was next examined. She said she had lived about twelve months in the Plaintiff's service, and had left it about two years and a half ago; during the time she lived with the Plaintiff, she recollected that Mr. Bott was twice there, and the first time he was there, her master was in London. From something that passed in the morning of the day, when Mr. Bott came to the house, she knew Mrs. Duckworth expected him: there was no other company in the house when he was there: she did not hear any thing that passed between them; they conducted themselves to each other like two lovers very freely. At that time there was no other

other servant at all in the house but her: Mr. Bott slept there that night; Mr. Bott's bed had been prepared for him a few days before he came; she warmed the bed for him about eleven o'clock at night: she went to bed before her mistress, and after she was in bed, she heard her mistress go into the back kitchen and shut the front-kitchen door, which was an unusual thing, as it used to stand open, that her mistress might hear the clock strike that stood in that kitchen. In consequence of that door being shut, she could not hear any thing that passed between her mistress and the Defendant: the rooms in which her mistress and the defendant slept were opposite to each other, and only separated by the passage. She got up the next morning before seven o'clock, and her mistress was up before her: she prepared breakfast for her mistress and Mr. Bott, in the dining-room; she then went up to her mistress's room, and put up the windows, and then went into Mr. Bott's room: her mistress and Mr. Bott were then below at breakfast. When she went into Mr. Bott's room, and put up the windows, she then put two chairs at the foot of the bed to make it: when she pulled off the clothes, she perceived some marks upon the under sheet; at that moment her mistress came into the room, and snatched that sheet out of her hand, as if she had been afraid she might perceive the marks upon it: the bed had the appearance of two persons having slept in it, and it was furnished with two pillows: she had no doubt from the appearance of the bed, that two persons had slept in it; and from the marks on the sheet, she had no doubt that a man and a woman had slept in it. There was no man in the house but the Defendant, and no woman but her mistress and herself, and she said she slept in her own bed. When her mistress snatched the sheet out of her hand, she said, this will do for Mr. Duckworth at night to sleep in when he returns from London: that was quite an unusual thing for her mistress to put sheets that any visitor had slept in on her master's bed: her mistress took the sheet from her, and carried it into the nursery. She then went down stairs; the curiosity of the witness led her to go into the nursery, and to examine the sheet again: she found it not folded up, but lumped up in a nook. After she had examined the marks upon it, she had no doubt that a man and woman had been in that bed: she then went into her mistress's bed room, the bed appeared just as if somebody had crept into it and gone out again; you could scarcely tell that any body had laid down in it; she could safely say, that nobody had slept in that bed that night. The washing came round in about a week after that, and her mistress gave her that pair of sheets, which she had formerly snatched out of her hands, observing to her at the same time, that it had come off Mr. Duckworth's bed: but the witness knew there was no truth in that, because she knew the sheet from the marks she had described: it was a finer sheet than that on Mr. Duckworth's bed; and her curiosity led her to examine the sheets on her master's bed, and she found them both on it. She shewed that sheet to Dorothy Wade, who was the wife of the man servant, who lived in a farm-house near, and who assisted her to wash.

In about four or five months after that, Mr. Bott was again at her master's country-house: her master was not then at home, but she did not recollect where he was. Mr. Bott and her mistress were in the

the dining-room, and she went in unasked, with some coals, when she found the defendant standing behind her mistress's chair, with his hands one on each side of her face: he appeared to be very much *fluttered*, and moved his hands away from that situation. He was not at that time performing any operation on her mistress's teeth in the way of his profession. Mr. Bott and her mistress dined alone that day, but he did not sleep there: after dinner the bell rang, and on going up stairs she found the door locked; her mistress asked who was there? She answered, Molly: she desired her, without opening the door, to bring her a decanter and a tumbler. When she carried them up, she heard her mistress unlock the door in the inside, and the door would not open, because it had also been bolted: when it was unbolted, she opened it so far as to admit the decanter and tumbler; the witness then perceived the defendant sitting by the fire; Mrs. Duckworth's head-dress, particularly her cap, was very much tumbled: she communicated what she had observed to her fellow-servant. Her mistress had a complete set of artificial teeth; she made no secret of it; they were made by the defendant, and she frequently used to take them out, and the witness cleaned them: she was then without any teeth. She said, the plaintiff always conducted himself as a good husband, and a good parent; he was extremely fond of his children.

On cross-examination, she said, that Mr. Duckworth was a very kind affectionate husband. When he was at home, he slept in his own room, and his bed was always at Mrs. Duckworth's service, but she was not always in a situation to sleep with him, when she was intoxicated with liquor, which she often was during the whole time she was in her service; and so intoxicated, that she was not fit to come into her husband's bed: that was frequently the case. Mrs. Duckworth was neither pleasing in her person, nor agreeable in her manners; Mr. Bott came there to look after her mistress's artificial teeth. The witness had seen her without teeth while she was cleaning them: Mr. Duckworth was a very handsome, well-looking man. As to the beauty of Mr. Bott, he was a tall fat-looking man, well stricken in years, and not a bad-looking man; he had the external appearance of a Quaker, and had an agreeable way with him.

Dorothy Wade confirmed the evidence of the last witness, as far as her evidence went. She had often seen Mrs. Duckworth intoxicated.

Dr. Collier spoke to the obligations the defendant was under to the plaintiff, for the kindness and friendship he had shewn him.

The next witness was a female of the name of Shuttleworth, who entered into the plaintiff's service in December 1799, and she had seen her mistress and the defendant on a sofa in the parlour in an indecent situation. When Mr. Bott was there, a towel used to be hung across the parlour window, and the reason assigned for it by her mistress was, that it was to keep out the sun, to prevent it from spoiling Mr. Bott's work when he was performing an operation on her teeth, and also to prevent the splinters from coming against the glass.

The Rev. Mr. Walker was acquainted with both these parties. The plaintiff was a most respectable attorney, and, for the last ten or twelve years, was in the very first line of business at Manchester. When this gentleman lived at Nottingham, Mr. Bott had been employed

ployed in his own family: he certainly had an idea, that he was a man very eminent in his profession, and carrying it on to a very considerable extent as to emolument.

The evidence for the plaintiff being closed, Mr. Percival, on the part of the defendant, made a very able speech in mitigation of damages.

Mr. Justice Le Blanc told the Jury, this was an action brought by the plaintiff, who is an attorney of character and credit at Manchester, against Mr. Bott, a dentist, at Nottingham, to recover a compensation for an injury Mr. Duckworth had sustained, in consequence of the misconduct of Mr. Bott, who had a criminal connection with his wife. Mr. Duckworth had received an injury in consequence of that, being by that act deprived of the comfort and society of his wife. The injury was a considerable one, when taken in the abstract, independently of any particular case to which it might be applied: but the extent of the injury which a man received from an act of this sort, must always vary from the injury which another received, inasmuch as the domestic happiness and comfort of one man varied from that of another; and therefore, it was impossible that the injury in any one case could be precisely the same with that in another; but each case must depend upon its own circumstances. The present was a civil action to recover a compensation for a civil injury: and, inasmuch as that compensation must be measured by money, the Jury, from the evidence laid before them, must decide on the quantum of the injury which the plaintiff had suffered. It was not easy to calculate the compensation, but it could only be made by damages of a pecuniary nature; and for that purpose the Jury would take into their consideration, in estimating these damages, all the circumstances of the parties: they would consider the situation in which the plaintiff and his wife were, and that sort of comfort and domestic happiness they enjoyed before the act complained of: they would compare that likewise with the situation of the party, who had been the cause of the interruption of that comfort and happiness. But his Lordship said, he could not well consider the defendant in this case, as standing before them for a crime, and to answer for it by a punishment; he was not before them to answer for a criminal charge, but he stood before them as a defendant in a court of civil jurisdiction, to answer for a civil injury. And when a party brought his action to recover a compensation for an injury, if, in such an action the Jury found the injury was slight, whatever opinion they might entertain of the offence abstractedly considered, according to the best judgment he could form, a plaintiff, who had received but a slight injury, was not entitled, by way of punishment on the defendant, for an act generally immoral, to recover from him greater damages than he had actually sustained. These observations were meant to direct the attention of the Jury to this point—namely, what compensation Mr. Duckworth was entitled to receive, and that must depend on the opinion which they should form of the injury he had sustained. His Lordship took it for granted, the Jury, on the evidence, would find the fact of adultery; and therefore the single question that remained, respected the amount of the damages.

His Lordship next summed up the evidence with great correctness and accuracy. The Jury then withdrew, and brought in a verdict for the plaintiff—damages 200l.

ANECDOTES OF THE EMPEROR PAUL.

THE following anecdotes are extracted from a *Ministerial Paper*. Our readers may recollect (sad experience and the evidence of facts prevent us from forgetting) that there was a time, when, to have published such anecdotes, might have procured an Editor some months residence *in Banco Regis:—*

Some time after his accession to the throne, Paul, going into the apartment of his daughters, began to joke with one of their maids of honour on the subject of her approaching marriage. "As to my daughter Alexandra (added he), she cannot be married, for her lover has not yet learned to write." The fact was, he had received a letter from the King of Sweden, whose Secretary had omitted in the address some of the Emperor's titles—among others, the perfectly new one of the Duke of Courland, &c. That no one in future might be guilty of this neglect, Paul issued a particular Ukase, in which he prescribed the manner in which he chose to be named: those by which it is his pleasure to be addressed, even in a petition, are sufficient to fill a good page.

A whim, which caused no little surprise, was the Imperial prohibition of wearing round hats, or rather the sudden order of taking them away, or tearing them to pieces on the heads of those who appeared in them. This occasioned some disgraceful scenes in the streets, and particularly near the Palace. The cossacks and soldiers of the Police fell on the passengers to uncover their heads, and beat those who, not knowing the reason, attempted to defend themselves. An English merchant going through the street in a sledge, was thus stopped, and his hat snatched off. Supposing it to be a robbery, he leaped out of the sledge, knocked down the soldier, and called the guard. Instead of the guard arrived an officer, who overpowered and bound him; but, as they were carrying him before the Police, he was fortunate enough to meet the coach of the English Minister, who was going to Court, and claimed his protection. Sir C. Whitworth made his complaint to the Emperor, who, conjecturing that a round hat might be the national dress of the English, as it is of the Swedes, said, that his order had been misconceived, and he would explain himself more fully to Arkarof. The next day it was published in the streets and houses that strangers, who were not in the Emperor's service, or naturalised, were not comprised in the prohibition. Round hats were no longer pulled off; but they who were met with this unlucky head-dress were conducted to the Police to ascertain their country. If they were found to be Russians, they were sent for soldiers; and woe to a Frenchman who had been met in this dress, for he would have been condemned as a Jacobin.

An officer walking the streets in a large pelisse, had given his servant his sword, which incommoded him, intending to put it on again, and to take off his pelisse when he got near the Palace. Unfortunately, before this took place, the Emperor met him, and, in consequence, he was reduced to the ranks, and his servant made an officer in his place.

Exercising his regiment of cuirassurs one day, the horse of an officer threw him. Paul ran furiously towards him, crying. "Get up, rascal!"—"Your Highness, I cannot,

cannot, I have broken my leg." Paul spat upon him, and retired swearing.

One Court day after the accession of Paul, Stanislaus, the deposed King of Poland, who was in his train, bending under age and fatigue, was obliged to sit down in a corner, while three or four hundred courtiers were kissing the hand of Paul. The Emperor, perceiving that the old King had seated himself during this ceremony, sent an Aide-de-Camp to him, to order him to keep on his legs.

It is the order of Paul, that whoever is permitted to kiss his hand is to make the floor resound, by striking it with his knee as loud as a soldier with the butt-end of his firelock. It is requisite too, that the salute of the lips on his hand should be heard, to certify the reality of the kiss, as well as of the genu-flexion.

One of Paul's first regulations was, a strict injunction of all tradesmen to efface from the front of their shops the French word *magasin*, and substitute the Russian word *lavka*, (shop) assigning as a reason, that the Emperor alone could have magazines of wood, flour, corn, &c. while a tradesman ought not to be above his condition, but *stick to his shop*.

The real cause of the disgrace of Suwarrow has never, we believe, been properly understood. The Emperor Paul, very soon after his accession to the Russian throne, ordered the dress of the Russian soldiers to be changed to the German fashion. Suwarrow, when he received orders to establish these novelties, with little sticks for models for the soldiers tails and side-curls, said, " hair-powder is not gunpowder, curls are not cannon, and tails are not bayonets." This sarcasm, which is not destitute of wit, and forms in the Russian language a sort of apothegm in rhime, soon spread from mouth to mouth through the army, and was the true reason that induced Paul to recal Suwarrow, and dismiss him from the service.

There is nothing so trifling to which Paul does not descend to shew disrespect to his mother's memory. The persons belonging to her wore rings, on which the date of her decease was enamelled. The Emperor expressed his dissatisfaction at it, and they are obliged to wear rings with the motto of *Paul consoles me*.

The person who has more immediate influence on his actions than his Ministers, or even his mistress will ever have, is a valet-de-chambre, by birth a Turk, made a slave in his infancy, and brought up in his house. To this Turk, named Ivan Paulovitch, the Generals and great men are eager to pay their court, as the real fountain of Paul's private favour. This Ivan is at present Counseller of State, and has the title of Excellency. Many lackeys, *Hof*, or *Kammer-fouriers*, Gentlemen of the Bed-Chamber, are every day rising to the highest posts.

Paul, in reviewing one of his regiments, one day, committed some blunder in the orders which he gave. Thinking that it ought to be punished, he ordered a drum to be placed end-ways on the ground. He then imposed upon himself the punishment of sitting upon it for half an hour without opening his lips, while the troops all the while marched round and round him. This ludicrous sentence upon himself was executed to the utmost.

THEATRE,

THEATRE, DRURY-LANE.

ON Saturday, December 12th, was performed, for the first time, a Tragedy called *Antonio*; or, *The Soldier's Return*. The characters were as follows:

Pedro, King of Arragon,	Mr. Wroughton
Don Antonio d'Almanza,	Mr. Kemble
Don Guzman, Duke of Zuiga	Mr. Barrymore
Don Henry, brother to Antonio	Mr. C. Kemble
Don Diego de Cordona,	Mr. Powell
Alberto,	Mr. Holland
Helena,	Mrs. Siddons.

This Tragedy, we believe, will not again be brought forward, which is a pity, as it afforded abundance of mirth. The effect of it, indeed, (for it is a very *deep* tragedy), was to throw the audience into a "most *humorous* sadness."

The fable and plot are extremely simple: *Helen*, the daughter of *Almanza*, a nobleman of the highest rank, had been promised in marriage by her father on his death-bed to *Rodrigo*, the friend of *Antonio*, her brother. During the absence of the latter, however, she marries *Guzman*, a man of the first family and merit, the object of her love, with the sanction of the King. *Antonio* returns, and finds his sister married. He had left *Rodrigo*, a prisoner at Milan, is pursuing means to procure his release, and had flattered himself with compensating his friend's misfortunes by marriage with his sister. Enraged to find his scheme disappointed, he applies to the King to dissolve the marriage. Being refused, he carries off his sister by force and stratagem, and places her in a convent. She is rescued from it; *Antonio* comes to Court, and insists on *Helen's* being sent back to the cloister. The *King* denies the request, and again sanctions the marriage with *Guzman*. *Antonio* endeavours to carry her off by force, but being prevented, he (to the utter astonishment and indignation of the audience at such an incident) plunges his sword into her bosom!!!

The whole interest of the piece is built upon the character of *Antonio*; but a more strange, uncouth, and unnatural combination of opposite sentiments and conduct never was patched together: It is a character with more than the high heroic madness of Don Quixotte, united to a degree of hardened villainy that would have disgraced a Cartouche. We suppose that the author meant to describe to what excess the proud, chivalrous honour of a Spanish grandee might be carried; but he must be utterly ignorant of the spirit and temper of the romantic, chivalrous principle. No extravagance, no distortion of it could have produced such conduct as that of *Antonio*, who, in other respects, is described as kind, humane, generous, and brave.— The honour of a Castilion, of a Knight, and a Soldier, might have been indignant at the breach of faith his sister had committed, and he would have been inexorable to her supplications of forgiveness. But that a brother, a soldier, and a cavalier, should demand the dissolution of an equal and an honourable marriage, sanctioned by love and authority; that he should tear his sister from her husband by low and unmanly stratagems; that he should insist upon her condemnation to a cloister; that he should become her murderer when thwarted in his cruel design, is something so incompatible with all virtue and honour; so irreconcileable with any thing noble or dignified, so absurd in the conception, so disgusting and odious in the representation, that we cannot but wonder how it entered into the heart of man to form such a monster, or to exhibit him to the public. The catastrophe is so detestable, that a universal cry of detestation burst from the audience on seeing it. It had the effect of surprising, indeed, because it was violent and extravagant, even for the preceding absurdities; it excited horror too, but not that sort of horror which is the legitimate province of the drama, when extraordinary scenes of difficulty are terminated by some awful crisis of distress, or when gigantic villainy crowns its career by some consistent act of atrocity. Unfortunately the principle of honour, at least in modern times, admits of an association with too many bad principles and too much bad conduct; but there are actions with which it can never be joined. Particularly is the behaviour of *Antonio* to a lady and his sister inconsistent with the spirit of chivalry in any possible modification of it. It is an unpardonable outrage upon this respectable sentiment, thus to describe it as capable of violating the curtesies due to the sex; fulfilling the dictates of honour by trampling on the tenderest rights of humanity and the fondest affections of nature; inspiring a conduct more unfeeling than that of the wildest barbarian; changing a soldier into a sophistical cut-throat, converting cruelty into duty, and the murder of a woman into an act of magnanimity worthy of a noble mind.

Upon this ridiculous personage, and the vagaries springing from all these inconsistencies, the whole piece depends. Of course the plot must be unnatural—the sentiments imputed to *Antonio* extravagant and unjust. The cant of honour and the conduct of a ruffian in the same man, afford some striking contrasts, or rather inconsistencies, because such they must appear in this instance. Contrast of opposite sentiments and conduct in the same person, may afford room for nice discrimination, and the display of great knowledge of the human heart. Yet, though they contrast, they should consist. But in *Antonio*, the difference between what is good, and that which is bad, is so prodigious, that the whole character is improbable and offensive; the two parts of it are so coarsely joined together, that it reminds us of the old pictures of the Devil, when, lest the upper part might deceive the spectator, the monstrous cloven feet are sure to be conspicuous. Such characters violate every rule——*Desinet in piscem, &c.*

The character of *Helen* is not disfigured by such wildness as this. She is attached to her brother, endeavours to smooth his resentment, and, when the victim of his injustice, assumes a becoming dignity. This, however, she does not maintain; she fluctuates between her love to her husband, and obedience to *Antonio's* violent caprice, so that she betrays her own cause, and weakens her claim to sympathy. The character of *Henry* is trifling and insignificant It seems as if the author intended to represent him as an artful, intriguing villain, but the sketch is very feeble. He does not appear to have any weight or influence in the contrivance or business of the plot, and in some places this part was quite unintelligible or ridiculous. The rest of the characters are not worth noticing.

The piece being destitute of incident, intrigue and bustle, abounds in declamatory speeches and sententious dissertations. The language will not compensate for the defects of the construction and characters. It is destitute of simplicity and elegance. There is in it a quaint-

a quaintness and affectation of style much aimed at by some in the present day. It is forced and unnatural, and when intended to be energetic, deformed by harsh and uncouth turns. In some places, indeed, when the sentiment was just, the language possessed vigour, and occasionally there was a happy application, if not great novelty of metaphor. Upon the whole, however, we don't think that good judges would consider the language pure and classical.

Kemble, Mrs. Siddons, and Barrymore, did all which could be done for their respective parts; but after some marks of disapprobation in the progress of this play, the last act was received with shouts and laughter.

The Prologue, spoken by Mr. C. Kemble, we could not hear. The Epilogue, spoken by Miss Heard, was a trite and not humourous description of a tradesman, who neglects his shop to go to the Play, but it had no more connection with the Tragedy than with the battle of Blenheim.

A PROPER BLOW UP.

[Extract of a Letter from the Captain of the ship Clyde, (which sailed from Liverpool to Jamaica in March last), to his friend in Edinburgh, dated Liverpool, 23d November.]

"I Have met with only one extraordinary accident since I saw you, which happened on the 11th of March last, at 2 A. M. My carpenter, (whom I had suspected of being deranged) two days after my leaving Martinico, with the convoy, being confined in the mate's cabin, broke through it into the next state-room, loaded a musket, put the iron rammer in, instead of a bullet, presented the piece close to my head, and blew me out of my hammock. I was found on the cabin-deck, bleeding, and in a state of insensibility; a few minutes, however, restored me, when I had him put on board the ship of war, our convoy. The rammer passed over the bridge of my nose and right eye-brow, cutting into the bone; the left side of my face was scorched, and a great quantity of powder yet remains never to be extracted, by which my countenance is somewhat altered."

A LEGAL DUEL.

A Few days ago an Officer confined in the King's Bench for debt, and a Gentleman in the same situation in Newgate, having each obtained a day-rule, met, and quarrelled in Drury-lane Theatre. A challenge was the consequence, and each obtained another day-rule to go and fight next day!

FOX HUNTING.

FROM the scarcity of hares in the neighbourhood of Putney and Wimbledon, as well as their speedy escape (when found) into the surrounding parks, the hounds of Mr. Chapman frequently hunt fox. Drawing Coombe Woods lately, they soon unkenneled, and after an excellent chase of three-quarters of an hour, *ran to earth*; a circumstance of great mortification to those who were in anxious pursuit, and eager expectation of *the brush*. Several coffee-houses were *bored* with a *recital* in the evening. The meeting place is the Obelisk, near the remains of Abershaw, every Monday morning at nine.

FEAST

FEAST OF WIT; OR, SPORTSMAN's HALL.

THE papers have prognosticated a fall in the price of *beef*, from the expected large importations of Hibernian *bulls*.—This *speculation* does not appear well grounded; for, in some parts of *this* country, an *advance* of price has been demanded for the *use* of that animal. —Poor *John Bull!* Some people seem to think they can never make *enough* of him.

The alteration of the times has been felt at Bristol:—During the last twenty years, Mr. Weeks at the Bush tavern, in that city, has annually, at Christmas, provided a larder furnished more abundantly and with greater variety, than perhaps any other tavern in the kingdom could have shewn; but this year, owing to the great pressure of the times, we understand, he prudently declines to make his accustomed exhibition.—Hence one of our quizzical correspondents remarks, that this is the age for producing *fat beasts* and *lean men!*

The officers of the 3d division of the East Middlesex regiment of militia, on their march through a country town, were waited upon after dinner by a surgeon of the town, (who had the care of a sick soldier, on account of getting him his pay) he was asked by them to sit down and take a glass of wine: after he had taken a glass or two, upon being asked by the President to give a military gentleman for a toast, he gave "*The Shank End of a Leg of Mutton.*" Upon his being asked for an explanation, he said it meant *General Boney-part*; on which the officers not chusing to drink to that toast, one of them gave the *Walley Part*, alluding to *General Wolfe*. The doctor left his stick behind him, and the officers the next day having amongst other things a *Leg of Mutton* for dinner, they sent the shank end of it to him tied to his stick. The doctor was in his shop at his pestle and mortar, when the stick was delivered to him by a soldier of the regiment, with the shank end of the leg of mutton tied to it; and he was observed to look *a little sheepish* on the occasion.

It has often been the Minister's triumph over the French, that they have no *money*; and now the enemy retort on us, that we have no *bread*. It would be very beneficial to both countries to exchange some of their superfluities, could their rulers be brought to think so!

Says a Gentleman to a Lady, the Bench of Bishops is the ugliest I know, for there is but one *Pretty-man* amongst them.—You forget, replied the Lady; surely there is one *More!*

A BULL.—On a late trial in Westminster-hall, one of the witnesses, bearing the defendant very severely reprobated by the Judge and Counsel, said, with great *naïvette*, " Now, by G—, is the time for the defendant to *shoot* himself *through the head*, if he ever *did so* in his *life*."

LEGAL CRITICISM.—Not long ago, an eminent special pleader was at the theatre seeing the play of Macbeth. In the scene where Macbeth questions the Witches in the cavern, what they had been doing, they answer, " a *deed* without a *name.*" This phrase struck the ears of the special pleader much more forcibly than the most energetic passages of the play, and he immediately remarked to a friend,

friend, who accompanied him, "a *deed* without a *name*," why 'tis void.

The legal gentleman who exclaimed the other night at Macbeth, that *a deed without a name* was absolutely void, made a similar comment at the representation of Othello. When the General was so loudly crying out "My handkerchief,"—"My handkerchief," he observed, that if it had been picked out of *Desdemona's* pocket, Mrs. Litchfield might be indicted for a *felony*, and Cooke as a receiver of *stolen goods*.

It seems that in the midst of hostilities raging around them, the Plenipotentiaries at Luneville are giving and receiving visits in the kindest manner. This proves at least, that if the two nations are incapable of the relations of *peace*, the Plenipotentiaries are disposed to those of *amity!*

Since the discovery that straw could be manufactured into paper, a new connection is formed between our *agriculture* and our *literature*. The man who raises a fine crop of wheat, may be furnishing the materials for a poem!

Thus, from the ingenuity of modern times, an author, after *threshing* his brains, may depend upon an allowance of *straw*, and the public will no doubt frequently be treated with mere *chaff!*

A wit observes, that if it be true that our late magnanimous ally, the Emperor of Russia, toasts Bonaparte's health *in his cups*, it is well for him that he is an *autocrat*. A man here, who would pledge the Emperor's toast, would be left to recover his *sober senses* in Cold-Bath-Fields!

The Master of the Wrestler's Inn, at Yarmouth, having solicited Lord Nelson to allow him to put up his arms, and change the name of his inn to the Nelson's Hotel, his Lordship returned for answer, that he was perfectly welcome to change the name of his inn; but that he must be sensible he had no *arms* to spare.

The *route* season is about to commence as well in this as in other countries, but with this difference, however, that in Germany and Italy, the routes will be given by the *men*, and in London by the *ladies*.

In the *crim. con.* case, Hoare *versus* ———, a wag lately observed it was rather hard, as the husband himself was the cause of *making his wife—a Hoare!*

An artisan lately calling upon a dealer in hard-ware, and asking him if he had any of the metal called pinch-back—*pinch-back!* exclaimed the other—No, no, I have nothing to do with *pinch-back* these *pinch-belly* times.

A wag has observed, that Mrs. Duckworth is certainly more to be pitied than blamed, for a frailty into which she fell—*in spite of her teeth:* and that her gallant *Nottingham Quaker* resembles Cassio, He is "framed to make women false"—teeth.

A late trial for *crim. con.* proves, that the *teething* season is sometimes no less fatal to the old, than to the young, and shews, too, that *false* teeth and *faux pas* have formed "a strange, uncouth, and unnatural connection!"

The whole fraternity of tooth-drawers are *au désespoir* at the conduct of one of the brotherhood. Not a beauty, they say, will visit one of them *alone* for the future, unless she has more regard for her teeth than her character. We think, however, it is a good trade still.

It is not true, that his Serene Highness the Stadtholder, has hired the Parsonage-house at *Sma-ring*.

SPORTING

SPORTING INTELLIGENCE.

BOXING MATCH.

BEFORE ten o'clock on Monday morning, December 22, above sixty post-chaises and hackney coaches, containing in the former two or three, and in the latter, five or six *well-dressed Gentlemen*, passed Hyde Park Turnpike, to be present at the pugilistical conflict between two Gentlemen—not of *Verona*—but of England and Ireland, by names *Belcher*, a noted pugilist from Bristol, and *Gamble*, an Irishman. The number of light carts, horsemen, and pedestrians, were, as a French General observes, *incalculable*. The battle took place on Wimbledon Common, for one hundred guineas a side.

Belcher was in the ring, walking about with his brother, for half an hour before Gamble made his appearance. The latter entered about twenty minutes before twelve o'clock; and, in the course of ten minutes, the champions stood forward in the middle of the ring, stript, and attended by their respective seconds and bottle-holders. Joe Ward was Belcher's second—Belcher, jun. his bottle-holder—and Tom Tring their deputy; Mendoza was Gamble's second—Coady his bottle-holder, and Crab their deputy. As if with intention to honour the manes of Abershaw, the field of battle was a short distance from his gibbet?

In the First Round—Gamble struck the first blow, which Belcher parried, and, quick as lightning, put in three in different parts of the face. They, then closed, and, from the Irishman's (Gamble's) superior strength, Belcher had the caution to drop. This confirmed the friends of Gamble, and five to four were betted with increased eagerness, though Belcher remained unhurt, whereas Gamble had received three several blows.

In the Second Round—Belcher advanced with great gallantry—Gamble retreated. Belcher then made a feint with his right hand; Gamble immediately guarded that side opposite, when the Bristolian hit him so severe a blow with his left hand, over the right eye, as to close it, and cause him to fall on the ground with such violence, that for a second or two he remained motionless. Bets were now two to one in favour of Belcher, and but cautiously accepted.

In the Third Round—Gamble still kept retreating: he hit Belcher several times in the body; but a severe blow on the nose drew the blood from Gamble. They then closed, when the latter threw Belcher with much violence on the ground, and fell across him. Bets were, however, four to one in favour of Belcher.

In the Fourth Round, which was uncommonly severe, the *Bristol Boy* displayed great coolness, intrepidity, and skill; and, after several very hard blows, Gamble, receiving one on the neck, again fell. The odds were ten to fifteen, nay even twenty to one.

The Fifth Round decided the contest, for the Irishman received so desperate a blow, put in on the stomach, that he fell backwards on the ground, and had scarce breath

breath enough to give in to Belcher.

The battle lasted nine minutes and three quarters. The umpire then declared that Belcher had won. The *Bristol Youth* gave a spring in the air, and was carried on the shoulders of his friends round the ring in triumph.

REMARKS.

When they stript, Gamble appeared so much the heavier man, that his friends backed him three to two. The general opinion, however, was against him, his bottom being suspected.

Previous to the appearance of the combatants in the ring, bets were seven to five in favour of Belcher; and before setting to, Ward offered twenty-five guineas to twenty, that he won, which was not accepted.

After the first round, Gamble was evidently afraid of Belcher, and constantly retreated from him.

Belcher laughed his antagonist to scorn during the whole of the battle; and used several motions both with his head and hand, to irritate him.

The opinion of the *knowing-ones* was decidedly in favour of Belcher. Gamble fought very badly, is a slow hitter, and shewed no courage.

Upwards of twenty thousand pounds was lost on the occasion. The landlord of the Crown and Punch Bowl, Seven Dials, won five hundred guineas by betting on Belcher.

After this bloody contest, much mirth was excited in the ring, by the following dialogue between Belcher and Mendoza, whilst the former was tying his shoes!

Belcher—Dan Mendoza!

Mendoza—Well, what do you want?

Belcher—I say, these were the shoes I bought to give you a thrashing in Scotland.

Mendoza—Well, well! the time may come.

Belcher—I wish you'd do it now.

Some friends interfered, and the contest was prevented. When Gamble was helped into the chaise he appeared to have a rib broken.

ANOTHER BATTLE.

Caleb Baldwin, a dealer in greens, and carman in Westminster, fought a battle for fifteen minutes with a shoemaker, of the name of Kelly, another Irishman, for twenty guineas a side. Baldwin was seconded by Ward, Crab, and Tring; Kelly by Coady and Burke. After a severe engagement for fifteen minutes, twelve rounds, victory was declared in favour of Baldwin, who gave his man a hearty drubbing.

In this time of scarcity, one of our fashions is somewhat useful, that of having little or no supper. The convenience of dining late produces in this instance the same effect, which poverty did at the close of the last century. Chamberlayne, in one of his editions, 1684, says of the English gentry—" In former times, their table was in many places covered four times a-day; they had *breakfasts, dinners, beverages,* and *suppers,* until the late troubles, wherein many eminent families being much impoverished by the prevailing revels, a custom was taken up by some of the nobility and gentry of eating a more plentiful dinner, but little or no supper."

A few days ago a part of a covey of partridges, which had been pursued by a hawk, exhausted by fear and fatigue, dropped down in the High-street of Dundee. Two of them took refuge in different shops.

Tuesday

Tuesday, as Mr. John Keene, who is totally blind, was going from Mear to Glastonbury, he heard the cries of a woman in the water, which was out to the edge of the road—he plunged into the water, and, directed by her screams, he waded to the spot, till he was up to his breast, when putting out his stick, she fortunately laid hold of it, and dragged her safe to the road. The woman was so exhausted, that she was unable to walk, and her poor blind deliverer absolutely carried her all the way to Glastonbury. Our readers must confess that Mr. K. bears a two-fold title to the attribute of "*feeling for another's woe.*"

A dramatic society is about to be established in Sweden, under the protection of the King, and under the inspection of the Duke of Sudermania: it is to be composed of the youth of the Court, and of other Nobles of both sexes. They are to perform before persons who may be invited, at the theatre which is to be constructed, the best French and Swedish pieces. The expences are to be supported by the subscriptions of the Court, and the most distinguished persons in the kingdom.

A swindler of great enterprize, and who like our celebrated highwayman Duval, not contented with depriving gentlemen of their purses, stole the hearts also of the ladies, was lately apprehended at the Opera in Paris: it appeared upon examination, that there are few countries, whether in alliance or at war with the Republic, of which he had not adopted the *costume*, and that in the disguise of a Dutch merchant, no dress very particularly adapted to the graces, he had been very successful in his amours. He was on the point of being married to his third wife when apprehended.

An over-driven ox lately tossed a woman who was walking on the pavement near the Poultry five or six times from the ground. Fortunately her petticoats saved her from being gored; and she was at length extricated from this danger by her petticoats being torn away, with which the ox ran off, carrying them in triumph on his horns. The woman was not materially hurt.—Thus it still appears that clothes are of *some* use!

On Monday, the 8th, a coursing match was run on Newmarket-heath, for ten guineas a side, between a greyhound of John Mosely, Esq. and one of Mr. S. Brook's, which was won by the former, after a very good course.

The farmers coursing meeting at Market Weighton, was well attended. The hares above Londesborough are not so plentiful as they used to be on the white grass there. It is supposed some very unfair means to destroy them have lately been practised.

During the late high wind, one of the chimnies at Horsham barracks fell through the roof, amongst four officers, who had just sat down to a *comfortable rubber at whist!*—The party providentially received no material injury; but were so alarmed by the sudden crash, that they all voluntarily declared they would never more touch the *Devil's Books* on the *Lord's Day!*

LUSUS NATURÆ.

The wife of Dominique Ledru, in Paris, has lately been delivered of a figure resembling an ape, having the horns of a goat, the foot of an ox, the tongue of a serpent, and the tail of an ass.

Mr. Cookson, well known on the turf, run his last *race*, and lost *dead hollow*, on the 25th of November.—*Death* took the *whip-hand* of him, and beat him completely out of the *field.*

POETRY.

POETRY.

THE HIGH COURT OF DIANA.

LINES,
OVER THE DOOR OF A PENNY BARBER.

UNDER this roof, there lives a Barber,
Who ne'er spares soap to raise a lather;
Whether your beards be thin or thick,
Or soft as down, or hard as brick—
Whether your jaws be plump or shrunk,
Or pimpled o'er from getting drunk;
 With razor keen,
 He'll shave you clean;
 And free from pain,
 Or bloody stain;
 And this in a trice,
 At a penny's price.
But if from home, he's call'd to shave,
Double the price he then must have,
And thrice the sum if in his bed
He lathers one that's sick or dead.
These are his terms he asks no more;
But he must have the brass before
The cloth's removed—he will not score!
    TIM. TRIM.

THE MOCK-BIRD AND RED-BIRD;
AN AMERICAN FABLE.

SOME birds (it is no news to tell)
Can sing, and in their songs excel;
Then, should we sometimes hear them speak,
What need we any wonder make?

The Mock-bird on a time, 'tis said,
Thus the sweet Red-bird did upbraid.

"Ah! hapless bird! with one poor note;
"One, and no more to swell thy throat;
"One, and no more, can'st thou repeat,
"To charm the Woods, or cheer thy mate;
"One, and no more, poor bird! whilst I
"Abound in sweet variety.
"Nor is't thy voice, thy voice alone,
"Thou simpleton! that I bemoan.
"Methinks your colour looks as mean;
"All of one hue—all red in grain
"Your topping's something gay, 'tis true,
"But that, even that, is red, poor you."

The Red-bird heard the taunting strain,
And answer'd without pride or pain.

"Poor me! say'st thou, proud gaudy bird!
"Thyself may better claim that word.
"They're poor who never are content,
"But still to steal from others bent.
"If all are poor that wear one hue,
"(Your pretty taunting to pursue)
"Then, po' r's the lily, tho' so fair,
"Or red rose that embalms the air.

"I wish not to grow proud or vain,
"By picking plumes of various grain;
"Nor would * feign'd song, by Rapine, raise;
"Content with my own native lays.
"My voice, thou mocker, 'tis well known,
"Such as it is, it is my own;
"And, if decided by fair votes,
"As sweet as all your mimic notes.
"But your small eyes can only see
"The beauties in yourself that be;
"And these, as little as they are,
"You magnify—and so prefer."

The Mock-bird cry'd—"Ha! my small eyes—
"But eyes are not to win the Prize.
"The question is of voice and colour,
"And not, whose goggle eyes are fuller.

* The Mock-bird has no song of its own, but can imitate every other bird it hears.

"Hark!

"Hark, have you ears?"—Each strain it
try'd,
And swell'd with music, and with pride;
Then would have spoke again, but
(chuak'd
With spite and spleen) it rather croak'd.
"My throat is hoarse,"—It scarce could
utter,
And yet seem'd something more to
mutter,
Then, taking flight, its weakness found,
And, fluttering, fell upon the ground.

The Red bird not insulting stood,
But wing'd, and warbled thro' the wood.

The MORAL, to be learn'd from hence,
Is pretty plain.—Let's have the sense,
Simplicity of life and heart
To love, and scorn delusive art;
Never, thro' pride or spite, in vain
Our breasts to vex, or throats to strain;
But shun all foolish ostentation,
And be contented with our station.

EPITAPH.

HERE lies that horse, PorBo's,
well yclept—
For he is goodly case his owners kept;
Oh! cou'd Potatoes at this time procure
Flesh on the bodies of the starving poor!
                        CAPTAIN SNUG.

THE WAY OF THE WORLD.

A familiar Epistle to a Friend in the
Country, requesting the Author to borrow him a few Hundreds from some
advertising Negociator or Friend.

HAPPY, dear Frank, could I obey,
    And meet your wishes in the way
Your letter points—but to be plain,
Experience shews it is in vain;
For let them promise what they will
They seldom have the cash, or will
To do the thing they advertise,
But fill you with amusing lies:
Unless indeed you are content
To yield them profits—cent. per cent.
And as few friends—e'en they you'll
find,
To self and usury inclin'd.
In proof—peruse the following rhymes,
They'll suit, you'll find, the modern
times.

The man you know—they say a plumb—
Tho' I believe—not half the sum.

With him I liv'd (as neighbours should)
Ready to do what's kind and good;
But Fortune, (fickle in her way,)
Sent me a Dun, I could not pay;
So, to my worthy neighb'ring friend
I went, not doubting he would lend;
But, to my wonder and surprise,
He flat denied me the supplies;
And said, "Why, surely you're in joke,
" And mean this trial as a cloak,
" To try me, if I'm such an elf,
" To love my neighbour—as myself."

" Then why profess!"—cried I, in turn;
" Be patient, Sir, and you shall learn.
" When first such language I profest,
" I thought you rich as——at least;
" But now I find you want a loan,
" It makes me change my former tone.
" For I'm, you know, a man in trade,
" Whence all my fortune I have made;
" And were it ever known on 'Change,
" (The world would think it wond'rous
    strange)
" That I, a man in years, should lend,
" My money, to a lord, or friend,
" Which, heaven knows, I ne'er, in-
    tend;
" But, if the present loan you want
" Can be secur'd by deed, or grant,
" Of one annuity or two,
" I'll try; my friend, what I can do.
" Or, if a banker here in Town,
" Whose name and character is known,
" Will join you in a bond or note,
" I'll give the thing a second thought;
" And may to issue soon be brought.

I thank you, Sir—but curse your pelf,
Your love, your friendship, and yourself;
And hope in future we shall be,
Tho' near—as distant, as Goree.

Thus, Frank, you see—how this world
goes—
How int'rest governs friends and foes;
And whatsoe'er man's profer'd will is,
Learn, with me—*nos credimus illos.*
But on yourself alone depend—
For there you'll find your only friend.

            * Virgil.

EPIGRAM.

JACK, an Acrostich made on Celia's
    name,
For which, to say the truth, he was to
    blame;
What, in return, deserves the poet Jack?
Why, like for like—a Stick-across-his-
    Back.

                                THE

THE POET's GARRET.

COME, sportive Fancy! come with
   me, and trace
The Poet's *attic* home! the lofty seat
Of th' heav'n-rapt'rd Nine! the airy
   throne
Of bold Imagination, rapture fraught,
Above the herds of mortals. All around
A solemn stillness seems to guard the
   scene;
Nursing the brood of thought;—a thriving
   brood,
In the rich mazes of the cultur'd brain.
Upon thy altar, an old worm-eat board,—
The pannel of a broken door, or lid
Of a strong coffer, plac'd on three-legg'd
   stool,
Stand quires of paper, white and beautiful!
Paper, by destiny ordain'd to be
Scrawl'd o'er and blotted; dash'd, and
   scratch'd, and torn,
Or mark'd with lines severe, or scatter'd
   wide
In rage impetuous! Sonnet, song, and
   ode,
Satire, and epigram, and smart *charade*;
Neat paragraph, or legendary tale,
Of short and simple metre, each by turns
Will there delight the reader.

            On the bed
Lies an old rusty suit of " solemn black"—
Brush'd thread-bare; and with brown,
   unglossy hue,
Grown somewhat antient. On the floor
   is seen
A pair of silken hose, whose footing had
Shews they are travellers, but who still
   bear
Marks, somewhat *bulky*. At the scanty
   fire
A chop turns round, by packthread
   strongly held;
And on the blacken'd bar a vessel shines
Of batter'd pewter, just half fill'd, and
   warm,
With Whitbread's bev'rage pure. The
   kitten purs,
Anticipating dinner; while the wind
Whistles thro' broken panes, and drifted
   snow
Carpets the parapet with spotless garb
Of vestal coldness. Now the sullen hour
(The fifth hour after noon) with dusty
   hand
Closes the lids of day. The farthing
   light
Gleams through the cobweb'd chamber,
   and the bard
Concludes his pen's hard labour. Now
   he eats

With appetite voracious! nothing sad
That he with costly plate, and napkin
   fine,
Nor china rich, nor fork of silver, greets
His eye, or palate. On his lyric board
A sheet of paper serves for table cloth;
An heap of salt is serv'd, Oh!—heav'nly
   treat,
On Ode Pindaric! While his tuneful
   puss
Scratches his slipper for her fragment sweet,
And sings her love-song soft, yet mourn-
   fully.
Mocking the pillar Doric, or the roof
Of architecture Gothic, all around
The well-known ballads flit, of Grub-
   street fame!
The casement, broke, gives breath ce-
   lestial
To the long dying-speech; or gently fans
The love-enflaming sonnet. All around
Small scraps of paper lie, torn vestiges
Of an unquiet fancy. Here a page
Of flights poetic;—there a dedication;—
A list of *Dramatis Personæ*, bold,
Of heroes yet unborn, and lofty dames
Of perishable compound, light as fair;
But sentenc'd to oblivion!

          On a shelf—
(Yclept a mantle-piece), a phial stands,
Half-fill'd with potent spirits!—spirits
   strong,
Which sometimes haunt the poet's restless
   brain,
And fill his mind with fancies whimsical.
Poor Poet! happy art thou, thus remov'd
From pride and folly!—for in thy domain
Thou can'st command thy subjects;—
   fill thy lines—
Wield the all-conqu'ring weapon heav'n
   bestows
In the grey goose's wing! which, tow'ring
   high,
Bears thy rich fancy to IMMORTAL FAME!
                             M. R.

On the MARRIAGE *of Mr.* J. BACCHUS,
aged 97, *to Miss* MARY WATSON, *aged*
27.

IF a man, when a century nearly is past,
   To encounter sweet wedlock doth pine,
'Tis a proof, and most positive e'en to the
   last,
Of the power of women and wine.

Some care must have been, though,
   adopted thro' life,
   (Our pleasures too much should not
   hook us)—
Or else how lamented the fate of poor wife,
And still more to be pity'd old *Bacchus*!

THE GREYHOUND.
A FABLE.

" Allura pasit opem res, et conjurat amice."
Hor.

IN times when animals could speak,
   With equal ease as men read Greek;
As o'er his prey a greyhound stood
Licking his lips upon his food—
Thus in himself he justly weigh'd,
Which of his limbs most merit praise.
The Tail suggests—I steer thee right;
The Legs reply, we bear your weight.
I, says the Nose the food must trace;
We, says the Eyes, direct the chace;
True, says the Mouth—but pray declare,
Can either of ye catch a hare?
Silence, says Spring, distraction smother,
For none subsist without another.
Thus statesmen, who for power are
   jarring,
The int'rest of the state are marring.

THE SPORTSMAN's MORNING.

THE night recedes, and mild Aurora
   now
Waves her grey banner on the Eastern
   brow;
Light float the misty vapours o'er the
   sky,
And dim the blaze of Phœbus garish
   eye;
The flitting breeze just stirs the rustling
   brake,
And curls the crystal surface of the lake;
The eager sportsmen snatch a short repast,
And to the field repair with anxious
   haste.

The active Pointer, from his thong
   unbound,
Impatient dashes o'er the dewy ground,
With glowing eyes, and undulating tail,
Ranges the field, and snuffs the tainted
   gale;
Yet 'midst his ardour still his master fears,
And the restraining whistle chearful hears.

See how exact they try the stubble
   o'er,
Quarter the field, and every turn explore;
Now sudden wheel, and now attentive
   seize,
The known advantage of th' opposing
   breeze;
At once they stop; yon careful dog des-
   cries
Where close and near the lurking covey
   lies,
His caution mark, lest e'en a breath betray
Th' impending danger to his timid prey;

In various attitudes around him stand,
Silent and motionless, th' attending band!

They rise!—they rise!—Ah yet your
   fire restrain,
'Till the mos'd birds a greater distance
   gain!
For, thrown too close, the shots your
   buyer elude,
Wide of your aim and innocent of blood;
But mark with careful eye their less'ning
   flight,
Your ready gun, obedient to your sight,
And at the length where frequent trials
   shew
Your fatal weapon gives the surest blow,
Draw quick.

THE SPORTSMAN's EVE.

WHEN the last sun of August's
   fervid reign
Now bathes his radiant forehead in the
   Main,
The *Panoply*, by sportive heroes worn,
Is rang'd in order for th' ensuing morn:
Forth from the summer guard of holt and
   lock
Come the *thick centre*, and the *furious
   flash*;
With curious skill the deathful *tube* is
   made,
Clean as the fireluck of the spruce parade,
Yet let no polish of the *Sportsman's* gun
Flash, like the soldier's weapon, to the
   sun,
Or the bright steel's refulgent glare pre-
   sume
To penetrate the peaceful forest's gloom;
But let it take a *brown's* more sober hue,
Or the dark lustre of th' enamell'd blue.
Let the close *pouch* the *wadded tow* con-
   tain,
The leaden *pellets* and the *vitreous grain*;
And wisely cautious, with preventive
   care,
Be the *spare flint*, and ready *turn-screw*
   there,
While the *slung net* is open to receive
Each *prize* the labour of the day shall
   give!

Yet oft th' experienced Shooter shall
   deride
This *quaint apparatus* of fastidious pride;
In some *old coat*, that whilom charm'd the
   eye,
'Till time had worn it into slavery;
His dusky gun, by spotted rust conceal'd,
Thro' rainy service in the sportive field,
He issues to the plain!

THE SPORTING MAGAZINE;

OR,

MONTHLY CALENDAR

OF THE

TRANSACTIONS OF THE TURF, THE CHASE,

And every other DIVERSION interesting to the

MAN OF PLEASURE, ENTERPRIZE, AND SPIRIT.

For JANUARY, 1801.

CONTAINING,

	Page
Ranelagh Masquerade	152
Sale of Mr. Cookson's Stud	ibid
Trial for a breach of promise of marriage—Protheroe v. Jones	ibid
Dog-Stealing	153
Singular Inscription	ibid
Account of the celebrated Lavater	154
Humorous account of the Death and Execution of a Corn-Buyer	155
Biography of Sir Edmund Mason	156
Necessary cautions and instructions to Young Sportsmen	157
Russian Manners	161
Russian Amusements	162
French Theatricals	163
Trick of a French Quack	164
Different Opinions on the Scarcity	165
The Bailiffs baffled	167
Modern Arabian Caravans	168
Trials at Clerkenwell Sessions	169
Assault in St. James's Park	170
Extraordinary Character	171
Extraordinary Incident	174
The Equestrian Philosopher	175
Extraordinary Sporting Intelligence	176
The Marquis of Exeter's State Bed	177
Mrs. Champney's Masquerade	ibid
Mirth in a Mask	ibid
Letter from Three Working Taylors to their Masters	178

	Page
Attempt to commit a Rape	178
Turkish Ceremony of laying a First Stone	180
Sale of a State Stud	181
Supernatural Campanology	182
Russian Manners	ibid
Scarcity and Plenty	184
The Utility of the Cow	185
Stylish Pickpocket	186
Speech of a Creek Indian, against the Use of Spirituous Liquors	187
A Dashing Imposter	189
A Female Swindler	ibid
Portraits of Horses	190
The Maid of the Hay-Stack	ibid
Desperate Enterprise	192
Adventures of a Traveller	193
Sporting Intelligence	194
Feats of Wit	198

POETRY.

	Page
Parody on " Ere around the Huge Oak"	201
Bayswater; or, The Whim	ibid
Sonnet to Peace	202
A Hungarian War Song	ibid
Harvest Home	ibid
Poor Tom	203
Prologue to the Siege of Belgrade	204

[Embellished with a beautiful Engraving of BRYAN O'LYNN, by SCOTT, and an Etching of THE HARE IN ITS FORM, by HOWIT.]

LONDON:

PRINTED FOR THE PROPRIETORS,

By Rider and Weed, Little-Britain.

And sold by J. Wheble, No. 18, Warwick-square, Warwick-lane, near St. Paul's; at John Hilton, Newmarket; and by every Bookseller and Stationer in Great Britain and Ireland.

(Price 1s. 6d.)

TO CORRESPONDENTS.

To all those who have expressed their wishes for Plates of different Racers of celebrity, we have but one answer, which is, That when it may suit them to furnish us with, or give us any information how we may obtain, any Equestrian Portraits or Drawings, for the use of the SPORTING MAGAZINE, the favour will be gratefully acknowledged, and improved to the best advantage.

Upon a review of our pages, we are sorry to find what the Printers call a *double*; that is, the appearance of the same article, "Upon French Dexterity," in two different parts of the impression. We assure our Readers, that in future we shall endeavour at no means of exculpation, upon any subject that may wear the least appearance of a want of care and attention.

THE SPORTING MAGAZINE,

For JANUARY, 1801.

EXPLANATION OF THE PLATE.

BRYAN O'LYNN.

BRYAN O'LYNN, of which a PLATE is here given, was got by Aston; his dam, by Le Lang; grand-dam, by Regulus; great grand-dam, by Partner,—Greyhound,—Curwen's Bay Barb.

This horse has been celebrated for his performances in Scotland, particularly at Ayr, where he last year, at four years old, won several Matches and Sweepstakes.—He is the property of Mr. Graham; and his name has been changed to BONAPARTE.

RANELAGH MASQUERADE.

THIS Entertainment (on Tuesday, January 20) was attended by a numerous and very genteel company. So many beautiful women have seldom appeared together.

The characters were much in the usual stile; *Housemaids, Footmen, Shepherdesses, Harlequins, Fruit Girls,* &c. &c.

Mr. D. and Mrs. E. of the Theatres, appeared as two *Quakers*: the male Friend was loquacious enough, but sister Ruth had not a word to say in support of her character. Three *Taylors* sang many glees in the stile of Professors. An *Indian* was very well dressed, and acted his part with much judgment. A *Mad Tom* was a good emblem of the rest of the company, and raved with characteristic propriety. A beautiful *Diana* was one of the best dressed characters in the room. There were several *Harlequins,* but only one who displayed much agility: another of them wore a very rich dress, spangled with silver.

The noise was equal to that of any former Masquerade, and the wit and good-humour of the company made the hours pass off quite agreeably.

Grimaldi, in throwing a summerset, severely sprained three of his fingers, the pain of which made him faint. A surgeon, one of the company, immediately gave his assistance. Grimaldi was supporting the character of a *Clown* with much humour.

The wines were of the best quality; and the supper was far beyond what could have been expected for the price, in these times.

The entertainment, altogether, went off with great glee, and detained a number of the visitors till a late hour.

SPORTING INTELLIGENCE.

SALE OF MR. COOKSON'S STUD.

THE late Mr. Cookson's Racing Stud has at last apparently found its destination. The following are its changes and chances since the death of its master:—

The advertisement for its sale reached Colonel Arthur Hyde, of Castle Hyde, near Kilworth, in the county of Cork, only the Wednesday preceding the day fixed for the auction at Tattersall's. He instantly dispatched a favourite groom with positive instructions to make his way to London, without a moment's delay, and to purchase *Sir Harry, Scrub,* and *Diamond;* the last at all events. The groom set out instantly for Dublin; but, not having a favourable passage, the day fixed for the sale had expired before he reached Holyhead. Not wishing to return an unsuccessful ambassador, he continued his journey in spite of the disappointment, and having arrived in town, communicated his mission to Mr. Taylor, in Warwick-square, his master's agent in London. An inquiry was immediately instituted for the purchasers of the horses, and *Diamond* was fortunately found in the possession of Mr. Thrupp, a dealer, in Bishopsgate-street, from whom he was bought on Colonel Hyde's account, for six hundred guineas. He was sold at Tattersall's for five hundred and twenty.—Mr. Thrupp had not had him many minutes in his possession, before he felt considerable alarm on his account: as the boy was bringing him home, he took fright in St. James's Park, and ran off at the top of his speed, down the Mall to the Horse Guards, where he stopped of his own accord, without meeting any accident.

Such was the fear of crossing or jockeying on the way, in case it was known when he should set out for Ireland, that both the time of his departure and his route were managed with more privacy than even a secret expedition. He went by way of Holyhead, as affording the shortest sea passage, and was insured before he was put on board. The little boy who attended him in Mr. Cookson's life-time rode him down; but notwithstanding the mutual attachment that subsisted between him and the horse, Mr. Hyde could not prevail on him to settle with him.

About one thousand people came to see the horse while he remained at Mr. Thrupp's; and very few in London but would have followed the example, had they supposed they could have got a sight of him.

The fate of the other two horses is also fixed; the one goes to the West Indies, and the other to Scotland.

COURT OF KING'S BENCH.
Wednesday, Jan. 28.

PROTHEROE v. JONES.

THIS was an action to recover a compensation in damages, for a breach of promise of marriage.—The Defendant is a Methodist Preacher, and is about sixty years of age; the plaintiff about twenty-eight.

It appeared, that, in the year 1799, the Defendant had paid his addresses to the Plaintiff, and, from a variety of letters (which were read in evidence) had promised her marriage; that, in the Spring of 1800, he had been on a journey into Denbighshire, but on his return refused to perform his promise, saying that his friends were averse to the match, and that a creditor, to whom he was indebted fifteen pounds, had threatened to arrest him, unless he gave up all thoughts of his "dear Winifred;" and that he could not marry her unless he sold all his houses, which in time of war would not fetch so much as in time of peace. This, however, appeared to be all a scheme in order to break off this intended match, as he soon after was married to another person. Upon his marriage he wrote to her, stating what he had done, and saying, "it was by command of God and his people."—It appeared also, that the Plaintiff had been seduced, prior to her acquaintance with the Defendant.

The letters were all written in Welch, and afforded much entertainment to a crowded court.

The Jury, after retiring near two hours, found a verdict for Plaintiff.—Damages *Fifty Pounds*.

PUBLIC OFFICE, BOW STREET,
Wednesday, Jan. 28.

DOG-STEALING.

THIS day *Jane Sellwood* and *Thomas Pallett* were brought before R. Ford and T. Robinson, Esqrs. on suspicion of having stolen and killed a great number of dogs for the sake of their skins.

Robert Townsend, one of the patrole, said, that he went yesterday morning (on information) to the house of the prisoner Sellwood, in St. George's Fields, and in a back room found about thirty carcases of dogs without their skins, piled one on another, and many more under the floor, most of them in a putrid state. Those in the back room appeared to have been lately killed, by being beat on the head with a hammer, as all their skulls were broken; and in the back room he found the hammer now produced, which no doubt had been used for the purpose, being covered with blood and dog's hair. In the front room he found the prisoners, whom he took into custody.

William Bagshaw, of Earl-street, London Road, deposed, that on the 14th of December last, he lost a pug bitch, and which he had every reason to believe was stolen from him; that on hearing yesterday morning of a number of dead dogs being found in the prisoner Sellwood's house, he went there, and among the carcases discovered that of his pug bitch, which he was enabled to swear to from a particular mark in its mouth, and being with pup at the time.

The prisoner Sellwood is an old woman; Pallett is a boy; neither of them having any thing satisfactory to urge in their defence, were committed for further examination.

During the time the prisoners were at the bar, a man came to give them a character, when three dogs in the Office immediately fondled about him; and had they not been prevented, would have followed him away, from which, and his appearance altogether, there was every reason to suppose he was one of the gang. Mr. Ford therefore ordered him out of the Office, or he should be taken into custody as a party concerned.

SINGULAR INSCRIPTION.

THE following is copied verbatim, from a sign over the door of a good house at Whalley, in Lancashire—in gold letters:—

Clegg—Surgeon, Apothecary, and Bone-setter—cures all sorts of cancers, wens, and wolves—old ulcers and the ague—Farrier and Cow Doctor—and drinks to be given to young Calves for striking of the *Hyes*. Also Colts and Pigs *Gelded*.

LAVATER.

LAVATER.

THE celebrated Physiognomist, who lately died at Zurich, has been, for many years, one of the most famous men in Europe.

He was an humble country-clergyman of good education, a warm fancy, and a natural acuteness of discernment. His perspicuity of intellect was associated with weaknesses of sensibility and imagination, not a little a kin to those of J. J. Rousseau.

In this situation, and with these qualities, he was accidentally led to turn his attention, in a particular manner, to the expression of human sentiment and character in the varied conformation of the countenance, head, and other parts of the frame, in the complexion, in the habitual motions and attitudes, in the temperament of health, &c. He perceived that in all these, not only transient passion, but even the more permanent qualities of character, are often very distinctly expressed. He carried his observations, in his way, much farther than any other person had before advanced. Success inflamed his imagination; and he became an enthusiast in the study of physiognomy. The opinions relative to it, which he propagated, were a medley of acute observation, ingenious conjecture, and wild reverie. They were divulged by him in conversation, and in a multitude of fragments, which he and his disciples soon assembled into volumes. Novelty, mystery, and the dreams of enthusiasm, have inexpressible charms for the multitude; every one was eager to learn to read his neighbour's heart in his face. In Switzerland, in Germany, in France, even in Britain, all the world became passionate admirers of the Physiognomical Science of Lavater.

His books, published in the German language, were multiplied by many additions. In the enthusiasm with which they were studied and admired, they were thought as necessary in every family, as even the Bible itself. A servant would, at one time, scarcely be hired till the descriptions and engravings of Lavater had been consulted, in careful comparison, with the lines and features of the young man's or woman's countenance. The same system was eagerly translated into the French language; and, as the insight into character and secret intention which it promised, was infinitely grateful to female curiosity, all the pretenders to wit, taste, and fashion, among the lively women of France, soon became distractedly fond of it. It was talked of as a science susceptible of mathematical certainty; and was applauded as capable of endowing man with the power of omniscient intuition into the hearts and intentions of his fellows.

But, even after the first charm had been dissolved, Lavater still retained many disciples. He continued to cultivate physiognomy, and was still eagerly visited by travellers passing near the place of his residence. By some of his adversaries he was idly and unjustly accused as an insidious Jesuit, who, under pretensions about physiognomy, pursued some vast and mischievous designs. His Theological Opinions took a colour from his Physiognomical ones; and he became the abhorrence of the orthodox. His private life was simple, and even devoutly pious. His wife had became, as well as himself, a great Physiognomist. He was always an early riser, and used never to take his breakfast, till he had, in his own mind, earned it by the performance of some literary task.

He was, at the dawn of the French revolution, not at all adverse to it. Even when it began to penetrate into Switzerland, he did not passionately declare against it; but when he saw his native country become a prey to the excesses of Jacobinism, his indignation was earnestly roused, and he wrote some eloquent pieces against the oppressions of the French. He favoured the momentary counter-revolution. He was cruelly attacked and wounded by the French soldiers when that counter-revolution was suppressed. His death was in consequence of those wounds. It may revive his fame, and excite a new curiosity for the perusal of his works.

HUMOROUS ACCOUNT OF THE DEATH AND EXECUTION OF A CORN-BUYER.

Extract of a Letter from Arundel, dated January 23.

THE following singular occurrence took place here, yesterday:—A lady passing along one of the bye streets, was greatly shocked on observing a man, decently apparelled, lying along, motionless, on a heap of rubbish. Conjecturing that he had fallen in a fit, the lady, who is philanthropy personified, caused the body to be immediately conveyed to a neighbouring house, and sent for a Surgeon to breath a vein. The practitioner having prepared his lancet, and the lady in the hurry and alarm of the moment, having loosed her garter for a bandage, the disciple of Æsculapius lifted up the arm, which fell again without sense or motion, and having in vain felt and refelt for a pulse, which was not to be found, declared, with an emphasis, "That it was no use at all at all! (for he is an Hibernian) for him to take blood from a man who had none in his veins; for sure enough the jontleman was no longer a member of our sublunary system!" The lady enquiring how long he supposed his patient had been dead, he replied, with great agacity, "that he was pretty certain he had ceased to exist from the moment the breath had gone out of his body." Having returned his lancet to its case, taken his fee, and made his bow, the Undertaker was sent for to perform the funeral obsequies, who, on going to measure the corpse, observed something sticking out through an opening in the waistcoat, which he immediately applied his hand to and dragged forth, exclaiming, "that the deceased had certainly been turned out to browse in the meadows, like Nebuchadnezzar of old, and that the heat of the stomach had turned the grass he had eaten into hay!" In a word, the poor gentleman, the subject of so much commiseration and alarm, proved to be no other than the effigy of a certain Corn-Buyer, which had, in the fore part of the day, undergone the discipline of a patibulary suspension on a gallows, erected in the market-place, with a placart, informing of the nature of the offence, viz. raising the price of corn at the market, by giving a greater price for what was offered at a less. This figure, after hanging for several hours, was ordered by the Magistrates to be cut down, and being thrown into a bye lane, gave rise to the foregoing ludicrous circumstance.—In the evening, a great number of boys and others with lighted torches, resembling, both by their appearance and horrid yells, a legion of imps from the regions below, claimed their destined prey; which having carried in procession through all the streets in the town, consigned it finally to the flames in the

the market-place, amidst the eve-eration of numbers of poor people; and, it being market-day, in the presence of numerous Corn-Buyers and Jobbers, on whom it is to be hoped it may have operated as a salutary admonition.

Biography of Sir Edmund Mason,

The Rival of Don Quixotte, and of the Emperor Paul.

DIED lately, at Leominster, in Herefordshire, Edmund Mason, a man remarkable, as being in spirit, integrity, disorder of imagination, and even a ray of intellectual ability, the living representative of the inimitable hero Cervantes. Though perfectly harmless, he was constantly accoutred in arms. He fancied himself the greatest General of the age; related deeds achieved by his arm in battle which no other mortal could equal; believed that Kings and Emperors—not accepting the Emperor Paul—had vied in conferring on him every imaginable title and badge of honour. Mason supposed, that he had enjoyed the confidential friendship and admiration of the late Great Frederick of Prussia. From his foreign correspondents, he told that immense remittances were sent for the support of his dignity; yet, he was ever without money—from the difficulty, as he told, of cashing bills of exchange for millions.

He was decorous and dignified in manners, cleanly in his person, temperate in his diet.

In love with the fancied Princess of some *undiscovered island*, he would not suffer one of the fair sex about him to touch even his little finger. His bed was a roomy wooden chest, from which his musket was constantly levelled. He was in his latter years confined; but the confinement was reconciled to his mind, by the persuasion that he resided in it as the governor of the Castle.

He was the author of the original plan for draining and enclosing the common of Widemarsh, near Hereford. He was by birth a gentleman.

The Hare in its Form.

THE present Month's Number will be found ornamented with two Copper-plates. That which is to be placed to face this page, is, *The Hare in its Form*. The manner in which this animal places itself to repose in the day, has always been noticed as singular; for he sleeps in his form or seat all day, and feeds and copulates in the night. In winter, he chooses a form exposed to the South, and in summer to the North. In summer a Hare will not sit in bushes, but in corn-fields and open places: in winter they sit near towns and villages, in tufts of thorns, brambles, &c. The Hare, though ever so frequently hunted, seldom leaves the place where she was brought forth, or even the form in which she usually sits. The Hare is supposed to emit very little scent, whilst quietly sitting in her form, as dogs have been known to jump over, and even tread upon her. The lips of the Hare continually move sleeping and waking, and the eye is too big and round for the lid to cover it, even when asleep; so that the creature sleeps, as it were, on the watch. In truth, the Hare is endowed with all those instincts which are necessary to its own preservation, and evince the wisdom and goodness of the Creator of all things.

NECESSARY

NECESSARY CAUTIONS AND INSTRUCTIONS TO YOUNG SPORTSMEN.

[*In a Letter to a Friend.*]

Learn to be wise from others' harms,
And you will do right well!

The writer of the following Letter might, perhaps, have made it more impressive, if he had collected into one view a number of the accidents which have happened, from the ignorance, or negligence, of those who take guns in hand; but he fears that any deficiency, on this melancholy head, will be but too readily supplied by most of his readers!

He has introduced the name of only one person, and that for the purpose of recording the good judgment of a keen and high-spirited Sportsman, whose apprehensions were well founded, as appears by one of the few accidents alluded to. That which relates to the blowing up of a powder-flask, in the act of loading, points out a source of danger seldom taken into consideration.

DEAR SIR,

IN answer to your questions on the subject of SHOOTING, and particularly referring yourself to my opinion on *double-barrelled Guns*, I shall endeavour to give you such hints as my experience may render of any service to you.

Whether a sportsman, who has the perfect management of a *double gun*, can kill more game with it in a season, than be or another person, *cæteris paribus*, can with a *single*, is not here the question; but whether the many circumstances of inconvenience and danger attending the *double*, do not overballance the advantages, admitted to their fullest extent; and whether, upon the whole, it is desirable for a young, or indeed any, sportsman, to use one.

You are aware that we adopted the double gun from the French; among whom the few who, under the old government, had the liberty of shooting, frequently got more shots in one day than you do in a month. From the abundance of game, they had the opportunity of picking their shots, which made very small charges answer their purpose; besides that, their shoulders could not have supported such as we find more effectual. The smallness of the charge required, admitted of the French guns being made so slight, that many persons in this country have supposed their iron of a quality superior to ours; but many of them have been burst here, with very moderate charges. I shall mention one instance of their extreme thinness—that I had once a double gun from the reputed best maker in Paris, in which the pattern of the ornaments chased on each side of the sight were distinctly seen indented, on looking through the barrels. Because the French guns are usually made too slight for our purpose, it does not follow that we cannot make them safe; but the fact is, that, from fear of over-weight, and of the breech being made so wide that the left cock should be reached with difficulty, we have made them so slight, that, I am sorry to say, I could furnish you with a well-attested catalogue of double guns, of English make, burst within these few years, attended with various injuries. It must, however, be acknowledged, that the objection of the locks being too far separated, is intirely removed by one of the patents now in force, by which the utmost strength required may be introduced at the breech.

That you may not suppose I recommend high loading, I must explain myself more fully, by observing that, if a man expects to get fifteen or twenty shots in a day, it will be of no advantage to him to use such a charge as would be more agreeable to his shoulder, in case he should get two hundred; and that one ounce and three quarters, or seven-eighths, of shot, will tell better in the field than the Frenchman's charge-meagre of one ounce. Two ounces of shot is the charge proposed in Page's ingenious treatise on "Shooting Flying;" you will therefore hardly think that my using one ounce and three quarters, can class me with those shooters against whom the following severe restriction was levelled: at the foot of an advertisement for pigeon-shooting, at Billingbear Warren-house—*N. B. No person to be allowed to load with more than four ounces of shot!*—A gamekeeper, to whom I mentioned this, laughed, and said, he thought it *a pretty fair allowance.* On my asking him what weight of shot he himself used, he answered, that he divided *one pound into five charges.*

A friend of mine, seeing his keeper equipping himself for a pigeon-match, was curious to examine the terrors of the prepared charge, and trying it with the rammer, expressed his surprize at finding it rather *less* than usual.— "Oh! Sir," replied the keeper, "I have only put in the *powder* yet."

Of this school are the wild-fowl shooters; in one of whose guns, of six feet barrel, I lately measured a charge to the height of *eleven fingers.*—" Sir, I likes to give my gun a belly-full."

He who gives a double gun the greatest advantage, has both locks cocked when he prepares to shoot, and discharges each barrel in succession, either at separate objects or the same, as circumstances may require, without removing the butt from his shoulder. Should only one trigger be drawn, there remains one lock cocked: and though there may be shooters who have never once omitted to let down the unused cock to the half-bent, I appeal to numbers, whether they have not, at some time or other, detected themselves in having loaded one barrel while the lock of that which remained undischarged was still cocked?—On making this discovery, in his own case, the late Sir George Armytage immediately laid aside the *double gun.* But there is a noted sportsman still fortunately alive in Yorkshire, who discarded it on still stronger ground; for, while he was loading one barrel, the charge of the other passed so near his body as to tear his waistcoat!

Though there may be some advantage in having both locks cocked, it is very practicable to take the gun down from the shoulder, on having missed a bird with the first barrel, cock, and kill the same bird with the second barrel.

If both locks are cocked, it is usual to pull the hinder trigger first. If the forward trigger is drawn first, there is a risk of the finger slipping over it when it gives way, and touching that behind. Whether this sometimes happens, or one is shaken off by the recoil, or the sears are made so long as to touch one another, it is certain that both barrels are sometimes unintentionally discharged by one pull. I was witness to this happening in the hands of a late keeper, in Berkshire, who, twice in succession, fired both barrels at once, at woodcocks. I was at the edge of the cover, and could just perceive an interval between the sound of the two explosions. On taxing him with the fact, he acknowledged it, but could give no account how it happened; and seemed well satisfied on producing his two birds, most completely peppered.

If

If only one lock is cocked, the wrong trigger may be drawn; and not answering the pull, whatever part of the work is weakest may be strained, or even broke.

From the practice of drawing the hinder trigger first, when birds are wild, and a second shot seldom to be had, I have seen persons shoot for several days together, without firing the right-hand barrel. By this means, it is evident that one barrel and lock will be worn out before the other. When only one half of a gun is thus brought into use, there seems to be no compensation for the extra weight: and surely a single-barrelled gun, with a reasonably larger charge, would make a better figure. Indeed, if your dogs are broke to lie down till you have reloaded, more shots may be frequently got with a single, than, where they are permitted to run in, with a double gun.

Whether the *aim* of a double or single gun suits your age best, must be determined by yourself. Though a random sight is more readily caught with the former, there seems a confusion in it, from the two muzzles, breeches, and locks, unfavourable to correctness; and it is so different from that of the latter, that, whenever you change from one to the other, you will hardly fail to find an inconvenience.

There is, indeed, a kind of double gun, known by the name of *Turnabout*, which, however little in use at present, has the following advantages over that which is in fashion:—

As there is no lock to be reached on the left side, there can be no plea for weakening the breech, by contracting its width.

There being only one trigger, no mistake can arise from it.

The aim being the same as with a single gun, no inconvenience can arise in changing, occasionally from one to the other.

The discharged barrel being regularly turned below the other, the two are equally used; as are also the hammers.

Those who never cock their gun till they raise it to the shoulder, cannot be guilty of loading with a lock cocked.

The muzzle of the barrel to be loaded being always uppermost, as the butt is on the ground, there is less probability of a charge being put into the wrong barrel; which, in loading hastily, sometimes happens. And I cannot but think that guns have actually been burst, from this mistake remaining undiscovered; all the blame being unjustly laid on the maker.

If, however, you should not be discouraged by the hazards which I have pointed out, the weight, and two-fold expence of a *double gun*, and its invidious name in case you should be reported to have trespassed on your neighbour with one in your hand, I shall give you a few hints on the management of it; concluding with some more general cautions.

If you have discharged only one barrel, and are reloading it, before you return the rammer be careful to secure the wadding of the unfired barrel, which, from the recoil, usually becomes loose. This is not only necessary, lest the shot should fall out, but for safety; as, in case of a space between the shot and wadding, the sudden resistance which the shot would meet with, on striking the wadding, might endanger the barrel. I know an instance of a hand being injured, a few years since, by a gun bursting, as it was judged, from this cause alone; for one barrel had been fired several times in succession, and this precaution

caution had not been taken with the other, which burst on the first discharge.

Whether you ram the unfired barrel before or after you have shotted the other, adopt one regular time for the operation, lest it should be entirely omitted. If you leave the rammer in the unfired barrel till you have poured shot into the other, be careful that none of it falls into that which holds the rammer, as it may jam, so as to give you considerable trouble.

If birds rise together, and near the shooter, it is not uncommon to see him spoil one, with the first barrel, that the other may be shot at a proper distance; and, if the first is shot well, the second has frequently got so far as to be only wounded, or missed. If there is a very small interval between the time of their rising, the *Turnabout* will answer your purpose as well as the common double gun; and I have shewn that it has some advantages over it.

Let me strictly enjoin you to forbear cocking your gun, till you are actually raising it to the shoulder: be assured, that it is perfectly unnecessary; and that if you are even in expectation of a rabbit crossing a narrow path before you, no advantage will be gained by it. But, if there should be any, a little reflection will convince you that it is too dearly purchased, by a practice which has given rise to so many accidents. I have a pleasure in considering that I have not only trained young sportsmen in the right way, but have reclaimed even old offenders from this dangerous habit.

I have seen a gun fired, unintentionally, by awkwardness in letting down the cock from the whole to the half-bent. To avoid this, be careful not to remove your thumb from the cock, till after having let it pass beyond the half-bent, and gently raising it again, you hear the sound of the sear catching the tumbler.

On account of guns being usually carried in the field with the muzzle pointed to the left, and the execrable practice of keeping them cocked, if you have occasion to shoot with a stranger, I shall advise you to plead for the right-hand station, that you *cannot hit a bird flying to the left*. With a gamekeeper, take the right hand without ceremony. In getting over a fence, except you are well assured of your new companion's care, it will be safer to compliment him with the honour of preceding you: an honour which, by the bye, in a thick black-thorn hedge, it may require some little speechifying to force upon his modesty. You will otherwise frequently find, that, while you were passing the hedge, his gun — cocked — had kept guard — with good aim at your back; and, except you file off as soon as you are clear, the same aim will be kept up till he is clear of the hedge likewise. Should you remonstrate, the usual answer is, "My dear sir, I assure you, I am remarkably careful."

Should he appear to consider a cocked gun as the best tool to beat bushes with, tell him you are too nervous to touch a feather in company, and get out of shot as fast as you can.

When you cross a ditch, be upon your guard, that, in case of falling, your muzzle may be immediately directed upwards. Few persons, indeed, have sufficient practice in falling, to bring this to a regular habit; but, remember that you *may* fall!

If you should think it necessary to put your gun into any attendant's hands, either for a time or to be carried home, let me recommend to you to secure the flint, or hammer, by some sort of case, which any man may invent and make of leather himself: or go a step farther, and draw the charge. I do not approve of shaking out the priming; in which case the gun will be considered as unloaded, except that the rammer is put into, and left in, the barrel. And it is a fact, that guns have been fired, when no priming has appeared in the pan.

I shall here point out a source of danger to which you are exposed, from the charge of powder which you are in the act of pouring into the barrel being inflamed, either by tow left in it after cleaning, or a part of the wadding remaining on fire within. I can hardly suppose this to have happened where card-wadding was used: it may from paper; but tow seems more hazardous. In some instances, the charge alone has been inflamed, the top of the flask having been removed in time, or the slider preventing communication with its contents. But it has happened that the whole flask has been blown up; and not many months since, in the case of a gentleman in a northern county, attended with the loss of sight. This hazard is easily obviated, by any method of detaching the measured charge of powder from the flask, before it is poured into the barrel.

In drying gunpowder, be careful to separate from your magazine, of whatever kind, the mere quantity which you wish to dry at once, suppose five or six charges: thus, in case of an accident, you may escape, like myself, with burnt eyebrows and eye-lashes.—But, should you pour into a shovel, unfortunately over heated, from your stock, even of a single pound, however *cerebri felicem*, nothing will save you.

I remember your laughing at my hyper-caution, when, handling various guns in the maker's shop, I shifted the muzzle, so that, at no one instant, any one was pointed at a limb of the several persons around us. I was not then exerting any particular care; the practice was habitual to me; and I wish to impress upon your mind, that, with respect to the muzzle being suffered, during the fraction of a second, to point towards any human being, *a gun should always be considered as loaded*. How have the numerous accidents happened, from the kitchen wit of terrifying the maids, by threatening to shoot them, but in presuming guns not to be loaded? In some of these cases, the trigger has been drawn unintentionally;—in others, with a view to study the passion of terror in the human countenance, (inexcusable thus, even in a painter) by snapping the lock;—sometimes, in a struggle, from persons interfering. This species of frolic, I fear, has not been totally confined to the kitchen;—but, on this head, I chuse to be silent.

I have not written thus, to deter you from a captivating amusement, but to enable you to enjoy it with greater security. Many of your friends could have told you all that I have done, and much more, but, till they shall take the trouble to do it, neglect-not what I have intended for your advantage.

RUSSIAN MANNERS.

Those who may conceive that the manners of the Russian take a tincture from his constitution, and that he is as rugged as he is hardy, will be astonished at the following account, which is given of them by a resident at Moscow:

THE gentleness of the Russians is universally remarked.— Would you believe that, in the
Play-

Play-house, the pit never hiss! They content themselves with not applauding bad actors; but, if the Play is not interesting, a conversation is begun, becomes almost general, and so noisy, that what is passing on the stage can no longer be heard; and if every person does not take part in it, those to whom it is disagreeable are too polite to shew their discontent.

I was yesterday at the Play-house. A Play of VISIN's was acted; it is one of the most favourite in the whole Russian collection; it is called the *Nidorost*, that is, "*The Scholar.*" I shall not carry you through all the details of this piece, which turns entirely upon the education which certain parents, ordinarily inhabiting the country, and lately arrived at Moscow for the education of their children, wish to give them. All the humour of the piece is founded on the industry of the son, the carelessness of the masters, and the blindness of the parents. The following is the *denouement*:—

The Aunt, a woman of accomplished manners, arrives to see her Nephew. They inform her of their incredible good fortune, in having found a French Preceptor, who is far above all praise. She wishes to see this admirable man.—He appears.—"What!" cries she; "This is the Coachman I had at Petersburgh."—"We are delighted that you know him!" say the parents." "He is then really a Frenchman!" and the latter, without troubling himself, advances to pay his respects to his *old acquaintance*—"He was, besides," says the Aunt, "a very good Coachman."—"Wonderful!" answered the parents; and, as it is much easier to manage a child than two horses, they are charmed with the acquisition they have made. The whole concludes with a general conversation, in which the metamorphosed Coachman takes his part, to the satisfaction of every person, &c.

RUSSIAN AMUSEMENTS.

Extract of a Letter from a Traveller, dated from Moscow.

FOR these three months have I now been traversing Russia, the only country in the world in which a man is worst received for money, and best by those whom he cannot pay; in which the innkeepers are the most slovenly and inattentive, and private families the most hospitable and kind. I know not well what to say of this contrast: I have found it sometimes just, and sometimes false; but, on the whole, I think that, for travellers, industry will still be better to be met with than hospitality.

At last I am at Moscow. Nothing can be more singular, in every respect, than the aspect of this city. It seems to contain two nations.—The one inhabit Palaces, speak French, converse about fashions and dresses, compose music, train horses to go to the Opera, give a thousand rubles a year for a house, and an hundred for a well-trained Canary-bird—The other lodge in huts, constructed in the manner of those of savages, wear long beards, know nothing of the Play-house, enervate themselves with drinking spirits, on Sundays quarrel about nothing like children, and are appeased in the same manner, as soon as two or three buckets of water are thrown on the disputants, which are always kept in readiness for this purpose, in the places where the people assemble. —On the one hand is civilization in all

all its luxury; on the other, the state which borders on barbarism. The difference of education thus forms the only cause of this most perceptible difference. Whoever he may be that presents himself to a Russian, will be well received, provided he can amuse. But the desire of amusement appears to be most powerful among the inhabitants of Moscow.

On the 1st of May, the whole city is in motion: all the carriages brilliant in appearance, all the liveries new and shewy, are on the promenade, called *The German Fables*, where they eat under tents and under trees. During the remainder of the summer, every person who has not fled from Moscow to the country, is to be seen constantly at the Vauxhall, in the Palace Gardens, in those of Count Orloff, of Paschkoff, &c.—But the winter is the true season of pleasure: on its approach, an hundred thousand persons return to Moscow: the streets, covered with snow, become so much the better: the ice of the Meska affords a new promenade; and the colds here have, as I am assured, a pleasantness altogether peculiar. I can, on Sundays, go and shew myself in a sledge or a carriage. In the street Pokroskaia, or figure away at the courses on the ice of the Meska.— " But take good care," said a man to me, who understood these things well, " that if your sledge is drawn by two horses, it is necessary that one of them should always gallop, and that his companion should at the same time trot, without disconcerting him."

However strange the above may appear to an Englishman, I have found that, if I neglected this generally observed regulation, I would do well, at least for a considerable time, not to shew myself in good company.

FRENCH THEATRICALS.

A New Play has been lately brought out in Paris, called *The Calvinists; or, Villars at Nismes*. The plot is as follows:—

A respectable Merchant, named *Daubusson*, has taken to his house the children of a proscribed Calvinist, and has collected the wrecks of their fortune. His son falls in love with the daughter of the proscribed Calvinist, and joins the troops of *Cavalier*, the chief of the rebels. *Daubusson*, though a Catholic, is exposed to great suspicion, and he is denounced to *Villars* as a favourer of the Calvinists.— This General, who assists with great reluctance in the measures which are taken against the Religionists, wishes to ascertain the truth of the charges against *Daubusson*, and fixes his head-quarters in his house. He immediately perceives him to be an honest man, and offers him his assistance; but *Daubusson*, who is conscious of the rectitude of his motives, persists in avowing all the charges brought against him. *Villars* is at a loss how to act, when the two children of the proscribed Calvinist throw themselves at his feet, and supplicate him in favour of their benefactor. The young girl pleads his cause with great earnestness, and at length succeeds. A perfidious friend, who had carried on a correspondence with the rebels, and who had secretly accused *Daubusson*, is detected by *Villars*, and punished. And, finally, *Cavalier* agrees to the propositions of the Marshal, and young *Daubusson*, who had been taken prisoner, is united to *Sophia*.

This piece was not very favourably received. Indeed the dreadful persecutions which have of late been experienced, make us feel but little interest in those of so remote a period.

TRICK

TRICK OF A FRENCH QUACK.

A Gentleman, after having ruined his fortune by extravagance, bethought himself of turning quack. He attempted at Paris without success, and then directed his views to the provinces. He arrived at Lyons, and announced himself as "*the celebrated Doctor Mantaccini, who can restore the dead to life!*" and he declared that, in fifteen days, he would go to the public church-yard, and excite a *general resurrection!*

This declaration excited violent murmurs against the Doctor, who, not in the least disconcerted, applied to the Magistrate, and requested he might be put under a guard, to prevent his escape, until he should perform his undertaking.

The proposition inspired the greatest confidence, and the whole city came to consult Doctor Mantaccini, and purchase his *Beaume de Vie*.

As the period for the performance of this miracle approached, the anxiety among the inhabitants of Lyons encreased. At length he received the following letter from a rich citizen:—

"The great operation, Doctor, which you are going to perform, has broke my rest. I have a wife buried for some time, who was a fury; and I am unhappy enough already, without her resurrection. —In the name of Heaven, do not make the experiment!—I will give you fifty Louis to keep your secret to yourself!"

In an instant after, two dashing *beaux* arrived, who, with the most earnest applications, entreated the Doctor not to revive their old father, formerly the greatest miser in the city; as, in such an event, they would be reduced to the most deplorable indigence. They offered him a fee of sixty Louis; but the Doctor shook his head in doubtful compliance.

Scarcely had they retired, when a young widow, on the eve of matrimony, threw herself at the feet of the Doctor, and with sobs and sighs implored his mercy. In short, from morn till night, the Doctor received letters, visits, presents, fees, to an excess that absolutely overwhelmed him. The minds of the citizens were so differently and violently agitated, some by fear, and others by curiosity, that the Chief Magistrate of the city waited upon the Doctor, and said—

"Sir, I have not the least doubt, from my experience of your rare talents, that you will be able to accomplish the resurrection in our church-yard the day after to-morrow, according to your promise; but I pray you to observe, that our city is in the greatest uproar and confusion, and to consider the dreadful revolution the success of your experiment must produce in every family. I entreat you, therefore, not to attempt it, but to go away, and thus restore the tranquility of the city. In justice, however, to your rare and divine talents, I shall give you an attestation in due form, under our seal, that you *can revive* the dead; and that it was our own fault we were not eye-witnesses of your power."

The certificate was duly signed and delivered, and Doctor Mantaccini went to work new miracles in some other place. In a short time he returned to Paris, loaded with gold; where he laughed at popular credulity, and spent immense sums in luxury and extravagance. A Lady, who was a downright *Charlatan* in love, assisted in reducing him to want; but he set out again on a provincial tour, and returned with a new fortune.

DIFFERENT

DIFFERENT OPINIONS ON THE SCARCITY.

"Quot homines, tot sententiæ."

To the EDITORS *of the* SPORTING MAGAZINE.

GENTLEMEN,

TO you, your readers, and the world in general, I announce, that it was only on Thursday last that I travelled in the stage-coach from Birmingham to London. That in the same coach were six others, namely, a child, two clergymen, a button-maker, an apothecary, and one more, who was neither a divine, nor an apothecary, nor a button-maker, but an old woman. We all appeared to be people of fine speculative dispositions, and deeply interested in what was passing in the world; yet, having nothing more to do with bread than to eat it; with the war than to support it; with taxes than to pay them; or with the laws than to obey them; it will naturally be supposed that such a party, in times so critical, with an opportunity so short of discussing subjects of importance, did not waste much of our time in silence, or compliments. The preliminaries were soon adjusted. The sun shone too bright to admit of a doubt that it was a very fine day; and the usual resolutions, that the road was dull, the coach uneasy, and the driver of it a tiresome dog, were carried with more unanimity than approbation. We then proceeded to take the sense of the coach upon the subject of the Scarcity of Corn. What was said on that occasion, I presume to transmit to you; and begin by informing you, that the conversation arose from one of my reverend companions asking of the button-maker, whether there was now any apprehension of disturbances at Birmingham?

Button-Maker.—All is quiet, Sir, at present; but God knows how long it may continue so—the price of corn does not fall. Those that have neither money, nor work, nor bread, must needs be poor, idle, and hungry; and if hunger breaks down stone-walls, no wonder if it breaks a baker's windows. But as long as the authors of these miseries find their account in the cause of them, the war must continue, I suppose; and the people starve on.

First Clergyman.—I am afraid the root of the evil is fixed more deeply than in the war. That, though long, can only be temporary; our's is a chronic disorder, and therefore more difficult to cure. Large farms, and the opulence of our farmers, are the cause of our distress. The quantity of corn in the country should regulate the market, and the market govern the farmer; whereas our farmers are now rich enough to direct the market, and the quantity of corn goes for nothing. The war has no more to do with it than——

Second Clergyman.—Your rich farmers! How singular it is, my dear Sir, that you so wilfully shut your eyes upon what forces it upon your observation! In the very nature of things, the rise and fall of corn in the market, must be as sure a sign of the scarcity or plenty of it, as the pointing of a weathercock is of the quarter from which the wind blows: one would think this proposition of itself sufficiently evident; even were it not supported in the present instance, by what every one who has eyes in his head, and walks about, must see, that the crop has this year been very deficient.

Apothecary.—I must confess, that what the gentleman says of his proposition,

proposition, no more meets my idea of the thing, than the sight, he alludes to, does the eyes, that I walk about with in my head. On the contrary, where I have observed, the corn has grown well, and perhaps was never got in in such good weather: and though the farmers have caught the fashion of complaining of the crop in general, ask them individually, and they will tell you they have no reason to be dissatisfied with their own. But will the gentleman account for the scarcity of other things by his short crop? Or will he say that cattle are scarce, or that feed is scarce? If the evil is general, the cause can never be so partial: and I am convinced, that it will be found to be nothing more or less than the increasing commerce and prosperity of the country, which having thrown an immense quantity of money into circulation, a depreciation of money, or, in other words, a rise of every thing must take place, of course; that rise naturally begins with the necessaries of life; but, in a little time, we shall see the price of labour, of manufactures, and the rent of land advanced in the same proportion; and then what cause will he have to complain, who pays double what he used to pay for his dinner, if he receives double wages for his work? The uneasiness we at present feel, is the sudden flush of health, the beginning of a universal glow.

Button maker.—Say, rather, the spasms of a general debility. It is the war that has given to those that had, and from those that had not it has——they have lost their nothing. It has made the poor less able to give a fair price, and the rich more able to ask an exorbitant one. The wealth you speak of, is an imaginary capital of funded debt, and so far from riches, is real poverty.

Old Woman.—My notion is, that till all forestallers are hanged, or, at least, a few for example's sake, we shall never get right again. And my husband says, he does not think the fault is in the farmers; for though they live well, they do not make fortunes, or they would leave off work, and live like gentlemen, as other folks do; but he says, it is the mealmen and cornfactors, who come in between those that grow the corn, and those that eat it, that do the mischief, and so I believe.

First Clergyman.—Indeed the farmers would not have it so much in their power to oppress the people, were it not for the country banks. These I look upon as great evils. He, who would otherwise be forced to sell his wheat immediately, to pay his rent, mortgages his stack to the banker, and having paid his landlord with the paper, waits till he can sell his corn at an enormous price. And the speedy communication now established between all parts of the country, together with the general diffusion of common learning, which enables farmers to correspond with each other more easily, tend to keep up the price uniformly throughout the kingdom.

Old Woman.—Aye: I always said what would come of all this reading and writing.

Second Clergyman.—The present distress can never be accounted for by any thing of so long standing as country banks. The sensation which they produced, would have been felt upon their first establishment; the crop of that year might have been delayed for a time; but upon the approach of the next harvest, the farmer must either have carried it there with precipitation, or lost the sale of it; and after

after that, the corn must have made its appearance in a regular manner, though perhaps some months later than before. The same reasoning applies to your other observation, and also to the method of selling corn by sample. No, Sir, it is a real scarcity, arising from a deficiency of two successive years.

Button-maker.—It arises from a bloody, expensive, unjust, and unnecessary war.

Clergyman.—It is not war, but famine.

Apothecary.—It is no famine, nor even scarcity.

{ *Old Woman.*— Those vile forestallers—
1st Clergyman.—Those pernicious country banks—
2d Clergyman—If there was not a real scarcity—
Apothecary.—The immense influx of wealth—
Button-maker.—To gratify a set of———
Myself.—All these, perhaps, may——— } *All together.*

But the confusion was now become general; and I could collect no more, for each was determined to discharge himself of his whole system, before he attended to what another had to offer. It is strange, that though all were speakers, no order should be kept; and impossible to say what might have been the issue of the debate, had not the loud cries of the terrified infant caused, perhaps, a very seasonable interruption of it. H. P.

THE BAILIFFS BAFFLED.

SOME few months ago, a Mr. C. a Frenchman, being much in debt, was beset continually by the Bailiffs; and being, one morning, informed by the maid of the house where he lodged, that the Philistines were hanging about the door, he immediately packed up every article he had of apparel, even to his shirt, hastened into bed, and requested the servant to secure his box in her room, telling her if they asked for him, to say he was at home. They knocked, and enquired; and being answered in the affirmative, were directed to his garret. Tapping at his door, they were told to come in; and, going to the bed-side, they asked if he was Mr. C.?

"Yes."

"Then we have a writ against you, for———"

"Ha! Ha!" said Monsieur.— "Let-a me see!—Ha! You take my *body!* your writ say."

"Yes; you must get up, and go with us.—Come, make haste, and dress yourself!"

"Begar, I have no dress!"

"No dress!—What do you mean by that?—Come, come, we can't loiter here: get up!"

"Upon my vard, all my dress at de pawnbroker.—You take my *body!* your writ say.—No dress." And immediately he sprang from the bed *in puris naturalibus*, and danced about the room. Being a perfect *Esau*, he made a most grotesque appearance.

The myrmidons in vain insisted on his dressing; while he reiterated "Take my body!"

"Why, who will take you in such a state?"

"I cannot tell," said he.—"You take my body!"

"D—n your body!—Come along, Flannagan!—We'll have him as yet, some how or other— D—n his body!" and for that time they left him.

The Frenchman hastily equipped himself, and instantly changed his lodging. In a few weeks after, the *powerful arrester of mortals* seized him, and for ever freed him from trouble.

MODERN ARABIAN CARAVANS.

The following account is given by Rosieres, one of the French Savants, in a letter dated from Suez, the 11th of November, of the manner in which the Arabs march and encamp, and of their customs and mode of living in the Desart.

THAT which surprised us most on our joining a Caravan of Mount Sinai Arabs, was the order with which the Arabs were encamped, which is not usual with the Turkish Caravans. Every tribe, and every section, is encamped separately. Each camp is divided into small parties of seven or eight Arabs, round a fire, preparing in common the provisions which will be necessary during the march of the next day.

These preparations occupy a part of the evening: they are principally employed in making bread. They mix their flour in a small wooden trough, and make paste without any leaven, with which they make most excellent cakes. In order to dress them, they make a hole in the ground, and, after having heated it, they put the cakes in, and then cover up the hole with camel's dung. They do not use copper plates, as the other Arab tribes do. With this bread they eat a few handfuls of beans, which are taken out of the provisions belonging to the camels, and which they boil in order to soften. This is their only nourishment during their journey. They take coffee regularly twice a day; and the necessary utensils for preparing it form a considerable part of their baggage.

These Arabs appear but little attached to the Mahometan religion: many of them know nothing more of the Koran than the name of Mahomet. Perhaps, when we know them better, we shall discover more information among them. They are almost all cloathed and armed in the same manner: their principal covering is a long large robe, open before, and without any sleeves: there are only two holes, through which they pass their arms. This garment is of coarse wool, and at the top it is striped black and white. The children have no other covering; but the men wear underneath it a kind of shirt of white wool, and about the waist they wear a leathern belt. Their boots are made of buffalo's skin, very clumsily, but they are sufficient to secure their feet from the flints, of which the road is full.— Every one of them, without exception, is armed with a two-edged dagger, very crooked, and some of them are very richly mounted; but the quality of the blades are nearly all alike. Those who have the best arms, are those who defend the Caravans, and they carry a match-lock.

They seemed very contented at our travelling with them over the mountains. Citizen Coutelle and I visited their encampments, and they shewed us the greatest kindness: they gave us coffee, and would force us to eat some bread dressed in camel's dung.—They seem, in general, very much contented with the treatment they experience from the French, and with the protection which is given to their trade. The Sheiks of the different tribes praised the magnificence of the Commander in Chief, who had made them presents of very fine pelices the evening of their departure. We are in as much security among them, as among the French.

In seven days we shall reach Tor, which is where we shall rest one or two days, before we set out for Mount Sinai. We are determined, if it is possible, to advance to the

Gulph

Gulph of Acaba: if we succeed, we shall be able to obtain pretty authentic information of the whole peninsula between the two gulphs, which terminate the Red Sea in the southern part.

CLERKENWELL SESSIONS.
Monday, January 13th.

THE business at this place commenced this day, before William Mainwaring, Esq.

CART-DRIVER.

Edward Thornton was indicted for assaulting Captain Durnford.—It appeared that Captain Durnford was in a one-horse chaise, on the evening of the 8th of November, near Kilburn Wells: there not being room to pass the cart of which the Defendant had the care, and he not being near it, Capt. D. was induced to touch the fore-horse, in order to be able to pass it. Immediately the Defendant coming up, abused Capt. D. and asked him what right he had to touch his horses. Capt. D. then offered to take his number, but was opposed by the Defendant, who struck him on the shoulder; upon which Capt. D. knocked him into a ditch, and told him he would stand over him until he told him where he lived, and the number of his cart, he having, previous to this, plastered it all over with mud, so that the name or number could not be perceived. Two men came out of a field, to the assistance of the defendant, and Capt. D. found it necessary to return to the chaise for his sword, with which he kept the assailants at bay until he made the man inform him who he was.

The Jury immediately found the Defendant—*Guilty.*

The chairman said, the public were much obliged to Captain Durnford, for having brought the Defendant's conduct before the Court; that drivers of carts had no right to prevent any person from looking at their number, whether they had been acting amiss or not, but in the present instance, the Defendant had acted in a very culpable manner. The court therefore sentenced him to be imprisoned in the house of correction for one month.

POACHERS.

Francis Mattenly and *James Mattenly* were indicted for assaulting William John Arabin, Esq. on the 15th of July, at Drayton, in Middlesex.

The Prosecutor stated, that, knowing the Defendants to be poachers, and seeing them, on the day stated in the indictment, with an unlawful net, fishing in a small river near Drayton, he immediately went up to them, being a Magistrate, and in the King's name demanded them to deliver up their net. They refused so to do, at the same time damning him and the King; on which he endeavoured to lay hold of the net, in order to wrest it from them, when he was immediately struck by the father, Francis Mattenly. He still persevered in endeavouring to obtain the net, but was unsuccessful; when the young Mattenly came to his father's assistance with a long pike, and made a thrust at the Prosecutor, in the same manner as a soldier does when he charges with fixed bayonet, and he was obliged to relinquish his purpose.

A witness was called to substantiate General Arabin's testimony. He stated, that he was upon a haystack at the distance of near a hundred yards, and that all he knew of the matter was, that they all appeared to be in a *bumbug.*

For the Defendants, Richard Bennet was called, who said, that he was in company with them when fishing; that General Arabin came up, and caught James Mattenly by the collar, saying, "You rascal! what business have you here?" To which he replied, "I hope I have not done any wrong! I did not mean to offend you."—The Prosecutor then said, "If I had my pistols, I would shoot you."— He then told his son, who was present, to fetch his pistols: they, however, were not brought.

This witness's testimony was confirmed by two other witnesses, with the addition of a Mr. Rolfe, who stated the water where they were fishing to be on his grounds; and that he had given permission to them to fish in it.

The Jury found the Defendants *Not Guilty.*

WESTMINSTER SESSIONS.

ASSAULT.

LAST month, *Dalleway, Clarke*, and *King*, three roaring sons of Bacchus, were indicted for an assault upon a sentinel in St. James's Park. It appeared these dashing heroes, one of whom is a Bankers' clerk, one the mate of an Indiaman, and the other a tradesman in the city, had indulged in copious libations at the shrine of the jolly god, and, hot with the Tuscan grape, were proceeding through St. James's Park, in their way to their head-quarters. It was at that hour when night is at odds with morning; and their noisy revelry rent the spheres, and awoke even the sober inhabitants of the Royal Palace. The sentinel, astounded at the unexpected invasion of these vociferous knights, or rather knights-errant, retarded their progress with fixed bayonet, and was preparing to convey them to *durance vile* till morning; but they, nothing dismayed, threatened to divest him of his arms and accoutrements, and exhibit him *in puris naturalibus.*— They would have carried this threat into instant execution, but that they were prevented by the arrival of the guard. The ensign, who commanded it, was at a loss how to deal with such determined opponents, and referred to the serjeant for advice. They told the ensign, they had bravely stood volleys of grape-shot the whole evening, and did not care for any he could fire at them: they added he was a s—y-nose boy, and advised him to go to school again. They were, however, secured, and delivered over to the secular arm.

These facts were all proved; but, as the delinquents had not exceeded threats, they were dismissed with a suitable lecture.

ANECDOTE.

A Person happening to call one day upon an acquaintance, found him exercising his wife with that discipline that *Jobson* tries in the Farce of the *Devil to Pay*; and, being hurt at the ungenerous task undertaken by his friend, he begged of him, by all the ties of honour, to forbear, at the same time asking him the occasion of such severe treatment.

"The occasion is," said the enraged husband, "that she will not be *Mistress in her own house.*"

His friend expressed great astonishment at the answer, and remarked, "that the omission was such as, he believed, no woman ever gave her husband occasion to thrash her for before."

"Ah! but, by G—d," said the husband, "my wife won't be *Mistress*, because she wants to be *Master!*"

EXTRAORDINARY CHARACTER.

Memoirs of Lord Rokeby.

MATTHEW Robinson Morris, eldest son of Sir Septimius Robinson, Knt. was born at Mount Morris, at his father's house, in Horton, near Hythe, in the county of Kent, in the year 1712. His early years were spent in this place, till he went to Westminster School, whence he was admitted at Trinity Hall, Cambridge, a pensioner, where he took his degree of bachelor of laws, and was soon after elected a fellow of the society, a place which he retained to the day of his death. It is not unusual at Trinity Hall, for men of large fortune to retain their fellowships. The society consists of twelve fellows, two of whom only are clergymen, and perform the regular and necessary duties of the college, such as those of tutor, lecturer, dean: but the other ten fellows seldom or never make their appearance in Cambridge, unless at the twelve days of Christmas, at which time the usual hospitality of that season of the year is conspicuous in the college; and the lay-fellows, having enjoyed good eating and drinking, and examined the college accounts, return to Doctor's Commons, the Inns of Court, or their country seats. Mr. Robinson, in the early part of his life, used sometimes to be of these parties, where his company was always acceptable, and his absence always regretted. As heir to a country gentleman of considerable property, he was not compelled to apply his abilities in the usual pursuits of a laborious and now almost technical profession; he enjoyed an introduction to the higher circles of life, and being possessed of the advantages of a liberal education and accomplished manners, he united the studies of the scholar with the occupations of a gentleman, and divided his time very agreeably between Horton, London, Bath, and Cambridge. In this period of his life, the celebrated peace of Aix-la-Chapelle attracted the attention of Europe; and the place appointed for negociation, at all times, from its waters, of great resort, was more than usually filled with good company. Soon after the ambassadors had here taken up their abode, Mr. Robinson escorted Lady Sandwich to this grand scene of gallantry and politics, where the classical taste of Lord Sandwich, the eccentricity of Wortley Montague, among his own countrymen, the prudence of Prince Kaunitz, the solidity of the Dutch deputies, and the charms of their ladies, for the Dutch belles carried away the palm of beauty at this treaty, afforded him an inexhaustible fund of instruction and entertainment. Having no official employment, and appearing in that once-envied character of an English gentleman, his company was generally sought after, and the ladies of the higher class thought their parties incomplete without his presence, and the *corps diplomatique* bowed to his credentials.

Among the women, none more sprightly, none more ready to join innocent mirth, or to be the subject of it, when a mistake in his language might give occasion to pleasantry; but foreigners admired the strength of his character, when his conversation was suited to graver subjects, and no man presumed to laugh at his mistakes, without repenting of his temerity. Respected by the men, and acceptable to the women, he was noted here for a singularity which he retained during his whole life, a remarkable attachment to bathing. He surprised the medical men by the length of his

his stay in the hot-bath, very often two hours or more at a time, and by going in and out without any of the precautions which were then usual, and which future experience has proved to be unnecessary. On his return to England, nothing particular happened to him till his election to Parliament by the city of Canterbury, which place he represented, and, we may add, really represented, for two successive Parliaments. His neighbourhood to Canterbury, had naturally introduced him to some of the higher classes of that city; but he had no idea of a slight acquaintance with a few only of his constituents, he would know and be known to them all. His visits to Canterbury gratified himself and them. They were visits to his constituents, whom he called on at their shops and their looms, walked within their market-places, spent the evening with at their clubs. He could do this from one of his principles, which he had studied with the greatest attention, and maintained with the utmost firmness,—the natural equality of man. No one was more sensible than himself of the advantages and disadvantages of birth, rank, and fortune. He could live with the highest, and he could also live with the lowest in society; with the forms necessary for an intercourse with the former class, he was perfectly well acquainted, and he could put them in practice; to the absence of these restraints, he could familiarize himself, and could enter into casual conversation with the vulgar, as they are called, making them forget the difference of rank, as much as he disregarded it: hence, perhaps, there never was a representative more respected and beloved by his constituents, and his attention to the duties of Parliament entitled him to their veneration. Independent of all parties, he uttered the sentiments of his heart; he weighed the propriety of every measure, and gave his vote according to the preponderance of argument. The natural consequence of such a conduct was, in the first Parliament, a disgust with the manners of the house; and he would have resigned his seat at the general election, if his father had not particularly desired him to make one more trial, and presented him at the same time with a purse, not such as has lately been thought necessary, for the party to pay his election expences. Mr. Robinson was re-elected, and what will astonish the generality of members, made no demand on his father for election bills; for, after paying every expence with liberality, he found himself a gainer, in a considerable sum, by the election. Corruption had not then made such dreadful havock in the mind, as it has been our destiny to lament in a subsequent period; yet Mr. R. found himself uneasy in the performance of his duty. He conceived that a Member of Parliament should carry into the house a sincere love of his country, sound knowledge, attention to business, and firm independence—That measures were not to be planned and adopted in a minister's parlour, nor the House of Commons to be a mere chamber of Parliament to register his decrees—That in the House of Commons every member was equal; that it knew no distinction of minister, county-member, city-member, or borough-member. That each individual member had a right to propose, to assist in deliberation, aid by his vote in carrying or rejecting a measure, according to the dictates of his own mind; and that the greatest traitors, with which a country could be curst, were such persons as would enter into Parliament without any intention

tion of studying its duties, and examining measures, but with a firm determination to support the minister or his opponents, according as the expectation or actual enjoyment of a place, pension, or emolument derived from administration, led them to enlist under the banners of one or the other party. Even, in his time,' he thought he saw too great confidence placed in the heads of party—too little reliance on private judgment—too little attention to parliamentary duties. The uniform success of every ministerial measure did not accord with his ideas of a deliberative body, and he determined to quit a place in which he thought himself incapable of promoting the public good; and where he was determined not to be aiding or abetting in any other measures. To the great regret of his constituents, he declined the offer of representing them at the next election; and no future entreaties could induce him to resume an occupation in which, as he told them, better eyes were required than his to see, better ears to hear, and better lungs to oppose the tricks of future ministers.

By the death of his father, in the second period of his parliamentary life, Mr. Robinson came into possession of the paternal estate, and had now a full opportunity of realizing his own schemes of life.— About twelve miles from Canterbury, on the ancient Roman road leading to the Portus Lemanus, the present Lympne, by turning a few paces to the left, the walker, who has been fatigued as much by the uniformity as the roughness of the road, feels, on a sudden, his heart expanded by a most extensive prospect, which he commands from a lofty eminence. Before him, and under his feet, at a distance of five or six miles, commences the vast flat, known by the name of Romney Marsh, which, with the Weald of Kent, is bounded to his eye by Dungeness, Beachy Head, and the hills of Sussex and Surrey, and the ridge of hills on a part of which he stands, and which runs through nearly the middle of the county of Kent into Surrey. Turning eastward, he perceives the sea, and has a glimpse of the coast of France. His view is bounded by hills still higher, as he turns to the north; but from the top of these hills, at half a mile distance from the spot on which he stands, he commands the same extensive prospect over the Marsh and West Kent, which is enriched on a fine day by the view of the coast of France from Boulogne to Calais, seeming scarcely to be separated from the island. At the bottom of these hills stands the family mansion, a substantial brick house, with offices suited to the residence of a man with four or five thousand a year. When Mr. R. came to the estate, there were about eight hundred acres round the house, partly in his own occupation, partly let out to tenants: they were allotted into fields of various dimensions, bounded by the substantial hedges so well known to be the ornament of Kent, but cutting the ground into too many minute parts for picturesque beauty. There was a garden walled in, and suitable roads to the house. Mr. R. took the whole of this land into his own occupation as soon as possible; and nature, with his occupancy, began to resume her rights. The only boundaries on his estate were, soon, only those which separated his land from that of his neighbours. Adieu to the use of gates or stiles in the interior; they were left to gradual decay. The soil was not disturbed by the labours of horse and man; the cattle had free liberty to stray wherever they pleased; the trees were no longer dishonoured

noured by the axe of the woodman; the pollards strove to recover their pristine vigour; the uniformity of hedges and ditches gradually disappeared; the richest verdure cloathed both hills and valleys; and the master of the mansion wandered freely in his grounds, enjoying his own independence and that of the brute creation around him.

The singularity of this taste excited naturally a great deal of curiosity, and, as usual, no small degree of censure. But, whatever may be objected on the score of profit, it is certain that the gain on the scale of picturesque beauty was, we might almost say, infinite. In a national view, the subject admits of much discussion; but the question has seldom been fairly stated and argued. The point is, could these acres have produced so much food, and cloathing, and implements for manufactures, if they had been subject to tillage and the usual mode of agriculture? In these times of agricultural curiosity, the question becomes interesting; but the present limits do not permit us to enter into the whole of Mr. R's views in the management of his affairs. But the gaps in the hedges, the growing up of the pollards, and the verdure of the grounds, might have been supportable, if the coach-roads also had not disappeared, the coach-house become useless, the gardens been trodden under foot by horses and oxen, and the hay-lofts superfluous. At the same time that nature resumed her rights over his fields, she took full possession of the master, and gave him the active use of his limbs. The family coach stirred not from its place to the day of his death: he seldom got into a chaise, and performed long journeys on foot. Naturally of a tender and delicate constitution, he thus became hardened to all weathers, and enjoyed his faculties and spirits to the day of his death. Indulging himself in these peculiarities, in which by the way, to say the worst of them, he was no man's enemy but his own, he kept up a considerable intercourse with his neighbours, and a correspondence with characters eminent in the political world: he published a pamphlet in the American war, replete with sound sense, and which procured, among other marks of respect, a journey from London to Bath, by a person with the express view, and extreme desire, of conversing with its author. He reprobated, during the whole of that unnatural contest, the conduct of administration; and the men of Kent, who were not at that time subdued by ministerial influence, listened with pleasure to its firm opponent, at their county meetings.

(To be continued).

Extraordinary Incident.

On Monday, the 5th Inst. the following very extraordinary Incident occurred at St. Ive's, in Cambridgeshire.

A Bullock walked into the passage of the Royal Oak public-house, in that town; and the stair-case door being open, it went up stairs into the dining-room, and run with such violence against the front window (which was a sash) as to drive the whole of the window-frame into the street, where the animal fell also (the height of more than ten feet), but, apparently, without receiving any material injury, although so much terrified that it ran with great precipitancy down to the bridge; and being stopped there, it leaped over the side thereof into the river, when it was carried down the current so rapidly, from a very high flood, that it has never since been heard of.

For

For the SPORTING MAGAZINE.

THE EQUESTRIAN PHILOSOPHER.

A Philosophical traveller, in his journey through the world, was my honest friend Jack Easy.— Jack came to a good fortune at the death of his father, and mounted his hobby without its ever having been properly broke in: he cantered over the plains of *Fancy*, went off in a full gallop to the road of *Dissipation*, and leaped over all the five-barred gates of *Advice* and *Discretion*. It may naturally be supposed, that, before long, his filly gave him a fall: poor Jack came down, sore enough; but he only shook himself, brushed off the dirt of the road, and mounted again in as high spirits as ever, excepting that he now began to sit firmer in the saddle, and to look about him. This, however, did not hinder him from getting into a swamp called a *Law-Suit*, where he remained a considerable time before he could get out. His fortune was now reduced from some thousands to a few hundreds; and, by this time, no man better knew the way of *Life* than my friend Jack Easy.— He had been through all the dirty cross-roads of *Business, Money-lending, Bankruptcy,* and *Law*; and had, at last, arrived at *a gaol*.

My friend Jack, however, did not despond. He consoled himself with the reflection that he was a single man: some of his misfortunes were the consequences of his own imprudence, others of unforeseen accidents, and most of them originated from his good-nature and generosity. He, however, *never excused*; he lumped them all together, took them in good part, and blamed nobody but himself: he whistled away his troubles, and repeated—

I am out of Fortune's power!
He, who's down, can sink no lower.

The Goddess, however, put on her best smiles, and paid Jack a visit in the King's Bench, in the shape of a handsome *legacy*. Jack smiled at the thing, being, as he called it, so extremely *apropos*, and once more mounted his nag. He now rode more cautiously, turning into the road of *Economy*, that led to a comfortable inn with the sign of *Competency* over the door. He had borrowed a martingale from an old hostler, called *Experience*; and he now, for the first time in his life, used a *curb*. He began already to find, that, though he did not gallop away as formerly, yet he went on his journey pleasantly enough.— Some *dashing* riders passed him, laughing at his jog-trot pace; but he had no occasion to envy them long; for, presently, some of them got into *ruts*, others were stuck fast in *bogs* and *quagmires*, and the rest were thrown from their saddles, to the great danger of their necks. Jack Easy, mean while, jogged on merrily: hot or cold, wet or dry, he never complained: he now preferred getting off, and opening a gate, rather than leaping over it; and smiled at an obstacle, as at a turnpike where he must necessarily pay toll.

The man who is contented, either to walk, trot, or canter through *Life*, has by much the advantage of his fellow-travellers: he suits himself to all paces, and seldom quarrels with the tricks which the jade *Fortune* is sometimes disposed to play him. You might now see Jack Easy walking his hobby along the road, enjoying the scene around him, with contentment sparkling in his eyes. If the way happened to be crowded with horsemen and carriages, you might observe him very readily taking his own side of the road, and letting them pass. If it began to rain, or blow, Jack only pulled up the collar of his great coat.

flapped his hat, and retreated to the little hedge, that *Philosophy* afforded him, till the storm was over.—Thus my friend, Jack Easy, came an with a jog-trot to the end of his journey, leaving his example behind him for the good of other travellers, as a kind of *finger-post*.

EXTRAORDINARY SPORTING
INTELLIGENCE, &c.

To the EDITORS *of the* SPORTING
MAGAZINE.

GENTLEMAN,

IF you think the following Sporting Occurrences worthy of insertion, by giving them a place in your entertaining Magazine, you will oblige, your's, &c.
A SUBSCRIBER.

"On Wednesday, the 24th of December, the hounds of Mr. Loder threw off at Eaton Furzes, and after drawing a large scope of heath country, were proceeding to Wytham Woods (belonging to the Earl of Abingdon), when they found an out-lying Fox, near Whitby-Farm, who, upon being roused, went off in high stile, the hounds close at him, over Cummer Meadow, Farnover Common, and through Stroud Coppice, to Wytham Great Woods; thence through Morley Wood, and across the open country to Stone's Heaths; thence through Brancomb Coppice, to Foxcomb Hill, and into those large extensive coverts known by the name of Bagley Woods. Refusing the shelter this covert offered, (the earth not being stopped he boldly passed through, and taking the open country again, made through the village of Wootten on to Besselsleigh, towards Tubney Wood, nearly reaching which, he was headed by some woodmen, and bent his course to Appleton Common; leaving which, he made again to Besselsleigh, and making for Tubney Warren, was run into, in a most gallant stile, near a farmyard, after a most severe chase of two hours and three quarters, and supposed to have run at least thirty miles.—Only eight of the original field in at the death."

DUKE OF GRAFTON'S HOUNDS.

Monday, January 5, 1801.

"FOUND at fifteen or twenty minutes past twelve, P. M. Unkennelled at Fakenham Wood, skirted Sapiston Groves, through Bardwell, to the left for Stanton Groves; through Dovehouse Wood, skirting Wicken, crossed the Grandel for Stanton High-wood, Hepworth North-common End, and Barningham Heath in a line for Fakenham Wood; then turned short to the right, through the inclosures between Coney Weston and Barningham, to Market Weston Fen. He was then headed up to Weston-church, and made from thence, round by Thelnetham, to Hopton Common. He then made away for the south end of Garboldisham Common, across the river to Garboldisham Old Plantation, skirted all the covers, and made the point to East Harling steeple; turned sharp to the right, and away by Uphall for the borders of Lopham Common; headed, and crossing Harling-hill Heath and Field, made for Quiddenham High Grove through Mr. Gooch's meadows, over the bridge between Eccles and Quiddenham, up to Wilby, over the warren to Buckenhammill; then pointing to Banham church, turned to the left for Buckenham New Inclosures. There tally-hoed, and ran him into a field to the east of Buckenham town, in Norfolk, and killed at half-past four o'clock."

On

On the Monday following, the same hounds unkennelled a fox at Pakenham Wood; which, after a chase of more than two hours and three-quarters, they killed in Hengrave Park.

THE MARQUIS OF EXETER'S STATE BED.

A subject of general conversation among the higher circles is, Lord Exeter's Bed, which is extraordinary for stile and elegance. The following particulars may not be unacceptable to our Fashionable Readers.

THE bedstead is, with a canopy top, at least eighteen feet high; the dome is of crimson velvet, the hangings of crimson satin lined with white satin, and a correspondent fringe of crimson and silver. Three fluted columns, with very highly finished Corinthian capitals, instead of a single pillar, appear at the foot of the bed, three on each side. The family arms are placed on the head-board, richly carved and gilt. On the returns of the cornice are likewise the arms; and the coronet is in the centre, in raised gold. The coverlet is of white satin, with a very magnificent embroidery in gold; the blankets of the finest swansdown, and the mattresses are finished in the same stile as the bed. The height is six feet, and the ascent is by steps affixed on each side. The bed is upon a retiring principle: by means of swivels, the whole paraphernalia of a *sanctum sanctorum* disappears, and then it exhibits a throne or state drawing-room, where the Marchioness may receive the Sons and Daughters of Fashion in appropriate *costume*.—The expence of this superb bed is said to be nearly three thousand pounds.

MRS. CHAMPNEY'S MASQUERADE.

AN elegant suite of apartments were thrown open at Orchardleigh-house, Bath, for the reception of masks, who, to the number of two hundred, assembled at an early hour. In order to heighten the hilarity of the entertainment, all dominoes were excluded. The characters were numerous; and these, by their frequent change of dress, added apparently to the catalogue of merry mortals. Among the most prominent were

A Jeffery Wild-Goose, in search of his daughter.
An Owl.
A lame Fidler.
Punch.
A most beautiful figure, in the dress of a Christ's Hospital Boy.
A Fury, clothed in the terrors of infernal paraphernalia, pursuing an Orestes.
Two chattering Barbers.
A Dancing Bear.
A pretty Milk-maid.
An elegant representative of a Fille de Patmos; and
A French Taylor, *bien babille*, galloping on a very magnificent goose.

The last mask was exquisite; and, by the drollery of its appearance, and the novelty of its accoutrements, preserved its fascination throughout the whole of the entertainment.

MIRTH IN A MASK.

AN original and comical scene, at the masked ball given on occasion of the marriage of the Dauphin to the Archduchess of Austria, afforded much diversion to Louis XV.

A beaufet, splendidly furnished, offered refreshments in profusion to the

the company at the ball.—A mask, in a yellow domino, came there frequently, and made dreadful havock among the cooling liquors and exquisite wines, and all the solid provisions. No sooner did this mask disappear, than he came back again, more thirsty and more hungry than ever. He was observed by some masks, who shewed him to others: the yellow domino became the object of universal curiosity. His Majesty wishing to see him, and anxious to know who he was, had him followed. It was found that this was a domino belonging in common to the Hundred Swiss, who, putting it on alternately, succeeded each other at this post, which was not the worst in the room.

It is well known, that one of the Hundred Swiss, who is equal to three or four men in corpulence, devours full as much as ten: so that it was just as if a thousand mouths had been fed at the beaufet.

LETTER *from* THESE WORKING TAYLORS *to their* MASTER, *respecting an Advance of Wages*.
SIR,

WE beg leave to say as how that your letter of *half a yard* long won't do. Your proposal is out of all *measure*. We are half starved, having nothing but *shreds* and *patches*, from Butchers stalls and Cooks shops, to maintain ourselves and little *minikin* babes. We should deserve a strait *waistcoat*, if we was to agree to what you have *cut out* for us. You may put yourself in a *pucker*, and make as great a *piece of work* as you please; but it won't *mend* matters, for we are resolved to remain stiff as *buckram* to our cause, even though not a *remnant* of us should be saved. We know you to be as sharp as a *needle*, and that you have not the heart to give us the value of a *skean* to eat, nor a *thimble*-full to drink, though we ply our *skirts* to your shop-board at least fourteen hours in the day. Once, indeed, you did give poor old Cuddy a drop of beer, when his fingers were bit by the *goose*; but it was so sour, that it gave the poor fellow a *stitch* in his side, and such a *twist* in his guts, that he has been ever since as thin as a *bodkin*. The Doctor thinks it has bred a *tape*-worm in him; but you laugh in your *sleeve* at his sufferings.

You say, that there *seams* to be a conspiracy among us. We have nothing to do with any such *seams*, but we are determined not to live in such *sheer* distress as we have done; and you shall find you may chance to *prick your fingers*, if you think it *fitting* to attack our *pockets* any further. Our *collar* is raised, and we would rather come to *cuffs* than give up a *needle* full of what we have asked. If it *suits* you to give enough to *line* our bellies properly, well and good: if not, we shan't care a *button* for your threats, though you tell us our existence hangs on a *thread*, and that you will have us *gather'd* in a prison.

So, sir, being *all of a cloth*, we find ourselves, your humble servants,

PETER CHEAPER,
CUTHBERT CABBAGE,
NEMO NINTH.

ATTEMPT TO COMMIT A RAPE.

Hicks's Hall, Clerkenwell, Jan. 13.

FREDERICK Sedgmond was indicted for an assault upon Elizabeth Bramwell, a young girl, apparently about fifteen years of age. The circumstances of this case, which excited a considerable degree

degree of sympathy towards the Prosecutrix, were these:—

She had for three years lived as servant in the family of the Earl of Besborough; and, during the whole of that period, her conduct had been modest and exemplary in every respect. The Defendant had been employed in the service of the same Nobleman, as porter, for the space of five years: and, till the present transaction, had deported himself with regularity and propriety.

On the 2d of November last, Lord and Lady Besborough were out upon a visit, and had most of their servants with them. Such female servants as were left behind had gone out, and left the house with no other persons in it than the Prosecutrix and the Defendant. The former had remained at home, because she expected some friend to call and drink tea with her.

About one o'clock she sat down to dinner by herself, when the Defendant entered the room. She was somewhat surprised at his intrusion, and asked him what he wanted. He made no reply, but seized hold of her, and was proceeding to take most unwarrantable liberties with her. Dreadfully alarmed at the dangerous situation she was in, she immediately lost all recollection, and fell into violent fits. How long she continued in them, she knew not; but, when she in some degree recovered, she perceived the Defendant close by her; and, from the disordered state of her own dress, as well as his, was but too well persuaded of the iniquitous purpose he had in contemplation.—He dragged her to a room in the back part of the house, and, holding a knife in one hand, and throwing his arm about her neck, threatened to take her life, if she refused to submit to his wishes.

Terrified at this action, she again relapsed into fits. When she had a second time recovered herself, she, by a violent effort, disengaged herself from the prisoner, and rushed up stairs to her room, where she locked herself in.—She looked out of the window, and in a short time saw the friend she expected at the door; upon which she went down, and let her in. Her agitation, at this time, was beyond all description. She related the cause of it to her friend, who remained with her until some of the servants returned.

As the evening advanced, she grew worse, and at length gave way to such strong hysterics, that it was with difficulty she could be held. She was conveyed to bed, and watched the whole night by one of the female servants. Till two o'clock she continued raving, calling upon her parents, and Mrs. Peters (the lady who was Lord Besborough's housekeeper), to save her. In her delirium, she repeatedly called upon them to keep Frederick away, who, she exclaimed, intended to murder her.

The woman who was with her having occasion to leave the room, in order to get a pillow to raise her head, found the defendant at the door of her chamber. He enquired how the prosecutrix was; and, upon being told her life was in danger, manifested the utmost degree of terror, and absconded from the house.—The prosecutrix continued so ill, that she could scarcely be moved in her bed. She received every necessary advice of the faculty, but it was near a fortnight before she perfectly recovered.

The evidence did not go the length of inferring that the last outrage had been committed on this unfortunate girl; on the contrary, the probability was, that the sufferings she experienced, after she had

had been put to bed, were the result of the violent agitation of spirits, while she was under the dominion of phrenzy. Such were the leading features of this case.

The defence consisted merely of such arguments as the ingenuity of the Defendant's Counsel could urge. The nature of the transaction did not admit of any witnesses being called in his behalf.

The Jury pronounced him Guilty,—and the court sentenced him to one years imprisonment.

FRENCH DEXTERITY.

SOME months ago, Mr. C——, a Frenchman, being much in debt, was beset continually by the Bailiffs; and being, one morning, informed by the maid of the house where he lodged, that the Philistines were hanging about the door, he immediately packed up every article he had of wearing apparel, even to his shirt, hastened into bed, and requested the servant to secure his box in her room, telling her, if they asked for him, to say he was at home—they knocked and inquired—and being answered in the affirmative, were directed to his garret: tapping at the door, they were told to come in, and going to the bed-side, they asked if he was Mr. C——. "Yes,"—"Then we have a writ against you, for"—"Ha! Ha!" said Monsieur.—"let-a-me see—ha! you take my *body!* your writ say."—"Yes; you must get up, and go with us—come, make haste and dress yourself."—"Begar, I have no dress."—"No dress!—what do you mean by that! come, come, we can't loiter here; get up."—"Upon my vard, all my dress at de pawnbroker—you take my *body*, your writ say—no dress,"—and immediately he sprang from the bed in *puris naturalibus*, and danced about the room. Being a perfect *Esau*, he made a most grotesque appearance. The myrmidons in vain insisted on his dressing, while he reiterated, "take my body!" "Why, who will take you in such a state?" I cannot tell, (said he) you take my body."—"D—n your body—come along Flannagan, we'll have him as yet some how or other.—D—n his body;" and for that time they left him. The Frenchman hastily equipped himself, and instantly changed his lodging; in a few weeks after, the *powerful arrester of mortals* seized him, and for ever freed him from trouble.

TURKISH CEREMONY OF LAYING A FIRST STONE.

THE town of Jaffa, in Syria, becoming a great depot for the Ottoman army, on account of the French in Egypt, and otherwise of the utmost consequence to the Turkish government, his Highness the Grand Vizier, embracing the opportunity of British officers serving in his camp, to further fortify and secure this important town against every future attempt, gave directions that plans to that effect might be prepared; which being done and approved, Saturday, the 30th of August, 1800, was fixed for laying the first stone of a large bastion, with all the pomp usual on great occasions in the East; and for which purpose, his Highness the Grand Vizier gave it every *eclat*, by honouring the work and its projectors, in laying the first stone himself, with the following ceremony, viz.—The Grand Vizier, with all the great state officers and attendants, guards, &c. came to the foundation of the new bastion about six o'clock in the morning, where they were met by Brigadier General

General Koehler, and all the other British officers. The salient angle stone being prepared to be set, it was done in his presence by one of the British Royal Military Artificers; when solemn prayers were performed by one of the Ulema, and parts repeated by all the Turks present, in a most devout manner; when a mallet, covered with blue velvet, was handed to the Grand Vizier, with which he struck the stone three times, saying a short prayer, which in like manner was repeated by all the great officers according to their ranks. During this part of the ceremony, five sheep were sacrificed, and the stone sprinkled with their blood. His Highness then retired with the State officers to a superb tent, pitched near the work for the occasion, where Brigadier-General Koehler, who commands the British military mission in the dominions of the Grand Signior, was invested with a sable pelice of the first order; and Major Holloway, the chief engineer, (who planned the bastion, as part of a system of works intended for the defence of the important depot at Jaffa and its environs) with a pelice of ermine; Major Fletcher, the second engineer, with a silk robe of honour; and some interpreters, &c. with castanes. Then the foregoing officers, being seated near his Highness the Grand Vizier, were served with coffee, &c.; after which the Grand Vizier, with the State officers, British officers, and all the attendants, who were very numerous, returned on horseback, sumptuously caparisoned, and with great dexterity riding, and throwing *djerids* in front.

Thus ended this memorable event; which, probably, is the first military work that ever was planned, and commenced by Englishmen in the Holy Land.

SALE OF A STATE STUD.

TO be Sold, on Thursday the 22d instant, (unless before then disposed of) in Palace-yard, the following well-known hacks, being the remains of a stud lately broke up in Ireland:—

Lot 1. DICK, a short-legged bitten hack, Galway bred; has had the mange, but is now recovered of it; stands fire well, but has a trick of braying like an ass, on which account he will be sold cheap. Sound.

Lot 2. SLOB, a large lobb-ear'd thick-hamm'd, heavy-quartered horse; has a blemish in his eye, which can be concealed by a winker; and has had a bad cold, which has brought on a *great discharge* from his mouth, on which account he will be sold cheap.— Not warranted.

Lot 3. KNIGHT, known to some by the name of School-Boy.— This hack, when very young, promised well; but is now, it is supposed, from having been kept on *too high feed*, become very skittish and vapourish. It was at first supposed he would answer for a Lady, but he cannot now at all be recommended for that purpose. Carries his head high.

Lot 4. HEARTH-MONEY.—This is the worst lot in the sale: he is a heavy, stumbling, and (to make use of an Irish expression) a thorough bred garron. He was a long time in training for the Patriot Stakes; but on the day of trial, in running over the Course, he started at a bit of paper, (proved after the Race to have been a Treasury Order) by which he threw his rider, and wheeled about. He has had the mange, but is sound.

Lot 5. BUBBLE AND SQUEAK.— This hack is only recommended

to Pig-drivers, and to such as require to be carried low.

Lot 6, is a tight-made black poney, called PETULANT. No certain account can be given of the origin of his breed; but it is supposed to have been of Limerick. Having gone through much dirty work and drudgery, he will be sold cheap.

COOKE, Dealer in Hacks in Ireland, has consigned the above to his friend ROSE, for sale in London; of whom farther particulars may be had.

SUPERNATURAL CAMPANOLOGY.

A letter from Cambridge, dated the 29th ultimo, contains the following curious Article:—

FOR some time past, the family of Dr. Apthorpe (resident in the house formerly occupied by the Bishop of Llandaff) has been much alarmed by the bells in the different rooms ringing without being pulled by any visible being. Every enquiry into the cause, that Reason and Philosophy could suggest, has been made, but to no purpose.

On Thursday evening, Dr. Cory, Master of Emanuel, and Mr. Dineaster, Fellow of Christ's College, were at the Doctor's, when the same merry inclination seized them again. These Gentlemen examined, with peculiar attention, the wires, cranks, and the appendages to these moving instruments, but could not discover by what means they had been set to work. A particular friend of mine called lately, on some business, when one solitary bell began its usual frolic, without any response from the rest; for, in general, they strike in concert.— The wire of one was cut, to prevent its joining the others; but that could not hinder its adding to the general chorus: another had neither pulley nor wire, yet that also refused to remain silent. Only last night the whole were very busy; but one, more noisy than the rest, rang with uncommon violence. I dare say some of your readers will be so sceptical as to laugh at and disbelieve this account; *but it can be attested by the most indubitable evidence.*

Something similar to the above is stated to have lately occurred in the mansion-house of a Gentleman in the country—where strange noises have been heard. The stove and fire-irons, indignant at confinement, have leaped from their recesses, and danced *cotillons* in the room—unasked—and unassisted, at least by any visible means: though strict search and anxious watching have been used to discover the cause, which, we will venture to say, is not preternatural.

RUSSIAN MANNERS.

Extract of a Letter from a Traveller, dated from Moscow.

I Have discovered a remarkable propriety in the Russian language. It is singularly adapted for the eloquence of popular disputes: there is not a term of infamy which has not its appropriate name; there is not an abusive idea which may not in it be expressed with energy, and without circumlocution. Hence, when you see two men disputing in the streets of Moscow, apostrophes crowd on each other—their voices are elevated, animation is in every gesture; but they will not pass a certain limit. In every country, the first blow is never given till the last abusive epithet is exhausted; and in this the vocabulary of the Russians

Russians is inexhaustible.—If, on the other hand, you attend to two beggars accosting one another, you will hear them mutually compliment each other on their health, and on their affairs: they will not forget any of the ceremonies of politeness, nor the forms of good manners; whereas, all the world knows that the Spanish beggars never accost each other, without asking, "Has your Lordship taken your chocolate?" And, at Paris, I have seen a beggar give alms to another, and the latter take off his hat to him.

I have been introduced into the best houses of Moscow; but it is in vain to look for any particular national character. A genteel Moscovite is a compound of all the nations of Europe. The French is his usual language: it is frequently a Swiss who has taught it him. His clothes are made by a German taylor. It is an Englishman who owns the Play-house, at which he spends many of his hours. The tales with which he amuses himself, are those of Marmontel, and his theatrical pieces are translated from Kotzebue. Kotzebue is the object of the enthusiasm of the Russians, and the Play the object of their ruling passion. There is scarcely a great Lord who has not in his castle his Theatre, and his company of Actors composed of his vassals, trained and formed for his own use. But this constitutes almost the whole of their taste for Literature. Karamsin (a young author at present fashionable) gives, indeed, every year, an Almanack of Fashions; but he wished to set up a Journal, and his attempt did not succeed. The inhabitants of Moscow content themselves with reading twice a week a news-paper, in which Authors sometimes insert advertisements of their works, with an extract made by themselves, and an eulogium, which the Bookseller takes care to add.

Without Journals, without new Romances, and without Translations, you will, perhaps, find it difficult to know how the Moscovites fil up their time, and contribute to habitual conversation; but play and the table supply every thing; It is a great merit, at Moscow, to keep a good table, and even to be able to speak scientifically on the subject; but it is a talent infinitely agreeable to play at Whist, and to be able to give an account, with extreme exactness, of the party of the preceding evening. I gained myself singular credit the other day, by correcting the recital of the facts of an important blow. I observed that the narrator must have mistaken the nine for the ten of Clubs, which made a great difference. The person whom I had set right thanked me for my information.

I think I shall soon leave Moscow. I shall carry with me a very pleasing idea of the happiness which strangers of every description enjoy there, with a very lively remembrance of the magnificence of some Moscovites, and of the air of grandeur which prevails in the use which they appear to make of their riches. If I have not always been equally struck with the delicacy of their taste—if I cannot reconcile myself to the *sebeken*, (that is to say, to a glass of spirits, accompanied with dried herrings and smoked meat, which is every afternoon served to the Russian ladies in place of tea) it still appears to me wonderfully pleasant to call to mind what it was in this country, that, scarcely a hundred years ago. Peter the Great was obliged to publish a decree, which prohibited Ladies in genteel life from getting drunk on assembly-days, and the men from being tipsey before nine o'clock in the evening, provided the assembly was to terminate at ten. But what, above all, I love to retrace, are the ancient Chronicles, in which I read that, even at the commencement of the seventeenth century, when the Czar intended marrying, the most beautiful women of his kingdom were assembled in his palace, where the Prince assisted at their games, at their conversations, and, attentive to every thing, carried (depend on the truth of it) his caution so far, as to go at night, and examine which of his subjects slept most gracefully, &c. &c.

SCARCITY AND PLENTY.

To the EDITORS *of the* SPORTING MAGAZINE.

GENTLEMEN,

THERE are so many mistaken opinions, which obtain very general credit, that you and I shall not be able to set the world right, upon all points, however earnestly we may wish and labour to do so. Nevertheless, as I am very ambitious to " deserve well of my country" (as they say in France), I am determined, when a gross error falls in my way, to attack it with all my might.

For some time past, I have not been able to pop my head into a Bookseller's shop, cast my eye upon a newspaper, or pay a morning visit to a friend, without meeting with doleful declarations that " Every thing is so scarce !— Now, Gentlemen, I do aver, that the complaint is for the most part groundless. True it is, that we have a *scarcity* of corn, a *scarcity* of good news from abroad, and a *scarcity* of good people at home. But then, how many things are abounding and even overflowing, among us ? We see *plenty* of room in our churches, *plenty* of people at the Play-houses, *plenty* of young ladies of age to be married, and *plenty* of young gentlemen very ready to marry them. We find *plenty* of new books to be bought, and *plenty*—no, no,—I forget myself,—we do *not* find *plenty* of money to buy them. Then, who does not know that there are *plenty* of patriots, willing to represent us in Parliament ; and *plenty* of poor curates, ready to take charge of the rich livings ?—if they could get them !

But, it is not only of *plenty* that we can boast ; in many instances we have an *excess*. For instance, our Literary Reviews exhibit *too much* partiality, and our Newspapers (no offence to the Gentlemen concerned) contain *too many* lies. Our Tradesmen have too many bad debts upon their books, and our Bankers issue *too many* bills. Doctors Commons has *too many* suits, and Jack Ketch has *too many* jobs. There are *too many* in gaol, that would be glad to get out ; and *too many* out of gaol, that ought to be put in.—In short, Gentlemen, (for I don't know when I should have done, if I went through the whole catalogue of our *professions*) we have *too much* trust in Providence to be afraid of the French ;—our sailors have *too much* courage to strike a flag to less than five times their force ; and I have *too much* respect for you, to omit subscribing myself, your very humble servant,

OBADIAH OVERPLUS.

P. S. If you think the above worthy a place in your entertaining Magazine, by giving it a corner you will much oblige a constant Reader, and may induce him to communicate with you at some future period.

On the Utility of the Cow.

Ye generous Britons, venerate the "Cow!"

To the EDITORS of the SPORTING MAGAZINE.

GENTLEMEN,

YOU cannot render a more important benefit to the public, and more especially to the lower orders of society, than by directing the serious attention of the Land-owners of this country to a disposition which, at this time, strongly manifests itself, amongst the principal occupiers of land, to banish that most valuable animal, the Cow, from their estates.

It is impossible to have observed, without concern, the numerous advertisements which have of late appeared for the sale of Dairies of Cows. Not in consequence of a change of occupiers; but because the occupiers prefer the Grazing to a Dairy system.— In the vicinity of a considerable market-town in Norfolk [Fakenham, it is supposed] no less than five dairies, consisting, together, of upwards of *one hundred cows*, have been lately annihilated! And various other instances, in different parts of the country, might also be mentioned.

Whatever motives may induce this change of system, whether proceeding from a prospect of present advantage—the trouble attending dairy-farms—the refinement of the sex—or to whatever cause it is to be imputed, its baneful effects to the public are the same; and though it is an evil which may, perhaps, in time effect his own cure, yet it is lamentable to observe, that it appears to increase, and to go hand-in-hand with the increasing wealth and prosperity of the Farmer!—Let those, however, who are disposed to commence Graziers, by the sacrifice of their dairies, be well aware (if the example they hold out should be generally adopted) how much they will be subjecting themselves to the exorbitant demands of the Scotch Drovers!—And, should the contagion of dropping Dairies extend itself throughout the kingdom, it may be asked, What, then, will they have to graze?

It is impossible to numerate the various advantages we derive from this valuable creature, the Cow. There is hardly an article of human subsistence that does not partake of her. In infancy, and in old age, the Cow best furnishes that kind of support which the weakness and infirmities of our nature then require; and at all times, and in all seasons, to the family of a poor man, the relief and comfort she affords are past all description. By an act of Providence it is, that, for a season, we ought cheerfully to submit to the scanty loaf; but let not the caprice or short-sighted policy of Farmers deprive the labouring poor, and others who have no conveniency of keeping a Cow, of all possibility of obtaining either cheese or butter—or even a little skimmed milk, to moisten their rice and potatoes.

To rescue this animal from banishment (though well worthy the attention of the Legislature) is peculiarly the province of Landlords. They most certainly possess the means; but without their interference, to object most likely to contribute, in its effects, to restore plenty in the land, will not be accomplished.

It is far from my wish to shackle occupiers with restrictions and stipulations, which may break in upon the general system and conduct of their farms; but the necessities, without adding the comforts, of the community.

community, call aloud for a check to be put to this serious grievance. To which end it seems extremely desirable, and it is meant here to be particularly recommended, that Landlords should, in future, introduce a covenant in their leases, obligatory on their tenants to keep a certain number of Cows upon their respective farms. The number may, in general, be proportioned by the rent; and in large farms there should, I think, be kept at least five Cows for every hundred pounds a year. The occupiers of small farms will most readily subscribe to a much higher proportion. I am, Gentlemen, your's, &c.

J. D.

STILISH PICKPOCKET.

AT the late Old-Bailey Sessions, *Joseph Parry*, a gay dashing Minion of the Moon, who, previous to his nocturnal depredations, occasionally sported his figure in the lobbies of the Theatres, was indicted for labouring in his vocation, by picking the pocket of Captain George Walsh of a gold watch.

The Prosecutor had been to Drury-lane Play-house, and had called a coach at the corner of Brydges street. He had a Lady with him, and had just handed her in, and was stepping in himself, when he felt his watch pulled from his fob. There was no person near him, who could have taken it, but the prisoner: he immediately laid hold of him, and accused him of the theft. The prisoner protested he was mistaken, advised him to be cautious how he imputed such a charge to a Gentleman, and expressed his readiness to be searched, observing that, if he had taken his watch, he must certainly have it about him.

Some of the Bow-Street Police Officers came up, and, having heard the accusation, took the prisoner into custody, conveyed him to the watch-house, and searched him; but the watch was not found.

The prisoner was next morning taken before Mr. Ford, the Magistrate, who, after duly weighing the evidence of the prosecutor against the prisoner's protestations of innocence, was of opinion there was not sufficient ground for submitting the matter to the investigation of a Jury, and accordingly the prisoner was on the point of being discharged; but, unfortunately for him, one of the Officers had been told, by somebody, that a link-boy had been heard to say, he had picked up a watch which a Gentleman had thrown away. The Officers, finding the Magistrate did not think the evidence of the prosecutor was sufficient, without its being corroborated by that of the link-boy, immediately proceeded in search of him. These useful ferrets of justice, with no other clue than that instinctive sagacity which seems peculiarly their own, scented their game, and unkennelled him, where he lay *perdue*, in a two-penny lodging, in Dyot-street, St. Giles's. He was committed to the safe keeping of the Governor of Newgate, in order that he might be forthcoming to throw a light upon the business.

Upon his being produced as a witness, he declared that he knew the prisoner perfectly well by sight, having frequently seen him at the Theatre. He was quite positive he was the person who took the prosecutor's watch: he observed him fling it away, and he immediately took it up.

The prisoner, in his defence, argued the inconsistency of the evidence of the prosecutor, contrasted with that of the link-boy. If it were true, that the prosecutor, the moment

moment he felt his watch go, seized him and pinioned his arms (as his evidence stated) then it was impossible he could have been capable of the action of flinging it away, as the link-boy had described. He declared his innocence, and contended that the link-boy had been tutored by the officers to swear in the manner he had done; and, therefore, he confidently looked forward to the acquittal of the Jury.

The Jury, however, gave a verdict of—*Guilty*.

SPEECH *of a* CREEK INDIAN, *against the Use of* RUM, *or other* SPIRITUOUS LIQUORS.

Oh! Countrymen,

I Will spare myself the ungrateful task of repeating, and you the pain of recollecting, those shameful broils, those unmanly riots, and those brutal extravagances, which the unbounded use of this liquor has so frequently produced among us. I must, however, beg leave to assert, that our prevailing love, our intemperate use, of this liquid, will be productive of consequences the most destructive to the welfare of the public, and the felicity of every individual offender. It perverts the ends of society, and unfits us for all those distinguishing and exquisite *feelings*, which are the cordials of life, and the noblest privileges of *humanity*.

I have already declined the mortification which a detail of facts would raise in every breast, when unpossessed by this *demon*. Permit me then, in general, only to appeal to public experience, for the many violations of civil order, the indecent, the irrational perversions of character, which these inflammatory draughts have introduced amongst us. 'Tis true, these are past; and may they never be repeated!—but tremble, O ye Creeks! when I thunder in your ears this denunciation—That, if the cup of Perdition continues to rule among us with sway so intemperate, *ye will cease to be a nation!* Ye will have neither *heads* to direct, nor *hands* to protect you!

While this diabolical juice undermines all the powers of your bodies and minds, with inoffensive zeal, the warrior's enfeebled arm will draw the bow, or launch the spear, in the day of battle. In the day of council, when national safety stands suspended on the lips of the hoary *Sachem*, he will shake his head with uncollected spirits, and drivel the babblings of a second childhood.

I hope I need not make it a question to say in this assembly, whether he would prefer the intemperate use of this liquor, to *clear perception, sound judgment*, and a *mind* exulting in its own *reflections*.—Yet there is not, within the whole compass of nature, so prevailing, so lasting a propensity, as that of associating, and communicating our sentiments to each other. And there is not a more incontestible truth than this—that *benignity of heart*, the calm possession of ourselves, and the undisturbed exercise of our *thinking* faculties, are absolutely necessary to constitute the eligible and worthy companion. How opposite to these characters Intoxication renders us, is so manifest to our own experience, so obvious to the least reflection, that it would be impertinent to enlarge farther upon it.

And now, O ye Creeks! if the cries of your country, if the pulse of glory, if all that forms the *hero* and exalts the *man*, has not swelled your breasts with patriot indignation against the immoderate use of this liquor;—if these motives are
insufficient

insufficient to produce such resolutions as may be effectual—there are yet other ties of humanity, tender, dear, and persuading.—Think on what we owe to our children, and to the gentler sex!

With regard to our children,—think how it must affect their tenderness, to see the man that gave them being, thus sunk into the most brutal state, in danger of being suffocated by his own intemperance, and standing in need of their infant arm to support his staggering steps, or raise his feeble head while he vomits forth the foul debauch!—Will not this gradually deprive us of all authority, in the families which we ought to govern and protect? What a waste of time does it create, which might otherwise be spent round the blazing hearth, in the most tender offices! It perverts the great designs of Nature, and murders all those precious moments in which the warrior should recount to his wondering offspring, his own great actions, and those of his ancestors!

But further, besides what we owe to our children, let us think on that delicate regulation of conduct, that soul-enobling *love*, which it is at once the happiness and honour of *manhood* to manifest towards the gentler sex. By the *love* of this sex, I do not mean mere desire of them. Those amiable creatures are designed not only to gratify our passions, but to excite and fix all the kind and sociable affections: they were not meant to be the slaves of our arbitrary wills in our brutal moments, but the sweet companions of our most reasonable hours and exalted enjoyments.—Heaven has endowed them with that peculiar warmth of affection, that disinterested friendship of heart, that melting sympathy of soul, that entertaining sprightliness of imagination, joined with all the sentimental abilities of mind, that tend to humanize the rough nature, open the reserved heart, and polish the rugged temper, which would otherwise make men the dread and abhorrence of each other.

Thus were women formed, to allay the fatigues of life, and reward the dangers we encounter for them. These are their endowments, these their charms. Hither Nature, Reason, Virtue call.—And shall they call in vain? Shall an unnatural, an unreasonable, a vicious perversity of taste, be preferred to those heaven-born joys of life? Will you treat the *Sovereign Principle of Good* with a thankless insensibility, and offer libations to the Spirit of all Evil? Will any Creek henceforth dare to approach those lovely creatures with unhallowed lips, breathing the noisome smell of this diabolical juice, or roll into their downy embrace in a state inferior to the brutes, losing all *that rapturous intercourse of Love and Friendship*, all those most exalted of human pleasures which *they, they* only, are formed capable of communicating to us?

Let me conjure you, by all these softer ties and inexpressible endearments—let me conjure you, as you yet hope to behold the *Tree of Peace* raise its far-seen top to the sun, and spread its odorous branches, watered by the dew of Heaven, over all your abodes, while you rejoice unmolested under its shade; and as you yet wish to behold the nations round about you, bound with the sacred *chain of Concord*, every hand maintaining a link:—by all these ties, by all these hopes, I conjure you, O Creeks! henceforward let the cup of Moderation be the crown of your festivities!—Save your country! maintain and elevate her glory!—Transmit to your posterity, *Health, Freedom,* and *Honour!*—Break not the great chain

of

of Nature; but let an honest, rational, and delicate intercourse, be the plan of social joy!—Let each domestic bliss wreathe the garland of connubial love!—Let truth and friendship sanctify the lover's with, and secure to the brave, wise, and temperate man, a felicity worthy his choice and his protection!

A DASHING IMPOSTOR.

To the EDITORS *of the* SPORTING MAGAZINE.

GENTLEMEN,

The following may be depended upon, as it recently happened to a respectable Counsellor in the neighbourhood of Gloucester-street, a friend of whom now requests you to insert his communication, as a warning to others to be aware of

An Impostor who now infests Town.

A Few nights ago, as Mr. —— was sitting in his study, reading some papers on which he was requested to give an opinion, the servant announced an unknown Gentleman, with some papers, which he had brought from a client of Mr. —— for his perusal. By the time that the stranger had drawled out his pretended message the servant had retired, when instantly the bundle of law was changed into more forcible arguments, and a pistol presented at Mr. ——'s head extorted from him his money. The sharper was civil, and prepared to take his leave, prudently walking off with one of the silver candlesticks, to *light himself* down stairs. No sooner was he out of the room, than the Gentleman rang the bell violently, and a servant running up to answer it, met the Impostor, who, with infinite presence of mind, told him that it was only to let him out, but that to save him (the servant) the trouble, he had taken the candle to let himself out; but that there was no farther occasion for it, and he would therefore put it down. The servant let him pass, and he made his escape.

A FEMALE SWINDLER.

A Few weeks since, a woman of genteel appearance, about thirty six years of age, middle sized, with a claret mark on her face, dressed in a dark riding-habit, and black beaver hat with a gold band, arrived at an inn in Salisbury, and afterwards took a lodging, where she ordered various articles of different tradesmen, some of whom incautiously sent them in: but it soon appeared that she had neither the intention nor the ability of paying any one; and, after a trifling bustle, she decamped on the Wednesday, having artfully engaged a post-chaise for Romsey, where she prevailed on an Innkeeper to satisfy the driver, and forward her immediately in another chaise for Gosport, where she said she had urgent business, and from whence she would send back the money for both. She called herself Mrs. Adams, widow of an Officer, and had a maid-servant with her; and, as she usually drank a bottle of wine a day, and lived otherwise in a similar stile, though so early detected, she defrauded different persons at Salisbury to the amount of fifteen pounds, or thereabouts.

Some time since she was three months at Dorchester, with her servant, whence they decamped in the night, without paying either for lodging or subsistence.

PORTRAITS OF HORSES.

To the EDITORS *of the* SPORTING MAGAZINE.

GENTLEMEN,

I Had great pleasure in seeing, in your excellent Magazine, the horse Dungannon; and I hope you will favour me, as soon as you can make it convenient, with an engraving of a son of Dungannon; and also of a mare, which you will find to have won many plates.— They at present belong to the Earl of Stamford, *viz.*

The horse George, a chesnut horse, got by Dungannon.

The mare, Petrina, a black mare, got by Sir Peter.

Your's, &c.
J. HARDY.

Manchester, Jan. 17, 1801.

P. S. You will find that, at Lincoln Races, in the year 1798, Petrina, by Sir Peter, (then four years old) beat several capital horses; and you will find George to have been a capital horse.

ON BOXING ATTITUDES.

To the EDITORS *of the* SPORTING MAGAZINE.

GENTLEMEN,

BEING a young Academician at this famed University, and at the present time ignorant and unskilled in the different avocations of life, &c. necessary for a Buck; and my father being a lover of the Pugilistic Science, I am quite at a loss to resolve a question put to me (at the coffee-house) on the origin, utility, &c. of the seconds, at all first-rate boxing matches, standing on each side the champions, in like attitude, as though they were likewise going to set-to, with their arms extended, and squaring. Now I hope those lovers of the pugilistic science, who have the good-will of some good fellows at heart, will resolve me (in your next) the above; flattering myself that, from the edification I shall receive, I shall not appear (when I attend boxing matches, or boxing conversations) so totally ignorant as at present.

I am, your's, &c.
E. L. C.

Oxford, Jan. 14, 1801.

N. B. A few evenings ago, two ladies of the Cyprian corps, having met by accident a certain gallant blade, and each being jealous as to the other, after letting flow a tolerable share of oaths, plentifully intermixed with words equally applicable, they (Belcher and Gamble like) stripped, and set-to. After half an hour's hard fighting, victory seemed doubtful, and they mutually agreed to put it off till the next morning, and then to fight it out for five shillings each. One of the championesses appeared on the ground at the appointed time; but the other, who had sacrificed too much at the shrine of jolly Bacchus, complained of incapability that day. Victory, of course, was declared in favour of a well known sporting female, Miss *Diana Grey.*

THE MAID OF THE HAY-STACK.

LATELY died in Guy's Hospital, the once unfortunately celebrated Louisa, or *Lady of the Hay-Stack;* who, about eighteen years ago, was found to have taken up her residence under *that shelter,* in the parish of Bourton, near Bristol, in a state of melancholy derangement. She then appeared to be under twenty years of age. —This very extraordinary woman, whose

whose "*Tale of Woe*" was first told to the public by Miss Hannah More, has naturally ceased, for a considerable time past, to interest the general curiosity.

During several days of her abode under the Hay-stack, (from which she at last permitted herself to be removed with reluctance) she was visited, and irregularly fed, by the country people, till the hand of more happy sympathy and compassion provided her better protection. As her name was unknown, she was immediately distinguished by that of Loisa. It may be gratifying to many on this occasion to learn, that during a considerable interval, in which she afterwards remained in retirement, and before she was admitted, as incurable, into the asylum in which she died, she was chiefly supported by a voluntary subscription, under the management of Miss Hannah More and her sisters. Those active advocates of humanity, who never yet began a good work and grew weary of well-doing, having lost the pecuniary assistance of most others, continued to supply the extra wants and accommodations of the poor solitary stranger, at the expence of more than ten pounds *per annum*, till her decease. They would be the last to wish that such an instance of benevolence should be publicly mentioned; but it is a tribute due, not less to them, than to the interest of society.

The same kind, and much the same degree, of mental derangement, which the "*Tale of Woe*" described, remained with Loisa to the last. In her general conduct, she exhibited the various common evidences of the men: confirmed insanity; which, in addition to the contraction of her limbs, from her exposure to cold in the open fields, and her future propensity to remain inactive, rendered her an object of the strongest pity. But her insanity was uniformly remarkable in this—that however disordered and childish her affections and resentments, she never could be drawn into any explanation respecting her family, her connections, or her country: however affable and unguarded she might sometimes appear, the moment any person put a question, directly or indirectly, relative to those topics, or made any allusion to them, however distant, she always changed countenance, assumed an air of suspicion, grew grave and inflexibly silent, or would instantly touch on some other subject. From her *accent*, she was undoubtedly of German origin; but, though she knew little of English, she avoided conversing in any foreign language. Her manners and occasional movements indicated superior rank; and her frequent exclamations of "*Dear papa!*" and "*Dear mama!*" in connection with ideas of equipage and ornaments, led to that conclusion.

Many endeavours were used, on the continent, to trace her family, by circulating her description and story in the public prints, but without effect. The mystery of this silence was too remarkable, not to confirm the first opinion of her being a person above the common classes, with the additional probability of some unhappy and treacherous seduction. This last opinion, from the whole of the distressful evidence, inclusive of the personal part which poor Loisa sometimes involuntarily furnished, is not doubted by those who, with the writer of this article, early saw and closely observed her.—The conviction that it is possible for any man, making pretensions to honour, or even of distinction, from a brutal nature, so to betray and so to abandon, in a foreign land, youth, beauty, the strongest sensibility, and perhaps the most engaging innocence, fills the mind with horror of the deed, and with shame and indignation for the character. Such profligacy, in this instance, may have been of foreign production; but comparatively happy would it be for *this* country, also, if instances did not abound, among *us*, of similar atrocity in those who, on inferior occasions, will make high pretensions to honour and principle, but who seek every opportunity of seducing from the abodes of paternal affection, or of innocent employment, whatever is the most fair and inexperienced,—rioting in its ruin for a short season, and then committing the greater crime of abandonment to infamy!—The theme is unhappily too common to need proof, and too mournful to dwell on.

The poor departed Child of Misery, whose story is here again revived, is too strong an instance of suffering, and excites too much feeling, to be permitted to pass, in the common course, to oblivion, if it could be avoided. Under this impression, permit me to attempt something in the character of an EPITAPH.—But, alas! poor Loisa's Tablet of Remembrance may only be found in the sympathetic bosom of a few surviving friends!

In yonder dust—unmark'd for public fame,
Low rest the relics of Loisa's frame!
Poor hapless suff'rer, of the Maniac line!
Thy wrongs no more a tortur'd breast confine!
Enough for thee, that ling'ring Sorrow's breath
Found final rescue in the boon of Death!
Consol'd be they, who sought thy soul's relief;
Tormented they, who overwhelm'd with grief!
Accurs'd the crime, that 'reft thy reason's ray,
Though thou be ransom'd for eternal day!
And where frail Innocence would Vice repel,
May guardian angels thy sad story tell!

Bath, Jan. 20, 1801.   W.M.

DESPERATE ENTERPRISE.

ON Sunday, the 1st November, a daring attempt was made by the convicts in the State Prison of New York, to effect an escape. Their plan was conceived with ingenuity, and conducted with a promptitude and boldness that surprised the caution, and rendered ineffectual the resistance of the keepers.

It originated with the Shoemakers in the fourth wing, who, first having seized the assistant-keeper, and Noah Gardner, who had charge of them, broke the bars across the chimney, and, after ascending to a certain height, knocked the bricks through, and thus made an opening into one of the front rooms on the second floor. This room being appropriated to one or two of the keepers, as a lodging chamber, was unguarded, and opened a passage to the whole building. The first thing they did, was to cut the bell-rope, to prevent any alarm being given: they then descended the stairs, rushed suddenly on the keepers, disarmed them, and seized their keys; after which, they secured all the arms they could possibly find.

Meantime Cap. Pray, the keeper of the prison, apprised of the circumstance, ran in, and attempted to seize some of them, but was himself knocked down, stabbed twice, and severely bruised. They then proceeded to the front gate, seized the keeper, wrested from him the key, opened the gate, sallied into the road, and even huzzaed as they proceeded to the shore. Having seized a boat, they rowed across the river, and landed a little above the Houboken Ferry-house, whence they proceeded forward in a body, setting the civil power at defiance.

ADVENTURES

ADVENTURES OF A TRAVELLER.

Among the literary productions of the last Leipsic Fair, in August, were the adventures of a German Traveller, which are curious and interesting.

C. F. Damberget, a poor German, a carpenter, and a fugitive soldier, was, in the year 1781, trepanned at Amsterdam, into the service of the Dutch East-India Company, as a common soldier. On account of illness, he was detained a while at the Cape of Good Hope, though enlisted and sent out from Holland, to serve in Batavia. Refusing to gratify the lewd desires of the wife of one of the Officers commanding at the Cape, he was, in consequence of her artifices and feigned complaints, ordered for Batavia a second time. He had been, ere this time, informed of the unwholesomeness of the climate of Java, and dreaded it as if he had been ordered for execution. He deserted; and as his desertion could not otherwise be concealed, took the desperate resolution of advancing into the interior wilds of Africa.

A carbine, a few pounds of gunpowder, some balls, a small sum of money, and a few other articles of indispensible necessity, were his only apparatus for the enterprize. He journeyed north-east from the Cape; passed onwards without interruption through the country of the kind, simple, and hospitable Hottentots; even among the fiercer and less humane Caffrarians, met with much more of gentle beneficence than of injury. With the narrative of the travels of Le Vaillant, he was before acquainted; and as he went on, he found continual occasion to detect the errors and fictions of that traveller.

He observed, among other things, that the Caffrarian matrons had the privilege of not being liable to be struck by their husbands; and yet, that married pairs lived there in enviable unanimity and peace. From the country of the Caffrees, he turned westward, and continued his journey in a north-west direction till he arrived in the kingdom of Angola. Among the Muborians, a race not more savage, but more egregiously vicious than any borde he had before visited, he discovered the bodies of five Europeans, who appeared to have been cruelly massacred; and was himself exposed to danger, from the unnatural lust of some wretches of that community.

He, however, escaped from their brutality, and, after long wanderings, came to Malemba, a walled town on the river Congo. Its King treated him at first with kindness; but was afterwards persuaded by the Prime Minister to reduce him to the condition of a slave, and use him cruelly. He at last escaped out of that King's service, travelled eastward, and then again backwards to the north-west, in a line of journey contiguous to those which are called by geographers, the Mountains of the Moon. After dangers almost incredible, he was made a slave by the Moors. A merchant of Mezzabeth, whose property he had become, sold him to another who was returning to Morocco with a caravan, from Mecca. He was carried by this man to the seaport town of Azaffe, in the Moorish dominions. A Mr. Vanderhaft, a Dutch gentleman, there ransomed him from servitude. He was brought on board a Dutch merchant ship to Amsterdam. The interposition of a Prussian ship-captain rescued him from detention in Holland. He took his passage with that Captain to Dantzick, and soon after arrived, in the year 1797, at his native town in the Prussian dominions, from which he had been more than sixteen years absent.

SPORTING INTELLIGENCE.

MR. EDITOR,

SEEING, a short time since, an interesting account of the Laws of the Chase, as they respected coursing in earlier days, probably the following ancient recommendatory document on the "Choice of Greyhounds, &c." written about the same period, may afford some useful information to the amateurs in the breed of Long Dogs. Your's, &c.   AN OLD COURSER.

ON THE CHOICE OF GREY-HOUNDS.

"Touching the shapes of Greyhounds (hope you will take the best collections for their goodness) they are certain and most infallible! therefore, touching greyhounds when they are puppies, or young whelps, those which are most rawboned, lean, large made, fickle, or crooked hought, and generally unknit in every member, are ever likely to make the best dogs, and most shapely; but such as in the first three or four mo:whs are round, and close hust, fat, strait, and as it were full sum'd and knit in every member, never prove swift, good, or comely.

"Now after your dog comes to full growth, as at a year and a half, or two years old, he would then have a fine, long, lean head, with a sharp nose, rush grown from the eye downward, a full clear eye, with long eyelids, a sharp ear, short and close falling, a long neck a little bending, with a loose hanging wizard, a broad breast, straight foreleg, side hollow, ribs strait, a square and flat back, short and strong fillets, a broad space between the hips, a strong stern or tail, a sound foot, and good large clefts. Now for the better help of your memory, I will give you an old rhyme, left by your forefathers, from which you shall understand the true shape of a perfect greyhound. Thus it is.

"If you will have a good pike,
Of which there are few like,
It must be headed like a *Snake*,
Neckt like a *Drake*,
Backt like a *Beam*,
Sided like a *Bream*,
Tailed like a *Rat*,
And footed like a *Cat*."

"These being the principal members of a good greyhound, if they resemble the proportions of the things above-named, the dog cannot chuse but be most perfect."

A waiter at one of the gaming-houses in St James's-street, got, in Christmas-boxes of the established clubs, above five hundred pounds. A nobleman, who in the course of the week had won eighty thousand pounds, gave him one hundred pounds of his winnings. Early one evening, the Peer lost all his money, and, as is not unusual, borrowed a sum from the waiter to begin again, and, as has been said, afterwards won the above sum.

A few days ago an over-drove ox entered the back yard of Brown's Hotel, in Alie-street, Goodman's-fields, when the family were just going to sit down to dinner; several persons endeavoured to turn him out, but in spite of every effort, he forced himself into the house; the passage being narrow, he could not be turned out.

The

The affrighted animal, seeing an opening before him, which descended into the cellar, went on, when he tumbled head-foremost to the bottom, with a dreadful noise by the breaking of the stair-case and the roaring that the poor creature made. The alarm of the people of the house was beyond description terrific: some butchers arriving, allayed their fears, by haltering the beast, and craning him out of the cellar.

Anecdote of the Emperor Paul.—To prove his knowledge of Scripture, he employed a singular expedient! Without any cause or preliminary, he gave a gentleman a violent blow on the face with his hand, and said to the astonished sufferer, "This salutation by the hand of me, Paul!"

Signior Pascal Carillez, the first violin at the Madrid Opera-house, lately performed at the Theatre de la Republique, in Paris. It was a concerto of Mestrino, which he attempted for his first essay; but he was so much hissed, that he ran away from the orchestra.

A simple fellow, who took Lord Hawkesbury's assertion, in the House of Commons, in a literal sense, "that Herrings were an excellent substitute for Bread," observed, that he had eat them, as such, with a buttock of beef, and, in his opinion, they did not *answer at all!*

A bet of one hundred guineas was made at the Duke of Bedford's sheep-shearing, at Woburn, in June last, that his Grace would shew a bull of the Hereford breed against one of the Leicester breed. The decision took place at Shiffnal, in Shropshire, last month, before a very numerous assemblage of Noblemen, Gentlemen, and Graziers, from all parts of the kingdom. The beasts were both remarkably fine; but the judge (Mr. Pistor, of Somersetshire) decided in favour of the Hereford bull, which was the property of Mr. Gwillam, near Ludlow: Mr. Honeyborne was the owner of the other bull.—Each of the beasts is supposed to have produced one hundred guineas, by being shown at one shilling each person.

Some cattle, we understand, have been introduced into Bengal from the island of Tinian, one of the Marians to the east of Canton. They are of a very singular and remarkable species, being all milk-white, except their ears, which are either brown or black. It is asserted, that there are ten thousand cattle of this species on the island of Tinian; nor can one be found to differ from the above description.

Longevity.—There is now living in Aberfeldy, Perthshire, one John Stewart, who has lived in three centuries, being 108 years old.—He was visited by a Gentleman from England on the 31st of December, who spent the evening, and brought in the new year and century with the old gentleman, much to his satisfaction.

Extraordinary Shooting.—Colonel Thornton made a bet that he killed 400 head of game at 400 shots.—The result was, that in the year 1800, he bagged 417 head of game (consisting of partridges, pheasants, hares, snipes and woodcocks) at 411 shots. Amongst these were a black wild-duck, and a white pheasant cock; and at the last point he killed a brace of cock-pheasants, one with each barrel. On the leg of the last killed (an amazing fine bird) was found a ring, proving that he had been taken by Colonel Thornton when hawking, and turned loose again, in 1792.

A few days ago, as the Earl of Shaftesbury was passing through Salisbury, on his way from Saint Giles's

Giles's House to visit the Earl of Newburg, in Sussex, having changed horses at the Antelope inn, the new-mounted drivers mistook the shutting of the carriage-door for a signal that all was ready, and drove off full speed with the empty carriage, his Lordship being in the house. A servant on horseback was dispatched after them, and his Lordship laughing heartily at the mistake, followed in a post-chaise; but so assiduous were the drivers to forward the noble Earl on his journey, that they drove eight miles before the servant could overtake them, and he had then some difficulty in getting them to listen to his account of their mistake.

An affair of honour took place a few days ago at Enniscorthy, between John Tottenham, Esq. commander of a yeomanry corps in the county of Wexford, and John Colclough, Esq. of Dublin, of the Attorneys corps, in which the latter gentleman was unfortunately shot in the first fire.

The fantastic shape of some of the fashionable carriages, from their being so round and small, has obtained them, in compliment to the Union, the appellation of the *Potatoes*.

A quadruped has lately been taken in the kingdom of Candy, of a most remarkable and extraordinary species. The animal is no larger than a common hare, but perfectly resembles a deer. It is delicately formed, and surprisingly fleet.

A few afternoons since two gentlemen in a gig, from Worthing, were, owing to the unruliness of the horse, overturned near Ashcombe turnpike-gate, but received no personal injury, though the carriage was broken to pieces. The horse, by plunging, disengaged himself, and, with one shaft hanging to the trace, galloped on, in the face of a whole regiment of soldiers, on their march from church to the barracks, whom he charged furiously in different directions, and put fairly to the route; after which he pursued his course to the town, where he placed several persons in great peril, till he was stopped by a projecting house, against which he ran with violence, and stunned himself.

A Correspondent tells us, that, "being at Kedlestone some years ago, nothing pleased him more in that beautiful house of Lord Scarsdale's, than the words "*Waste not ! Want not !*" painted in large letters over the fire-place in the kitchen." Words which, he thinks, ought at this time to be put up in every kitchen and dining-room; for all kinds of provisions are so very scarce and dear, nothing should be wasted; and every body, of what degree soever, that wastes, ought to want. —Our Correspondent adds, that "dining a few days ago in a large company, he observed that some of them were particularly saucy, taking and tasting of every thing on the table, but sending away on their plates more than they eat, which probably would go to the dogs or swine."—As this Correspondent seems to be a good, natured Quiz, we have inserted his remarks.

Another Jane Gibbs.—A woman lately appeared at the Police Office, Whitechapel, to present a charge against two soldiers of the Tower Hamlet militia, for having violently assaulted her, and carried off from her person a considerable quantity of wearing apparel. In the course of the examination, however, it having appeared that this same woman had several months ago lodged a similar complaint against a respectable tradesman in Hackney parish, which turned out to be utterly malicious and false, the two soldiers

soldiers were acquitted, and the accuser dismissed with a severe reproof and admonition to amend her conduct.

Among the many instances that have been given of the prolific nature of hogs, the following is, perhaps, the most extraordinary.—Mr. Baker, farmer, of Spray's Bridge, in the parish of Westfield, has now a sow, fourteen years old, which has produced him *five hundred pigs!*

Caution.—Last week two valuable horses, the property of Mr. Owen, of Penaant, Shropshire, were found dead in their pasture.—On opening their stomachs, which were much swelled, and had a slight appearance of inflammation, a large quantity of the small sprigs of yew-tree were found, which was the cause of the death.

Colonel Pelham's Cup.—This silver vessel, lately presented to Mr. John Ellman, of Glynde, in Sussex, value thirty pounds, was purchased, not from the general fund of the Sussex Agricultural Society, but by a voluntary subscription entered into by its members, at the head of whom stand engraven on the cup, His Grace the Duke of Bedford, Earl of Egremont, Lord Pelham, Lord Viscount Gage, Lord Sheffield, &c. &c. who presented it to Mr. Ellman, in token of the merit they ascribe to him for his successful exertions in the improvement of the breed of South-down Sheep. It is a handsome piece of plate, very neatly wrought, and exhibits on one side the figure of Mr. Ellman's prize ram, engraved from a drawing of Scott's; and on the other, an appropriate inscription, ornamented with a pretty device, containing, in oblique compartments, the names of the donors; names that, no doubt, will for ages to come, be drank with grateful remembrance, whenever the cup shall be brought forth with its beverage sparklingly alive, to glad the eyes and cheer the hearts of Mr. Ellman's posterity, and their friends.

Captain Aylmer, of Rye, has now in his possession a fine Ostrich, lately landed from Africa. This bird stands upwards of six feet high, though only ten months old, and is in excellent health, and beautiful plumage. The extraordinary digestive powers of this species of the feathered race are daily exemplified by this bird, which swallows numerous iron nails, pieces of broken crockery, and other hard substances, without the least apparent injury.

Among the higher circles, there are three head-dresses in vogue— The *Tiara*, worn by ladies, who wish for *three strings* to their bow; the *Diadem*, by those who aspire to *royalty*; and the *Grecian*, by those who are deep in the *Aristotelian philosophy*.

Died lately, aged fifty, Mr. Isaac Perringe, of Manchester, engine-worker.—A man, who to a lion-like strength of body, united the disposition of a lamb. Perringe will be remembered from the circumstance of his having fought, for a considerable sum, the late well-known Johnson, the pugilist, a battle that engaged the attention of the amateurs more than any other ever fought in this kingdom. He fell, by the hand of that prime pugilist, Death, a sacrifice to cold and fatigue, brought on by overstrained exertions at the late dreadful fire in that town.

Sporting.—The Bradwell and Tillingham Coursing Club, in Essex, had their first meeting this season, on Monday, the 12th instant, when the following matches were run, which afforded excellent diversion, viz.

1. Mr. Dudley's *Madam*, beat Mr. Wakefield's *Delilah*.

2. Mr. C. Parker's *Pizarro*, beat Mr. Pattison's *Twist*.

3. Mr.

3. Mr. Dudley's *Friday*, beat Mr. P. Wright's *Crazy*.
4. Mr. C. Parker's *Dashaway*, beat Mr. J. Tuffnell's *Catch*.
5. Mr. Dudley's *Miss*, beat Mr. Wakefield's *Norfolk*.
6. Mr. Pigott's *Driver*, beat Mr. Wakefield's *Sampson*.
7. Mr. Dudley's *Terling*, beat Mr. Wakefield's *Sweepstakes*.
8. Mr. Bawtree's *Cayan*, beat Mr. P. Wright's *Scurvy*.
9. Mr. G. Bird's *Crazy*, beat Mr. P. Wright's *Kaiterfelto*.
10. Mr. G. Wright's *Teazer*, beat Mr. Pigott's *Primrose*.
11. Mr. Wakefield's *Quiz*, beat Mr. Dudley's *Trull*.
12. Mr. J. Tuffnell's *Playmate*, beat Mr. Cawston's *Slut*.

After the above Subscribers' matches were run off, several others succeeded. The hares ran stoutly, and gave a fine day's sport to a numerous field.

FEAST OF WIT; or, SPORTSMAN's HALL.

THE Hyde Parker, which recently brought to the Onslow frigate by a connubial shot, though one of our old *sixty-fours*, is stout in her timbers, and well manned. The Onslow is only pierced for a *twenty-four*, and was *armé en flute* when she struck.

Forty-three years is rather a long period to intervene between the age of a husband and his wife, but in the case of a gallant Admiral, it is quite in character, who regards the *superior force* of the enemy!

Some idea of the population of London may be formed from the immense number of taylors in the metropolis, even upon the computation of *nine to a man*.

During Lord Malmesbury's negotiations at Lisle, there was published in a Manchester Paper an advertisement of the sale of an estate, in which the advertiser announces—" That he is appointed *plenipotentiary* to treat in this business; that he has ample *credentials*, and is prepared to *ratify his powers*; that he will enter into *preliminaries* either on the principle of the *status quo*, or *uti possidetis*; that he is ready to receive the *projet* of any person desirous of making a purchase or exchange, and to deliver his *contre projet* and *sine qua non*, and even at once to give his *ultimatum*, assuring the public, that as soon as the *definitive treaty* shall be *concluded*, it will be ratified by his constituents, and duly guaranteed."

Two honest tars were conversing the other day on the foreign places they had visited, and the various customs that prevailed. One of them said, "I have been five or six times in France, but I never knew how many *saints* they had:— they say they have *one* now."— "Not know that! (said the other) —why, you lubber, they had one for *every day* in the year, and *one to spare* ;—and they called him *All Saints*."

Anecdote.—While a carpenter and a taylor were exercising their political abilities, upon our rupture with Russia, the carpenter observed, "There is not the least doubt but we should soon beat the Russians at sea, but the great difficulty lies in bringing them into action." To which the taylor boldly replied, "You know nothing of the matter. —After the brave Lord Nelson passes the Darning-needles (meaning the Dardanelles), and gets fairly

fairly into the Black Sea, it will be ALL over with them."

A correspondent observes, that the public have, perhaps, as great a right to complain of the present combination among the journeymen taylors, as the masters of those obstinate *heroes of the goose*. The cessation of the *needle* has caused such general inconvenience, that most people begin to call aloud for *redress*.

A bad memory.—A man was lately tried at the Old Bailey, for *privately* stealing a pint pot, by hiding it in his *breeches*. In his defence he assured the Court, " that he did not know, at least could not *remember*, how the pot got into that part of his dress." One of the Counsel observed, " that it might have got in by *mistake*." " True," added the prisoner with the most sedate and unaltered countenance, " it *might*."

Lately died, at his house at Ringmer, in Sussex. Mr. Thomas Pain, a considerable farmer, of that place. Had the majority of our farmers entertained the same sentiments which influenced the conduct of the deceased, we should have had a famine indeed, for he held it a SIN to waste wheat by throwing it into the ground, when it bore such an extravagant price, and was so much wanted for food; he, therefore, would not the last or present year, sow a single grain, though he had in his possession several hundred acres of good land, a considerable portion of which he suffered to remain uncultivated, rather than to burthen his conscience with such a crime!!

The appearance of the ship's names, suggests the idea, that the number of *Saints* in the Russian fleet, and a war with Paul, will not be a war *for* religion, but *against* it.

A Genoese Journal, contains a most violent philippic against English country-dances, and denounces such persons who so amuse themselves of *being sold to England*, and enemies to their country and to liberty. Its patrons have not confined themselves to mere declamations against English country dances, but when to the *bal de Turc*, threatening to throw the dancers out of the window if they did not desist from English country dances. Some of the ringleaders, however, have been arrested, and their journal suppressed.—Punch also being an *English liquor*, it is added, that some of these patriots could not drink it without *horror*.

An Irishism.—George Faulkner.—This was one of the worthy Alderman's remarks on the weather.—" *There* is a fine *day*, this *evening*. I thought it would have been snow *to morrow*: but it *has turned out* quite different:—very *fine* indeed."

Is it possible, says a wit, that foreigners will think us *starving*, when they shall hear that the Countess of Clonmell has one *sheaf of wheat* that would sell for five thousand pounds?

Some military gentlemen, a few Sundays since, having found the pews in S———m church very difficult of access, took under their arms their camp stools, and seated themselves in the aisle during the whole time of divine service. We know not whether the inhabitants took this as a gentle rebuke, for their want of politeness to strangers, but we understand the gentlemen have never since been under the necessity of loading themselves with their seats!

The *mitre*, the *sheaf of wheat*, &c. hitherto the favourite signs for inns, are now the *signs* worn by our fine women, and with the same signification—" Good entertainment for man, &c."

Sir Hyde Parker's appointment to a command in the North Seas, has converted his *honey-moon* into a sort of *ague*; a complaint always attended with a sudden transition from a *hot* to a *cold* fit.

Conundrum.—One of the most ridiculous, and therefore best things of this sort, is the following:—What Tradesman is he, that is most *likely* to set the *alphabet a galloping?* Answer, The *Glass-blower*; for he makes the D *canter*.—But what Tradesman is he that shall *stop* them? Answer, The *Hair-Dresser*; for he *ties up* the Q. and puts the *Two P's in irons!*

Previously to the last rhodomontade of *Russian insanity*, Paul actually returned, unopened, the dispatches sent to him by our Government, containing terms of conciliation, after piercing them in many places with the *Imperial pen-knife*.

Moorfields, according to the History of Tournaments in this country, was formerly a great theatre of action, and if the emperor Paul should persist in his *challenge*, a more appropriate place for the decision of the contest could not well be chosen, for *his* accommodation!

The French author St. Pierre, now an old man, lately married a young girl of twenty. The following compliment, by a young widow of his acquaintance, was on that occasion presented to him, on a visiting card:—" Long shall his children know a mother's tenderness. The person, like the works of the immortal author of *Paul and Virginia*, remains for ever in its prime. Nature owes new youth and beauty to his pencil; and, in return, she commands Time to flutter over him with light downy pinions, and to strew only roses on his head. To explain the flux and reflux of the tides, he imagined mountains of ice at the poles.—Life, too, has its poles; but, for St. Pierre, these poles are without ice!"

A punster who frequently sees omens and dire potents in names, assures us, that the embargo laid by Russia on the English shipping, is a much more serious evil than we at first imagined. From a list of the vessels, it appears, the emperor has by it provided himself with *Admiral Nelson*, *Lord Rodney*, *Earl Howe*, and several others of our best Admirals. Thus supported no wonder he has taken from us our *Commerce* our *Prosperity*, our *Perseverance*, *Industry*, and *Resolution*; leaving us without *Fortune*, *Friendship*, *Union*, *Concord*, *Peace*, *Amity*, or *Hope*. He has parcelled out all *Albion*, and possessed himself of *Manchester*, *Bedford*, &c. deprived us of the *Prince of Wales*, *Lord Carrington*, and a long train of fashionable *Nymphs*, *Betseys*, *Annes*, *Fannys*, *and Marys*.—Even the winds of heaven are not suffered to visit us, as he has seized upon *Zephyr*, *Boreas*, &c. In this situation we are left without *Expedition*, *Enterprize*, or *Chance*.

Among the motley groups at the Ranelagh Masquerade, there were but few parts ably supported; there were, indeed, men of all characters, and women without any character at all—several Harlequins, one of whom was lame—savages out of costume and language, except in a brawl—and a fat-headed butcher, who was not aware that he ought not to be " as dull as Leadenhall," but that to support his dress at a masquerade, his wit should have been as polished as keen; as cutting and as pointed as his own knife—while he thought it enough merely to

'Hang a calves skin on his recreant limbs.'

A wit has observed, since her Majesty's birth-day, that the mutiny among the *taylors* had its effect on the birth-day gala. Some gentlemen actually appeared with *coats* that had been *turned!*

POETRY.

POETRY.

THE HIGH COURT OF DIANA.

To the EDITORS *of the* SPORTING MAGAZINE.

GENTLEMEN,

Should the following attempt be thought worthy a place in your Magazine, I shall be happy to exert my feeble powers, at any future period, for the amusement of your numerous readers.

I am, most respectfully, your's,
A SUBSCRIBER.

PARODY
On "ERE AROUND THE HUGH OAK."

ERE the sinewy shank, that supports my brown mare,
  The fierce iron had dar'd to embrace;
Ere the ring-bone had first laid her coronet bare,
  Or a wind-gall her tendons had grac'd;

Could I number the *brushes* by her born away,
  Or the deeds in the field she has done!
E'en the cup I now drink from, in life's early day,
  Her fam'd grandsire at Doncaster won.

To his son be transferr'd all his beauty and speed,
  Which next by my mare were possess'd;
For her colt they're preserv'd, and by Fate 'tis decreed,
  He with victory oft shall be blest.

Cambridge, Jan. 20, 1801.   A.W.W.

BAYSWATER; OR, THE WHIM.

WHILE some post to *Brighton* to take a salt dip,
And others at *Cheltenham* the sun'd waters sip;

Give me the delights which our good *London* yields,
Give me the delights of gay *Paddington's* fields!

For there 'tis my pleasure on Sundays to stray
Through fields clad with corn, and thro' sweet-scented hay;
Each passer looks cheerful, each lassie as fair,
Complacency smiles on her youth debonnaire.

But when with my ramble I 'gin to grow tir'd,
My pipe, ale, and biscuit, are always required;
I hasty to regale me, retir'd from Sol's gleam,
Beneath the green willows of *Bayswater's* stream.

Rich men may boast of a Summer's retreat,
Each Noble may vaunt his old family seat;
I envy them neither their riches nor power,
So I smoke my pipe beneath *Bayswater's* bower.

There, smiling, the married take coffee or tea,
While children, well pleas'd, climb the lov'd parents knee;
The batchelor quaffs the enlivening glass,
While others breathe love to the listening lass.

Some skittles delight in, some quoits, some the bowl—
I view all their pastimes; then with joyful soul,
At eve homeward stray, and there, on my pillow,
I dream of *Bayswater's* pure ale and cool willow.

CONTENT.

SONNET

SONNET TO PEACE.

FRIEND of Mankind! by whose in-
    dulgence train'd,
The softer virtues blossom into life;
    At whose approach, ambition, mortal
    strife,
And havoc, with the blood of nations
    stain'd,
Back to their native hell desponding
    fly.
Friend of Mankind, return!—the wi-
    dow's cry;
The wailing peasant, stinted of his bread;
The lazar's inmost groans; the virgin's
    sigh
For her lov'd hero, numbered with the
    dead,
Or wasting life in sad captivity.—
These are the ills that on thy absence wait!
That Season and the virtues all deplore;
O! come again! Bind round the brows of
    Hate
Thy flowers—O come, fair Peace, to
    part no more!

LOUDHON's ATTACK.

A HUNGARIAN WAR SONG.

RISE, ye Croats! fierce and strong,
    Form the front and march along!
And gather fast, ye gallant men
Of Nona, and of Warrasden;
Whose sunny mountains nurse a line
Generous as her fiery wine.
Hosts of Buda, hither bring
The bloody flag, and eagle wing!
And ye that drink the rapid stream
Fast by walled Salankeme!
Ranks of Agos, head and heel,
Sheath'd in adamantine steel!
Quit the woodlands, and the boar,
Ye hunters wild, on Drava's shore!
And ye that hew her oaken wood,
Brown with lusty hardihood;
The trumpets sound, the colours fly,
And LOUDHON leads to victory!

Hark! the summons loud and strong—
"Follow, soldiers— march along!"
Every Baron, sword in hand,
Rides before his gallant band;
The vulture, screaming for his food,
Conducts you to his fields of blood,
And bids the sword of valour seek,
For nurture, to his gory beak!

Men of Austria! mark around,
Classic fields and holy ground;

For here were deeds of glory done,
And battles by our fathers won—
Fathers who bequeath'd to you
Their country and their courage too!
Heirs of plunder and renown,
Hew the squadrons—hew them down!
Now ye triumph!—Slaughter now
Plows the fields with bloody plough;
And all the streamy shore resounds
With shouts, and shrieks, and sabre
    wounds!—
Now your thunders carry fate—
Now the field is desolate—
Save where *Loudhon's* eagles fly
On the wings of Victory!

This is glory! this is life!
Champions of a noble strife,
Moving like a wall of rock
To stormy siege or battle shock!—
Thus we conquer might and main,
Fight, and conquer o'er again.
Grenadiers, that fierce and large,
Stamp like dragons to the charge—
Foot and horseman, serf and lord,
Triumph now, with one accord!
Years of triumph shall repay
Death and Danger's troubled day:
Soon the rapid shot is o'er,
But glory lasts for evermore—
Glory, whose immortal eye
Guides us to the victory!

HARVEST HOME,

(FROM BLOOMFIELD's FARMER's BOY)

A RURAL POEM.

" *A Shepherd's Boy—he seeks no better name.*"

NOW, ere sweet Summer bids its long
    adieu,
And winds blow keen, where late the
    blossom grew,
The bustling day and jovial night must
    come—
The long-accustom'd feast of HARVEST-
    HOME.
No blood-stain'd victory, in story bright,
Can give the philosophic mind delight;
No triumph please, whilst rage and death
    destroy:
Reflection sickens at the monstrous joy.
And where the joy, if rightly understood,
Like cheerful praise for universal good?
The soul, nor check, nor doubtful anguish
    knows,
But, free and pure, the grateful current
    flows.

Behold

Behold the sound oak table's massy
   frame
Bestride the kitchen floor! The careful
   dame,
And gen'rous host, invite their friends
   around;
While all that clear'd the crop, or till'd
   the ground,
Are guests by right of custom.—Old and
   young,
And many a neighbouring yeoman, join
   the throng;
With artizans, that lent their dext'rous
   aid,
When o'er each field the flaming sun-
   beams play'd.

Yet Plenty reigns, and from her bound-
   less hoard
(Tho' not one jelly trembles on the board)
Supplies the feast with all that Sense can
   crave—
With all that made our great forefathers
   brave,
Ere the cloy'd palate countless flavours
   try'd,
And cooks had Nature's judgment set
   aside.
With thanks to Heaven, and tales of rustic
   lore,
The mansion echoes when the banquet's
   o'er:
A wider circle spreads, and smiles abound,
As quick the frothing horn performs its
   round;
Care's mortal foe, that sprightly joys im-
   parts,
To cheer the frame, and elevate their hearts.

Here, fresh and brown, the hazel pro-
   duce lies
In tempting heaps, and peals of laughter
   rise;
And crackling Music, with the frequent
   thump,
Unheeded bear the midnight hour along.
I—
Here, once a year, Distinction low'rs its'
   crest,
The master, servant, and the merry guest,
Are equal all; and round the happy ring,
The Reaper's eyes exulting glances fling,
And, warm'd with gratitude, he quits his
   place,
With sun-burnt hands, and ale-enliven'd
   face,
Refills the jug, his honour'd host to tend,
To serve, at once—the master and the
   friend;
Proud thus to meet his smiles, to share his
   talk,
His nuts, his conversation, and his ale.

For the SPORTING MAGAZINE.

POOR TOM.

'TWAS for a crime, no matter small
      or great,
Whether against the people or the state,
Poor Workhouse Tom got into dismal
   limbo.
Thomas, like other Britons, hated chains,
And much about disgrace and wrong com-
   plains;
   When, with a surly air, and arms a-
      kimbo,
Thus spoke the tender-hearted Gaoler—
   "How!
" Why what an empty-pated rogue art
      thou,
   " To think a chain the badge of igno-
      miny,
" When the Lord Mayor, and the Shrieves,
      i'fecks!
" Wear chains themselves, and even round
      their necks;
   " But thou wear'st thine upon thy leg,
      thou ninny!"

Tom thought their Honours had a curious
   turn,
To bend their necks to what he'd gladly
   spurn;
   Nor thought their wearing chains made
      his less galling.
" Besides," cries Tom, " they walk about
      at will,
   " But poor Pill Garlic lies in prison still;
" Which, I confess, I see no fun at all
      in!"

At length Tom's tried, and sentenc'd to
   be hang'd;
When, with much logic, thus his friend
   harangu'd,
   'Galmer Tom's unwillingness to wear a
      halter—
" Halters no more than hempen collars are,
" And collars, Lords and Courtiers gladly
      wear!
" Why, therefore, let thy noble courage,
      faulter?"
" Alas!" sigh'd Tom, " thy far-fetch'd
      comfort ceose,
" Nor seek, by nominals, my woes t'ap-
      pease!
" 'Tis not the rope I'mind; to that I'm
      callous;
" But 'tis the death it brings!—Ah! could
      I change
" My collar for a Courtier's, then 'twere
      strange
" If I, altho' a rogue, should fear the
      gallows!"   NAMO.

FANTOCCINI.

FANTOCCINI.

PROLOGUE TO THE SIEGE OF BELGRADE.

Written by one of the Company, and delivered by Harlequin, at the Taylor's Hall, Tuesday, 10th January.

LADIES and Gentlemen!—'tis somewhat queer,
That such a *motley* fellow should appear,
And thus with heart o'erflowing come before ye,
To tell a true though lamentable story.
But first, my worthy patrons! bending low,
I greet you all with my best dancing bow.
  [*Bows.*
You smile—and I perceive that each one feel,
My genius lies not *here* [*pointing to his head*] but in my *heels*.
Yet there's no help for't; so, to be explicit,
I'll tell you all the cause of this odd visit.
Little Rebecqui was in anxious doubt
How you would like the piece that's coming out,
And look'd so sad, that we perceiv'd his pother,
And held a consultation with each other.
Each wish'd to serve him, if he knew the way,
But how to do it—not a soul could say.
At length cried one, " Let some bold dashing dog
Step forth and speak a Pro- or Epi-logue!"
But next arose this question—" Who should write it?"
Or, what was worse by far—" Who should indite it?"—
For though we have amongst us Queens and Kings,
We are not much accustom'd to these things.
Some thought the Conjuror, demure and cragie,
Ought to enchant the audience with his magic.
" Och, blood and 'ounds—cried Darby—how you'd wonder
If I should hit it off without a blunder!
Arrah! send Pat the soldier on the stage;
He's the dear boy to please this warlike age:
Besides, 'tis known to all the world, his trade is .
Not *to fight* only—but *to court the Ladies*."
Others said, " Push our green *Abomtique*,
And let old Blue Beard for the puppets speak."

But this was over-rul'd, lest, like his wives,
The maidens should all tremble for their lives
Three Tails propos'd to send out old *True Blue,*
(Knowing he was a favourite with you;)
And thus all eyes were fix'd on Heart of Oak:
But honest Jack did not admire the joke,
" Avast! avast!—shall I, like a landlubber,
Cringe, bow, talk nonsense, pipe my eye and blubber?
No, dam'me if I do!—I love my wench,
And hate the Dutch, the Spaniards, and the French;
And since the Danes and Swedes will make a rout,
We'll pepper well their jackets *scribabout*;
D—n *their Neutralities!* Let's drink and sing,
True to ourselves, our Country, and our King!!!"

Thus, though each wish'd him well, each little elf
Cunningly push'd the burthen *from himself*;
And poor Rebecqui, 'midst his odds and ends,
Was, like Gay's Hare, " among her many friends."
What, then, if I turn champion to the cause,
And boldly dare to ask for your applause?
Plead for the blunders that may hap' to sight
Among our wooden actors in the fight?—
Consider, Sirs! my minster needs your aid
To fortify and *to maintain* BELGRADE.
Pray do not let him, then, at any rate,
First slacken fire—and then capitulate;
For if you do—there is not half a doubt
But garrison and all *will be udrav'd out*;
For though our Lilliputians do not mind
Being on *short allowance*, yet you'll find
Others behind the scenes, who cannot bear,
Like your cameleon—to live on air.
Come, then, my friends! bring succours to the town,
Nor let the Critics' cannon beat it down—
Look on our faults with a forgiving eye,
And let our errors, with the moment, die!

[*Bows and his going—returns.*]

One gentle hint, good folks! before I go;
Now and then join your hands together,
so— [*Claps.*
You take the joke, I see—aye that's the way
To make us " push on" briskly through the Play.

THE SPORTING MAGAZINE;
OR,
MONTHLY CALENDAR
OF THE
TRANSACTIONS OF THE TURF, THE CHASE,
And every other Diversion interesting to the
MAN OF PLEASURE, ENTERPRIZE, AND SPIRIT.

For FEBRUARY, 1801.

CONTAINING,

	Page		Page
The Wild Ox	207	An Eccentric Dog	237
The late Arrival of Diamond in Ireland	ibid	Peculiar Winter Diversions in Russia Described	ibid
The Berkley Hounds	208	A Horse Cause—Lemon v. Ferguson	239
Malton Coursing Meeting	ibid	Boxing Combats, and the Humanity of the English Character, described by a French Traveller	240
Crim. Con.—Hoare v. Allen	209		
An Assault—Hackett v. Bloxham	ibid		
Account of the New Historical Drama—Deaf and Dumb; or, The Orphan Protected	210	Rustic Simplicity	242
		Oxfordshire Sporting, with Harriers	243
		Origin of planting Yews in Churchyards—Gaming—Isle of Dogs	244
Melancholy Occurrence	212		
Cherubim Shooting	ibid	Essex Coursing	ibid
Memoirs of Lord Rokeby	213	Cynographia Britannica	245
Cursing Enemies, offering Horses, &c. in Wales	216	Account of the New Comedy of The Poor Gentleman	247
The Indian Sportsman	217	Gaming Debts—Whaley v. Southcot	249
Manners and Customs of the Welsh	219		
Account of the Patent Organ	223	Sporting Intelligence	252
A Civil Action	224	Feast of Wit	256
Matrimonial Battery	ibid		
Tim Tape's Journal	ibid	POETRY.	
On Perfection and Imperfection	225		
Account of the New Operatic Farce of The Veteran Tar	226	The Chairman—a Song	257
		A Song for St. Patrick's Day	258
Arundel Castle Described	229	A Hint to a Friend	ibid
Anecdotes of German Authors and Authoresses	230	Lines on Will Abdy, Huntsman	259
		Antient G'ee, composed in 1501	ibid
Preachers—Sunday Sports, &c. under the Head Miscellanies	233	Verses by the Right Hon. R. Fitzpatrick	ibid
Humourous Account of Decoys, in use near Calais	234	A Batchelor's Prayer, by Anthony Pasquin, Esq.	ibid

[Embellished with a beautiful Engraving of THE WILD OX, by SCOTT, and an Etching of CHERUBIM SHOOTING, by HOWITT.]

London:
PRINTED FOR THE PROPRIETORS;

And Sold by J. WHEBLE, Warwick Square, Warwick Lane, near St. Paul's; C. CHAPPLE, 66, Pall-mall, opposite St. James's Place; J. BOOTH, Duke Street, Portland Place; JOHN HILTON, at Newmarket; and by every Bookseller and Stationer in Great Britain and Ireland.

W. JUSTINS, PRINTER, PEMBERTON ROW, GOUGH SQUARE.

Hunting the Wild Ox
from Ridinger.

THE SPORTING MAGAZINE,

For FEBRUARY 1801.

EXPLANATION OF THE PLATE.

THE WILD OX.
AN ENGRAVING, FROM RIDINGER.

THIS untameable animal, endowed with a degree of strength and swiftness not to be paralleled, is no longer to be found, at large, in the forests of Germany, but only in the parks and enclosures of the great Lords, where it is preserved for pleasure, or as a rarity.

RIDINGER was a celebrated German Draughtsman and Engraver; and whose Life we shall give in some future Number, meaning to furnish more Engravings from his inimitable Works.

DIAMOND.
HIS SAFE ARRIVAL IN IRELAND

ALL the Sporting World, whose hopes and fears this celebrated horse has so often and so powerfully excited, must feel some interest in his fate. It is with pleasure, then, we announce his safe arrival, at twelve o'clock on the 17th inst. at Castle Hyde, in the county of Cork, the seat of Colonel Arthur Hyde, his new master.

DIAMOND was two days and two nights on his voyage from Holyhead to Dublin, during which time he encountered much boisterous weather. Notwithstanding this disadvantage, and that horses suffer very much at sea at all times, he reached his destination in as good health and condition as when he set out from London. No better proof can be urged, of the fineness of his temper, and the excellence of his constitution. Had Alexander's *Bucephalus*, or the favourite of Nero, risen from the dead, and appeared in Dublin, they could not have excited more curiosity than his arrival in that city. During his stay there, the milliners shops were deserted for the stables, and the Ladies vied with the Gentlemen in number and eagerness to see him. Every village, through which he passed, resounded with nothing but his name, and praises of his beauty: some, indeed, would rank him in mind, as in form, superior to the rest of his species; for they assure us, that, in passing over the Curragh of Kildare, he seemed perfectly sensible he was upon his *own ground*.

From this account, DIAMOND is not likely to have reason to complain of Irish hospitality. At all events, (considering the numerous accidents to which such a spirited animal was liable) Colonel Hyde may consider the journey as a sort of *Diamond Lottery*, and himself the fortunate holder of the *Prize Ticket*.

SPORTING INTELLIGENCE.

THE BERKELEY HOUNDS.

A Most extraordinary circumstance happened with the Berkeley Hounds, on Tuesday the 10th instant:—

Meeting the company to throw off at Hodgmoor, they soon unkennaled, and went away in the highest stile imaginable, crossing a considerable scope of country, with breast-high running for two hours. They at length reached Pollard's Wood, where the field of horsemen was very much reduced: here Reynard, finding himself severely pressed by the pack, (which was close at his brush) jumped into what is called a *gravel-pit*, of ten or twelve feet deep, and was immediately followed down the obscured precipice by the body of hounds, who were completely lost to view, and the very few horsemen, that were near, left in a state of the utmost consternation.

Tom Oldaker, (the Huntsman) and one *Whipper-in*, being up, the latter permitted himself to be let down into the dreary abyss, from whence, by the most incessant exertion and incredible fatigue, he extricated and got to the surface *seven* couple,—then *the fox*, and, with a persevering Herculean labour, the remaining *fourteen* couple, many dreadfully bruised, and the last, a favourite leading hound, (which it is supposed went down close to the fox) *quite dead*. Previous to the conclusion of this arduous and dreary task, the Whipper-in had earnestly implored assistance for extrication, and had no sooner reached the surface (nature being quite exhausted with bodily fatigue) than he fainted, and his recovery was for some time doubtful. To use Oldaker's own words, "It was the most shocking sight he ever was a witness to, and hopes never to see the like again."

We are happy to afford our Sporting Readers early and authentic information, that these hounds will hunt the Berkshire district the first week in March. On Monday, the 2d, they throw off at Kidgeham Copse, near Wokingham; and on Wednesday, the 4th, at the Shoulder of Mutton, Binfield.

MALTON COURSING MEETING,

February 3.

IN consequence of the numerous matches that were run at this meeting, the sport continued till Friday afternoon.

The first Silver Cup was run for over the Wharham Grounds: the entry for it as follows—

Sir Rowland Wynn, a dog named.
Major Topham - 1
Mr. Plumer - 1
Mr. Croft - 1

But in consequence of all the dogs, except Sir Rowland Wynn's, being slipped before the signal, the cup was adjudged to Sir Rowland.

Mr. Plumer was the chief winner of matches. His dogs distinguished themselves much. His famous dog, *Speed*, died shortly after his match, the last meeting, with *Snowball*.

WEDNESDAY.

Mr. Duncombe's fox-hounds threw off at Settrington Wood. No fox found. The hounds appeared in a gallant stile.

THURSDAY.

Various matches were run; and the dogs beat the hares, who did not run well.

FRIDAY.

The second large silver cup was run for by seven dogs. Here, again, a singular circumstance occurred:—

curred:—Mr. Darley's bitch (unanimously allowed to be the best) disqualified, by starting before the signal. Mr. Lee, of Grove, was the winner. The cup was contested on the Duggleby Grounds.

The meeting was very numerous, and the weather uncommonly fine. More hares were killed than ever were known at a February meeting.—The matches made for the next November meeting exceed in number any before made: among the rest, seven of the blood of *Snowball*, against seven capital dogs that have won every thing, bred from a famous bitch of Mr. Croft's, which won the cup seven years ago.

LAW INTELLIGENCE.

CRIM. CON.

COURT OF KING'S BENCH,
Saturday, Feb 21.
Before Lord Kenyon and a Special Jury.

HOARE v. ALLAN.

THIS very interesting cause to-day again came before the Court. We shall, however, now give but a very short statement of it, as we detailed all its circumstances at great length when it was first tried, and as the result of the two trials is exactly the same.

The parties are both Gentlemen of large fortune and great respectability. The action was brought for criminal conversation. That Major Allan had lived with Mrs. Hoare, it was clearly proved; but it could not be made out, that there had been any improper intercourse between them till after Mrs. Hoare had left her husband's house. She had become acquainted with Major Allan in India, many years ago, and had then conceived an incurable passion for him; but till October last, when he returned, she had never violated the laws of decorum.

It was attempted to be made out, that Mr. Hoare was altogether ignorant of his wife's intentions, and that he believed she was going on a visit to her uncle, Major Cooke. The attempt was not successful; and, notwithstanding the evidence of Mr. Clarke, who described them both to be in the most dreadful state of distress when they parted, the Jury, with Lord Kenyon's approbation, found a verdict for the Defendant.

All hope of Mr. Hoare being able to procure a divorce, *à vinculo matrimonii*, is thus taken away.

SLIGHT OF HAND.—ASSAULT.

COURT OF KING'S BENCH,
Monday, February 23.

HACKET v. BLOXAM.

MR Garrow stated, that the Plaintiff in this case was sitting in the Red Lion public-house, Islington Road, with several other persons, attending to the exhibitions of a Slight-of-hand professor. After he had concluded his performance, the company gave him a gratuity of a penny each, except the Plaintiff, who, being much delighted with his amusing tricks, rewarded him with six-pence. Seeing this, the Defendant said he was in colleague with the Juggler, to cheat and defraud the public; that he was concerned also with a banditti of robbers infesting the neighbourhood, and had robbed him a few nights before. On this the Plaintiff replied, and the Defendant immediately struck him in the face, beat out

out two of his front teeth, and otherwise much bruised him.

This statement was confirmed by the evidence of one witness, an Attorney, who happened to be present during the transaction.

Mr. Mingay observed, he should not call any witnesses on the part of the Defendant, as he was of opinion the Jury saw the business in the light that he did, which was—a *Juggler* exhibiting his *tricks*, in order to *cheat* the gaping throng out of their pence; while an honest Attorney was taking notes of a drunken squabble, to shew *his tricks* in Westminster Hall. He trusted the Jury had found him out, and were of opinion, with him, that *one penny* was damages enough to give; and that the Plaintiff's witness, who was his real Attorney in the cause, though another name appeared on the record, might go home with his client, and part their gains.

The Jury gave a verdict for the Plaintiff—Damages *Forty Shillings*.

NEW DRAMA.

DEAF AND DUMB; or, THE ORPHAN PROTECTED.

THEATRE-ROYAL, DRURY-LANE, *Feb. 24.*

THIS evening, this new Historical Drama, in five acts, was performed here for the first time. The principal characters were thus represented:

MEN.

Julio of Haraucour (Theodore)	Miss De Camp.
Darlemont	Mr. Wroughton.
St. Alme	Mr. C. Kemble.
Franval	Mr. Barrymore.
De l'Epeé	Mr. Kemble.
Dupre	Mr. Banister, jun.
Pierre	Mr. Palmer.
Dominick	Mr. Suett.
Servants—Mr. Trueman, Mr. Chippendale, and Mr. Maddocks.	

WOMEN.

Madame Franval	Miss Pope.
Marianne	Mrs. Mountain.
Claudine	Mrs. Sparks.

This interesting piece is a translation from the German of Kotzebue, adapted to the English Stage, by Mr. Kemble. It may be considered an handsome compliment to the humane institution established at Paris, for the instruction of the Deaf and Dumb, of which fame has spoken so highly. Of the merits of the establishment the following description, given by the Abbe de l'Epée, the Founder of the Seminary, may afford some idea. "If the peasant," says he, "feels delight when he beholds the abundant harvest which rewards his industry; judge what must be my sensations, when I stand in the midst of my pupils, and see how the unfortunate beings emerge by degrees from darkness; how they become animated by the first beam of heavenly light; how they step by step discover their powers, impart their ideas to each other, and form around me an interesting family, of which I am the happy father." An institution such as this must be a fruitful source of anecdote, and accordingly we find the author has, in the present instance, availed himself of one long familiar to the public, and not the less interesting from its being founded on fact. The fable is the simplest that can be conceived; but its simplicity is the simplicity of nature, and the most successful appeal to her force and influence. *Julio*, an interesting youth, born deaf and dumb, the orphan heir to the first Magistrate of Toulouse, is brought to Paris by *Darlemont*, his uncle and guardian,

Deaf and Dumb; or, The Orphan Protected. 211

guardian, and exposed in a mean attire. Here he is received into the Philanthropic Asylum for unfortunates of his kind, under the name of *Theodore*. His manners, so ill corresponding with the meanness of his dress, at once induce the discerning *De L'Epee*, to suspect that his pupil is the victim of fraud and injustice, and the quick intelligence of the youth soon confirms this suspicion. He accordingly sets out with him for the South of France, from some city of which his observations on the conduct of the boy lead him to conclude he has come. Arrived at Toulouse, the extravagant joy exhibited in the looks and gestures of his companion, satisfies the Abbe that he has reached the sought-for place. It is here the scene opens with a view of Toulouse, and *Theodore*, recognizing the habitation of his father, now usurped by his uncle.—His restoration to his fortune constitutes the interest of the plot, of which the means by which that end is accomplished form the principal ingredients. *Julio* recognizes the old domestics of his father, and is recognised by them in return. Proofs rise on proofs of his identity; but it is not until after a most obstinate resistance to their force that the uncle confesses his guilt, and restores his property to the injured *Julio*.

There is also an underplot, judiciously blended with the main story. It consists of the love of *St. Alme*, the son of *Darlemont*; but his reverse in disposition for *Marianne*; all obstacles to which are removed by the generosity of *Julio*, whose first act, after he obtains possession of his fortune, is to settle half of it upon his cousin. From the recital of this story, the reader might not suppose it a source of great interest. It is therefore impossible to speak of it in adequate terms of praise, without the suspicion of over-rating its merits. We must, however, assert, that of all the productions of this celebrated author, which have yet appeared in an English garb, the present is equal in interest to any, and superior in purity of sentiment and moral to all. The ground which he has chosen, has the advantage of novelty, but it has also the disadvantage of being extremely difficult. Of this he seems to have been perfectly aware, for the *Abbe* tells *Franval*, the advocate, whom he engages in his pupil's cause, that " a person who is deaf and dumb, always creates distressing sensations;" and that he was therefore afraid the presence of his pupil might not be pleasing. With such a knowledge of his subject, Kotzebue must have been afraid that the infirmities of nature were dangerous subjects for theatrical exhibition. That the attempt has succeeded in the present instance, is owing to the great delicacy and skill with which it is managed. Perhaps too the manner in which Miss De Camp sustained the character of *Julio*, contributed not a little to its success. Her fine expressive countenance supplied the deficiencies of speech and hearing. The presence, therefore, of *Julio*, was interesting, but not distressing. In all the incidents and situations the author has been peculiarly happy: they are all of the most simple, natural, and domestic kind; they are such as come home to men's business and their bosoms; they are such as they may every day see in the families of others, and tremble for in their own, connected and embellished with all those affecting scenes which render injured innocence doubly interesting by the helplessness of its situation, and all those sentiments of humanity which flow from the peculiar nature of the subject.

The adaptation of this Piece to the

the English Stage does not appear to have been a difficult task. It is one, however, which is executed with great care, taste, and judgment. Except that the portrait of *Julie* is more relied on as a principal proof of his identity, all the other incidents are the same as in the original. The characters and the plot also suffer no variation; but in the language, and the turn of the sentiment, there are many alterations, all of them improvements.

The humane, philosophic Abbe *De l'Epée*, was well sustained by Mr. Kemble; and Mr. Wroughton, in the proud and guilty *Darlemont*, was uncommonly energetic and impressive. Mrs. Mountain, in *Marianne*, the heroine of the piece, had a gentle, delicate part, of no great compass. She was in full voice, and executed a pleasing air allotted to it, with great sweetness: this charming air was composed by Kelly. All the other characters were supported with like success.

The Prologue, which stated the claims of the Piece to public favour on the grounds of novelty, and nature, was delivered with considerable feeling and judgment by Mr. Powell; and Miss De Camp, in the Epilogue, made some pleasing allusions to the recovery of her speech, and the grand charter of the sex.

The House was filled with an elegant audience, and the piece was heard throughout, and announced for future representation, with the most ardent and uniform approbation.

MELANCHOLY OCCURRENCE.

ON Saturday morning last, two soldiers, of the 3d Lancashire Militia, on furlough, travelling between Durham and Auckland, were so fatigued and distressed by the inclemency of the weather, that one of them, on entering a public house near Butcherraw, and warming himself by the fire, fell backward and expired. The other was found dead under the park-wall, near Auckland, by a butcher coming to Durham market.

EXPLANATION OF PLATE II.

CHERUBIM SHOOTING.

(An Etching, by Mr. Howitt.)

TWO Cockneys went on a shooting party to some little distance from Town, and were to sleep at an alehouse, and rise early to their sport in the morning.—Trudging to their quarters in the dusk of the evening, a large looking bird came sailing round the corner of a barn, at which one of them put up his gun; he shot, and the bird fell;—but, oh horror! what was the surprize and dread of him and his companion, when running up in a great hurry to pick up his game, he found a pair of full bright eyes in a comely round face, with a pair of snow-white wings extended, and fluttering in agonies?— Away they ran to the house, when the shooter instantly fainted; and, on the earnest enquiry of mine Host into the cause of their alarm, his fellow Sportsman, with a tremulous voice, cried —" Ah! poor creature! Heaven " forgive him!—But he has had " the misfortune—I am sure it was " unintentional—to shoot a Che-" rubim!"

However, as Boniface and his Hostler were not quite satisfied with this account, they took a candle and lanthorn to the spot, and there found the supposed Cherubim to be only a poor unfortunate Owl.

Memoirs of Lord Rokeby.

(Concluded from page 174.)

ABOUT that period, he either formed the opinion, or began to express it with an unusual degree of confidence, that the Bank of England would break during his life-time. He was so firmly convinced of it in his own mind, that it became a pretty constant topic with him; and, when he met with opponents, he defended it with such strength of argument as could not easily be resisted. One day the conversation on this subject ended in a singular wager, which was taken down in writing, purporting that the heirs and executors of Mr. Robinson should pay to the other party, an alderman of Canterbury, the sum of ten pounds, if the Bank did not break during the life-time of the former; and, on the other hand, that the alderman should be similarly bound to pay the sum of ten pounds, if the Bank did break in Mr. R.'s life-time.—The proof was to depend on a 10l. Bank-note being offered at the Bank, and not producing in return ten pounds in specie. Every year added strength to the singularity of Mr. R.'s opinion, and he maintained it as firmly as another on a philosophical subject, which he defended with great vigour of mind, and, when past eighty years of age, supported by quotations from the classics, repeated with the utmost energy and classical taste—*The future destruction of the earth by fire.*—On this question, he solicited no aid from the arguments sometimes used in the pulpit on the same subject; for the path to his church was overgrown, and his pew left to the same decay as his coach-house. Yet this circumstance led to a trait in his character, which was better discovered by his own recital of the anecdote, than it can be by the pen of the writer.

A little time before the death of the archbishop of Armagh, he made a visit into Kent, to see his relations, and, among them, him who was to inherit his title. "The archbishop told me," said Mr. R. "that he would dine with me on Saturday. I gave orders for dinner, and so forth, for my cousin, the archbishop; but I never thought, till he came, that the next day was Sunday. What was I to do? Here was my cousin, the archbishop, and he must go to church;—and there was no way to the church,—and the chancel-door had been locked up for these thirty years,—and my pew was certainly not fit for my cousin, the archbishop. I sent off immediately to Hythe, for the carpenters, and the joiners, and the drapers; and into the village for the labourers, the mowers, and the gravel-carters. All went to work: the path was mowed—the gravel was thrown on and rolled—a gate made for the church-yard—the chancel-door opened and cleaned—a new pew set up, well lined and stuffed, and cushioned; and the next day I walked by the side of my cousin, the archbishop, to church, who found every thing right and proper. But I have not been to church since, I assure you."—This singularity, in abstaining from the places of religious worship, arose partly from the exalted view which he entertained of the nature of the Deity, whose altars, he used emphatically to say, were Earth, Sea, Skies; from the little regard he paid to the clerical or ministerial character; and from the disgust in his mind at the stress laid by Divines upon trifles, their illiberality in wishing every one to rely upon them for their faith, their frequent persecution

persecution of others, and from a strange opinion of the great inefficacy of their preaching. Religion he conceived to be a mere personal concern between the creature and the Creator: and the Supreme, in his opinion, was degraded by being made a party in questions often political, and on the mode of his existence being made a barrier between the natives of the same island. Yet, with these opinions, he could converse with the Clergy, of all descriptions, as freely as with other men; and, where they were men of liberal education and enlightened minds, was much gratified by the pleasure of their company.

In the year 1794, Mr. R. became, by the death of the archbishop of Armagh, Lord Rokeby; and it is natural to ask, What difference the title made in his manners?—Precisely none. He was now addressed by the title of Lord instead of Sir; and, as he used to say, they are both the same in the Latin. Yet the accession to his title gave him rights in Ireland; and his letter to Lord Castlereagh shewed that he was not unworthy of them, and that, if age and infirmities had presented no obstacles, the Irish House of Lords would have been dignified by the presence of a man who assumed for his motto, on this occasion, what he really possessed in his heart, *Independence*. Very fantastical notions accompany, in some persons minds, the titles of the peerage: they think of fine dress, splendid carriages, haughty demeanour, something differing from the many. Such persons were much embarrassed at the sight of Lord Rokeby:—a venerable man with a long beard, sallow complexion, furrows on his forehead, the traces of deep thinking, fore part of the head bald, from the hinder flowing long and lank locks of white hair, a white or blue flannel coat and waistcoat and breeches, worsted stockings, and shoes tied with black strings. The ruffles at his wrists, and the frill sewed to his waistcoat, were the only linen about him. His body was rather bent; but, till he was near his end, his pace was firm, and he was seen walking in this manner from his house to Hythe or back, or, which was more gratifying to his friends when they caught a first view of the house, walking up and down the pavement before his door.—"How can this man be a Lord?" said the vulgar. "Would to God more Lords were like this man!" said the man of sense. "I wish we were all as attentive to good-breeding!" said the man of fashion.

From the time of his accession to the title to the day of his death, Lord Rokeby seldom went farther from home than Hythe; but he would have thought that he had forfeited all regard to his principles, if he had not gone to Maidstone to vote for his friend, Filmer Honeywood, the staunch advocate for the independence of the county; and a contested election for the city of Canterbury drew him again from his retirement. This election took place just after the famous stoppage of the Bank; and, after a visit to his friends at the hall, and shouts of congratulation from all the freemen, he walked to the alderman's house, with whom the wager had been laid, proffered some notes for cash, presented the written agreement on the wager, and demanded of the alderman the sum of ten pounds.

The question, as might naturally be expected, staggered a little the alderman, who was also a Banker; and as the words admitted of some debate, and Lord R. had not with him

him documents of the refusal, at the Bank, of cash for a ten-pound note specifically proffered, the payment was deferred; and, whether it has been made, or not, the writer cannot determine.

On returning to the hall, Lord R. came again on the hustings, by the side which is appropriated for persons to return who have voted, and for the infirm and the friends of the candidates, or the officers of the court. The sheriff very politely offered to take here his lordship's vote, who with his usual good humour declined it. "I am not so old, neither," says he, "that I cannot do like the rest of my brother citizens!" and instantly went down the stair, where he met an old man ascending, who had given him a vote nearly fifty years before, mixed with his brother citizens, went up the proper stairs with them, and gave the last proof of his political connection with Canterbury in a manner worthy of himself and his principles.

We might recount a variety of anecdotes expressive of his character, but the limits will not permit us; yet we must not pass over the subject of his food, which has been so much the object of enquiry and misrepresentation. He has been said to live on raw flesh, and to be, in short, little better than a cannibal. This was by no means the case; and to understand this, as well as the other parts of his character, we must look to his leading principles, *Nature and Independence*. He thought that this island produced within itself sufficient food for his nourishment. Wheat he considered as an exotic; besides, it was fermented: two reasons sufficient to expel it from his nourishment. Foreign coffee, for the same reason, was rejected; and he tried various experiments with burnt beans, peas, &c. Remarkably fond of sweet things, he used honey as a substitute for sugar. But it is to be observed, that he was not a scrupulous observer of his general rule; and when it was hinted to him that he was eating the crust of a pie, or similar things in the ordinary cookery, he turned it off with a good-humoured laugh, adding, " Where is the man that lives as he preaches?"—His appetite was remarkably strong, which he satisfied at times by boiled beef, or rather beef kept for a considerable time in boiling water; and his table was amply provided with every thing in season, exceedingly well dressed, and of which he partook, off a wooden platter, like any other person. He drank no wine; and he gave the best proofs of the excellence of his diet, by the length of his life. No one was more hospitable to his guests: they were desired to order just what they pleased; and, in return, were requested and expected to permit the host to eat what and when he pleased.

He never willingly omitted bathing a single day, and had made, for that purpose, a bathing-house of considerable length and breadth, glazed in front, to a south-eastern aspect, and thatched at top. This, probably, is the most comfortable bath-house in England, as, after bathing, you may run up and down to dry yourself, and do not feel that disagreeable cold common in the small elegant bath-houses of marble, where you freeze in cold magnificence. Lord R.'s bath-house was boarded and matted. In this bath-house, and a wood at a small distance from it intersected with walks, and, at proper intervals, having wooden seats and benches, his lordship spent considerable time, frequently committing to paper his valuable reflections.

His memory was prodigious. In conversation

conversation, if any thing occurred which afforded room for difference of opinion, he would frequently run on the sudden to his library, bring back a folio or two, and point the passage on which the whole depended. He was a great reader, as well as deep thinker, and preserved the use of his eyes to the last. For writing, he very frequently availed himself of the help of an amanuensis.

In so singular a character, it is natural that persons little acquainted with it should make very erroneous conjectures. Covetousness was represented to be his prevailing feature: but this was not perceptible in his domestic arrangements, where, in every article of good living, there was superfluity; and his parlour fires of wood and coal, which would be sufficient for half a dozen common rooms, did not countenance the idea of a frugal disposition: besides, his conduct to his tenants (for there was no where to be found a milder landlord, and perhaps, indeed, he carried this propensity to indulge them to almost blameable excess) is a sufficient proof that his thoughts were not bent, with any degree of anxiety, on the acquisition of wealth. Yet he was tenacious of his property, when once it had come into his hands, and he made a joke himself of his fondness for a new guinea: but this may be accounted for from his idea of the nature of paper credit, and the firmness of our Bank; and the quantity of money found in his house, at his death, was the natural result of these opinions.—He was an excellent master and a good neighbour, just in all his dealings, of strict honour, firmly attached to the liberty of his country, of a most enlarged mind, a true free-thinker, and, with all the singularities in his dress and manners, he united to his love of Nature and Independence all the good qualities which constitute a perfect gentleman.

CURSING ENEMIES, OFFERING HORSES, &c. IN WALES.

I Have heard (says Mr. Bayley) of a strange custom that prevails in some part of North Wales; which, no doubt, the Clergy study to abolish, as much as lies in their power.—When any person supposes himself highly injured, it is not uncommon for him to repair to some church, dedicated to a celebrated saint, as Llan Elian in Anglesea, and Clynog in Carnarvonshire, and there, as it is termed, to *offer* his enemy. He kneels down on his bare knees in the church, and offering a piece of money to the saint, utters the most virulent imprecations, calling down curses and misfortunes upon the offender and his family for generations to come: all which they have a firm belief will come to pass. Sometimes, instead of a church, they repair to some of the sacred wells that are dedicated to the saints. Mr. Pennant mentions his being threatened by a fellow, who fancied he had been injured by him, with "the vengeance of St. Elian, and a journey to his well to curse him with effect."

Some of these wells are in great repute for the cure of diseases, by means of the intercession of the saint. The saints are also applied to when any kind of goods are lost, and are made the instruments of recovering them, or of the thief who has stolen them.

St. George had formerly, in the parish of Abergele, in Carnarvonshire, his holy well, at which this British Mars had his offering of horses; for the rich were, at certain times, accustomed to offer one, to secure his blessing on all the rest. St George was the tutelar saint of those animals; and all that were distempered were brought to this well, sprinkled with the water, and had this blessing bestowed—*Rhad Duw a Saint Sior arnat!* "The blessing of God and St. George be on thee!"

In the churches, when the name of the Devil occurred, an universal spitting used formerly to seize the congregation, as if in contempt of that evil spirit; and whenever Judas was mentioned, they expressed their abhorrence of him, by smiting their breasts.

If a *Ffynnon Vair*, or Well of our Lady, or any other saint, was near, the water for baptism was always brought from thence; and after the ceremony was over, old women were very fond of washing their eyes with the water of the font.

Upon Christmas-day, about three o'clock in the morning, most of the parishioners assembled in the parish church, and after prayers and a sermon, continued there, singing psalms and hymns, with great devotion, till it was day-light: and if, through age or infirmity, any were disabled from attending, they never failed having prayers at home, and carols on our Saviour's nativity. The former part of the custom is still in some places preserved, but too often perverted into intemperance. This act of devotion is called *Pulgen*, or *The prowling of the cock*.—It has been a general belief, among the superstitious, that instantly,

"at his warning,
"Whether in sea, on fire, in earth, or air,
"The extravagant and erring spirit hies
"To his confine,"

THE INDIAN SPORTSMAN.

Mr. Howitt has just put forth a very singular and highly interesting Prospectus of a series of Designs, to be intituled "*The Indian Sportsman*," and to be designed, drawn, and etched by himself. His account of the undertaking is as follows:—

THIS truly novel and interesting Work is now proceeding, under the care and direction of an Officer who has served upwards of Twenty Years in Bengal. It is admitted, by a number of Gentlemen who have resided there, to be a most faithful delineation, not only of the sports in general, but of the costume of the natives, as well as of the appearance of the country, &c.

Mr. HOWITT intends this notice merely to ascertain how far he may hope to be patronised in so arduous and expensive an undertaking.—Judging from the high encomiums, and the subscriptions with which he has already been honoured, he flatters himself that its circulation will exceed his most sanguine expectations.

The Plates are all 18 inches by 13, and will be aqua-tinted and coloured in such manner as to imitate the Drawings as closely as possible; which, of course, must render them highly ornamental for furniture, as well as suited to the folio, or to bind in volume.

The whole will be published in pairs, with all possible expedition. Price, to Subscribers, Two Guineas per pair; payable on delivery.—Ladies and Gentlemen may subscribe for any number, or for any Plates they may select.

The following List of subjects now in hand is subjoined, that the Public may judge of the nature of the work. Mr. Howitt will do himself the pleasure to exhibit and explain, to those who may honour him

him with their commands at his residence, the several Drawings which are finished, and which are in the Catalogue marked thus *.— Those in a forward state, but not yet fit for exhibition, are marked thus †.— The whole of the Drawings are expected to be complete by the end of April; before which period some of the Plates will, in all probability, be published. The first impressions will be delivered to the earliest subscribers.

CATALOGUE OF DRAWINGS.

NO.
*1 Hunters going out in the Morning.
*2 Beating Sugar Canes for a Hog.
*3 The Chase after the Hog.
*4 Hog-Hunters coming by surprize on a Tigress and her Cubs.
†5 Hog chased thro' a Village.
*6 Hog at bay.
*7 The dead Hog.
*8 The Return from Hog-hunting.
*9 A Tiger prowling through a Village at Night.
†10 A Tiger seizing a Bullock in a Pass.
*11 Shooting a Tiger from a Platform.
*12 Driving a Tiger out of a Jungle with Elephants.
*13 Chasing a Tiger across a River with Elephants.
*14 The Tiger at bay.
*15 The Tiger springing on an Elephant.
*16 The dead Tiger.
*17 Shooters coming by surprize on a Tiger.
*18 A Tiger hunted by Wild Dogs.
†19 A Tiger killed by a poisoned Arrow.
*20 Shooting a Leopard from a Tree
†21 Exhibition of a Battle between a Buffalo and a Tiger.
†22 Buffaloes rescuing a Calf from a Tiger.
†23 Hog-hunters chased by Buffaloes.
†24 Hunting a Buffalo.
†25 The Buffalo at bay.
†26 The dead Buffalo.
*27 Peacock Shooting.
†28 Duck Shooting.
†29 Snipe Shooting.
*30 Shooting at the Edge of a Jungle.
†31 Driving a Bear out of Sugar Canes.
*32 Death of the Bear.
*33 Hunting a Kntauss, or Civet.
*34 Jackalls rescuing a hunted Brother.
†35 Chase after a Wolf carrying off a Lamb.
†36 The common Wolf-trap.
*37 Smoking Wolves from their Earths.
†38 Digging out a Fox.
*39 The Ganges breaking its Banks, with Fishing, &c.
*40 Killing Game in Boats, at the Inundation of an Island.
†41 Doreeahs, or Dog-keepers, leading out Dogs.
†42 Sices, or Grooms, leading out Horses.
†43 Running a Hog-Deer.
†44 The Hog-Deer at bay.
*45 Driving Game into Nets with Elephants.
*46 Driving Elephants into a Kedduh.
*47 Koomkies, or Decoy Elephants, catching a Mule.
†48 Koomkies leaving the Male fastened to a Tree.
†49 Rhinoceros attacking Horses at their Pickets.
†50 Rhinoceros bayed by Elephants.

N. B. With every Print will be delivered a descriptive Ticket, intended to be pasted on its back, when framed. A great variety of other subjects are sketched; but it is Mr. Howitt's intention to confine his labours, for the present, to those enumerated in the Catalogue.

MANNERS AND CUSTOMS OF THE WELSH.

From Bingley's Tour round North Wales.

THE manners of the Welsh people have had many singular and striking features, from the earliest periods of their history. Driven into this obscure corner near fourteen centuries ago, they have, from the mountainous nature of their country, and their own dispositions, been ever since almost entirely excluded from all commerce with their neighbours, and prevented from settling any connections with them.—They, therefore, we find, prejudiced in favour of their own institutions, and their own customs, retained many of them for several centuries afterwards. From their seclusion they also contracted new and different habits, different modes of life, and many other customs, which remained long unknown to their neighbours; some of these have been transmitted to us by their historians.

Sylvester Giraldus Cambrensis, Archdeacon of St. David's and Brecknock, who, in the year 1187, travelled through Wales, his native country, with Baldwin, Archbishop of Canterbury, to preach the crusades, has left us, though mingled with superstition, and many of those incredulous stories, which were common in those dark ages, a very accurate detail of the character of the Welsh people.

Pride of ancestry and nobility, were, he says, at that time, points held by them in the highest estimation; and so deeply rooted was this spirit, that even the very lowest of the people carefully preserved the genealogy of their families, and were able, from memory, to recite the names of their ancestors, for several generations.

They were keen in their resentments, and revenged most deeply any insult committed on their family. They were vindictive and bloody in their anger, and too prompt to avenge, not only recent injuries, but even those committed at very remote periods.

They did not in general reside in cities, villages, or camps, but led solitary lives in the woods. On the borders of their forests, the lower class formed their dwellings, by twisted ozier coverings, suited to the different seasons of the year, but with as little art as expence.

They had no beggars in their whole country, for their hospitality was extended to every one.

They esteemed liberality, and particularly hospitable entertainments, as preferable to every other virtue. By a mutual return of civilities, this habit was so common, that whenever a traveller entered a house, upon delivering his arms to the guard, some of the domestics brought a vessel of water to him; and such was the custom, that if he suffered his feet to be washed, he was considered as a lodger for the night. The offering of water was their mode of invitation; but, if he refused their kindness, he was considered only as desiring a morning's recreation.

The strangers who arrived in the morning were entertained through the whole day, and till the evening, with the conversation of young women and the music of the harp, for almost every house was provided with both of these; from whence it appears, says Giraldus, that this people were not, like the Irish, given to jealousy. Every tribe or family possessed the skill of playing upon the harp beyond any kind of learning; and the Welsh excelled, in the wit and ingenuity of their songs, and extemporaneous effusions of genius, all the other Western nations.

In the evening the strangers being all assembled, an entertainment was provided for them, according to their number and rank, and according to the ability of the host. The kitchen was not loaded with much profusion, nor with delicacies, or with incentives to gluttony; nor had they tables, table linen, or napkins; nature was always studied more than splendour.

The guests were placed by threes at supper, and the dishes were placed on green and fresh rushes. They had also thin and broad cakes of bread, that were always baked the same day.

At the same time that the whole family, with a kind of emulation in their civilities, were waiting on their guests, the host and hostess in particular, always remained standing, that they might overlook the whole, and see that none of the dishes were taken away, till every one had finished; so that if any one had not sufficient, it might be his own fault.

When the hour of rest approached, a large bed of rushes, thinly spread, and covered with a hard and rough cloth, the produce of the country, was ranged lengthways along the sides of the room. On this they all laid down together, in the same dress they had worn during the day, which consisted of a shirt and small cloak. The fire was always kept burning at their feet during the night; and either when they found themselves starved, or the bed uneasy, from its hardness, they hasted to it, to seek a remedy against those inconveniencies; then, returning again to their bed, they alternately presented one side to the cold, and the other to the hardness.

Both sexes of this nation took particular care in preserving their teeth. These they kept perfectly white, by continually rubbing them with a green hazel and a woollen cloth; and what tended much to their preservation, they invariably abstained from every kind of hot food, using only such as was cool and temperate.

The men, who were chiefly occupied in military affairs, shaved their beards, leaving only a whisker on their upper lip. The youth went by clans and families, with their chief at their head; and they were so prompt in the defence of their country, that they were permitted to enter the houses of every person with the same security as their own.

In the time of Howel Dda, Howel the Good, about nine hundred years ago, and near three hundred before the time of Giraldus Cambrensis, the royal mansion consisted merely of a noyadd, or hall; an ysdasell, or parlour; and a bywythy, or buttery; an yslable, or stable; a cynhordy, or dog-kennel; and an ysgubaur, or granary; an odyn, oven or bake-house; a tybychan, or little-house; and a hundy, or bed-room.

The fire-pan was of iron, and the fuel of wood; and the bed was only of straw, as it continued to be, even in the royal bed-chambers of England, till so late as the conclusion of the thirteenth century.—The King's own dress was a mantle and tunic, shirt, breeches, shoes, stockings, and gloves, and a cap of skins.—The Queen's was nearly the same, differing only in her having fillets under her cap.

The great officers of the court were, Penteulu, the Mayor of the Palace; Effeirad-teulu, the Domestic Chaplain; Y Dysdain, the Steward of the Household; Penhebogydd, the Head Falconer, or Master of the Hawks; and Brawdur Llys, the Court Justiciary; Pengwasdrawd, the President of the Grooms; Pencynydd, the Chief Huntsman;

Huntsman; Gwas Dysdein y vrenhines, Steward of the House to the Queen; Edeirad y vrenhines, the Queen's Chaplain; Barddteulu, or the Court Poet: Gosdegwr, or the King's Serjeant, who had to command silence in the King's hall, at dinner, by striking on a particular pillar; Drysawr y neuadd, the Door-keeper of the Hall; Drysawr Yr Ystasell, the Door-keeper of the Chamber; Pencenydd, or the Master of the King's Hounds; Meddwyd, or the King's Cellarer; Meddyg, or the Physician to the Household; Trulliad, or the Butler; Drysawr, or the Porter, who had to provide straw for all the beds, and to kindle all the fires in the Court; the Cog, or Cook; the Cantrwllyd, the Curator of Lights; Morwyn Ystasell, the Chambermaid; Gwastrawd Arwyn, the Groom of the Rein to the Queen.

In this establishment we see the head of the falconers, the chief of the grooms, the poet laureat, and the cook, all ranked immediately among the great officers of state. Such a precedence was naturally given them in a Court, generally devoted, as all originally were, and as in all illiterate ages ever will be, to the pleasure of the feast, and the diversions of the chace.

In the absence of the King, the authority of the Court was vested in the Domestic Chaplain, the Steward of the Household, and the Judge of the Palace, conjointly.

Their different ranks of society were, Brenin, or Teyrn, the King; Twysog, or Duke; Jarll, or Earl; Arglwydd, or Lord; Harwn, or Baron; Uchelwr, or Squire; Gwrcang, or Yeoman; Alltud, or Vassal; and last of all, the Caeth, or Slave.

The King had reserved to him, the right of commanding every person to join his army; and once a year, if it were necessary, to go with him out of the country; but, in his own country, he had the power of calling them together whenever he pleased.

The Welsh people are naturally inquisitive and curious, but this is by no means a circumstance peculiar to this country. In all wild and unfrequented parts of the world it is the same, and it is only in such parts of Wales that this disposition is most observable. Dr. Franklin has told us, that this curiosity prevailed so much in America, that when he travelled in that country, if he only wished to ask the road, he found it expedient to save time by prefacing his question with—" My name is Benjamin Franklin — by trade a printer—am come from such a place—and going to such a place; and now—which is my road?"—In all travels, through unfrequented countries, we find it very common; and, from the inquisitive dispositions of men in general, where novelty lays such hold upon their attention, it would seem strange were we not to find it so.

They are much inclined to superstition.—But in all countries, there are weak and foolish people; in England, many of our peasantry are ready to swallow, with the most credulous avidity, any ridiculous stories of ghosts, hobgoblins, or fairies. In Wales it is more general, and the people are certainly more credulous than the generality of the English.—There are very few of the mountaineers, who have not by heart a whole string of legendary tales of those disembodied beings.

The Roman Cavern, in Llanymynech-hill, called Ogo, has been long noted, as the residence of a clan of the fairy tribe, of whom the villagers relate many surprising and mischievous tricks. They have listened at the mouth of the cave, and have sometimes even heard them in conversation, but always in such low whispers, that their words have been never distinguishable. The stream that runs through it is celebrated as being the place in which they have been heard to wash their clothes, and do several other kinds of work.

These busy little folk seem to be somewhat allied to what are called *knockers*, which by the Welsh are believed to be a species of aerial beings, that are heard under ground, in or near mines, who, by their noises, direct the miners where to find a rich vein. The following extraordinary account of them, is from a letter of Mr. Lewis Morris, to his brother, Mr. W. Morris, Comptroller of the Customs at Holyhead, dated October 14th, 1754. I will make no comment upon it, and only preface it by observing, that Mr. Morris was a very learned and sensible man, and a person whose judgment is esteemed of great weight by every one who has been either acquainted with him or his writings.

" People who know very little of the arts or sciences, or the powers of nature, (which, in other words, are the powers of the author of nature) will laugh at us Cardiganshire miners, who maintain the existence of *knockers* in mines, a kind of good-natured impalpable people, not to be seen, but heard, and who seem to us to work in the mines; that is to say, they are types, or forerunners of working in mines, as dreams are of some accidents which happen to us. The barometer falls before rain or storms. If we did not know the construction of it, we should call it a kind of dream, that foretells rain; but we know it is natural, and produced by natural means, comprehended by us.—Now how are we sure, or any body sure, but that our dreams are produced by the same natural means?—There is some faint resemblance of this in the sense of hearing: the bird is killed before we hear the report of the gun. However this is, I must speak well of these *knockers*, for they have actually stood my very good friends, whether aerial beings, called spirits, or whether they are a people made of matter, not to be felt by our gross bodies, as air and fire, and the like.

" Before the discovery of Esgair y Mwyn, mine, these little people, as we call them here, worked hard there day and night; and there are abundance of honest sober people, who have heard them, and some persons who have no notion of them or of mines either; but after the discovery of the great ore, they were heard no more.

" When I began to work at Llwyn Llwd, they worked so fresh there for a considerable time, that they even frightened some young workmen out of the work. This was when we were driving levels, and before we got any ore; but when we came to the ore, they then gave over, and I heard no more talk of them.

" Our old miners are no more concerned at hearing them *blasting*, boring holes, landing *deads*, &c. than if they were some of their own people; and a single miner will stay in the work, in the dead of night, without any man near him, and never think of any fear or harm they will do him; for they have a notion that the *knockers* are of their own tribe and profession, and a harmless people who mean well. Three or four miners together shall hear them sometimes, but if the miners stop to take notice of them, the *knockers* will also stop; but let the miners go on at their own

own work, suppose it is *boring*, the *knockers* will go on as brisk as can be, in landing, *blasting*, or breaking down the *lode*; and they were always heard, a little from them, before they came to the ore.

"These are odd assertions, but they are certainly facts, though we cannot, and do not pretend to account for them. We have now very good ore at Llwyn Llwd, where the *knockers* were heard to work, but have now yielded up the place, and are no more heard. Let who will laugh, we have the greatest reason to rejoice, and thank the *knockers*, or rather God, who send us these notices."

An intelligent friend of mine informs me, that those noises, the *knockers*, as they are called, have very lately been heard in the parish of Llanfihangel Yscelfiog, in Anglesea, where they continued at different intervals for some weeks. In accounting for these noises it has been observed, that they probably may have proceeded either from the echo of the miners at work, or from the dropping of the water; but these seem by no means sufficient, if Mr. Morris's assertion be true, that while the miners are going on with one kind of work, they are going on with another: while for instance, as he says, the *miners* are *boring*, they are *blasting*, the former certainly cannot be true, and the blasting entirely puts the latter conjecture out of the question, for droppings of water could never produce any effect of that kind. As I am only acquainted with the subject from report, I am under the necessity of leaving the elucidation of these extraordinary facts to some who have better opportunities of enquiring into them. I have only to express a hope that the subject will not be neglected, and that those who reside in the neighbourhood where they are heard, will enquire into them carefully, and, if possible, give to the world a more accurate account of them than the present.

(To be continued.)

THE PATENT ORGAN.

IN the drawing-rooms of people of fashion, organs are now introduced upon a new principle.—They are made in the form of a commode, with a marble top: in the front, brass wire doors, with green silk curtains. Each organ has twelve tunes, which, when set agoing, will play through the whole without further assistance. The pipes are much superior to the generality of those articles; the sounds are soft and full of harmony. The plan upon which they are introduced is as singular as novel: the organ is placed in such a position, as to give music to two rooms at once by the following ingenious contrivance:—In the drawing-room it is a fixture over the convex mirrors, and on it are placed *or moulu* girandoles, &c. candelabras are set on each side; a communication is cut through the floor; a pipe is there introduced from the organ, which extends through the ceiling of the eating parlour below, and there it appears in the shape of a gilt trumpet. To give additional effect to the deception, a transparent lamp is suspended from the trumpet, by four gilt chains, and that is not without its use, being the means of giving additional light to the sideboard placed underneath.

The elegance of the article, the peculiar melody of its tones, and the singularity of the plan upon which they are introduced make much noise in the fashionable world, as it is a most *unique* and tasteful appendage

appendage to the apartments of the great and opulent.

A CIVIL ACTION.

A Few nights ago, as Mr. —— was sitting in his study, reading some papers, in which he was requested to give an opinion, the servant announced an unknown gentleman, with some papers, which he had brought from a client of Mr. —— for his perusal. By the time that the stranger had drawled out his pretended message, the servant had retired. When instantly the bundle of law was changed for more forcible arguments, and a pistol presented at Mr. ——'s head, extorted from him his money. The sharper was civil and prepared to take his leave, prudently walking off with one of the silver candlesticks to *light himself* down stairs—No sooner was he out of the room, than the gentleman rang the bell violently, and a servant running up to answer it, met the impostor, who, with infinite presence of mind, told him, that it was only to let him out, but that to save him (the servant) trouble, he had taken the candle to let himself out. There was no farther occasion for it, and he would therefore lay it down. The servant let him pass, and he escaped.

MATRIMONIAL BATTERY.

A Cause extremely interesting to the rights of married ladies was discussed at the County Dublin Sessions the 19th of January last, in the prosecution of Elizabeth Quinn, against Robert Quinn, her husband, for assault and battery. After much argument on the case, the Chairman strenuously recommended the prosecutrix to settle amicably with her husband, and return to her family. The counsel for the defendant, to induce such compromise, offered, on the part of their client, to settle on her three hundred pounds, in case she should survive her husband, and enter into security of one thousand pounds, never more to molest her, on returning to the loving and penitent affections of her tender husband. The lady modestly alledged the risk of her life in cohabiting with him; and her Counsel tendered a proposal of a separate maintenance, as the condition of dropping the prosecution. The trial was then adjourned, *sine die*, to consider of the terms of accommodation—in the mean while the lady remains under proper protection, to secure her safety.

TIM TAPE'S JOURNAL.

" Instructs the fiery steed, and trains him to his hand."—ADD.

THOUGH the noble art of Horsemanship was sedulously cultivated among the antients, I much doubt if it ever attained that perfection which it has at present acquired. Alexander tamed the fierce Bucephalus; but I am inclined to think he could not have bestrode one of our Sunday hacks, with half the ease and elegance of attitude exhibited by those gentlemen, who have studied under the immortal Gambado. Innumerable have been the feats performed on horses with *four* legs; but it was reserved for the present enlightened age to make those go that possess but *three*; nay, so wonderful has been our improvement that I have even known a journey of seven miles accomplished in two hours! and that on a steed, which,

in

in the jockey phrase, hadn't *a leg to stand on.*—Oh! the persuasive powers of whip and spur!

I was induced to these reflections by a walk which I took last Sunday on the Highgate road; where, whilst admiring equestrian exertion in its highest excellence, I picked up the following paper, which, after the correction of a few orthographical errors, is now submitted to the perusal of my readers:—

"Rose at seven—Spent an hour in balling doe-skins, colouring boot-tops, &c. &c.—Stupid boy had lost one of my spur-leathers—obliged to use packthread—Got to the stable by nine—Spurs wrong put on—Gave ostler a pint of beer to alter 'em—Mounted on the off-side in such a hurry, that, losing my balance, I pitched over head foremost into the horse-trough—Got out half suffocated: wig so wet, was forced to take it off and dry it—Stable-boys laughed, dogs barked, I swore; but at length, being mounted by the help of a step, set off, and reached Tottenham-Court Road without any material accident, except that a hackney-coach splashed me all over—*N. B.* Took his number.—Whilst paying the turnpike, dropped my glove—afraid to get off, for fear of not being able to mount again, so rode on, putting my naked hand in my pocket.—*Mem.* It's genteel to sit easy.—Just by Mother Red-Cap's, horse made a trip - pulled at him with all my might, but, breaking the rein, fell backwards, and came to the ground with my foot in the stirrup—Luckily, horse was no run-away—Mended the rein with my garter, and led my horse till I came to a mile-stone, where with some difficulty I remounted—Finding that I should be too late for the ordinary, squared my elbows, turned out my toes, flourished my whip, stuck in the spurs, and away I trotted—By the time I had gone a mile, found myself very sore, though I rose in the stirrups at least a foot every second—however persevered, and by two o'clock reached Highgate Hill, at the bottom of which, as the Devil would have it, the saddle turned round, and down I came once more—To compleat my misfortune, the girth (for there was but one) broke; so, with the saddle on my back, and leading my horse, I fagged up the hill, and at length reached the inn, followed by all the rabble of the place.—After dinner, discovered I had lost all my money by my fall—Obliged to leave my watch for the reckoning.—Girth being mended, I mounted about eight in the evening; but, being dreadfully galled, borrowed a crown of the landlord, and giving it a man to take my horse home, returned to Cheapside in the stage, delighted with my ride, and the pleasures of the country!

"*Sunday night.* TIM TAPE."

Should TIM TAPE be inclined to make any more of these excursions, an account of his adventures cannot fail to amuse the public.

VALCOUR.

On PERFECTION *and* IMPERFECTION.

To the EDITORS *of the* SPORTING MAGAZINE.

GENTLEMEN,

DO we not frequently hear of such a character as a *perfect blockhead?* And are there not men who can talk (I will not say when or where) for an hour together, the most *perfect nonsense*; nay, and publish the said perfect nonsense, too, in the very teeth, and in open defiance, of Messieurs the Monthly Critics

Critics and Reviewers? But this is not all: I have heard, since the commencement of the present war, that some men high in authority (I do not say in what country) have, more than once, committed a *perfect blunder*, to the great detriment of the nation.—I do remember some lines illustrative of this kind of perfection, that were written many years ago, which, if the *rhime* may be pardoned, are no bad illustration of our modern opinions of perfection. They were written in a tavern—

" The poor have some things perfect,
  some the rich:
And here's our landlady, a perfect ——!"

How egregiously was Pope mistaken, when he asserted, that

" Whoever thinks a *perfect* work to see,
  Thinks what ne'er was, nor is, nor e'er
  shall be!"

Strange that a man, who knew the world as he did, should hazard such a contradiction in terms. What would he have said, had he lived in our days, and beheld the various instances of perfection with which we are surrounded?—Beheld some who had attained a *perfect* knowledge of the *chase line*, others *perfect* in the *manual exercise*—some restored to *perfect* health by a single pill, and others *perfectly blind* from their infancy—some *perfect* in the *Latin* and *Greek*, and others in the management of a *dairy*—some who have attained a *perfect friendship*, and others who have made considerable progress in a *perfect hatred*. But I check my pen, lest you should suppose I was not so *perfectly correct* in my ideas of what space ought to be allowed for the lucubrations of, Your's, &c.

OXONIENSIS.

P. S. I was very much shocked, on going into the Clarendon Printing-Office the other day, and hearing about several *bundles* of the *Imperfections* of the Bible. I always thought that one of the *most perfect* of books, although of the *old school*.

DRURY-LANE THEATRE.

THE VETERAN TAR.

A New Operatic Farce, called *The Veteran Tar*, (the Music by Dr. Arnold, the Drama by his son) was performed, the first time, on Friday the 30th of January.

PERSONS OF THE DRAMA.

Tom Sturdy,	-	Mr. Bannister, jun.
Philip,	-	Mr De Camp.
Doctor Gossamer,	-	Mr. Wewitzer.
Farmer,	-	Mr. Suett.
Henry,	-	Mr. Trueman.
Tom Cluelive,	-	Mr. Chippendale.
Ben Bowling,	-	Mr. Webb.
Margery,	-	Mrs. Sparks.
Lisetta,	-	Miss Stephens.
Cicely,	-	Mrs. Mountain.

Chorus of Sailors and Villagers.

STORY.

A cutter is wrecked on the coast of England.—Near the shore is a village inhabited by good peasants of different ages, married and unmarried, merry and out of humour, following their labours, and enjoying their simple pleasures, plagued by a conceited apothecary, a Dr. *Gossamer*, who insists on surfeiting them all with his physic. A Farmer's family, consisting of the *Farmer* himself, his wife *Margery*, and his daughter *Cicely*, are selected from among the rest to perform conspicuous parts in the piece. A happy new-married couple, *Henry* and *Lisetta*, are the only others of the villagers brought forward into the action. *Tom Sturdy* presents himself as the late commander of the cutter, and, in his own supposition, the only survivor of the shipwrecked crew. He laments his gallant messmates, and is miserable

able for the loss of his son *Philip*, among them. The villagers console and entertain him. He searches for his son; and resolves to divert his sorrow by going again as soon as possible to sea. His son, in the mean time, presents himself, as having escaped to the rocks of the shore, near where his father is in search of him. They meet, and joyfully recognize each other. The son meets also with the Farmer's daughter, *Cicely*, falls in love with her at sight, and quickly wins her affections. His father disapproves his passion, as incompatible with the fearless, careless, adventuring spirit of a Tar. The *Apothecary* is his rival with *Cicely*; and the *Farmer* will not have his child to marry a wandering Sailor. A French privateer alarms the coast, and threatens the village. *Philip*, joined by his messmates, (who were supposed to have perished) puts out to sea, boards the privateer, makes her his prize, and returns in triumph. By this gallantry, he reconciles all parties to his marriage with *Cicely*. The piece thus ends with the general triumph and happiness of all the characters, except the ridiculed and disappointed *Apothecary*.

The chief merit of this piece, is its adaptation to the state of the country at the present moment, and its tendency to animate the patriotic feelings of Englishmen. If there is nothing new in the Fable or the Characters, there is a vigour and spirit in the Dialogue, which is, in that respect, above the ordinary run of such compositions. Many of the sentiments are noble, and yet appropriate: none of them are extravagant, and most of them are impressive.

As it was necessary to diversify the characters, the author has introduced, among his Seamen, a *Farmer* and a *Doctor*; but the scenes, in which the two latter are engaged, are by no means so well conceived as those which relate to his honest Tars. Those characters, however, though less efficient, give the others a more forcible influence by contrast.

Several of the patriotic effusions were warmly received by the audience, particularly one which imported that the English Tars would soon exert their prowess on the French, the Swedes, the Danes, and the Russians.

The piece was very well sustained, particularly by young Bannister, who played the *Veteran Tar* with admirable force and feeling. Young De Camp also distinguished himself very well. Such made as much of his part as it admitted; and Mrs. Sparks was successful in the *Farmer's Wife*: her *rustic* ran very much diverted the audience.

Mrs. Mountain sung delightfully, though, considering the situation of the part she sustained, a little more simplicity would have been more characteristic.

The piece was received with great applause by a crowded and a loyal audience, who seemed to glow in sympathy with every patriotic sentiment; and it was announced for the ensuing evening with a hearty consent.

The Drama itself was written by Mr. Arnold, the son of the respectable composer, Dr. Arnold, who furnished the Music, which is altogether highly creditable to his taste, science, and genius.

The following Songs were all encored:—

SONG.—CICELY.

YES, I'll die an old maid, if a man I can't find
That my fancy has pictur'd as quite to my mind—
His heart shall be open, his countenance too,
And lib'ral his hand—or he never will do!

In short, to convince me he's this thing
 and that,
"My heart, when I see him, must bounce
 —pit-a-pat.

I care not for cash, or for acres in store,
 With a man that I love I can never be
  poor!
Nor with one I detest, can I happy be
 made,
Tho' I daunted in sattins, in silks, and
 brocade!
In short, I'll ne'er wed in this world, and
 that's flat,
Till my heart says—"that's he!" with
 a bounce—pit-a-pat.

DUET.—LISETTA and CICELY.

HARK, hark! the village bells delightful sound,
  In cadence sweet they die along the
   vale;
Now lowly murmuring o'er the broken
 ground,
  Now loudly swelling on the travelling
   gale!

Hark! low they echo round the rocky
 shore;
  Now, soft they steal responsive on the
   ear;
Now, caverns deep rebellow to the roar,
  In sounds harmonious, audible and clear.

SONG.—CICELY.

WHEN storms are sunk to rest,
 And thunders roll no more,
The Sailor's heart, how blest,
Who seeks his native shore!

That shore, where many a fair
 His cheering spirit warms;
All crowd his smiles to share—
Snug moorings follow storms!

Then rage, ye faithless winds!
 Ye foaming billows roar!
The Tar a welcome finds
Upon his native shore.

Though tempest-tost at sea,
 Ashore affection warms:
A sailor's creeds agree—
Snug moorings follow storms.

SONG.—LISETTA.

THE Sailor who ploughs the salt wave,
 Far absent from love and from home,
Tho' he fears not a watery grave,
 Yet he sighs from his charmer to roam.

Tho' the tempest howl loud o'er the main,
 Yet he fears not the wind's dreadful
  roar;
For those winds will soon waft him again
 To the arms of his Nancy ashore.

SONG.—TOM STURDY.

ODDS, life! when a Sailor gets bother'd
 with love,
  He's all one as a ship without rudder or
   sails,
That the roaring of buffeting billows must
 prove,
  And must drive at the mercy of thun-
   d'ring gales.
His cargo's afloat, all his masts by the
 board,
  A sheer-hulk, without ballast, she heavily moves!
"Helm a-weather!" he whimpers; he
 sighs, "his adore'd!"—
  " Betsy, boys!"—A lubber, he pipes
   out "he loves!"

But see him tight-rigg'd, and for duty
 agog;
  A light-hearted, jolly, brisk crew man
   the shrouds;
He springs upon deck, he distributes his
 grog,
  Pipes all hands from below, and his
   light canvas crowds;
No thoughts cross his mind, but of drubbing our foes,
  The proud flag of Britain in triumph
   unfurl'd,
A signal, a breeze boys, three cheers, and
 he goes,
  Takes his prize—and is gaz'd by a
   wond'ring world.

The Monsieurs love to dance, let 'em dance
 o'er the main,
  With Mynheer and the Don; tho' they
   'scape a salt dip,
Why the French we'll soon teach how to
 dance back again!
  And tho' rubbers can't dance, we'll soon
   teach 'em to skip!
Let our navy be ready, with canvas unfurl'd;
  For when England is threaten'd, we always are ready;
And our dear little England defies all the
 world—
  To our King and our Country, still
   steady boys, steady!

LISETTA.

LHETTA, GYPSY, and HENRY.

High on a rock, by ocean lash'd around,
  Britannia sits upon her well fix'd throne;
Views the vast main, and bids her waves
    resound,
  And calls unmov'd the vast expanse her
    own.
Bids the swoln waters heave their angry
    heads,
  Securely smiling 'mid the bellowing
    deep,
Drives back the wild waves to their bil-
    lowy beds,
  Till winds are hush'd, and storms are
    lull'd to sleep.

ARUNDEL CASTLE DESCRIBED.

ARUNDEL Castle, which is said to confer upon its owner, by the mere fact of its possession, the Earldom of Arundel, is now receiving such repairs and embellishments, as must render it the chief of ancient residences in England. Perhaps no other building of equal date has been retained in a habitable condition, without having its appearance, and the style of its construction, in some degree perverted by additions and alterations inconsistent with the taste of the age in which it was built. Arundel Castle, on the contrary, is but maintained and continued by its present exterior improvements, vast as they are; the design of the original founder is still obeyed; the new walls have risen upon the ancient model, and correspond with the old ones in solidity of fabric, as well as dignity of ornament. The successor of the Montgomerys, the Albeneys, and the Fitz-Alans, has respected their taste, and that of the ages in which they here held dominion over their ample territories. An entire new front of massy stone differs from the others only in exhibiting the insignia of the Howards, mixed with those of their predecessors. In raising this front, the duke has taken an opportunity to enlarge the house, and appears to have gained the space now occupied on the basement story, by a long range of servant's offices, including a new kitchen, with two fire-places, and grates twelve or fourteen feet long. A new dining-room, or rather hall, on the principal floor, is also in this part of the building. The floor of this apartment is not yet fully laid, nor the walls stuccoed, but a skirting of mahogany has been run along them, to the height of four feet, and a music gallery at the bottom is complete. This is one of the most sumptuous and appropriate of the interior improvements. It is constructed entirely of mahogany, richly carved with the foliage of the oak and the vine, and is supported by solid pillars of the same valuable material, embraced by similar ornaments. A beautiful marble chimney piece also displays some bacchanalian imagery; but this is intended to be removed, being of a shape somewhat too modern for the style of the apartment, the stucco of which will be a deep brown. The prince, it is said, will be present at the first dinner that *adorns* this room. But of all the modes of liberal and dignified expence displayed in this mansion, that which is peculiar and distinguishing, is the use of the richest mahogany in almost every decoration, and for purposes to which ordinary wood is thought sufficient in the finest houses. Thus the walls, being more than six feet thick, form a kind of frame for each window, which is five feet deep on the inside; and the whole of this spacious case, not excepting the top, is lined with mahogany of more than an inch in thickness. The window-frames which hold the magnificent plate-glass panes, three feet each in height, are of course of the same material; and the solid mahogany doors are held

held in cases, which the thickness of the inner walls renders, perhaps, four feet deep, all lined with pannels of the most beautiful grain. It was once intended to floor all the best rooms with this costly wood; but, when it was tried in one apartment, the effect was found to be too gloomy.

ECCENTRICK.

Anecdotes of German Authors, and Authoresses, residing at Weimar, in Saxony.

VON GÖTHE, privy counsellor to the Duke of Saxe-Weimar, intendant of the ducal mines, of the theatres, of the Academy of Painting, &c. the Apollo of the German Parnassus, has attained in his political, as well as literary career, a splendid eminence. Göthe is a native of Frankfort. When the Duke of Weimar passed through that city on his way to Darmstadt, to be betrothed to a Hessian princess, he became acquainted with young Göthe, then already resplendent with the rays of glory reflected upon him, from his " Werther," and his " Götz von Berlichingen." He had, about that time, written against Wieland's review of the Alceste of Euripides, a satyrical farce, entitled, " Gods, Heroes, and Wieland." Wieland answered the Frankfort satyrist in the same style. The duke, who was no stranger to the warfare carried on by the two poets against one another, asked Göthe if he had no commission to his good friend in Weimar, or whether he would not rather go there himself, to finish the contest in a personal interview? Göthe answered, " if you will make something of me in Weimar, I shall most willingly go thither."—" It shall be done."—" But you must make me something worth the while."—" That too shall be done." —The young poet accordingly accepted the duke's offer.

The tumultuous genial epoch, which, on his arrival, commenced at Weimar with walking on stilts, horse-racing, skating, banquets where the guests drank out of skulls, cudgelling, boxing, and other wild pranks and overflowings of a genial humour, and thence spread, together with the fashion to dress *à-la-Werther*, like a whirlwind over all Germany, is sufficiently known and decried. Lessing immortalized this stormy period, by the following energetic and characteristic saying, " If any one," exclaimed he, " call me a *genius*, I shall give him so severe a box in the ear, that he will believe there were two of them." The madness had at last risen to such a height, that poor Lenz, who afterwards died insane in Russia, when his unlucky stars led him to Weimar, into the midst of the whirlpool, broke out into these disgusting words, on seeing some cowdung lying in the sun: " What bliss to be a cow-t—d basking in the sun!"—There was such noise, bustle, and stamping, after the new genial fashion, that the then yet sober, prosaic ground of Weimar, quaked and smoked, and the timid nymphs of the Ilm took refuge in their grottos. The rage for theatrical exhibitions, in particular, was indulged to a great excess. The duke and his courtiers acted on a private stage the satyrical farces of Göthe, before the chief inhabitants of Weimar. The age of Aristophanes, and of the old comedy in Athens, seemed to have returned. Every one laughed at the follies and failings of his neighbours, which were here held forth to public view; and unexpectedly found his own exhibited in his turn. Many allusions

allusions in Göthe's earlier plays, which were afterwards published with many omissions, but still so that many passages stand in need of a secret key to disclose their meaning, cannot be explained, except by referring to the history of that period of gaiety. Thus, for instance, he then wrote an imitation of the *Birds* of Aristophanes, which was acted on a small stage at one of the duke's hunting seats. At that time too he produced his *Faust*, or the Adventures of a Necromancer, who is at last carried off by the devil. The greater and most interesting part of those high entertaining and festive productions is not yet printed. Many of the plays were exhibited in the woods and valleys; every place near and around Weimar was consecrated to the service of the Comic Muse; and the surrounding country every where exhibits the ruins of that golden age of mirth and genius. They endeavoured to draw Wieland into the vortex of wild tumultuous diversion; but the mild Wieland shuddered at their break-neck leaps and pranks; and, in consequence, he had the mortification to see himself, a few days after, exhibited on the stage in the most ridiculous costume.

But soon these wild ebullitions of youthful spirit subsided; and a dignity and manliness succeeded, which rendered Göthe the more worthy of esteem. It is said that then, and even at a later period, he possessed an almost magic power over the affections of the fair sex; and that, however, no woman could boast to have held him, either as a youth or a man, enslaved in the fetters of her charms. He still converses with the ladies in that easy and dandling playful manner with which we are wont to treat children; and even now, the ladies emulously either hate or love him. Göthe is of opinion, that the wings of genius would be hindered from expanding by the too strict domestic bonds. His ideas of women are most strongly expressed, in his last novel, entitled, *Wilhelm Meister*, in which the pretty Philinia, is his heroine, and in his Love Elegies, which are written with all the voluptuous fire of a Propertius, and have been again reprinted, last year, in the seventh volume of his works. Göthe has acted perfectly consistent with these notions, in never marrying. He cannot, however, be accused of licentiousness in his amours; and gives a very proper education to his only son, whom he had by his housekeeper, a Demoiselle Vulpius.

In the mean time, our poet, equally the favourite of Fortune and of the Muses, rapidly rose from dignity to dignity; he now appeared like a beneficent genius at the side of the duke, over whom he possessed the most unbounded influence; and few things of importance were done, which were not either planned or executed by the new minister. When he went to Italy, he resigned the management of *part* of the numerous affairs connected with his high office, that he might have the more leisure to dedicate to the Muses. Even at present, however, his Sovereign does nothing without previously consulting him; and in the campaign against the French, in 1792, Göthe was obliged to accompany him to the army.

The external appearance of this great man, forms a striking contrast with Wieland's: that of the latter full of mildness, modesty, and friendliness; and that the former indicating pride, arrogance, and defiance. But through this forbidding outside, there shines forth a firmness and elevation of character, to which no one, on a nearer acquaintance, can refuse his esteem.

Göthe, like Wieland, entertains no very high opinion of mankind in general; only it would seem, that what is merely disgust in the latter, is become in the former a settled habit of contempt. To him, mankind appear interesting but only in one point of view, namely, as furnishing a subject for the exertion of his poetical talents.

Jena is the favourite abode of Göthe's muse. In the castle of that place, our poet often resides and pursues his studies for weeks together; probably, because he can there enjoy undisturbed peace and tranquillity, which is denied him at Weimar. His Iphigenia was composed in a wood near Weimar, which particularly recommended itself to him, when, in the moments of inspiration, he sought for solitude. On the wall of the hermitage, whence came forth the Iphigenia, the following verses were inscribed by Göthe, and may still be read there:—

"Ueber allen Wipfeln ist Ruh !
Jn allen Zweigen horst du
Keinen Hauch !
Die Vögel schlafen in Walde,
Warte nur, balde
Schläfst du auch !"*

In his person, Göthe exhibits the fullness and rotundity of health and good living: he is a true Epicurean god, up to the neck, which supports a Platonic head. Wicked wits have said of him, that he poetises best in the banqueting-room; but, according to his own confession, it is in the lap of Beauty. Götho interests himself with enthusiasm for the improvement of the fine arts, especially painting; to which the *Propyläen*, published by him, bear honourable testimony.

Many of the best artists now living at Weimar (as, for instance, Krause, who is president of the academy of painting, Horny, and others) owe their first establishment there, and after success, chiefly to his fostering patronage. The Italian Muses, whom he has several times visited in their own charming country, have decorated his house with their choicest gifts. Göthe possesses a mind extremely eager after knowledge: he loves, and, as far as he can, pursues the study of all the sciences. He has formed himself by the contemplation and enjoyment of the beautiful, and by the constant endeavour to see and investigate every thing himself—the character of great and original writers in every branch of literature.

To enable us to pronounce a proper judgment on the merits of Göthe, we must distinguish three periods of his life, and of the therewith intimately connected emanations of his genius. The first is the boisterous stormy period, which closes with his "Clavigo." Many passages of "Wilhelm Meister," however, which were then already written, are stamped with the same character—as likewise the noted *Xenia*, or biting epigrams on most of the German authors and learned societies, which appeared in Schiller's Poetical Almanack for 1797. The second period comprehends his Iphigenia, his Tasso, his Egmont, and other mature works of his genius, which then received the highest classical polish in Rome, Naples, Sicily, where he lived four years. It closes with his idyllic poem, entitled "Hermann and Dorothy." —The third period, in which he at present is, is that of the arts. The mighty creative Genius now seldom swings his flaming torch on high ; in his stead has succeeded the imitative and reasoning Muse. During this

---

* * Calmness reigns o'er the tops of the trees ! not a breath is heard among the branches !—The birds are asleep in the grove—wait but a little while, and thou also sleepest."

this latter period, Göthe has given a modern metrical dress to the old satyrical poem entitled "Reynard the Fox;" and lately, he has fitted for the German stage, several of Voltaire's tragedies. He now instructs us in the laws of the fine arts, in his *Propyläen*, a periodical publication, whose excellence will not be wholly comprehended till some later period. Most praiseworthy is the prize-exhibition for the works of German artists, which he two years ago, out of his own pocket, instituted at Weimar. The candidates for last year's prize seat, from various parts of Germany, twenty-seven pictures, which were for fourteen days exhibited to the Weimar public.—Further information relative to this prize-exhibition may be found in the *Propyläen*, of which six numbers have appeared.

(*More of the Literati of Wiemar in our next.*)

MISCELLANIES.

PREACHERS.

MANY a man (says Dr. South) would have made a very good pulpit, who would have made a very bad figure if he had been put into it himself.

SUNDAY SPORTS.

It is a singular circumstance, that an act, allowing dancing, &c. on a Sunday, should have passed in the reign of Charles I. who, his greatest enemies must allow, had at least every exterior of religion; and that an act for keeping holy the Sabbath-day should be passed in the reign of Charles II. who, his best friends must acknowledge, had no more religion, nor regard to its forms, than one of his own coach-horses.

Account of two Centenarians,

Extracted from a Literary Journal of 1740.

The pictures of two Centenarians are brought to Compeigne.

The first is the picture of John Rovin, aged 172, and Sarah Dessen, aged 164: they were born in the Banyat of Temeswar, in Hungary, where they still live. They have been married near 147 years, and have two sons and two daughters living: their youngest son is 116 years old, and has two great grandsons, one 35, and the other 33.

The second picture is that of Peter Zorton, a peasant in the same Banyat, who died Jan. 25th, 1724, aged 185. His youngest son is still living.

Opposite Consequences from the same Cause.

SPILLER, the Comedian, for whose benefit Hogarth engraved a ticket, was, about the year 1720, in such estimation, that he had what was then deemed a very handsome salary; but, had it been double what it was, his improvident disposition and unbounded extravagance (especially in his amours) would have kept him poor—and very poor he was. With his poverty he was frequently reproached, and once with some severity by a female performer, who having a good person and a very tender heart, contrived to make a figure with a very inferior salary. Of this she boasted, and asked him—*Why he could not manage in the same way?* "Madam," replied the irritated performer, "Madam, that which makes you rich, keeps me perpetually poor!"

HUMOUROUS

HUMOUROUS CEREMONY OF DECOSSE, IN USE NEAR CALAIS.

ON Midsummer-day in particular, a festival is observed by the inhabitants of this country, to which they give the appellation of *Decosse*. This ceremony bears a strong resemblance to the wakes which are celebrated in Ireland. Mark is a little village about two leagues distant from Calais; its appearance is mean and wretched: the only thing in it worthy of notice, is its church, which is passable for a country church. Every village has some particular saint for its patron, on the anniversary of whose day, the inhabitants have merry meetings; the people of the village, and the peasants who inhabit the country adjacent, invite their friends to these; these friends are likewise at liberty to invite as many of theirs, as they think proper. I happened to be admitted into one of these companies by a second invitation, and must acknowledge, that the peasant and his wife shewed more civility to me, than to him that invited me: I observed the same distinction made with regard to others, in the same case with myself. This instance of country politeness does not require a comment. As soon as the company was all assembled, the good woman of the house brought in a large pewter dish, into which she poured a bottle of brandy: she then put a large pewter spoon into the dish, and then began at the right side, by presenting the dish, with the brandy and spoon in it, to a gentleman who was acquainted with the custom. I was particularly attentive to observe what was to be done with this dish of brandy; he took up a spoonful of the brandy, and drank the healths of all present: this every body present was obliged to do in his turn, which proved rather disagreeable to me. This ceremony being over, she presented every body present with a piece of cake, big enough to serve a plowman, but it would have given great offence to have refused. Then the company retired, some to walk, some to dance, according as their inclinations led them, till such time as dinner was ready. Their manner of dining is one of the oddest ceremonies I ever saw in my life. The cloth was laid on two old crazy tables, with a plate for each person, or one for every two of the guests. The same economy was observed with respect to chairs and forks, but there was but one knife at the table, and that was for him that had the office of carver. It would be considered as a breach of decorum for any lady, or any person belonging to the family, to undertake this office. The ladies were first accommodated with seats, and every thing else which was to be had at this extraordinary entertainment; but the guests of the other sex were so entirely neglected, that they were obliged to shift for themselves as well as they could; except the ladies compassionately condescended to lend them part of what they had taken possession of. Each guest was obliged to find his own knife; such as had none, were obliged to wait till their neighbours had done, in order to borrow theirs. Thus were we obliged to manage at this country entertainment: and in all my life, I never met with any thing more ludicrous, or that made me laugh more, than what I saw in this day's excursion, especially the brandy and dinner. The strangers were accommodated with wine; but the friends and acquaintances of the peasant were obliged to put up with beer. Dinner being over, the peasant's wife entered with a cake, and what the French call a *Tarte.*

Tarte. The former was tolerably good in its kind, but the latter was quite disagreeable to all the English present, as well as to myself. It is made of a kind of sour cream, covered over with a piece of dough which has leaven in it. The French are so fond of this cake, ordinary as it is, that they defer eating till it is brought in. We were regaled next with *creme bouilli*, or boiled cream; the ingredients which enter into the composition of the *beverage* are sour cream, eggs, and milk hot from the cow, with a little rennet; we were served with it in pans, with a spoon to sip it, and sugar was given to such as chose it. I found this *beverage* agreeable enough; it is a good refreshment upon a hot summer's day. The dinner, upon these occasions, consists of soup and boiled meat, with a third course of roast meat, which is generally veal.

When dinner is over, and all things removed, the fidler is introduced. I shall give the reader as particular a description as possible of this ball, as he may likely be curious to see one of these *Decosses.* If he should, I would recommend it to him, to endeavour rather to see it at a farmer's house, than a public house; as it is to be seen in its perfection in the former, but not in the latter. The ball was opened by the gentleman who had carved for us at table. He took a lady out to dance; and, as soon as he had walked a minuet with her, led her back to her seat, and requested the same favour of another lady. As soon as he had danced a minuet with the second lady, he sat down, and she chose a partner for herself. The example of the first gentleman is followed by all the rest of the company in their turns. With regard to the dance, I must here give a friendly caution to those who may happen to be present at one of these country entertainments. Let your partner be ever so disagreeable, you must, by no means, offer her your hand, till she thinks proper to give you her's, and put an end to the minuet. In the second place, you are upon no account to dance with your wife at one of these ceremonies: and lastly, let who will ask you to dance, you are by no means to refuse. This would be looked upon as a high instance of ill manners, and an affront to the company in general. My reason for giving the first caution is, that a person's giving his hand to his partner would be considered as a sign of his being tired of his partner, and desirous of shortening the minuet. This would not fail to give great umbrage to the peasant who entertains you, who would look upon it as a demonstration that you think his friend unworthy of your company. With regard to the second caution, your taking your wife, looks like a symptom of jealousy, and shews, that you think no lady present a suitable partner for you. With regard to the last caution, the reason of it is, that, at these meetings, all the guests are upon a footing; and, as the peasant treats both his friends, and the friends of his friends, you must not take exception to any one person, as that would affront both him and his friends. In case the weather happens to be fine, they dance without door; if it happens to be windy or rainy, within. Upon this occasion they make the greatest parade of finery that they possibly can, and do all possible acts of charity. The poor flock in crowds to the ceremony, and, let their multitude be ever so great, they are all made to eat and drink; none are sent away empty.

Upon the 29th of June, which is

St.

St. Peter and St. Paul's day, a *Decosse* is celebrated in the *Basse Ville*; but it is not like the ceremony above described; it is conducted in a much genteeler and more polite manner. It is not remarkable enough to require a particular description; but the curious traveller may depend upon meeting with amusement even here. What is most worthy of observation at this ceremony is, the ancient custom of Shooting at the Bird, of which I shall here subjoin a circumstantial account.

CURIOUS CEREMONY OF SHOOTING AT THE BIRD.

First, those that are to be the marksmen, march from the places where they had paraded. They march in ranks two by two, with some of the principal inhabitants at their head as officers; after the officers, comes a man carrying the bird that is to be shot at. It is placed at the top of a stick, and over it a sheet of tin, six or eight inches distant from the bird. This tin is placed over it in order to render the mark more conspicuous to the view. This figure of a bird which is to be shot at, is made of iron, and in size about as big as a sparrow. The marksmen march through the *Basse Ville* till they arrive at the place where the bird is fixed up to be shot at. This place is on a common, or, as the French term it, *La plaine*. When they arrive here, the governor, general commandant, grand major, or some of the principal officers belonging to Calais, cause the bird to be fastened to a spindle with the sheet of tin over it. This spindle is driven into a pole about twelve or fourteen feet long, which pole is fastened to the blade of a windmill, and put into a perpendicular position, by turning the blade round. The governor, or whatever person of quality happens to be present, is obliged to shoot at it first. The peasants that are candidates for the prize, afterwards shoot at it in their turns, and they then continue to shoot till such time as some one amongst them has knocked it off the spindle. Whenever any of the candidates hit any part of the bird, the drum beats; but he that has the good luck to knock it off entirely, is rewarded with a pair of white gloves, and a silver cup. This he hangs to his button-hole by a red ribband, and is honoured with the first place in the procession when it marches back again. The order of the procession at its return, is the same as has been described above; drums beating, colours flying, &c. during this whole time. The peasant that wins the prize is honoured with the title of King of the lower town till that day twelvemonth, and is exempt from paying all taxes during that year. He is entitled to many other privileges and exemptions. He cannot be compelled to do the King's work, or repair the high roads; nor is he liable to have any soldiers quartered on him. The perpendicular height of the mark, including the pole and the blade of the wind-mill, from the plain place where the peasants shot from, which was a hollow, could not be less than fifty yards high. Every person was obliged to shoot with a single ball, and an equal charge of powder. I will frankly acknowledge, that I never met with persons of an equal dexterity at shooting; for, notwithstanding the smallness of the mark, and its great distance from them, few or none of them missed the sheet of tin, and many of them hit the bird itself.

So great is the antiquity of this custom, that you can hardly meet with two persons in this country, that

hat are agreed with regard to its first institution. The only account any way satisfactory that I ever received of it, was given me by an old gentleman that resides there. He told me, that he remembered having met with an account of its origin, which was as antient as Baldwin's time. He gave me to understand, that the intention of this prize annually, was to encourage the peasants to become marksmen; and that the prize was confined within the limits of *La Basse Ville*, or the lower town, as it still continues to be. This is the only account of the origin of this ceremony, which carries with it any appearance of probability; I shall therefore content myself with this, and not trouble my readers with the other fabulous accounts which I have heard of the origin of this antient custom. The ceremony being over, the inhabitants and their friends adjourn to their houses, where the rest of the day is spent in eating and drinking, and the night in dancing; so that upon this occasion the peasants indulge their genius, and seem to conform to the precept of Horace,

Nunc est bibendum, nunc pede libero
Pulsanda tellus——

It is but doing the people of this country justice, to acknowledge, that they neglect no means in their power to promote the pleasure and general satisfaction of their company. This is to be understood only of private houses; for, with regard to the manner in which these ceremonies are conducted in public houses, I am an utter stranger to it, as I never had the curiosity to visit any of those places. During the summer season there scarce passes a week but the ceremony, called *Ducasse*, is celebrated in some of the villages in the neighbourhood of Calais.

AN ECCENTRIC DOG.

THE following recent advertisement is among the eccentricities of the day.—To be disposed of, a handsome, well proportioned Dog, four years old, twenty-six inches high; is between a mastiff and Newfoundland. This valuable animal possesses every desirable quality peculiar to his species; he has saved four men from drowning, is a most excellent watch-dog, and his sagacity is such, though poison has been laid in his kennel several times, he refused the same; added to which, his ferocity and watchfulness at night are such, that he killed two robbers in the Isle of Wight, who had the temerity to attack his master's house.

Also, a true-bred Game Cock, two years old next month, his equal not to be met with; his sire has won twelve battles.

The cause of their being sold is on account of their master's going abroad.

Both warranted to answer the above description.

PECULIAR WINTER DIVERSIONS IN RUSSIA DESCRIBED.

SOME of their amusements are peculiar to the climate. One of the chief is that of riding in a light open sledge for pleasure, which is very common, because very agreeable when the weather is not too severe. Skating may be mentioned as another; but the weather is often too severe for that, and therefore it is by no means so general in Russia as in milder climates, such as Holland, Germany, &c. But of all the winter diversions of the Russians, the most favourite, and which is peculiar to them, seems to be that of sliding down a hill. They make a track on the side of a steep hill, mending any little inequalities with snow or ice; then at the verge of the hill, sitting on a little seat not bigger than, and much resembling a butcher's tray, they descend with astonishing velocity. The sensation is indeed very odd, but to myself, for I often had the curiosity to try it, I cannot say it was agreeable; the motion is so rapid, it takes away one's breath: nor can I give an idea of it, except desiring you to fancy you were to fall from the top of a house without hurting yourself, in which you would probably have some mixture of fear and surprize. The Russians are so fond of this diversion, that at Petersburgh, having no hills, they raise artificial mounts on the ice on the river Neva, for the purpose of sliding down them, particularly on holidays and festival seasons, when all the people, young and old, rich and poor, partake of the sport; paying a trifle to the persons who constructed the mount, each time they descend.

I call this peculiar to Russia as a diversion: for though it is practised at the place known by the name of the Ramasse, the descent of Mount Cenis to Lanebourg, which in some seasons of the year is in a state that admits of travellers sliding down it in the same method, as is described in most books that treat of the Alps, yet this may be considered rather as necessity or convenience than merely amusement.

The late Empress Elizabeth was so fond of this diversion, that, at her palace of Zarsko Zello, she had artificial mounts, of a very singular construction, made for this purpose. These have been called, by some Englishmen who have visited that country, "The Flying Mountains," and I do not know a phrase which approaches nearer to the Russian name. You will observe that there are five mounts of unequal heights; the first and highest is full thirty feet perpendicular altitude; the momentum with which they descend to this carries them over the second, which is about five or six feet lower, just sufficient to allow for the friction and resistance; and so on to the last, from which they are conveyed by a gentle descent, with nearly the same velocity over a piece of water into a little island.. These slides, which are about a furlong and half in length, are made of wood, that they may be used in summer as well as in winter. The process is, two or four persons sit in a little carriage, and one stands behind, for the more there are in it the greater the swiftness with which it goes; it runs on castors, and in grooves to keep it in its right direction, and it descends with wonderful rapidity. Under the hill, is a machine worked by horses for drawing the carriages back again, with the company in them. Such a work as this would have been enormous in most countries for the labour and expence it cost, as well as the vast quantity of wood used in it. At the same place, there is another artificial mount which goes in a spiral line, and in my opinion, for I have tried it also, is very disagreeable; as it seems always leaning on one side, and the person feels in danger of falling out of his seat.

They are able also to go out a hunting; and as the country abounds with game, it furnishes a large part of their provisions during the seasons when they are permitted to eat it; for the fasts of the Greek church, taken together, interdict animal food full half the year. The method the common people use in hunting is with snow shoes, which are nothing more than a piece of wood half an inch thick, five or six feet long, and about four inches broad,

broad, turned up at the end, which they fasten at the bottom of their feet, and by means of them they run, or rather skate over the snow with a pole in their hands, faster than the hare or any game they pursue, which are apt to sink in.

They enjoy also the profitable diversion of fishing, notwithstanding the water's being covered with ice; and one manner of it with a drag-net, is very particular, though I doubt if I shall be able to describe it so as to give you an idea of it. There is a hole about four feet by two cut in the ice, to let down a common drag-net; opposite to this, at the distance they mean to pull up the net, is another hole, about four feet square: they then cut a number of small round holes at about four yards distance from each other in a circular form, from the hole where the net is let down, to that where it is taken up. At the ends of the two strings, that is, the upper and lower strings which drag the net, long poles are tied: these poles will reach from one round hole to another, where they are directed and pushed under the ice, as they swim at the top of the water, till they come to the biggest square hole, at which they draw them out, and by this means the net, inclosing the fish it has surrounded; for the upper part of the net is floated at the top of the water under the ice, and the lower part of it sunk by leads, in the same manner as when the river is open; the ingenuity of the operation consists in the contrivance of dragging under the ice.

COURT OF COMMON PLEAS, FEB. 14.

Sittings after Term before Lord Eldon.

A HORSE CAUSE—LEMON v. FERGUSON.

THIS was an action to recover somewhat above Sixteen Pounds, stated to be the amount of the sum due for the work and labour of two horses for one month, and for other expences necessarily incident during that period.

It was alledged on behalf of the plaintiff, that these horses were hired by the defendant at a particular sum for a year, that, at the end of a month, they were returned to him without any sufficient reason, and that he was therefore entitled to recover for the time they had been employed. To substantiate his case, a number of witnesses were called, who deposed that the horses used by the defendant were capable of undergoing any moderate degree of work, and that the charges made by the plaintiff were not more than were fair and just, at the time the transaction took place.

In addition to this, one witness was produced, whose testimony went to prove that the defendant, on a particular occasion, had given him authority to say to the plaintiff, that he would pay his account, as the plaintiff might be useful to him in buying or selling horses.

On the other hand, the defendant avowed that the contract expressly admitted, that he should have the power of returning the horses, and getting them exchanged for others, if they were not found on experience to be adequate to his service. On this principle he had taken the horses with him to Cheltenham, and from his experience on this journey of their being unable to perform his work, he had returned them to the plaintiff. At the time that this complaint against the sufficiency of the horses was made, it was further contended, that the plaintiff had agreed to exchange them, though, at a subsequent period, he refused to do this, unless a considerable addition was made to the sum specified in the contract.

To prove these allegations, four witnesses were called. The evidence of two of these witnesses particularly respected the insufficiency of the horses to perform the journey to Cheltenham; and the testimony of the others referred to the promise made by the plaintiff, to supply the defendant with such horses as would be sufficient for performing any work in which he should have occasion to employ them.

After Lord Eldon had summed up the evidence, and explained the law of the case with very great ability, the Jury retired for an hour and a half, and then brought in a verdict for the plaintiff—*Forty Shillings*.

Boxing Combats,
And the Humanity of the English Character,
Described by a French Traveller, in 1763.

WHATEVER is not an immediate infraction of the public peace, or has no tendency to endanger the liberty or lives of the citizens, does not fall under the cognizance of the Police; which, of consequence, leaves full liberty to the combats that frequently happen at London, between the lower sort of people, and sometimes between persons of condition, who, by way of recreation, chuse to engage in a bruising match.

The mob are the supreme judges of these combats; and they have traditional laws, the first of which is, that the combat is to last till one of the parties acknowledges himself conquered, either by begging for quarter, or lying upon the ground without stirring, and rejecting the assistance of the spectators, who are always ready to raise the vanquished.

These combats are managed by blows with the head and fisty-cuffs. These bruisers, when they enter the lists, take off their clothes, and often even strip themselves to the skin: it is but politeness in an Englishman to act in this manner, when he has a foreigner to contend with. The combatant shews thereby, that he is not afraid of blows, and that he has nothing upon him that can either ward them off, or deaden their effect.

This species of combat is, no doubt, congenial to the character of the English. It has always been practised in England, and from thence adopted by the inhabitants of Bretagne in France, who have constantly retained it, and still practise it with certain modifications. It was a genteel diversion amongst Englishmen of the first rank. In the famous interview between Francis the First and Henry the Eighth, at Boulogne, the latter one day took the King of France by the collar, and proposed wrestling to him: the challenge being accepted, Henry gave the French monarch two trips, which Francis recovered from, and laid the English King sprawling upon the ground, giving him (says Fleurange) a surprizing toss.

This taste is so inherent in English blood, that at Eaton, Westminster School, and other places of the same sort, the children of the greatest noblemen often challenge one another to combats of this kind, and box according to all the rules and punctilios of honour. " Why should I not fight?" said one of these boys to me. " Am I not a match for any other of my age? If I decline the combat, or own myself worsted in it, the rest of the boys will have an advantage over me ever after: my adversary will have a right to say, *I have beat that fellow, I am therefore his better.*"

These

These young noblemen, notwithstanding, had never an opportunity of learning lessons and examples of this species of ferocity amongst the lower sort of people.

It extends even to women, at least among the vulgar. I saw, in Holborn, a woman engaged with a man, who, taking all sorts of advantage, flew at her with a rage of which the most frightful symptoms were conspicuous in his attitude and all the features of his face. Having struck her with his utmost force, he retreated back, and roused himself, by pouring out torrents of abuse, to return again to the attack. The woman, who appeared less furious than he, seized these intervals to fall upon his face and eyes with her hands. I was witness to five or six bouts of the combat; which surprized me the more, as the woman had, upon her left arm, an infant a year or two old, which was so far from crying out, as it is natural for children to do even in circumstances of less danger, that it did not so much as seem to knit its brow, but appeared to attend to a lesson of what it was one day to practise itself.

The Police takes no cognizance of these combats of individuals, which keep up the bravery of the people, but without fortifying their minds against the fear of sharp weapons. It allows men to revenge, upon the spot, an insult which they have not given occasion to. I once saw, in Parliament-street, one of the low fellows that infest the foot-paths of that neighbourhood fall foul of a gentleman, who was passing by, give him the most opprobrious language, and even lift up his hand to strike him: the gentleman thereupon applied his cane so violently to the skull of the aggressor, that he fell to the ground insensible; and the gentleman very quietly walked on. I was given to understand, that the insult which he had received was entirely unprovoked, and that he would have had no prosecution to fear, even if he had killed the man.

Happening another time to be taking a walk in St. James's Park, I saw a tolerably well-dressed Englishman come into the middle of the mall, to attack a person who had the air of a foreigner, and wore a sword. He had the insolence to stand in his way, and, without touching him, made a shew of a few allonges at him in tierce and quarte. The foreigner, provoked at this behaviour, clapt his hand to the hilt of his sword; at which the Englishman instantly took to his heels. A lawyer, with whom I was then walking, assured me, that if the foreign gentleman had that instant run the fellow through the body, the insult he received was so public that he would have been in no danger from the law.

Murder is, nevertheless, looked upon in England as the greatest and most heinous of all crimes. The prepossession which the laws have established, in this respect, has so universally prevailed in the minds of men, that even highway-men seldom go so far as to kill those whom they rob. As soon as the heat of the bloodiest revolutions subsides, this prepossession again coming in force, preserves the lives of persons who, in any other country, would, without mercy, be sacrificed to reasons of state.

Thus Richard Cromwell, Fairfax, and all the chiefs of the anti-royal party, survived the re establishment of monarchy, and spent the remainder of their days unmolested. I was shewn, at court, the grand-daughter, or great grand-daughter, of Cromwell; a connection which is not so much considered as a mark of infamy, as it is of honour and distinction.

The

The city of London, destitute of troops, guards, or a patrole of any sort, peopled by unarmed men, (for few wear swords, except physicians, and officers, when they are in their regimentals) reduced in the night to the superintendancy of old men without arms, is guarded only by the divine commandment, *Non occides!* "Thou shalt not kill!" and by laws enacted against murder, severe and rigidly observed, without distinction of rank or persons,—whether it be that the law had some influence upon the character of the people, or that the national character facilitates the exact observance of the law.

London is the only great city in Europe where neither murders nor assassinations happen. This I found by experience, as far as it was possible for me to find it. Returning from the play house late at night, I chose, in preference to great streets, narrow passages, very indifferently lighted, like those which, at Paris, lead from the street of St. John de Beauvais to St. Michael's Place, through St. John of Latran, St. Benoit, and the Sorbonne. I told those who asked me the reason of my giving this preference, that I was desirous of knowing, by my own experience, whether it was fact that there were no assassinations in London; and I had, in this respect, as full and satisfactory information as I desired. Even in the most violent disturbances, when I was in the midst of the mob, I have seen them threaten weakly, plunder some houses obnoxious to them, throw a few stones, and, though surrounded by troops, remain in a kind of awe, as well as the soldiers, through mutual fear of the effusion of blood.

In a word, the people of London, though haughty and ungovernable, are in themselves good-natured and humane; which holds even amongst those of the lowest rank. This appears from the great care which they take to prevent the frays, almost unavoidable, amidst the eternal passing and repassing of carriages in the most frequented streets, some of which are exceeding narrow. If, notwithstanding the great care of the coachmen and carmen to avoid them, there arises some confusion and perplexity, their readiness to turn aside, to retire, to open, to lend each other a hand if there be occasion, prevents this confusion from degenerating into one of those bloody frays which so often happen at Paris.— Let us even add, to the honour of English coachmen, that I have seen four hundred coaches together, at Ranelagh, which placed themselves in a file, passed each other, and were always ready at the first word, without either guards or directors to keep them to order.

At public festivals, and all ceremonies which attract a crowd, let it be ever so great, children and persons low in stature are seen to meet with tender treatment; all are eager to make room for them, and even to lift them up in their arms, that they may have an opportunity of seeing. The passages and doors of the place, where the festival is celebrated, are guarded by persons who have no guns, partisans, or halberts for their arms; but long hollow staves, which, when they make use of them (a case that happens very rarely) make a great noise, and do but little hurt.

RUSTIC SIMPLICITY.

The following whimsical circumstance, we are assured, have recently happened:—

A Farmer, not accustomed to large dealings, in the county of Chester, brought to Stockport market

market a quantity of oatmeal to sell; and an article which forms a great part of the subsistence of the lower orders of society, in that neighbourhood, soon found a purchaser. It being usual for the middle-man, as he is called, to pay in a good bill of two months, the bargain being struck, and the bill produced, the Farmer immediately raised an objection to take such a piece of paper for money; but an appeal to custom soon decided against him. However, not being perfectly satisfied, he applied to a Shopkeeper to have it put into cash, and was told it might be done for *ten shillings*; which he at length agreed to give, but was again astonished to find the *cash* was likewise composed of paper, commonly called *young Newlands*. An appeal a second time to *custom* obliged him to submit; but, still unwilling to be disappointed, he applied to another person to know if he could get these scraps of paper put into KING GEORGE's guineas, and was told, that, by paying *two-pence* each for them, that might be done. A third bargain was struck, at the expence of *eight shillings and fourpence*: but, just before he left the town, it came into his head that some of these guineas might be light, and that possibly they might not do so well for hoarding; he therefore had them tried in the balance, when, unfortunately for him, *twenty-three* were found wanting.—Here it was in vain urged, by his friends, that *custom* had rendered the weighing of gold quite useless in that neighbourhood and he positively gave *eleven shillings and sixpence* in exchange for *twenty-three* that were full weight, and went home, after all these deductions, with more than *four times* the sum the same quantity of that article (oatmeal) would have produced to him two years ago.

OXFORDSHIRE SPORTING.

To the EDITORS *of the* SPORTING MAGAZINE.

GENTLEMEN,

The distinguished honour you did me, in inserting the Sporting Intelligence I troubled you with, induces me, as opportunity offers, to transmit you any matter, of the sporting kind, that occurs in and near this city and neighbourhood, worthy of recital in your celebrated Magazine. Your attention to the following will oblige

A SUBSCRIBER.

Oxford, Feb. 7, 1801.

ON Friday, the 23d of January, a pack of Harriers, kept by subscription at Bolton, near Wheatly, Oxon, threw off in a turnip-field near the suburbs of this city, and, after beating it without success, were informed, by a man at work, of a Hare in her seat, in a thick hedge-row called Divinity Walk; proceeding to which, they started Puss, and clapping the hounds at her, she went off at a stile that beggars all description, taking them a ring of near six miles in circumference, through the parishes of Headington, Barton, Stanton, Garsington, Sandford Breaks, and across the river Isis, above Sandford Ferry: making a sharp turn to the right, she nearly made to Bagley Woods, but the staunch pack kept rattling so close to her that she, to avoid submitting, recrossed the river; and making for where she first started, she had nearly reached the spot, when she fell a glorious victim to the superior fleetness of her pursuers, after a fine chase of two hours and ten minutes. She is supposed to have run twenty-five miles, beating half the field the first hour's running; and run in a most capital stile, as a cast-net, if thrown, would have nearly covered them most part of the chase.

For the SPORTING MAGAZINE.

GLEANINGS.

Origin of Planting Yews in Church-Yards.

THE planting yews in church-yards (being places fenced from cattle) originally arose from an attention to the materials from which bows were made for archery; nor do we hear of such trees being planted in the church-yards of other parts of Europe.

GAMING.

GAMING had been introduced into England before the time of Edward the Fourth, as Chaucer speaks thus of it:—

"As hazard, riot, stewes and tavernes,
"Whereat, with lutes, harps and geternes,
"They dauncen, and plaien at dice, night and days."

And again,

"For in the cities, was there no pretense
"That fairer couth *entries a pair of dice*"

CHAUCER in the COOK's TALE.

IN the following reign (of Henry the Seventh) Caxton, in one of his Prefaces, addresses his readers—

"What do ye now, but play at dice?"

ISLE OF DOGS.

THIS island, opposite to Greenwich, obtained the name of the *Isle of Dogs* from the King's spaniels being kept there.—Edward the Third, in the twenty-first year of his reign, ordered the Sheriffs of Essex and Hertfordshire to build bridges in the neighbourhood of Waltham, that he might enjoy the amusement of Falconry. He also forbids any one hawking in those parts, without his special licence.

Feb. 11. J. J. B.

ESSEX COURSING.

THE last meeting, for this season, of the Bradwell and Tillingham Club, was held on Wednesday, Thursday, and Friday, the 4th, 5th, and 6th instant, when the following matches between the members were run, which afforded excellent diversion to the *amateurs* in Coursing, viz:

FIRST DAY.

1. Mr. Evans's *Jupiter* beat Mr. Williams's *Primrose*.
2. Mr. J. Tuffnell's *Princess* beat Mr. Wise's *Chace*.
3. Mr. Pattisson's *Dart* beat Mr. Wakefield's *Bashful*.
4. Mr. Tweed's *Fly* beat Mr. P. Wright's *Crazy*.
5. Mr. C. Parker's *Smut* beat Mr. Dudley's *Merlin*.
6. Mr. Pattisson's *Twist* beat Mr. P. Wright's *Windsor*.
7. Mr. Wakefield's *Blue Nose* beat Mr. Wilson's *Monk*.
8. Mr. Wilson's *Cheesecake* beat Mr. P. Wright's *Cayenne*.
9. Mr. J. Wright's *Fly Cap* beat Mr. P. Wright's *Ruby*.
10. Mr. J. Tuffnell's *Playmate* beat Mr. Wright's *Wonder*.
11. Mr. Dudley's *Trull* beat Mr. Wilson's *Gossip*.
12. Mr. Wakefield's *Dalilah* beat Mr. Dudley's *Merlin*.
13. Mr. Wakefield's *Sampson* beat Mr. P. Wright's *Katerfelto*.
14. Mr. Tuffnell's *Pickle* beat Mr. Wilson's *Monk*.

After which several *bye* matches were run.

SECOND DAY.

Winning Dogs of this and the last Meeting, being matched by lot, ran for the CLUB CUP, in classes, till they were reduced to a brace, whose final course determined the contest, viz.

Cynographia Britannica.

CLASS 1.
1. Mr. Pigott's *Driver* beat Mr. Wakefield's *Sampson*.
2. Mr. Pattison's *Twist* beat Mr. Wilson's *Cheesecake*.
3. Mr. C. Parker's *Dashaway* beat Mr. Tuffnell's *Playmate*.
4. Mr. Evans's *Jupiter* beat Mr. J. Wright's *Fly Cap*.
5. Mr. Dudley's *Madam* beat Mr. Tweed's *Fly*.
6. Mr. Dudley's *Friday* beat Mr. Pigott's *Helen*.
7. Mr. Dudley's *Miss* beat Mr. Wakefield's *Blue Nose*.
8. Mr. Wakefield's *Dalilah* beat Mr. Pattison's *Dart*.
9. Mr. Dudley's *Terling* beat his own *Trull*.
10. Mr. C. Parker's *Pizarro* beat Mr. Tuffnell's *Pickle*.

CLASS 2.
1. Mr. C. Parker's *Pizarro* beat Mr. Dudley's *Madam*.
2. Mr. Dudley's *Miss* beat his own *Friday*.
3. Mr. Evans's *Jupiter* beat Mr. C. Parker's *Dashaway*.
4. Mr. Pigott's *Driver* beat Mr. Pattison's *Twist*.
5. Mr. Dudley's *Terling* beat Mr. Wakefield's *Dalilah*.

CLASS 3.
1. Mr. Pigott's *Driver* beat Mr. C. Parker's *Pizarro*.
2. Mr. Evans's *Jupiter* beat Mr. Dudley's *Terling*.
3. Mr. Dudley's *Miss*, as undrawn, ran a course single-handed.

THIRD DAY.
CLASS 4.
1. Mr. Evans's *Jupiter*, and Mr. Dudley's *Miss* a *dead course*.
2. Mr. Dudley's *Miss* beat Mr. Evans's *Jupiter*.
3. Mr. Pigott's *Driver*, as undrawn, ran with and beat Mr Cawtro's dog *Ruby*.
4. Mr. Dudley's *Miss* beat Mr. Pigott's *Driver*, and consequently won the Cup.

After which some good bye matches were run; which terminated three fine days sport, and as sharp running as the oldest Coursers remember.

CYNOGRAPHIA BRITANNICA.

ON the blue paper cover of our Magazine for the present month, is advertised the First Number of a work, entitled, Cynographia Britannica, consisting of Coloured Engravings of the various breeds of Dogs, existing in Great Britain, drawn from the life, and coloured under the immediate inspection of Sydenham Edwards, with observations on their respective properties and uses, price Seven Shillings and Six-pence. Sold by White, Bookseller, in Fleet-street, &c. &c.

A publication so applicable to Sporting, could but excite our notice and curiosity. It is printed on fine wove Royal Quarto Paper, and two coloured Plates, given in this Number; first, the Newfoundland Dog; and secondly, The Beagle. The author might have said, *Dogs* and *Beagles*, as there are two of the former, and three of the latter. They are characteristically, naturally, and tastefully drawn. The subject commences with an introduction, and which we shall take the liberty of here presenting to our readers.

"In the following pages I propose to give a more satisfactory account of the Dogs found in England, with their uses, habits, and appearance, than has hitherto been offered to the public.

"The description of each kind is accompanied with a figure delineated from the living animal, which has been attended with great trouble and expence, as it was necessary, for the correctness of the work, that each portrait should be carefully made from some distinguished individual Dog of each particular breed: and, in the execution of the portraits, much study and attention has been paid, to represent as strongly as possible, the peculiar character and manners of each respective race. Thus far I may venture, perhaps, without incurring the charge of ostentation, to speak of the nature of my labours; the rest is submitted with the greatest deference to the judgment and indulgence of a discerning public.

"The descriptive part is occasionally interspersed with some account of the Dogs formerly used in this island, which have been superseded by others more useful, or better suited to the wants or fashion of the times, as may be exemplified in the Blood-hound which was commonly in use at a period, when, as an emblem of war, our restless ancestors pursued the wild boar, wolf, or red deer; on mountainous wastes or wilds, covered with forests and thick underwoods, he was employed to trace the wounded game to its concealment, and the midnight thief, or blood-stained robber, to his secret cave. When our country was cleared, the larger game was destroyed, or only preserved in the parks of our nobles; and the thief, or robber, found a surer protection in the crowded city, than the solitary glen: the services of this animal being no longer useful or necessary, he is lost to us, or suffered to degenerate and sink into obscurity.

"In like manner the mechanical arts have superseded the use of the Turnspit; and the introduction of new kinds, with various modes of protecting property, the Mastiff, and other breeds, once frequent, are for similar reasons lost. I would be a matter of great curiosity, could their history be pursued to periods more remote; as we might, from the Dogs in use, deduce the sports and character of times past; but for this I lament the want of satisfactory materials.

"The Dog may be considered as not only the intelligent, courageous, and humble companion of man, but he is often a true type of his mind and disposition; the hunter's Dog rejoices with him in all the pleasure and fatigues of the chase; the ferocious and hardy disposition of the Bull dog, may commonly be traced on the determined brow of his master: nor does the Dog of the blind beggar look up to the passing stranger, but with suppliant eyes. Always the ready and affectionate servant, an excellent companion when human society is wanting, the faithful and incorruptible guardian of his master's person and property.—'Dogs are honest creatures, they never fawn on those they love not, and I'm a friend to Dogs.'—England has been long eminent for the superiority of her Dogs and Horses, now preferred in almost every part of the world. Whether this superiority arises from the climate, or from the pains taken in their breeding, education, and maintenance, I do not undertake to determine. The Fox-Hound and the Bull-dog, out of this island, are said to lose their properties in a few years; if so, then there must be some local cause of their perfection in this country, and their degeneration in others.

"The attachment of our countrymen for ages, to the sports of the field, has given them health and vigour of body, and a gallant contempt of danger, the uniform effect on those nations that have cultivated them.

Romanis

"Romanis solenne viris opus
Utile lanæ, vitæque, et membris."
HORACE.

"The chace was, by our sires, esteem'd
Healthful, and honourable deem'd."
FRANCIS.

"Without pursuing these remarks any farther, I will now enter into a short historical dissertation on the Dogs cultivated in this country, as far back as any certain account of them can be traced, which is not more distant than the reign of Queen Elizabeth. Of the Dogs existing at this period, we have an excellent catalogue from the able pen of the illustrious Dr. Cajus, and, according to him, there were then known in England sixteen species, or rather varieties of Dogs; for all the different breeds, it is imagined, are merely varieties from one original stock; to which, Mr. Pennant, and Mr. Hunter, have added of late years, the Wolf, the Fox, the Hyæna, and the Juckall, considering them as offsprings of the same stock. To Dr. Cajus, succeeded Merret, Ray, Topsell, and Pennant; they have, however, added but little to his invaluable remarks.

"The species enumerated by Dr. Cajus, are contained in the following list: Terrare, Harier, Blud hunde, Gasehunde, Grehunde, Leviner or Lyemmer, Tumbler, Spaniel, Setter, Water-spaniel or Fynder, Spaniel-gentle or Comforter, Shepherd's Dog, Mastive or Bandedog, Wappe, Turnspit, and Dancer. Some of these are wholly extinct, or only a few individuals preserved by the curious.

"For the same reasons that some breeds have become extinct, new ones have been formed, and a great number of these changes from fashion and caprice, take place in a short period of time; the principal, however, still do, and probably ever will remain.

"It is not the purpose of this undertaking to give every possible mixture and variety of Dogs, which, by repeated crossing in various breeds, become almost infinite, but to adhere to what are termed the permanent, as the mixtures or crosses may be referred to the original races.

"The artist also may find these figures useful, by exhibiting the outline and character of these animals, when the originals are not at hand.

"It is hoped the whole will form an useful and entertaining work for the public, and the information given, will be collected from the most authentic sources, but chiefly from my own investigation of the different subjects."

COVENT GARDEN THEATRE.

ON the evening of the 11th, was performed, for the first time, at this Theatre, the Comedy of, "THE POOR GENTLEMAN," written by George Colman, Esq.

The following are the principal characters in this Drama:—

Lieut. Worthington, the Poor Gentleman,	Mr. MURRAY.
Sir Robert Bramble, a testy old Baronet, fond of argument, & full of humanity,	Mr. MURDEN.
Farmer Harrowby, an honest hearted English Yeoman,	Mr. TOWNSEND.
Mr. Stephen, the Farmer's Son, somewhat military mad,	Mr. EMERY.
Mr. Lollipop, an Apothecary, and a Corner in the Volunteer Cavalry,	Mr. FAWCETT.
Sir Robert Crafty, a dissipated young man of fashion,	Mr. FARLEY.
Mr. Frederick Bramble, nephew to Sir Robert, a wild, warm hearted young man, just arrived from Russia,	Mr. LEWIS.

Corporal,

Corporal, the Lieutenant's Servant, the Trim of Tristram Shandy,	Mr. KNIGHT.
Humphrey, Sir Rob. Bramble's Servant, who loves and contradicts his master,	Mr. BATTERTON.
The Hon. Miss Lucretia Mac Tab, ridiculous for family pride, weakness of understanding, and selfishness of heart,	Mrs. MATTOCKE.
Miss Emily Worthington,	Mrs. GIBBS.

THE SCENE—A farm house, Gentleman's mansion and grounds, in the neighbourhood of Tunbridge.

THE FABLE.

Which is original, is as follows:—*Lieutenant Worthington*, after having his wife killed in his arms as he lay in his tent, losing himself an arm in the famous defence of Gibraltar, living for a number of years with his only child *Emily*, in the wilds of Canada, comes at last to reside in England at a farmer's house near Tunbridge. His daughter *Emily*, his late wife's aunt, *Miss Lucretia Mac Tab*, and a faithful old Corporal, his servant, are his companions in this retreat. Scarcely had they settled in the farmer's house, when *Sir Charles Craftly* comes to pursue, with the aid of *Lollipop* the village apothecary, his insidious designs against *Emily's* virtue. *Sir Robert Bramble*, and his nephew *Frederick*, newly arrived from Russia, are about the same time, introduced as friends and protectors to the Lieutenant and his daughter. His misfortunes, however, thicken. A friend, for whom he was engaged to the amount of five hundred pounds dies; and the Lieutenant, unable to discharge the debt, is in danger of sudden imprisonment. *Sir Charles Craftly*, after striving in vain to seduce *Emily*, prepares to carry her off by force; but, *Frederick Bramble* rescues her from *Sir Charles's* attempt. *Sir Robert Bramble*, and his nephew, make eager offers of their friendship. The alarming debt is secretly discharged by *Sir Robert*. *Frederick* and *Emily* discover a mutual attachment, and *Sir Robert* consents to make them happy. *Sir Charles* owns his error, and is forgiven. The *Lieutenant* sees his daughter provided for, and his debt freely discharged. *Miss Mac Tab*, after some quarrels and ill humours, still retains the Lieutenant's kindness; and the inferior persons are gratified in seeing the felicity of the patrons to whom they are attached. The time in which the whole passes does not much exceed twenty-four hours.

REMARKS.

THE author's object, in the composition of this piece, has been to combine the power of sentiment, and of the familiar pathetic, with that of wit and humour. These he endeavours to display, partly in the delineation of character, and in sentiments respectively appropriated to the different characters—partly in general, and, in some sort, unappropriated sentiments and manners—and in part, by the effect of changes of fortune, incidents, and situations. The character of *Lieutenant Worthington* is marked with honour, dignity, tenderness, fortitude, and by a sorrow that commands respect, on account of the virtuous affection from which it springs: but it is not all new to the stage; it is a common species, and, even of that species, quite a common individual. *Sir Robert Bramble* is a character not hackneyed on the stage, not unallied to real-life; formed, we believe, from hints or descriptions to be found in some of our classical periodical papers.—Mr. Colman has not made the most of the idea; he has not sufficiently marked

marked with the delicate touches of nature that strong caricature which was necessary for stage effect; yet he has made the character a very pleasing one, rich in humour and pathetic sentiment, and even not destitute of wit. The military passion of *Master Stephen*, the Farmer's son, is highly entertaining: it is borrowed, in part, from the *Trim* of *Tristram Shandy*; but the application is in some degree new, and certainly fortunate. There is no novelty, but much admirable humour and satire, in the character of the *Honourable Miss Lucretia Mac Tab*. The Corporal has the fidelity, spirit, and kind-heartedness of *Trim*, and nothing more. The Apothecary and *Frederick Bramble* have little merit, but that they were written for Fawcett and Lewis, and endowed with a liveliness and bustle which London audiences have been much accustomed to applaud.—The general unappropriated sentiments and manners bespeak honour, honesty, British generosity and courage, gallant respect for the fair sex, the just feelings of natural affection, all the tenderness of melting humanity. These sentiments occur in every modern drama; are justly and invariably applauded; and, to say the truth, are almost the only recommendations which the majority of our late Tragedies and Comedies possess.—The succession of the incidents, and the various situations, are almost, without exception, skilfully contrived; they are generally natural, yet adapted to produce a powerful stage effect.—The piece has more of genuine and original wit than any late Comedy we have seen; yet it is not free from stale jests, which Mr. Colman's taste and fertility of genius might have taught him to avoid. Why put into the mouth of the young lady, *Sterne's* old joke of "Ever since he was a puppy?"—On the whole, this piece, though not of first-rate excellence, is greatly above comparison with the Farce of Dibdin.

Mrs. Mattocks's representation of *Miss Mac Tab* was such as to deserve every praise: Emery had first-rate merit in his exhibition of the part of *Mr. Stephen*. Munden, in *Sir Robert Bramble*, contributed much to the success of the piece. Mrs. Gibbs, though not uniformly correct, was often very interesting, in *Emily Worthington*. Fawcett excited much merriment in the Military Apothecary; and in this, as in former instances, we are ready to do homage to the force and vivacity of his comic powers. Mr. Lewis was, as usual, ardently and very justly applauded. Mr. Murray is a very able representative of the *Poor Gentleman*.

An Epilogue, in dialogue, was spoken with good effect. The piece also continues to be a favourite with the Town.

GAMING DEBTS.

COURT OF KING'S BENCH, FEB. 16.

Sittings before Lord Kenyon and a Special Jury of Merchants.

WHALEY, v. SOUTHCOTT.

THIS case occupied the attention of the Court and Jury a great part of the day, and therefore we can only give the outlines of it.

The pleadings were opened by Mr. Raine.

The Attorney General stated to his Lordship, and the Gentlemen of the Jury, that this action was brought by Mr. Whaley, who was a Gentleman of considerable family, connections and fortune, in Ireland, against Sir Thomas Southcott,

cott, Bart. to recover several sums of money which were owing to him by way of loan, and also the price of several horses that had been sold to him. The whole amounted to 1788l. 19s. 7d. for which Sir Thomas had given Mr. Whaley a warrant of attorney, to confess judgment, and on which judgment had been entered up; and Sir Thomas, being a prisoner on that account, applied to the Court of King's Bench to have the proceedings on that warrant of attorney set aside, the warrant of attorney itself to be delivered up, and he himself to be discharged on finding common bail. Sir Thomas made that application to the Court on the ground that the consideration of that warrant of attorney was merely won at play; and, it that was so, the Attorney General admitted that his client could not recover. After this business had been laid before the Court considerable doubts rested upon it, and therefore the Court, with great propriety, referred it to the consideration of a Jury. They ordered that an action should be brought on the original demand for which the warrant of attorney was given, and which consisted of a variety of sums, amounting in all to 1788l 19s. 7d. When sums of money were lent between parties who had a mutual confidence in each other, there might be some difficulty in making out a demand in a Court of Justice, since parties in such a situation might not be so strict in taking regular vouchers. He should produce an account, which the Plaintiff thought was lost when this business was before the Court of King's Bench: that account comprehended all the items for which the warrant was given, and was regularly signed by the Defendant. He should not rest it on the account stated alone, but he should be able to prove that demand also by living witnesses, on whose credit it would rest that several of these sums were advanced by the Plaintiff to the Defendant in their presence. The Attorney General stated chiefly what each of the witnesses would prove.

Mr. Prescott, the first witness, proved the signature of Sir Thomas Southcott to the account, &c.

Mr. Cox, an Irish gentleman, said he had seen Mr. Whaley and Sir Thomas Southcott together, in Mr. Whaley's house; that they appeared to be acquainted; that one day after dinner, at Mr. Whaley's, he recollected a message sent by Sir Thomas to Mr. Whaley, and that Sir Thomas himself came in about half an hour. Mr. Whaley then went out of the room, and returned with some Bank notes in his hand. He counted them over, and then delivered them to Sir Thomas, when he counted them. Mr. Whaley said they amounted to 520l. or 530l. Sir Thomas said they were very right.—Some of this gentleman's evidence did not accord exactly with one or two parts of the Plaintiff's affidavit.

Mr. Jefferys, the Member for Coventry, said, he witnessed the execution of a power of attorney, and also of a warrant of attorney, by the Defendant, Sir Thomas. That was in August, or September, 1799. Mr. Whaley called on him, and requested he would give him five minutes of his time, by calling at his lodgings to witness the assignment of some property. He saw Sir Thomas Southcott sign his name. At desire of the Plaintiff, he asked Sir Thomas, if he knew what he was signing; if he had received the consideration; and if he was satisfied? Sir Thomas said, he knew what he was signing, and was perfectly satisfied. He then saw him sign it.

Mary Thompson said, she had been in the service of Mr. Whaley, and

and spoke to the different sums of 150l. and 120l. or 130l. which Sir Thomas had received from her mistress by the direction of Mr. Whaley.

Mr. Dupler spoke to the finding of the account made up of all the items of which the Plaintiff's demand consisted, and signed by the Defendant. It was found in one of the Plaintiff's trunks, which stood in his house, in the beginning of January last. It also appeared from the evidence, that the Defendant had purchased two horses of the Plaintiff, for 500l.

There were two drafts produced by the clerks of Messrs. Walwyn and Co. Bankers, for five hundred guineas, which were payable to one Barnly, and paid by the Plaintiff for the Defendant. There were other two drafts for 46l. each, payable to the Defendant himself, and also paid by the Plaintiff's Bankers.

It was observed, that there was no objection to Mrs. Whaley's being examined; and this lady proved 20l. and 10l. of Mr. Whaley's money, which she delivered to Sir Thomas.

The Plaintiff's case being closed, the leading counsel for the Defendant made a very elegant speech, reprobating in strong language every species of gambling, as well as the conduct of those who were parties to this transaction. No man should deter him, in the discharge of his professional duty, from calling things by their proper names. He considered, in their order, the various items of which the Plaintiff's demand consisted, and did not admit any of them, except the 20l. and 10l. which Mrs. Whaley swore Sir Thomas had of her, of Mr. Whaley's money: he said he was in no condition to deny these two sums; but all the rest he hoped the gentlemen of the Jury would reject.

The Defendant called no witnesses.

The noble and learned Judge, after having directed the attention of the Gentlemen of the Jury to the most material parts of this case, concluded with observing, that, when a man came into a Court of Justice, it was incumbent upon him to make out, if not to demonstration, yet to the fair conviction of a Jury, the justice of his demand, before he could entitle himself to their verdict. How far that had been done in this case, they would judge: the constitution and jurisprudence of this country had left the decision of it to them, and his Lordship had no doubt that they would do justice between the parties.—The Jury withdrew near half an hour, and returned with a verdict for the Plaintiff, for 298l.

Lord Kenyon.— As something was said about duelling, in the course of this cause, it may not be useless to observe what is enacted by 9 Anne, c. 14, sect. 8. "And, for the preventing of such quarrels as shall and may happen upon the account of gaming, be it further enacted by the authority aforesaid, that in case any person or persons whatsoever shall assault and beat, or challenge or provoke to fight, any other person or persons whatsoever, upon account of any money won by gaming, playing, or betting at any of the games aforesaid, (cards, dice, &c.) such person or persons assaulting and beating, or challenging or provoking to fight, such other person or persons, upon the account aforesaid, shall, being thereof convicted upon an indictment, or information to be exhibited against him or them for that purpose, forfeit to her Majesty, her heirs and successors, all his chattels and personal estate whatsoever, and shall suffer imprisonment, without bail or mainprize, in the common jail of the county where such conviction shall be had, during the term of two years.

SPORTING INTELLIGENCE.

A Saddler of Chelmsford, has invented a saddle and stirrup to prevent the foot hanging in the latter, in the event of a fall, and is about to obtain a patent for them.

In Brussels, and some parts of France, Professor Hygge observes, that a very whimsical species of travelling equipoge has been adopted; it consists of a light curricle drawn by large dogs; sometimes four, and sometimes six of these animals are used as substitutes for horses.

Two boxing matches have been made lately; the first, between Bartholomew, and the Butcher who beat Seabrook a short time since, for one hundred guineas; and the other, between the noted Caleb Baldwin, and Robert Watson, a Bristol man, for twenty pounds a side. The latter, we hear, has forfeited his stake.

February 3, a match for ten guineas, two miles, was trotted on the Norwich Road, between Setch and Lynn; between Mr. Robson's poney Filch, and Mr. Scarse's poney Fidler, which was won with great ease by the former, he having trotted over the ground at the rate of eighteen miles an hour.

February 1st, died, Mr. J. Langhorn, of the City Repository, Barbican.—N. B. Some account of the life of this old and very eminent horse-dealer, by any of our correspondents, will be esteemed a favour.

"He was a favourite dog," said a gentleman to a friend who was enquiring after him, "but I was obliged to part with him."—"How so, sir."—"Why he took into his head to *kill his own master*."

February 7.—A few days since a lad, aged about fourteen, only son of a merchant, at Minehead, took a gun, with an intention to shoot some blackbirds, adjoining the town; to his parents surprize, he did not return that evening; next morning search was made for him, and about a quarter of a mile from the house, he was found quite dead. It is supposed, that as he was going over a hedge, the gun accidentally went off, and lodged its contents in his stomach.—Verdict—Accidental Death.

Sherborne, February 3.—Tuesday last, a gun was carelessly left loaded in a house behind a door of Mr. Dodderidge, at Minehead; on opening the door, the gun fell and went off, and part of the contents was lodged in the legs and hips of one of his children, a boy about four years old; but there are no hopes of his recovery.

Citizen Basterreche, who has been endeavouring to persuade the French to abandon the use of gold, may be compared to Seneca writing his Treatise on the Contempt of Riches in the bosom of opulence. This Citizen has married a niece of Cambaceres, a young lady of great beauty, on whom he has settled a jointure equal to Thirty Thousand Pounds sterling. This Citizen may, however, dispense with his wife much more easily than the French people can dispense with their gold, as he is a cripple, and has lost the use of nearly all his limbs. A machine has been invented for him, by which he is raised in his chair to the height of his bed, and is, by means of a spring, thrown upon it.

A few

A few days since, the cock-loft of Mr. Adams, a famous game-cock breeder, at Pevensey-sluice, was broken open, and thirty-eight young cocks, (denominated stags) stolen therein. Mr. Adams, we understand, estimates his loss at upwards of one hundred pounds.

A few days ago, as Mr. Whiteman, a respectable yeoman at Keymer, was taking the diversions of the gun, in company with a young gentleman of his acquaintance, he sprang and shot a partridge, which his companion, who was close at his heels, also intended to shoot at, but like all young and inexperienced sportsmen, being over eager, he so incautiously discharged his gun, that the whole of its contents entered the back part of Mr. Whiteman's hat, and actually passed under the crown of it, and out at the front part without touching his head, or doing him the least injury.—It may therefore be said literally, that he experienced—*an hair's breadth escape!*

In a coursing match lately at Newmarket, the hare ran with such velocity against a partridge as to strike it down, and it was afterwards taken up by a gentleman who was engaged in the sport.

From the repeated experience of the Courts, there seems to be something in *horse dealing* very fatal to *veracity.* It is *neck* and *neck* with the *evidence!*

A fellow who waited on Thursday at a public-house in the Old Bailey, to give evidence against a woman who had robbed him of some articles, but which had all been returned to him, got so intoxicated before the trial was called, that, on entering the witness's box, he could hardly stand, and when questioned by the Recorder, respecting what were the contents of a bundle which he held under his arm, he stammered out, "What is that to you, Old Big Wig?"—He was of course immediately ordered into custody, and the woman was discharged.

Girardami, a Tyrolese peasant, and self-taught artist, who now resides at Vienna, has invented an air-gun, which may be discharged fifty times without pumping again. The first twenty shots penetrate through a board at an uncommon distance. Girardami makes these air-guns himself, and likewise very good wooden watches.

A fox, hard pressed by the hounds some days since, made for the village of Gamlingay, Cambridgeshire, and entering the house of Mr. Woodham, ran up stairs, and passing from one of the attic windows to the roof, lay there till the pursuit was at an end, when he again passed through the house, and escaped.

A desperate engagement took place a few nights since, on Mr. Penruddock's manor in Wiltshire, between two poachers and two of the keepers; after a contest of nearly half an hour, a third keeper came up, and the two poachers were secured. One of the keepers was severely wounded in the head by the butt-end of one of the poacher's guns.

The French papers contain a marvellous account of a child of twelve years old having been the cause of the death of a furious wolf, with a pruning hook. This wolf, like the Dragon of Wantley, had already destroyed a number of children, " that could not with him grapple;" when he had the misfortune to meet with Master Etienne Trouva. The wolf was engaged with a young man of eighteen, for whom he was more than a match, when this boy came up, thrust his hand, Lysimachus like, into the throat of the wolf, cut his nose, knocked out his teeth, and forced him to take to his heels. He was pursued and shot.

The following venerable coincidents took place in Bath a few days since:—A gentleman now in his seventy-fourth year, sat down to a Rucker's harpsichord, full one hundred and fifty years old, upon a chair which belonged, at least two hundred and fifty years ago, to one of the Monks of Glastonbury, and played some music published above two hundred years since by Pallestrina and Bird; so that the aggregate age of the performer, the instrument, the seat, and the music, amounted to six hundred and seventy-four years!

There is now living at Cloves, in the parish of Alves, Murrayshire, James Watson, who has seen part of three centuries. He was born in March 1699. His farthest journey from his native spot was once to Keith, a village about twenty miles distant. He was at his son's harvest home in October last, and after spending the evening with much glee, walked home to his own house, a distance of a mile and a half, where he was born, and within a hundred yards of where his father was born, who died at the advanced age of ninety-nine years.

PARISIAN AMUSEMENTS.— "I have," says a Correspondent, "been to see the parade of the Carousel, to which no person is admitted without cards.—Never did Berlin present to strangers, (which is saying a great deal), any thing so worthy of admiration. All Paris run to it, at least all who have it in their power. It is held every Quintidi, that is to say, every ten days and has never been more grand than after the event of the 25th of December.—The Chief Consul was saluted with cries of "Long live Bonaparte!"—His horse and foot grenadiers are magnificent. They are the conquerors of Marengo (in part renewed and filled up by choice youths).—Nothing is to be seen but gold and silver. Never have the Generals been so brilliant and well clothed. Their uniform is superb, and there were twenty of them seen together. In order to form a proper judgment of this parade, it is absolutely necessary to see it. It almost always consists of from four to five thousand men.

"Never had the comic opera been more rich in productions of its kind; but, on the other hand, the Great Opera is on its decline, and is in want both of actors and authors. The ballets are uniformly beautiful. At the Oratorio, the pit tickets cost fifteen, and even eighteen livres; those at the orchestra, at twenty-four livres, were all taken in the morning; they would have been at three louis, if it had been possible that the place could have held more. *The Enchanted Flute*, a German opera, of which the music is delicious, is soon to be given under the name of, *The Mysteries of Isis*. You know that it will be necessary to make some alterations. *Don Juan*, *The Marriage of Figaro*, &c. pieces of which the music is generally relished in Germany, have been given and applauded. On the whole, music, or to speak more properly, the art of composition, has been carried so far within the last ten years, that the French will soon have no cause to envy their rivals in this respect. This is said without the least exaggeration. The number of little excellent performances which the Italian comedians have in their possession, is unaccountable. Some Italian performers are expected, but it is thought that they will not succeed, if it be not from their novelty.

"Larive is the best French performer,

ormer, though great attention is paid to Lafond, his rival. It is to the latter that we are indebted for the full impression of that affecting hemistich—*Zaire vous pleurez*, which has never been well given since the famous Le Kain.

"I have paid a short visit to the Museum, and have there admired the master-pieces of antiquity, which the Conquerors of Italy have brought within the walls—The *Apollo of Belvidere*, the *Venus de Medicis*, the *Laocoon*, &c. Besides the antiquities which are presented at the Louvre to the public curiosity, in marbles, pictures, bronzes, &c. Paris presents in many other rooms to public admiration, all that the moderns have opposed to the most beautiful works of antiquity. (This is, perhaps, saying too much, as London, Vienna, Madrid, Berlin, and Dresden, also present many remarkable performances well worthy of being attended to.) Versailles has also a magnificent Museum. In fact, when a person has traversed and examined these different rooms, he feels himself penetrated with a holy respect, and thinks that he finds himself all at once in the midst of an ancient Grecian Temple, in which are crowded at his feet marbles taken from the quarries in the neighbourhood of Athens."

A Cumberland paper informs us, that two gentlemen, riding a few days ago in a gig, between Egremont and Calderbridge, observed a sparrow hawk pursuing a lark; the latter, after several narrow escapes from its enemy, at length was reduced to the necessity of taking refuge in the carriage! the hawk, thus deprived of its expected prey, disappeared in a few minutes; and the lark, soaring upwards, appeared to pour out its lively notes, in gratitude to its protectors.

FEAST OF WIT; OR, SPORTSMAN's HALL.

HOBBY-HORSES.

STERNE says, "Every man has his hobby-horse; and, by observation, we find *to be talked of* seems to be the *summum bonum* of this life. Few men of rank will glide through life without a distinguished rage; and almost every man of figure determines, on setting out in life, in what line of life to *sport* himself, and that choice is called his *hobby-horse*. One makes the turf his scene of action; another drives about in tall phaetons, to peep into his neighbours garret-windows; and a third rides his *hobby-horse* in Parliament, where it jerks him, sometimes on one side and sometimes on the other, sometimes in and sometimes out, till at last he is jerked out of his *honesty*, and his constituents out of their *freedom*.

Bon Mot.—A cobler in Dublin lately refused his wife the comfort of *a dish of tea*. The woman vented her complaint to a neighbouring lady, who promised to allow her a trifle for that enjoyment. The woman exultingly told her husband, that she had found *a friend* who would provide her with *tea*. "Very well," said the man, "then I will keep you in *hot water*."

A report, says a wit, is current, that Mr. Pitt is going to be married, and the reason assigned is curious, "now that he has *done* with *business*."—It is more likely, that it is because he has parted with the *lady which he kept in Town in* &c.-*street*.

The Emperor of Russia, it is observed, now suffers so much from the assaults of his ministerial persecutors, that it seems fair that he should receive the protection of the laws against *bear-baiting!*

An Irish Member said, "I feel myself here so strange, not having my old friends about me, and not knowing the streets and the ways of people, that I am like *a fowl out of water!*"—but, recollecting himself, added hastily, "I mean *a fish in the water!*"

Curious Explosion.—One of the late French papers tells us of a lady of the name of Lanjunais, near Bourdeaux, who was extremely addicted to drinking brandy. With this spirit it seems her body was so inflammably impregnated, that on the 3d Frimaire, attempting to blow out the candle, the flame caught her breath, and she *blew up like (une fusée volante) a rocket!!!*

"The high price of *corn,*" said a wag, "is not so much to be wondered at, when it is considered that a *single wheat-sheaf* is valued at *five thousand pounds,* though it is so small that the Countess of Clonmell sticks it in her hair as an ornament!"

We are informed the *Je ne sçais quoi* Stays are constructed upon the ingenious principle of the *Patent Coffin;* and that, in both cases, there is no possibility of getting *at the body.* They have been so much approved by many husbands and guardians, that an ingenious artist has applied for a patent for a *Je ne sçais quoi* Petticoat; and, in order to make assurance double sure, he has invented a *Je ne sçais quoi Fichè,* and a *Je ne sçais quoi Chemise.*

A late Shrewsbury Chronicle has an advertisement, in which one George Robinson humbly begs pardon, for having charged the wife of a publican, of Wedingborough, with *making* in the midst of divine service at church, and singing the song of "Tally Heigh O, the Grinder!"

A Swinish Trick.—A few days ago the servants of a Farmer, a little on the other side of Shoreham river, adopted quite a novel mode of expressing their disapprobation of the coarse bread; which being first introduced to them at supper, they partook of very cordially and plentifully, but afterwards, instead of going to bed, went unperceived to the HOG-STY, (the cabin of which they had previously well littered over with clean straw) and there took their repose for the night. At the hour of labour the next morning, the Farmer, not hearing his men about as usual, got up to enquire the cause, and on going into the yard, was by a strange kind of *grunting* led to the sty, where he found his men, on their hands and knees, in rank before the feeding-trough, intimating, by signs and gruntings, that to be the most proper place for the reception of such food as they had henceforward to expect at his hands. The Farmer endeavoured to get an explanation, but in vain; he, however, took the hint and departed, which produced the desired effect; for, on sending his son to the men, with a promise of better bread in future, they instantly cast off the *swinish* character, and went cheerfully to their labour.

A young man at Lavenham in Suffolk, for a wager of six guineas, a short time since undertook to pick up three hundred stones, and to return with each to the point from which he started, within seven hours; but after six hours violent running, in which it is computed he went fifty-one miles, he was obliged to give up the bet.

POETRY.

POETRY.

THE HIGH COURT OF DIANA.

For the SPORTING MAGAZINE.

THE CHAIRMAN.

A SONG.—TUNE—MRS. CASEY.

OF soft Signora's famous squall,
  I own myself no sharer,
Nor yet expect to hear me bawl
  In pitch of Madam Mara;
Is mirth and glee your better choice
  I'll suit you to a hair, man,
Like Teague, I'll handle with my voice,
  The title of a Chairman!
    Here's fun and frolic,
    Ye melancholic,
    Nor libel fear nor treason;
    With friendship glowing,
    Soul int'rest flowing,
    This is the feast of Reason.

I'd sing of Kings, and Queens, and Lords,
  But fear and prudence hinder,
Much mischief comes of naughty words,
  To all but *Peter Pindar!*
The Devil nam'd, his horns appear,
  With perr'wig'd lumps to scare man,
And pill'ries tingle in the ear,
  Decreed by legal Chairman.
    For fun and frolic, &c.

To humbug all with lott'ry sop,
  And prove that snow is black, Sir,
Take taxes on, and income lop,
  By help of choral pack, Sir,
To lead us on thro' thick and thin
  Would make a parson swear, man,
Then jump bo-peep behind the screen,
  Becomes a nation's Chairman.
    There's fun and frolic, &c.

The patriots bluff, with jerkin blue,
  Lead on the people's battle,
With equal zeal (you'd swear, 'twas true)
  Their tongues and dice-box rattle,
To very rags with thund'ring sound,
  They right divine will tear, man,
Yet *charter'd rights,* scarce safely found,
  When patriot was our Chairman.
    What fun and frolic, &c.

With turtle cramm'd, and fish and fowl,
  Big as their Guildhall giants,
High ranks each Corporation owl
  In epicurean sciences;
Lo! London's knights in order rang'd,
  Shrieves, Aldermen, and May'r, man,
Till guzzling soon's to guzzling chang'd,
  As swigs the city Chairman.
    Drinks fun and frolic, &c.

The liq'rish prude, who turns askance,
  Nor e'er looks up where male is,
Tho' longing still for Hymen's dance,
  Of husband still her tale is;
In secret tried, both good and bad,
  Black, tawny, brown and fair, man,
Prefers the Tipperary lad
  The six foot Irish Chairman.
    For fun and frolic, &c.

Should wilful nature chance to stray,
  And trip with neighbour's spouses,
For peeping now you dearly pay
  When legal fury rouses;
A thousand pounds, a standing price,
  The bizzard should you dare man,
For furiously against this vice,
  Declaims each black-rob'd Chairman.
    Hates fun and frolic, &c.

Ye sons of mirth, assembled here,
  May nought our pleasures shorten;
By youthful beauty blest, ne'er fear
  That wrinkled hag, Mis—Fortune;

May health and ease and senses keen,
(And who but joins my prayer, man)
Attend ye all in ev'ry scene
So hopes your humble Chairman.
    And fun and frolic, &c.

    GIDEON JUVENAL, Junior.
Leven, Jan. 14, 1801.

A SONG
FOR ST. PATRICK'S DAY.

IT has long been agreed by all persons
    of learning,
Who in stories of old have a ready dis-
    cerning,
That in every country which travellers
    paint,
There has always been found a Protector
    or Saint,
        Derry down, &c.

St. George for Old England, with target
    and lance,
St. Andrew for Scotland, St. Denis for
    France,
St. David for Wales, who on goats us'd to
    ride,
And St. Patrick, Hibernia's patron and
    pride,
        Derry down, &c.

St. Denis gives soup, and St George the
    sirloin,
While St. Andrew on oatmeal will fre-
    quently dine;
With leeks the fair board of St. David are
    crown'd,
And St. Patrick's for rivers of claret re-
    nown'd,
        Derry down, &c.

He was gallant and brave, as a Saint
    ought to be,
For St. George was not braver or better
    than he;
He'd drink and he'd sing, and he'd rattle
    like thunder,
Tho' 'tis said he was now and then given
    to blunder,
        Derry down, &c.

He'd tell you how certain he'd meet you
    behind,
And he'd follow before you as quick as
    the wind;
To a tavern he'd go for a temple of prayer,
And he'd drink to the lass with the strait-
    colour'd hair,
        Derry down, &c.

But the jeers of his friends he took in good
    part,
For the blunders were nought but th' ex-
    cess of his heart,
Though there was but one blunder he ever
    would own,
And that was—when he saw all the liquor
    was gone,
        Derry down, &c.

He'd fight for his country's religion and
    laws,
And when beauty was injur'd he took up
    the cause;
For the gallant St. Patrick, as ev'ry one
    knows,
Was fond of a pretty girl, under the rose,
        Derry down, &c.

So many his virtues, it would be too long
To rehearse them at once in a Ballad or
    Song;
Then with laughter and mirth let us hal-
    low his shrine,
And drown all his bulls in a bumper of
    wine,
        Derry down, &c.

United with Britain, Hibernia shall be
One Nation, One People, the brave and
    the free;
Then in vain shall the thunders of Denis
    be hurl'd,
And St. George and St. Patrick give laws
    to the world,
        Derry down, &c.
        AN OLD ENGLISHMAN.

A HINT TO A FRIEND.

FROM Barnstaple, as you declare,
    Arriv'd your letter and a hare;
I know the gift you did intend
Should please a very early friend,
But when the charges I did pay,
The pleasure was all done away;
Nine pence your letter cost, ('tis true)
Your hare to London shillings two,
Fourteen-pence more, I do declare
I paid when I receiv'd the hare;
Nearly four shillings in the whole,
It is too much upon my soul.
It brings this adage to my thought,
(That is) far fetch'd and dearly bought.
However, if you'll be content,
A letter and a hare I've sent;
If you should pay as much for these,
Our equal shares must equal please;
In obligations no arrears,
In future let each keep his hares.
Feb. 10.   I. L. B.

LINES,
BY THE LATE LADY TYRCONNEL,

ON WILL ABDY, HUNTSMAN.

(From the Room at Medley, Herefordshire, where the Members of a Hunt frequently dined.)

READER! behold a genuine son of
    Earth!
Like a true Fox-hound Sportsman, from
    his birth,
O'er hills and dales, o'er mountains, woods
    and rocks,
With dauntless courage, he pursued the
    Fox!
No danger stopp'd him, and no fear dis-
    may'd;
He scoff'd at *Fear*, and *Danger* was his
    trade.
But there's a bound—no mortal e'er can
    leap,—
Wide as eternity, as high, as deep:
Hither, by Death's unerring steps pur-
    su'd,
By that sagacious scent which none elude,
By a strong pack of fleetest years run
    down,
He leaves his whip—where Monarchs leave
    their crown.
No shift, no double, could the hero save,
Earth now his kennel,—his abode the
    grave.

    Still let us listen to his warning voice,
That sound which once made all the fields
    rejoice;
Still Easton's plains, and Walcot hills, re-
    sound
With the shrill note that cheer'd the
    drooping hound;
Hark forward, mortals!—mortals, hark
    away!
Hark to the summons of that awful day,
When the great Judge of Quick and Dead
    shall come;
And wake the mould'ring corpse to meet
    it's doom!
For this important hour let each prepare!
'Midst all enjoyments, this your constant
    care!
Above this world let your enjoyment
    live,
Nor seek on earth—what Earth can never
    give!
With stedfast faith, and ardent zeal, arise,
Leap o'er Time's narrow bounds, and reach
    the skies!

ANCIENT GLEE,
COMPOSED IN THE YEAR 1501.

ADAM BELL, CLYM o' THE CLOUGH,
AND WILL CLOUDISLEE.

I.
WE three, archers be,
    Rangers that rove through
    the north country;
Lovers of ven'son and liberty,
That value not honours, or money.

II.
We three, good fellows be,
That never yet run from three times three;
Quarter-staff, broad-sword, or bow-
    manry;
But give us fair play for our money.

III.
We three, merry men be,
At a lass, or a glass, under green-wood
    tree;
Jocundly chaunting our ancient glee,
Though we have not a penny of money.

VERSES
INSCRIBED IN THE TEMPLE OF FRIEND-
SHIP, AT ST. ANNE'S HILL.

By the Right Hon. R. FITZPATRICK.

THE Star, whose radiant beams adorn
    With vivid light the rising morn,
The season chang'd—with milder ray
Cheers the calm hour of parting day.
So Friendship (of the generous breast
The earliest, and the latest, guest)
In youthful prime with ardour glows,
And sweetens Life's serener close.

Benignant pow'r! in this retreat,
O! deign to fix thy tranquil seat;
Where, rais'd above the dusky vale,
Thy favourites brighter suns shall hail;
And, from *Life's* busy scenes remote,
To thee their cheerful hours devote;
Nor waste a transient thought, to know
What cares disturb the crowd below!

A BACHELOR's PRAYER.
By ANTHONY PASQUIN, Esq.

Nec sum qualis eram bonæ sub regno Cynaræ.
    HOR. Ode I. Ad Venerem.

WHAT is a Bachelor?—a thing,
    A non-descript without a sting;

A pipe unfill'd with joy's mundungus,
A mule—a manakin—a fungus ;
A sterile rush ; or seedless grass,
A rusty key—a nought—an ass.
I'll have a Co, if I can get her ;
Who would be thus, who could be better ?
I'm full of gout, or bile, or grief ;
Faith I'll turn o'er another leaf ;
As Nature's ebb'd to half my term,
I'll take a partner in the firm.
The cunning, in their cautious will,
Would, with a prop, descend the hill :
I've pass'd the sultans of wealth,
I've topp'd the height of manly health,
And, as I gaze adown the steep,
I see the human phantoms creep,—
The lame—the pestilent—the blind,—
And I'm not many leagues behind.
Oddsniggins, what a truth to know,
The more we are, the more's our woe !
Squeeze the ripe clusters in my glass,
I'll drown the thought, and hail my lass ;
I'll inundate my bane in wine ;
No statute bids the heart repine ;
We'll circle Hope, and scorn to stie,—
Despair's, at best, a sniv'lling cur ;
Tho' Bergen's poor, and Newport garish,
There's happiness in every parish.
I'll have a spic'd house ker, be to eat ;
I want some pickles to my meat.
Time gnaws me, (ah ! that I could noose him)
While I, a blockhead, but abuse him !
The tyrant scuds, like Dian's hounds,
But even as he runs, he wounds ;
He mars my vitals—spoils my geer,
Yet still my motto's " NEVER FEAR ! "
Those hours we waste, for Love design'd,
Proclaims the folly of our kind.
What are we at ? The deuce is in it,
That either sex should slip a minute :
The orbs of Beauty lose their rays,
And man, imperial man, decays !
I'll quit these templts, which we sin in ;
I want a Dame, to darn my linen,
To read the Bible, warm my slops,
Tuck up the bed, and broil my chops ;
Lead me from error, like a fairy,
And skim the cream in Passion's dairy ;
To share the nectar of my bowl,
And smooth the angles of my soul ;
'Tis woman, lovely woman, gives
The zest to him who truly lives :
Though cynics satirize and flout 'em,
By Jove, we cannot do without 'em.
Now Joans and Zantippes are rare,
Women are better than they were !
That is, if they've been had at all,
Which yet is problematical ;
And infant states, the Magi say,
Exact new shoots as trees decay ;

Should nymphs live spinsters, like old Celia,
Pray who will people the Ohio !
I'll have my fill of nuptial pleasure,
Honour and arms demand the measure ;
Where shall I meet the rosy maid ?
I'll seek Circassia's spicy glade,
Or Lesbian bow'r, or Greek alcove,
Or Caidos' amaranthine grove,
The Sophi's blazoning Seroll,
The Paphian grot, or Egypt's vale,
Or Tempe, where the Sylvans dwell ;
But, sounds ! New-York will do as well.
" Marry," says Impulse. Tell me,
Hymen,
(For you're accustom'd long to try men)
How I shall choose a loving wife,
Who'd fan the breezes of my life !
We all are vain and frail, yet each
Affects the other sex to teach ;
Though Polly counteracteth' opinion,
Yet men and women love dominion ;
The difference 'tween 'em (I'll maintain it)
Is, only how they each may gain it,
Direct me, genial god, to woo !
But recollect—I'm forty-two.
" Advance," said Cupid, " on with brav'ry ! "
But he's a rogue, and full of knav'ry ;
I think his agency not wise ;
Besides, the boy has lost his eyes.—
There's Kate and Delia, Bell and Bess,
Would take a snack at Rapture's mess ;
A relic too, both sleek and kind,
Pregnant with sweets as either Ind ;
These hussies play about my station,
And heat my dull imagination.
Eliza's flush'd with youth and beauty,
But who can tell her map of duty ?
Cudgers inveigle nymphs too late,
Then blame those faults themselves create !
Your moralists may preach and tire,
But cannot damp the bosom's fire ;
And he's a varlet, who'll pretend
To separate the cause and end.—
Bella's a nymph whose radiant charms
Would draw the Thund'rer to her arms :
She trips, as Atalanta gay ;
She warbles like the Siren's lay ;
But ever ogling, nodding, gadding,
And that in wedlock, sets us madding ;
Her coquetry's made many sick—
She broke the heart of honest Dick !
I must not venture there, because
The gypsey's shun'd Discretion's laws.—
The pretty Dowager, they say,
Breathes odours like the florid May :
Her hazel orbs announce new blisses ;
Her pulpy lips are wet with kisses ;
She smacks their ruby dew, and seems
To relish Mem'ry's brilliant dreams :

(*The remainder in our next.*)

THE SPORTING MAGAZINE;

OR,

MONTHLY CALENDAR

OF THE

TRANSACTIONS OF THE TURF, THE CHASE,

And every other DIVERSION interesting to the

MAN OF PLEASURE, ENTERPRIZE, AND SPIRIT.

For MARCH, 1801.

CONTAINING,

	Page
Sussex and Surrey Sporting	263
Essex Sporting	264
A Successful Race	ibid
Surprising Attraction of Fowls	ibid
Law Cases	265
Singular Mode employed by the Mahrattas for the Recovery of Debts	ibid
A Strange King	266
Another Hunks	ibid
Nathaniel Bentley—An Eccentric Character	267
Hog and Man Race	268
Badger-Hunting	269
Sporting Observations on National Habits	270
Pennant's Journey from London to the Isle of Wight	272
Manners and Customs of the Welsh	274
Mr. Tuffnell's Hunt	277
Boxing in Grain—a Law Case	278
French Stonehenge	279
On the Advantage of the present Female Fashions	280
Account of the New Pantomime of the Desolated Island	281
None of us can tell how Things happen	282
Account of the King's Cock-Crower	283
Natural History for Sportsmen	284
Fox and Hare Hunting	285

	Page
New Game Laws at the Cape of Good Hope	286
Diamond Cut Diamond	287
A Modern Proteus	ibid
Supernatural Dogs, Asses, &c. in Britany	288
Lioness at Paris	ibid
A Counterfeit Dragon	289
Singular Method of playing at Shuttlecock in Cochin China	ibid
Swindling Females	292
Pigeon Shooting	293
Sporting Advertisement	294
A Boisterous Sportsman	ibid
Death of a Sportsman	297
Festival of the Carnival at Paris	298
Grand Main of Cocks	301
Pedestrianism	ibid
Anecdote of Farinelli, the celebrated Singer	ibid
Horse without Hair	ibid
Eccentric Characters	302
Feast of Wit	304
Sporting Intelligence	306

POETRY.

The Agriculturist's Lamentation	309
Fashionable Riding	ibid
A Batchelor's Prayer, concluded	310
The Cracked Sixpence	311
Paddy's Portbase	312

[Embellished with a beautiful Engraving of BROOD MARES AND FOALS, by SCOTT, and an Etching of HOG AND MAN RACE, by HOWITT.]

London:

PRINTED FOR THE PROPRIETORS;

And Sold by J. WHEBLE, Warwick Square, Warwick Lane, near St. Paul's; C. CHAPPLE, 66, Pall-mall, opposite St. James's Place; J. BOOTH, Duke Street, Portland Place; JOHN HILTON, at Newmarket; and by every Bookseller and Stationer in Great Britain and Ireland.

W. JUSTINS, PRINTER, PEMBERTON ROW, GOUGH SQUARE.

TO CORRESPONDENTS.

The cowardly assassin, who, under the signature of *A Sporting Gentleman*, sent us two *ill-spelled* letters, censuring the conduct of our Magazine, may now have a *literal proof* that the 'Cobler cannot go beyond his Last,' without detection,—otherwise he would not have dated from FINSBURY SQUARE, when he might have known that the *Post mark* upon his letters would have betrayed his real residence, in some alley near BUNHILL ROW.—To these objections of disappointed malignity, we urge no other answer than a reference to the increasing patronage and sale of the SPORTING MAGAZINE.

G. W. L. is respectfully informed, that an account of the decease of Mr. LAMB, of Gaytonthorpe, in Norfolk, had reached us some days previous to the reception of his friendly communication.

Respecting G. W. L.'s hint for a Plate on the subject of Mr. LAMB's Death, can he procure, or furnish our Engraver, with a Drawing?

The Readers of this Publication are requested to accept our best thanks for past favours, and to be assured of the most determined exertions, on the part of the Proprietors, to render it still more worthy of their patronage. —The consideration, however, of the advance of every article in Printing, will compel the Proprietors, next month, to raise the price of their Magazine to

EIGHTEEN PENCE EACH NUMBER.

This, nevertheless, will not take place without a due attention to improvement in every department of our Miscellany; and which will be better evinced in the performance, than by any professions we may here offer.

THE SPORTING MAGAZINE,

For MARCH 1801.

EXPLANATION OF THE PLATE.

THE subject of the Frontispiece to the Seventeenth Volume, given in the present Number, is Brood Mares and Foals.

SUSSEX SPORTING.

THE Duke of Richmond is forming a Race Course at Goodwood, where it is intended to have three days Racing annually. Cups are already proposed to be run for; and the 7th, 8th, and 9th of April, are said to be the days fixed for the sport.

On Monday, the 9th instant, Lord Egremont's hounds unkennelled a Fox near Muntham, which produced a chase superior to any the Field had before experienced since the commencement of the season. Reynard made complete jades of all the horses, and got safe to earth, after a very hard run of an hour and forty minutes.

The next day a Fox was unkennelled near Bramber Castle, by the Truly Harriers, whose pursuit Reynard so little regarded, that he actually stopped, during the chase, to regale himself with a fowl which he had stolen in the farm-yard of the Rev. Mr. Whistler, of Newtimber. The dogs, however, afterwards kept at a less respectable distance from his brush, and followed him almost to Rodmel, near Lewes, where, being totally exhausted, they left Reynard to exult in his victory, and make the best shift he could for himself; but being seen licking his brush, and gambling on the declivity of the Downs, he had there to engage afresh with two Greyhounds that were brought to course him: they soon drove him into Rodmel Street, where, to escape, he climbed a house; but his cunning did not altogether avail him, as, on his descent, he was taken alive, and reserved for a future day's sport.

SURREY SPORTING.

On Monday, the 23d instant, Mr. Snow's Surrey Fox-hounds had a very fine chase. They cast off at Huckley Wood, where they quickly found two Foxes, one of which took directly up the Merstham hills to Ninwood, near Coulsdon: the other ran along the valley, over Tupwood Common, and down to Godstone, where he was killed close to the kennel of his enemies, after a fine run. They then went in search of part of the pack at Ninwood, where, having joined, poor Reynard was driven back, against the wind, down into the valley; and, being very hard run, got into a stone-quarry below Bletchingley, from which the terriers were not able to draw him. It was a very fine day; and there was a most brilliant field of Sportsmen.

men. The hounds were hunted in a capital style by West.

ESSEX SPORTING.

The little pack of Harriers, belonging to Messrs. Davis, Andrews, and Rutland, at Hempstead, which consists of but *six couple*, have lately performed wonders. There wants no greater proof of their being uncommonly staunch, fine-nosed, fast, and well hunted, when we learn that it is no uncommon thing for them to kill a *brace* of foxes, in one day. Tuesday the 24th instant, they found a brace of foxes, and killed, after a severe run of more than twelve miles.

As a proof of the courage of those in the field, nine horsemen started with the hounds, and eight of them were in sight when the fox made his *exit*.

A SUCCESSFUL RACE.

A Few days since, Mr. Robert Tiffin, a respectable Farmer at Outwell, in the county of Norfolk, undertook, for a wager of Twenty Pounds, to run from the toll-gate at Outwell, five miles on the road to Wisbech, and back again, in an hour and an half; which he accomplished, with perfect ease, in an hour and eleven minutes.

SURPRIZING ATTRACTION OF FOWLS.

To the EDITORS *of the* SPORTING MAGAZINE.

GENTLEMEN,

IN my attentive perusal of your Magazine, it has surprized me not a little, that I have not seen related a circumstance which now occupies the attention of the inhabitants of the North, and of which their prints are full: —

On the 20th of January last, a violent explosion took place in a mountain at the foot of Skiddaw, which emitted vast columns of fire and smoke, and threw fragments of rock to the great distance of four miles. It continues to burn with the greatest fury, and is a complete Mount Ætna in miniature. The most serious consequence is, that it renders all the adjoining country perfectly uninhabitable. Its suffocating smell has already created the greatest alarm, even to those who live at the distance of twenty miles. But a very curious circumstance, and that which is more especially entitled to your notice, is, that it possesses peculiar attractive powers, and animals of every kind seem allured towards it. Every species of birds, and more particularly Moor-game, have been frequently observed to precipitate themselves into its flames. The most gloomy prospects present themselves to all the Sportsmen, as well as to the other inhabitants of the country; and I understand a Bill is going to be brought into Parliament, for the relief of those who have been ruined by its contagious influence.

If you think this account worth a place in your Magazine, (a publication which I have ever esteemed and recommended, from my considering it to be as necessary to form a true Sportsman, as it is entertaining to the curious observer) you will again oblige one whose communications you have hitherto kindly inserted, and who has now the honour to subscribe himself,

Your most obedient servant,
T. WILSON.

London, March 19, 1801.

We have given place to this letter, but strongly suspect it to be altogether an effort at the MARVELLOUS, and as such we must consider it, until convinced to the contrary.

LAW

LAW CASES.—GAME LAWS.

When men conceive themselves injured, the opportunity of retaliation comes some time or other. From the report of the first of the following Trials, and, indeed, as it is therein hinted, the action was not brought from any enmity in the Plaintiff towards the Defendant, but to pay off an old score to Mr. Thellusson, for his former great efforts, in prosecuting the Plaintiff for a breach of the Game Laws;—at least, so we understand it.

SUFFOLK ASSIZES.

ALSTON (qui tam) v. the Reverend SAMUEL HENLEY, Rector of Rendlesham.

THIS action was brought for the recovery of eleven penalties for non-residence on his benefice. The learned Defendant pleaded his own cause in a most able manner; but the law on the case being very explicit, a verdict was given for the Plaintiff for One Hundred and Ten Pounds.—This cause was tried at the last Summer Assizes, when the Plaintiff was nonsuited, and took its origin more from a personal dispute with Mr. Thellusson, relative to the Game Laws, than any enmity towards Mr. Henley, Mr. T. having hired the parsonage house of the Defendant, and it seemed to be understood that the damages must be made good by Mr. T.

CLARK v. LEE, qui tam.

An action upon the Game Laws, for snaring a hare. The Plaintiff's case was supported by two game-keepers, who swore that the Defendant was the person who took up the snare. The Defendant produced a witness, who swore *he himself* took it up. The Jury gave credit to the game-keepers, and found a verdict for the Plaintiff for Five Pounds, being the amount of one penalty.

The world has lately been favoured with a Publication in Two Volumes, Octavo, of which the following is the Title:

THE LIFE, ADVENTURES, and OPINIONS, of COLONEL GEORGE HANGER.— Written By HIMSELF. To which is added,

Advice to the Prelates and Legislators, how to correct the Immorality and Jacobinism of the present age, and at the same time increase the Revenue.

Advice to the lovely Cyprians, and to the Fair Sex in general, how to pass their Lives in future to their better satisfaction, and to enjoy, with discretion, the three Cardinal Virtues.

On Matrimony, Compulsive Wedlock, and on Polygamy.

On the Misery of Female Prostitution.

The History of the lovely Ægyptia, the Pamela of Norwood, and Paragon of the Ægyptian Race; the Author's Marriage with her; and her cruel infidelity and elopement with a Travelling Tinker: and a History of the King's Bench Prison, written by the Author during his Custody under the Marshal of that Prison; descriptive of the miseries endured by the Prisoners, and the extravagant expence incident to their confinement.

" *Insanire parat, certa ratione modoque*
" *Nudus agris, nudus nummis.*"

We have perused a part of the above work, and shall, in our future Numbers, furnish some extracts from it.

SINGULAR MODE employed by the MAHRATTAS for the RECOVERY of DEBTS.

WHEN a Mahratta has tried in vain to obtain payment of a debt, as the last and most effectual expedient, he sits in *Dherna* on his debtor. The consequence of this is, that the debtor, be he who he will, even though the ch of man of the state, is not permitted to eat or drink, or wash or pray, is not suffered to remove from the spot where he sits or stands, at the time the Dherna takes place, till the money be paid, or security for payment given.

Sometimes a still more violent method of Dherna is resorted to. The creditor goes to the door of his debtor, and demands payment or security. If neither is given by the debtor, he stands up in his presence with an enormous weight on his head, which he brings with him for the purpose; swearing never to alter his position, or allow the weight to be removed, until satisfaction be given; denouncing, at the same time, the most horrid execrations on his debtor, should he suffer him to expire in that situation. This seldom fails to produce the desired effect; but, should he actually die in Dherna, the debtor's house is razed to the ground, and he and his family sold, for the satisfaction of the creditor's heirs.

A STRANGE KING.

The following very singular event lately happened at Basle:—

IN the wall of the spire, beneath which people pass on the bridge over the Rhine, at Basle, there stood formerly, below the clock, a large opening, in which there was a head, which thrust out its tongue every minute. It was called by a German name, which signifies *King Thrust-out Tongue*. At the beginning of the Helvetic revolution, a patriot of Basle removed this head, by his own authority, and fixed in its place a Tree of Liberty. The Helvetic Government having ordered all the Trees of Liberty to be removed, and only one to be left in each place, this one met with this fate. The Clock-maker who had the care of the clock then replaced the head. In the morning it was perceived;—a great clamour was raised, that *King Thrust-out Tongue* had re-appeared. " It is a sign of counter-revolution," said some. " There is a wish to re-establish the ancient order of things," said others. " Surely it is by order of the Municipality! Can it be done in concert with the Oligarchists?"

The clamour became so great, that the Prefect gave notice to the Municipality of their responsibility, and that it was in agitation to call in the military. At last, after a long examination, the Head of the King was taken away for ever, and all the heads of the people of Basle were set at rest.

ANOTHER HUNKS.

A Few days ago, as the workmen were unflooring an old house in Capel-court, Bartholomew-lane, (the spot on which the new Stock Exchange is to be erected) they discovered a small box, containing upwards of two hundred and ninety guineas, half-guineas, half-crowns, and shillings, wrapped in pieces of rags and tied in the feet of old stockings, supposed to have been accumulated by an old man, who died about two years ago on the premises, and who, for some years previous to his death, lived in the most abject state of human wretchedness, allowing himself barely sufficient of the coarsest food to support his body. It is believed he actually died for want of the support he was so well enabled to provide himself with, as he was one morning found dead in his bed, having gone to it, on the preceding evening, very much enfeebled, from the want of nourishment.

NATHANIEL

NATHANIEL BENTLEY.

An Eccentric Character.

THIS inhabitant of a well known dirty shop in Leadenhall-street, has for many years past excited the surprise and risibility of passengers in general, and the inhabitants likewise. Every mouth is filled with enquiries, why and wherefore, there should be such an uncommon appearance of plenty and parsimony?—A number of ridiculous stories it is certain have been fabricated, about his being bound down by his father's will never to have his house repaired, &c. However, as the following is the best account we can collect of him, we submit it to our readers, together with an Ode addressed to him by some Wag, whose observation he had drawn upon him in common with the rest.

Nathaniel Bentley, (son of a respectable hardwareman of that name, who died about 1770) resides at the corner of the Old Crown Tavern, Leadenhall-street, and is one of the most eccentric characters this day living. His father, who kept a carriage, and lived in stile, gave him a good education. It is said, indeed, that he speaks not only French, but Italian, fluently. Previous to his father's death, and for several years after, he was called the Beau of Leadenhall-street, and was seen at all public places dressed as a *Man of Fashion*. He attended, in a most elegant suit, the Fete at Ranelagh, given by the Spanish Ambassador on the King's recovery. His manners in company, in short, bespeak the Gentleman; yet his appearance in business is little short of disgusting.

Many anecdotes are, of course, circulated about this phenomenon, and many of them, no doubt, illiberal and unfounded; but on the truth of the following circumstances we believe the reader may rely:—

Mr. Bentley has not had a female servant in his house for more than twenty years past.

When any of his windows are broken, he places an old japanned waiter against the aperture; remarking, that it is the cheapest method of repairing the damage.

His answer to a gentleman who ventured to give him advice for correcting the slovenly appearance of his person, was, "It is of no use, Sir; for if I wash my hands to-day, they will be dirty again to-morrow."

It has been said, that his neighbours, particularly those opposite to his house, have frequently offered to defray the expence of painting and white-washing the front; but this he constantly refuses; alledging, that his shop is so well known abroad by the denomination of *The Dirty Warehouse*, that it would ruin his trade with the Levant, &c.

His expence in coals must be very trifling; for, except when absolutely indispensable, he considers fires as extravagant: but as his feet, from age, or other circumstances, are chilly in the winter season, he fills a box with straw, and stands in it.

He keeps no servant; but when he goes out in the day-time, he fastens the door, and gives a poor woman a trifle to wait *outside* till his return.

His favourite dress in his beauish days was blue and silver, *chapeau de bras*, &c.

We believe the house will soon be pulled down, to make way for India warehouses. Mr. Bentley has had offers from the India Company, who wish to purchase it; what his determination is, has not transpired.

ODE

ODE, *to the Inhabitant of a well-known Dirty Shop in Leadenhall Street.*

WHO has not seen (if he can see at all)
'Twixt Aldgate's well-known pump and Leadenhall,
A curious Hardware Shop, in general full
Of wares, from Birmingham and Pontipool?—
Begrim'd with dirt, behold his ample front,
With thirty years' collected filth upon't:
See festoon'd cobwebs pendant o'er the door,
While boxes, bales, and trunks, are strew'd around the floor.

Behold, how whistling winds, and driving rain,
Gain free admission at each broken pane,
Save where the dingy tenant keeps them out
With urn or tray, knife-case, or dirty clout!
Here, snuffers, waiters, patent screws for corks;
There, castors, card-racks, cheese-trays, knives and forks!
Here, empty cases, pil'd in heaps on high;
There, packthread, papers, rope, in wild disorder lie.

O say, thou enemy to soap and towels!
Hast no compassion lurking in thy bowels?
Think what the neighbours suffer by thy whim,
Of keeping self and house in such a trim!
The Officers of Health should view the scene,
And put thy Shop and Thee in quarantine.

Consider thou, in Summer's ardent heat,
When various means are tried to cool the street,
What must each decent neighbour suffer then
From noxious vapours issuing from thy den?

When fell disease, with all her horrid train,
Spreads her dark pinions o'er ill-fated Spain,
Behoves us doubly now to keep our dwellings clean.

Say, if within the street where thou dost dwell,
Each house were kept exactly like thy cell,—
O say, thou enemy to brooms and mops!

How long thy neighbours could keep open shops,
If, following thee in taste, each wretched elf,
Unshav'd, unwash'd, and squallid, like thyself,
Resolv'd to live?—The answer's very plain!
One year would be the utmost of their reign:
Victims to filth, each vot'ry soon would fail,
And one grand jail-distemper kill them all.

Persons there are, who say thou hast been seen
(Some years ago) with hands and face quite clean;
And, would'st thou quit this most unseemly plan,
Thou art ('tis said) a very comely man,
Of polish'd language, partial to the fair——
Then why not wash thy face, and comb thy matted hair?
Clear from thy house accumulated dirt,
New paint the front, and wear a cleaner shirt!

EXPLANATION OF PLATE II.

Hog and Man Race.

(An Etching, by Mr. Howitt.)

A Wager was lately laid between a noted Runner and a Butcher, that the Butcher, on that day month, should produce a Hog, which should beat the Runner in a race of two hundred yards, on the adjoining common. The Butcher put his Hog in training, by feeding him every day at the place agreed on for the winning-post, keeping him at the starting-post till his meal was ready. The man, who depended on the Hog's natural restiveness, and that he would never keep the course, (being previously unacquainted with the mode the Butcher intended to pursue) found himself mistaken, and was fairly and easily beat.

BADGER.

BADGER HUNTING.

To the EDITORS *of the* SPORTING MAGAZINE.

GENTLEMEN,

ON reviewing some of the former volumes of your justly admired Miscellany, I was highly pleased with the elegant representation of *Badger Hunting*, in January 1800.—In order to illustrate this beautiful Engraving, I have transmitted you an account of the manner of Hunting that animal, as I have observed it in some of the western counties of this kingdom.

Your's, &c.
J. J. BRAYFIELD.

IN Badger Hunting, you must first seek the earths and burrows where he lies, and, in a clear moonshine night, go and stop all the burrows except one or two, and therein place some sacks fastened with drawing-strings, which may shut him in as soon as he straineth the bag. Some use to set no more than a hoop in the mouth of the sack, and so put it in the hole; and as soon as the Badger is in the sack, and straineth it, the sack slippeth off the hoop, and follows him into the earth; so he lies tumbling therein till he is taken.—These bags being thus set, cast off the hounds, beating about all the woods, coppices, hedges and tufts, round about, for the compass of a mile or two; and what Badgers are abroad, being alarmed by the Hounds, will soon betake themselves to their burrows:—and observe, that he who is placed to watch the sacks, must stand close, and upon a clear wind, otherwise the Badger will discover him, and immediately fly some other way into his burrow: but, if the Hounds can encounter him before he makes his sanctuary, he will then stand at bay, like a Boar, and make good sport, grievously biting and clawing the Dogs; for the manner of their fighting is lying on their backs, using both teeth and nails; and by blowing up their skins, they defend themselves against all bites of the Dogs, and blows of the Men upon their noses. And, for the better preservation of your Dogs, it is good to put broad collars, made of Badgers skins, about their necks.

When the Badger perceives the Terriers begin to yearn him in his burrow, he will stop the hole betwixt him and them; and, if they still continue baying, he will remove his couch into another chamber, or another part of the burrow, and so from one part to another, barricading the way before him, as he retreats, until he can go no farther.

If you intend to dig the Badger out of his burrow, you must be provided with the same tools as for digging out a Fox; and, besides, you must have a pail of water, to refresh the Terriers when they come out of the earth to take breath and cool themselves. It will be also necessary to put collars of bells about the necks of your Terriers, which, making a noise, may cause the Badger to bolt out.—The tools used for digging out the Badger, being troublesome to be carried on mens backs, may be conveyed in a cart.

In digging, you must consider the situation of the ground, by which you may judge where the chief angles lie; or else, instead of advancing the work, you will retard it. In this order you may besiege them in their holds and castles, and may break their platforms, parapets, and casements, and work them with mines and countermines until you overcome them.

Having taken a live and lusty Badger, if you would make good sport,

sport, carry him home in a sack, and turn him out in your court-yard, or some other inclosed place, and there let him be baited by your Terriers.

The flesh, blood, and grease of the Badger, though not good for food, is very useful for oils, ointments, salves, and powders, for shortness of breath, the cough of the lungs, for the stone, sprained sinews, colt-achs, &c.; and the skin, being well dressed, is very warm and comfortable for ancient people who are troubled with paralytic disorders.

SPORTIVE OBSERVATIONS ON NATIONAL HABITS.

NEVER did so light a subject excite such grave and general attention. We read arguments *à priori* upon an apron; arguments *à posteriori* upon a train. There is not a plait in a Lady's sleeve that does not produce a conundrum; her very shoes are pointed with epigrams; nor can she even mount a new wig, without bringing down on her head a host of sermons, satires, anathemas, and *bulls*. The true length of her waist induces more learned anxiety than the discovery of the longitude; and her bosom is explored with more optical industry than the milky way. On this part of the subject, every Bond-street lounger fancies himself a Herschell, and talks of *concave* and *convex lens* with all the gravity of a Newton, or a Galileo. We never hear of the position of the *zones*, but of the place of the *cestus*; nor is it any longer a question, how the planets move in their orbits, but—how a new cap, or a new bonnet, holds its course in the circle of Fashion?—whether that which is the rage of the present hour shall remain stationary, or quickly pass away?—whether it be a comet or a fixed star? Venus may rise in splendour, and set in clouds, unnoticed and unknown; but no dashing Cyprian can put down her chariot without attracting a thousand eyes, and producing a thousand observations. The elongation of the moon is not half so much thought of as an elopement; a superior conjunction among the heavenly bodies, as a fashionable wedding; and, in the place of constellations, eclipses, the music of the spheres, and the signs of the zodiac, modern conversation has substituted routs, masquerades, operas, and cards.—But, in the midst of this monopoly of learned attention, Female Fashion has much cause for complaint: while it endeavours to dazzle and captivate, by the most enchanting display of natural beauties, all ranks and descriptions of men are unanimous in their hostility; millions of gentle claims and pleas, in mitigation, are lost in unrelenting prejudice, which, like the deaf adder, listeneth not to the voice of the charmer. The paragraph of the Witling, the cruelty of the Caricature, the morality of the Pulpit, the eloquence of the Bar, the wisdom of the Senate, the thunders of the Vatican, are all levelled against Female Fashion's devoted head.—In such a cause, ten thousand pens should leap from their cases, to avenge her wrongs, and to maintain her rights. Let mine be the first. The enterprize could not be undertaken at a more seasonable moment. Spring is the time when all nature begins to assume a new and beauteous livery. What time, then, more proper to bestow our care on the dress of the fairest of her creation.

The grand objection to Fashion is, that it is the child of Whim and Caprice, irreducible to any fixed standard or rule of Reason.—In

answer

answer to this charge, it may be sufficient to cite the new Pope's bull of the 16th of October. In this famous state-paper, we find that the rise and fall of a Lady's petticoat are exactly in the same degree with the morality of the country; that a loose dress is the external symbol of a loose character, and a muslin transparency the clearest evidence of a *faux pas*. His Holiness accordingly calls upon all Tailors, Haberdashers, Milliners and Men Milliners, Hair-dressers, (these are the precise words of the Bull) Ladies Maids and Chambermaids, all Priests, Confessors, Overseers, Churchwardens and others, to oppose themselves to the voluptuous tendency of Female Fashions. Nay, he goes farther: he constitutes these heterogeneous particles the *Custodes Morum* of his dominions, and erects them into a Supreme Court of Dress, with power to excommunicate all who shall offend against its ordinances, even to the sticking of a pin, upon the same principle as the English law, which requires (for the benefit of the staple manufacture) that every corpse shall be buried in woollen.

The French, whose sovereignty in the empire of Fashion has never been disputed, having so long made a fool's cap of the Papal tiara, it was natural to expect (and the event has proved it) that the head of his Holiness would have been turned, in the first place, to the important article of Female Fashion. —On this ground alone, we might safely rest the proposition, that Dress, so far from being a matter of whim and caprice, uniformly and strictly accommodates itself to the moral state of the country; but, to preclude [all possible] scepticism on the subject, one argument more will be sufficient.

The dress of Eve was a leaf. The dress of Europe, new from the hand of Nature, was a leaf also. This was her primitive state. Kingdoms and realms, empires and principalities, only constitute the various articles of artificial dress superinduced on her person by man in society. A female in sex and form, (as all geographers admit, from Cellarius to D'Anville) it might not be difficult to show that the dress of Europe, and of our females, have had a mutual relation from the beginning; that a change never takes place in the costume of a *fashionable*, without a similar one in the geography of Europe; that the instant Poland was shamelessly torn off her bosom, away went our Ladies neck-handkerchiefs; that the instant our females mount the Union Cap, up starts a Northern Confederacy. This would, however, lead into too wide a field of argument: a more confined sketch will answer the purpose.

To begin, then, with Italy, the *leg* of Europe; when that country was rich, and luxuriously cloathed, a peep at a neat English ancle was as difficult to obtain as a peep into the Conclave. Now that it is stripped, and naked to the very Gulf of Venice, what with transparent clocks and a short petticoat, the female leg is exhibited to the very garter.

France, the *Dicky* of Europe, while that kingdom was confined within its antient limits, never used to presume much above the hip, or below the knee; but what is the case now? The instant that kingdom, actuated by a spirit of revolution and aggrandizement, overran all the neighbouring states, the Dicky did the same,—threw off all superiority, became one and indivisible, and, to the utter destruction of all other petticoat controul, usurped the *waist*, and encroached upon the *leg*.

In former times, the Ladies wore

wore a pad and pockets. What was the state, then, of the seven United Provinces, with which they correspond in local situation? The United Provinces then cut a swelling figure: they were the carriers of Europe, and its most prominent state: they had colonies in the East and in the West; but, the moment the Dutch ceased to be the carriers of Europe, away went the pad; and the instant John Bull cut off St. Thomas and Ceylon, away went the pockets after it.—It would be an easy task to pursue the parallel much farther:—to shew how Turkey, the train of Europe, is liable to be rent and torn in pieces, and more exposed to be trampled on, than any other state:—how Prussia, with its line of demarcation, sympathizes with the Braces, in its endeavours to fix limits to its ambitious neighbours, and preserve the due proportions of the body of Europe:—how Russia, extending her views downwards, seeks to exchange her old bear-skin spencer for a new-fashioned Opera coat:—how Sweden and Denmark have thrown off all disguise, as our Ladies ceased to wear any covering on their bosoms;—and how the kicks and insults of Bonaparte have been directed to Germany, as being the seat of Honour.

This statement, however, may suffice for the leading point of this interesting question, and clearly demonstrates that Female Fashions are regulated by great political and moral principles; that there is no whim, no folly, no caprice, in the system; but that a Lady, while choosing a cup or a bonnet, actually holds the balance of Europe in her hands.

―――― Facies non omnibus una,
Nec diversa tamen; qualem decet esse sororum.

MODESTUS.

ENTERTAINING REVIEW OF A JOURNEY FROM LONDON TO THE ISLE OF WIGHT.

BY THOMAS PENNANT, Esq.

ON the 7th of May, 1787, the late Mr. Pennant sailed from the Temple Stairs down the Thames, in company with his son, the present David Pennant, Esq. on a voyage or journey from London to Dover. With his wonted vigilance of enquiry, as an Antiquarian, a Naturalist, a Friend to the Useful and Fine Arts, he suffered no considerable object to escape from under his observation, before he had particularly examined it, and noted down his remarks for future use. Many objects of curiosity met his eyes, on both sides of the river, from the very moment of his entering the boat. The flatness of the grounds on the Surrey side suggested the conjecture that these might have been formerly covered by an expansion of the river. Embankments have been, for these four hundred years, necessary, to prevent it from again inundating them. Of the Isle of Dogs, he was induced to note, that it was the scite of the Royal Dog-kennel, when the Kings of England kept their court at Greenwich.—He could not pass Deptford, without recollecting that Cowley the Poet, Evelyn the Botanist, and the Russian Czar, Peter the Great, had honoured it with their residence.—Upon a wager (as he tells us) of 300ol. Sir Puckington, in the reign of Queen Elizabeth, engaged to swim from Whitehall Stairs to Greenwich, but was prohibited, by the Queen's command, from making an attempt so perilous. The famous Duchess of Chevreuse, the favourite of the mother of Louis XIV.

of France, actually swam across the Thames, when she was in England, in the year 1635. From the accession of William of Normandy to the reign of William of Orange, Greenwich was a residence of the Sovereigns, or of some part of the royal kindred. Henry VIII. Elizabeth, Anne the wife of James I. Henrietta Maria the wife of the unfortunate Charles I. and her son Charles II. delighted much in Greenwich, and altered or enlarged its buildings, at a great expence. It was appropriated by William III. in the year 1694, as an Hospital for the reception of aged and wounded Seamen.—Of Woolwich, several curious anecdotes were collected by Mr. Pennant and his companion. He remarked, that the convicts at work in chains by the river, and belonging to the hulks, were well clad and well fed, but utterly shameless.—The *white-bait*, which to the joy of the luxurious fill the river in July, and the *sprats*, which are from the beginning of November to March the great relief of the poor, were remembered, as he passed those parts of the river where they are chiefly caught. He learned that, at Dagenham, in Essex, multitudes of Welsh, Scotch, and Lincolnshire sheep, of old Norfolk ewes, of cows and oxen, are fed for the London market from Michaelmas to the end of November.—At Westwood, he saw vast decayed trunks of chesnut trees. These trees grow not together, in woods, in any English county but Kent: they were common here, before Britain was subdued by the Romans: their timber was much valued by the ancient Britons.—He recollected the insurrection under *Wat Tyler*, at Dartford, where it first began. The cherry-orchards and hop-gardens of Kent engaged much of his notice. Of the uses of the chalk and flints, so abundant in that county, he was induced to collect the history. At Tilbury, at Rochester, at Feversham, he gathered much information to gratify curiosity. He went on shore at Margate, and learned the history of the house of entertainment named *Dandelion*.— Canterbury presents much to interest an antiquarian. Mr. Pennant's enquiries collected a variety of important anecdotes respecting St. Augustine's monastery, and other objects of that city. Concerning the Cinque Ports, his enquiries were equally diligent and successful. At sight of Dover Cliff, he revered the picturesque power with which it has been described by Shakespare.

From Dover, he proceeded to the Isle of Wight.—Sandgate Castle, Winchelsea, Brighton, Arundel Castle, Caresbrook Castle, Yarmouth, &c. were in his progress successively visited by him. Curious anecdotes in history, remarkable appearances of nature, the establishment of the arts, and facts in the biography of eminent men, he every where eagerly gleaned, in this, as in the former part of his tour.

The result of all his enquiries and observations was, with his usual diligence, committed to writing, for publication. He lived not to give them, himself, to the public; but his manuscript was lately put, by his worthy son, into the hands of a competent Editor. It has been made public since the beginning of the present year: we have read it with uncommon pleasure and instruction; and have written the foregoing sketch of its contents, for the purpose of suggesting to the literary readers of the SPORTING MAGAZINE, that, in the Tour itself, they will find an ample fund of highly amusing information, on the topographical curiosities of one of of the most interesting portions of the British coast. The style and mode of composition are distinguished by all the beauties of Pennant's former writings.

The work is illustrated by two maps, and by a number of other curious and well executed engravings, &c.

MANNERS AND CUSTOMS OF THE WELSH.

From Bingley's Tour round North Wales.

(Continued from page 223.)

AS soon as it is dark, on the evening before Michaelmas-day, the Welsh people kindle great fires near their houses, and generally, where they can have it, on a large stone upon an eminence. These they call *coelcerth*, or bonfires; and Rowlands, in his *Mona*, supposes this custom to have originated with the Druids, and to have been intended by them as an offering of thanksgiving for the fruits of the harvest. The Druids had also another, at the vernal equinox, to implore a blessing from the Deity on the fruits of the earth. On Michaelmas Eve, several hundred of these fires may sometimes be seen at once, round each of which are numbers of labouring people dancing hand-in-hand, "in merry glee," shouting and singing in the most riotous and frantic manner. In many places, they retain the custom of each throwing stones or nuts into the flame, by which they pretend to foretell the good or ill luck that will attend them the ensuing year.

On the eve of St. John the Baptist, they fix sprigs, of the plant called St. John's Wort, over their doors, and sometimes over their windows, in order to purify their houses, and by that means drive away all fiends and evil spirits, in the same manner as the Druids were accustomed to do with vervain.

They have a firm belief in witches! and consequently many old women, merely because they happen to be old and ugly, are forced to bear all the blame of the cows not yielding milk, or of the butter not forming in the churn. They are also believed to possess the power of inflicting any disorder they think proper, on man or beast, and that they never neglected to do it, if they have been offended. There are now living two celebrated conjurors, or fortune-tellers, who are consulted by all the neighbours, when their goods, horses, or cattle, are missing: these are, Sionet Gorn, of Denbigh, and Dick Spot, of Oswestry.

The young people have many pretended modes of foretelling their future sweethearts; but most of these being customary among the peasantry of our own country, it would be useless to repeat them.

I have been informed, that a disorder similar to St. Anthony's fire, called Yr Eryr, "the eagle," is supposed by the labouring people to be always cured by the following kind of charm:—a man or woman, whose father, grandfather, or great grandfather, have eaten the flesh of that bird, is to spit upon the part affected, and rub it, and they say it will go away. A servant girl belonging to a friend of mine, who resides in Wales, says she was cured of this complaint by an old man, whose grandfather had eaten of the eagle's flesh; he made use of some words, to assist in the charm, which she did not comprehend.

There is an opinion, very commonly received within the diocese of St. David's, in Pembrokeshire, that, a short time before the death of any person, a light is frequently seen proceeding from the house,

and

and even sometimes from the bed where the sick person lies, and pursues its way to the church where the corpse is to be interred, precisely in the same track in which the funeral is afterwards to follow. This light is called *Canwyll Corph*, or "the Corpse Candle."

The lower class of people of Carnarvonshire, Anglesea, and part of Merionethshire, have a mode of courtship which, till within these few years, was scarcely ever heard of in this kingdom:—The lover generally comes under the shadow of night, and is taken, without any kind of reserve, into the bed of the fair one. Here, as it is generally understood, with part of his clothes still on, he breathes his tender passion, and "tells how true he loves."—This custom seems to have originated in the scarcity of fuel, and in the disagreeableness of sitting together in cold weather without fire. Much has been said of the innocence with which these meetings are conducted: it may be so, in some cases; but it is certainly not an uncommon thing for a son and heir to be brought into the world within two or three months after the marriage ceremony has taken place. No notice seems, however, to be taken of it, provided the marriage is over before the living witness is brought to light.—As this custom is entirely confined to the labouring people, it is not so pregnant with danger as it otherwise might be supposed; for both parties being poor, they are constrained to marry, in order to secure their reputation, and, by that means, a method of getting a livelihood.

Their weddings are generally attended with noise and riot, being dedicated by the guests to little else than drinking and singing. On the appointed day, as many of the neighbours and friends as can be collected together, attend the couple to church, and from thence, after the ceremony, home again. Here a collection is made among the guests, to defray the expences of the occasion, and frequently to aid in establishing the new-married couple in the world. At these times they are often so extravagant, that many of them have literally to starve, perhaps for near a month afterwards, in order to make up a sum they thus foolishly expend; and it is from imprudencies of this kind, and the smallness of their earnings, that the people are kept so miserably poor.

In South Wales, previous to their weddings, a herald, with a crook or wand adorned with ribbands, sometimes makes a circuit of the neighbourhood, and makes his *bidding*, or invitation, in a prescribed form. But the knight-errant cavalcade on horseback—the carrying off the bride—the rescue—the wordy war, in rhime, between the parties, &c. which formed a singular spectacle of mock contest at the celebration of nuptials, is now almost, if not altogether, laid aside, through every part of the principality.

The funerals are also attended by great crowds of people, all the relatives and neighbours of the persons deceased being invited. The custom of the congregation making offerings of money on these occasions, is, I believe, peculiar to North Wales, and has, no doubt, been retained from the Roman Catholic religion, where money was given for singing mass for the soul of the deceased. It is now only considered as a mark of respect paid to the clergyman; for, if he is not liked, the offerings are made on the coffin, at the door of the house where the person resided, and distributed among the poor relatives. But, when they are made in the church, the morning or evening service for the day is first read; the clergyman reading two prayers for the funeral service, and then the general thanksgiving, and the rest of the service, at the altar table. When the prayers are concluded, the next of kin to the deceased comes forward, and puts down sixpence or a shilling, if they are poor; but where they are more opulent, half a crown or a crown, and sometimes even so much as a guinea. This example is followed by the other relatives, and afterwards by the rest of the congregation that are able, who advance in turns and offer. After the offering of silver is ended, there is a short pause, when those who are not able to afford more come forward, and put down each a penny (a halfpenny not being admitted). The collections thus made amount sometimes to ten or fifteen pounds; but, where the relatives are indigent, to not more than three or four shillings. If the relatives are poor, but particularly where a man or woman is left with a number of children, the money is usually given to them by the clergyman. After the collection is entirely finished, the remainder of the burial service is read, and the awful ceremony is closed. The offerings at Llanbublic and Carnarvon are said, upon an average, to amount to seventy-five or eighty pounds a year.—I have been told, that it is the intention of the clergy of North Wales to abolish this custom, if possible.

It is usual in Caernarvonshire, and some other parts of North Wales, for the nearest female relative of the deceased, be she widow, mother, sister, or daughter, to pay some poor person of the same sex, and nearly of the same age with the deceased, for procuring slips of yew, box, and other ever-greens, to strew over and ornament the grave, for some weeks after the interment; and, in some instances, for weeding and adorning it on the eves of Easter, Whitsuntide, and Christmas, and some other particular days, for a year or two afterwards. The money is given to the person on a plate, at the door of the house where the body is standing on a bier. This gift is called *Diodlys*; for formerly, instead of it, the person used to receive from the hand of the female relative, a cheese, with a piece of money stuck in it, and some white bread, and afterwards a cup of drink: but this practice is now entirely discontinued: the gift, however, still retains its old name.—When this ceremony is over, the clergyman, or in his absence the parish clerk, says the Lord's Prayer, after which they proceed with the corpse. Four of the nearest of kin take the bier upon their shoulders; a custom considered as the highest respect that filial piety can pay to the deceased. If the distance from the house to church is considerable, they are relieved by some of the congregation; but they again take it, in order to carry it in and out of the church. I have been told, that it is usual in some parts to set down the bier at every cross-way between the house and the church, and again repeat the Lord's Prayer, and to do the same when they enter the church-yard. They generally sing Psalms on the way, by which the still of rustic life is often broke into in a manner finely productive of religious reflections.

In some places, it was customary for the friends of the dead to kneel and say the Lord's Prayer over the grave for several Sundays after the interment, and then to dress the grave with flowers.

Among the Welsh, it was reckoned fortunate for the deceased if it should rain while they were carrying

rying him to church, that his bier might be wet with the dew of heaven.

I have observed, that in many parts of Wales, as well as England, the relations most ridiculously crowd all into that part of the church-yard which is south of the church; the north, or, as they term it, the *wrong side*, being accounted unhallowed ground, and fit only to be the dormitory of still-born infants and suicides.

Mr. Pratte has given us a most animated and enchanting description of the neatness of the Welsh church-yards, and of the care that is taken, by the relations, of the graves of their kindred; but I am sorry to say, that (if this gentleman has stated facts) they must be, not (as he has asserted) in general, but completely local. I never saw, nor could ever, during the whole of the three months I spent in Wales, hear of the graves being weeded every Saturday; of their being "every week planted with the choicest flowers of the season;" or that, if a nettle or weed were seen on the Sunday morning, the living party, to whom the grave on which it was seen belonged, "would be hooted, after divine service, by the whole congregation."—Mr. P. throughout the whole of the volumes, seems to have mingled too much of the novelist with his observations. To this there would be less objection, if, by some previous hint, he could apprise us of the entire of the former: the characters, which ought never to be confounded, might thus be kept distinct. But when a writer, who seems to think himself entitled to credit, (and in general, perhaps, not without reason) in relating his real adventures, condescends to embellish his account with fiction, however I may admire his abilities, I cannot help reprobating his practice.

The clergy of North Wales are, in general, very respectable men, and their churches pretty well attended. Their livings are in general rectories, and the incumbents, for the most part, men that have been educated at one of the Universities. These circumstances place them upon a much more respectable footing than those of the southern division of the principality, whose stipends, I have been told, are so slender as to render their situations almost worse than those of the labouring class of the community.

Mr. Tuffnel's Hunt.

We beg leave to apologize to the Correspondent who sent us the following account, the insertion of his favour having been delayed merely through accident.

ON Saturday, the 30th January, Mr. Tuffnel's pack was thrown off at the seat of Sir H. Mildmay, near Chelmsford. The morning proved rather unfavourable; and the hounds not arriving till near two o'clock, instead of half past ten, as appointed, the consequence was, that the Field was not honoured with the presence of Sir Henry, as was intended. After drawing several fields and hedge-rows round the mansion without a challenge, the hounds were thrown into the Thrift which adjoins Galleywood Common. It was some time ere the musical sound, which elates the Sons of Nimrod, so as to defy their opposers, (hedge, ditch, and gate) greeted the ear: it, however, at last came; and although the hounds have not been accustomed to hunt foxes, yet, too high mettled to lose the opportunity of smelling a *brush*, a general crack ensued, and Reynard (who had but a few hours before been seen to enter the cover, was at last obliged to quit it, which ho did with the greater part of the hounds in view, leading them through Stock, and from thence to Cray's Hill, when he headed and came back to Runwell Wood, where he was lost, after near three hours hard breast-high running and when the evening was very far advanced.

BOXING IN GRAIN.

GUILDHALL, LONDON,
FEB. 28.

Sittings before Lord Kenyon, and a Special Jury of Merchants.

BRICKWOOD v. DUNKIN.

THIS was an action of assault and battery, opened by Mr. Attorney General, who observed, that whatever complaints might be made of our morals and good conduct, yet our manners and improvement in civilization were such, that it seldom happened that a Gentleman had to complain of gross and brutal treatment at the hands of another. The insult exhibited in this case was accompanied with severe bodily injury, which prevented the Plaintiff, for a time, from transacting his business: the insult that had been offered this Gentleman was offered on the public Corn Exchange, in the presence of all his fellow-citizens resorting there on that public occasion, and accompanied with every sort of outrage and aggravation this species of injury was capable of. Mr. Brickwood, he said, had a stand at the Corn Exchange, and was a Gentleman of great respectability. Mr. Dunkin was a considerable dealer, and made purchases at the Corn Exchange for Government. On the 1st of December last, when this assault was committed, they were talking about the price of peas; which conversation produced the assault, and which we shall state shortly from the evidence of the witnesses.

Mr. Haines, the first witness, said, he was clerk to Mr. Brickwood, who attends the Corn Exchange every day. Mr. Dunkin, the Defendant, on the 1st of December last was speaking to the Plaintiff about peas: they were in conversation about five minutes: he thought they were joking, and took no notice of it. Mr. Dunkin asked Mr. Brickwood, what he meant by bidding for some samples of peas which belonged to Messrs. Sayer and Williams? Mr. Brickwood said, he had only bid for three or four of the best samples, at 5l. 8s. Mr. Dunkin said, he had raised the market, by bidding for the whole. Mr. Dunkin wanted Mr. Brickwood to go to Sayer and Williams, to have this business explained, which Mr. Brickwood refused to do. Mr. Dunkin then repeated again, that Mr. Brickwood had raised the price of the whole market. Mr. Brickwood said the contrary; that he had only bid for three or four of the best samples. Mr. Dunkin had before said, that he bade for the whole. Mr. Dunkin said, "Do you mean to give me the lie?" Mr. Brickwood answered, that he only bade for three or four of the best samples, and did not want the whole. Mr. Dunkin said, a second time, "Do you mean to give me the lie?" Mr. Brickwood gave him the same answer. Mr. Dunkin said, the third time, "Do you mean to give me the lie?" and before Mr. Brickwood could make any answer, Mr. Dunkin knocked him down, and struck him five or six times. He gave him a blow on the nose, three or four on the face and eyes, and one on the side. Mr. Dunkin is a tall man, and of the age of between thirty and

and forty. Mr. Brickwood was much hurt: his face was all covered with blood: he was confined for eleven days, and could not come out.

On cross examination, the witness said, the Plaintiff dealt in all kinds of corn. It was well known that Mr. Dunkin was an agent for Government. When Mr. Dunkin repeated that the Plaintiff had raised the price of the whole market, the Plaintiff asserted the contrary, and did not say it was false; but the witness thought he said it was untrue.

Joseph Branley was at the Corn Exchange on the 1st of December, when this affray happened, and saw the Defendant strike the Plaintiff, who did not fall, but supported himself by the stand.

On cross examination, he said, there was not a better natured fellow than the Defendant in the whole kingdom.

Mr. Gibbs, of Counsel for the Plaintiff, said, they had to complain of him, that he was too prodigal of his right-hand.

Mr. Jones said, he was a Surgeon, and attended the Plaintiff. He found his face very much disfigured: one of his eyes was almost closed up: the Plaintiff was exceedingly affected with it. He thought he never saw a greater impression made on any man's face: he could not well go out, and was certainly obliged to keep his house. He could not have conceived the injury was done with the fist.

Mr. Erskine made an eloquent speech, on the part of the Defendant, in mitigation of damages, in the course of which he observed,— that Mr. Dunkin was an agent of Government; that he had no personal interest whatever in the rise of the price, as he was paid a commission: that he had been told by Sayer and Williams what had been asserted to the Plaintiff; and that the market had been raised upon him *six hundred and twelve pounds*: this, as a servant of the public, he resented. This Gentleman was the Captain of a Volunteer Corps; and a more honourable man, or a more faithful servant of the public, did not exist.

The Lord Chief Justice observed, that the Gentlemen of the Jury were in possession of the whole of the case, and would decide it on the evidence they had heard. His Lordship said, he could not forbear just observing, that the first witness seemed to enhance the nature of this assault: he swore that the Defendant knocked the Plaintiff down. In that he was not supported by the rest of the evidence.

Verdict for Plaintiff—Damages *One Hundred Pounds.*

FRENCH STONEHENGE.

A traveller in Brittany gives the following account of the celebrated CARNAC, on the coast of Vannes; a relique of antiquity, to all appearance of the same kind with our Stonehenge, on Salisbury Plain:—

THIS is an immense colonnade of stones, about four thousand in number, planted in the form of a quincunx, exactly in even parallel lines, and fixed upon the loftiest part of the coast, near the town of Carnac, in full view of the sea, occupying a space of a thousand toises (two thousand yards) long, and fifty in breadth. There are eleven rows, with unequal intervals of two to six toises between them; and the distance between each column is likewise irregular, being from eighteen to twenty-five feet. The height of each varies from a few feet to eighteen or twenty above ground, and the thickness in proportion.

proportion. What is very singular, almost all the columns are somewhat conical in form, and are fixed with the point downward, so as to give the appearance of a vast block of stone resting on a pivot. No inscription is to be found, to give the least information as to the period of their erection, or their designation; nor does history throw any light on the subject: but, from their great antiquity, and the rude method of their construction, they have all the appearance of Celtic monuments.

ON THE ADVANTAGES OF THE PRESENT FEMALE FASHIONS.

To the EDITORS *of the* SPORTING MAGAZINE.

GENTLEMEN,

I have long regretted the abusive language which has been lavishly bestowed on the Fair Sex, in consequence of the present fashionable mode of dressing, or rather of *un*-dressing, prevalent in the metropolis and other parts of the kingdom; and as you have frequently joined in propagating the popular clamour, I hope you will be candid enough to give my defence of them a place in your Magazine. I am induced to take this liberty, because I have my reasons for believing that even you, Gentlemen, secretly prefer a continuance of the present fashion, to the revival of the obsolete method of encumbering the body with a load of useless cloathing, whatever you may aver or insinuate to the contrary.

The principal design of dress is, I conceive, Gentlemen, to display the beauties of the person to the greatest advantage; and not, by an old fashioned attention to what goes under the name of *Modesty*, to conceal those exquisite graces and perfections which Nature has so lavishly bestowed on the Female Sex. If experience, therefore, has proved, to the satisfaction of the Ladies, that an unreserved disclosure of their charms ensures them a greater degree of admiration and homage, it would be arbitrary, in the highest degree, to endeavour to oblige them, either directly or indirectly, to adopt a different line of conduct.

Many unanswerable arguments might be urged in support of the reigning fashion; and, in point of economy in particular, it seems to deserve universal encouragement. But a still more honourable motive has been assigned for its prevalence. My friend *Jack Rattle*, who is intimately acquainted with several leaders of the mode, assures me, that they are actuated solely by a desire to relieve the wants of their distressed fellow-creatures, by a sacrifice of their own superfluities; and that they thus voluntarily discard the parade and expence of cloathing, in order that their inferiors may be enabled to perceive its inefficacy and inutility.—Although, without any irony, Gentlemen, I am fully persuaded of the benevolence of our fair countrywomen, I am scarcely inclined to credit my friend's account; yet, surely, the bare possibility of its being accurate, ought to put a stop to the licentious declamations of their enemies.

If we view the subject in another light, we may consider the conduct of the Ladies as an incontestible proof of their candour, and detestation of hypocrisy. Personal defects are very frequently hidden from the world by means of artificial disguises; and nothing, in my opinion, more evinces the fortitude and noble-mindedness of our Females, than their contempt of the sneers and sarcasms of the world at their

their publicly exposing blemishes of this kind, when put in competition with the benefits likely to result, from their conduct, to society at large.

Hoping these hints may prevent any future insults being offered to the sex, I remain, your's, &c.

TOM TRIM.

NEW PANTOMIME.

THE DESOLATE ISLAND.

THEATRE ROYAL, COVENT-GARDEN.

OF the new piece produced this evening, (February 28) the celebrated and unfortunate French Navigator, PEROUSE, furnishes the name, but nothing more. With a few exceptions, the incidents are neither such as his history does, or could furnish.

The scene opens with a view of *Perouse* making his escape from a wreck, on the shore of a luxuriant but desolate country. Here he meets a species of Ouran-Outang, or Wild Man of the Wood, with whom he becomes familiar, and whose fidelity and attachment constitute the principal interest of the piece. Shortly after, a canoe full of Savages comes on shore, and *Umba*, the mistress of their Chief, falls in love with *Perouse*. A battle ensues, excited by the jealousy of the Indian Chief, in which the savages, defeated by *Perouse*, fly to their native island, leaving *Umba* behind. In their absence, a Frenchman of war arrives, and sends its boat on shore, with Madame *Perouse* and her infant son, in search of her husband. A meeting shortly after takes place between them: but its joy is on the eve of being destroyed by the return of the savages with fresh forces, thirsting for revenge, when their designs are interrupted by the address of the Wild Man of the Wood, and finally defeated by the arrival of the crew from the French ship.

In the conduct of this piece, there is much to remind the audience of *Robinson Crusoe* and his man *Friday*. In the present story, the Ouran-Outang occupies the same place as *Friday*, in relation to *Perouse*; and by his activity, ingenuity, and various tricks, constitutes a substitute for the mechanical devices and changes which generally form the most important part of this species of entertainment. What, therefore, the present piece may want in those artificial devices which astonish and surprise, it makes up in interesting views of nature. The effect of the one is produced on the mind; of the other, in the heart.

The little *Wild Man of the Wood* was admirably sustained by Master Monage; and Mrs. Mills (who is the life of every piece in which she performs) displayed much attitudinarian grace, and in every other respect pourtrayed *Umba* in a most capital stile.

All these particulars, however, are only subordinate in the description of this Pantomime. Its *forte* principally lays in the scenery, which is extremely rich and luxuriant. The perspective of the coast, with the French vessel in full sail, is beautifully painted. The internal views of the island, of which there are many, are also finely conceived, and well executed. The dresses and decorations are in a corresponding style of splendour.

The piece was received throughout with applause; but its effect would be rendered much stronger, and more impressive, by a little retrenchment.

The following is a specimen of the poetry:—

SONG—(*Umba*)—Mrs. Mills.

MY name be *Umba*—you shall hear
 How true me love a comely stranger:
My native island, parents dear,
 Me leave to watch white man in danger.
Sweet as the morn his face to me,
 Wild mountain-berries when me bring him;
And while the sun sinks under sea,
 On this fond breast to sleep me sing him.
  Sing tra la, my true love!
  Sing tra la!

But, oh! poor *Umba* sometimes sigh;—
 For sighs of love be hard to smother;
White man, for whom me gladly die,
 In this country love another!
Of wife at home he often speak—
 It almost break my heart to hear him;
But, as the tear steal down my cheek,
 Me try to smile, and sing to cheer him.
  With tra la, my true love! &c.

NONE OF US CAN TELL, HOW THINGS HAPPEN!

To the EDITORS *of the* SPORTING MAGAZINE.

GENTLEMEN,

IT has been asserted, by ill-natured people, that mankind in general are backward in confessing their ignorance. However true this may prove on some occasions, I have met with many instances of a most engaging ingenuousness, which do infinite honour to the parties concerned. I have often admired the candour with which very sensible persons, when stating a fact, have acknowledged their inability to account for it, by saying, "*I don't know how it happens!*"— Thus a toping fellow, whom I have met with, protests that he *does not know how it happens*, that he has always such a dismal head-ach.—My neighbour, the Silk Mercer, who has long been in the habit of keeping a country house, driving a curricle, and washing down a dinner of two courses with claret, does *not know how it happens*, that he is under the necessity of becoming a bankrupt.—My maiden aunt, who has seen the wrong side of fifty, does *not know how it happens*, that the Gentlemen of this age are less civil and attentive to her, than those of the last; and her pretty niece, (my cousin Caroline) who fully conforms to the present fashion of scanty dress, does *not know how it happens*, that she has always a violent cold, and feels chilly from morning to night.—I correspond with a most worthy and pious Curate, who, after passing forty years at the foot of one of the Welsh mountains, in a patient performance of the duties of his function, does *not know how it happens*, that he has never been made a Bishop, nor even presented to a living.—I have seen a country Apothecary, who, though ignorant of the first rudiments of the medical art, does *not know how it happens*, that all his patients die before he has time to cure them.—I know the Landlord of a public house, who is always swallowing his own fat ale, yet does *not know how it happens*, that he grows as large as his biggest beer-barrel; —and I have heard of a light-fingered fellow, who, after picking pockets for ten years with impunity, wondered *how it happened*, that he came at last to the gallows.

I might illustrate the position which I set out maintaining, by producing other instances; but these will probably be sufficient for my purpose. I therefore shall conclude with adding, that, though I *know not how it happens*, I am,

Your very obedient servant,
TAUTOLOGUS.

THE KING'S CROWER.

To the EDITORS *of the* SPORTING MAGAZINE.

GENTLEMEN,

THERE was, till within the last century, retained within the precincts of the royal palace of Westminster, a solemn officer, stiled the King's Cock-crower; whose duty, during the whole season of Lent, was to *crow* the hour, instead of crying it, as is the present practice of Watchmen.

The intention of crowing the hour of the night was, undoubtedly, to remind waking sinners of the august effect the third crowing of the cock had on the guilty apostle St. Peter: and the limitation of the custom to the season of Lent was judiciously adopted; as, had the practice continued throughout the year, the impenitent would become as habituated, and as indifferent to the crowing of the mimic cock, as they are to that of the real one, or to the cry of the watchman.

The adaptation to the precincts of the Court seems also to have had a view, as if the institutor (probably the Royal Confessor) had considered that the greater and more obdurate sinners resided within the purlieus of the Palace.

Many reasons concur for restoring the office of Royal Cock-crower. One is, that it would not now be a sinecure. As we have turned night into day, the officer in question could not sleep on his post; and, as courtiers do not at present retire to rest till morning, the Cock-crower would have much more chance of striking terror into their guilty minds, (as happened to Saint Peter) than by giving his warning to men fast asleep:—the only mistake which the institutor seems to have made in so religious an establishment! How awfully would it strike a Noble Lady, as passing through the streets to a Rout or a Gaming-table, with a row of footmen and torches, to hear a chanticler, of sonorous lungs, crow "Past four o'clock, and a cloudy morning!"—Peter wept; her Ladyship might drop a tear.

As the national concerns, too, are often agitated in the Senate after midnight, might not the venerable Senators themselves receive devout mementos of their mortality, on meeting, in the Broad-way at Whitehall, as they return from their duty, a body of Cock-crowers iterating the past hour; could we suppose that any of those Legislators had, like St. Peter, been denying their master, or, like his comrade Judas, been selling their conscience for a bribe?—But I recollect that the office remained in force long since debates lasted past midnight, and even since Bribery and Corruption had taken root; and yet it is not recorded that any Member, of either House, ever imitated St. Peter, at the voice of his Majesty's Cock-crower, and repented.

I am founded in this bold assertion, by an anecdote dated soon after the accession of the present Royal Family:—On the first Ash-Wednesday, as his late Majesty George II. (then Prince of Wales) sat down to supper, a person advanced, before the Chaplain said grace, and crowed "Past ten o'clock!" The astonished Prince, not understanding English, and mistaking the tremulation of the crow for mockery, concluded that this ceremony was an insult, and was rising from table in great heat, till informed that what his Royal Highness took for an affront, was nothing but an etiquette of the Palace, which had been practiced in the presence of all preceding princes, Plantagenets, Tudors, and Stuarts.

Stuarts.—The practice, however, was discontinued, from that time, within the walls of St. James's, and no other part of the ceremony observed, than that of our Sovereign's washing the feet of the poor, on Maundy Thursday, in person.

J. J. BRAYFIELD.

Charles Street, March 9.

NATURAL HISTORY, FOR SPORTSMEN.

To the EDITORS *of the* SPORTING MAGAZINE.

GENTLEMEN,

AS the two following Instances of the extraordinary perseverance and courage of animals of the Weasel and Stoat kind, may contribute to the amusement of some of your Readers, and may also tend to shew them why they frequently miss the Game, where they are confident it could not have been shot or netted, I shall be happy to see the publication of them in your next Magazine. You may insert them in any shape you please; and I beg to assure you, that you may depend on their authenticity.

Expect to send you, in a little time, the particulars of two days Racing, &c. &c. on the Hanaways, which is countenanced by his Grace the Duke of Richmond, and which will happen in April. I have been so much employed lately, as to prevent me the pleasure of handing you any thing; but for the future, whatever occurs, I shall be happy to forward it, if I think it worth your notice. Your's, &c.

J. C.

Chichester, March 6, 1801.

A few weeks since, as Mr. Clarke, of Horndean, was going a few miles on foot, in the forest of Bere, to visit a friend, he observed a Hare come into the green road before him, which seemed to be listening, and looking back for something which pursued her. He stood still, and hearing no dog, was curious to discover the cause of her alarm; when, to his great surprize, he discovered the object of it to be a small yellow-red and white Stoat, which hunted her footsteps with the utmost precision. He, wishing to know if so diminutive an animal could have a chance of coping with the great speed of the Hare, retreated to a holm-bush hard by, where he was an attentive observer of this silent hunt for nearly two hours, during which he is certain to have seen both Hare and Stoat at least forty times. They were frequently gone for five or ten minutes; but the Hare, still unwilling to leave the place where she was found, came round again, and her little pursuer sometimes, close at her heels. Toward the end of this remarkable chase, which became uncommonly interesting, the Hare took advantage of the thickest covert the place afforded, and made use of all her cunning and strength to escape, but without effect; till at length, wearied out by the perseverance of the Stoat, Mr. C. heard her cry for some time. At last, the cries coming from one point, he concluded she was become the victim of the chase; on which he went to the spot, where he found the Hare quite dead, and the Stoat so intently fastened on her neck, as not to perceive his approach. The Stoat, in its turn, now fell a victim to Mr. C.'s stick; after which he proceeded, with both Hare and Stoat, to the house of his friend.

Mr. K. C. of Hunston, looking over his ground, he observed a large brown Hawk to pounce a Blackbird.

bird, and fly with him into a hedge. Mr. C. who was about an hundred yards distant, immediately ran to the spot, where he found the Hawk had already become the prey of a Stoat, which had seized him by the shoulders, and was at that moment shaking him with the utmost violence; but, being disturbed by Mr. C.'s appearance, the Stoat made off.—Mr. C. has affixed the Hawk and Blackbird at the end of his barn, as a memento of the circumstance.

SPORTING INTELLIGENCE.

COURSING.

FLIXTON WOLDS.

THE extremely bad weather having delayed this Meeting for nearly a fortnight, the Cup was not run for till Tuesday, March 3.—Twenty of the best Greyhounds, that money or interest could procure, were entered for it; which, being divided into five classes of four dogs each, were started according to ballot. The five winning dogs, after five most severe courses, were declared to be as follow:

Major Topham's black dog *Snowdrop*, a son of *Snowball*.
Mr. Best's black bitch *Young Snowball*, a daughter of ditto.
Mr. Hart's blue bitch *Defia*, (winner of the last Flixton cup) a daughter of ditto.
Mr. Dade's black and white bitch, *Eagle*.
Mr. Darley's brindled and white bitch, *Dart*.

On the above five dogs being started for the cup, Mr. Darley's bitch was the favourite, both from the extreme speed she discovered, and from her having had a much less severe course than the others.—If any doubt could have been entertained of the immense superiority of the Flixton hares, it would have been made certain on this occasion, as, before five of the best dogs that England, perhaps, ever produced, the hare ran above three miles and a half!

The tryer then declared them as below:

Mr. Dade's *Eagle* 1 (winner of the cup)
Major Topham - 2
Mr. Best - 3
Mr. Darley - 4
Mr. Hart - 5

Mr. Dade's bitch was so overcome when she killed the hare, that she lay for many minutes to all appearance dead, and was, with great difficulty, so far recovered as to be carried off the field alive.

The numbers on the ground were not so great as at the last Meeting, and much more orderly and regulated; so that every course was well seen, and none of the horsemen crossed on the dogs. On the whole, it was allowed to have been a day of the best sport ever seen in the country; and it was observed, that there had been more great matches of Greyhounds this year than ever had been known.

Mr. Watersworth was the winner of the cup at Market Weighton; and two or three of the best dogs of that country were brought to Flixton.

FOX AND HARE HUNTING.

AT the beginning of this month, Major Wilson's fox-hounds were hunting the country in Cambridgeshire, formerly licensed by Mr. Panton. Their head-quarters were at Linton, where they had very excellent sport.—The hounds, which are said to be the handsomest in the kingdom, have proved themselves entitled to equal credit for their excellence.

The Sporting Gentlemen at Belvoir Castle sprung abundance of game

game in that neighbourhood, and the chase has been attended by some serio-comic events.

On Tuesday, March 3, a bag-fox was turned out before the Brighton hounds, on the Downs, near the Race-Course, which afforded a most excellent chase, being killed in an osier-plat near Lewes.

On Wednesday the 4th, a bag-fox, saved by the Brighton Hunt, and reserved for a future day's sport, was again turned out, and killed, after a chase of about fifty minutes.

On Friday the 6th, another fox was turned out before the same hounds, and, after a chase of some hours, Reynard was taken alive, and reserved for a future day's sport.

The Prince's harriers, on the same day, hunted a hare so gallantly to the edge of Lewes river, near Landport, that poor Puss, to escape them, found herself compelled to cross the water; but, being followed by the Huntsman, and some others of the field, she at last fell a victim to her keen pursuers.

The same day the Brookside hounds killed a leash of hares, and ran a fourth so hard that she was taken up alive, and is now in keeping for the diversion of pedestrian hunters, before whom she is shortly to be turned out on the Downs.

NEW GAME-LAWS AT THE CAPE OF GOOD HOPE.

PROCLAMATION,

By his Excellency the Governor.

NOTICE is hereby given, that, notwithstanding the orders contained in the Proclamation of the 15th of July last, respecting Game, by which it is strictly prohibited and forbidden to take, kill, or destroy, any Hares, Deer, or Antelopes, between the 1st of September and the 1st of January, his Excellency the Governor and Commander in Chief is graciously pleased to grant permission to the Farmers residing in the districts of Roggeveld and Bokkeveld, to protect their corn and pastures from the damages they may otherwise sustain from the vast herds of Spring Bocks and other Deer, that, owing to the drought which has prevailed in those parts, have been forced to seek for food in the cultivated lands of the colony: they are therefore hereby permitted, for this season only, to shoot, kill, and destroy, the said Spring Bocks, whenever they either have sustained, or are likely to sustain, any damage from the same.

Leave is likewise hereby given, to the Farmers in the neighbourhood of Saldanha Bay, and in that part of Swartzland adjoining to it, to take, kill, or destroy, any Hartebeests that may be found in their corn; but not to hunt the same for their diversion, until the time fixed by the proclamation before alluded to.

In consequence of the vast numbers of Wild Peacocks which have unexpectedly made their appearance in the colony this year, (which was otherwise ordered to have been a jubilee one, in which none were to have been killed) it is now to be considered as an open one; and leave is hereby given, as soon as the season commences, to shoot the same, as well as other game.

By command of his Excellency the Governor and Commander in Chief.

(Signed) A. BARNAD, Secretary.

Castle of Good Hope, 6th Nov. 1800.

DIAMOND

DIAMOND CUT DIAMOND;

Or, An Anecdote of the late Mr Muilman and Constantia Phillips.

IN the early part of Mr. Muilman's life, he became enamoured with Constantia Phillips; and, finding he could not procure her as a mistress, resolved to venture upon her as a wife. They were accordingly married; but, as their dispositions were not *exactly* similar, they were not *superlatively* happy.

"Mr. Muilman," said Constantia, after they had been married about three months, "Mr. Muilman, I believe you are heartily tired of me, and I am heartily tired of you; so, if you will settle five hundred pounds a year upon me for life, I will put you in a way of dissolving our marriage."

He eagerly embraced this proposal, and gave her his bond for performance of the contract; when she produced a certificate of her *previous* marriage with a Pastrycook, who lived in Maiden-lane, Covent-Garden. This point being ascertained, Mr. Muilman refused to pay her the promised annuity; and, to her sorrow, she found that there was a flaw in the drawing up the bond, which put it out of her power to compel him to pay it: she therefore told him, that, unless he entered into a new and legal engagement to pay it, she would take a step that would render her marriage *with him* perfectly legal.—He laughed at her; but she performed her promise, by bringing a certificate, and producing a register, by which it appeared that the Maiden-lane Pastrycook, *previous to his marriage with her*, had married *another woman*, who was still alive.

This disconcerted the Merchant, who, however, got quit of her importunities, by giving her a considerable sum on condition of her going to Jamaica, where she settled as keeper of a coffee-house, and died soon after.

A MODERN PROTEUS;

Or, An extraordinary Instance of the Flexibility of the Human Frame.

JOSEPH CLARK, a well-made man, and rather stout, exhibited, in the most natural manner, every species of deformity and dislocation to which the human form is liable. He frequently diverted himself with the Taylors, who came to measure him for clothes, by changing his posture, and apparently his shape, when the clothes were brought home.

He could dislocate the vertebræ of his back, and other parts of his body, and resume their proper form, at his pleasure. He once presented himself in this situation, as a patient, before Molins, a famous Surgeon, who, shocked at his appearance, refused to attempt the cure.

He often passed for a cripple, with persons who had but a few minutes before been conversing with him. Upon these occasions, he would not only change the position of his limbs, but alter his features and countenance.

He could assume all the professional, characteristic, and singular faces, which he had observed at the Theatre, at the Quakers Meeting, or any other place of public resort.

He was, by profession, a Posture Master, and died about the commencement of the reign of King William.

Supernatural Dogs, Asses, &c. in Britanny.

The following are some of the oral and written Traditions which are current among the Bretagners:—

AT the castle Roche Maurice, a dragon devours men and animals. King Brislonus pacifies him, by delivering to him, every Sunday, one unfortunate victim, on whom the lot has fallen.

The celebrated Saint Gueurie takes his sister's eye from the stomach of a goose which had swallowed it, and replaces it in its socket, without its beauty or lustre being diminished.

The necklace of Szint Sanè strangles on the spot those who are guilty of perjury.

St. Vincent Ferrier, who is saying mass at Vannes, searches for his gloves and his parapleu in Rome, without his absence being observed.

A wolf had devoured the ass of a poor man. St. Malo forces the glutton to perform the work of the animal which he had eaten.

Jon Gaut Y Tan (John and his Fire) is a kind of dæmon, who in the night carries five lighted candles on his five fingers, and whirls them about with great rapidity.

The repeated cry of the cuckoo indicates the year of marriage.

They dip the shirts of children into certain wells. If the shirt sinks to the bottom, the child infallibly dies before the expiration of a year; if it swims, it is a sign that the child will live a long time; and the wet shirt is put on the poor creature, to preserve it from every kind of evil.

In one place, a number of stories are told about a small staff, which is changed into a black dog, an eagle, or a lion: in another, they believe that eagles, by the command of a genius, carry men up into the air.

A sudden noise, three times repeated, foretells an impending misfortune. The nocturnal howling of a dog is a certain fore-token of death.

In the roaring of the distant main by night, and in the whistling of the wind, they hear the voice of drowned persons demanding a grave.

Subterraneous treasures are guarded by giants, ghosts, and fairies: some of these hobgoblins are called *Teuss.*

The *Trassorpoulict* appears in the shape of a dog, a cow, or some other domestic animal, and performs all menial services.

The blood freezes at hearing the dreadful tales about the car of Death, (*cariquel Ancou*) which is covered with a winding-sheet, and drawn by skeletons. The rumbling of its wheels is heard when a person is on the point of dying.

Under the castle of Morlaix there are a number of little mannikins, not above a foot high, who from time to time dry a large quantity of gold in the sun. Whoever modestly approaches them, receives as much as he can hold in one hand; but he who comes with a sack to fill it with gold, is ill-treated, and sent away empty-handed.

Lioness at Paris.

THE Lioness in the National Menagerie having lately whelped three living cubs at her full time, an opportunity has been afforded of observing several particulars, relative to the propagation of this animal, with more accuracy than has been done hitherto.—Both the parent animals were taken by the Arabs, between Bonn and Constantine,

Constantine, when only six months old, and were believed to be of the same litter. They were brought into France by C. Felix, one of the keepers of the Menagerie. By his great attention to them, they are now in perfect health and vigour; and the male is, perhaps, the finest of this kind in Europe. They are at present six years and a half old. The female has been pregnant once before, but being irritated in her den by some imprudent visitors, she hurt herself, and miscarried. The fœtus were then only two months old, and were without hair. Fifteen days afterwards she became in heat, and received the male several times. As the last time was the 23d of July, it is probable that the time of conception may be dated from this period, and this fixes the time of gestation at one hundred days, and not six months, as Buffon has mentioned from the authority of Philostratus and Wredt.

On the day of her delivery, the Lioness appeared languid, and dragged her food within her den without tasting it. However, she made no kind of cry, nor appeared less mild to her keeper than usual. She dropped her first whelp on the evening of the 9-10 November, at ten o'clock; the second, three quarters of an hour after; and the third, two hours after midnight. When first born, they were as big as full-grown cats (and, not six or seven inches in length, as some have pretended); their head, however, was larger in proportion. They differ much from full-grown lions: their skin is of a red-brown, marked with blackish spots and burs; the tail is marked with black rings on a tawny ground: the males have no mane; their eyes were open from the first, and they walk dragging their legs: their cry is a loud mewing, like a cat when irritated. The mother takes the greatest care of them, carries them in her mouth when she wants to change their place, licks them constantly, and takes great care not to trample on them when she is moving.

A COUNTERFEIT DRAGON.

MR. Jacob Bobart, formerly Botany Professor, or keeper of the physic garden, at Oxford, found a dead rat, to which, by altering its head and tail, and distending the skin on each side by sharp taper sticks, to resemble wings, he gave the appearance of the common picture of Dragons.—Having left it to dry hard, it was produced, and immediately pronounced by the learned to be a Dragon. An accurate description of this phenomenon was sent by one of them to Dr. Magliabecchi, Librarian to the Grand Duke of Tuscany. Several fine copies of verses were written in honour of so rare a production; till at length Mr. Bobart owned the cheat. The Dragon was, however, deposited as a master-piece of art, in the Museum, or Anatomy School, where it remained many years.

SINGULAR METHOD OF PLAYING AT SHUTTLECOCK IN COCHIN CHINA.

SEVEN or eight young men, standing in a circle, were engaged in a game of Shuttlecock. They did not employ the hand or arm any way in striking it; but, after taking a short race, and springing from the floor, they met the descending shuttlecock with the sole of the foot, and drove it up again with force high into the air. It was thus kept up some time, the players seldom missing their stroke, or failing to give it the intended direction.

SWINDLING

SWINDLING FEMALES.

TWO *fashionable Females*, who, for upwards of twelve months, lived in the most *dashing* style of elegance, in the neighbourhood of Blackheath, have disappeared within the last three weeks, leaving their several trades-people unpaid. One of the *artful* Fair Ones bears the appropriate name of *Sharp*; her partner in *dexterity* is a Miss Robinson. Their debts are supposed to amount to little short of Fifteen Thousand Pounds. All the articles which they left upon the premises have been sold by auction. Some of their gowns were of so rich and elegant a description, as to sell, at second-hand, for Thirty Pounds a-piece; and the looking-glasses alone, which they obtained upon the credit of their appearance, were worth upwards of Fifteen Hundred Pounds. They constantly rode about in a very fashionable carriage, and lived in every respect in a most extravagant style. They originally kept a boarding-school on Blackheath, but that concern not answering their dashing purposes, they invented a story of an immense East India fortune, and thus succeeded in establishing, for a considerable time, an extraordinary system of deception.

All that can be learnt respecting these Female Swindlers is, that the principal of them is a Miss Robertson. This impostor had a boarding-school, on Croome-hill, two years, during which time she kept her carriage, and represented herself as heiress to several large estates, particularly to that of an uncle in Scotland, on whose demise she should come into possession of One Hundred Thousand Pounds.

Under the impression of these high-sounding appearances, she assumed all the consequence attached to birth, fortune, and expectations; and, from the manner of address, and the lofty stile which she assumed, the people in the neighbourhood of Blackheath and Greenwich, really believed every thing she thought proper to advance.

In May last, she sent to a Mr. Creasy, of Greenwich, a man of property, by trade a currier, whom she informed, that her uncle, Alexander Stuart Robertson, of Fascally, was dead, and begged he would accompany her to a respectable attorney, in Crane-court, Fleet-street, to arrange matters preparatory to her taking possession. Mr. Creasy complied, and went with her to the gentleman's house in question; Miss R. in stating the business to the attorney, desired he would make out a factory (the usual process for conveying Scotch property) for Sixteen Hundred Pounds a year, on the estate of her late uncle, Alexander Stuart Robertson, of Fascally, and a bond for Five Thousand Pounds, to be drawn on the agent who had the superintendance of the estate, and who she said had been appointed to receive her rents. A few days after this transaction, she again sent to Mr. Creasy, and knowing him to be a man of property, asked him to lend her Two Thousand Pounds, until the settlement of her affairs at Fascally. Mr. Creasy not having the slightest suspicion of any part of what had been advanced being untrue, readily complied, and likewise recommended her to all the tradespeople in the town. Desirous of an elegant house, she fixed upon a very handsome one in the Paragon, which was in an unfinished state: this house she purchased on credit; and, through the recommendation of Creasy, engaged bricklayers, carpenters, and painters, to finish the premises in the most expensive stile imaginable; and ordered Mr. Driver,

Driver, the nurseryman, to spare no expence of planting the shrubberies, and improving the pleasure grounds.

While these improvements were going forward, Miss Robertson, set up three carriages, a coach, sociable, and post-chariot; and, while the house and grounds were finishing, she, and her sister, Miss Sharp, (who lived with her) continued at Cnoome-hill, from whence they made frequent excursions to London.

The latter end of June, they set off for Brighton, where they figured away with four horses and outriders. The horses they had on job from a stable-keeper at Greenwich, and the carriages from different coachmakers in London.

On their return in August last, Miss Robertson went to Hatchett's, and desired him to make her an elegant chariot, with silver mouldings, and raised coronets of the same. Mr. Hatchett treated his customer with much respect, and hastened to complete the order by the time promised, the Queen's Birth-day, her cousin, Mr. Secretary Dundas, intending, on that day, to introduce her at Court.

About this time, the house was finished, but not furnished: having heard that Mr. Oakley, in Bondstreet, was remarkable for the elegance of his ware-rooms, she applied to him, through the medium of a man of respectability, at Blackheath, and, from the representations made to Mr. Oakley, he agreed to furnish the house for Four Thousand Pounds. Things then went on in a flourishing way; the drawing rooms were painted in water colours by one of the first artists in the kingdom; the walls in landscape, and the cieling composed of clouds, and appropriate devices. The looking glasses to the floor were in burnished gold frames, richly carved, with statuary marble slabs, and ormolu ornaments. These six mirrors came to Eleven Hundred Pounds. On the marble slabs in the principal drawing-room were placed a pair of Egyptian candelabras, the price of which was Two Hundred Guineas; the principal bed Five Hundred Pounds, and every other article equally magnificent.

During the three months that the furnishing of the house was going forward, Mr. Oakley had frequent conferences with his employer, Miss Robertson, when she frequently mentioned that she had great expectations from rich relations in India, and was continually receiving presents of great value. Among the number lately arrived, was a marble chimney-piece, then lying at the India House, worth, in that country, Eleven Hundred Pounds, and added, that it was her intention to build a room on purpose to erect it in, adapted for balls or music. Mr. Oakley, not being perfectly satisfied with appearances, requested, when half the order had been completed, the sum of One Thousand Pounds. Miss Robertson felt herself hurt, and said, if he had any doubts of his having his money, when her affairs were settled at Fascully, he might apply to her sister, Lady Paget, or to her cousin, the Bishop of London.—"If you have any further doubts (added Miss Robertson), apply to Sir Richard Hill, who has known me from infancy, Sir Edward Law (the present Attorney General) can speak to my respectability."—From these bold assertions, Mr. Oakley proceeded with the order, but when nearly completed he judged it proper to wait upon the Bishop of London, and Sir Richard Hill; both those gentlemen said they had no farther knowledge of a Miss Robertson, than by a card, which

which a person of that name had been in the habit of leaving at the houses of persons of distinction.

Upon this discovery, in February last, Mr. Oakley took out a writ, and with proper officers, his own men, and several carts, went down to Blackheath, and laid in wait till nine o'clock (being informed that Miss Robertson dined out), when the carriage came home, but no Miss Robertson. From this circumstance it appeared that she had received intimation of what was going forward, and would not return. Mr. Oakley, finding he could not take the body, contrived to get into the house, and let in his men, who disrobed the mansion of its furniture by six o'clock the next morning, having worked hard all night. At nine o'clock in the morning came in an execution, under virtue of which, the remaining part of the property was sold by auction on the premises.

No discovery has yet been made as to the place of residence of this swindler. Mr. Pearse, haberdasher, of St. Paul's Church-yard, met her on Saturday, the 14th instant, in Bishopsgate street, dressed in man's clothes and boots, with Miss Sharp leaning on her arm.—The following persons have been defrauded to a large amount:—At Greenwich, the Carpenter, of Fourteen Hundred Pounds—the Bricklayer, of Nine Hundred Pounds—the Painter and Glazier, of Seven Hundred Pounds—the Stable-keeper, who lent the horses, of Three Hundred Pounds.—The Nurseryman, for lawns and pleasure-grounds, of Four Hundred Pounds.—Mr. Clark, of Fleet-street, silversmith, a superb sideboard of plate.—Messrs. Ord and Morris, and Mr. Pearse, of St. Paul's Church yard, are among the number defrauded.—A Milliner, in Bond-street, for dresses and laces, of Two Hundred and Sixty Pounds.

This female Proteus pretended to great sanctity in religion, with a devotee, and attended several Presbyterian and other meetings, where she worked upon the Christian bowels of the compassionate and liberal, by borrowing money in the way of loan, representing herself as a person of family in distressed circumstances. In person she is plain, much marked by the small-pox, about five feet two inches in height, insinuating in her manners, and speaks in an elevated tone of voice.

PIGEON SHOOTING.

DETAILED account of what has been called in the newspapers, the famous Match of Pigeon Shooting, at Wrotham, on the 5th of March, 1801, by —— Barton, Esq. and —— Myers, on the one side, and the Hon. W. Coventry, and —— Robinson, the cricketer, on the other, for the sum of One Thousand Guineas. Each person had twelve shots, and the birds were liberated from him at the distance of eighteen yards only.

MYERS'S SHOTS.

1st shot.—Brought the bird to the ground dead.
2d do.—Brought the bird to the ground dead.
3d do.—Did neither kill nor wound the bird.
4th do.—Did neither kill nor wound the bird.
5th do.—Brought the bird to the ground by pinioning it.
6th do.—Brought the bird to the ground by pinioning it.
7th do.—Did neither kill nor wound the bird.
8th do.—Did not kill, but slightly wounded the bird.
9th do.—Brought the bird to the ground by pinioning it.
10th do.

10th shot.—Brought the bird to the ground dead.
11th do.—Did neither kill nor wound the bird.
12th do.—Brought the bird to the ground by pinioning it.
Total killed by Myers, agreeable to the rules, is six birds.

—— BARTON, ESQ.'S SHOTS.

1st shot.—Brought the bird to the ground dead.
2d do.—Did neither kill nor wound the bird.
3d do.—Brought the bird to the ground by pinioning it.
4th do.—Did not bring the bird to the ground, but slightly wounded it.
5th do.—Brought the bird to the ground by pinioning it.
6th do.—Brought the bird to the ground by pinioning it.
7th do.—Brought the bird to the ground dead.
8th do.—Did neither kill nor wound the bird.
9th do.—Brought the bird to the ground by pinioning it.
10th do.—Did not bring the bird to the ground, but slightly wounded it.
11th do.—Did not bring the bird to the ground, but slightly wounded it.
12th do.—Did not bring the bird to the ground, but slightly wounded it.
Total killed by —— Barton, Esq. is six birds.

—— ROBINSON'S SHOTS.

1st shot.—Did neither kill nor wound the bird.
2d do.—Brought the bird to the ground by pinioning it.
3d do.—Brought the bird to the ground by pinioning it.
4th do.—Did neither kill nor wound the bird.
5th do.—Brought the bird to the ground dead.
6th shot.—Brought the bird to the ground dead.
7th do.—Did not kill, but slightly wounded the bird.
8th do.—Brought the bird to the ground dead.
9th do.—Did not kill the bird, but wounded it so as to cause it to fall to the ground, soon after which it rose again and flew away.
10th do.—Did not kill, but slightly wounded the bird.
11th do.—Brought the bird to the ground dead.
12th do.—Brought the bird to the ground dead.
Total killed by Robinson, agreeable to the rules, is seven birds.

HON. W. COVENTRY'S SHOTS.

1st shot.—Did neither kill, nor wound the bird.
2d do.—Did neither kill, nor wound the bird.
3d do.—Brought the bird to the ground by pinioning it.
4th do.—Did neither kill nor wound the bird.
5th do.—Did neither kill nor wound the bird.
6th do.—Did neither kill nor wound the bird.
7th do.—Did not kill, but only slightly wounded the bird.
8th do.—Did not kill, but only slightly wounded the bird.
9th do.—Brought the bird to the ground by pinioning it.
10th do.—Did neither kill nor wound the bird.
11th do.—Did not kill, but slightly wounded the bird.
12th do.—Brought the bird to the ground dead.
Total killed by the Hon. W. Coventry, is three birds.

The abstracted account of the number of birds killed by each party will be as under:
—— Myers, 6; —— Barton, 6; —Total, 12.
—— Robinson, 7; Hon. W. Coventry, 3;—Total 10.

The difference will be two in favour of —— Barton, Esq. and —— Myers.

SPORTING ADVERTISEMENT
From an Edinburgh Paper.

TO SPORTSMEN.

GLENDYE Shooting Quarters to be Let from Whitsunday first, for such a period as may be agreed on. The house consisting of four rooms and a kitchen, is new, substantially built, and neatly fitted up; stands nearly in the centre of a meadow, surrounded on one side by a bank covered with wood, and on the other by the Water of Dye, which passes along the margin of the meadow, in a course nearly semicircular almost touching the house, at the point, where it runs through the arch of Bridge of Dye, and having its banks fringed with birches, the whole lying near the base, and having the high-featured mountain of Clock-na-Baine in full view: forming, altogether, something not a little picturesque; situated almost in the middle of that district of the Grampion Mountains about twenty-five miles from Aberdeen, but not exceeding twenty from either of the market towns of Montrose or Brechin, and only five or six from a post office at Banchory. The military road to the North, over the Cairn of Mount, passes very near the house.—Within less than a mile of the quarters, in each of three different directions, commences an exclusive privilege of grouse shooting, extending all around for many miles, and such as to afford, even to a middling shot, opportunity of killing from ten to twenty brace a-day.

The water of Dye affords excellent trout fishing: on the Teugh, about three miles distant, grilsing in July, August, and September; and a little farther on the river Dee, what is reckoned among the best stations in Scotland for killing salmon with the rod. The proprietor's exclusive property extends, including the forestry of Blackhall, over a surface of from nine to ten miles square, comprehending the whole course of the water of Dye, nearly that of the Teugh, and above six miles of the south bank of the river Dee, all conterminous.

To a gentleman sportsman will be made over, not only the exclusive right of shooting and fishing on the whole property, and of hunting and killing deer and roe in the forest of Blackhall, but also of protecting the game of all kinds, with the exception of a very few privileged friends of the proprietor's, whose society in sporting, and aid in protecting, will be found equally pleasant and useful, &c. &c.

A BOISTEROUS SPORTSMAN.

To the EDITORS *of the* SPORTING MAGAZINE.

GENTLEMEN,

OF all the various characters delineated in your entertaining Miscellany, none, I believe, for extravagance, can equal the following, I mean the latter of the two. The first I choose to call Sophronius, for his prudence; the second, or my principal hero, I call Orson, for his ruder manners. I must own I had devoted a day to quiet enjoyment; and therefore you will guess what my feelings must have been, not being acquainted with Orson before, after having met with Sophronius, a man the most congenial to my own cast, of any that I know. But now to my narrative.

I could

I could not have wished for a better opportunity than I have had lately, of seeing how differently two people, of pretty equal fortunes, contrive to make use of them.—I dined at Richmond, with the celebrated Sophronius, a man of good sense, affability, and good-nature, every thing about him, his house, his garden, and furniture, all constructed in the most elegant and refined taste, gave me a secret pleasure, which the bare appearance of wealth and grandeur can never bestow: there is nothing superfluous in his whole system of domestic economy, and yet not a jot wanting of real magnificence; his business is the enjoyment of life, and his pleasures the means of that enjoyment, none of which are inconsistent with reason, humanity, and benevolence. His knowledge of mankind makes him seldom misapply his favours, and his studies are sweetened with the pleasures of having discovered how to be more useful to others.—His intimate acquaintances are select, and his distant ones universal.—He makes no man his confident, nor lays himself under obligations to any, lest he should be angry with them for deceiving him, as he is not willing to forfeit a friend, because subject to the failings of human nature; and has too much spirit to let an injury pass unresented. Thus lives Sophronius, master of himself and his fortune, deserving well of all; and, in return, meeting with no enemies but such as envy to his superior merit, or an hatred to virtue itself raises him.

Orson, with whom I supped, is strangely reversed to this my host at noon.—I had no sooner alighted from my horse, at his gate, and was walking up the area to the door, but, coming behind me, he saluted me with the most violent slap on the back, seizing instantly hold of my hand, and shaking my arm as if he intended to separate it from my body. He had, it seems, been lounging, if I may use the expression, round about his house and garden walls, as if he had entertained some felonious intent of breaking in at night, and was looking out beforehand for a convenient place to execute his design. His observations, however, were disturbed by my arrival, and he immediately ran to receive his visitor. We went into a parlour—the servants were summoned with great clamour—in an instant the table was covered with glasses and bottles, and I was commanded to drink.—I obeyed, and after having been asked for news, and returning the common answer, there is none stirring, we fell into discourse upon indifferent subjects; in which, happening to ask my friend how he diverted himself, or spent his time in the country, he began to give me a detail of his exercises; at most of which, I expressing some dislike, he told me, he was sure my disapprobation could proceed from nothing but my ignorance of them, and, therefore, he insisted upon my taking a *smack*, as he called it, of one or two of them. I would gladly have been excused, but that availed little—he had said I should, and so I should.

Orson's favourite sport, it seems, was ringing, which I was first to see; he, therefore, dispatched a servant to Tom Spade the sexton, bidding him order Dick Skittle, Tom Ding, Will Clapper, and Harry Bellmettle, to meet him at the Church, to join in a peal with him; telling me, at the same time, they were five as clever fellows as ever pulled a rope; and, together with himself, could tip you a bob-major as clean as any fellows in England.—The coach was next ordered out, and we drove away for the belfry; where Dick, Will, Harry, and the two Toms, were already assembled over a gallon, which, it seems, was their allowance for attending his honour.

They all stripped immediately, and to work they went: his honour, out of a bravado, because I was witness of it, taking on himself alone the management of the tenor or largest bell. After being stunned with the most confused and hideous noise I had ever heard, for about an hour, they gave over, and we returned home. Orson all the way endeavouring to give me, but in vain, a good opinion of this manner of diversion, and telling me, he had made the Parish a present of those Bells, chiefly for his own amusement. Not omitting, at the same time, to mention the necessity and the use of bells to parishes in general.

We had not sat down above five minutes before a servant entered with word, that Mr. Rubbadub, of Barbican, had brought home his honour's drum. It was ordered to be sent in; and, notwithstanding I told him several times, I had an utter aversion to such kind of musick, he persisted in making trials of its goodness, beating the "Grenadier's March," "Drunk or sober go to Bed Tom," "Round-about Cuckolds," and several other elegant pieces of the same stamp.

After this, protesting the drum had a good sound, he laid it down, and began to inform me of the proficiency he had made in drum-musick, assuring me he could make it speak as plain as a Christian; and that I should attend him to his summer-house, in the garden, looking on to the Thames, where I might hear it.

We presently went thither, where I had a fresh instance of the improvement of my friend's taste; for, since I had been there, he had got this little saloon painted, in the imitation of the gayest-coloured marble all over, wamscot, window-shutters, and even the ceiling not excepted. This he much boasted of, asking me if I thought there was such another room in England, to which I replied, *I really believe not*; an answer that gave him a great deal of satisfaction, as he thought it a mark of distinguishing approbation.

Here he now braced the drum, and after many significant dubs, first with one end of the sticks, and then the other, he gave a flourish, and asked me if I knew what it said.—I protested I did not, as was really the case; at which, with evident tokens of surprize, he cried, *No! I wonder at that—you are thick of hearing sure!*—I told him no, I was not quite so happy at that instant. He looked at me as if he did not understand what I had said; then crying, *now*, gave another flourish, and asked me, if I did not hear it say, *King George the Second*.—I still maintained my inability of comprehending it so; which somewhat disgusting him, I began to acquiesce in the probability of the resemblance of its sounds, which, however, I denied were to be distinguished articulately. He repeated the word, articulately, and, with a loud laugh, asked me, if I expected the drum to talk grammar; upon which, giving another flourish, he swore it spoke as plain and as sensibly as he could himself, in which I did not think proper to contradict him.

The drum was now laid aside, and we amused ourselves in looking across the Thames, over the beautiful prospects on the opposite shore, where a fisherman having placed himself by the side of the river, took a pipe and tabor out of his pocket, and began a very sprightly air. My friend, Orson, was at this highly displeased, and immediately
hallooed

hallooed out and bid him be quiet with his tooting.—The fisherman did not hear what he said, or would not regard him, and therefore played on; upon which, calling out for two of his servants, he ordered them to launch the punt into the river, and he himself would go over and make him quiet. The fellows obeyed the orders, but gave notice to the piper, by some means or other, to desist; so that before we were half over the river he put up his musick and walked away; at which my friend's choler in some degree abated; and he observed it was very well for the fellow, that he went away before he came up to him, or else he would have taught him to pipe with a devil to him. All this while Orson was pushing a flat-bottomed boat upon the water, by means of a long pole which reached to the bottom of the river, while his servants, among other people, were staring at us from the Banks. Having now no business across, he put his pole into the boat, which letting float along the stream, he sat himself down, and pulled a black shaggy dog, of the bear kind, that was swimming after us, into the boat; who, as soon as ever he found a resting place for his feet, began to shake himself, and besprinkled us all over; for which breach of ill manners, Shock was thrown again into the river, and made to dive for pebbles; at which kind of business he was very ingenious; when, upon testifying my satisfaction of his performances, Orson, without delay, called to his men to throw in the speckled duck, and to turn loose Diver and Dash after her.—Hereupon followed an elegant scene of duck-hunting, to the infinite satisfaction of my friend, who kept us still upon the river, varying our situation, with wonderful ease, for the more commodious prospect of the game. After the duck was pretty well tired, Orson ordered her up; and we adjourned to the house, followed by all the company of dogs, who, with much ado, I prevailed on him not to permit in company any longer.

I staid to sup with him, and it being a fine evening, rode home to bed, not a little admiring the contrast of the two characters I had visited.

DEATH OF A SPORTSMAN.

ON Saturday, Feb. 28, died, in the 25th year of his age, Mr. John Lamb, late a very considerable farmer, at Geytonthorpe, in Norfolk.

The circumstances incidental to the death of this much respected and lamented young man, are peculiarly, and almost beyond precedent, poignant and affecting.—On Friday, the 20th ult. he went out to course in Geytonthorpe Fields, in company with his neighbour Mr. Kendall, jun. whose humane offices towards, and deep concern for the melancholy fate of his friend, are pointed testimonies of his sensibility and goodness of heart. In the heat of the chase, Mr. Lamb's mare plunged her off fore foot into a sand-gall, and instantly fell with such aggregated violence and impetuosity, as to be forced fourteen yards on her knees before her unfortunate rider came to the ground, when the animal doubled upon him and crushed him in a manner too horrible for description! In this dreadful state he languished nine days, when it pleased God to call him to "another and a better world!"

The person whose painful office it is to record this tale of woe, had long been on terms of friendship and intimacy with the deceased; and, conscious of his innate worth, and exemplary

exemplary conduct, feels himself assured that there is no one who truly knew him, but must ever retain the most affectionate respect for his memory, and sometimes shed a friendly tear of regret at the recollection of his premature and melancholy fate!

Festival of the Carnival at Paris.

Our Readers know that the present is the time of the Carnival at Paris; dances, illuminations, masquerades, jeux d'esprit, plays, operas, vaudevilles, &c.— The present Carnival has been rendered more gay than usual, by the peace with Austria, the intelligence of which arrived just at the commencement of it.

"FOR ten years," says one of the Paris Journalists, "the Carnival had lost its powerful dominion. Revolutions and Gaiety seldom go hand-in-hand; but the Revolution is at an end, and Gaiety again makes her appearance. Never did the *Rue Honoré* afford so animated a spectacle of what is called Masquerade: the balls were numerous and brilliant, and no event happened to disturb the joy of the people. At the beginning, however, of the Carnival, Deshayes got a terrible sprain in dancing, in the ballet of the *Noces de Gamache*: he is now much better. Never was there a greater affluence seen than at the Opera. The last masked ball was as numerously attended as the famous ball last year, the first that had taken place for some years. If a stranger were to enter Paris now, for the first time, he would think that all the inhabitants had nothing to do but *rire, chanter, boire, et s'amuser*."

Some lively and pleasant adventures have taken place at the Carnival:—Many of the officers returned from the army to Paris during the Carnival, and were resolved to try the affections of their mistresses. The following event actually occurred at a celebrated house near the Rue Honoré:—A young officer had formed the determination of trying the constancy and the affections of his mistress. The lady, by some means or another, became acquainted with his determination, and resolved to punish him for his injurious doubts. The lover appeared in masquerade, with a letter from himself, in which he informs her, that he has found a fairer and a dearer mistress in Italy, and takes his leave of her for ever. He expected that this news would have affected the lady: no such thing—she smiled, said it was a strange coincidence, declared that her affections had also undergone a change, and presented him a letter for her former lover, announcing the intelligence. The officer immediately threw off his disguise, to upbraid her with perfidy. The fair one laughed—the lover stormed—till at length an explanation took place, in which he found out that his mistress had adopted this expedient only to punish him.

This adventure has been made the subject of a song, and the officer has not escaped without some pretty severe jokes, upon having the tables so turned upon him.

In addition to this slight sketch, we beg leave to present our Readers with the following more elaborate and circumstantial account of these holidays; not taken from books, but from a Gentleman who was an eye-witness to what he relates.—Our Readers, however, should recollect, that it is a Country Carnival here described; and it may therefore differ as much from the refinements of Paris, as the humours of our morrice dancers, or those of a country fair, in comparison, with a ball at St. James's.

"Carnival begins in France and Flanders the week before Lent;

Lent; but *Dimanche gras, Lundi,* and *Mardi,* as they are called by the French, (which signify, in English, fat Sunday, Monday, and Tuesday) are the days peculiarly consecrated to the celebration of this festival: upon other days, it is only celebrated in private families, by way of recreation and amusement, those principal days being for the populace, and such as choose to be seen in public.

"The Carnival, or Carnaval, is a scene of mirth and rejoicing, observed with great ceremony by the Italians, particularly at Venice. At the last mentioned city, it is so pompous and fine a sight, that strangers of the first quality flock thither to see it from all parts of Europe. It was not my good fortune ever to see this ceremony celebrated at Venice:

" Non cuivis homini contingit adire
  Corinthum.   Hor.

"But, if I may be allowed to form an idea of it from what I have seen in this country, it is a sight which, to use an expression of Shakespeare, ' beggars all descrip-
' tion.' Carnival time, in these countries, commences from Twelfth Day, and continues till Lent. It is a time when all people indulge their genius, and give their souls a loose to joy and merriment. It is a season which, to use the expression of one of the English poets, ' seems to be marked for triumphs ' and rejoicing;' and at this time the maxim of Horace, *Dulce est decipere in loco,* seems to be adopted by people of all ranks; for, upon this occasion, none choose to be grave, or too severely wise. Treats, balls, operas, concerts of music, intrigues, marriages, &c. are chiefly celebrated in Carnival time, so that we may not improperly apply to it the expression of Mr. Rowe:

" Happy lovers ever keep it sacred,
" Chuse it to bless their joys, and
   crown their wishes."

"The word is formed of the Italian *carnevale,* which, according to the opinion of M. du Lange, is derived from carn-a-val, which etymology denotes that the flesh then goes to pot, to make amends for the season of abstinence ensuing: he observes accordingly, that, in the corrupt Latin, it was called *Carnelevamen,* and *Carnispri-oium;* and the Spaniards at this day denominate it *Carnis tollendas,* which implies that meat is then to be taken.

"There is not one circumstance relating to the Carnival, which renders it more amusing, than that of the various disguises worn upon this occasion. A Carnival may be properly considered as a general masquerade of the whole species, and a city where it is celebrated has some sort of resemblance to a theatre, where every individual acts his peculiar part, and assumes a habit suited. Such a variety of different disguises and personages does a Carnival afford, that, when I saw it, I was tempted to exclaim, with Shakespeare,

" All the world's a stage,
" And all the men and women mere
  players."

"Notwithstanding all the boasts of antiquity concerning the Olympic games, the Pythian games, the Floralia, and many more, I do not apprehend that any of them surpassed a modern Carnival.

"In the convents, monasteries, &c. but particularly in the former, they will not suffer any boarder, or any person under the roof with them, to put on any mask; as they look upon it as a heinous sin, and consider all such disguising as defacing the image of God: however, upon the three last days already mentioned, they will allow of changing dresses, as French for English, and English for French; and in some convents, they indulge their

their boarders so far as to allow them the nuns habits to disguise themselves. During the grand and public days of Carnival, people are at liberty to mask themselves, and assume any disguise they think proper, in order to prevent their being known: nor is any body to be seen walking the streets without a masking-dress; even children of two or three years old have some sort of disguise upon them. Dresses are to be hired for the Carnival, from three livres (about two shillings and seven-pence halfpenny) to as many guineas. When a stranger receives a dress, he is obliged to deposit the value of it in money at the place where he hires it; and, at the same time, he must give an account where he lodges, and with whom. This precaution is always thought necessary, except where the landlord of the stranger accompanies him, or sends a person with him. When an inhabitant of the town hires a habit, these precautions are not observed.

"At the time of Carnival, it is dangerous for a person to be seen walking the streets without some disguise or odd habit. Those who walk the streets without a disguise are sure of receiving some insult, and having their clothes spoiled; so that a disguise, upon this occasion, is as necessary as a wedding garment was formerly to those invited to a wedding. Those whose ill fortune it is to be insulted, or to have their clothes spoiled, do wisely to pocket the affront and walk off, as it is not customary to resent it upon any account.

The time of Carnival is a time of general hospitality, as every one is at liberty to go into any house he thinks proper, without exception, and, if in a genteel dress, is sure to be made welcome, and entertained as a friend, with wine, sweetmeats, and other good things. This they never fail to do, if they suspect who you are, or have any knowledge of you; and at some houses which I have gone to, though they were entire strangers to me and my company, they sent for music, and danced with us. It is customary for people at a Carnival, just as with us at a masquerade at the Haymarket, to disguise their common tone of voice: this is a custom you are under an indispensable obligation of complying with, otherwise you are soon known; and if they discover who you are, they immediately depart the house, or pull your mask off, which I observed to be customary upon such occasions. If there happen to be any eatables or liquor in your way, you may carry them off, if you have a mind to play the rogue: if you should, they dare neither stop you, nor pull off your mask; if they do, they are liable to a penalty of six hundred livres. However, none but blackguards are guilty of the scandalous meanness of keeping any thing taken in this manner. These jocose thefts are intended solely to create diversion; and those that have taken any thing in this merry way, immediately return it. If they happen to catch a person at dinner or supper, he is sure to have his plates, dishes, &c. according to the number of the company, taken away; these they keep as long as they think proper, but not so long as to prevent your eating your victuals with satisfaction, except they happen to be persons of no principle or honour. I must, however, frankly confess, that I have seen the jest carried too far; and the tricks played upon these occasions were sometimes too like plundering in good earnest.

(*To be continued.*)

GRAND

GRAND MAIN OF COCKS.

ON Monday, March 2, a grand Main of Cocks was fought at Hallion's Tennis-court, Rose-street, Edinburgh, between the Hon. Mr. Maule, and Mr. Oswald of Auchencruive. The following is a statement of the different battles:—

Forty-one pair of cocks, out of which 38 pair fought; and 10 bye battles.

Feeders—Sanly, for Mr. Maule; Small, for Mr. Oswald.

		Main.	Byes.
Monday,	Mr. Maule	1	2
	Mr. Oswald	4	0
	One drawn battle.		
Tuesday,	Mr. Maule	4	1
	Mr. Oswald	2	1
Wednesday,	Mr. Maule	3	2
	Mr. Oswald	3	0
Thursday,	Mr. Maule	3	0
	Mr. Oswald	3	2
Friday,	Mr. Maule	5	1
	Mr. Oswald	2	0
Saturday,	Mr. Maule	3	0
	Mr. Oswald	4	1

Mr. Maule winning by one battle, and the byes by two.

PEDESTRIANISM.

THE bet between Mr. Barclay, of Ury, and Mr Fletcher, of Ballingshoe, so much talked of, was lately decided. Mr. Barclay had wagered two thousand guineas, against the like sum from Mr. Fletcher, that he would walk ninety miles in twenty-one hours and a half. He accomplished sixty-seven miles in about thirteen hours; but, having exerted himself too much at first, he became so much fatigued that he was obliged to give it up: of course, he lost the wager. At setting out, the general opinion was in favour of Mr. Barclay.

A few days since, Mr. Fletcher walked, on Doncaster Race-ground, sixty miles in sixteen hours and a half, being within the time betted.

ANECDOTE.

FARINELLI, the celebrated singer, who made so much noise in this country about half a century ago, having acquired a very considerable fortune here, settled in Spain, where he became so great a favourite with the Queen (consort of Ferdinand) that he for a while not only governed her councils, but, at her intercession, was made a Knight of Caravalla.

The Spanish Nobles felt this disgrace so much, that on the day of installation, while the *gold spurs* were putting on *Farinelli*, a Grandee asked Lord Stair, who happened to be present at the ceremony, "Whether it was the fashion in England to do so much honour to their *castrate* singers?" Upon which his Lordship (who felt, by sympathy congenial to great minds, the indignity put upon the Spanish Nobles) quickly replied, and loud enough to be heard, "No, my Lord. We put *spurs* on our *Game-cocks*, 'tis true, but never on our *Capons!*"

HORSE WITHOUT HAIR.

Citizen LASTERIE has just published a description of a Horse, (taken from the Turks, and purchased at Vienna) apparently about twenty years of age, which he considers as forming a variety in the species, and whose state is neither the effect of art nor of disease.

HE eats the same food, and about the same quantity, as other horses; is lean, and very easily affected by the cold. There is not upon the whole body any hair, except the eye-lashes of the lower eye-lids. His skin is black, bordering upon grey, with some white spots under the fore-shoulders and in the groin, soft to the touch, glossy, and a little unctuous. The bones of the nose are depressed, which embarrasses his respiration, and produces a noise each time that he takes in or emits air.

ECCENTRIC

ECCENTRIC CHARACTERS.

Of an Army in General.

AN army is the very reverse of a church; and, as we learn piety in the one, 'tis ten thousand to one, but we are taught profaneness in the other. As all religions concur, and meet in Amsterdam, so all vices center in an army. The oaths of the private men rattle louder than their drums, and may be heard almost at as great a distance as their cannon.

But, hold! the devil is not so ugly as he is painted. An army is an hospital, where you may certainly meet with a cure for the wounds of the mind, however you endanger the body. Are you troubled with an undutiful parent, with a relation who lives longer than he should do, or with a termagant devil of a wife? here's a remedy. Are you plagued with wants, bailiffs, and lawyers? here's a cure for them too; a brace of pills, and a little gun-powder, will effect the business better than all the prescriptions of Rock, or Ratcliff.

They cannot be reckoned among the children of Rechab; for though they pay obedience to their general, who ought to be looked on as their father, and live in tents, yet they drink abundance of wine.

'Tis a rendezvous of beasts of prey; and as the ark contained creatures wild and tame, so you have here variety of the first; but if you expect any of the other sort, you may be mistaken, unless a few female warriors, that come now and then to visit an uncle, brother, or cousin-german, may be reckoned in that number.

The scholars will have it, that an army is *ultima ratio regum*, the last reason which kings usually offer; and that when other arguments fail, they make use of this, as most irresistible and convincible. But the politicians may talk what they will of the matter, if a plundered boor was to preach of reason to his landlord, a dragoon, Lord bless us! how the landlord in red would lay him over the noddle! Or suppose a gentleman of the long robe should cant of reason to a carcass piping-hot from that terrible engine a mortar-piece, I cannot but think what a dash in the chops 'twould give the poor fellow; 'tis ten pounds to a shilling, 'twould so spoil his countenance, he'd never look like an honest man afterwards.

'Twould be a good whim for some fearful fellow to talk of peace over his cups at a sutler's; he might chance to meet with a good drubbing for his folly. For my part, I'd no more be in his case, than in that of a saucy rascal's, who should have the impudence to offer a reference, or arbitration in Westminster Hall.

'Tis a sanctuary for insolvent debtors, where an honest fellow, over a glass of gin, may laugh at the several colleges of the King's Bench, Fleet, and Newgate; and no more value an escape warrant, though granted by my Lord Chief Justice himself, than the scoundrel did the Lord Mayor of this honourable city, whom he bid kiss his a—, when he had got upon Highgate Hill.

An army is the true resemblance of the lion's den in the fable; 'twill puzzle the mathematical head of a Flamstead, to tell you the numbers that go thither; but a crop-hair'd school-boy, who has learned but three months to write, and cast accounts, will easily reckon the numbers which return, without endangering his hand by the *ferula, Restigia pauca retrorsum.*

It resembles, in one sense, the pool of Bethesda, mentioned in the holy gospel; there's abundance of cripples to be found there, but with this

this difference, to those unhappy wretches; from the first they drew their cure, and the last reduced them to this maimed condition.

This, like all other great bodies, moves heavily; but if you attack it with a superior force at the postern gate, it will march as nimbly as an overseer of the poor to a parish cullation.

Though the army deals in wounds and bastinadoes, sorts of scurvy commodities, yet they are a civil, courteous people, in one respect, for they seldom refuse any body into their society; and you need no other qualifications to rig you out with, than want, impudence, and folly. But the devil of it is, a man often pays too much for his *sex partite* alcove; and if he escapes with his head, and a brace of members, from the fortune of war, he has a good title to Chelsea College, or to demand contribution from well-disposed Christians; and despise at once both constables and beadles.

It is true, they are not the best Christians; but no men follow the rule of not providing for to-morrow, better than themselves; and to speak the plain matter of fact, they are in the right of it; for to-morrow takes care of them, and either provides them with plunder, and other appurtenances of war, or shovels them amongst that mass of matter, where they have no occasion for their daily bread.

They say, no grass grows wherever the Grand Seignior's horse sets his foot; if so, our squadrons have much the better of it; for no sooner are our inquisitive dragoons in an enemy's country, but they can raise, as it were out of the dust, corn, hay, and all manner of contributions.

The inhabitants towards the West of England, have an odd way of burning their ground to make it fruitful. I verily believe, they have communicated their secret to our armies; for no sooner are forty or fifty acres of corn set on fire by one modern Sampson, but there ensues an immediate plenty in the camp, and the farmers in red always reap an extraordinary harvest.

Astræa, they say, is banished from the court, bench, and bar; from gentlemen, traders, and physicians; but if you are at a loss for the sculking maid, you may meet with her in a camp; for, from high to low, they deal justly, curse themselves, and each gives the devil his due.

It was a pleasant sort of a battle, when the giants and Jove pelted one another with hills and vallies. —Here an earth-born monster snatched up a town, people, and all, and swung it at the head of the tyrannical thunderer. Jove, in a passion, returned the compliment, by throwing back an island at the rebel. But if those unexperienced warriors had known the use of cannon, they might have laughed at the thunder of their enemy, and have served him as Saturn did his father, have deposed him first, and afterwards cut off the representatives of his manhood.

Yet as terrible as the cannon is, the smoak of it is very fructifying; and a Burgher's wife, who goes two or three times a week to smell gunpowder, is as sure of a receipt against barrenness, as a good woman who makes a journey to Tunbridge, Epsom, or the Spaws in Yorkshire.

Juno kept her chariot at Samos. Venus her magazine of love's artillery on the delicious plains of Cyprus; but the devil builds his arsenal of death in an army, and from thence shoots far and wide his destructive arrows.

Our men at arms are mightily changed from the knights of antiquity.

quity. In those fighting days, the sons of Mars never minded their bellies, and we never read of the least provision that they carried with them over barren sands and deserts, whilst they were in search after their glorious adventures. Alas! those good men had no stomach, but to fight; and our modern blades perfectly reverse the scene, and have little stomach but to eat.

After all, it must be acknowledged, that, since cannons, bombs, carcasses, and red-hot bullets have been in fashion, a soldier has but a scurvy time of it. Before, a two-handed fellow, such as Achilles in Homer, had nothing to do, but to implore some divine blacksmith to make him a suit of armour; with the assistance of which impenetrable steel, and a scull as impenetrable, the heroic lubber would make no more of breaking through a regiment, than a modern soldier would of devouring a capon.

FEAST OF WIT; OR, SPORTSMAN's HALL.

A Person lately mentioning that a new set of Philosophers had risen up, remarkable for their silence, replied, "Well, and what do they hold?"—"Hold," said the relator, "why they *hold their tongues!*"

A person methodistically inclined lately left a favourite preacher, merely through learning where he resided, which till then had been a secret: but hearing that this dear good man resided in *Rotten Row*, he determined upon leaving him, observing, "that living in *Rotten Row*, he was afraid he did not preach *sound doctrine*."

Of the Female Swindlers at Blackheath, it has been wittily observed, that they *paid nothing but visits*.

One of the Morning Papers, a few days since, after stating that a fine gelding had been stolen from a certain stable, very reasonably presumed, that the robbery had been committed by some *horse-stealer!*

Focus of Ennui!—A respectable Evening Paper, lately mentioned, that from the moment the Grand Fleet assembled at Yarmouth till its departure, that town has been the *focus* of all the fashion, curiosity, and *ennui*, of the district for several miles round.

An unlettered gentleman stood up to preach in a country meeting-house, and in reading the chapter from which he took his text, came to that passage, "I am that I am." The first part of the sentence, viz. "I am," happened to be at the bottom of the page; unfortunately, in turning over, the leaves stuck together, and the first words on the second leaf were, "an ass," which he very innocently repeated; but immediately perceiving his mistake, he hastily separated the leaves, and finished the first sentence, so that the whole ran thus—"*I am an ass that I am.*"

Our dramatic authors give their works a title, that seems an appeal to the *humanity* of the public. We have a *Poor Gentleman*; and there is in preparation at one House, "The *Blind* Girl," and at the other, the "*Deaf* and *Dumb*."—It is impossible to reject the claims of such candidates!

The following spirited and whimsical letter was written by the Captain of Hume Castle, to Colonel Fenwicke, who summoned it in the name of Oliver Cromwell:

"Right Honourable—I have received a trumpeter of yours, as he tells me [*], to render Hume Castle to the Lord General Cromwell. Please you I never saw your General, nor know your General. As for Hume Castle, it stands upon a rock.

"Given at Hume Castle this day before seven o'clock. So resteth, without prejudice to his native country, your most humble servant,

"JOHN COCKBURN."

A young clergyman, of great modesty, preaching before Charles II. took for his text the 13th verse of the 139th Psalm—"I am fearfully and wonderfully made."—Apprehension, rather than the warmth of the weather, having caused him to perspire, he had, just before naming the text, wiped his face with one of his hands, on which was a new black glove, and the consequence may easily be imagined. The Duke of Buckingham, one of his audience, on comparing the words of the text with the figure of the preacher, was seized with a fit of laughter, in which he was joined by Sir Henry Bennet and several of the courtiers, nor was the King, who loved a jest, to the great discomfiture of the preacher, able to resist the contagion.

Dulkhuk, a celebrated droll of the court of Sultaun Mamhood, had been guilty of a crime. The Sultaun commanded him to be ex-

[*] The trumpeter had left his pass behind him.

ecuted in his own presence. The executioner waved his scymetar round the head of the criminal, who trembled with apprehension; on which some pert Lords of the Court said, "Thou wretched coward, man came into the world in an instant, and must go out of it as suddenly."—"That is very true," said poor Dulkhuk, "but as I am just now not prepared for my exit, and your Lordships are, suppose one of you take my place." The Sultaun could not help laughing, and pardoned poor Dulkhuk.

A loose fellow was brought as an evidence in a Court of Law, on a point of religion. One of the Judges asked him if he knew any thing of religious ceremonies. "Yes," replied he, "I understand them all."—"Well," said the Judge, "didst thou ever wash a corpse for the burial?"—"My profession is that of a washer of the dead," said the man.—"What dost thou repeat in prayer, whilst thou art dressing the corpse?" rejoined the Judge.—"Why I always first say to the corpse, Happy fellow, thou hast now escaped the chance of being cross-questioned before a Judge."

A covetous, but very vain nobleman, employed an architect to erect for him a splendid mausoleum.—When it was finished, he said to the builder, "Is there any thing wanting to complete it?"—"Nothing but your Lordship's corpse," replied the architect.

A pretended wit was very free in playing his tricks upon a modest man, who told him, that he would do well not to make himself ridiculous.—"My friend," said the wit, "the materials of my composition are such, that I cannot help being so."—"No," replied the other, "thou art formed of good materials, but they want to be well beaten into decent form."

An importunate beggar went to a miser, and asked for a garment, saying, that his object was to have something to remember him by.— "My friend," said the miser, "as thy end is to remember me, I shall give thee nothing; for I am sure thou wilt remember a refusal much longer than a gift."

A poor man once came to a miser, and said, "I have a boon to ask."—"So have I," said the miser; "grant mine first, then I will comply with thine."—"Agreed," said the petitioner.—"Well, then," said the miser, "my request is that thou ask me nothing."

Mr. Burr, who is spoken of as likely to succeed to the Presidency of the United States of America, is so little known in this country, that a North Country Gentleman, on being asked the other day, who he was, replied, that he knew nothing at all about him, unless he was one of the *Burrs of Newcastle!*

Discoveries.—Among the inventions of the present period, are those of two Hair-dressers of this Metropolis, one of whom has obtained a Patent for his *Spring Perukes*, and the other for his Transparent, Elastic, Fur Friz *Tetes*. An improvement in placing the garter has been made by the Ladies, who now pin it close under the left ear; and an Irishman has just found out a new mode of furnishing the Nation with *news!* He has published his proposals for printing a Newspaper near the Land's End; says he is situated at the very fountain head of intelligence, and will circulate his news *backward*, for the benefit of the Cornish.

SPORTING INTELLIGENCE.

ON Thursday, March 12, Major Wilson's hounds unkennelled a bitch fox in a wood near West Wratting, Cambridgeshire, which went off in a fine style through the different woods and fields; when, after a hard run of one hour and thirty-five minutes, the fox was so fatigued that she laid down in a ploughed field, and, being taken up by a labourer, died in his arms.—Between eighty and ninety horsemen started from the cover, but very few were in at the death.

On Friday, March 27, another grand match of Pigeon Shooting was to take place at Foot's Cray, in Kent, the Hon. T. W. Coventry and Robinson the cricketer, against ——— Barton, Esq. and Fry, (Myers having declined the match) for two hundred guineas a side.

Wednesday, March 12, Mr. John Kett, a butcher, of Norwich, rode his own horse from St. Stephen's Gate to the twenty-five mile stone, on the Newmarket Road, and back again for a bet of one hundred guineas. He was to perform the journey between the hours of twelve at noon and four in the afternoon; he, however, completed it in three hours fifty-nine minutes and five seconds, with apparent ease to horse and rider.—From a miscalculation of the time with the rider, the horse had only ten minutes to go the last three miles.

There are at this time more horses in training for the ensuing Spring Meetings at Newmarket, than have been seen for some years; amongst which are some from Yorkshire, Cheshire, Gloucestershire, Oxfordshire,

Oxfordshire, and Surrey. Great sport is expected.

A few days since a valuable coach-horse was stolen out of the stables of Dr. Cline, in Lincoln's-Inn Fields; it is supposed by some Horse-dealers, who have of late committed similar robberies in London and its environs.—It frequently happens, that the very thief himself, confident in his own art, is the first to avail himself of the reward offered in these cases.

A catastrophe of a very singular nature lately happened to a respectable Farmer in the neighbourhood of Woodton:—As he was offering his daily sacrifice in a temple dedicated to *Cloacina*, which was built over a pond, he, being a very corpulent man, and the foundation of the structure being rotten, was suddenly immersed into an excrementitious element; and, had it not been for the timely assistance of his servants, he must inevitably have perished.

Noverre, the celebrated Ballad Master, who is now said to be reduced to a state of indigence in France, was once in the highest repute in his profession.—He possessed the mind of a poet, and was profoundly learned in every subject that related to his art. Voltaire thought highly of his talents, and paid many a flattering tribute to his genius and learning. The great fault of Noverre was his prodigality in bringing forward his Ballads, for the honour of which he thought no expence was excessive. Therefore, notwithstanding all their beauty and interest, they never indemnified a Manager for the expence of preparing them, and hence the Conductors of Theatres were afraid to employ Noverre, with all his acknowledged skill in his art.

The following are the particulars of the death of a Gentleman, near Mallow, in the County of Cork, which we insert as a warning to others.—As he was leaning over the pallisades adjoining his house, and his cattle were driving into the place where they were usually kept, a favourite bull happened to strike him in the soft part of his hand, near the thumb, with his horn, which gave him some little pain, but not perceiving any inconvenience from it, he went to a fair the next day, when he felt it painful, and applied to a physician, who saw that there was a mortification, and amputated the thumb; but the mortification communicated to his arm, and appeared likewise in his throat, in consequence of which death ensued in the course of six or seven days after the accident.

In a house in Paris, the first floor is dedicated to a *Gaming Club*; on the ground floor is a *Pawnbroker's shop*; and on the second floor, a *Maker of Pistols*. The coincidence is curious.

The Boston Gazette, of the 8th January, says, " A few days since passed through Holden, to a new settlement, from Portland, a gentleman and his wife, with *twenty* sons, born at *eight* births, viz. fifteen at the five first, four at the two next, and one at the last.

There are now at Boddlewiddan, in Flintshire, three oxen, bred by Sir John Williams, Bart. which are supposed to be the largest of the Welsh breed that have been seen for some years past. One is fifteen hands two inches high, and nine feet six inches round; another, fifteen hands two inches high, and nine feet seven inches round; the third, sixteen hands high, and ten feet round.

On the 27th of February a match was run in Dallingham-field, Cambridgeshire by a brace of greyhounds, for one hundred guineas, one the property of Mr. Margetts,

Sporting Intelligence.

sen. of Hemmingford, near Huntingdon; and the other belonging to the Rev. J. Stevenson, Fellow of Trinity College. The course was clearly decided in favour of the former. The winning dog was bred by Mr. T. Ind, of Chesterton, in that county.

Recipe to disperse Rats and Mice.—Throw a quantity of the parings of the hoofs of mules, cut off in shoeing, on burning coals, so as to excite a strong fumigation; and vermin will fly the place.—N. B. This recipe is given in the Moniteur and Citoyen Françoise: but it may be asked, Why the hoofs of mules are necessary to the scent? Would not parings from the hoofs of horses be equally efficacious? and will any scent long avail? We believe that nothing but an incessant hunt by dog, cat, ferret, poison, and gun, will keep them down, much less extirpate them, in the country.

A few days ago, a man in Glasgow undertook, for a bet of ten guineas, to run ten miles in one hour, upon the Greenock road; which he performed, with great ease, in thirty-two seconds less than the time.

The three young lion-whelps in the Menagerie at Paris continue to grow fast; they have already got their cutting teeth, and jump and play round their dam. No change has yet taken place in the marks of their skin. The mother has so much confidence in C. Felis, the keeper, as to allow him to take them from her, and to convey them out of her sight.

A recent Advertisement.—Lost, a dark Tortoishell Cat, spotted with black and yellow, with a white breast and black face. Whoever will bring the same to Berkeley-street, shall receive One Guinea reward, and no more.

The Lady of a Suffolk 'Squire has lately quitted her home, in consequence of a *sincere regard* for a certain Military Officer. The subject of this elopement is expected to afford a plentiful harvest to the Gentlemen of the Long Robe in Westminster Hall.

Celestial Intelligence, from a Morning Paper.—Dr. ———, New Compton-street, Soho, having given the greatest satisfaction in all astrological enquiry, may be consulted on Planetary Influence, *gratis*. He teaches Astrology, and the whole art of calculating Nativities, in the most compendious manner, at 2s. 6d. per lesson. Likewise instructions in an advantageous mode of speculating in the Lottery.—In answer to the Gentleman who wrote to me in the signature of G. L. desiring to know when a *General Feast* would be proclaimed; for the resolve of his problem, I refer him to those who proclaimed the *Fast*.

Extraordinary Race against Time.—A few days ago Mr. Alexander Bulloch, Flesher in Glasgow, undertook for a bet of thirty guineas, to ride fifteen miles in an hour, with his face to the horse's tail; which he performed with astonishing ease. He started from the first mile-stone leading to Kilmarnock, and rode sixteen miles in fifty-eight minutes. A considerable number of other bets were also gained by him. He rode without spurs, had a cloth in place of a saddle, the bridle round his waist, and a belt fixed to the crupper to hold by. Several other horses started; but only one rider, although he had three different horses, could keep sight of Mr. Bulloch, and he arrived even two minutes behind him. The road upon which this bet was decided is very rugged, and mostly up and down hill.

POETRY.

POETRY.

THE HIGH COURT OF DIANA.

For the Sporting Magazine.

THE AGRICULTURIST's LAMENTATION.

YE powers above, who feel for human
    woe,
Look down with pity on my griefs below;
Ten Thousand Pounds is all my store of
    gold,
Three Thousand Acres all the Land I hold!
Two Thousand Sheep along my pastures
    feed,
My Stock of Cattle very small indeed.
One Pipe of Port is all my winter's stock,
I've Twenty Dozen of the best Old Hock.
I'm forc'd to purchase Butter, Milk, and
    Cheese,
(For keeping Cows would much my wife
    displease)
How much it would conduce to make me
    warm,
Would my kind Landlord leave me one
    more Farm.
Oh! when I join the splendid troop, I
    ride—
(My massy sabre rattling by my side)
Heavens! how I tower above the vulgar
    throng,
As my bay Charger bears me swift along!
Aye, let the rabble murmur, let 'em grin,
While Silver shines without, and Gold
    within.
Oh! how I'd seek the Church, and *pray*
    and fast,
Could I sell Wheat at *Hundred Pounds* at
    last.
Vain hope! alas! Associations spread,
And aim their spleen on my devoted head.
Unhappy! I must sell my hoarded store,
Monopoly's sweet gains are mine no more;
The Miller buys his Corn beyond the sea,
And gives the hungry, Bread, in spite of
    me.

Oh! Britons! had I power to burn thy
    Mill,
Bid the Wind cease to blow, the Stream
    stand still,
Then would I hoard up mighty heaps of
    Grain,
And every Market should be mine again!
                  G. GRASPALL.

FASHIONABLE RIDING.

" The *fashion* of the new Chariots is *mean*
" and *contemptible*
" The shape is exactly like a *Tub*.—"
                  Vide Newspapers.

NOW ponder well, ye Censors grave,
    Who make this strange hubbub,
Because, forsooth, our *Belles* and *Beaux*
    Go riding in a *Tub*.

Let each forbear, nor clamorous be,
    Nor tasteless as a scrub,
As if they never yet had heard,
    Of good things in a *Tub*.

The Conqueror of the World, we know,
    Received a moral rub,
When wise Diogenes of old,
    Preach'd to him from a *Tub*.

" What can I do," the Conqueror cried,
" For thee, thou snarling scrub?"—
" Hide not from me the Sun," said he,
" Nor come too near my *Tub*.

" 'Tis all the favour thou canst grant,
" For thou art but a grub,
" And soon like me shalt find thy home
" Within a little *Tub* !"

Fair Virtue in a cottage bides,
  Beneath the flowery shrub;
Truth's residence they say's a well,
  Philosophy's a *Tub*.

And now our Dukes, and Lords, and
  Squires,
Quick eels, or dull as chub,
Before they're worms, themselves confine
  Within a little *Tub*.

And when the King, for service meet,
  A worthy knight doth dub,
That worthy knight, 'tis ten to one,
  Begins to roll his *Tub*.

Wine, brandy, rum, and sugars sweet,
  For which we gayly club;
And brilliant beauty, fair and kind,
  Came to us in a *Tub*.

Then he for whom a *Tub*'s no charms
  Is but a silly cub;
And sure his head's no better thing
  Than is an empty *Tub*.

When in her teens, Miss rakes about,
  Mama begins to snub;
But she with Bob to Gretna Green
  Goes rolling in a *Tub*.

When I see Stanhope* in a cask,
  Like a sweet syllabub,
I'd give the world to be within
  That pretty little *Tub*.

But let it not forgotten be,
  That froth's no syllabub;
And nought but *foam* is sometimes seen
  Within a painted *Tub*.

Full well we know a cask conceal'd
  The projects of a Club;
And meal and treason once were mix'd
  Within a silent *Tub*.

And now, in later times we find,
  An Anti-Tyrant Club
Reveal their private sentiments,
  From a loud thundering *Tub*.

Because the Corsican, they say,
  Is an usurping scrub,
They thought that he was proper stuff
  To pickle in a *Tub*.

The cunning Corsican, in wrath,
  Doth kill, transport, and drub
The men that chose to speak their minds
  From that *infernal Tub*.

* Lady Anna Maria.

May British casks *good things* contain,
  Or else sound dub-a-dub
To Loyalty—and Honour grace
  The *fashionable Tub!*

                TRIM.

A BACHELOR's PRAYER.
By ANTHONY PASQUIN, ESQ.

Non sum qualis eram bonæ sub regno Cynaræ.
    Hor. Ode I. Ad Venerem.

(*Concluded from page 260.*)

SHE calls on men for love's devotion,
  And all her atoms are in motion;
She's got a farm and land, I hear,
Besides three hundred pounds a year;
Some oxen too, in wild Kentucky;
Rin horns, in marriage, are unlucky:
She's plump and buxom, rich and glowing,
But then your widows are so knowing,
They'll have the payment, when they've
  said it,
Young traders, take a bill on credit!—
Kitty has wit, but what of that,
I'll have no witty wife, that's flat;
I have but little Heaven knows,
And e'en that little's made me foes!—
Delia, ah Delia, she's my choice,
When she appears the lads rejoice;
She does not pout, because she knows,
It lays the germ of unborn woes;
She views life, as an April day,
That's partly stormy, partly gay!
And when she gets a sweet ingredient,
Will make the most of joys expedient;
Delia's good humour'd, ev'n when warm,
Good humour rides out many a storm;
Should care assail in ruin's garb,
She'd search my soul and draw the barb;
To peace she dedicates her youth;
Her faith to God—her love to truth:
Infuses balm to the distrest,
And is divine, and pure and blest;
Now social charity is blind,
I'll leave this burning world behind,
To policy I give her imps,
That vile, perturbed haggard limps;
In shades to Delia, I'll incline,
Be comfort and the muses mine:
Bring me the Zone from Nepthe's side,
Sweet Hebe's vest—the Persian's pride;
The lucid gem—the sapphire plume;
A mantle from the Tyrian loom,
Yet this is frivolous and vain,
Delia's most charming when most plain.
Too good to hate, or to be hated,
'Tis piteous such a girl's not mated:

                Ditto.

Hirbes then Hymen, with your aid,
I'll lay my fortunes at her feet;
I'll have her (tell the gods) with glee,
That's entreated us if she'll have me!
New York, April 1, 1799.

THE CROOKED SIXPENCE.
An Imitation of the Splendid Shilling,
Written by J. Phillips.

HAPPY the School-girl, who exempt
   from cares
That cloud each future project, and elate
With present blessings, heedless of the
   morrow,
Boasts in the corner of her pocket hid
In ribban purse, or coat y'cleped balloon
Of red Morocco, and with clasp of steel,
A Crooked Sixpence. She with pleasure
   hears
At Evening's closing hour, the punctual
   call
Of Cake and Tart-women; if here indeed
Within these gloomy walls, where beauty
   buds
Like blushing roses in the desert air
A Tart-woman admittance finds; nor
   fear'd
As vent'rous Knight disguis'd in mean at-
   tire.
If such her cruel fate, how doubly blest
To watch the happy moment when un-
   barr'd
The massy gates grate harsh discordant
   sounds,
And steal unseen and silently along
To where the well-known shop inviting
   spreads
Its varied treasures; here with eager eye
She views the sweet assemblage, doubtful
   which
To call her own, or where to fix her
   choice,
Whether the Macaroon more charms can
   boast
Propp'd on it's silv'ry base, or Ratafia
Call'd Matrimony, as uniting in itself
The bitter with the sweet; or Custard rich
With luscious cream, and India's choicest
   spice
Thickly o'erspread; whose high indented
   walls
Look like a mural crown; on all the
   dwells
With rapture, and enjoys the quick repast.
Whilst such her stol'n delight, how dif-
   ferent far
My hapless fate, compell'd by adverse
   times,

To try my aching grinders 'gainst the
   strength
Of dry and tasteless Cod, or else to dine
On hard-boil'd dumplings of coarse-sifted
   meal.
Nor this my sole complaint, for whilst I
   sit
Beneath my humble roof, and court the
   Muse,
(The Muse who smiles with pity on the
   puns,
And scorns the pride of riches) or indite
Epistles breathing forth a Brother's love;
As thus intent I write, quick rushes in
With grizely beard, and filthy unkempt
   hair,
A lounger, worst of thieves, the thief of
   time,
And this the worst of loungers; down
   he drops
On the first vacant seat, and thence begins
His ceaseless senseless prattle. How of
   late
Wheat had advanc'd, what crops of peas
   he grew,
How much his Bullocks cost, and how be
   hoped
A London market amply would repay.
Next he enlarges on his wondrous feats
Perform'd in early youth; what leaps he
   took
Before th' astonish'd field, and how he
   left
The proudest Hunters lagging far behind.
Stunn'd by his thund'ring voice I answer
   nought—
But umph! and ah! and with averted
   eyes
Now ken the fire, and now direct my looks
To the unfinish'd paper. Not a hint
Alas he takes, but scrapes his dirty shoes
Upon the polish'd fender, nor regards
A Housewife's cleanly care; he cocks
   his hat
In careless stile, and launches out again
On prodigies perform'd; what miles be
   rode
(More to the credit of the beast than him)
Without a pause. Exhausted I mean-
   while
Cease to attend, and give my thoughts full
   play.
At length, each subject to the very dregs
Drawn out, wearied, or anxious to retail
   again
His vast atchievements at another's door,
He spits, and clears his throat, and then re-
   tires.

So pass my morning hours—our happier
   seems
The howling mongrel to whose tortur'd tail

Some wicked wit a cannister has hung,
Or puff'd-up bladder fill'd with rattling
  peas,
When first a friendly post, or pointed nail,
Or deeply-piercing thorn affords relief,
And frees him from th' incumbrance.
  Quickly round
He turns his head with sharp erected ears
And looks of gratitude; but nought de-
  scries,
No cause of joy or torment; yet he barks
A note of extasy, rolls o'er and o'er,
And wonders greatly at this sudden
  change.
Just so reliev'd, I quit my elbow chair
With sudden spring, and pace my humble
  floor
With many a giant stride; I seem to
  breathe
A purer air, and feel myself again
A free-born man, and Monarch of a shed.

But when calm Evening o'er the wearied
  world
Unfurls her dusky veil, bids labour cease
And whispers comfort to the poor man's
  heart,
Then, when 'midst higher orders lustres
  glare,
When Play-houses and Operas abound
With all the charms that art and nature
  boast
I strive to husband well my frugal fire
With gather'd chips, and sifted cinders
  heap'd.
Around my little family are plac'd
With looks of joy, nor murmur when I
  cut
With sparing hand from off the coarse
  brown loaf
(Ah! now how dearly priz'd) th' allotted
  share.

Retir'd to rest, (and slumbers soon o'er-
  take
The tranquil mind) I then begin to feel
A new existence. Fancy, wont to play
The flatt'rer's part, then quickly conjures
  up
A diff'rent scene of things. Fresh honours
  rise.
Instead of dead small beer, I deeply drink,
Forgive, O Pye, the thought! thy gen'-
  rous sack.
I feel myself a Poet, and aspire
E'en at thy envied crown; but when I
  thus
In agitation seiz'd the proffer'd boon,
Away the phantom flies, the thread is
  snapt,
I grasp at air, and finds the whole a dream.
So (as those tales record which, when a
  boy

I read with ceaseless rapture and delight)
Some simple maiden in her frothing pail
Sees all her future greatness, skips with
  ease
O'er intervening years, to when the hopes
Th' accumulated gain must surely bring
A lady's title, and a lady air;
Exulting at the thought, she apes too soon
Each proud demeanour, and with scornful
  foot
O'erthrows the source whence glided pros-
  pects rise.
Aghast she views the milky deluge spread
It's foaming tide around; and, dire mis-
  chance,
Sees honours, titles, fortune, vanish all
In smoke, and irretrievable despair.

PADDY's PURCHASE.

IT chanced, on a time, that an Irish
  Dear Honey,
Who had lately received a "*small trifle*"
  of money,
Took it into his head to dispose of his
  riches,—
In what he crush wanted—a good pair of
  breeches;
In these *modish* days they've acquired a
  new name;
But *breeches*—or *small clothes*—why, sure,
  they're the same.

His purse stuff'd with chink, (and his
  heart full of glee)
Pat so a found a shop to his mind, do you
  see.
On a *prime piece* of stuff, now his eyes
  quickly casting,
And asking the name, he was told "*everlasting,*"
"If in he *everlasting*, (quoth Pat with a
  stare)
"Then—Erin go-brach!—"faith, I'll
  purchase *one pair!*"

THE ESSEX MAN's APOLOGY FOR
BEING A CALF.

IN every quarter of this world so wide,
  John Bull means Englishman—this
  same world's pride;
Proud may an Essex Calf then surely be;
A true descendant of John Bull is he,

INDEX to Vol. XVII.

A.

ACTION, a civil, 224
Advertisement, curious, 55
Advice, Swiftean, to the Collegians of Dublin, 121
Agricultural Societies, Trait Hits upon the, 53
Agriculturist's Lamentation, Lines on the, 109
Alfred and Jupiter, Pedigree and Performances of, 11
Amusements, Russian, 162
Anecdote, 97, 170, 301
Arabs, Roscica's Account of the, 168
Arundel Castle, described, 229
Assault, Slight-of-hand, 209
Attitudes, Boxing, 190

B.

Badger-hunting, some Account of, 269
Bailiffs, the, baffled, 167
Batchelor's Prayer, 259, 310
Battery, Matrimonial, 224
Bentley, Nathaniel, an eccentric Character, Particulars relating to, 267
Billiard playing, 50
Blow-up, a proper, 139
Boxing, 97
——— Matches, &c. described, 240
Boxing, a Trial in the Court of King's Bench in consequence of, 278

C.

Campanalogy, supernatural, 182
Carnival at Paris, Account of the, 298
Cause, Crim. Con. 122, 130, 209
Ceremony, Turkish, of laying a first Stone, 180
Character, Extraordinary, 54, 171
Characters, Description of, 302
Clerkenwell Sessions, Trials at, 162
Cocks, Main of, Statement of the Battles fought by a, 301

Cock-crower, the King's, Account of, 283
Cookson's Stud, Sale of Mr. 152
Corn, pertinent Pleasantries on the Price of, 59
Corn Buyer, humorous Account of the Death and Execution of a, 153
Cow, on the Utility of the, 185
Cricket, 26, 27, 28, 29
Cruelty and Avarice, outwitted, 24
Custom, Heraldic, 81
Cynographia Britannica, 243

D.

Dean Swift, Instructions in the Manner of, 23
Dream, humorous Account of a, 235
Desolated Island, Account of the new Pantomime of the, 261
Devonshire Epistle, 72
Dexterity, French, 180
Diamond and Water, 4
———, his safe arrival in Ireland 207
Diamond cut Diamond, an Anecdote, 287
Dog, an eccentric, 257
Dog-stealers, 153
Dogs, &c. in Britanny, Account of supernatural, 288
Dragon, Description of a counterfeit, 289
Duel, a legal, 139

E.

Eccentricities, Chronicle of, 17
Enterprise, a desperate, 192

F.

Farinelli, Anecdote of, 801
Feast of Wit, 38, 82, 140, 198, 255, 304
Female Fashion, Advantages of the present, 290
Fowls, surprizing Attraction of, 263

Fu

INDEX.

Fox-hunting, 139
Fox and Hare Hunting, Account of, 285
French Quack, Trick of a, 164

G.

Game Laws at the Cape of Good Hope, Account of, 286
Gamester, Journal of a, 7
Gaming, on the Abuse of, 107
——— Debts, 249
German Universities, Blackguardism of the, 71
Gleanings, 244
Guy Vaux, 67

H.

Hair-cropping in England, real Origin of, 80
Harlequin in Italy: or, A Flight over the Alps, 111
Hay-stack, the Maid of the, 190
Hog and Man Race, an Etching, 268
Horse-stealing, 54
———, Cause of a, 239
Horse without Hair, curious Description of a, 301
Horses, a philosophical and practical Treatise on, 19, 77, 116
———, on Trotting, 68
———, Portraits of, 190
Household Servants, curious Regulations for, 15
Human Frame, extraordinary Instance of the Flexibility of the, 247
Hunks, another, 266
Hunt, Mr. Tuffnell's, Account of, 277

I.

Impostor, a dashing, 189
Incident, extraordinary, 174
Inscription, taken literally from a Shew-board, 100
Isle of Wight, Account of Pennant's Journey from London to the, 272

J.

Jerusalem Whalley, Account of, 108
Journal, Tim Tape's, 224

K.

King, a strange, Account of, 266

L.

Lavater, 154
Lionesses at Paris, several Particulars relative to the, 288
Longevity, American, 81

M.

Mahrattas, singular Mode of recovering Debts by the, 266
Manners, Russian, 161, 182
Margate, Aquatic Excursion to, 16
Mason, Sir Edmund, Biography of, 136
Masonic Mummery, 30
Masquerade, Ranelagh, 111
———, Miss Champney's, 177
Mirth in a Mask, 177
Miscellanies, 233
Modern Characters, Journal of, 67
Moralities, Sportive, 25

O.

Occurrence, Melancholy, 212
Organ, the Patent, 223
Oxfordshire Sporting, 243

P.

Paddy's Purchase, Lines on, 312
Park, St. James's, an Assault in, 170
Paul, Anecdotes of the Emperor, 135
Pedestrianism, a Wager of 2000 gs. decided by, 301
Perfection and Imperfection, on, 225
Philosopher, the Equestrian, 175
Pigeon-shooting, Account of, 291
Pickpocket, aillish, 186
Poaching, a Case of, 5
Poetry, 41, 89, 145, 201, 237, 309
Post-Master, Epitaph on a German, 25
Pretty French Woman, Cash Account of a, 68
Punishments, on Medical and Surgical, 101

Q.

Quere, a strange, Observations on, 50

Races,

INDEX.

R.

Racers, Deaths of, 49
Rape, an Attempt to commit a, 179
Riding, Lines on Fashionable, 309
Rokeby, Memoirs of Lord, 213
Rains, magnificent in Egypt, 115
Russia, peculiar Winter Diversions in, 287

S.

Scarcity, different Opinions on the, 165
Scarcity and Plenty, 184
Shooting at the Bird, curious Ceremony of, 236
Shopkeepers, Apprentices, &c. Instructions for, 57
Shuttlecock at Cochin China, singular Method of playing at, 289
Simplicity, Rustic, 242
Singular Inscription, 153
Sixpence, crooked, Lines on a, 311
Skaiters, Norwegian Corps of, 105
Spirituous Liquors, Exhortations against the Use of, 187
Sporting, in Surrey and Sussex, 263
Sporting Advertisement, curious Description of a, 294
Sporting Intelligence, 33, 47, 85, 95, 143, 191, 208, 255, 308
Sporting Intelligence extra, 9, 176
Sporting Observations, some Account of, on National Habits, 276
Sportsman, the Indian, by Mr. Howitt, 217
Sportsman, Account of the Death of a, 297
Sportsmen, Account of the Characters of two, 295
Sportsmen, Natural History for, 284
Sportsmen, Cautions and Instructions to young, 157
State Bed, the Marquis of Exeter's, 177
Stonehenge, French, Account of, 272
Stud, Sale of a State, 141
Swallows, the Submersion of, 61
Sweating Sickness, humorous Account of the late, 14
Swindler, a Female, 189
Swindling Females, Account of, 290

T.

Taylors Letter, 178
Theatricals, 6, 62, 98, 137, 210, 226, 247
——, French, 63, 163
——, in Edinburgh, 109
Traveller, Adventures of a, 193

V.

Various Pedigrees, Nimrod on, 48
Veterinary Science, Thoughts on the, 9, 73

W.

Wales, strange Customs in, 216
Wardrobe, Tippoo Saib's, 76
Warter, Pedigree and Performances of, 120
Wedding, a Bidding to, 4
Welsh, Manners and Customs of the, 74, 219
Welijie, Death of Mr. 8
Wills, curious Abstracts from Original, 114
Wolves, ferocious, in France, 16
Woman, a dangerous, 82

Y.

Yankee Wit, a Specimen of, 97

DIRECTIONS

DIRECTIONS TO THE BOOKBINDER.

1. Brood Mares, Frontispiece to the Volume, to face the Title.
2. Johnny — — — — 3
3. The Fox and his Prey — — — 8
4. Dungannon beating Rockingham — — 47
5. Battle between Rooks and Herons — — 52
6. Farrier's Shop — — — — 95
7. Wild Cat and Spaniels — — — 100
8. Brian O'Lin — — — — 151
9. The Hare in its Form — — — 156
10. Hunting the Wild Ox — — — 207
11. Cherubim Shooting — — — 212
12. Hog and Man Race — — — 263

RACING CALENDAR at the end.

RACING CALENDAR.

SHREWSBURY.

ON Tuesday, September the 16th, a Maiden Plate of 50l. for all ages; four yr olds, 7st. 7lb. —4-mile heats.

Ld Stamford's b. c. Alfred, by John Bull, 4 yrs old   1 1
Sir W. W. Wynn's gr. c. Doctor O'Liffey, 4 yrs old   -   2 dr

Sweepstakes of 10g. each, for three and four yr olds. (4 Subscribers).

Mr. Heming's br. c. Kill Devil, 3 yrs old, walked over.

On Wednesday the 17th, 50l. given by Sir W. Pulteney, Bart. and the Hon. W. Hill, free for any horse, &c.—4-mile heats.

Mr. Lockley's b. b. Sloven, by Alexander, 6 yrs old, 8st. 10lb.   2 1 1
Mr. Saunders's br. f. by Cœur de Lion, 3 yrs old, 5st. 10lb.   1 2 3

Mr. Heming's b. h. Ploro, 5 yrs old, 8st. 6lb.   4 3 2
Sir W. W. Wynn's gr. c. Doctor O'Liffey, 4 yrs old, 7st. 3lb.   5 4 4
Sir T. Mostyn's ch. c. Chicken, 3 yrs old, 5st. 10lb.   -   3 dr

On Thursday the 18th, 50l. for three and four yr olds;—heats, twice round.

Mr. Heming's Kill Devil, by Rockingham, 3 yrs old, 8st.   1 1
Sir T. Mostyn's ch. c. Heart's Ease, 4 yrs old, 8st. 10lb.   2 2

STOCKTON.

ON Wednesday, September the 17th, Sweepstakes of 10gs each, for three yr old colts, 8st. and fillies, 7st. 12lb.—two-mile heats. (9 Subscribers.)

Sir H. Williamson's b. f. by

Sir Peter, out of Mother
  Red Cap - 1 1
Mr. Hutchinson's b. f. Mary 2 2
Sir T. Gascoigne's b. c. by
  Delpini, dam by Garrick 3 3
Mr. Baker's br. c. Sowerby,
  (lame) . 4 4

A Maiden Plate of 50l. for three yr olds, 6st. 10lb. four yr olds, 7st. 11lb. five yr olds, 8st. 6lb. six yr olds and aged, 8st. 12lb.—3-mile heats.

Mr. Cornforth's ch. c. by
  Pipator, dam by Le Sang,
  3 yrs old - 1 1
Sir R. Winn's br. c. Bilham,
  by Clown, 3 yrs old 2 2
Mr. Hopper's ch. c. Hazard,
  by Windlestone, 3 yrs old 3 dr

On Thursday the 18th, 50l. for three yr olds, 7st. 4lb. and four yr olds, 8st. 4lb. that never won above that value at one time. A winner of one fifty, 3lb. extra, of two or more, 5lb.—3-mile heats.

Mr. Riddell's ch. c. by
  Walnut, 3 yrs old 1 3 1
Mr. G. Bainlet's b. c.
  Coniac, four yrs old 4 1 3
Mr. Fletcher's b. c.
  Jemmy, 4 yrs old 2 4 2
Mr. L. Seymour's b. f.
  Hyale, 3 yrs old 3 2 4

On Friday the 19th, 50l. free for any horse, &c. except the winner of a Great Subscription at York, or the Cup at Richmond.

No race, for want of horses.

BURFORD.

ON Friday the 19th of September, His Majesty's Plate of 100g.s, for five yr olds, carrying 9st.—3-mile heats.

Sir F. Poole's b. h. Worthy,
  by PotBo's 1 1
H. R. H. the P. of Wales's
  br. h. Knowsley 2 2
  2 to 1 on Knowsley.

The Cup, a Subscription of 10gs each, for three yr old colts, 8st. 5lb. and fillies, 8st.—New Course. (6 Subscribers.)

Mr. Hallett's bl. f. Wowski, by
  Mentor, out of Waxy's dam 1
Mr. Coventry's br. c. by King
  Fergus 2
Mr. Snell's b. c. Gallant Sidney,
  by Fortunio - 3

NORTHAMPTON.

ON Tuesday, September the 23d, 50l. for three yr olds; —heats, about a mile and half each.

Mr. Bettison's br. c. by
  Rockingham, 8st. 5lb. 3 1 1
Mr. Heming's br. c. Kill
  Devil, 8st. 9lb. 0 4 2
Mr. Hallett's bl. f.
  Wowski, 8st. 3lb. 4 2 dr
Mr. Bott's b. f. Miss
  Totteridge, 8st. 7lb. 0 3 dr

On Wednesday the 24th, the Town Plate of 50l. free for all horses;—4-mile heats.

Mr. Sitwell's br. g.
  Cockboat, by Overton, 4 yrs old, 7st. 11lb. 4 1 1
Marquis of Donegall's
  br. h. Trifle, 5 yrs
  old, 8st. 4lb. 1 2 3
Mr. Bettison's ch. c. by
  Erasmus, 4 yrs old,
  7st. 11lb. 2 3 2
Major Snell's b. h. Eyford, 6 yrs old, 8st.
  12lb. - 3 dis

AYR.

ON Tuesday, September the 23d, 50l. for all ages; three yr olds, 3st. 10lb. four yr olds, 7st. 7lb. five yr olds, 8st. 3lb. six yr olds, 8st. 10lb. and aged, 9st. The winner of one 50l. this year, carrying

RACING CALENDAR.

carrying 3lb. of two, or a King's
Plate, 6lb. extra.—4-mile heats.

Mr. Graham's b. h. Duncan, by Stride, 5 yrs old	2	1	1
Mr. Fletcher's ch. h. Master Robert, aged	1	2	2
Mr. Baird's c. yrs old	3	3	dr

Sweepstakes of 20gs each, for
three yr olds, 8st. 1lb. and four
yr olds, 8st. 1lb.—2-mile heats.
(9 Subscribers.)

Mr. Cunningham Graham's b. c. Buonaparte (late Bryan O'Lynn) by Aston, four yrs old	1	1
Mr. Fletcher's ch. c. Logie O'Buchan, 4 yrs old	2	2
Mr. Kincaid's Master Bagot, yrs old	3	3
Mr. Boswell's c. yrs old	5	4
Mr. Oswald's f. yrs old	4	dr

On Wednesday the 24th, 50l.
on the same terms as the Tuesday's Plate.

Mr. Fletcher's Logie O'Buchan,
walked over.

On Thursday the 25th, the Ladies Plate of 50l. for three yr olds,
carrying a feather; four yr olds,
7st. 2lb. five yr olds, 8st. six yr
olds, 8st. 7lb. and aged, 8st. 10lb.
—extra weights as on Tuesday.
—4-mile heats.

Mr. Graham's Buonaparte, 4 yrs old	1	1
Mr. Fletcher's Master Robert, aged	2	2
Mr. Boswell's br. h. Pensioner, 5 yrs old	3	3

On Friday the 26th, the Handicap Plate, 10gs entrance, making
in the whole 80gs.—2-mile heats.

Mr. Kincaid's Master Bagot, 8st. 2lb.	3	1	1
Mr. Fletcher's Rosalind, 8st. 10lb.	1	2	3
Mr. Graham's Wirley, 8st. 4lb.	2	3	2
Mr. Baird's colt, 8st. 2lb.	4	4	dr
Major Cathcart's Star filly, 7st. 7lb.	5	dr

Besides the above, there were
five Matches, of which we expect
to be able to give the particulars
in our succeeding number.

DONCASTER.

ON Tuesday, September 23d,
a Sweepstakes of 200gs
each, h. ft.—four miles. (3 Subscribers.)

Ld Fitzwilliam's ch. c. Idler, by Overton, out of a Phœnomenon Mare, 8st. 2lb.	1
Mr. Wentworth's Roxana, 8st.	2

The St. Leger Stakes of 25gs
each, for three yr old colts, 8st.
2lb. and fillies, 8st.—two miles.
(17 Subscribers.)

Mr. Wilson's b. c. Champion, by Pot8o's, out of Huncamunca	1
Sir H. T. Vane's br. c. Rolla, by Overton	2
Sir H. T. Vane's b. c. by Walnut, out of Skelton's dam	3
Ld Darlington's br. c. Agonistes	4
D. of Hamilton's b. f. by Walnut, out of Tickle Toby's dam	5
Mr. J. Lonsdale's b. c. by Sir Peter, out of Queen Mab	6
Mr. G. Crompton's c. Lignum Vitæ	7
Mr. Heming's ch. c. Sir Sidney	8
Sir T. Gascoigne's gr. c. by Delpini, dam by Garrick	9
Mr. T. Robinson's b. f. Belle-fille	10

2 to 1 agst Champion, 2 to 1
agst Agonistes, 5 to 1 agst
Sir H. Vane's Walnut colt,
and 6 to 1 agst Rolla.

The Corporation Plate of 50l.
for horses, &c. of all ages; three
yr olds, 5st. 2lb. four yr olds, 7st.
5lb. five yr olds, 8st. 3lb. six yr
olds,

olds, 8st. 11lb. and aged, 9st. Maiden horses, &c. allowed 3lb. The winner of any of the Subscription Plates at York this year, to have carried 4lb. extra.—4-mile heats.

D. of Hamilton's b. m. by Walnut, five yrs old   1 1
Mr. Johnson's b. c. Sir Solomon, 4 yrs old   2 2
Mr. Hewett's ch. h. Wouder, 6 yrs old   3 dr

Mr. Hewett's Wonder, by Phœnomenon, 8st. beat Mr. Wentworth's Tartar, 8st. 3lb.—four miles, 100gs, h. ft.

Mr. P. G. Burk's gr. h. Win if be Can, by Snake, dam by Blank, beat Mr. T. Raywood's b. m. by Ruler, 9st. each, one mile, 100gs, h. ft.

On Wednesday the 24th, the Gold Cup, value 100gs, free for any horse, &c. Three yr olds to carry 6st. four yr olds, 7st. 7lb. five yr olds, 8st. 3lb. six yr olds, 8st. 12lb: and aged, 9st. The winner of any Subscription Plate at York this year, to have carried 4lb. extra. of any two, 7lb.—four miles.

Mr. Garforth's b. h. Dion, by Spadille, 5 yrs old   1
Ld Darlington's b. c. Haphazard, 3 yrs old   2
Ld Fitzwilliam's br. f. Fanny, 4 yrs old   3
Sir H. T. Vane's b. c. by Walnut, 3 yrs old   4

Even betting, and 5 to 4 on the field agst the Walnut colt.

The second year of the renewed Doncaster Stakes of 10gs each, with 20gs added by the Corporation of Doncaster, for any horse, &c. bona fide the property of a Subscriber, or his declared confederate; three yr olds, 6st. four yr olds, 7st. 7lb. five yr olds, 8st. 3lb. six yr olds and aged, 8st. 10lb. —four miles. (14 Subscriber).

Sir H. T. Vane's br. c. Cockfighter, by Overton, 4 yrs old   1
Mr. Garforth's ch. c. Hyacinthus, by Coriander, 3 yrs old   2

10 to 1 on Cockfighter.

Sweepstakes of 20gs each, for two yr olds,—the last mile and three quarters; 8st. each.

Ld Darlington's ch. c. Muly Moloch, by John Bull, out of Misseltoe   1
Mr. G. Crompton's b. c. Dotterel   2
Sir T. Gascoigne's b. c. Doodle, by Restless, out of Tippet   3

Muly Moloch the favourite

On Thursday, the 25th, One Hundred Pounds for three and four yr olds; three yr olds, 7st. 5lb. four yr olds, 8st. 7lb. Maiden cults allowed 2lb. Maiden fillies, 3lb. The winner of any Subscription or Sweepstakes, 4lb. extra—two-mile heats.

Mr. Wentworth's b. c. Chance, by Lurcher, 3 yrs old   1 1
Mr. Johnson's b. c. Sir Solomon, 4 yrs old   5 2
Ld Darlington's b. c. Haphazard, 3 yrs old   2 3
D. of Hamilton's b. c. by Walnut, 4 yrs old   7 4
Mr. Garforth's ch. c. Hyacinthus, 3 yrs old   4 5
Ld Fitzwilliam's ch. c. Idler 4 yrs. old   6 6
Mr. Hewett's b. c. Commodore, by Admiral, 3 yrs old   3 dr

10 to 1 agst Chance.

Sweepstakes of 20gs each, with 20gs added by the Corporation of Doncaster, for three yr old fillies, carrying 8st.—two miles. (9 Subscribers)

Mr. G. Crompton's b. f. Anniseed, by Coriander, dam by Highflyer   1

Ld Fitzwilliam's

RACING CALENDAR.

Ld Fitzwilliam's b. f. Lap-wing,
 by Overton - 2
D. of Hamilton's b. f. by Walnut, out of Tickle Toby's
 dam - 3
Mr. Alderson's b. f. Vanguard,
 by Walnut, dam by Young
 Marske - 4

Even betting between Anniseed
and the field.

Sweepstakes of 10gs. each, for
hunters, carrying 12st. each;—
four miles. (5 Subscribers.)

Mr. C. Cholmondeley's b. h.
 Collector, by Spadille, out
 of Rosalind, 5 yrs old 1
Mr. J. S. Foljambe's b. g. Proteus - 2

4 to 1 on Collector.

MORPETH.

ON Tuesday, the 23d of September, 50l. given by the
Earl of Carlisle, for three yr old
colts, 8st. and fillies, 7st. 11lb. A
winner of Plate or Stakes since
the first of March, carrying 3lb. of
two or more, 5lb. extra.—2-mile
heats.

Mr. Riddell's ch. c. by
 Walnut, 3 yrs 1 1
Capt. Lidderdale's br. c. John
 O'Groat - 4 2
Sir H. Williamson's b. f. by
 Sir Peter, 3 yrs old 2 3
Mr. Hopper's ch. c. Hazard 3 4

On Wednesday, the 24th, 50l.
for four yr olds, 7st. 3lb. five yr
olds, 8st. six. yr olds, 8st. 5lb.
and aged 8st. 9lb. A winner of
Plate or Stakes, since the first of
March, carrying 3lb. of two or
more 5lb. extra. Mares allowed
3lb. geldings 2lb—4 mile heats.

Mr. Wilson's ch. h. Apple-
 garth, by Stride, 5 yrs old 1 1
Mr. W. Fletcher's Camper-
 down, 5 yrs old 2 2
Sir H. Williamson's ch. h.
 Stripling, 5 yrs old 3 3

Mr. Elliott's b. c. 4 yrs old
 (fell) - dis
On Thursday, the 25th, the
Members' Plate of 50l. for all
ages; three yr olds to carry 6st.
4lb. four yr olds, 7st. 9lb. five ye
olds, 8st. 5lb. six yr olds and aged,
8st. 9lb. A winner of Plate or
Stakes, since the first of March,
carrying 3lb. of two or more, 5lb.
extra.—Mares allowed 3lb. geldings, 2lb.—3-mile heats.

Mr. W. Fletcher's Cam-
 perdown, by Delpini,
 5 yrs old 3 1 1
Mr. Wilson's Apple-
 garth, 5 yrs old 1 2 2
Mr. Ilderton's ch. g.
 Bashful (late Billy)
 aged - 2 3 ds
Mr. Hopper's ch. m. Lit-
 tle Betsy, by Comer,
 out of Magpie's dam,
 4 yrs old, fell and
 broke her neck in run-
 ning.

The Hunters' Sweepstakes of
10gs each, 12st.—3-mile heats. (6
Subscribers.)

Mr. W. Hutchinson's b. h.
 Sling, by Highflyer 1 1
Mr. Hunter's br. h. Hutton 3 2
Mr. Davison's ch. h. High-
 flyer - 2 3

NEWMARKET.

ON Monday, the 29th of September, the Sweepstakes of
200gs each, h. ft. for three yr olds,
carrying 8st. 3lb. Across the Flat.

Ld Grosvenor's b. c. by John
 Bull, out of Nimble 1
Sir F. Standish's b. c. brother
 to Spread Eagle 2
Ld Grosvenor's b. c. by John
 Bull, out of Kiss my Lady pd ft.
Mr. Cussans's b. c. by Pegasus,
 out of Sweetheart pd ft.
Sir C. Bunbury's gr. c. by
 Whiskey, out of Grey Do-
 rimant - pd ft.

5 to

5 to 2 and 3 to 1 on Ld Grosvenor's colt.

Mr. R. Heathcote's ch. f. Georgiana, by John Bull, 3 yrs old, 8st. beat Mr. Panton's gr. c. Grey Falcon, 4 yrs old, 7st. 7lb. Ab. M. 50gs.

5 to 4 on Grey Falcon.

Mr. Adams's b. f. Cuckoo, by Woodpecker, 7st. recd. 20gs from Mr. Heathcote's b. f. Lady Jane, 8st. 2lb. Two yr old Course, 100gs. h. ft.

Mr. Cookson's br. h. Diamond, by Highflyer, 7st. 13lb. recd. ft. from Mr. Heathcote's b. Warter, 8st. 6lb. B. C. 500gs. h. ft.

Mr. Howard's br. f. by Whiskey, out of Sybil, 7st. 10lb. recd. 70gs. from Mr. Perrin's br. f. by Trumpator, out of Cinderella, 8st. Two yr old Course, 100gs.

Mr. Howorth's ch. c. Pet, by Buzzard, 8st. agst Mr. Heathcote's ch. c. Popinjay, 7st. 5lb. Ab. M. 100gs.—Off by consent.

On Tuesday, the 30th, Ld Clermont's b. c. by Meteor, 4 yrs old, 8st. 2lb. beat Mr. Wilson's b. c. Surprize, 3 yrs old, 8st. R. M. 20gs.

6 to 4 on Surprise.

Mr. Heathcote's gr. h. Symmetry, by Delpini, 5 yrs old, 8st. 1lb. beat Sir C Bunbury's bl. c. Sorcerer, 4 yrs old, 8st. Across the Flat, 500gs, h. ft.

5 and 6 to 4 on Symmetry.

Fifty Guineas, free for any horse, &c. four yr olds, 7st. 4lb. five yr olds, 8st. 5lb. six yr olds, 8st. 11lb. and aged 9st. B. C.

Mr. Adams's b. c. Humbug, by Precipitate, 4 yrs old   1
Mr. Cookson's br. h. Sir Harry, 5 yrs old   -   2
Sir C. Bunbury's bl. c. Sorcerer, 4 yrs old   -   3
Mr. Lake's b. h. by Spadille, dam by Mungo, 5 yrs old   4

D. of Grafton's b. f. Hornby Lass, 4 yrs old   5
Ld Clermont's b. h. Cadet, 5 yrs old   -   6

13 to 8 agst Sir Harry, 5 to 2 agst. Sorcerer, 5 to 1 agst Hornby Lass, and 50 to 6 agst Humbug.

On Wednesday, the 1st of October, Mr. R. Heathcote's ch. f. Georgiana, by John Bull, 8st. 7lb. beat Mr. Adams's ch. f. Ephemera, by Woodpecker, 7st. 10lb. both three yrs old, Ab. M. 50gs.

2 to 1 on Georgiana.

The Town Plate of 50l. for three yr old colts, 8st. 7lb. and fillies, 8st. 3lb. D. I.

N. B. The late Mr. Peiram, by his will, directed his Executors to pay 30gs to the winner of this Plate.

Mr. Heming's br. c. Kill Devil, by Rockingham   1
D. of Grafton's b. c. First Fruits   -   2
Mr. Wilson's b. c. Surprize   3
Mr. Dawson's b. f. Canary   4
Mr. Cookson's ch. c. Scrub, by PotSo's   -   5

6 to 5 on First Fruits, 5 to 1 agst Surprize, 5 to 1 agst Scrub, and 6 and 7 to 1 agst Kill Devil.

On Thursday, the 2d of October, Mr. Ladbroke's bl. c. Whiskerandos, by Whiskey, 7st. 11lb. beat Ld Clermont's f. Noisette, 7st. 5lb. Two yr old Course, 25gs.

3 to 1 on Whiskerandos.

Sir C. Bunbury's b. f. Thaïs by Trumpator, 7st. 11lb. beat Mr. Windham's br. c. by Fidget, 8st. Two yr old Course, 100gs, b. ft.

7 to 4 on Thaïs.

The King's Plate of 100gs, for four yr olds, carrying 10st. 4lb. five yr olds, 11st. 6lb. six yr olds, 12st. and aged, 12st. 2lb. R C.

Sir F. Poole's b. b. Worthy, by PotSo's, 5 yrs old   1

Sir

Sir C. Bunbury's bl. c. Sorcerer, 4 yrs old 2
Mr. Adams's b. c. Humbug, 4 yrs old - 3
Mr. Golding's b. h. Boaster, 5 yrs old - 4

2 to 1 on Worthy, 9 to 2 agst Humbug, 7 to 1 agst Sorcerer, and 10 to 1 agst Boaster.

A Handicap Plate of 50l. D. I.

Mr. Howorth's gr. h. Trust, by Pilot, 6 yrs old, 8st. 7lb. 1
Mr. Lake's b. h. Quatorze, by Spadille, 5 yrs old, 8st. 6lb. 2
D. of Grafton's b. f. Hornby Lass, 4 yrs old, 7st. 10lb. 3
Sir C. Bunbury's b. c. Gig, 3 yrs old, 6st. 8lb 4
Ld Clermont's b. h. Cadet, 5 yrs old, 8st. 5l. 5

6 to 4 agst Truss, and 3 to 1 agst Quatorze.

Mr. R. Heathcote's ch. m. Hippona, by King Fergus, 6 yrs old, 8st. 9lb. beat Mr. Windam's ch. c. by Woodpecker, out of Platina, 3 yrs old, 6st. 8lb. R. M. 300gs, h. ft.

7 to 4 and 2 to 1 on Hippona.

BOROUGHBRIDGE.

ON Wednesday, October the 1st, a Sweepstakes, of 10gs each, for three yr old colts, 8st. 2lb. and fillies, 8st.—two miles.— (5 Subscribers,)

Mr. G. Crompton's b. f. Annixed, by Coriander 1
Sir H. T. Vane's br. c. by Coriander, dam by Magnet 2

The Members' Plate of 50l. for all ages; three yr olds, 6st. 3lb. four yr olds, 7st. 7lb. five yr olds, 8st. 3lb. six yr olds, 8st. 10lb. and aged, 8st. 12lb. A winner of one 50l. Plate this season, carrying 3lb. extra, of two, 5lb.—3-mile heats,

Mr. Hutton's b. c. Heart of Oak, by Windlestone, 4 yrs old 1 1
Mr. Coulson's gr. g. Pushforward, 5 yrs old 3 2
Sir H. Goodricke's b. m. Stella, 5 yrs 2 3

On Thursday the 2d, 50l. for three yr olds, 7st 10lb. and four yr olds, 8st. 8lb. The winner of one 50l. this season, carrying 3lb. extra.—2-mile heats.

Mr. Robinson's b. c. Ambo, by Overton, 3 yrs n'd 3 1 1
Mr. Bamlett's b. c. by Coriander, 4 yrs old 2 3 2
Sir H. Hogbton's ch. c. by Buzzard, 3 yrs old (fell lame) 1 2 dr

On Friday the 3d, a free Plate of 50l. for all ages,

Not run for, for want of horses.

ENFIELD.

ON Monday, the 22d of September, 50l. for three and four yr olds;—heats, two miles and a quarter.

Mr. Durand's bl. f. Ramschnondra, by Sir Peter, 4 yrs old, 7st. 12lb. 1 1
Mr. Hallett's ch. c. Provisional, 3 yrs old, 6st. 10lb. 3 2
Sir F. G. Smyth's br. c. Omen, 4 yrs old, 8st. 10lb. 2 3
Mr. Goodisson's ro. c. Silvertail, 3 yrs old, 6st. 12lb. 4 4

On Tuesday the 23d, a Sweepstakes of 15gs each, by horses that never won above the value of 25l. —3-mile heats. (7 Subscribers.)

Mr. Fletcher's b. g. Magog, by Magog, 5 yrs old, 9st. 4lb. 1 1
Mr. Munslow's b. m. Tanner-Collin, by King Fergus, 5 yrs old, 9st. 1lb. 2 2

Mr.

RACING CALENDAR.

Mr. Webb's b. m. Country-
wench, by Meteor, aged,
9st. 4lb. - 2 3
Mr. Ridout's br. h. Fox, by
Highflyer, aged, 9st. 7lb. 4 dis
Mr. Johnson's b. g. Sprightly,
by Jubilator, 8st. 11lb. dis
Mr. Goldham's br. h. Tal-
ly-O! by Satellite, aged,
9st. 7lb. - dis

On Wednesday the 24th, the
Ladies' Plate of 50l. for all ages;
—4-mile heats.

Mr. Durand's b. f. by Sir
Peter Teazle, out of the
Yellow mare, 3 yrs old,
5st. 11lb. - 1 1
Mr. Barkey's b. h. Play or
Pay, aged, 8st. 7lb. 2
Mr. Edwards's b. m. Du-
chess, 5 yrs old, 8st. 7lb. 6 3
Mr. Abbey's ch. h. Com-
modore, 6 yrs old, 8st. 5lb. 5 4
Mr. Wixcy's b. c. Tea-
boy, 4 yrs old, 8st. 4 5
Mr. Dockeray's b. f. Steel-
lips, 4 yrs old, 8st. 3 dis

MALTON.

ON Tuesday, October the 7th,
a Sweepstakes of 20gs each,
for all ages; three yr olds, 7st. four
yr olds, 7st. 10lb. five yr olds, 8st.
4lb. six yr olds and aged, 8st. 10lb.
Mares allowed 3lb.—two miles.
(5 Subscribers.)

Mr. Peirse's b. h. by Walnut,
dam by Young Marske, 5 yrs
old - 1
Capt. Pigot's ch. c. Slap-bang,
4 yrs old - 2
6 to 4 on Mr. Peirse's horse.

Sweepstakes of 20gs each, for
three yr old colts, 8st. 2lb. and
fillies, 8st.—two miles.—(9 Subscribers.)

Ld Darlington's c. Agonistes,
by Sir Peter 1
Ld Strathmore's b. c. by Walnut, out of Little Scot's dam 2

Mr. Garforth's ch. c. by Coriander, out of Rosalind 3
Mr. Robinson's b. f. Belle-fille 4
Ld Fitzwilliam's b. f. by Coriander, out of Matron 5
7 to 4 on Agonistes.

Hunters' Sweepstakes of 10gs
each, wt. 12st. three miles. (5
Subscribers.)

Mr. Parkhurst's b. h. by Jupiter, dam by Leviathan 1
Mr. W. Hutchinson's b. h.
Sling 2
Mr. Lumley Savile's b. m. Sa-
bella 3
2 to 1 on Sling.

On Wednesday the 8th, a
Sweepstakes of 10gs each, for
three yr old fillies, carrying 8st.—
two miles. (5 Subscribers.)

Mr. G. Crompton's b. f. Anniseed, by Coriander 1
Ld Fitzwilliam's b. f. by Coriander, out of Matron 2
Very high odds on Anniseed.

Fifty Pounds for all ages; three
yr olds, 6st. 6lb four yr olds, 7st.
6lb. five yr olds, 8st. 1lb. six yr
olds, 8st. 7lb. and aged, 8st. 9lb.
A winner of one 50l. in Plate,
Match or Sweepstakes, this year,
carrying 3lb. of two, or a King's
Plate, 5lb. extra. Mares allowed
2lb.—3-mile heats.

Sir G. Armytage's ch. h.
Tartar, by Phœnomenon,
6 yrs old 1 1
Mr. G. Crompton's b. m.
Stella, 5 yrs old 2 2
6 to 4 on Tartar.

On Thursday the 9th, a Sweepstakes of 20gs each, for two yr
old colts, 8st. and fillies, 7st. 11lb.
—the last mile. (3 Subscribers.)

Mr. Robinson's b. f. Swallow,
by Wessel 1
Mr. G. Crompton's b. c. Dotterel 2
2 to 1 on Dotterel.

Fifty

Fifty Pounds for three yr olds, 7st. 11lb. and four yr olds, 8st. 7lb. winners carrying extra, as on Wednesday;—2-mile heats.

Ld. Strathmore's b. c. by Walnut, out of Scot's dam, 3 yrs old — 1 1
Ld Darlington's b. c. Haphazard, 3 yrs old — 2 2

PENRITH.

ON Thursday, the 9th of October 50l. given by the Gentlemen of the Inglewood Hunt, for three and four yr old colts, &c. that never won more than the value of 50gs, in Match, Plate, or Sweepstakes; three yr olds, 7st. 4lb. four yr olds, 8st. 2lb. A winner of fifty pounds, or guineas, carrying 3lb extra.—2-mile heats.

Ld Belhaven's ch. c. by Star, 4 yrs old, 8st. 2lb. — 2 1 1
Mr. Hutton's b. c. Coniac, 4 yrs old (1 Plate) 8st. 5lb. 1 2 2
Mr. Lucock's ch. f. Rebecca, by Walnut, 3 yrs old, 7st. 4lb. 3 dr

On Saturday, the 11th, 50l. given by the town of Penrith, for horses, &c. of all ages; three yr olds, 6st. 7lb. four yr olds, 7st. 7lb. five yr olds, 8st. 4lb. six yr olds, 8st. 11lb. and aged, 9st. A winner of 50l. in the present year, carrying 2lb. of two, 4lb. and of three or more, 6lb. extra.—4-mile heats.

Mr. I'Anson's b. c. John O'Groat, by Overton, 3 yrs old, 6st. 9lb. 1 0 1
Mr Lucock's b. c. Richard Hughes, by Windlestone, 4 yrs old (two Plates) 7st. 1lb. — 2 0 2
Mr. Hutton's b. c. Coniac, 4 yrs old (1 Plate) 7st. 9lb. 3 dr

NEWMARKET.

ON Monday, the 13th of October, Mr. Cookson's ch. c. Scrub, by Pot8o's, 3 yrs old, 6st. 4lb. beat Ld Clermont's Meteor c. 4 yrs old, 8st. Ab. M. 25gs.

5 to 4 on the Meteor colt.

Sweepstakes of 100gs each, h. ft. by three yrs old colts and fillies (warranted totally untried at the time of naming) colts, 8st. 2lb. fillies, 8st. Across the Flat.

Mr. Watson's br. c. Triumver, by Volunteer 1
Mr. Ladbroke's ch. c. Lazarus 2
Mr. Heathcote's c. by Pegasus, out of Cinderwench pd
Ld Clermont's b. c. by Trumpator, out of his youngest Highflyer mare, out of his Othea pd
Sir F. Standish's brother to Spread Eagle pd

6 to 4 on Lazarus.

Sir C. Bunbury's bl. c. Sorcerer by Trumpator, 4 yrs old, 8st. 9lb. beat Mr. Wilson's b. c. Surprize, 3 yrs old, 6st. 12lb. D. I. 200gs, h. ft.——13 to 8 on Sorcerer.

Mr. Heathcote's ch. c. Popinjay, by Buzzard, 8st. recd. ft from Mr. Adams's b. f. Cuckoo, 7st. 12lb. R. M. 100gs, h. ft.

Mr. R. Heathcote's Hippona, 8st. 9lb. agst Mr. Howorth's Truss, 7st. 2lb. Two yr old Course, 300gs.—Off by consent.

On Tuesday, the 14th, a Sweepstakes of 100gs each, h. ft. for two yr old colts, 8st. 3lb. fillies, 8st. Two yr old Course. Those out of untried mares allowed 2lb. (8 Subscribers.)

Mr. Wilson's b. f. Sophia, by Buzzard, out of Huncamunca, an untried mare) 1
Ld Clermont's br. c. by Volunteer, bought of Mr. Kingsman 2

b Ld

Ld Grosvenor's ch. c. by John
Bull, out of Maid of all
Work - 3

4 and 5 to 1 on Sophia.

Mr. Wilson's b. c. Surprize, by
Buzzard, 3 yrs old, 7st. beat Mr.
Howorth's ch. c. Pet, 4 yrs old,
8st. Ab. M. 25gs.

5 to 4 on Surprize.

Fifty Pounds, for two yr old
colts, carrying 8st. 2lb. and fillies,
8st. Two yr old Course.

Mr. Wilson's b. f. Sophia, by
Buzzard - 1
D. of Grafton's ch. c. Flambeau 2
Ld Grosvenor's b. c. by John
Bull, out of Ariadne 3
Mr. Sitwell's ch f. Harpy, by
Phœnomenon, out of Hor-
net - 4
Mr. Bullock's b. f. by Javelin,
out of Mouse's dam 5
Mr. Cookson's b. c. Jack
Chance, by Fortunio, out of
Brandy Nan 6
Mr. Panuwell's ch. c. by Rock-
ingham, out of Miss Dun-
combe - 7
5 to 4 agst Sophia, and 13 to 8
agst Flambeau.

Sweepstakes of 25gs each, Two
yr old Course.

Mr. Hallet's bl. f. Wowski, by
Mentor, 3 yrs old, 8st. 4lb. 1
Mr. Ladbroke's bl. c. Whis-
kerandos, two yrs old, 6st.
2lb. - 2
Mr. Wyndham's br. c. by
Fidget, 2 yrs old, 6st. 3lb 3

Even betting and 5 to 4 on Whiskerandos, 2 to 1 ags Wowski,
and 3 to 1 agst the Fidget colt.

On Wednesday, the 15th, Mr.
Cookson's br. h. Diamond, by
Highflyer, beat Mr. R. Heathcote's ch. m. Hippona, 8st. each,
the last three miles of B. C. 200gs.

11 to 8 on Hippona.

Mr. R. Heathcote's ch. f. Georgiana, by John Bull, 3 yrs old,
7st. 12lb. beat Mr. Howorth's
Truss, 6 yrs old, 8st. 9lb. Ab. M.
50gs.

5 and 6 to 4 on Truss.

The Town Plate of 50l for
three yr olds, 7st 4lb. four yr olds,
8st. 4lb. five yr olds, 8st. 11lb.
six yr olds, 9st. 1lb. and aged, 9st.
4lb. Two Middle miles of B. C.—
Whh this condition, that the winner was to be sold for 53gs. if demanded, &c.

Mr. Adams's ch. f. Ephemera,
by Woodpecker, 3 yrs old 1
Mr. R. Heathcote's b. h. Piccadilly, 6 yrs old 2
Mr. Goodisson's ro. c. brother
to Admiral, 3 yrs old 3
Mr. Watson's br. c. Gloucester,
3 yrs old - 4

13 to 8 agst Ephemera, and 5 to 2
agst Piccadilly.

The first year of the renewal of
the October Oatlands Stakes of
30gs each, B. M. (18 Subscribers.)

Sir C. Bunbury's bl. c. Sorcerer, by Trumpator, 4 yrs
old, 9st. - 1
Mr. Cookson's ch. c. Scrub, 3
yrs old, 6st 12lb. 2
Mr. Howorth's Truss, 6 yrs old,
8st. 11lb. Mr. Lake's Quatorze,
5 yrs old, 8st. 4lb. Ld Clermont's Cadet, 5 yrs old, 8st.
2lb. Mr. Adams's Humbug, 4
yrs old, 8st. 2lb. Mr. R. Heathcote's Georgiana, 3 yrs old, 7st.
11lb. D. of Grafton's First
Fruits, 3 yrs old, 7st. 6lb. and
Mr. Wilson's Surprize, 3 yrs
old, 6st. 11lb. also started, but
the Judge could place only the
first two.

11 to 5 agst Sorcerer, 4 to 1 agst.
Georgiana, 5 to 1 agst Humbug, 7 to 1 agst First Fruits,
and 8 to 1 agst Scrub.

The

The following having declared ft. within the time prescribed, paid only 10gs each.

Mr. Heathcote's Symmetry, 5 yrs old, 9st. 7lb. Mr. Golding's Boaster, 5 yrs old, 8st. 12lb. Mr. Howorth's Chippenham, 4 yrs old, 8st. 11lb. Sir F. Standish's b. c. Eagle, brother to Spread Eagle, 4 yrs old, 8st. 11lb. Mr. Howard's Weymouth, aged, 7st. 11lb. Ld Clermont's Meteor c. 4 yrs old, 7st. 10lb. Mr. Watson's Triumvir, 3 yrs old, 7st. 5lb. Mr. Norton's c. Mittimus, by Ruler, 3 yrs old, 7st. and Mr. Cussans, who did not name.

Mr. Norton's b. c. Mittimns, by Ruler, 3 yrs old. 8st. 7lb. beat Ld Clermont's Noisetta, 2 yrs old, 7st. Two yr old Course. 25gs.

5 to 1 on Mittimns.

On Thursday the 16th, Mr. Parkhurst's b. h. Welter, by Jupiter, beat Sir Wheeler Cuffe's br. h. Old England, 13st. each, B. C. —Mr. Parkhurst staked 2cogs to 150gs.—13 to 8 on Welter.

Subscription Plate of 50l. for two yr olds, 7st. 4lb. and three yr olds, 9st. Two yr old Course. With this condition, that the winner was to be sold for 200gs, &c.

Mr. Bullock's b. f. by Javelin, out of Mouse's dam, 2 yrs old   1
Sir C. Bunbury's b. c. Gig, 3 yrs old   -   2
Mr. Sitwell's ch. f. Harpy, 2 yrs old   -   3

Even betting on Mr. Bullock's filly, and 2 to 1 agst Gig.

Mr. R. Heathcote's Hippona, 8st. 9lb. beat Mr. Howard's Weymouth, 6st. Ab. M. 50gs.

5 to 2 on Hippona.

Sweepstakes of 100gs each, h. ft. Across the Flat.

Mr. Heathcote's ch. c. Popinjay, by Buzzard, 7st. 9lb. recd. ft. from Sir H. T. Vane's c. by Coriander, 8st. 1lb. and Mr. Ladbroke's Lazarus, 8st.

HOLYWELL HUNT.

ON Tuesday, October the 14th, Sir T. Mostyn's f. Hedera, by Creeper, 8st. 10lb. beat Sir W. W. Wynn's c. Doctor O'Liffey, 9st. two miles.

2 to 1 on Hedera.

Mr. E. L. Lloyd's Highflyer mare, 12st. beat Sir W. W. Wynn's Volunteer mare, 10st. two miles.

Sweepstakes of 25gs each.

Sir E. Lloyd's Chicken, by Microscope, 3 yrs old, 8st,   1
Mr. E. L. Lloyd's c. by Symmetry, 3 yrs old, 8st.   2
Sir W. W. Wynn's Llangedwyn, 3 yrs old, 8st. 3lb.   pd

The second year of a Sweepstakes of 15gs each, for three yr olds, 6st. four yr olds, 7st. 7lb. five yr olds, 8st. six yr olds and ageds 8st. 7lb.—four miles. (7 Subscribers.)

Sir W. W. Wynn's ch. g. Alexander the Great, by Alexander, out of Medea, walked over.

The Plate was not run for, Mr. Cholmondeley's br. m. Roaring Meg, by Highflyer, being the only one entered.

On Thursday the 16th, a Handicap Sweepstakes of 5gs each.— (8 Subscribers.)

Mr. E. L. Lloyd's c. by Symmetry, 3 yrs old, 8st. 5lb.   1   1
Sir W. W. Wynn's Volunteer, aged, 9st. 10lb.   2   2
Mr. Cholmondeley's Devil among the Taylors, aged, 10st. 4lb. (bolted)   ds
Sir E. P. Lloyd's Chicken,   3 yrs

3 yrs old, 9st. 1lb.
(bolted) - dis

NORTHALLERTON.

ON Thursday, the 16th of October, a Sweepstakes of 10gs each, with 30gs added, for all ages; two miles. (5 Subscribers.)

Mr. Harrison's b. h. by Trumpator, aged, 9st. 1

Mr. J. Ackers's br. c. Beulevane, by Soldier, 3 yrs old, 7st. 3lb. - 2

Mr. l'Anson's ch. h. Applegarth, five yrs old, 8st. 8lb. 3

A Maiden Plate of 50l. for three yr olds, 6st. 7lb. four yr olds, 7st. 10lb. five yr olds, 8st. 3lb. six yr olds and aged, 8st. 8lb.—two-mile heats.

Sir H. T. Vane's br. c. by Coriander, 3 yrs old 4 1 1

Mr. Alderson's f. Vanguard, three yrs old 1 2 2

Mr. Hullock's ch. c. by Antæus, 3 yrs old 5 3 3

Mr. Fenton's b. f. by Lurcher, 3 yrs old 2 dr

Mr. Dodsworth's gr. f. by Walnut, 3 yrs old 3 dr

On Friday the 17th, 50l. for three and four yr olds, that never won above that value, at any one time;—3-mile heats.

Mr. Cornforth's colt, by Pipator, 3 yrs old, 7st. 5lb. 3 1 1

Mr. Riddell's c. by Walnut, 3 yrs old, 7st. 10lb. 1 2 3

Mr. Fenton's b. f. three yrs old, 7st. 3lb. 2 3 2

On Saturday the 18th, 50l. for three yr olds, 6st. 4lb. four yr olds, 7st. 11lb. five yr olds, 8st. 9lb. six yr olds, 8st. 12lb. and aged, 9st. Mares allowed 3lb. A winner of one fifty since the first of March, carrying 3lb. of two, or a King's Plate, 5lb. extra.—4-mile heats.

Sir G. Armytage's ch. h. Tartar, by Phœnomenon, 6 yrs old 4 4 1 1

Mr. J. Ackers's br. c. Beulevane, 3 yrs old 1 5 6 2

Mr. Milbank's b. c. Takamahaka, 3 yrs old 5 1 5 3

Mr. Harrison's b. h. by Trumpator, aged 6 2 2

Mr. Robinson's b. c. Ambo, 3 yrs old 2 3 3

Mr. Fletcher's gr. h. Camperdown, 5 yrs old 3 6 4

IRELAND.

CURRAGH SEPT. MEETING, 1800.

ON Monday, September the 8th, a Sweepstakes for two yr olds, 50gs, h. ft.—Two yr old Course.

Mr. Hamilton's b. c. Sweet William, by Tugg, on St. Bridget, 8st. 1

Mr. Kirwan's gr. c. by Master Bagot, on York's dam, 8st. 2

Mr. Whaley's br. c. Abomelique, by Fennelly's Highflyer, on Struggler's dam, 7st. 13lb. 3

Mr. Taylor's ch. c. by Tugg, on Conductress, 7st. 13lb. 4

Mr. Daly's c. by Chanticleer, on a Mambrino mare, 8s'. pd ft

Even betting Abomelique agst the field, who lost ground et starting.

Sir H. T. Vane's br. m. Lady Sarah, by Fidget, 6 yrs old, 8st. 5lb. beat Mr. Whaley's gr. m. Duchess of York, by Delpini, 5 yrs old, 7st. 12lb. four miles, 200gs, h. ft.

Both

Both horses having run on the wrong side of a post, the race and all bets declared void.

5 to 4 on Duchess of York.

Mr. Kirwan's b. c. brother to Toby, 5 yrs old, beat Mr. Daly's ch. c. Chicken, by Chanticleer, 5 yrs old, 8st. each, over the course, 100gs each, p. p.

2 to 1 on Toby.

Mr. Whaley's ch. h. Challenger, by Tugg, 5 yrs old, 8st. beat Mr. Daly's ch. h. Dawdle, by Master Bagot, 5 yrs old, 7st 11lb. Red Post, 100gs, h. ft.

3 to 2 on Challenger.

On Tuesday the 9th a Handicap Plate, 50gs;—Post on the Flat, home heats.

Mr. Ormsby's br. h. Cornet, by Tugg, aged, 8st. 9lb.   1 1
Mr. Whaley's ch. c. Peewcet, by Tom Turf, 4 yrs old, 8st. 1lb.   2 2
Mr. Hamilton's c. Little Bowes, 2 yrs old, 5st. 10lb. 3 dr

5 to 2 agst Cornet, 2 to 1 agst Peewcet, and 5 to 4 agst Little Bowes.

On Wednesday 10th, the King's Plate of 100gs, for any horse, carrying 12st.—4-mile heats.

Mr. Kelly's b. m. Katty Flanagan, by Queensberry, aged   -   1 1
Mr. Whaley's gr. f. Duchess of York, by Delpini, 5 yrs 2 2
Ld Barrymore's gr. h. Warrior, by Chocolate, 6 yrs 3 dr
Mr. Daly's ch. h. Jonquille, by Master Bagot, 6 yrs old (restive) - dis

Even betting Katty Flanagan agst the field, 4 to 1 agst Duchess of York, 5 to 2 agst Warrior, and 7 to 4 agst Jonquille.

On Thursday the 11th the King's Plate of 100gs, for three yr olds, 8st. each,—one 2-mile heat, 3lb. to mares.

Mr. Kirwan's ch. c. Traveller, by Chanticleer   -   1
Mr. Hamilton's gr. e. George, by Armstrong   -   2
Mr. Edwards's c. Bagatelle, (late Little Jemmy) by Douglas 3
Col. Lumm's gr. c. Selim, by Honest Tom   4

5 to 4 on Traveller, 3 to 1 agst George, 4 to 1 agst Bagatelle, and 5 to 2 agst Selim.

On Friday the 12th the King's Plate of 100gs, for mares, 10st each—4-mile heats.

Sir H. T. Vane's br. m. Lady Sarah, by Fidget, 6 yrs old 1 1
Mr. Kelly's b. m. Katty Flanagan, by Queensberry, aged   -   2 2

At starting, 5 to 4 on Katty Flanagan; after the heat, 3 to 2 on Lady Sarah.

On Saturday the 13th, the Lord Lieutenant's Plate of 100gs, wt. for age, viz. four yr olds, 7st. 11lb. five yr olds, 1st. 8lb. six yr olds, 8st. 13lb. and aged, 9st.—one 4-mile heat.

Mr. Daly's b. h. The Hank (late Sir Horatio) by Master Bagot, 5 yrs old   -   1
Mr. Kelly's ch. c. Honest Ralph, by Master Bagot, 4 yrs 2
Mr. Whaley's b. c. Swordsman, by Prizefighter, 4 yrs old 3
Mr. Kirwan's b. c. Toby, by Chocolate, 4 yrs old   4

2 to 1 agst The Hank, 2 to 1 agst Ralph, 2 to 1 agst Swordsman, and 4 to 1 agst Toby.

Tit Stakes (first year, renewed for three years) for two yr old colts, 7st. fillies, 6st. 10lb. the present Two yr old Course, 25gs each, 15 forfeit.

Mr. Kelly's b. c. Peter, by Master Bagot, on Courtezan   1

Mr.

Mr. Hamilton's b. c. Sweet
 William, by Tugg, on St.
 Bridget. - - 2
Mr. Edwards's b. f. sister to
 Commodore - 3
Col. Lumm's ch. c. by Honest
 Tom, on Lady Mary 4
Mr. Daly's b. c. by Chanticleer,
 on a Mambrino mare pd
Mr. Daly's ch. f. by Chanti-
 cleer, on Bess pd
Mr. Kirwan's b. c. by Plough-
 boy, dam by Aurelius, on
 Divone's dam - pd

5 to 4 on Peter, 6 to 4 agst Sweet-
William.

Mr. Whaley's br. c. Abomelique, by Fennelly's Highflyer,
7st. beat Mr. Kirwan's c. by
Ploughboy, on Ophelia, 7st. 2lb.
50gs, h. ft. Two yr old Course.

2 to 1 and 5 to 2 on Abomelique.

On Monday the 15th, (after the
Meeting) a Sweepstakes, 15gs.
each;—Red Post, home.

Mr. Daly's ch. h. Dawdle, by
 Master Bagot, 5 yrs old, 8st.
 1lb. - - 1
Col. Lumm's gr. c. Selim, by
 Honest Tom, 3 yrs old, 6st.
 9lb. - - 2
Ld Barrymore's gr. h. Warrior,
 by Chocolate, 6 yrs old,
 7st. 12lb. - 3
Mr. Whaley's ch. f. Peeweet,
 by Tom Tuft, 4 yrs old,
 7st. 4lb. - 4
Mr. Taylor's ch. f. Little Pickle,
 by Chanticleer, 3 yrs old,
 5st. 1lb. - 5

Little Pickle came in fourth, but
ran the wrong side of a Post.
—Even betting the field agst
the fillies, 3 to 1 agst Dawdle,
4 to 1 agst Selim, 7 to 1 agst
Warrior, 3 to 1 agst Peeweet,
and 3 to 1 agst Little Pickle.

On Thursday the 18th, Mr. Daly's ch. h. Dawdle, by Master
Bagot, 5 yrs old, 7st. 5lb. beat
Mr. Whaley's ch. h. Challenger,
5 yrs old, 8st. over the Course,
50gs. each.

5 to 4 on Challenger.

CARLISLE.

ON Tuesday the 14th of October, 50l. given by the Earl
of Carlisle, for all ages.

No race, only one horse being
entered.

On Thursday the 16th, 50l.
given by J. C. Curwen, Esq. and
Sir F. F. Vane, Bart. Members
for the City, for three yr olds, 7st.
7lb. and four yr olds, 8st. 4lb. A
winner of one fifty pounds or
guineas, since the first of March
last, carrying 3lb. of two, 5lb.
and of three or more fillies, 7lb.
extra, a Sweepstakes considered
as a fifty;—2 mile heats.

Ld Belhaven's ch. c. by
 Star, 4 yrs old (1 plate) 1 1
Mr. Lucock's b. c. Richard
 Hughes, 4 yrs old (2 plates) 3 2
Mr. l'Anson's b. c. John
 O'Groat, 3 yrs old (2
 plates) 2 3

John O'Groat the favorite.

On Saturday the 18th, 50l.
given by the Members of the
Cumberland Hunt, &c. four yr
olds, 7st. 7lb. five yr olds, 8st.
3lb. six yr olds, 8st. 9lb. and aged
horses, &c. 8st. 12lb.—extra
weights as on Thursday;—3 mile
heats.

Ld Belhaven's ch. c. 4 yrs
 old (2 plates) 1 1
Mr. Lucock's b. c. Richard
 Hughes, 4 yrs old (2
 plates) - 2 2

2 to 1 on Ld Belhaven's colt.

HOLY.

HOLYWELL HUNT.

[CONCLUDED]

ON Saturday the 18th of October, Sir W. W. Wynn's ch. g. Alexander, the Great, by Alexander, 5 yrs old, 10st. beat Mr. E. Lloyd's b. m. by Highflyer, aged, 12st.—two miles, for 100gs.

Sir T. Mostyn's b. f. Hedera, by Creeper, 4 yrs old, 9st. beat Sir W. W. Wynn's m. by Volunteer, aged, 8st. 9lb.—two miles, 100gs.

A Handicap Sweepstakes of 5gs each;—two miles. (9 Subscribers.)

Mr. E. Lloyd's b. m. by Highflyer, aged, 9st. 1lb.	1
Sir W. W. Wynn's Alexander the Great, 5 yrs old, 8st.	2
Sir T. Mostyn's Heart's-ease, 4 yrs old, 9st.	3
Mr. E. Lloyd's c. by Symmetry, 3 yrs old, 7st. 7lb.	4

CALEDONIAN HUNT.

AT HAMILTON.

ON Monday, the 20th of October, Mr. Fletcher's Delamere, by Highflyer, aged, 13st. beat Mr. Graham's Duncan, 5 yrs old, 12st. 8lb.—two miles, 500gs, b. ft.

Even betting, and 5 to 4 on Duncan.

His Majesty's Plate of 100gs given to the Caledonian Hunt, free for any horse, &c. carrying 12st.—4 mile heats.

Mr. Hopp's Delamere, by Highflyer, aged	3	1	1
D. of Hamilton's c. by Walnut, 5 yrs old	1	2	dr
Mr. Fletcher's Master Robert, aged	2	dr	

On Tuesday, the 21st. the Gold Cup, value 100gs, the residue in specie, being a Subscription of 25gs each (9 Subscribers.)

Mr. Graham's Bonaparte, by Aston, 4 yrs old, walked over.

Fifty Pounds given by the Hunt, for all ages;—4-mile heats.

Mr. Hopp's Delamere, aged, 9st. 9lb.	1	1
D. of Hamilton's gr. c. by Walnut, 4 yrs old, 7st. 8lb.	2	2
Mr. Boswell's Pensioner, 5 yrs old, 8st. 8lb.	3	3

On Wednesday the 22d, a Sweepstakes of 200gs each, N. P. four yr olds carrying 8st. five yr olds 8st. 12lb.—four miles. (4 Subscribers)

Mr. Graham's b. h. Duncan, by Stride, 5 yrs old	1
Mr. Graham's Bryan O'Lynn, 4 yrs old	2
Mr. Fletcher's Logie O'Buchan, 4 yrs old	3

4 to 1 on Bryan O'Lynn, and 11 to 1 agst Logie O'Buchan.

Fifty Pounds given by the Caledonian Hunt.

D. of Hamilton's b. c. Little Bob, by Spadille, 4 yrs old, walked over.

Mr. Oswald's Phlegon, beat Mr. Maxwell's Brown Jug, 12st each, four miles, 100gs.—Rode by the owners.

On Thursday the 23d, Fifty Pounds, the gift of his Grace the D. of Hamilton;—four miles.

Mr. Hopp's Delamere	1
D. of Hamilton's c. by Spadille	2
Mr. Fletcher's Logie O'Buchan	3

Capt. Maxwell's Brown Jug, beat Mr. Graham's horse, 12st. each, four miles, 200gs.

NEW-

NEWMARKET

THIRD OCTOBER, OR HOUGHTON MEETING.

ON Monday, October 27th Mr. Heathcote's gr. h. Simmetry, by Delpini, beat Mr. Cookson's br. h. Diamond, 8st. each, Across the Flat, 200gs.

5 to 4 on Diamond.

Mr. Heathcote's ch. c. Popinjay, by Buzzard, beat Mr. Wyadham's ch. c. by Woodpecker, out of Platina, 8st. each, R. M. 200gs.

4 to 1 on Popinjay.

D of Grafton's ch. c. Flambeau, by Skyscraper, or Grouse, 2 yrs old, 6st. 6lb. beat Mr. R. Heathcote's Georgiana, 3 yrs old, 8st. 7lb. Two yr old Course, 200gs. h. ft.

11 to 8 on Georgiana.

Mr. C. C. Smith's b. h. Florist, by John Bull, out of Florella, gnt. beat Lord Milsintown's Whitethorn, 10st. 7lb. D. I. 50gs.

6 to 4 on Florist.

Mr. Howarth's gr. h. Truss by Pilot, 8st. alb. recd. from Ld Donegall's Flugelman, 8st. 7lb First three miles of B. C. 50gs.

Mr. Turner's br. h. Oscar, by Saltram, 7st. 3lb. recd. ft. from Mr. Heathcote's Warter, 8 st. 8lb. Across the Flat, 500 h. ft.

Mr. R. Heathcote's Georgiana, 8st. 7lb. agst Mr. Adams's Lazarus, 7st. 12lb. Two yr old Course, 200gs, b. ft.—Off by consent.

On Tuesday the 28th, Mr. Wilson's b. c. Surprize, by Buzzard, 8st 7lb. beat Mr. Norton's b. c. Mittimus, 8st. Ab. M. 50gs.—Even betting.

Mr. Hallett's bl. f. Wouski, by Mentor, 3 yrs old, 8st. 7lb. beat Mr. Bullock's b. f. by Javelin, 2 yrs old, 6st. 3lb. Two yr old Course, 50gs, h. ft.—6 to 4 on Mr. Bullock's filly.

Mr. Wyndham's br. c. by Fidgit, out of Cælia, 8st. 7lb. beat Mr. Perren's br. f. by Trumpator, out of Cinderella, 7st. 7lb. both two yrs old, Two yr old Course, 100gs.

11 to 8 on the filly, who ran out of the Course.

Mr. Panton's b. c. Snuff-box, by Pot8o's, 7st. 7lb. beat Mr. R. Heathcote's Piccadilly, 8st. 8lb. Ab. M. 50gs.

9 to 4 on Snuff-box.

Mr. R. Heathcote's ch. m. Hippona, 8st. 9lb. and Ld. Clermont's Paynator, 7st. 7lb. Two yr old Course, 100gs, ran a *dead heat.*

5 to 2 on Hippona.

Fifty Pounds for two yr olds, carrying a feather; three yr olds, 7st. 5lb. four yr olds, 8st. 9lb. five yr olds, 9st. 3lb. six yr olds, 9st. 7lb. and aged, 9st. 10lb. the last three miles of B. C.—With this condition, that the winner was to be sold for 300gs, if demanded, &c.

Mr. Wyndham's br. c. by Fidget, out of Cælia, 2 yrs old	1
Mr. Girdler's b. h. Capricorn, 5 yrs old	2
Mr. Lockley's ch. f. Rushlight, (late Ephemera) 3 yrs old	3
Mr. Panton's b. c. Snuff box, 3 yrs old	4
Mr. Cookson's b. c. Jack Chance, 2 yrs	5
Mr. Bullock's b. f. by Javelin, out of Mouse's dam, 2 yrs old	6
Mr. Golding's b. c. Skyrocket, 3 yrs old	7

5 to 2 agst Snuff-box, 5 to 2 agst Skyrocket, 3 to 1 agst Rushlight, 8 to 1 agst Mr. Wyndham's colt, and 6 to 1 agst the Javelin filly.

On Wednesday the 29th, Ld Clermont's b. c. by Meteor, 8st. beat Mr. Hurt Sitwell's Huntingdon, 8st. 3lb. R. M. 25gs—2 to 1 on the winner.

Mr. R. Heathcote's ch. f. Georgiana, by John Bull, 8st. beat Mr. Hallett's bl. f. Wowski, 7st. 1lb. both 3 yrs old, Ab. M. 50gs.

6 to 4 on Wowski.

Mr. Howorth's b. c. Chippenham, by Trumpator, 4 yrs old, 8st. 7lb. beat Mr. Wilson's Surprize, 3 yrs old, 7st. 5lb. R. M. 50gs.

2 to 1 on Chippenham.

Mr. Heathcote's ch. c. Popinjay, by Buzzard, 8st. 3lb. beat Mr. Adams's Lazarus, 8st. Two yr old Course, 10ogs, h. ft.

3 to 1 on Popinjay.

Mr. Heathcote's gr. b. Symmetry, by Delpini, 8st. 9lb. beat Mr. Adams's Humbug, 7st. 9lb. D. I. 50gs.—5 to 2 on Symmetry.

D. of Grafton's b. c. First Fruits, by Grouse, 8st. 2lb. beat Mr. Wilson's Surprize, 8st. B. C. 50gs.—11 to 10 on First Fruits.

Mr. R. Heathcote's ch. f. Georgiana, by John Bull, 8st. 3lb. recd. 75gs from Mr. Whaley's b. f. Tuneful, 8st. Two yr old Course, 200gs. h. ft.

On Thursday the 30th, Mr. Norton's b. c. Mittimus, by Rules, 3 yrs old, 8st. 7lb. beat Mr. Perren's br. f. by Trumpator, out of Cinderella, 2 yrs old, 7st. Two yr old Course, 50gs.

6 to 4 on Mittimus.

D. of Queensberry's ch. h. Egham, by Dinned, 5 yrs old, 6st. 4lb. beat Mr. R. Heathcote's ch. m. Hippona, 6 yrs old, 8st. 4lb. Clermont Course, 50gs.

3 to 1 on Hippona.

Sweepstakes of 50gs each, Two yr old Course.

Mr. Wyndham's ch. c. by Woodpecker, out of Platina, 8st. 7lb. - 1
Ld Clermont's c. by Volunteer, 6st. 13lb. - 2
Mr. Norton's b. c. Mittimus, 7st. 8lb. - 3

6 to 4 on the winner, 5 to 2 agst Mittimus, and 7 to 2 agst Ld Clermont's Colt.

Mr. Panton's b. c. Snuff-box, by Po80's, 3 yrs old, 8st. 4lb. beat Mr. Ladbroke's bl. c. Whiskerandos, 2 yrs old, 7st. The last three quarters of a mile of Clermont Course, 50gs.

11 to 8 on Snuff-box.

A Subscription Plate of 50l. for two yr olds, carrying 5st. 2lb. three yr olds, 7st. four yr olds, 8st. 2lb. five yr olds, 8st. 9lb. six yr olds and aged, 8st. 13lb. D. I.—With this condition, that the winner was to be sold for 150gs, if demanded, &c.

Mr. Cookson's b. c. Jack Chance, by Fortunio, 2 yrs 1
D. of Queensberry's ch. b. Egham, 5 yrs old 2
Mr. Girdler's b. h. Capricorn, 5 yrs old - 3
Mr. Golding's b. h. Boaster, 5 yrs old - 4
Ld Clermont's br. c. Carlo, 4 yrs 5.

6 to 4 agst Capricorn, 5 to 2 agst Egham, 3 to 1 agst Carlo, 6 to 1 agst Jack Chance, and 6 to 1 agst Boaster.

Mr. Howorth's b. c. Chippenham, by Trumpator, 7st. recd. from Mr. R. Heathcote's Hippona, 8st. 11lb. R. M. 200gs.

On Friday, the 31st, Mr. Delme's bl. m. Gavlass, by Gay, 8st. 5lb. beat Ld Milsintown's Whitethorn, 8st. 7lb. D. I. 200gs.

4 to 1 on Gaylass.

Sir Wheeler Cuffe's b. c. Huntingdon, by Pegasus, 4 yrs old, beat Mr. Parkhurst's h. h. by Jupiter, dam by Leviathan, 6 yrs old (rode by the owners) 13st each, Across the Flat, 100gs.
5 to 4 on Huntingdon.

Ld Milsintown's b. c. Folly (late M.ttimus) by Ruler, 7st. 1lb. beat Mr. Delme's Gaylass, 8st. 5lb. The two yr old Course, 25gs.
5 to 2 on Gaylass.

LINCOLN.

ON Thursday the 30th of October, His Majesty's Purse of 100gs, for four and five yr old mares; four yr olds, 7st. 11lb. and five yr olds 8st. 7lb. A five yr old mare having won a Royal Plate at four yrs old, and not started since, carrying 4lb. extra, but but if started this year, and not won a Plate of 50l. value, no extra. weight. Winners of a Royal Plate this year, carrying 4lb. of two, 7lb. extra. Any mare that has not won a Plate of 50l. this year, but has started for a Plate, and been once beat, allowed 3lb. if twice beat, 5lb.—2-mile heats.

Mr. G. Crompton's Stella, by Phœnomenon, 5 yrs   1   1
Mr. Hutton's b. f. by Windlestone, 4 yrs old   2 dr
Mr. T. Fisher's Duplicity, 4 yrs old   3 dr

CARLISLE.

ON Thursday the 6th of November, his Majesty's Plate of 100gs, for five yr olds, carrying 10st. each;—3-mile heats.

Mr. Lidderdale's ch. h. Applegarth, by Stride   1   1
Mr. Graham's b. b. Duncan   2   2
Mr. Fletcher's gr. h. Camperdown   -   3   3
5 to 4 on Duncan; after the heats even betting between Applegarth and Camperdown.

TARPORLEY HUNT,

ON CRABTREE-GREEN.

ON Thursday, November the 6th, a Sweepstakes of 15gs. each, for all ages; five yr olds, carrying 11st. gls.—heats, twice round. (10 Subscribers.)

Mr. C. Cholmondeley's b. h. Collector, by S, adiik, 5 yrs. old   1   1
Mr. Langford Brooke's b. g. by Drone, 5 yrs old   2   2

Sweepstakes of 5gs each—heats once round. (7 Subscribers.)

Mr. Cholmondeley's b. g. Cheshireman, by Drone, 5 yrs, 11st. 12lb.   4   1   1
Col. Broughton's br. c. Mobberly Crab (late Vanguard) 4 yrs. old, 11st. 7lb.   1   3   4
Sir W. W. Wynn's ch. g. Alexander the Great, 5 yrs. 11st. 12lb.   2   4   2
Mr. E. Lloyd's b. m. by Highflyer, aged, 12st. 2lb.   3   2   3

Sweepstakes of 10gs. each, thrice round. (5 Subscribers.)
Mr. C. Cholmondeley's Collector, 5 yrs old, 8st. 9lb. walked over.

EXTRA

Intelligence Extra.

NEWMARKET.—FIRST SPRING MEETING, 1801.

MONDAY.—Col. Mathew's Folly (late Mittimus) 8st. agst. Mr. Cox's Cocoa Tree, by Woodpecker, 7st. 11lb. D. I. 100gs. h. ft.

Sir C. Bunbury's Sorcerer, 8st. 9lb. agst Mr. Concannon's Richmond, by Walnut, 7st. 7lb. B. C. 100gs. h. ft.

SATURDAY.—Sir C. Bunbury's Sorcerer, 8st. 10lb. agst Mr. Concannon's Richmond, 7st. 5lb. Two middle miles, 100gs. h. ft.

Major Rooke's Dick Andrews, 8st. 4lb. agst Mr. Heathcote's Popinjay, 8st. D. I. 260gs.

SECOND SPRING MEETING, 1801.

MONDAY.—Sweepstakes of 200gs each, h. ft. Across the Flat.

	st.	lb.
Mr. Heathcote's Symmetry	8	9
Mr. Concannon's Richmond	7	6
Mr. Cox's Cocoa Tree	6	8

Mr. Watson's Triumvir, 8st. 7lb. agst Col. Mathew's Folly, 7st. 6lb. Across the Flat, 100gs. h. ft.

JULY MEETING, 1801.

MONDAY.—Mr. Heathcote's Warter, 8st. agst Major Rooke's Jack Andrews, 6st. 13lb. First three miles of B. C. 200gs. h. ft.

FIRST OCTOBER MEETING, 1801.

Mr. Elton's gr. c. by Porto's, out of Brighton Belle, agst Major Rooke's b. c. by Precipitate, dam by Mercury, out of Wren, 8st. each, Across the Flat, 100gs. h. ft.

FIRST SPRING MEETING, 1803.

MONDAY.—Sweepstakes of 100gs each, h. ft. for colts carrying 8st. 4lb. and fillies, 8st. now foals, R. M.

D. of Grafton's ch. c. by Buzzard, out of Garland

Mr. Watson's b. c. by Buzzard, dam by Dungannon, out of Rutland's dam

Lord Grosvenor's b. c. by John Bull, out of Esther

Lord Grosvenor's b. c. by John Bull, out of Tulip

Lord Grosvenor's ch. c. by John Bull, out of Dido

Lord Grosvenor's br. c. by John Bull, out of Olivia

Sir F. Standish's brother to Spread Eagle

Sir F. Standish's brother to Stamford

Mr. Whaley named Ld Camelford's own sister to Allegranti

Mr. Lockley's b. c. Herschell, by Telescope, out of Maid of Ely

JULY MEETING, 1803.

TUESDAY.—The Produce of Mr. Bullock's dam by Ralpho, covered by Buzzard, 8st. 2lb. agst the Produce of Ld Camelford's Nelly, covered by Pegasus, 7st. 12lb. Two yr old Course, 200, h. ft. no produce, no forfeit. Notice

tice to be given to Mr. Weatherby, within a month after foaling, or forfeit 25gs.

₊ Besides the Oatland Stakes there will be three Handicaps, on the same plan as last year; viz. one for three yr olds, Across the Flat; one for four yr olds, D. I. and another for five years old and upwards, D. C. the particulars whereof will be sent to the proprietors as soon as the weights are fixed.

EPSOM, 1801.

THURSDAY.—Sweepstakes of 20gs each, for fillies, then two yrs old, 7st. 5lb. each, the last mile: the winner to be sold for 150gs, if demanded, &c.

H. R. H. the P. of Wales's b. f. by Volunteer, out of Trumpetta
Mr. Whaley's f. by Sir Peter, out of Editha
Ld Egremont's b. f. by Woodpecker, out of Albatross's dam
The M. of Donegall is a Subscriber, but did not name.

MONTROSE, 1801.

FIRST DAY.—Mr. Graham's Wiley, agst Mr. Barcklay's Tally-ho, 12st. each, ten miles, 400gs, h. ft.

Races to Come.

NEWMARKET CRAVEN MEETING, 1801.

MONDAY, APRIL 6.

THE Craven Stakes, a Subscription of 10gs each, for all ages; two yr olds carrying 6st. three year olds, 8st. four yr olds, 8st. 9lb. five yr olds, 9st. 1lb. six yr olds, 9st. 5lb. and aged, 9st. 7lb. Across the Flat.

Sir F. Standish's sister to Stamford, agst Sir G. Heathcote's f. by Delpini, out of Faunus's dam, 8st. each, Across the Flat, 200, h. ft.

Mr. Heathcote's Warrer, 8st. 7lb. agst Sir H T. Vane's Cockfighter, 8st. Two middle miles of B. C. 1000gs, h. ft.

Ld Sackville's Expectation, 7st. 10lb. agst the Marq. of Donegall's Flugelman, 7st. 3lb. B. C. 200gs, h. ft.

Marq. of Donegall's Fortitude, agst Major Rooke's Dick Andrews, 8st. each, D. I. 100gs, h. ft.

Mr. O'Kelly Wrangler, 8st. 4lb. against Major Rooke's Jack Andrews, 8st. Three last miles of D. C. 100gs, h. ft.

Mr. Heathcote's Popinjay, 8st. 6lb. agt Mr. Whaley's Tuneful, 8st. Ab. M. 200gs, h. ft.

TUESDAY—The Oatland Stakes of 50gs each, h. ft. except those declaring forte t to Mr. Weatherby, at Newmarket, or in Oxenden-street, on or before the 14th of January, 1801, who are to pay only 10gs. each. To run from the Ditch-In.

Sweepstakes of 200gs each, h. ft. 8st. 4lb. B. C.

Mr. Dawson's Jack a-Lantern.
Ld Grosvenor's b. c. by John Bull, out of Nimble
Mr. Cussan's b. c. by Pegasus, out of Sweetheart
Sir F. Standish's brother to Parisot.

www.ingramcontent.com/pod-product-compliance
Lightning Source LLC
Chambersburg PA
CBHW020320240426
43673CB00039B/865